DATE DUE

NOV 21 '91			

DEMCO 38-297

Communication et Culture:
un début

Anne Slack   Harvard University

Marise Thompson   Framingham State Teacher's College

Marlies Mueller   Harvard University

HOUGHTON MIFFLIN COMPANY   BOSTON

Dallas   Geneva, Illinois   Hopewell, New Jersey   Palo Alto   London

Acknowledgments

The authors and publisher wish to thank the following instructors for their thoughtful reviews of the manuscript of *À Propos!* and for their valuable suggestions.

Edmund J. Campion   University of Tennessee

Margaret Clark   University of Arkansas

Joan Dargan   University of New Mexico

Robert A. Fischer   Southwest Texas State University

Michel Fougères   Carnegie-Mellon University

David R. Green   Concordia College

Harriet Hutchinson   Bunker Hill Community College

Bernice Melvin   Austin College

Helene Neu   University of Michigan

Gloria M. Russo   University of Virginia

Components of *À Propos!*
Student text (hardbound)   Instructor's Guide
Workbook/Laboratory manual   Recordings

Printed in the U.S.A.

Student text ISBN: 0-395-33167-6

Instructor's guide ISBN: 0-395-33168-4

INTRODUCTION

To the Instructor

À Propos! Communication et Culture: un début is a comprehensive college-level program for first-year French, with the following components: student text, instructor's guide, workbook/lab manual, recordings (cassette or open reel), and tapescript.

The components of the program provide a thorough and systematic development of the basic skills (listening and reading comprehension, speaking, and writing).

Aims and methodology

Aims: The primary objectives of *À Propos!* are (1) to provide effective means for students to learn to communicate in French—that is, to make active, spontaneous use of the structures and vocabulary under study and (2) to help students gain an appreciation of contemporary French culture. **Methodology:** In learning another language, students have two basic tasks: understanding new structures and vocabulary, and using them appropriately. Students assimilate information at different rates of speed, but once they have absorbed the information, they can converse at nearly the same rate. Thus in *À Propos!* the student text provides step-by-step self-teaching explanations of grammar, and contextual exercises that students complete outside of class at their own learning speed.

The Instructor's Guide provides a wealth of field-tested classroom activities that focus on vocabulary acquisition, practice of grammatical structures, and open-ended communication, enabling students to put to use the information explained in the student text. In both the text and the guide there is continuous review and integration of previously-learned material with new material.

The underlying methodology of the program draws on the best features of a number of language-teaching methods (audio-lingual, functional-notional, direct method, and grammar-translation) and incorporates insights from the communicative competence approach and cognitive theory.

Student Text

The student text contains twelve *Phases* that are divided into *Préparations*. Each Phase begins with a section called *Qu'est-ce que vous allez apprendre?* that states the contextual theme of the Phase and the sorts of meaning students will be able to convey with the new structures and word sets.

A typical Préparation contains the following elements:

Presentation material: a dialogue, narrative, poem, essay, etc., that presents new structures and vocabulary contextually.

Échange d'idées: a set of open-ended situations and activities intended primarily for in-class use. The *Échanges* help students integrate new structures and vocabulary, and encourage student-to-student participation.

Numbered sections: explanations of grammar and practice with new vocabulary, reading comprehension, and writing, in a step-by-step format. Since many students may have forgotten what they once knew about grammar terminology, the student text defines basic terms (verb, object, etc.) and illustrates their use in both French and English.

À Propos!: a brief question that helps the student use in an active, personalized way the grammatical structure or word set just practiced.

Note Culturelle: a cultural note related to the theme of the Phase (in English in Phases 1–7, in French in Phases 8–12), often accompanied by a photo.

Note Linguistique: a note introducing some aspect of the French sound-spelling system (Phases 1 and 2 only).

Vocabulaire: a reference list of new words and expressions presented in the Préparation or in class, with English equivalents.

The text also contains realia with captions, maps,

verb appendices, a French-English vocabulary, an answer key for the self-correcting exercises, and an index.

Instructor's Guide

The Instructor's Guide contains Suggested Teaching Plans (STPs) that are closely coordinated with the topics in the student text. Detailed yet flexible, the STPs offer activities that provide pattern practice, exploitation of presentation material, communication activities, and other strategies for effective teaching. (Refer to the Introduction to the Instructor's Guide for a detailed description.)

Benefits of À Propos!

Communication: Students of *À Propos!* are engaged in meaningful communication from the beginning of the course. The student text and the Instructor's Guide work together to build a sound foundation of structures and vocabulary, and to stimulate the spontaneous use of language, through a variety of means: questions and answers in programmed format; questions asking for personal interpretation and observation; dialogues with authentic language and situations that are often amusing or thought-provoking; contextual exercises; pattern practice; debates; role-playing; games; discussion.

Students experience the satisfaction of being able to understand spoken French in everyday situations, to read an uncomplicated newspaper or magazine article, and to communicate their own thoughts and attitudes in simple spoken and written French.

Culture: *À Propos!* helps students break out of the confines of ethnocentricity and open the door to the culture of the Francophone world by means of up-to-date language and culturally-infused situations in the dialogues, and through the frequent cultural notes, photographs, and realia.

Flexibility: *À Propos!* is suited to a variety of instructional situations. The Instructor's Guide, with its plentiful supply of well-coordinated activities, offers both the experienced and the inexperienced instructor assistance in planning and implementing a sound course structure with interesting substance. The student text, with its programmed format, permits use in intensive programs, courses for proficiency in reading, independent study and re-view, individualized instruction, and continuing education courses.

An emphasis on culturally-based material, communicative fluency, and continuous review and integration—like that in *À Propos!*—has been proven to help build students' confidence and satisfaction in language learning. But no program—no matter how thorough and imaginative—will of itself guarantee the success of a class; there will never be a substitute for the creative teacher. The authors hope that *À Propos!* will be an inspiration to teachers and students alike.

To the Student

When will you use your French outside of class? No one can predict. Perhaps you will use it studying or working abroad, or when you meet a French-speaking visitor here; you will need it for work in business or in social services.

As the amount of contact between countries increases through business and vacation travel, the opportunities to use a foreign language increase daily. But even if you should have little occasion to use French actively after your college years, you will have deepened your understanding of the functioning of language (including your own). Your horizons will be wider because of what you have learned about the French language and the culture of the people who speak it, and you will have another window for looking out at the world.

Is it easy to learn another language? Not particularly—but it is quite possible for you to acquire a good basic knowledge of French by working at it one step at a time.

In *À Propos!*, the explanations of how the French language system and its grammatical structures function are introduced to you step by step in homework assignments called Préparations, rather than in class lectures. You study the Préparations at your own speed on a regular basis. In class, you use what you have learned in the Préparation to convey to others what you want to say. Refer to the section called *Student Text* on p. iii for the organization of a typical Préparation.

The sense of mastery and accomplishment you will feel when you converse in French will be exhilarating! So, be adventurous in French, and enjoy yourself. *Bonne chance!* (Good luck!)

Contents

Phase 3   Pas d'accord   *112*

Préparations

Dialogues et Échanges d'idées

Structures et usage

Notes Culturelles

Phase 4   Loisirs   168

Préparations

Dialogues et Échanges d'idées

Structures et usage

Notes Culturelles

Notes Linguistiques

Phase 5   À Table!   200

Préparations

Dialogues et Échanges d'idées

Structures et usage

Notes Culturelles

Phase 6   Modes   276

Préparations

Dialogues et Échanges d'idées

Structures et usage

Contents

Phase 7   Au Sénégal   330

Préparations

Dialogues/lectures et Échanges d'idées

Structures et usage

Notes Culturelles

Phase 8   À Paris   381

Préparations

Contents

Contents

Structures et usage

Notes Culturelles

Phase 12   À vous la parole   560

Préparations

Dialogues/lectures et Échanges d'idées

Structures et usage

Notes Culturelles

Révision *604*

Lecture et Échange d'idées

Vive le cyclisme! 604

Structures et usage

Phase 1

Salutations et Rencontres

Qu'est-ce que vous allez apprendre?

This title means *What are you going to learn?* This section at the beginning of each Phase tells you the topics you will discuss, attitudes and states of mind you will be able to express, the grammatical structures and word sets you will learn to use, and the cultural content with which you will become familiar.

Communication

You will learn how to make a polite get-away, how to introduce yourself, how to express your likes and dislikes for certain fields of study, how to react to receiving a gift, how to express frustration (when something does not function), and how to react to someone who is absent-minded. To help you accomplish this, you will:

Learn to recognize cognates.
Use courtesy titles and ways of address.
Use definite and indefinite articles.
Conjugate *-er* verbs and the verb *être* (to be).
Use negation *ne...pas.*
Use word sets referring to classroom objects and prepositions to describe locations.
Learn French numbers from 0–69.
Use several adjectives of personality to describe people.
Learn basic French sounds and intonation patterns.

Culture

French ways of greeting, *le français dans le monde,* French numbers, *la douce France,* Creoles and Acadians in Louisiana, and *formules de politesse.*

PRÉPARATION 1

Philippe est pressé

Philippe Boivin est pressé d'arriver au match de football de son équipe. En chemin il rencontre une voisine qui adore bavarder.

Mme Chenaud: Bonjour, Philippe!
Philippe: Bonjour, Madame. Comment allez-vous?
Mme Chenaud: Pas mal, merci, et toi?
Philippe: Très bien, merci. Excusez-moi, Madame. Je suis pressé. Je suis en retard. Au revoir, Madame.
Mme Chenaud: Au revoir, Philippe. Quel garçon impoli! Il est toujours pressé quand je lui parle.

Philippe is in a hurry

Philippe Boivin is in a hurry to get to his team's soccer game. On the way he meets a neighbor who loves to chat.

Hello, Philippe.
How do you do (good morning), Mrs. Chenaud. How are you?
Not bad, thanks. And you?
Very well, thank you. Excuse me, Mrs. Chenaud. I'm in a hurry. I'm late. Good-by.
Good-by, Philippe. What an impolite young man! He is always in a hurry when I talk to him.

This section (to be done in class) gives you the opportunity to use words and phrases in the dialogues and readings, to talk with your classmates, and to talk about yourself. Use lots of expression when you speak, and don't be afraid to experiment a little with what you know. Your instructor will help you. *Amusez-vous bien!* (Enjoy yourself!)

1. Greet your neighbor and ask how he/she is. Reply, and then say good-by.
2. With a partner, take the roles of Philippe and Mme Chenaud, but use your own names and genders. Refer to the dialogue, but do not read from it. Remember the context: you greet, ask how things are going, one of you says he/she is late, you say good-by, and the other complains about the impoliteness.
3. Greet your instructor, ask how things are going, and then excuse yourself and say good-by.

1. How to do a Préparation

A Préparation prepares you to participate actively in class. It provides information that you need to know in order to spend most of your class time using French actively. Cultural notes and photographs give you glimpses of the people and customs of the French-speaking world. (See also *Student text* and *To the student* in the Introduction.)

Each Préparation has several parts and each part is made up of numbered frames. In a typical frame, the first portion gives you information and asks you to supply an answer to a question. The second portion gives you the answer. You do not have to wait until the next class to find out if you were right.

Here is a sample frame, followed by an explanation of how to work with it.

1. The French word for *green* is *vert*. The name of a New England state is made up of two French words, and its nickname is *The Green Mountain State*. The name of the state is _____. |

Here is how you work with a *Préparation*.
Cover the page with a sheet of paper or a 5″ x 8″ card, and slide it down until you come to the mark | at the end of the final sentence of the frame. Read the frame as far as the mark |, then write the answer on a separate worksheet. Your answer to frame 1 would be:

1. Vermont

Slide the cover sheet down past the answer and check to see if your response was correct. Now try frames 2–4.

2. The names of many American cities contain the French word for *city*. Three examples are Charlottesville, Jacksonville, and Nashville. What is the French word for *city* in each of these names? |

    ville

3. Two of the Great Plains states have capitals with French names. What is the capital of Iowa? And the capital of South Dakota? |

    Des Moines; Pierre (*Pierre* is a common French name, equivalent to *Peter.*)

4. You've probably seen an expert baton twirler leading a parade. *Baton* comes from *bâton,* a French word meaning *stick.* The capital of Louisiana has a French name meaning *red stick.* What is the name? |

    Baton Rouge

If your answer to any frame was incorrect, draw a circle around it on your worksheet. This circle will tell you to look at the frame again when you have completed the Préparation. Now go to frame 5.

5. If *Baton Rouge* means *red stick,* then what is the French word for *red*? |

    rouge (It is believed that French settlers named the town after red cypress trees that formed a boundary between Indian tribes.)

Often additional information is given in parentheses after an answer, as in frame 5 above; you are not expected to supply it.

6. There are many French place names in Louisiana (named after Louis XIV) because French colonists were among the first people from Europe to settle there. Look at the map.

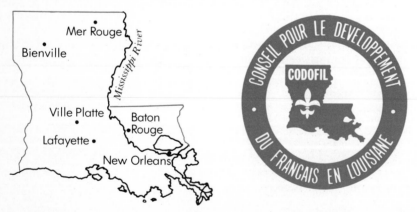

Comprenez-vous (do you understand) le logo?

Which famous Louisiana city is known for its jazz bands and its Mardi Gras festival? |

    New Orleans (Named after the city of Orléans. French street names and handsome wrought-iron balconies in the "old quarter" are attractive reminders of the French colonists.)

7. Which city has the same name as the French general who fought during the American Revolution? |
   Lafayette

How long it takes to do a Préparation depends on your particular abilities and needs as a language learner. If you take the time *you* need to do each assignment well, you will be well prepared for the next class. It is important that you do the Préparations regularly. If you fall behind in your work in a language course, it is very difficult to catch up. Your success depends on regular contact with the material.

2. Recognizing cognates

Many English words and most French words come in part from the same parent language—Latin—and thus many English and French words are related. Words that have the same parent word are called *cognates.*

Look at the relationship between the words below:

Latin:	spiritus	adventura
English:	spirit	adventure
French:	esprit	aventure

English and French cognates are often easy to recognize in print because their spelling is similar or identical, but they are harder to recognize in conversation because they do not sound alike in the two languages. If you can learn to recognize these related words, you can have thousands of French words "for free."

1. Compare these English and French words for fields of study.

geometry	*biology*	*geography*
la géométrie	la biologie	la géographie

a. The English words end in the letter _____; the French words end in the letters _____. |
   -y; -ie

b. What word appears with *géométrie, biologie,* and *géographie?* |
   la (The article *la* is one equivalent for *the.* The others are *le, l',* and *les,* and you will see them with other nouns in this section. French often uses an article where English does not. The article is part of the noun phrase and you must learn it when you learn a new noun.)

2. Many English words ending in -*y* have a French equivalent ending in -*ie.* Write the French words for *philosophy* and *astronomy,* with the articles: *la* _____, *l'* _____. |
   la philosophie, l'astronomie

À Paris. Jeune couple au Jardin du Luxembourg.

3. Look at the English and French names for these subjects.

music	*gymnastics*	*mathematics*
la musique	la gymnastique	les mathématiques

Many English words ending in *-ic* or *-ics* have French equivalents ending in _____ or _____. |
-ique, -iques

4. What is the French equivalent of *physics? la* _____ |
la physique (no *-s* in French)

5. Your study of French will be easier if you learn to recognize patterns in English and French spelling.
Note the spelling patterns in these pairs.

senator	*actor*	*doctor*
le sénateur	l'acteur	le docteur

Many English words ending in *-or* have French equivalents ending in _____. |
-eur

À Propos!

À *Propos!* means *appropriate* or *suitable*. It also means *by the way...*, implying a connection to the previous topic of conversation. These sections give you a chance to try your wings with new material you have just learned.

1. Read this sentence, then answer the questions.

Le cours de mythologie est fantastique!

What course is this student taking? What does she think of it?

2. Try this one.

Le directeur de la compagnie de matières plastiques est très sarcastique.

What is this man's job? What is his personality like?

3. Vocabulary recall

Alas, it takes time and effort to learn vocabulary in a foreign language, but you can't speak without it.
1. Spend a few minutes now looking at the vocabulary list on pp. 12-13. Look at the French, and look at the English equivalent.
2. Now cover the English, say the French aloud, and say or write the English equivalent.
3. Now write the complete English equivalent for the following.
Je suis en retard: *I am* _____.

Phase un

Au revoir: _____.

La chimie: _____.

J'aime assez la physique: *I like* _____. (*Assez = somewhat; well enough.*)

Merci beaucoup: _____.

De rien: _____.

4. To *recall* French words is a more difficult task than to recognize them when you see them. Go back to the list on p. 12 and cover the French. For each English expression, recall the French equivalent and say it aloud.

4. Accent marks and the cedilla

In written French, some letters have special marks that help to tell the reader how to pronounce them.

Accent aigu *(acute accent)*	Only on *e:* été
Accent grave *(grave accent)*	On *e:* algèbre
	On *a:* voilà
	On *u* only in the word *où*
Accent circonflexe *(circumflex accent)*	On all the vowels, usually as a sign that, in an earlier form of the word, an *s* used to follow the vowel:
	a: tâche *(task)*
	e: bête *(beast, animal)*
	i: île *(island)*
	o: hôte *(host)*
	u: août *(August)*
Cédille *(cedilla)*	Only on *c* followed by *a, o,* or *u* (it indicates that ç is pronounced like *s*): français, leçon

1. One word in each pair of school subjects below should have an accent or cedilla. Pick out that word and rewrite it correctly.

   Modèle: l'histoire, la geographie

   la géographie

   a. la musique, les mathematiques

   les mathématiques

   b. l'algebre, l'espagnol

   l'algèbre (Make sure your accent mark goes in the correct direction.)

   c. l'anglais, le francais

   le français

2. Copy these words and add the correct accent marks (two *accents aigus,* one *accent grave*): geometrie, algebre |

géométrie, algèbre

Accent marks on capital letters: In traditional French usage, acute and grave accent marks were rarely used on capital letters. In current French usage they may occur. In this text, they are used on capitals to help students learn spelling and to guide pronunciation.

As you write, adopt the habit of stopping at a letter which needs an accent and putting it on, rather than waiting until the end of the word. You will run less risk of forgetting the accent, which is an integral part of the spelling.

5. Ways to say "you": *tu* and *vous*

In every culture there are elaborate rules that govern how people are to interact. Often there are codified rules on how people are to speak to each other: lawyers address a judge in court as *Your honor,* diplomats have handbooks on how to address foreign dignitaries. In some cultures women use different forms of speech from men. Similarly, there are many features in the ordinary speech of any language which clearly mark different kinds of social and personal relationships. The president of a U.S. corporation, Mr. Peter R. Hollister, might address his secretary as Betty or Tom. She or he would generally not call the boss Pete or Peter but Mr. Hollister.

Some religious groups still use the old English forms *thou, thee,* and *ye* when speaking to members of their family and church, but use *you* when addressing strangers or people who are not members of their group.

In French, you have to choose between the pronouns *tu* and *vous* when you speak to someone. The choice depends on many conditions. Two important factors are the relationship between the speakers and their ages.

Vous is usually used:

With a person you don't know well.
To indicate respect (toward an older person who's not related to you, for instance).
In formal situations.

Tu is usually used:

By a child, a teenager, or students, in talking with a friend.
Between a child and a parent or relative.
By an adult speaking with a child, a close relative, or a close friend.
By anyone speaking to an animal.

10

Note Culturelle
French ways of greeting

In France, adults who are not close friends usually shake hands each time they meet and each time they say good-by. In business offices, people usually shake hands every morning and at the end of the day. Young people greet adults who are not relatives or close friends of the family with a handshake. The French handshake consists of a light, firm grasp with a slight upward stroke, then one downward stroke—unlike the American handshake, which often includes a vigorous pumping up and down. Most French students greet each other with a simple *bonjour* or *salut*. If they are good friends, they may kiss on both cheeks.

Philippe est pressé illustrates some differences in the way French and American people greet each other. In America, people use the family name after the courtesy title (*Mr., Ms.,* etc.): *Good morning, Mrs. Smith.* In France, however, the courtesy title is used alone: *Bonjour, Madame.*

In France, two adults who don't know each other very well always use courtesy titles. For instance, in a store the salesperson and the client would say *Bonjour, Madame.* In America, it is perfectly proper for a child to greet an adult by saying *Hi!* or *Hello!* In France, a child or a young adult greeting an older person who is not a relative is expected to use a courtesy title: *Bonjour, Mademoiselle.*

À St. Amont. L'ancien (former) président Valéry Giscard d'Estaing embrasse sa tante (aunt).

1. Use the information above to decide whether to use *tu* or *vous* in the following situations. Write *tu* or *vous* on your worksheet.

   a. You're speaking to the dean of a university. |
      vous

   b. You're talking with a classmate. |
      tu

   c. You're talking to your neighbor's dog Milou. |
      tu

   d. You're asking a policeman for directions. |
      vous

   e. A Christian is praying to God. (This one may catch you!) |
      tu (In most cultures, people feel very close to their God. In English, the Lord's Prayer addresses God in the familiar form: *Thou art, Thy will be done,* etc.)

   f. A man is very angry at a motorist who is blocking traffic. He wants to insult him. |
      tu (Using *tu* to an adult stranger suggests that he is inferior.)

2. If you were a student in France, how would you ask *Do you like math?* of your classmate Paul? *Vous aimez les maths?* or *Tu aimes les maths?* |
   Tu aimes les maths?

À Propos!

Think of five friends and acquaintances and write their names. Would you address them with *tu* or with *vous* in a French context?

Vocabulaire

At the end of many Préparations, you will find a list of some of the French words and expressions you have used or will use in class or in the Préparation. It is important for you to spend a few minutes each day studying new words and expressions. Be sure to learn the articles along with nouns. When *l'* is used, *m.* and *f.* indicate gender.

Noms
l'équipe *f.*   team
le football   *soccer*
le garçon   *boy*
le match   *game*
le voisin/la voisine   *neighbor*

Les cours
l'algèbre *m.*   *algebra*
l'anglais *m.*   *English*
l'anthropologie *f.*   *anthropology*
la biologie   *biology*
la chimie   *chemistry*
l'espagnol *m.*   *Spanish*
le français   *French*
la géographie   *geography*
la géométrie   *geometry*

STAGE D'ÉTÉ juillet
COURS INTENSIFS
ANGLAIS   CÉRAMIQUE
PHOTOGRAPHIE
PEINTURE
SCULPTURE
MUSIQUE   DANSE
CUISINE
SÉRIGRAPHIE
PARIS
AMERICAN
ACADEMY
9, rue des Ursulines, 75005
Tél. : 325.35.09 - 325.08.91

la gymnastique   *physical education*
l'histoire *f.*   *history*
l'italien *m.*   *Italian*
les mathématiques *f.pl.*   *mathematics*
la musique   *music*
la physique   *physics*
les sciences économiques *f.pl.*   *economics*
les sciences naturelles *f.pl.*   *natural sciences*
les sciences politiques *f.pl.*   *political science*

Adjectifs
impoli/e   *impolite*
pressé/e   *in a hurry*

Salutations
à demain   *see you tomorrow*
au revoir   *good-by*
bonjour   *hello, good morning, good afternoon*
bonsoir   *good evening*
comment allez-vous?/comment vas-tu?   *how are you?*
comment ça va?   *how is it going?*
je vais bien, et vous/toi?   *I'm fine, and you?*
pas mal   *not bad; pretty good*
salut   *hi, hello (informal)*

Expressions de politesse
avec plaisir   *with pleasure*
de rien   *you're welcome; not at all*
excusez-moi   *excuse me*
madame (Mme)   *ma'am; Mrs.*
mademoiselle (Mlle)   *Miss*
monsieur (M.)   *Mr.*
merci   *thanks; thank you*
merci beaucoup   *thanks a lot*
s'il vous plaît/s'il te plaît   *please*

Expressions employées en classe
je m'appelle   *my name is*
il s'appelle   *his name is*
elle s'appelle   *her name is*
comment vous appelez-vous?/comment t'appelles-tu?   *what is your name?*
et lui?   *and he?*
et elle?   *and she?*
et vous?   *and you?*

Autres mots et expressions
beaucoup   *a lot; very much*
bien sûr!   *of course! naturally!*
en retard   *late*
toujours   *always*
très   *very*
un peu   *a little*

PRÉPARATION 2

Une Rencontre

Philippe rencontre un autre étudiant à une boum à Ivry.

Philippe: Bonjour!
Jean: Salut!
Philippe: Tu es d'Ivry, toi aussi?
Jean: Non, je suis de Versailles. Je m'appelle Jean Dupont.
Philippe: Moi, je suis Philippe Boivin. Dis, tu connais ces deux filles là-bas? Elles ne sont pas mal, hein?
Jean: Ce sont des amies de mon camarade de chambre. La blonde est en lettres; la brune fait son droit, je crois.
Philippe: Elles sont chouettes. On va dire bonjour?
Jean: D'accord.

A Meeting

Philippe meets another student at a party in Ivry (a city close to Paris).

Hello!
Hi!
Are you from Ivry, too?
No, I'm from Versailles. My name is Jean Dupont.
I'm Philippe Boivin. Say, do you know those two girls over there? They're not bad, eh?

They're friends of my roommate. The blond one is in liberal arts and the brunette is studying law, I think.
They're pretty nice. Shall we say hello?

O.K.

Échange d'idées

The English version of a dialogue does not give a word-by-word translation, but an equivalent thought in idiomatic English. For example, *Je m'appelle Jean = I'm Jean* or *My name is Jean.*

1. Greet your partner, tell your name, and where you're from. Find out where your partner is from.
2. Find out if your partner knows two other classmates you point out. Ask if you should both go say hello.
3. Ask your partner what some of the people in the class are studying. Use *en lettres, en maths, en sciences, en sciences po.*

1. More on *tu* and *vous*

1. In Préparation 1, you learned that the choice between *tu* and *vous* depends on a number of conditions. Would the people in these situations use *tu* or *vous* to speak to you?

14   Phase un

a. You are a young adult and you work as a sales clerk in a bakery. Someone your own age whom you don't know comes in and asks you for some pastry. |

> vous (Store employees address customers with *vous* and vice versa.)

b. A student meets you at a campus party. |

> tu (You're both young, and students.)

c. You've won a national science contest, and the director is about to give you an award before a large audience. |

> vous (He doesn't know you well, and the situation is a formal one.)

2. So far, the situations have involved the speaker and only one other person. What about this sentence? *Philippe et Marie, vous êtes en retard aujourd'hui.* Is *vous* used to speak to one person, or to more than one? |

> more than one

3. In French, when you speak to more than one person, you always use *vous*. It doesn't matter what your relationship is to them. Would you use *tu* or *vous* in the following situations?

a. You ask your mother and father if they will let you borrow the car. |

> vous

b. You ask your mother whether she will let you borrow the family car. |

> tu (although in some families of the upper middle class and the aristocracy children may address their parents with *vous*)

4. Students automatically use *tu* with each other. With other adults, however, it may be difficult to tell if you know someone well enough to use *tu*. Should you use *tu* or *vous* in a doubtful case? |

> vous (It is better to use *vous* than to risk offending someone by using *tu*.)

À Paris. Renseignements (directions) à un motocycliste.

2. The indefinite articles *un* and *une*

1. A word that refers to a person, a place, a thing, or a concept or idea is called a noun. Look at the list below and write the nouns.

man   sing   restaurant   my   enter   tree   liberty |

> man, restaurant, tree, liberty (*Man* refers to a person, *restaurant* to a place, *tree* to a thing, and *liberty* to a concept.)

2. If you use certain words in front of a noun, you give different kinds of information. For example:

It's a shoe.   (You identify the shoe as belonging to a group of things known as shoes.)

It's the shoe.   (You're talking about a shoe that you have referred to before.)

It's my shoe.   (You're talking about a shoe that belongs to you.)

The words *a* and *the* belong to a group of words called *articles* (sometimes also called *markers* or *determiners*).

Which words below can be used to complete *It's _____ apple?*

slowly   an   his   bread   this   the   run |

an, his, this, the (These are all determiners.)

3. In English, the singular indefinite articles are *a* and *an*. The choice of *a* or *an* depends on whether the noun begins with a vowel *(a, e, i, o,* or *u)* or a consonant *(b, c, d,* etc.). Which article goes with each noun here—*a* or *an?*

car   apple   woman   adult |

a car, an apple, a woman, an adult

4. All nouns in French are either masculine or feminine, whether they refer to people or to things. (When words are referred to as being masculine or feminine, they are said to have *gender.*) In French there are two singular indefinite articles: *un* and *une. Un* is masculine, *une* is feminine.

Would you use *un* or *une* if you were talking about the following people in French? (Answers appear at right.)

a. an uncle |

b. a sister |

c. a policeman |

d. a female flight attendant |

a. un

b. une

c. un

d. une

5. a. What determines the choice of *un* or *une?*

   (a)   Whether the noun begins with a consonant or vowel.
   (b)   Whether the noun is masculine or feminine in gender. |

   (b)

   b. Is *un crayon* a masculine noun or a feminine noun? |

   masculine (*Un* tells you the noun is masculine.)

6. In French, there is no simple way to tell whether a noun is masculine or feminine. Therefore, it is very important to learn the article when you learn the noun. Spend a few moments reviewing the names of useful objects in the list on p. 22.

7. Now identify each picture you see on p. 17 by writing the correct indefinite article and noun.

   Modèle: u _ l _____ |

   un livre

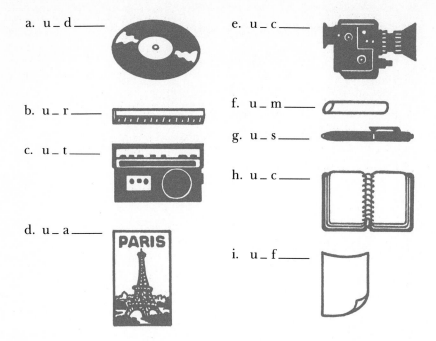

a. u _ d _____

b. u _ r _____

c. u _ t _____

d. u _ a _____

e. u _ c _____

f. u _ m _____

g. u _ s _____

h. u _ c _____

i. u _ f _____

a. un disque   b. une règle   c. un transistor   d. une affiche   e. une caméra
f. un morceau de craie   g. un stylo à bille   h. un cahier   i. une feuille de papier

Indefinite articles

un   **un** disque, **un** écran   a record, a screen
une **une** affiche, **une** gomme   a poster, an eraser

3. Subject pronouns and *être* (to be)

1. What is the English equivalent of each sentence?
   a. Je suis Philippe Boivin. |
      I'm (I am) Philippe Boivin.
   b. Tu es de Versailles? |
      You're from Versailles? (Are you from Versailles?)
   c. Vous êtes pressé aujourd'hui! |
      You're (You are) in a hurry today!

2. In English, the words *I* and *you* are subject pronouns. The words *am* and *are* are verb forms. A verb form must "match" or go with the right subject pronoun. This matching is called agreement.

Some forms of être (to be)

je **suis**   I am
tu **es**   you are (familiar)
vous **êtes**   you are (formal; plural)

Write the verb form that agrees with each subject pronoun.

a. vous |

      êtes (Remember the *accent circonflexe.*)

b. je |

      suis

c. tu |

      es

3. Write complete French equivalents for each sentence.
   a. I am from Versailles.   _____ de Versailles. |

       Je *suis* de Versailles.

   b. You *(vous)* are late today!   _____ en retard aujourd'hui! |

       Vous *êtes* (remember the *accent circonflexe*) en retard aujourd'hui!

   c. You're *(tu)* from San Francisco?   _____ de San Francisco? |

       Tu *es* de San Francisco?

   d. You're Paul and Jean Dupont?   _____ Paul et Jean Dupont? |

       Vous *êtes* Paul et Jean Dupont?

4. Refer to the chart below.

More forms of être

il **est**   he/it is
elle **est**   she/it is
ils **sont**   they are (masculine; mixed)
elles **sont**   they are (feminine)

   a. Do both *il* and *elle* and *he* and *she* tell you whether the person referred to is male or female? |

       yes

   b. Do *ils* and *elles* tell you whether the people are male or female? |

       yes

   c. Does *they* tell you whether the people are male or female? |

       no

5. Now look at this pair of sentences.

   Georges et Marie sont en retard. Ils sont en retard.

a. In this case, does *ils* refer to two males or to a male and a female? |

> a male and a female (*Ils* can refer to males only, or to a mixed group of males and females.)

b. Suppose a friend is waiting for some people, and he/she says *Ils sont en retard aujourd'hui.* Does the word *ils* give you enough information to tell if there are women in the group? |

> no (You would need to hear the names of the people, or be able to see them.)

6. Write the subject pronoun that would replace each name: *il, elle, ils,* or *elles.*

a. Madame Chenaud | a. elle
b. Jean Dupont | b. il
c. Beatrice et Florence | c. elles
d. Guy, Henri et Nathalie | d. ils
e. Monsieur Fleury | e. il
f. Jeanne, Sylvie, Suzanne et Laurent | f. ils

À Propos!

Say that you are late today. Say what town or city you are from. Be prepared to ask your classmate if he/she is from your town.

4. The present tense of *être* (to be)

Être is one of the most useful and most frequently used verbs in French. Use the chart of subject pronouns with present-tense forms of *être* to help you do frames 1 and 2. Check your spelling carefully.

je	**suis**	nous	**sommes**
tu	**es**	vous	**êtes**
il/elle	**est**	ils/elles	**sont**

1. Write the subject pronouns with the matching verb forms. Some verb forms agree with more than one subject pronoun.

   Modèle: est |

   > il est, elle est

   a. êtes |

   > vous êtes (Remember the *accent circonflexe*.)

   b. est |

   > il est, elle est

   c. sommes |

   > nous sommes

d. es |

        tu es

e. sont |

        ils sont, elles sont

f. suis |

        je suis (Unlike English *I*, *je* is not capitalized unless it is the first word in a sentence.)

2. Write an English equivalent for each sentence.
   a. Nous sommes d'Ivry. |

        We're from Ivry.

   b. Vous êtes monsieur Chardin? |

        You're Mr. Chardin?/Are you Mr. Chardin?

   c. Tu es très en retard! |

        You're very late!

   d. Je suis très pressé! |

        I'm really in a hurry!

3. Write complete sentences with *être* to say where the people below come from, whether they are late, in a hurry, or who they are. (When no answers appear on the page, check your work with the answer key at the end of the book.)
   Modèle: Pierre/pressé aujourd'hui. |

        Pierre est pressé aujourd'hui.

   a. Jeanne/de Chicago   d. Jeanne et Paul Dupont/d'Ivry
   b. Nous/d'Ivry   e. Vous/monsieur Chardin?
   c. Tu/très en retard!   f. Je/très pressé!

À Propos!

Correct these false assumptions. Begin your reply with *Non* followed by a positive statement.

1. Vous êtes français? (Non, je suis américain.)
2. Vous êtes de Versailles?
3. Vous êtes Jeanne Dupont?

5. Vocabulary recall

Spend a couple of minutes looking at the adjectives of nationality on p. 23 and saying them with the tape, if available. Many are cognates; use the resemblance to English to remind you of the French word.

Most French adjectives have a masculine form and a feminine form. In the list, the order is *masculine, feminine: américain, américaine.* Complete the French equivalent and indicate its gender with *m.* or *f.*

    Modèle: American: _____aine |

        américaine *f.* (Remember: small initial letter and accent marks.)

1. French: _____ ais
2. Portuguese: _____ aise
3. Canadian: _____ ien
4. Swiss: _____ e
5. German: _____ ande
6. Japanese: _____ aise

1. français *m.*
2. portugaise *f.*
3. canadien *m.*
4. suisse *m.* and *f.*
5. allemande *f.*
6. japonaise *f.*

Note Culturelle

Le français dans le monde

The French language is spoken by millions of people throughout the world. Its official status, however, is changing in some countries. In the former French colonies of Vietnam, Cambodia, and Algeria, for example, the use of French as an essential second language is gradually disappearing. On the other hand, in the former French territories of Morocco, Tunisia, and Senegal, French retains its importance because of commerce and tourism, or because it continues to serve as the official language in a country whose inhabitants speak many dialects. In the Canadian province of Quebec, the spirit of nationalism is prompting the use of French in government and commerce.

Traditionally, France's beauty and its vigorous artistic and intellectual life have attracted intellectuals, artists, and students from many nations. Among them were American statesmen like Benjamin Franklin and Thomas Jefferson, who said *Chaque homme a deux pays, le sien et la France* (Every man has two countries, his own and France); American writers, like Ernest Hemingway and James Baldwin; and musicians, like the American composer Aaron Copland. France has also opened its doors to refugees and foreign workers. Since the beginning of the 20th century, France has taken in more foreigners than any other European country. Roughly 35,000 foreigners are naturalized every year.

The French and English languages are constantly exerting their influence on each other. English has adopted French words from such fields as fashion and cosmetics: *lingerie, rouge, eau de cologne;* food and cooking: *restaurant, menu, cuisine, à la carte;* art, music, and dance: *aquarelle, collage, prelude, pas de deux.* Similarly, in modern times French has adopted from America words such as: *le jean, le rock, le marketing, le drugstore.*

Note Linguistique

The sounds of French: consonants

When you hear any foreign language, you are probably struck by the strangeness of its sounds. You may wonder if you would ever be able to duplicate them. Of course you can! You can duplicate any human sound, just as you did when you were a baby learning your mother tongue. What stands in the way now that you are an adult is the training your speech organs have had for many years in making the sounds of English. You have to learn to use your lips, tongue, gums, vocal cords, and even your nasal passages in slightly different ways; and you must listen carefully, imitate, and practice.

A note: Symbols from the International Phonetic Alphabet (IPA) are used to refer to the sounds of French. The IPA provides one symbol for a sound, no matter how many ways it may be spelled. For instance, the letter c in cat, q in queen, k in kid all represent the sound /k/. The IPA was devised in France at the turn of the century to improve the teaching of English by sorting out dis-crepancies between spelling and actual pronunciation.

These consonants are identical in both languages:

	English	French
/f/	foe	faux
/g/	garage	garage
/m/	mud	mode
/n/	no	non
/s/	salt	sel
/v/	vigor	vigueur
/z/	bizarre	bizarre

These consonants have an additional degree of tenseness in French that is not obvious to a beginning learner.

	English	French
/b/	bed	bête
/d/	dough	dos
/k/	cash	cache
/p/	pale	pâle
/t/	tea	thé
/l/	bell	belle

Vocabulaire

Objets utiles

une affiche   poster
une bande   tape
un cahier   notebook
une caméra   movie camera
une cassette   cassette
un crayon   pencil
un disque   record
un écran   screen
une feuille de papier   sheet of paper
une gomme   eraser
un livre   book
un morceau de craie   piece of chalk
une règle   ruler
un stylo (à bille)   (ballpoint) pen

un transistor   radio

Noms

un ami/une amie   friend
un blond/une blonde   blond man/woman
un brun/une brune   brown-haired man/woman
un/une camarade de chambre   roommate
un étudiant/une étudiante   student
une fille   girl
une boum   party (for young people)
une rencontre   meeting, encounter

C'est un dollar
américain?

Adjectifs de nationalité

allemand/e   *German*
américain/e   *American*
anglais/e   *English*
canadien/ne   *Canadian*
français/e   *French*
japonais/e   *Japanese*
portugais/e   *Portuguese*
suisse   *Swiss*

Adjectifs

autre   *other*
blond/e   *blond*
brun/e   *brown, brown-haired*
capitaliste   *capitalist*
chic   *chic*
chouette   *great, nice*
communiste   *communist*
difficile   *difficult*
formidable   *wonderful, great*
gentil, gentille   *nice, kind*
idéaliste   *idealist*
intelligent/e   *intelligent*
intéressant/e   *interesting*
optimiste   *optimistic*
pessimiste   *pessimistic*
réaliste   *realistic*
socialiste   *socialist*

Verbes

j'aime   *I like*
je n' aime pas   *I don't like*
être (de)   *to be (from)*
être en lettres   *to be in Liberal Arts*
tu connais   *you know*
je crois   *I believe, I think*
je déteste   *I hate*
vous détestez   *you hate*
dis,...   *say,...*
j'étudie   *I study*
je n'étudie pas   *I don't study*
vous étudiez   *you study*

Expressions utilisées en classe

c'est (Valérie)   *it's (Valérie)*
c'est un (livre)   *it's a (book)*
ce n'est pas (Hugues)   *it's not (Hugues)*
ce n'est pas une (règle)   *it's not a (ruler)*
demandez-moi si   *ask me if*
je ne comprends pas   *I don't understand*
je ne sais pas   *I don't know*
où est... ?   *where is... ?*
présent, présente   *present*
qu'est-ce que c'est?   *what is it?*
qui est-ce?   *who is it?*
répétez, s'il vous plaît   *please repeat*

Autres mots et expressions

aujourd'hui   *today*
aussi   *too*
ça va? ça va bien?   *How's it going?*
d'accord   *O.K.*
droit: je fais mon~   *I study law;*
   il/elle fait son~   *he/she studies law*
là-bas   *over there*
pas mal   *not bad, pretty good*
très bien   *very well*
un autre, une autre   *another*

Articles et pronoms

elles/ils   *they*
le, la, l', les   *the*
nous   *we*
vous   *you*
un, une   *a, an*

Prépositions

à côté de   *beside, near*
derrière   *behind*
devant   *in front of*
entre   *between*
près de   *close to, near*

PRÉPARATION 3

Qu'est-ce que c'est?

What is that?

Martine est en train d'ouvrir un cadeau que Pierre vient de lui offrir.

Martine is opening a present that Pierre has just given her.

Martine: Qu'est-ce que c'est?

Pierre: C'est une surprise!

Martine: Pour moi?

Pierre: Mais oui, bien sûr!

Martine: Tiens! C'est une cassette de Gilles Vigneault. Comme tu es gentil! On va l'écouter tout de suite... Oh, zut!

Pierre: Quoi? Qu'est-ce qu'il y a?

Martine: Le magnétophone ne marche pas.

Pierre: Fais voir. Humm... Je ne comprends pas.

Martine: Attends, j'ai une idée. Donne-le-moi.

Pierre: Une fille qui connait la mécanique? Quelle blague!

Martine: Une blague, hein? Tiens, regarde. La cassette est mal placée. Tu vois, ça marche maintenant! Alors, les filles et la mécanique? Pas si mal, hein?

Pierre: Mille excuses, Mademoiselle l'ingénieur!

What is it?

It's a surprise!

For me?

Yes, of course!

Look! It's a cassette by Gilles Vigneault. How sweet of you! We're going to listen to it right away... Oh, darn!

What? What's the matter?

The recorder doesn't work.

Let me see... I don't understand.

Wait, I have an idea. Give it to me.

A girl who knows about machinery? That's a laugh (What a joke)!

A laugh, huh? Take a look. The cassette isn't in right. See, it's working now! So what about girls and machinery? Not so bad, huh?

A thousand pardons, Madam Engineer!

Échange d'idées

The abbreviations S1 and S2 stand for *student 1* and *student 2*. They indicate that you work with a partner.

1. S1: On a piece of paper, write the name of a record, and fold the paper.

   S2: Respond. Open the paper and express pleasure or displeasure. Be polite or sarcastic.

2. (S2: Have some mechanical object in mind.)

   S1: You see that your partner is having trouble with an object. Ask what's wrong.

S2: Tell what's not working.

S1: Ask to see the object. Either say it's working now, or admit you don't understand.

S2: Respond by expressing pleasure or sarcasm.

1. Identifying things and people

1. Refer to the chart to answer frames 1–4.

Things	People
Qu'est-ce que c'est?	**Qui est-ce?**
C'est une boîte.	C'est Brigitte.
Ce n'est pas une étagère.	Ce n'est pas Christine.

   a. Which question means *Who is it?* |

         Qui est-ce? (Remember to put the hyphen in *est-ce*.)

   b. Write the French for *What is it?* |

         Qu'est-ce que c'est? (It's tricky; check your spelling!)

2. Ask someone to identify the following for you. Use *Qui est-ce?* and *Qu'est-ce que c'est?* to ask your question.

   a. a new kind of airplane   d. a container to put things in
   b. your new math professor   e. your friend's lab partner |
   c. a place to put books

         a. Qu'est-ce que c'est?   b. Qui est-ce?   c. Qu'est-ce que c'est?   d. Qu'est-ce que c'est?   e. Qui est-ce?

3. Answer the questions with the information in parentheses. Use *un* or *une* when appropriate.

   a. Qu'est-ce que c'est? (cassette) |

         C'est une cassette.

   b. Qui est-ce? (Brigitte) |

         C'est Brigitte.

   c. Qu'est-ce que c'est? (crayon) |

         C'est un crayon.

4. Write the negative of c'est. |

         ce n'est pas (The French equivalent of *not* has two parts: *n'* and *pas.*)

5. Contradict these statements.

   a. C'est Sylvie. |

         Ce n'est pas Sylvie.

   b. C'est un tableau. |

         Ce n'est pas un tableau.

6. Answer each question below with *ce n'est pas* and tell what the pictured item is.

    Modèle: C'est une règle? |

        Non, ce n'est pas une règle, c'est un disque.

  a. C'est un transistor, n'est-ce pas? |

        Non, ce n'est pas un transistor, c'est une caméra.

  b. C'est une chaise? |

        Non, ce n'est pas une chaise, c'est une table.

  c. C'est une Peugeot, n'est-ce pas? |

        Non, ce n'est pas une Peugeot, c'est une Renault.

  d. C'est une feuille de papier? |

        Non, ce n'est pas une feuille de papier, c'est un morceau de craie.

  e. C'est une fenêtre ou *(or)* une boîte? |

        Ce n'est pas une boîte. C'est une fenêtre.

2. Vocabulary Review: Classroom objects

Identify the items you see. If you can't remember the names or the spelling of some words, review the *vocabulaire* on p. 22. (See key.)

    Modèle: |

        C'est une affiche.

1.    2.    3.   4.   5.

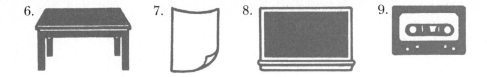

6. 7. 8. 9.

3. More about subject pronouns

In any conversation, there is a speaker, a person spoken to, and often a person or thing spoken about. Speakers use a different pronoun to refer to each person.

1. Read the following exchanges, and then answer the questions.

> *John:* Are you early? *Mary (with Jack):* Are we late?
> *Susan:* Yes, I am. *Alex:* Yes, you are.

a. John uses *you* in his question. Susan replies with the pronoun

———. |

b. Mary uses *we* in her question. Alex replies with the pronoun

———. |

> you (In English, you hardly have to think about changing pronouns and verb forms when you respond to a question. To speak French with ease, you must practice shifting pronoun and verb forms until the procedure becomes automatic.)

	Singular	Plural
Person speaking (1st person)	je I	nous we
Person spoken to (2nd person)	tu/vous you	vous you
Person spoken about (3rd person)	il/elle he/she/it	ils/elles they

2. Identify the subject pronoun in each sentence as the person speaking, the person spoken to, or the person or thing spoken about.
   a. Je suis en retard. | a. person speaking
   b. Tu es gentil. | b. person spoken to
   c. Il est d'Ivry? | c. person spoken about
   d. La gomme? Elle est sur le bureau. | d. thing spoken about
3. Write the English meaning of *La gomme? Elle est sur le bureau.* |

> The eraser? It's on the desk. (When *il* or *elle* refers to a thing, the English equivalent is *it*.)

4. Write the complete answer to this question, and begin with *Oui . . .*: *Tu es en retard, Philippe?* |

5. Choose the correct answer to each question below. Say the English equivalents of your answers.

    Modèle: Je suis en retard, Irène? — Oui, je suis en retard.
                                — Oui, tu es en retard. |

  a. Marc et Suzanne, vous êtes en retard? — Oui, nous sommes en retard.
                                       — Oui, vous êtes en retard. |

  b. Je suis en retard, Mme Longe? — Oui, je suis en retard.
                                   — Oui, vous êtes en retard. |

  c. Nous sommes en retard, Sophie? — Oui, je suis en retard.
                                   — Oui, vous êtes en retard. |

4. Vocabulary recall: *Qu'est-ce que c'est?*

Check your answers against the dialogue on p. 24.
1. *Ask a friend if what she is holding is a present.* C'est ____?
2. *Ask if it's for you.* C'est ____ moi?
3. *Explain that it's a cassette. Say how nice your friend is.*
    Ah, c'est ____! ____ tu es ____.
4. *Exclaim to show that you're frustrated.* ____!
5. *Your friend asks you what's wrong.* ____ il y a?
6. *Explain that the tape recorder isn't working.* ____ marche pas.
7. *Get your friend's attention.* ____, regarde.
8. *Say that it's working now.* Ça marche ____.

5. Practice with *être*

1. Use the correct form of *être* to make complete sentences. (See key.)
  a. Marie/une fille.
  b. Nous/derrière Marc.
  c. Tu/pressé.
  d. Robert et Marie/de New York.
  e. Je/Stéphanie Romain.
  f. Vous/en retard!

2. If you make any mistakes, go back to Préparation 2, Part 4, and spend a few minutes reviewing. Then complete these sentences with the correct form of *être*. (See key.)

a. Je _____ de Paris.
b. Vous _____ devant le tableau.
c. Où _____ le crayon d'Alice?
d. Nous _____ en retard aujourd'hui.
e. La bande et le livre _____ là.
f. Tu _____ de Chicago?

6. The numbers 0 to 32

Here are the written forms of the numbers 0 to 10 in French.

0 zéro	1 un	3 trois	5 cinq	7 sept	9 neuf
	2 deux	4 quatre	6 six	8 huit	10 dix

1. Some simple addition problems will help you practice the numbers. Write the missing work, then write the equation in numerals. *Font,* which rhymes with *sont,* means *makes* or *equals.*

   Modèle: Un et un font _____. |
      deux 1 + 1 = 2

   a. Deux et quatre font _____. |
   b. Quatre et _____ font sept. |
   c. Un et huit font _____. |
   d. Trois et _____ font cinq. |
   e. Quatre et _____ font quatre. |
   f. Neuf et _____ font dix. |

   a. six 2 + 4 = 6
   b. trois 4 + 3 = 7
   c. neuf 1 + 8 = 9
   d. deux 3 + 2 = 5
   e. zéro 4 + 0 = 4
   f. un 9 + 1 = 10

2. Read aloud each equation on your worksheet.
3. Read these numbers aloud or repeat with the tape.

11 onze	16 seize	20 vingt	25 vingt-cinq	30 trente
12 douze	17 dix-sept	21 vingt et un	26 vingt-six	31 trente et un
13 treize	18 dix-huit	22 vingt-deux	27 vingt-sept	32 trente-deux
14 quatorze	19 dix-neuf	23 vingt-trois	28 vingt-huit	etc.
15 quinze		24 vingt-quatre	29 vingt-neuf	

4. Write out the following equations in numbers. *Et* stands for $+$, *moins* for $-$.

   a. Huit et six font quatorze. |
      $8 + 6 = 14$
   b. Onze et quatorze font vingt-cinq. |
      $11 + 14 = 25$
   c. Trente et un moins dix font vingt et un. |
      $31 - 10 = 21$
   d. Vingt-sept moins onze font seize. |
      $27 - 11 = 16$

Confirm or correct the accuracy of the arithmetic.
1. Dix et onze font trente et un.
2. Vingt-cinq moins dix font quinze.

Note Culturelle
French numbers

The number seven was originally written *7* , to show seven angles. This came from the Arabic practice of writing a figure that showed the same number of angles as the number itself. Part of this symbol remains as the French *sept*: *7* . The French write the number *un* as *1* , and often interpret an American 7 as the number one. Here are the numbers 0 through 9 as a French person would write them. Which ones are different from the way you write?

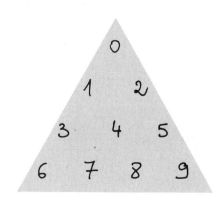

Note Linguistique
The sounds of French: oral vowels

French vowels have only one sound, very clear and precise. This contrasts with the English tendency toward diphthongs, or a glide between two sounds, like *ay* and *ee* in *day*.

	English	*French*
/i/	Lee	*lit*
/e/	baby	*bébé*
/ɛ/	bet	*bête*
/a/	cat	*chat*
/ɔ/	Paul	*Paul*
/o/	dough	*dos*
/u/	do	*doux*
/œ/	lull	*seul*

The schwa /ə/ as in *le, je te,* is often called *mute e.* It is a much more definite sound than English schwa. Keep lips rounded as you say it.

/ə/	*petit*	*donne-le-moi*
	regardez	*le disque*

At normal conversational speed, mute e often disappears entirely. Listen for and imitate patterns like these:

Je n'sais pas.   J'suis d'Versailles.
C'n'est pas.   Voilà l'disque.

Vocabulaire

Noms

la blague *joke;*
   quelle ~! *what a joke!*
la boîte *box*
le bureau *desk*
le cadeau *present*
le/la camarade *classmate*
la chaise *chair*
le crayon-feutre *felt-tip pen*
l'élève *f./m. pupil*
l'enfant *m./f. child*
l'étagère *f. shelf*
la femme *woman*
la fenêtre *window*
l'homme *m. man*
l'idée *f. idea*
l'ingénieur *m. engineer*
le lycéen/la lycéenne *high school student*
le magnétophone *tape recorder*
la mécanique *mechanics, machinery*
le singe *monkey*
la surprise *surprise*
la table *table*
le tableau *chalkboard*
la télévision *television*
le tiroir *drawer*

Adjectifs

égoïste *selfish*

Verbes

attends *wait*
ça marche *it's working*
chercher *to look for*
écoutez et répétez *listen and repeat*
fais voir *let me see*
font *equals*
tu vois *you see*

Expressions employées en classe

comment dit-on... en français? *how do you say... in French?*
demandez à... *ask...*
dîtes à... *say to...*
écoutez et regardez *listen and look*
maintenant, tout le monde *now, everybody*
que veut dire... en anglais? *what does... mean in English?*

Autres mots et expressions

alors *so*
assez *enough*
comme tu es gentil! *How nice you are!*
dans *in*
mais *but*
moi, je... *I (emphatic)*
pas du tout *not at all*
pour *for*
qu'est-ce qu'il y a? *what's the matter?*
qu'est-ce que c'est? *what is that?*
quoi? *what?*
sous *under*
sur *on*
tiens! *look*
toi, tu... *you (emphatic)*
tout de suite *right away*
zut! *darn!*

Nombres 0–31

zéro *0*
un *1*
deux *2*
trois *3*
quatre *4*
cinq *5*
six *6*
sept *7*
huit *8*
neuf *9*
dix *10*
onze *11*
douze *12*
treize *13*
quatorze *14*
quinze *15*
seize *16*
dix-sept *17*
dix-huit *18*
dix-neuf *19*
vingt *20*
vingt et un *21*
vingt-deux *22*
trente *30*
trente et un *31*
trente-deux *32*

PRÉPARATION 4

Où est le disque?

Irène entre dans le salon et voit son frère
Charles en train de chercher quelque chose.
Charles est très agité.

Charles: Zut, zut et zut!
Irène: Qu'est-ce qu'il y a? Qu'est-ce que tu
  cherches?
Charles: Le disque de Paul. Je ne sais pas où
  il est.
Irène: Oh toi, tu perds tout! Tu ne sais pas
  où tu as la tête!
Charles: Oh, ça va, tais-toi et aide-moi à
  chercher le disque.

Where is the record?

Irene walks into the living room and sees
her brother Charles looking for something.
He is very upset.

Darn, darn, darn!
What's the matter? What are you looking
  for?
Paul's record. I don't know where it is.

Oh, you, you lose everything. You don't
  even know where your head is!
Oh, that's enough, be quiet and help me
  look for the record.

Irène: Mon dieu, que tu es bête! Regarde sur la télévision!

My goodness, you're so stupid! Look on top of the T.V.

Charles: Ah, ça alors! Voilà le disque! Pas possible.

Oh, good grief! There's the record. Unbelievable!

Échange d'idées

1. With a partner, act out the dialogue. Choose a different lost object, and a different location for it. Refer to the dialogue, but do not read it aloud. Recall what you want to say, thought by thought.

   S1: You express frustration.
   S2: You ask what's wrong, what your partner is looking for.
   S1: You tell what you're looking for.
   S2: You express your frustration at your partner's absent-mindedness.
   S1: You tell your partner to be quiet and help you look.
   S2: You say your partner is stupid, and tell him/her where to look.
   S1: You express your frustration and disbelief.

2. With a partner, imagine you have lost track of your little sister at a big party. Use elements from the dialogue to express your frustration, ask for help, and eventually find her.

1. The definite articles *le, la, l'*

1. The *indefinite* article often identifies an item for the listener. The *definite* article often talks about an item that has already been identified or mentioned.
   Write English equivalents: *C'est un magnétophone. Le magnétophone ne marche pas.* |

   This (It) is a tape recorder. The tape recorder doesn't work.

2. Refer to the chart.

Singular definite articles

Masculine	le garçon, le cadeau, l'écran
Feminine	la fille, la table, l'affiche

   a. Which article goes with *garçon: le* or *la?* |

   le (*Le* is used with a masculine singular noun.)

   b. Does *la* go with a masculine or a feminine noun? |

   a feminine noun

c. The nouns *écran* and *affiche* begin with what kind of sound—
vowel or consonant? |

> vowel (*Le* and *la* drop their vowels when they occur before a noun beginning with a
> vowel sound. The French name for this is *élision*.)

d. Can you tell by looking at the article *l'* if the noun is masculine
or feminine? |

> No (*L'* goes with any singular noun that begins with a vowel sound.)

3. The letter *h* is always silent in French. In the French word *homme*,
the first sound you hear is a vowel sound. Is the article *le* or *l'*
used with *homme*? |

> *l'* (Most nouns beginning with *h* use *l'*. There are some exceptions such as *le héros*,
> hero.)

4. Rewrite each noun with the correct article: *le, la,* or *l'.*

a. une table | a. la table
b. un homme | b. l'homme
c. un morceau de craie | c. le morceau de craie
d. une affiche | d. l'affiche
e. un cadeau | e. le cadeau

5. Use these prepositions to describe the location of each item.
(See key.)

devant	*in front of*	sous	*under*	entre	*between*
derrière	*behind*	sur	*on top of*		

Modèle: garçon: entre |

> Le garçon est entre la chaise et l'écran.

a. professeur: derrière   d. écran: entre
b. morceau de craie: sous   e. feuille de papier: sur
c. professeur: devant

2. Expressing possession with *de* + a name

1. Compare the pattern for expressing possession in English and French.

Possession

Name + 's + item owned: This is Paul's notebook.
Item owned + **de** + name: **C'est le cahier de Paul.**

In French, which word connects the item owned with the name of the owner? |

de (The preposition *de* is often used to connect one noun with another.)

2. *C'est la cassette d'Alice.* What happens to *de* when it precedes a vowel sound? |

De becomes *d'*. (This dropping of e before a vowel sound is another example of *élision*.)

3. Imagine that you have borrowed some things, and now it's time to return them. Tell who owns each item.

Modèle: écran/Charles |

C'est l'écran de Charles.

a. règle/Marie |

C'est la règle de Marie.

b. transistor/Georges |

C'est le transistor de Georges.

c. gomme/Édouard |

C'est la gomme d'Édouard. (Did you remember to write *d'*?)

d. caméra/M. Laval |

C'est la caméra de M. Laval.

4. Give the French equivalents for the following sentences. (See key.)

   a. It's Marc's camera.
   b. It's Valerie's transistor radio.

5. Identify each item, and explain that it belongs to your French professor. You may abbreviate. (See key.)

Monsieur = M.   Madame = Mme   Mademoiselle = Mlle
   Modèle: |

C'est une chaise. C'est la chaise de M. Belfort.

a.    b.    c.    d.

3. Saying *not*: *ne . . . pas* with *être*

Negation with être

je	**ne**	suis	**pas**	nous	**ne**	sommes	**pas**
tu	**n'**	es	**pas**	vous	**n'**	êtes	**pas**
il/elle	**n'**	est	**pas**	ils/elles	**ne**	sont	**pas**

1. *N'* is another example of *élision*. Write the negative forms of *être* that use *n'*. |

   > tu n'es pas, il/elle n'est pas, vous n'êtes pas

2. Say that these people are not from Paris. Check your verb forms against the chart.

   Modèle: je |

   > Je ne suis pas de Paris.

   a. vous
   b. elle
   c. tu

   d. nous
   e. ils
   f. M. Rimbaud

3. Contradict these statements. *Mais non!* means *of course not!* Say your answer aloud before you write.

   Modèle: Tu es pressé, Robert! |

   > Mais non, je ne suis pas pressé!

   a. Paul et Jean sont sous la table? |

   > Mais non, ils ne sont pas sous la table!

   b. Nous sommes en retard! |

   > Mais non, vous n'êtes pas en retard!

   c. Je suis très réaliste. |

   > Mais non, tu n'es pas très réaliste!

4. Answer each question, and correct it by adding the information in parentheses. (See key.)

   Modèle: Mlle Boivin, vous êtes de Versailles? (Non, Ivry) |

   > Non, je ne suis pas de Versailles. Je suis d'Ivry.

   a. C'est une cassette? (Non, bande)
   b. Anne et Marie, vous êtes très en retard? (Non, seulement un peu: *only a little*)
   c. La jeune fille est belge? (Non, française)

Tell a little about yourself. Use the negative if appropriate.

Vous êtes allemand/e?
Vous êtes réaliste? pessimiste?
Vous êtes souvent *(often)* **en retard?**

4. Basic intonation patterns

1. Intonation is the rise and fall of the voice in speaking. The intonation pattern of a sentence helps to determine its meaning. For example, say *I'm going home* as if you were very happy. Now say it as if you were very angry. Finally, say it as if you were very tired. Did you use the same intonation each time? |

> no (Intonation varies with the meaning you convey.)

2. Say these sentences aloud. *Is it a present? It's a present.*
   a. Did your voice rise or fall at the end of the question? |

   > It rose.

   b. Did your voice rise or fall at the end of the statement? |

   > It fell. (In both English and French, there are two basic intonation patterns for sentences: rising and falling.)

3. This question has rising intonation. *Vous êtes de Chicago?* Would a one-word answer of *oui* or *non* make sense here? |

   > yes (A *oui-non* question has rising intonation.)

4. This question has falling intonation: *Où est Chicago?* Would a one-word answer of *oui* or *non* make sense? |

   > no (It asks for additional information. Information questions have falling intonation.)

5. Read this statement aloud: *Je m'appelle Jean Dupont.* Does it have rising or falling intonation? |

   > falling (Most statements have falling intonation.)

   Of course, intonation in French or English is much more varied than simple rising or falling. When you repeat with speakers in the taped dialogues, listen for and imitate the intonation of phrases and sentences. Try to use the right melody in your French sentences.

6. Read each sentence aloud, then say what kind it is—*oui-non* question, information question, or statement—and whether the intonation would be rising or falling.

   Modèle: Tu es pressé? |

   > *oui-non* question; rising intonation

   a. C'est un cadeau pour moi? |

   > *oui-non* question; rising intonation

   b. Qu'est-ce que c'est? |

   > information question; falling intonation

c. Qui est-ce? |

information question; falling intonation

d. C'est Jean-Paul. |

statement; falling intonation

5. Verb form

Verbs are an important part of a sentence. Some express an action: *to run, to swim.* Some express a state: *to be, to stay.* Some express a process: *to become, to think.*

1. a. In *The children run,* which word tells who runs? |

children (*Children* is the subject of the sentence. The subject performs the action of the verb.)

b. Which word tells what the subject does? |

run (The verb tells the action.)

2. a. Compare: *The children run. The child runs.* Does the verb form change when the subject changes from plural to singular? |

yes

b. Does the *-s* ending of *runs* give you information about whether the subject is singular or plural? |

yes (The ending *-s* indicates that the subject is singular.)

3. Most verb forms are composed of two basic parts: a *stem* and an *ending.* In *runs,* the stem is *run* and the ending is *-s.* Which part tells you what the action is—the stem or the ending? |

the stem (run)

6. The present tense of *chercher*

Present:	je	cherch	**e**		nous	cherch	**ons**
	tu	cherch	**es**		vous	cherch	**ez**
	il/elle	cherch	**e**		ils/elles	cherch	**ent**

1. *Chercher* means *to look for.* Can you think of three English equivalents for *Je cherche?* |

I look for; I am looking for; I do look for (English expresses the present tense in more than one form.)

2. Most French verbs, like English verbs, are composed of a stem and an ending. What is the stem of *chercher?* |

cherch-

3. In French, a verb form that has one sound in speech may have several written forms. The *je, tu, il/elle* and *ils/elles* forms of *chercher* are all pronounced the same way. Their written present tense endings are silent in speech, and so you just hear the stem *cherch-*.

Write the endings that complete each written form of *chercher*.

a. tu cherch _____ | -es
b. Robert cherch _____ | -e
c. je cherch _____ | -e
d. Marie et Irène cherch _____ | -ent
e. Irène, Jean et Paul cherch _____ | -ent
f. Mlle Chenaud cherch _____ | -e

4. Write the endings for the *nous* and *vous* forms of *chercher*. |

                  -ons, -ez (These endings are heard in speech.)

5. *Chercher* has three spoken forms in the present tense. How many written forms does it have? |

             five (The *je* and *il/elle* forms are spelled the same.)

6. Write the subject and the matching form of *chercher* for each sentence.

    Modèle: Je _____ la gomme de Marie. |

           Je cherche

a. Tu _____ un crayon?
b. Vous _____ Philippe Verlut?
c. Lisette _____ un stylo.
d. Nous _____ l'écran.
e. Georges et Paul _____ le cahier de Paul. |

     a. *Tu cherches*   b. *Vous cherchez*   c. *Lisette cherche*   d. *Nous cherchons*
     e. *Georges et Paul cherchent*

7. Write French equivalents. (See key.)
    a. I'm looking for Jacqueline.
    b. Is he looking for a pen?

7. What is a regular verb?

Now that you know the present tense forms of *chercher,* you can apply the same knowledge to other French verbs.

1. In French, the infinitive form of a verb has a stem (which gives the meaning) and an infinitive ending.

The stem of *chercher* is *cherch-*. What is the infinitive ending? |

            -er (Verbs may be identified by their infinitive endings. To get the stem of an *-er* verb, drop *-er*.)

2. Verbs that follow a predictable pattern based on the infinitive are called regular verbs. Every *-er* verb except *aller* (to go) is regular.

a. *Parler* (to speak) is a regular *-er* verb. Write its stem. |

parl-

b. The *je*-form of *chercher* is *je cherche*. What is the *je*-form of *parler*? |

parle

c. The *nous*-form of *chercher* is *nous cherchons*. Write the *nous*-form of *parler*. |

parlons

3. Not only can you predict the forms of *-er* verbs, you can often guess their meanings, because many *-er* verbs are cognates. Give the English equivalent, the stem, and the *je*-form of each verb. (See key.)

   Modèle: changer |

to change; chang-; je change

   a. guider   c. remarquer

   b. résister   d. vérifier

4. Not all French verbs are regular. Do *suis, es,* and *sont* look like their infinitive *être?* |

no (*Être* is irregular. You can't predict its forms by looking at the infinitive.)

8. *Ne... pas* with *-er* verbs

1. You know that *ne* and *pas* are used to make a sentence negative. Rewrite this sentence in the negative: *Martine cherche le cadeau de Pierre.* |

Elle ne cherche pas le cadeau de Pierre.

2. Answer these questions in the negative.

   a. Ils cherchent le magnétophone? |

Ils ne cherchent pas le magnétophone.

   b. Le magnétophone marche? |

Le magnétophone ne marche pas.

3. Eric isn't interested in dancing the tango, and neither is anyone else. Convey that information. (See key.)

   Modèle: Éric, vous dansez le tango? |

Non, je ne danse pas le tango.

   a. Paul et Sara dansent le tango?

   b. Toi et moi, nous dansons le tango?

   c. Et Brigitte?

   d. Et moi? (non, vous . . .)

Note Culturelle
La douce France

France, celebrated in poetry and song for its gentle beauty, is in fact a country of endless variety and fascination. Physically, France is shaped like a hexagon, a characteristic which accounts for the name *l'Hexagone,* used at times to designate metropolitan France. France covers 550,000 square kilometers (about the size of Texas) and ranks as Europe's second largest country (after the Soviet Union). Its coastline faces three different bodies of water: *La Manche* (the English Channel) to the north, *l'océan Atlantique* (the Atlantic Ocean) to the west, and *la Méditerranée* (the Mediterranean Sea) to the southeast. Its terrain includes great mountain ranges, such as *les Pyrénées* and *les Alpes,* smaller mountains, such as *les Vosges,* and a mixture of the two, like *le Jura.* France also has plateaux and massifs, such as *le Massif Central,* and plains that cover more than half the country. Five great rivers flow over the hills and plains.

Situated well within the temperate region of Europe, France merits the title of *la douce France.* Yet its physical features create different types of climate: the oceanic or maritime climate, with mild winters and slight changes in temperature; the Mediterranean climate, with its luminosity and hot summer days; and the continental climate, with its severe summer-winter contrasts.

Some regions of France are reminiscent of areas in the United States. Brittany, with fresh summers and sandy beaches, recalls the charm of New England; the gently rolling hills and soft climate of the Loire valley are not unlike those of Virginia. The French Alps, like the Rockies, attract skiers in win-

ter and alpinists eager to climb the Mont Blanc in summer. Like California, the French Mediterranean coast is a haven for painters and sunlovers. Northern France might bring to mind similar industrial areas in this country, and *La Camargue,* a warm, swampy region of Provence, might well remind one of some areas of Texas or Florida. *La Camargue* is famous for large herds of sheep that winter there and summer in the Alps; for its horses, left free to run wild under the surveillance of guards called *gardians;* and for its black, agile bulls featured in Provençal rodeos called *courses à la cocarde.*

Vignobles (vineyards) autour d' (around) un joli village.

There are a few typically French sounds that have no counterpart in English (including the nasal vowels), and whose mispronunciation will automatically brand you as a non-native speaker. It is worth your time and effort to learn them well. Then, whatever you say in French will immediately appear polished and right, and you will sound well traveled without ever going away.

The nasal vowels are:

/ã/   *as in* Jean, présent
/ɔ̃/   *as in* blond, mon
/ɛ̃/   *as in* canadien, bien
/œ̃/   *as in* un, brun

An increasing number of speakers use /ɛ̃/ in place of /œ̃/.

Your lips should not utter even a trace of a consonant /n/—except in linking with a following vowel as in *un‿ami.*

Vocabulaire

Noms

le chiffre   *digit*
le frère   *brother*
le nombre   *number*
le professeur   *professor, teacher*
le salon   *living room*
la tête   *head*

Adjectifs

agité/e   *agitated*
bête   *stupid*
jeune   *young*
belge   *Belgian*

Verbes

admirer   *to admire*
aider (à)   *to help*
changer   *to change*
chercher   *to look for*
danser   *to dance*
entrer   *to go in, enter, to come in*
examiner   *to examine*
guider   *to guide*
marcher   *to work (machinery)*
parler   *to speak, to talk*
placer   *to place*
préparer   *to prepare*

regarder   *to look at, to watch*
remarquer   *to remark; to notice*
résister   *to resist*
trouver   *to find, to think*
utiliser   *to use*
vérifier   *to verify*

Autres mots et expressions

ça alors!   *good grief!*
comment est . . .?   *how is . . .?*
de   *of; from*
être en train de   *to be in the process of;* ~ chercher   *to be (in the process of) looking for*
mais non!   *no! (emphatic)*
oh, ça va!   *that's enough!*
ou   *or*
pas possible!   *unbelievable!*
un peu   *a little*
quelque chose   *something*
seulement un peu   *only a little*
souvent   *often*
tais-toi/taisez-vous   *be quiet*
tout   *all, everything*
tu ne trouves pas?   *don't you think?*
voilà le disque   *there's the record*

PRÉPARATION 5

1. Practice with -er verbs

1. Say that these people are working.
    Modèle: je |
                Je travaille.

  a. Sylvie |
                Sylvie travaille.

  b. nous |
                Nous travaillons.

  c. Alain et Marc |
                Alain et Marc travaillent.

2. Express your surprise that these people don't speak English.
    Modèle: il |
                Il ne parle pas anglais?

  a. vous   b. tu   c. elles |
                a. Vous ne parlez pas anglais?   b. Tu ne parles pas anglais?   c. Elles ne parlent pas anglais?

À Propos!   Répondez *(answer):* Vous préparez la leçon de français?
                Vous dansez bien?

2. Verbs in -*ger* and -*cer*

1. In French, when the letter *g* is followed by the vowels *e, i,* or *y,* it has the soft sound /ʒ/ as in *gentil.* When followed by *a, o, u,* or a consonant, *g* has the hard sound /g/ as in *garçon.*
Read these words aloud and write them in two lists, "hard" and "soft," according to the sound of the *g: girafe, magazine, gomme, gymnastique, angle, manger* (to eat), *grave, langue* (language *or* tongue), *Gilbert, géographie.* |
      "Hard": ma*g*azine, *g*omme, an*g*le, *g*rave, lan*g*ue, *g*éographie
      "Soft": *g*irafe, *g*ymnastique, man*g*er, *G*ilbert, *g*éographie

2. Look at the forms of the verb *manger*.

je **mang**	e		nous **mange**	ons
tu mang	es		vous mang	ez
il/elle mang	e		ils/elles mang	ent

The written stem of *je mange* is the same as the infinitive stem *mang-*. What is the stem of the *nous* form? |

> mange- (In the *nous* form, an *e* is added so that the written *g* represents the same sound as in the other present tense forms. *Changer, arranger,* and all other verbs in *-ger* are conjugated like *manger*.)

3. Tell about the eating habits of these people. (See key.)
   a. Je ne/pas aujourd'hui.
   b. Nous/à midi *(at noon)*.
   c. Tu/en classe?
   d. Christine et moi, nous/beaucoup.
   e. Mon grand-père/peu.
   f. Vous/avec nous aujourd'hui?

4. When the letter *c* is followed by *i, e,* or *y,* or is written *ç,* it has the soft sound of /s/ as in *cinéma*. When *c* is followed by *a, o, u,* or a consonant, it has the hard /k/sound as in *cadeau*.
   Read these words aloud and write them in two lists, hard and soft, according to the sound of the *c: caméra, cinq, coiffeur, cuisine, français, cédille, garçon, commencer* (to begin). |

> Hard: caméra, coiffeur, cuisine, commencer
> Soft: cinq, français, cédille, garçon, commencer

5. Look at the forms of *commencer*.

je **commenc**	e		nous **commenç**	ons
tu commenc	es		vous commenc	ez
il/elle commenc	e		ils/elles commenc	ent

Write the *nous* form of *commencer*. How does the *nous* stem differ from the other stem? |

> nous commençons; *commenç-* has a *cédille* (In all the other forms, the stem is followed by an *e,* and thus the *c* is soft. All *-cer* verbs are conjugated like *commencer*.)

6. Say that one group is doing something but we are not. (See key.)
   Modèle: commencer à parler |

> Vous commencez à parler. Nous ne commençons pas à parler.

   a. commencer la leçon
   b. remplacer *(to replace, to get another)* le cadeau
   c. menacer *(to threaten)* le professeur

3. Descriptive adjectives

In order to describe someone or something in French, you need to know how to use adjectives.

1. An adjective is a word that *describes a noun* (a person, a place, a thing, or an idea). Write the adjectives from these sentences.

   Sharon is usually optimistic. New York is a complex and varied city. |

   optimistic; complex, varied

2. In English, an adjective does not change form to match the gender of the noun it describes. Most French adjectives, however, have two different forms in the singular—a masculine form and a feminine form. Compare the adjectives here:

   Le garçon est petit.   La fille est petite.

   a. Which goes with the masculine noun, *petit* or *petite?* |

   petit

   b. Which form matches the feminine noun? |

   petite

3. The written feminine form of many French adjectives is the masculine form + *e: petit* + *e* = *petite*. Write the feminine forms of *absent, grand, américain.* |

   absente, grande, américaine (Be sure to use a small letter *a* for *américain*, and to write the *accent aigu*.)

4. The spoken feminine form of most French adjectives ends in a consonant sound. For example, *petite* ends in the consonant sound [t]. Say aloud each pair of adjectives below. Then write the feminine form and underline the pronounced consonant.

   Modèle: présent, présente |

   présente

   a. absent, absente |

   a. absente

   b. française, français |

   b. française

   c. américaine, américain |

   c. américaine

5. Sometimes the written feminine form doubles the consonant before the final *e*. For example, *bon* becomes *bonne*. Write the feminine form:

   a. gentil |

   b. canadien |

   c. norvégien |

   d. bon |

   a. gentille
   b. canadienne
   c. norvégienne
   d. bonne

**Tourisme** Québec

Combien de (how many) fleurs-de-lys voyez-vous? (do you see?)

Two Spoken Forms

Masculine	**Feminine**
Vowel sound	*Consonant sound*
petit	petit**e**
français	français**e**
Nasal vowel sound	*Consonant sound*
grand	gran**de**
canadien	canadie**nne**

6. With some adjectives, both the masculine and feminine written forms end in *e*. They are pronounced the same: *superbe, magnifique, formidable*. Complete this sentence: *Paul est belge, et Marie est _____ aussi.* |

   belge

7. A masculine adjective that ends in *é* or another vowel adds an *e* in the written feminine form, but there is no change in the spoken form. Complete with the correct form of *pressé*.

   a. Philippe n'est pas _____ aujourd'hui. | a. pressé
   b. Mme Chenaud est très _____ aujourd'hui. | b. pressée

One Spoken Form

Masculine	**Feminine**
-e	**-e**
suisse	suisse
optimiste	optimiste
-é	**-ée**
fatigué	fatiguée

8. Describe the people below in complete sentences, using the cues. If you are unsure about the feminine form of an adjective, refer to frames 3–7.

    Modèles: Véronique/être/gentil |

               Véronique est gentille.

        Pierre/ne . . . pas être/absent |

               Pierre n'est pas absent.

  a. Mlle Bonnard/être/pressé aujourd'hui
  b. Le livre/être/magnifique!
  c. Catherine/ne . . . pas être/très gentil
  d. Louise/ne . . . pas être/pessimiste |

          a. Mlle Bonnard est pressée aujourd'hui.   b. Le livre est magnifique!   c. Catherine n'est pas très gentille.   d. Louise n'est pas pessimiste.

4. Practice with *ne...pas* and adjectives

Below are pictures of some people. Say that each has the first characteristic indicated, but not the second one. Remember to use the correct masculine or feminine form of each adjective.

    Modèle: Bob (américain/français) |

          Bob est américain. Il n'est pas français.

1. Irène (grand/petit) |

          Irène est grande. Elle n'est pas petite.

2. André (riche/pauvre) |

          André est riche. Il n'est pas pauvre.

3. Stéphanie (blond/brun) |

          Stéphanie est blonde. Elle n'est pas brune.

4. Monique (français/américain) |

          Monique est française. Elle n'est pas américaine.

À Propos! Describe your roommate or another person you know well. Identify the person by the first name. Use *très* or *assez* (somewhat, rather) to shade your judgments. Say your answers aloud, then write them.

Modèle: C'est Bob. Il est (assez) gentil. Il n'est pas très réaliste. Il est intelligent. Il n'est pas portugais, il est canadien.

5. Sound-spelling practice

1. Write each word or expression with the correct accents or marks. (See key.)
   a. *Accent aigu:* camera, present, presse, television
   b. *Cédille:* francais, garcon, ca alors!, ca va?
   c. *Accent aigu:* mathematiques, etudiante, geometrie, americaine
   d. *Accent circonflexe:* bien sur!, vous etes, bete, fenetre
   e. *Accent grave:* ou est . . .?, regle, tres bien, a demain
   f. *Accents aigu et grave:* eleve, Helene
2. In your next class your instructor will dictate some sentences for you to write. To practice associating the sound of words with the way they are written, decode each sentence and figure out which letters belong in the blanks, then write the complete sentence. (See key.)
   a. C'es_ l_ st_lo d_ Ph_lip__.
   b. C_ n'__t pa_ un_ gom__.
   c. J_ ch_____ _'a__iche d_ M_r_e.
   d. Tu par___ fr___ais.
   e. N__s tr_v__ll___ b___coup.
   f. H_l_ne __garde _eanne.
   g. V___ ec_____ le pr___ss__r?

6. Vocabulary recall and writing practice

Use the letters and the number of blanks to help you recall words and phrases from *Qu'est-ce que c'est?* and *Où est le disque?* Do your best to spell them correctly. Then check your spelling with the dialogues printed on pages 24 and 32.
1. Catch someone's attention: T__ns! Reg_r__ . . .
2. Get more information: Qu'est-__ q__ c'___? Qu'___-ce qu'__ y _?
3. Show annoyance: _ut, ___ et ___! Ç_, a_or_! Oh, ça__! Qu_ tu __ b_t_!
4. Be skeptical: Pa_ poss____! Qu_ll_ b__gu_!
5. Show your gratitude: ___ci. _omme tu es __ntil.

6. Does the recorder work or not? L_ ma__ ét _ ph _ ne n_ mar __ pa _? _ a m __ che m ___ tenant.

7. Admit that you don't know: Je __ c __ prends _ as. Je ne _ ais ___ où il ___.

Note Culturelle

Creoles and Acadians in Louisiana

The French originally used the term *créole* to distinguish between French settlers in the New World and French people in France. In the strictest sense, the term was applied to the descendants of French settlers in the West Indies and the southern United States, especially Louisiana. A Creole dialect, based on French and African languages, came about as a result of the need for communication between French plantation owners and the African-born slaves. Other French dialects evolved for similar reasons in Martinique and Haiti, islands which the French had colonized in the 17th century.

The French used the term *Acadien* (Acadian) to refer to French settlers on the northeast coast of Canada. The *Acadiens* were driven out of Canada by the British in 1755 and sought refuge, for the most part, in Louisiana. The American name *Cajun* is a modified form of the word *Acadien*.

Do you know the origin of the word *Dixieland*? A widely used ten-dollar note, issued before the Civil War by the Citizens' Bank of Louisiana, showed a large *F. dix* in the center of the reverse side; hence the South became known as the land of the "dixies" or Dixie Land.

Today there are about 600,000 French-speaking people in Louisiana, many of them descendants of *Créoles* or *Acadiens,* and French is officially the second language of the state.

Une cour intérieure à la Nouvelle-Orléans.

Note linguistique

The sounds of French: difficult consonant sounds

The consonant /R/comes from the back of your tongue against the back of your throat (like a German *ch* in *Bach*).

> /R/   *Ravel, Ivry, regarde, d'accord*

The letters *ch* in English often sound like *tch*, as in *chair*. In French, they are pronounced like English *sh*, as in *share*. English *j* and *g* often sound like *dj* as in *judge* or *jet*. In French, they are pronounced like the *s* in *measure*.

English	French
Charles	/ʃ/ *Charles*
George	/ʒ/ *Georges*

In French, the letters *gn*, as in *Vigneault* and *magnétophone*, are pronounced like the *ny* in *canyon* (the English transcription of the Spanish *ñ* in *cañon*).

English	French
ignorant	/ɲ/ *ignorant*

The semi-consonants are part consonant, part vowel. French /j/ begins with a bit of the vowel /i/. French /w/ begins with a bit of the vowel /u/.

> /j/   *Yougoslavie, fille*
> /w/   *oui, toi*

Vocabulaire

Noms
le cousin/la cousine *cousin*
le grand-père *grandfather*
la leçon *lesson*

Adjectifs
absent/e *missing*
amusant/e *amusing*
belge *Belgian*
bon/bonne *good*
cultivé/e *cultured, refined*
fatigué/e *tired*
grand/e *tall*
gros/se *fat*
joli/e *pretty*
laid/e *ugly*
magnifique *magnificent*
maigre *thin*
mince *slim, slender*

norvégien/ne *Norwegian*
pauvre *poor*
petit/e *small*
riche *rich, wealthy*
superbe *superb, beautiful*
triste *sad*

Verbes
arranger *to arrange*
commencer (à) *to begin (to)*
manger *to eat*
menacer *to threaten*
remplacer *to replace*
travailler *to work*

Autres mots et expressions
à midi *at noon*
qu'est-ce qu'elle/il a dit? *what did she/he say?*

PRÉPARATION 6

1. The alphabet

1. Repeat with the tape or read aloud. The pronunciation of each letter is shown in IPA (International Phonetic Alphabet).

A /a/   H /aʃ/   N /ɛn/   U /y/
B /be/   I /i/   O /o/   V /ve/
C /se/   J /ʒi/   P /pe/   W /dubləve/
D /de/   K /ka/   Q /ky/   X /iks/
E /ə/   L /ɛl/   R /ɛʀ/   Y /igʀɛk/
F /ɛf/   M /ɛm/   S /ɛs/   Z /zɛd/
G /ʒe/   T /te/

2. Spell in French: France, Canada, Angleterre. (For *rr,* say *deux r.*)

À Propos!   Spell in French your name and your home town.

2. Review of subject pronouns

Write the subject pronoun that agrees with the verb form and any adjective. (See key.)

1. _____ êtes américain?   4. _____ est américaine.
2. _____ suis derrière le bureau. 5. _____ mangeons bien.
3. _____ es pressé aujourd'hui?   6. _____ parlent anglais.

3. Review of *chercher* and other *-er* verbs

1. Write the form of *chercher* that goes with each subject. (See key.)

   a. je _____   d. tu _____   g. M. Dubois _____
   b. nous _____   e. vous _____   h. elle _____
   c. ils _____   f. Monique _____   i. Paul et Charles _

2. Write the correct form of each verb. (See key.)
   a. Je _____ le cahier d'Hélène. (*vérifier*)
   b. Tu _____ la caméra de M. Delmas? (*admirer*)
   c. Vous _____ le transistor de Philippe? (*réparer*)
   d. Marie-Hélène _____ le livre de Pierre. (*accepter*)
   e. Il _____ beaucoup. (*travailler*)
   f. Vous _____ bien français! (*parler*)
   g. Philippe et Jean _____ Marc. (*aider*)
   h. Nous _____ le magnétophone sur la chaise. (*placer*)

3. Say that these people don't talk much in class. (See key.)
   Modèle: tu |
   Tu ne parles pas beaucoup en classe.
   a. Thierry
   b. toi et Luc, vous
   c. toi et moi, nous
   d. Lucie et Georges

4. Use the infinitive phrases below to give a French equivalent for each sentence.

   chercher
   danser souvent
   écouter
   parler (bien) français

   étudier la leçon
   regarder le professeur
   travailler

   a. Marc is looking at the teacher.
   b. Are you *(vous)* listening?
   c. I'm not listening.
   d. We're working.
   e. They're not working.
   f. Robert is studying the lesson.
   g. I'm looking for Annick.
   h. You *(vous)* don't speak French?
   i. They *(elles)* don't dance often.
   j. You *(tu)* speak French well. |

   a. Marc regarde le professeur. b. Vous écoutez? c. Je n'écoute pas. d. Nous travaillons. e. Ils ne travaillent pas. f. Robert étudie la leçon. g. Je cherche Annick. h. Vous ne parlez pas français? i. Elles ne dansent pas souvent. j. Tu parles bien français!

4. Review of *être*

1. Say that everyone is late. (See key.)
   a. tu
   b. nous
   c. Danielle
   d. nous deux, nous
   e. Eric et Jean
   f. je

2. State that these assertions are not true. (See key.)
   Modèle: Stéphanie est petite. |
   Stéphanie n'est pas petite.
   a. Mme Chenaud est pressée.

b. Philippe est poli.

c. Jean et Jacques sont de Versailles.

d. Tu es bête!

5. Review of indefinite and definite articles

1. Write the correct indefinite article, *un* or *une*, in the space provided. (See key.)

a. _____ homme
g. _____ règle
b. _____ femme
h. _____ table
c. _____ garçon
i. _____ bureau
d. _____ fille
j. _____ cahier
e. _____ livre
k. _____ enfant intelligent
f. _____ feuille de papier
l. _____ enfant intelligente

2. Write the correct definite article, *le, la,* or *l',* in the space provided. (See key.)

a. _____ stylo
f. _____ homme
k. _____ gomme
b. _____ écran
g. _____ transistor
l. _____ caméra
c. _____ crayon
h. _____ chaise
m. _____ élève
d. _____ tableau
i. _____ femme
n. _____ étudiante
e. _____ télévision
j. _____ affiche
o. _____ enfant

6. The numbers 40–69

40	quarante	50	cinquante	60	soixante
41	quarante et un	51	cinquante et un	61	soixante et un
42	quarante-deux	52	cinquante-deux	62	soixante-deux
45	quarante-cinq	55	cinquante-cinq	65	soixante-cinq
49	quarante-neuf	59	cinquante-neuf	69	soixante-neuf

Repeat the numbers with the tape. Then write out the following problems. *Combien* means *How much?*

1. Combien font *soixante-quatre moins vingt-cinq?*

$$64 - 25 = 39$$

2. Combien font *cinquante-cinq moins douze?*

$$55 - 12 = 43$$

3. Combien font *quarante-trois et dix-sept?*

$$43 + 17 = 60$$

4. Combien font *treize et seize moins douze?*

$$13 + 16 - 12 = 17$$

baseball

Quel est (what is) le score?

St-Louis?
Cincinnati?

Texas?
Kansas City?

Ligue Nationale
Jeudi
Los Angeles 8, Montréal 2
Atlanta 6, Pittsburgh 1
St-Louis 10, Cincinnati 1
Philadelphie 3, San Francisco 0
San Diego 5, New York 2
Hier soir
Chicago à Montréal
St-Louis à Atlanta
Los Angeles à New York
San Diego à Philadelphie
San Francisco à Cincinnati

Ligue Américaine
Jeudi
Texas 2, Kansas City 0
Détroit 9, Milwaukee 1
Seattle 8, New York 6
Californie 7, Baltimore 5
Hier soir
Texas à Kansas City
Toronto à Minnesota
Cleveland à Chicago
Détroit à Milwaukee
Boston à Seattle
Baltimore à Oakland

7. Review of forms of adjectives

1. Describe each person below. Write a complete sentence with the correct form of the adjective in parentheses. (See key.)

   Modèle: (gentil) Marie est _____.

   Marie est gentille.

   a. *(grand)* l'homme est _____.
   b. *(française)* Anne est _____.
   c. *(pauvre)* M. Martelli n'est pas _____.
   d. *(riche)* Mme Martelli est _____.
   e. *(petit)* La fille est _____.
   f. *(présent)* Elisabeth n'est pas _____ aujourd'hui.
   g. *(laid)* La femme est _____.
   h. *(élégant)* Le monsieur est _____.
   i. *(intelligent)* L'étudiant est _____?
   j. *(beau)* L'affiche est _____.

8. Review of possession with *de*

1. Tell who owns the item mentioned, then write the sentence. (See key.)

   Modèle: règle/Georges

   C'est la règle de Georges.

   a. affiche/Martine
   b. disque/Annick
   c. enfant/M. Marteau
   d. caméra/Bernard

2. Write complete sentences, using the cues given. In each case, you will have to connect a noun and a name by using *de* or *d'*. Make all other necessary additions and changes. (See key.)

   Modèle: L_ cassette/André/être/dans l_ tiroir *(drawer)*

   La cassette d'André est dans le tiroir.

   a. où/être/l_ gomme/Jacques?
   b. je/chercher/l_ caméra/M. Teyssier
   c. tu/ne . . . pas/écouter/l_ cassette/Mme Legrand?

9. Reading Comprehension

Read the following dialogue, then answer the questions. (See key.)

Jeanne et Laura sont dans le salon.

Laura: Ah, ça alors. Je ne sais pas où est mon livre de zoologie.
Jeanne: Il n'est pas sur la télévision?
Laura: Mais non, il n'est pas là. Tu m'aides à chercher?
Jeanne: Non, je suis pressée.
Laura: Oh, tu n'es pas très gentille, tu sais!
Jeanne: Je regrette, mais je suis très en retard.

1. Where are Jeanne and Laura?
   (a) kitchen
   (b) back yard
   (c) living room
2. What is Laura looking for?
   (a) the zoo
   (b) her book about zoos
   (c) her zoology book
3. Is the book on the T.V.?
   (a) yes
   (b) no
4. What does Laura ask Jeanne to do?
   (a) leave now
   (b) help her look
   (c) look for help
5. Does Jeanne agree to help?
   (a) yes
   (b) no

10. Review of *tu* and *vous*

Tell whether you would use *tu* or *vous* in the following situations. (See key.)
   1. You are talking to both your parents.
   2. You are talking on the phone to your best friend.
   3. You are talking to a teller in the savings bank.
   4. You are talking to another college student you have met at the beach.

5. You are talking to your younger sister and a classmate of hers.
6. You are talking to the manager of a supermarket about a job for the summer.
7. You are talking to three cousins who have just come to town.
8. You are talking to a small child you see in the park.
9. You are talking to two of your roommate's friends.
10. You are talking to a stranger who asks for directions.
11. You are talking to two other students in your French class.

Note Culturelle
Formules de politesse

When two French-speaking people are introduced to each other, they shake hands and say *bonjour* with *monsieur, madame,* or *mademoiselle.*

The most common expression for *please* is *s'il vous plaît. Merci, merci bien,* and *merci beaucoup* are common ways to say *thank you.* When someone says *merci,* the proper equivalent for *you're welcome* is usually *de rien* (literally, *it's nothing*), or the slightly more formal phrase *je vous en prie* (literally, *I beg of you*). To say *excuse me,* a French speaker often uses *pardon, excusez-moi,* or *excuse-moi.* When someone sneezes, one can say jokingly *à vos amours, à tes amours (to your loves* or *may you have love).* The normal response, however, is *à vos souhaits* or *à tes souhaits (best wishes* or *may your wishes come true).*

Note linguistique
The sounds of French: difficult vowel sounds

The vowel /y/ is very tense. Keep your lips rounded, your tongue tip behind your bottom front teeth, and your tongue raised when you say it.

/y/   *tu, salut, Luc, rue*

The vowel /ø/ also requires that you keep your lips rounded. It resembles the vowel in English *blur,* but /ø/ should have absolutely no consonant /R/.

/ø/   *deux, bleu, peu, mon dieu!*

The semi-vowel /ɥ/ begins with a bit of the vowel /y/ before blending into /i/.

/ɥ/   *suis, lui, huit*

11. Writing Practice

Make up a *brief dialogue* between Roger and Alice. Roger wonders what it is that Alice is looking for but cannot find. (to find = *trouver*)

Vocabulaire

Adjectif
beau/belle   *beautiful*

Verbes
accepter   *to accept*
écouter   *to listen*
regretter   *to regret*
réparer   *to repair*

CHATEAU

Chillon - Montreux
Suisse

C'est un beau château? Il est grand ou petit?

Phase 2

Question d'opinion

Qu'est-ce que vous allez apprendre?

In this Phase you will learn how to express your likes and dislikes, focusing on music; how to talk about advantages and disadvantages of life in a small town or a large city; and how to tease a jealous friend. You will learn how to make small talk about current affairs, professions and occupations, nationalities, and family relationships, and you will learn a very useful flavoring word expressing indifference.

Communication

In order to accomplish these objectives you will study:
Use of the present tense.
Verbs in *-re* and *-ir*.
Question formation.
Demonstrative adjectives *ce, cet, cette* (this, that).
Connecting two phrases with the relative pronoun *qui*.
Numbers 70 and higher.
Pronunciation of nasal vowels and consonants.

Culture

A letter from France; French Canada; the ancient provinces; age and legal privileges; administrative France; Aimé Césaire.

PRÉPARATION 7

On aime ou on n'aime pas...

André et Valérie parlent de ce qu'ils aiment et de ce qu'ils n'aiment pas.

André: Tu aimes danser?
Valérie: Oui, beaucoup. Et toi?
André: Pas du tout. Je déteste danser.
Valérie: Mais tu aimes la musique?
André: Oh oui, j'aime bien écouter le rock, le jazz...
Valérie: Et la musique classique, tu aimes?
André: Ah oui, j'adore Mozart, Rameau et surtout Chopin.
Valérie: Moi aussi. Mais je n'aime pas tellement Ravel ou Debussy.
André: Moi non plus.

You like or you don't like...

André and Valérie are talking about what they like and what they don't like.

Do you like to dance?
Yes, very much. Do you?
Not at all. I hate to dance.
But you like music?
Oh yes, I like to listen to rock, jazz...

Do you like classical music?
Oh yes, I love Mozart, Rameau, and especially Chopin.
Me, too. But I don't care very much for Ravel or Debussy.
I don't either.

1. Tell whether you like or hate dancing. Be emphatic. Ask a class-mate if he/she likes dancing.
2. Work with a partner. One of you act the part of Mme Chenaud. Greet each other. Mme Chenaud asks you about some of your likes and dislikes. Answer a few of her questions, but then make a polite get-away.

1. The pronoun *on*

1. In the title *On aime ou on n'aime pas* and in the verb chart, you see the pronoun *on. On* is a third person singular pronoun subject. It refers to people when no particular individual is referred to, very much like English *one* as in *In winter, one must dress warmly.* In American English, *one* is considered quite formal and is rarely used. *On,* however, is used very frequently in French. It is equivalent to *people, they, you,* and *we.*
Write an English equivalent: *En France, on parle français.* |

   In France, people speak (they speak, you speak, one speaks) French.

2. Use *on* to ask if people like baseball in France. |

   On aime le baseball en France? (French people play and watch soccer, volleyball, and basketball—but not baseball.)

2. The present tense of *aimer*

1. Look at the chart of the present tense of *aimer* (to like).

j'	**aim**	**e**	nous	aim	ons
tu	aim	es	vous	aim	ez
on/il/elle	aim	e	ils/elles	aim	ent

   a. Which form is used with *aime: je* or *j'?* |

      j'

   b. Before a verb beginning with a vowel sound, the form *j'* replaces *je,* another example of *élision.* Which pronoun form is used before *écoute: j'* or *je?* |

      j' (*j'écoute:* I'm listening *or* I listen)

2. Compare the pronunciation of the subject pronouns below:

ils cherchent	elles cherchent	nous cherchons	vous cherchez
ils aiment	elles aiment	nous aimons	vous aimez

a. The subject pronouns end in *-s*. Is the *s* pronounced when the pronouns are used with the forms of *chercher?* |

no

b. With the forms of *aimer?* |

yes (When these subject pronouns are used before any verb beginning with a vowel sound, the written *s* is pronounced, and the subject and verb are pronounced as if they were one word.)

c. Does the *s* sound like /s/ in *salut* or /z/ in *chaise?* |

/z/ in *chaise* (Linking of a final consonant with a beginning vowel is called *liaison*.)

3. One way to indicate linking visually is with a link mark between the subject pronoun and the verb: *nous aimons.* This link mark is *not* a part of French spelling.
Read the following verb forms aloud. Write those that have linking sounds when they are spoken, and insert link marks in the correct places.

| nous parlons | ils échangent | j'aime | vous cherchez |
| nous écoutons | ils admirent | je suis | vous utilisez | |

nous écoutons, ils échangent, ils admirent, vous utilisez

4. Write sentences according to the model, then say your answer aloud.

Modèle: Ask David if he likes rock music. |

David, tu aimes le rock?

a. David replies no, he likes classical music. |

Non, j'aime la musique classique.

b. Ask your professor if he or she likes television. |

Monsieur/Madame, vous aimez la télévision?

c. Write the reply: No, but I like the movies *(le cinéma).* |

Non, mais j'aime le cinéma.

d. Ask a friend if Hélène and Marie like to dance: _____ *danser?* |

Hélène et Marie aiment danser?

e. Complete the answer: Non, mais _____ écouter le jazz. |

Non, mais elles aiment écouter le jazz.

5. In *Elles aiment écouter le jazz,* is *écouter* in the *elles* form or in the infinitive form? |

infinitive (When a conjugated verb form is followed by another verb, the second verb is in the infinitive form. The only exceptions are in the compound tenses, which will be presented later.)

Here is *aimer* in the negative.

je	**n'**	aime	**pas**	nous	**n'**	aimons	**pas**
tu	**n'**	aimes	**pas**	vous	**n'**	aimez	**pas**
on/il/elle	**n'**	aime	**pas**	ils/elles	**n'**	aiment	**pas**

6. When *ne . . . pas* is used with *aimer,* what happens to *ne?* |

> It becomes *n'.* (*Ne* contracts to *n'* before any verb form beginning with a vowel sound—
> another example of *élision.*)

7. Tell or ask what the following people don't like by using *ne... pas*
   and *aimer.* Say each sentence aloud before you write it. (See key.)

   Modèle: Je/ne... pas/histoire |

   > *Je n'aime pas l'histoire.*

   a. Ils/ne... pas/histoire
   b. Georges/ne... pas/géographie
   c. Anne et moi, nous/ne... pas/espagnol
   d. Vous/ne... pas/tricoter, Madame?

À Propos!   Make a statement about a school subject: do you like it or hate it?
Say that you don't know if a friend of yours likes or dislikes it: *Je ne
sais pas si* (if)...

3. Definite articles with *aimer, détester*

1. Sort the following nouns into three groups: what you love, what
   you hate, and what you like somewhat. *J'aime..., Je déteste...,
   J'aime assez....*

   > la biochimie, la physique
   > le chinois, le français
   > le sport, le golf, le tennis
   > le vin, le champagne, la bière
   > la politique, l'histoire, la littérature, la sculpture

2. One noun from the list has the article *l'*. Which noun is it? |

   > *l'histoire* (The article *l'* is used with most nouns that begin with *h*.)

3. Write the French equivalent: Antoine and Michel like physics, but
   they hate biology. |

   > *Antoine et Michel aiment la physique, mais ils détestent la biologie.* (In the English
   > sentence, no articles are used with *physics* and *biology,* i.e. with nouns taken in a
   > general sense. The French equivalent, however, requires the definite article.)

4. Write the French equivalent: *I like wine, but I hate beer.* |

   > *J'aime le vin, mais je déteste la bière.*

5. Tell what these students said that they like and hate. (See key).

   Modèle: Paul et Frédéric/musique/sport |

   > *Paul et Frédéric aiment la musique, mais ils détestent le sport.*

   a. Monique/tennis/golf
   b. Jean et moi, nous/biochimie/histoire
   c. Antoine et Michel/physique/sculpture

4. French and English equivalents of verb forms

Sometimes it takes two or three English words to express the equivalent of a single French word and vice versa. In this section, you will practice using verbs whose English equivalents are longer and more complex than the single French form. This chart shows English equivalents of some present tense forms of *chanter*.

> **je chante**   I sing/I'm singing
> **je ne chante pas**   I'm not singing/I don't sing
> **tu chantes?**   are you singing?/do you sing?

1. Compare the French sentence with its English equivalent.

   Je cherche un crayon.   I am looking for a pencil.

   The French verb form is one word: *cherche*. The English equivalent is ____. |

   > am looking for (English often uses a form of *to be* and the *-ing* form of the verb where French uses a single verb form. Also, many English verbs are followed by a preposition while the French equivalent is not: *to listen to* a record, *écouter un disque,* etc.)

2. Now compare these negative sentences:

   Marie n'aime pas le jazz.   *Marie doesn't like jazz.*

   The French verb form *n'aime pas* is equivalent to ____. |

   > doesn't like (In negative sentences, English uses *doesn't* or *don't* with most verbs.)

3. What happens in interrogative sentences? Compare:

   Tu chantes?   Do you sing?

   In this example, the single verb form *chantes* is equivalent to two English words: ____ + ____. |

   > do + sing (There are other ways to formulate a question in French; they will be presented later.)

4. a. Give two English equivalents of *je cherche.* |

   > I look for, I'm looking for

   b. Give two English equivalents of *je ne cherche pas.* |

   > I'm not looking for, I don't look for

   c. Give two English equivalents of *tu cherches?* |

   > are you looking for? do you look for?

5. Give French equivalents for these sentences. (See key).
   a. Do you (*vous*) watch television?
   b. He's not listening.
   c. Don't you (*tu*) like golf? |

5. The numbers 70–100

Listen to the recording if available, then use the numbers below to answer the questions in this part.

70	*soixante-dix*	89	*quatre-vingt-neuf*
71	*soixante et onze*	90	*quatre-vingt-dix*
79	*soixante-dix-neuf*	91	*quatre-vingt-onze*
80	*quatre-vingts*	99	*quatre-vingt-dix-neuf*
81	*quatre-vingt-un*	100	*cent*

1. From 20 to 69 the pattern of counting in French is the same:
   vingt, vingt et un, vingt-deux...; trente, trente et un, trente-deux....
   After 69, the pattern changes.

$$69 = 60 + 9, \text{ or } soixante\text{-}neuf$$
$$70 = 60 + 10, \text{ or } soixante\text{-}dix$$
$$71 = 60 + \underline{\hspace{1cm}}, \text{ or } \underline{\hspace{1cm}} \quad |$$

   11, *soixante et onze* (Whenever *et* is used, there are no hyphens.)

2. Using what you know about counting in French, write out the numbers 72, 75, and 77 in words. |

   soixante-douze, soixante-quinze, soixante-dix-sept

3. *Eighty* in French is expressed as four 20s: *quatre-vingts*. Look at the chart above for the French word for 81, then write it. |

   quatre-vingt-un (After *quatre-vingts*, the numbers in the eighties have no *s* at the end of *vingt*. *Quatre-vingt-un* is the first number ending in the digit 1 that uses hyphens instead of *et*.)

Note Culturelle
A letter from France

This letter (p. 66) was written by a French girl of fifteen who had been studying English for four years. She was writing to an American girl who planned to visit her as part of an exchange program. The picture shows a rural house in the province of Berry, two figures wearing traditional costumes, and a heraldic shield.

As you read the letter, you will probably feel as if you are reading English written with a French accent. An "accent" like this occurs when someone uses words from the new language in a sentence pattern from his or her own language. You can see phrases in which the writer struggled with the English sound-spelling system, with verb tenses, and with the differences between English and French word order: burthsday, a hole bedroom,... if you want to do absolutely something..., a fireighner (foreigner) friend. Few people find it easy to learn a second language perfectly!

Saturday, February 28th.

Hello Carolyn !

I knew a few days ago that you'll come home during your staying in France and I am very glad of this. My teacher gave me your letters; I also 15 years old but when you'll come, I'll be 16 : my birthday is on March 28th. I have a sister and a brother but both are older than me and the one lives in a study in Paris near her university and the other got married in December. So I live with my parents and we'll give you a hole bedroom when you'll come.

I went back home a week ago: I spent my holidays in the South-West of France : in the mountains of Pyrénées, where I can ski with friends. It's a pity that it was not longer than a week! I like this sport very much. In Paris I play a little tennis. At school we have only three ours of sport a week and it is not a lot! I learn English (you'd have guess it!), German, Latin, Mathematics, history et geography of France, chimie and Physic. I like listening to music very much but especially classic music and "chansons" (songs?). Do you like this? If you do you'll come with us to a concert... If you want to do absolutly something during your staying at home, you must write me what. It's the first time, I have a freighner friend and I don't know exactly what I must do!

I hope to receive soon a letter from you
Best wishes.

Phase deux

Vocabulaire

Noms

la bière   *beer*
la biochimie   *biochemistry*
le champagne   *champagne*
le chinois   *Chinese*
le cinéma   *movies*
le golf   *golf*
le jazz   *jazz*
la littérature   *literature*
la musique   *music*
la politique   *politics*
le rock   *rock and roll*
la sculpture   *sculpture*
le sport   *sports*
le tennis   *tennis*
le vin   *wine*

Verbes

aimer   *to like, to love;* ~bien   *to like (something) quite a bit*
adorer   *to adore, to love*
chanter   *to sing*
détester   *to detest, hate*
tricoter   *to knit*

Autres mots et expressions

et   *and*
je ne sais pas si   *I don't know if*
moi aussi   *me too*
moi non plus   *me neither*
on   *people, we, you, they (subj. pron.)*
pas tellement   *not very much, not really*
toi aussi   *you too*
surtout   *above all, especially*

Les jours de la semaine

lundi   *Monday*
mardi   *Tuesday*
mercredi   *Wednesday*
jeudi   *Thursday*
vendredi   *Friday*
samedi   *Saturday*
dimanche   *Sunday*
le lundi   *on Mondays*
le jour   *day*
la semaine   *week*

Nombres 70–100

soixante-dix   *70*
soixante et onze   *71*
soixante-dix-neuf   *79*
quatre-vingts   *80*
quatre-vingt-un   *81*
quatre-vingt-neuf   *89*
quatre-vingt-dix   *90*
quatre-vingt-onze   *91*
quatre-vingt-dix-neuf   *99*
cent   *100*

PRÉPARATION 8

Ville ou campagne?

Véronique Lebeau, une jeune Canadienne, est étudiante aux États-Unis. Charles, un reporter du journal de l'université, lui pose quelques questions.

Charles: Vous habitez à Montréal?
Véronique: Non, j'habite à Saint-Pierre. C'est un petit village.

Charles: Un petit village? Ce n'est pas toujours très agréable, non?
Véronique: Mais si, c'est agréable. L'air est pur, il n'y a pas de pollution et pas de bruit.
Charles: Oh là là! Le retour à la nature, comme Rousseau!
Véronique: Pourquoi pas? C'est un type bien, Rousseau! Les grandes villes, c'est pas mal de temps en temps, mais y habiter, non, merci!

City or country?

Véronique Lebeau, a young Canadian, is a college student in the United States. Charles, a reporter for the university paper, asks her some questions.

Do you live in Montreal?
No, I live in Saint-Pierre. It's a small village.

A small village? That's not always very pleasant, it is?
Oh, yes it is, it's very pleasant. The air is pure, there's no pollution and no noise.

Oh, my! The return to nature, just like Rousseau!
Why not? Rousseau is a great fellow! Big cities aren't bad once in a while, but to live there? No thank you!

Échange d'idées

1. Work in a small group or with a partner. Find out where the others live, whether they come from large cities, small towns, or villages, whether they like where they live, and why.
2. S1: Ask if your partner likes some of the activities listed on page 70, frame 3.
   S2: Answer according to the intensity of your reaction.

   Oui, beaucoup./J'adore ça *(that)*.
   Pas tellement./C'est pas mal de temps en temps.
   Non, pas du tout./Je déteste ça.

3. Take a poll. Report the number of answers to each question.

   Qui (who) préfère habiter dans une grande ville?
   Qui préfère ne pas habiter dans une grande ville?
   Qui sait qui est Rousseau? Qui ne sait pas?

Phase deux

Petit village dans la province de Québec.

1. Practice with *habiter* and other *-er* verbs

1. To express where people live, the French use the verb *habiter:*
   J'habite à Montréal. Vous habitez à Québec, n'est-ce pas?
   a. Does *habiter* begin with a vowel sound (like *aimer*) or with a
      consonant sound (like *chercher*)? |
         a vowel sound (The *h* is not pronounced.)
   b. Why is the *e* dropped from *je* in *j'habite?* |
         Because *je* precedes a verb form that begins with a vowel sound.
   c. When you say *Vous habitez,* do you pronounce the *s* in *vous?* |
         yes (The *s* of *nous, vous, ils,* and *elles* links with a verb that begins with a vowel sound.)
   This chart shows the present tense forms of *habiter.*

j'	**habit**	**e**	nous	habit	ons
tu	habit	es	vous	habit	ez
on/il/elle	habit	e	ils/elles	habit	ent

2. Is *habiter* a regular *-er* verb? |

3. Tell where these people live.
    Modèle: Serge: Paris |

   a. Nous: Nice
   b. Tu: Bordeaux
   c. Paul: Montréal
   d. Je: Bruxelles
   e. Louise et Michel: Genève |

In the remaining frames you will use *habiter* and the other regular *-er* verbs listed below. Remember that they all use the same endings.

aimer	chanter	chercher	danser	détester	écouter
nager	manger	patiner	tricoter	regarder	

Remember that several English equivalents have a preposition where the French verb has none: *chercher* (to look for), *écouter* (to listen to), *regarder* (to look at).

4. Complete the French equivalents by writing the subject pronouns and matching verb forms. Be sure to include *ne (n')... pas* in the negative sentences. (See key.)
    Modèle: Does he like to dance? _____ danser? |

   a. *Claire and Marcel, are you singing in French?* Claire et Marcel,
      _____ en français?
   b. *She's living in London.* _____ à Londres.
   c. *We don't listen to the radio.* _____ la radio.
   d. *Do you like living in New York?* Vous _____ à New York?
   e. *I don't sing often.* _____ souvent.

5. Write complete sentences with these cues. Use the correct verb forms, and add articles where necessary. (See key.)
    Modèle: Je/ne... pas habiter/à Paris |

   a. Jean-Claude et Philippe/écouter/radio
   b. Richard et Martine/ne... pas danser/rock
   c. Tu/aimer/danser?
   d. Marc/détester/jazz

6. Write affirmative or negative answers, according to the cues. (See key.)
    Modèle: Vous aimez danser? (non) |

Phase deux

a. Béatrice et Marie aiment la vie à la campagne? (non)

b. Denis et Pierre, vous habitez à Saint-Louis? (non)

c. Thierry aime habiter à Ivry? (oui)

7. Write the correct forms of these verbs. (See key.)

a. *(nager)* Tu _____ bien!

b. *(ne... pas/danser)* Nathalie et Alain _____ beaucoup.

c. *(ne... pas/manger)* Je _____ aujourd'hui.

d. *(patiner)* Il aime _____.

e. *(tricoter)* Vous _____ bien.

f. *(regarder)* Tu _____ l'affiche?

À Propos!   Ask a classmate if he or she swims well, and if he/she likes to watch television. Be prepared to answer for yourself.

2. Definite vs. indefinite articles

In this section, you'll learn more about the use of definite articles in French.

1. The definite articles *le, la,* and *l'* are used in sentences expressing a like or dislike of something in general. In sentences like this, English does not use any article.

> *François déteste la musique.*   François hates music.

a. What is the article in the French sentence? |

> *la*

b. How would you say *Marie-France loves classical music?* Marie-France adore _____. |

> Marie-France adore la musique classique.

2. Express your feelings about these topics. Begin each sentence with one of these phrases: *J'adore, J'aime, Je n'aime pas,* or *Je déteste.* Use the appropriate article: *le, la,* or *l'.*

a. baseball (m.) |

> (J'adore) le baseball.

b. musique classique (f.) |

> (Je n'aime pas) la musique classique.

c. français (m.) |

> (J'aime) le français.

d. golf (m.) |

> (Je déteste) le golf.

3. Sound and spelling: -é, -er, -ez

This section will help you learn to write the forms of verbs when you hear them.

1. Say these words aloud: *télé, regardez, danser.* Write the three words, and in each one underline the letters that spell the sound /e/. |

   télé, regardez, danser

2. Which words below contain the sound /e/?

   a. cinéma   règle   cassette   élève   géographie   bête |

   cinéma, élève, géographie

   b. chanter   habiter   monsieur   cahier   bonjour   fenêtre |

   chanter, habiter, cahier

   c. cherche   mangez   aiment   assez   regardez   entre |

   mangez, assez, regardez

3. Read the following sentences aloud, and write the words that contain the sound /e/. Remember that the /e/ may be spelled in three different ways.

   a. Qu'est-ce que vous tricotez? |

   tricotez

   b. Gérard Leduc habite à Montréal. Il adore patiner. |

   Gérard, Montréal, patiner

4. Below are phrases whose missing letters spell the sound /e/. Write the whole words, and be careful about spelling.

   a. un cahi_ _, agr_able, vous n'_cout_ _ pas |

   cahier, agréable, écoutez

   b. une _cole, j'aime _cout_ _ de la musique, vous tricot_ _ |

   école, écouter, tricotez

4. The verb *avoir* (to have)

If *être* (to be) is the most-used verb, *avoir* is a close second. Here are the present tense forms of *avoir*.

j'	**ai**	nous	**avons**
tu	**as**	vous	**avez**
on/il/elle	**a**	ils/elles	**ont**

1. Yvette needs to borrow something to write with and is asking Jacques.

> *Yvette:* Tu as un stylo?
> *Jacques:* Non, mais j'ai un crayon.

a. Write the English equivalent of the dialogue. |
   —Do you have a pen? —No, but I have a pencil.

b. Write the subject-verb phrases that mean *I have* and *you have.* |
   j'ai, tu as

2. *Avoir* is an irregular verb. Its forms do not follow a pattern of infinitive stem + ending. Which of the following verbs is also irregular—*aimer, être,* or *parler?* |
   être (In many languages, the verbs that are used most frequently are irregular. *To be* and *to have* are irregular in English, too.)

3. a. A linking sound occurs between the subject pronoun and the verb in *ils ont, elles ont, nous avons, vous avez.* Is this sound like /s/ in *salut* or /z/ in *chaise?* |
      the /z/ in *chaise*

   b. Which two of these forms sound exactly alike: *ai, as, a?* |
      as and a (The final *s* is not pronounced.)

4. Tell how many pencils each person has. Say each sentence aloud, then write it.
   Modèle: Alain: un crayon |
   Alain a un crayon.

   a. Nous: deux crayons |
      Nous avons deux crayons.

   b. Tu: trois crayons |
      Tu as trois crayons.

   c. Sylvie: quatre crayons |
      Sylvie a quatre crayons.

   d. Ils: cinq crayons |
      Ils ont cinq crayons.

   e. Je: six crayons |
      J'ai six crayons.

   f. Vous: beaucoup de *(a lot of)* crayons |
      Vous avez beaucoup de crayons!

5. Ask if each person has these classroom objects. (See key.)
   Modèle: Eric: feuille de papier |
   Eric a une feuille de papier?

   a. tu: cahier
   b. le professeur: magnéto-phone
   c. vous: livre
   d. Pierre et Robert: deux stylos

À Propos!

Vous avez combien de *(how many)* stylos-feutre?
Vous avez un ami français? Comment s'appelle-t-il?

5. Numbers 101 and above

First study the list of numbers in the Vocabulaire on p. 76. Note that in French a period is used to separate columns: 10.000 (ten thousand). A comma marks decimals: 1,5 (one and five-tenths.) From what you know of French numbers, write out the following numbers in French.

1. 101　|

　　　cent un (In speech the *t* is not linked with *un*.)

2. 102　105　110　150　|

　　　cent deux, cent cinq, cent dix, cent cinquante

3. a. 300?　|

　　　trois cents (Note the *s* on multiples of *cent*. This *s* drops again if another number follows.)

　　b. How would you write: 305 and 527?　|

　　　trois cent cinq, cinq cent vingt-sept

4. 1000　2000　|

　　　mille, deux mille (Mille has no plural form.)

5. 1001 (like *cent un*)　|

　　　mille un (No *et* is used.)

6. 1.000.000　|

　　　un million

7. 1.000.000.000　|

　　　un milliard

8. Read aloud, then write these dates: *treize cent soixante-sept, dix-sept cent soixante-dix-neuf, dix neuf cent quatre-vingt-treize*　|

　　　1367, 1779, 1993

9. Dates are also read like this: *1367, mille trois cent soixante-sept.* Read aloud beginning with *mille:* 1779, 1993.　|

　　　mille sept cent soixante dix-neuf; mille neuf cent quatre-vingt-treize

10. Write the year of your birth in words, once beginning with *dix-neuf cent...* and once with *mille neuf cent... .*

Vous aimez la cuisine japonaise? Quelle est (what is) l'adresse de ce restaurant?

Phase deux

Note Culturelle
French Canada

Most French Canadians live in the province of Quebec, but there are substantial numbers of French-speaking Canadians in other regions of Canada, particularly in Ontario, New Brunswick, and Manitoba. They have maintained their language, traditions, and customs. French Canadians have their own newspapers, books, radio and TV networks, particularly in the province of Quebec. Called *La Belle Province* because of its natural beauty, Quebec is the largest Canadian province in size and the second largest in population after Ontario.

Of the 6,000,000 inhabitants of Quebec, 5,000,000 are French Canadians (*Québecois*). The province's largest city, Montreal, is one of the largest cities in Canada. Quebec City, the seat of government for the province, retains much of the charm of the old world. It has kept the French flavor in its architecture and way of life.

Just as American English has become different from British English, Canadian French has evolved differently from the mother tongue. Canadian French differs slightly from Metropolitan French (the standard French spoken in France) in both pronunciation and vocabulary. From the early French settlers, it has preserved some words and expressions no longer in use in France.

La Place Royale, Québec, P.Q.

1. Read aloud the approximate number of inhabitants of Montreal: *1.222.000.*
2. Where are these things in your book?
   Où est la Préparation 8? (Elle est à la page...)
   Où est la note culturelle sur le Canada français?
   Où est l'Index?

Vocabulaire

Noms

l'air *m.* *air*
le baseball *baseball*
le bruit *noise*
la campagne *countryside*
le journal *newspaper*
la nature *nature*
la pollution *pollution*
la radio *radio*
le reporter *reporter*
le retour *return*
le théâtre *theater*
le type *guy, fellow*
l'université *f.* *university*
le village *village*
la ville *city*

Adjectifs

agréable *pleasant*
classique *classical*
faux, fausse *false*
pur/e *pure*
vrai/e *true*

Verbes

avoir *to have*
habiter *to live*
nager *to swim*
patiner *to skate*
poser une question *to ask a question*
préférer *to prefer*

Autres mots et expressions

aux États-Unis *in the United States*
ça *that (indefinite pron.)*
comme *like, as*
de temps en temps *once in a while, sometimes*
aujourd'hui *today*
demain *tomorrow*
hier *yesterday;* ~c'était... *yesterday it was...*
il n'y a pas de... *there is no...*
mais si *yes, on the contrary*
oh là là! *oh my!*
pour *for; in order to*
pourquoi (pas)? *why (not)?*
quel jour est-ce aujourd'hui? *what day is today?*
qui sait...? *who knows...?*

Les douze mois de l'année

janvier *January*
février *February*
mars *March*
avril *April*
mai *May*
juin *June*
juillet *July*
août *August*
septembre *September*
octobre *October*
novembre *November*
décembre *December*
l'année *f.* *year*
le mois *month*

Nombres 101 et +

cent un *101*
cent deux *102*
cent dix *110*
deux cents *200*
deux cent un *201*
mille *1000*
deux mille *2000*
un million *1.000.000*
deux millions *2.000.000*
un milliard *1.000.000.000*
deux milliards *2.000.000.000*

PRÉPARATION 9

Une belle voiture, c'est important?

Jacques taquine Roger, qui voit sa petite amie parler avec un jeune homme près d'une belle voiture.

Roger: Qui est ce type qui parle avec Anne?

Jacques: C'est François Galant. Il est beau, hein?

Roger: Beau? Avec cette barbe? Ah non, alors!

Jacques: Avec une belle voiture un homme est toujours beau!

Roger: Oh, ça va, ça va!

Jacques: Dis donc, Roger, tu es jaloux?

Roger: Moi, jaloux? Tu plaisantes!

A beautiful car: important or not?

Jacques is teasing Roger, who sees his girl-friend talking with a young man next to a beautiful car.

Who is that guy who's talking with Anne?

It's François Galant. He's handsome, isn't he?

Handsome! With that beard? Not at all. (Not in the least.)

With a beautiful car, a man is always handsome!

O.K., O.K.! (Cut it out!)

By the way, Roger, are you jealous?

Me, jealous? You've got to be kidding!

1. S1: Pick a character from the comics, television, or a play. Identify the character, and comment on how beautiful or handsome he/she is.

   S2: Express agreement or disagreement by commenting on a feature of the character's appearance. Let your intonation express your attitude.

ce visage *(face)*	ce sourire *(smile)*
cette bouche *(mouth)*	ces cheveux *(hair)*
ce nez *(nose)*	cette moustache

   S1: Ask if your partner is jealous.

   S2: Reply.

2. S1: Ask your partner if he/she does certain activities well *(bien)*. (See list p. 70, frame 3.)

   S2: Let your intonation express your attitude toward your skill or lack of skill.

   Oh, oui, très bien. *(pride, enthusiasm, or sarcasm)*
   Pas très bien. *(indifference or disappointment)*

1. More feminine forms of adjectives

1. You have learned that the feminine forms of some descriptive adjectives end in a consonant sound. Look at this sentence: *André est français; Marthe est française.* Which written combination contains a consonant sound when spoken—the masculine *-ais* or the feminine *-aise?* |

   the feminine *-aise*

2. Most French adjectives have a masculine form that ends in a written consonant. In the feminine form, all French adjectives end in the written vowel *e*. Write the correct form of the adjective in parentheses to complete the sentences below.

   Modèle: Vous êtes _____, Mademoiselle? (français) |

   française

   a. Madeleine est _____. (grand) |

      grande

   b. Est-ce que le garçon est _____? (américain) |

      américain

   c. La fille est _____. (petit) |

      petite

3. Some adjectives have masculine and feminine forms that sound alike. Read the following pairs of sentences aloud.

M. Dupont est riche.	Mme Dupont est riche.
M. Saunier est pauvre.	Mme Saunier est pauvre.

a. Both forms of these adjectives end with the written letter
_____. |

e

b. Do these adjectives end in a vowel sound or a consonant
sound? |

consonant sound

c. In which pair of adjectives do both forms sound the same?

américain, américaine   moderne, moderne   petit, petite |

moderne, moderne

4. Write a short dialogue in French in which you pretend that you
are talking to a friend about M. Blondeau.
   a. You ask your friend whether M. Blondeau is tall. Then your
   friend says no, he's very short. |

—M. Blondeau est grand? —Non, il est très petit.

   b. Continue by asking whether Mme Blondeau is short. Your
   friend says no, she's very tall. |

—Mme Blondeau est petite? —Non, elle est très grande.

2. Talking about occupations and religions

The word *professions* in English implies work requiring advanced education; the French word *professions* has the wider meaning of *occupations*. Familiarize yourself with the words below, then continue. In
the list of cognates, notice differences in spelling between the French
and English words.

Cognates

l'architecte *m.*   *architect*
le/la dentiste   *dentist*
le/la journaliste   *journalist*
le pilote   *pilot,* la femme
pilote
le/la secrétaire   *secretary*

le directeur/la directrice   *chief
    administrator; principal (of a school)*
le médecin *doctor*
le photographe   *photographer*
le professeur   *teacher, professor*

Other

l'avocat/e *m./f.*   *lawyer*
le comptable   *accountant*
l'écrivain *m.*   *writer*
le gérant/la gérante   *manager*

l'infirmier/infirmière   *nurse*
l'ingénieur   *engineer*
l'ouvrier/ouvrière   *manual
    worker; blue-collar worker*

1. These sentences tell what two people do for a living: *M. Durand
   est dentiste. Mme Roule est journaliste.*
   a. Write the English equivalents. |

Mr. Durand is a dentist. Mrs. Roule is a journalist.

b. In English, an indefinite article is used after *to be* with an occupation: He's *a* dentist; she's *a* journalist. Are indefinite articles used in the French equivalents? |

no (after *être* + a noun of occupation, the article is usually omitted.)

2. Write the French equivalents:
   a. You *(Vous)* are a dentist? |

Vous êtes dentiste?

   b. I'm an accountant. |

Je suis comptable.

3. As in English *actor, actress,* the names of some occupations in French have feminine forms when they refer to women.
   a. Alain est ouvrier. Alice est _____. |

ouvrière (Remember the *accent grave.*)

   b. Jean-Paul est infirmier. Jeannette est _____. |

infirmière (There's that accent again.)

4. Match the picture cues with *avocat, pilote, dentiste, médecin, photographe* and write what people do for a living. Check your spelling carefully.

   Modèle: M. Labouche

M. Labouche est dentiste.

a. Arthur Laprise

Arthur Laprise est photographe.

b. Tu

Tu es pilote.

c. Je

Je suis médecin.

d. Elle

Elle est avocate.

5. In English, an indefinite article is often used to describe someone's religious or political affiliation: *He is a Moslem. You are a Republican.* In French, adjectives are used. Write equivalents.
   a. He is a Catholic. *(catholique)* |

Il est catholique.

   b. You are a Gaullist? *(gaulliste)* |

Vous êtes gaulliste?

3. Forming questions: *qui, où, qu'est-ce que?*

Information questions (which generally have a falling intonation pattern) often begin with a question word or expression like *qui* (who?), *où* (where?), or *qu'est-ce que* (what?).

1. Read the following questions aloud.

> Où est Marie-Claude? Qui habite à Paris?
> Qu'est-ce que tu regardes?

   a. Which question asks *what?* |
> Qu'est ce que tu regardes? (What are you looking at?)

   b. Which one asks *where?* |
> Où est Marie-Claude? (Where is Marie-Claude?)

   c. Which question asks *who?* |
> Qui habite à Paris? (Who lives in Paris?)

2. Below are partial questions and their answers. Figure out whether each question should begin with *qui, où,* or *qu'est-ce que,* and write the complete question.

   a. —_____ tu écoutes?   —J'écoute un disque de jazz.
   b. —_____ aime danser?   —Moi! J'adore danser!
   c. —_____ est le disque de rock?   —Il est sur la table. |
> a. Qu'est-ce que tu écoutes?   b. Qui aime danser?   c. Où est le disque de rock?

3. Write French equivalents. (See key.)
   a. Where is Philippe?
   b. Who's singing?
   c. What are you eating? |

À Propos!

Ask who has a piece of paper.
Ask where two of your friends are.

4. The demonstrative adjectives *ce, cet,* and *cette*

In English, the adjectives *this* or *that* make clear which person or thing you're talking about.

1. Here's a conversation that might take place at an auto show.

> *Paul:*   Do you like this sedan?
> *Jeanne:*   No, I like that station wagon better.

This and *that* are demonstrative adjectives. What kind of word accompanies an adjective—a noun or a verb? |
> a noun

2. a. Write the demonstrative adjectives in these sentences.
Ce garçon est Jean-Michel. Cet homme est M. Giraud.
Cette fille est Marie-Claire. |

ce, cet, cette (Each adjective can mean either *this* or *that,* depending on the context. When the differentiation is not obvious, *-ci* (this) or *-là* (that) is added to the noun: *cet homme-là,* that man.)

b. Which form of the adjective is used with a masculine noun beginning with a consonant sound? |

ce

c. Which form is used with a masculine noun beginning with a vowel sound? |

cet (The word *homme* actually begins with a vowel sound and the *t* links with the vowel.)

d. Which form is used with a feminine noun? |

cette

3. Write the form of the demonstrative adjectives that completes each of these statements.

a. _____ avocat est de Bordeaux. |

Cet

b. _____ avocate est Mme Rochemont. |

Cette

c. _____ photographe est américain. |

Ce

4. How can you tell whether to write *cet* or *cette* when you hear *cet avocat, cette avocate*—by the gender of the noun or by the sound you hear? |

by the gender of the noun

5. Rewrite the noun phrases, changing the indefinite article to the demonstrative adjective.

Modèle: un stylo, un comptable |

ce stylo, ce comptable

a. une classe, une secrétaire |

cette classe, cette secrétaire

b. un écran, un homme |

cet écran, cet homme

c. une étagère, une enfant |

cette étagère, cette enfant

d. un ouvrier, une ouvrière |

cet ouvrier, cette ouvrière

e. un mois, une année |

ce mois, cette année

À Propos!

Name a record you have and ask a friend if he or she likes this record.

5. The relative pronoun *qui*

This section explains how to use the word *qui* to combine two statements.

1. You already know the word *qui* as an interrogative pronoun. Write the English equivalent: *Qui est cet homme?*

     Who is that man? (*Qui* is used to ask questions about people.)

2. Here are two sentences that each give information about a person.

     Anne is talking with a man.   The man is an architect.

     It's possible to combine the two sentences into one. Write the word that is needed to join the two statements.

     Anne is talking with a man _____ is an architect.

     who (The relative pronoun *who* replaces *the man*.)

3. Here are the French equivalents.

     Anne parle avec un homme. L'homme est architecte.
     Anne parle avec un homme *qui* est architecte.

     Which word corresponds to *who?*

     qui (Like *who*, the relative pronoun *qui* always replaces the subject of a sentence. Here, *qui* replaces *l'homme*. It can also replace a feminine noun or a plural noun.)

4. Combine these two sentences into one: *Nathalie parle avec une femme. Elle est médecin.*

     Nathalie parle avec une femme qui est médecin.

À Paris: Montmartre, quartier des artistes. Une femme chante. Comment s'appelle sa chanson?

5. Give the French equivalent: *David is talking with a man who is a nurse.* |

David parle avec un homme qui est infirmier.

6. See how these sentences are combined.

Monique is looking for the record.
The record is under the chair.
Monique is looking for the record that is under the chair.

Here the relative pronoun is _____ instead of *who.* |

that (*Who* is used only for people. *That* and *which* refer to people or to things.)

7. Now look at the French sentence: *Monique cherche le disque qui est sous la chaise.*
   a. What noun phrase does *qui* replace? |

le disque

   b. True or false? The relative pronoun *qui* refers only to people. |

false (*Qui* can also refer to things.)

8. Monique has a few friends who are as absent-minded as she is. Write complete sentences to tell what each is looking for and where it actually is.
   Modèle: Monique/le livre/sur la table. |

Monique cherche le livre qui est sur la table.

   a. Jacques/la cassette/derrière la télévision. |

Jacques cherche la cassette qui est derrière la télévision.

   b. Colette/la feuille de papier/sous le bureau. |

Colette cherche la feuille de papier qui est sous le bureau.

9. Read the sentences below.

Cette jeune fille est grande.
La jeune fille qui chante maintenant est grande.

Does *grande* agree in gender with *jeune fille* in both sentences? |

yes (The occurrence of the *qui*-clause does not change the need for agreement between the noun and the adjective.)

10. Tell the nationality of each person living in the cities below. (See key.)
    Modèle: cet homme/Milan/italien |

Cet homme qui habite à Milan est italien.

    a. cet homme/Munich/allemand
    b. cette femme/Wichita/américain
    c. cette femme/Aix/français

À Propos!

Using only French vocabulary you are familiar with, say something about a friend of yours: *J'ai un/e ami/e qui...*

Note Linguistique
The melody of French

You have been practicing the sounds of many vowels and consonants which are quite different from the same letters when they are used in English. But there is something else to notice: the melody of the sentence. The way individual syllables are strung into words, and words into sentences, obeys different rules or habits. Knowing what constitutes the melody of your own language will help you hear and imitate the melody of French.

1. In English, some vowels are long, some are short: i.e. *bin* is shorter than *bean*. In French each vowel sound is about the same length: *je, suis, pas, bien, mer-ci.*

2. In English, some syllables are stressed more than the others: family, fa*mi*liar, famil*i*arity. The vowel in the stressed syllable is much clearer than the unstressed vowel. Unstressed vowels become neutral, blending into an indistinct schwa /ə/ sound like *a* and *i* in *hospital*.

In French, every syllable receives *equal* stress. In *familiarité*, every *a*, *i*, and *é* retains a clear, distinct sound. No vowel disappears into an unstressed schwa sound. Sometimes you might think that the French speak faster. They do not; but in a twenty-syllable sentence in French there will be twenty stressed segments, while in English there might be only half as many. French has an even staccato rhythm, while English slows down or speeds up:

Equal stress

Il est ar- ri- vé à six heures.

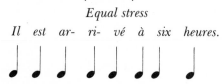

Unequal stress

He came at six o' clock.

However, in French, the last syllable of a group receives a slightly stronger stress: Bon*jour*. Bon*jour*, Ma*dame*.

3. In English, one word is usually separated from another by a brief break: six//o'clock, he//is, my//eyes. This gives English a somewhat choppy rhythm. In French, any final consonant sound is carried over to begin the next word in what is called *liaison*. This tends to make French sound smoother than English. Compare:

An English speaker says:
Sam/ate/an/old/apple.

A French speaker says:
Sa may ta no ldapple.

Words flow into each other: consonants link with the following vowel, and vowel links to vowel until a breathing pause is needed. This produces a pleasant smoothness, but it can hinder your comprehension until you learn to recognize the boundaries of words by their meanings instead of by sound.

By listening for and imitating these features of French—clear, distinct vowels; equal stress on each vowel; linking words in a smooth, even flow—you will speak well and you will find it easier to understand what you want to hear, whether it is a conversation in class or the dialogue of a movie.

Vocabulaire

Noms

l'étagère *f.*   *shelf*
le petit ami   *boyfriend*
la petite amie   *girlfriend*
la voiture   *car*

Les professions
l'architecte *m./f.*   *architect*
l'avocat/e   *lawyer*
le/la comptable   *accountant*
le/la dentiste   *dentist*
le directeur/la directrice   *chief
     administrator; principal (of a school)*
l'écrivain *m.*   *writer*
le gérant/la gérante   *manager*
l'infirmier/infirmière   *nurse*
l'ingénieur *m.*   *engineer*
le/la journaliste   *journalist*
le médecin   *doctor*
l'ouvrier/ouvrière   *manual worker;
     blue-collar worker*
le/la photographe   *photographer*
le pilote/la femme pilote   *pilot*
le professeur *m.*   *teacher, professor*
le/la secrétaire   *secretary*

Le visage

la barbe   *beard*
la bouche   *mouth*
les cheveux *m.pl.*   *hair*
la moustache   *moustache*
le nez   *nose*
le visage   *face*

Adjectifs

catholique   *Catholic (a Catholic)*
ce, cet, cette   *this, that
     (demonstrative adj.)*
gaulliste   *Gaullist (a Gaullist)*
important/e   *important*
jaloux/jalouse   *jealous*
moderne   *modern*
musulman   *Moslem (a Moslem)*

Verbes

plaisanter   *to joke*
taquiner   *to tease*

Autres mots et expressions

ah non, alors!   *not in the least
     (emphatic no!)*
avec   *with*
dis donc   *say, now; by the way (to get
     immediate attention)*
hein?   *don't you think? what?*
qui   *who, which (relative pron.)*
je voudrais   *I would like*
tu voudrais   *you would like*
il/elle voudrait   *he/she would like*
vous voudriez   *you would like*

PRÉPARATION 10

1. Nasal consonants and nasal vowels

1. A nasal sound is one that is produced when air passes through the nose as you speak.
   a. To find out if a word contains a nasal consonant, pinch your nostrils shut while you say the word. If there's a nasal consonant, you will have trouble saying the word because you are blocking the passage of air through your nose. Which of the following words contain nasal consonants?

   murmur   dawdle   noon   history   mystery |

   murmur, noon, mystery

   b. The two nasal consonants are represented by the letters _____ and _____. |

   m, n (These two nasal consonants occur in both French and English.)

2. In French, there are nasal vowels as well as nasal consonants. Place your fingers lightly on the sides of your nose as you say these words aloud: *beau, bon* (good).
   a. For which word do you feel a strong vibration in your fingertips? |

   bon (The vibration occurs because air is passing through your nose and mouth at the same time. The *-on* of *bon* represents a nasal vowel sound.)

3. Look at these words with nasal vowels emphasized.

   *un   an*glais   médec*in*   bo*n*jour   scie*n*ce   *im*porta*n*t
   co*m*ptable   *em*pire

   In written French, a nasal vowel sound is represented by a vowel *(a, e, i, o,* or *u)*, plus the consonant _____ or _____. |

   m, n

4. Here are the same words with letters missing. Complete each word by adding the letters that represent the nasal vowels.
   a. b _ _ jour, médec _ _, sci _ _ ce, _ _ glais |

   bonjour, médecin, science, anglais

   b. _ _ port _ _ t, _ _ pire, c _ _ ptable |

   important, empire, comptable

5. English speakers tend to close nasal vowels into nasal consonants. Try saying these words syllable by syllable, keeping the nasal vowels open.

André /ã dRe/   important /ɛ̃ pɔR tã/   grande /grã d/

2. More practice with adjectives

This chart shows some adjectives you have used so far to describe people. Refer to the chart to answer the questions below.

Adjectives: Masculine and Feminine Forms

Sound and spelling are different	Sound and spelling are the same	Sound is the same: spelling is different
américain, américaine	bête	pressé, pressée
beau, belle	célèbre	joli, jolie
bon, bonne	classique	
français, française	jeune	
gentil, gentille	maigre	
grand, grande	moderne	
gros, grosse	pauvre	
intelligent,	riche	
intelligente	stupide	
jaloux, jalouse	moche	
laid, laide	sociable	
petit, petite	optimiste	
vieux, vieille	réaliste	
	idéaliste	

1. a. In writing, the feminine form of many adjectives is made by adding *e* to the masculine form. Select those adjectives from the chart above, and write both forms. |

   américain, américaine; français, française; grand, grande; intelligent, intelligente; laid, laide; petit, petite; pressé, pressée; joli, jolie

   b. Sometimes the written feminine form is just like the masculine except that the final consonant is doubled before the final *e* is added. Which adjectives in the chart are like this? |

   gentil, gentille; gros, grosse; bon, bonne

   c. Often a masculine adjective ends in a written consonant, and a feminine form ends in a written vowel. Which form—masculine or feminine—ends in a *vowel sound*? |

   masculine form (for example, *petit, petite*)

2. Three of the adjectives are irregular—that is, the sound and spelling of the feminine form are different from the masculine, and the difference doesn't fit a predictable pattern. Write the irregular adjectives. |

beau, belle; vieux, vieille; jaloux, jalouse

3. You have learned quite a few adjectives that have the same sound and spelling in the masculine and feminine forms. Try to write those below without looking at the chart.

b_te   r_ch_   st_pid_
c_lèbr_   m_d_rn_   cl_s_iq_e
_aigre   p_uvr_   j__ne |

bête, riche, stupide, célèbre, moderne, classique, maigre, pauvre, jeune

4. The first sentence in each pair makes a statement about a person. Complete the second statement with the opposite adjective.

Modèle: Henri n'est pas petit. Il est _____. |

grand

a. Philippe n'est pas stupide. Il est _____. | a. intelligent
b. Josette n'est pas laide. Elle est _____. | b. belle
c. Marcel n'est pas gros. Il est _____. | c. maigre
d. Monique n'est pas vieille. Elle est _____. | d. jeune

5. Serge and Monique are much alike. Write the appropriate form of the adjective to complete the description of the other.

Modèle: Serge est grand. Monique est _____ aussi. |

grande

a. Monique est belle. Serge est _____ aussi. |

beau

b. Serge est jaloux. Monique est _____ aussi. |

jalouse

c. Serge n'est pas gros. Monique n'est pas _____ non plus *(not . . . either).* |

grosse

6. Rewrite each sentence below so that it describes the person named in parentheses. (See key.)
   a. Paul Bertrand est très beau et très célèbre. *(Sylvie Duval)*
   b. M. Lesage est très vieux et très intelligent. *(Mme Lesage)*
   c. Pierre est gros, laid et jaloux. *(Christine)*

À Propos!

Pick five adjectives from the chart and think of someone you know who can be described by that word. Write the name and any of these relationships that apply:

ami/amie; camarade; parent (relative);
voisin/voisine; collègue (colleague, co-worker)

3. Vocabulary recall: occupations

Figure out the French word for the people described by the cues.

1. a. A male singer |
   b. A female singer |
2. A person who writes books and articles |
3. a. A man who plays a role in a drama |
   b. A woman who does the same |
4. a. A woman who plays an instrument |
   b. A man who does likewise |
5. a. A female dancer |
   b. Her partner |
6. a. A man who helps a doctor |
   b. The female counterpart |
7. a. A woman who works in a factory |
   b. The male counterpart |

1.a. un chanteur
  b. une chanteuse
2.   un écrivain
3.a. un acteur
  b. une actrice
4.a. une musicienne
  b. un musicien
5.a. une danseuse
  b. un danseur
6.a. un infirmier
  b. un infirmière
7.a. une ouvrière
  b. un ouvrier

COMPAGNIE D'ASSURANCES A BRUXELLES-CENTRE
recherche pour son service « INFORMATIQUE »

UN PROGRAMMEUR
COBOL & ASSEMBLER

Exigences :
— 35 ANS maximum ;
— libre service militaire ;
— graduat en informatique minimum,
— préférence bilingue.

Est-ce que vous êtes qualifié/e pour cet emploi (job)?

4. Demonstrative adjectives: practice

1. What are the two English equivalents for *ce, cet,* and *cette*? |
   this, that
2. Which form—*ce, cet,* or *cette*—is used with a singular noun that is:
   a. feminine? |
   b. masculine and begins with a vowel sound? |
   c. masculine and begins with a consonant sound? |

   a. cette
   b. cet
   c. ce

3. Complete the sentences below. (See key.)
   a. _____ fille est française.
   b. _____ enfant est anglais.
   c. _____ gérante parle espagnol.
   d. _____ livre est beau.
   e. _____ directeur est de Québec.
   f. _____ enfant est belle.
   g. _____ homme est infirmier.
   h. _____ magnétophone est petit.

5. The present tense of *-re* verbs

This section introduces a group of verbs whose infinitive ending is *-re*.

1. Your uncle Bernard is almost deaf. One day your friend Monique comes to visit and you tell her about the problem. You say: *Tu sais, il n'entend pas bien.*

   a. Write the English equivalent of *il n'entend pas bien.* |
      he doesn't hear well

   b. The infinitive ending of *entendre* is *-re*. Write the infinitive stem. |
      entend- (This is also the present tense stem.)

   The verb *entendre* can serve as a model for all regular *-re* verbs.

j'	**entend**	**s**	nous	entend	**ons**
tu	entend	**s**	vous	entend	**ez**
on/il/elle	entend		ils/elles	entend	**ent**

2. Only two forms have pronounced endings. Write these forms with their subject pronouns. |
   nous entendons, vous entendez

3. Say all the forms aloud. Is the *-d-* of the stem pronounced in the singular forms, or in the plural forms? |
   in the plural forms

4. Study all the forms of *entendre* for a few moments, then test yourself by completing the sentences below. Write both the subject and the verb. Check your answers against the chart.

   a. On _____ l'orchestre.
   b. Vous _____ la voiture?
   c. Elle _____ la musique.
   d. Je n'_____ pas la radio.
   e. Est-ce que tu _____ le télé-phone?
   f. Nous _____ le bruit *(noise)*.

5. There are many regular *-re* verbs.

   a. Write the stems of *vendre* (to sell) and *répondre à* (to answer something or someone). |
      vend-, répond-

   b. Can you write out what this abbreviates? R.S.V.P. |
      Répondez, s'il vous plaît (often seen on formal invitations)

   c. *Vendre* has an English cognate: a _____ing machine. |
      vending

6. Each of the following sentences can be logically completed with *vendre* or *répondre (à)*. Write the correct form of the appropriate verb on your worksheet.

   a. Nous _____ la question.
   b. On _____ des jeans en France.

   a. répondons à
   b. vend

c. Est-ce qu'ils _____ cette maison?
d. Philippe ne _____ pas _____ cette question.
e. Vous _____ cette auto?
f. Comment est-ce que tu _____ cette accusation?

c. vendent
d. répond à
e. vendez
f. réponds à

Here are some other verbs whose forms are like those of *entendre,* *vendre,* and *répondre.*

attendre *to wait (for)*
défendre *to defend; to forbid*
rendre (à) *to give something back*

descendre (de) *to descend, go down, step down from*
perdre *to lose*

7. Complete each statement with the correct form of a verb from the list above. (See key.)
   a. Les spectateurs _____ le match de football avec impatience.

Note Culturelle
The ancient provinces

Before the French Revolution of 1789, France was divided into thirty provinces, each with distinctive traditions and privileges, and each with its own administrator, called *intendant (de province),* who was appointed by the king. The responsibilities of the *intendant* included maintaining order and justice, and promoting the general welfare of the province. The power and influence of the *intendants* grew significantly under King Louis XIV when appointments were made permanent. The intendancies were abolished in 1791 by the first French Republic, which divided the provinces into *departements* and smaller administrative districts. Today, although they have no legal status, the ancient provinces play a vital part in the lives of all French people, who are strongly devoted to and appreciative of the diverse customs and qualities of each region.

Dans la province d'Alsace. C'est un lac ou un canal?

b. Les voyageurs _____ du train.
c. L'armée _____ la ville.
d. Nous _____ toujours à la loterie.
e. Martine _____ ce disque à Paul.

À Propos! Answer, and be prepared to ask a classmate:
Vous perdez la tête *(go crazy, lose your head)* quand *(when)* vous avez un examen?

6. Practice with *avoir*

Charles perd tout. Où sont les disques, la cassette, le cadeau et le magnétophone? Use the proper form of *avoir* to tell with whom Charles has left these things. (See key.)

1. Irène _____ le disque.
2. Pierre et Martine _____ le cadeau.
3. Je _____ la cassette.
4. Vous _____ le magnétophone.
5. Nous _____ les disques.

Vocabulaire

Noms

l'acteur *m.*   *actor*
l'actrice *f.*   *actress*
l'armée *f.*   *army*
l'athlète *m.*   *athlete*
l'auto *f.*   *car*
le chanteur/la chanteuse   *singer*
le/la collègue   *colleague, co-worker*
le danseur/la danseuse   *dancer*
l'examen *m.*   *exam*
la fin   *end*
l'impatience *f.*   *impatience*
la loterie   *lottery*
la maison   *house*
le musicien/la musicienne   *musician*
le/la parent/e   *parent, relative*
la porte   *door*
le spectateur/la spectatrice   *member of the audience, spectator*
le train   *train*
le voyageur/la voyageuse   *traveler*

Adjectifs

célèbre   *famous*
idiot/e   *stupid, idiotic*

impatient/e   *impatient*
moche   *ugly*
patient/e   *patient*
sociable   *sociable, outgoing*
stupide   *stupid*
timide   *shy*
vieux/vieille   *old*

Verbes

attendre   *to wait (for)*
défendre   *to defend; to forbid*
descendre   *to go down; to get out (of a vehicle)*
entendre   *to hear*
perdre   *to lose;* ~la tête   *to go crazy, lose one's head*
rendre à   *to give back to*
répondre (à quelqu'un)   *to answer (someone)*
vendre   *to sell*

Autres mots et expressions

en France   *in France*
ne... pas non plus   *not... either*
quand   *when*

PRÉPARATION 11

1. *Le voilà, la voilà*

1. Read this short dialogue.

> —Où est le livre?
> —Le voilà.
> —Ah, merci!

What does *Le voilà* mean? |
There it is./Here it is.

2. In *Le voilà* in frame 1, *le* refers to the noun phrase *le livre*. If the noun phrase is *la cassette,* you use a different word before *voilà.*
—Où est la cassette? —_____ voilà. |
La (*Le* is used to replace a masculine noun; *la* replaces a feminine noun.)

3. Now look at this dialogue.

> —Où est Marie?   —La voilà.

a. What's the English equivalent of *la voilà* this time? |
There she is./Here she is.

b. How would you say *There he is* in French? |
Le voilà. (You can use *Le voilà* and *La voilà* to talk about things or about people.)

4. Suppose your instructor is ill and another instructor or teaching assistant has your class for the day. The new person needs help finding people and things in the classroom, so you point them out. Write *Le voilà* or *La voilà* in response to the questions.

a. Où est la bande? | a. La voilà.
b. Où est Michel Auriol? | b. Le voilà.
c. Et Nancy Barbery? | c. La voilà.
d. Où est le cahier de M. Roland? | d. Le voilà.
e. Où est l'écran? | e. Le voilà.
f. Et l'affiche? | f. La voilà.

2. Asking questions with *n'est-ce pas?*

1. The expression *n'est-ce pas* (literally, *isn't it?*) is often used after a statement to turn it into a question. The French expression is

invariable; the English equivalent can vary from sentence to sentence. Complete the English equivalents below.

a. C'est un disque, n'est-ce pas? *It's a record, _____?*

isn't it

b. Daniel est français, n'est-ce pas? *Daniel is French, _____?*

isn't he (The English equivalent of *n'est-ce pas* depends on the subject and the tense of the verb in the statement.)

2. Write the French equivalents, using *n'est-ce pas.*

a. They (*Ils*) are speaking Italian, aren't they?

Ils parlent italien, n'est-ce pas?

b. She's listening to a Dany Leclerc record, isn't she?

Elle écoute un disque de Dany Leclerc, n'est-ce pas?

3. Jean-Luc, a French student in the U.S., is trying to remember things about his new American classmates, but he isn't having much luck.

—Chuck, tu n'aimes pas le jazz, n'est-ce pas?
—Mais si, j'aime le jazz.

Give the English equivalent of the exchange.

—Chuck, you don't like jazz, do you?

—Yes, I *do* like jazz. (*Mais si* is used to contradict a negative statement.)

4. Write Jean-Luc's questions with *n'est-ce pas,* and answer for his classmates with *mais si.*

a. Bob/ne pas habiter à Clinton

—Bob, tu n'habites pas à Clinton, n'est-ce pas?

—Mais si, j'habite à Clinton.

b. Debbie/ne pas aimer patiner

—Debbie, tu n'aimes pas patiner, n'est-ce pas?

—Mais si, j'aime patiner.

À Propos!

Give your opinion of a particular record, and ask a classmate to agree with you:
Le disque de _____ est bon, n'est-ce pas?

3. *Qui suis-je?*

In class you will be playing the game *Qui suis-je?* in which one person plays the role of a mystery guest and another guesses the identity by asking *oui-non* questions. This part of the Préparation will prepare you to play.

1. You may want to know whether the mystery guest is a man, woman, or child. Write the indefinite articles that complete these questions.

a. Tu es _____ homme?
b. Tu es _____ femme?
c. Tu es _____ enfant? _____ enfant? |

a. un   b. une   c. un, une

2. You may want to ask the guest whether he or she is American.
   —Tu _____ américain?
   —Non, je ne _____ pas américain. |

   es, suis

3. If you guessed the wrong nationality, you may want to try again. This time ask whether the mystery guest is French.
   —_____ _____ français?
   —Oui, _____ _____ français. |

   tu es, je suis

4. You'll probably want to know the occupation of the mystery guest. Remember that when *être* is followed by the name of an occupation, the indefinite article is usually omitted.

   Modèle: architecte (non) |

   —Tu es architecte?
   —Non, je ne suis pas architecte.

   a. écrivain (non) |

   —Tu es écrivain?
   —Non, je ne suis pas écrivain.

   b. acteur (oui) |

   —Tu es acteur?
   —Oui, je suis acteur.

5. Find out more about the mystery guest. Ask in French:
   a. Do you live in Paris?
   b. Do you speak French?
   c. Do you like to sing? |

   a. Tu habites à Paris?   b. Tu parles français?   c. Tu aimes chanter?

À Propos!

Think of the people who sit to your left and right in class. Identify them by gender and hair color, and tell their names. For example, *La fille brune s'appelle Julie.*

4. Practice with *qui? où? qu'est-ce que?*

Suppose a group of Americans is in Europe on vacation. The sentences below tell which places they are visiting and some of their reactions. For each sentence, write a question with *qui*, with *qu'est-ce que*, with *où*.

Modèle: Donna visite le Kremlin à Moscou.

   a. qui

   b. qu'est-ce que

   c. où |

a. Qui visite le Kremlin?   b. Qu'est-ce que Donna visite?   c. Où est le Kremlin?

1. Nancy visite le Louvre à Paris.

   a. qui

   b. qu'est-ce que

   c. où |

a. Qui visite le Louvre?   b. Qu'est-ce que Nancy visite?   c. Où est le Louvre?

2. Robert aime Buckingham Palace à Londres.

   a. qui

   b. qu'est-ce que

   c. où |

a. Qui aime Buckingham Palace?   b. Qu'est-ce que Robert aime?   c. Où est Buck-
ingham Palace?

3. Mathieu admire le Parthénon à Athènes.

   a. qui

   b. qu'est-ce que

   c. où |

a. Qui admire le Parthénon?   b. Qu'est-ce que Mathieu admire?   c. Où est le Par-
thénon?

5. *Avoir + ans* to express age

1. Compare the following sentences.

> J'ai 17 ans. *I'm 17 years old.*
> My tante a 32 ans. *My aunt is 32 years old.*

   a. Which verb is used in English to express age—*to be* or *to have?* |

to be

   b. Which verb is used in French to express age—*être* or *avoir?* |

avoir

2. French uses *avoir + ans* (years) to express age: *Il a huit ans.* Does French also use the equivalent of *old,* as in *He is 8 years old?* |

no

3. It may help you remember *avoir + ans* if you think of age as accumulated experience in living. For example, *Roger a douze ans:* Roger has 12 years (of experience in living).

   Tell how old each of these people is, and write out each number.

   Modèle: Monique Larue: 20 |

Elle a vingt ans.

a. Henry Dupont: 17 |

> Il a dix-sept ans.

b. Édouard Dupont: 12 |

> Il a douze ans.

c. Jacqueline Dupont: 15 |

> Elle a quinze ans.

d. Charles Larue: 18 |

> Il a dix-huit ans.

4. Someone asks how old Jacqueline is. Read the question and answer.

> —Jacqueline a seize ans?
> —Non, elle n'a pas seize ans, elle a quinze ans.

Someone else asks how old Henri is. Complete the answer.

> —Henri a seize ans?
> —Non, _____, il a dix-sept ans. |

> il n'a pas seize ans

5. Et vous, vous avez seize ans? |

> Non, je n'ai pas seize ans. J'ai . . . ans.

Vocabulaire

Noms
la chanson *song*
la femme *woman; wife*
le restaurant universitaire *university restaurant, cafeteria*

Adjectifs
blond cendré *ash-blond*
blond doré *golden blond*
châtain (inv.) *chestnut (hair)*
châtain clair *light brown*
colombien/ne *Columbian*
crépu/e *frizzy*
indien/ne *Indian*
mexicain/e *Mexican*
raide *straight*
roux, rousse *red (haired)*
russe *Russian*

Autres mots et expressions
avoir... ans *to be... years old*
la/le voilà *there it/he/she is*
n'est-ce pas? *isn't that so? right?; doesn't he? don't you? etc.*
qui suis-je? *who am I?*

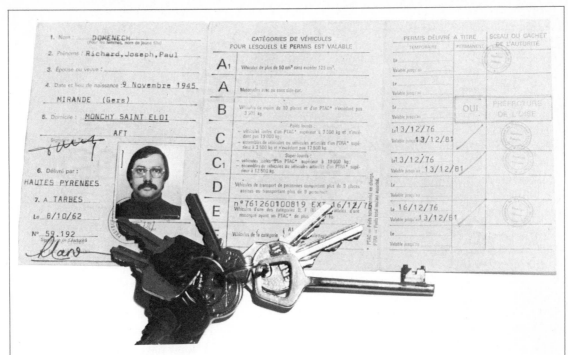

Note Culturelle
Age and legal privileges

A young person in France is legally an adult at the age of eighteen. Although sixteen is the minimum age for obtaining a license for a *mobylette* (motorized bike or motor scooter), one must be eighteen to have a driver's license (which, once obtained, is good for life). At eighteen one may vote, and marry without parental consent. Young men of eighteen are subject to required military service for one year. The concept of a "drinking age" does not exist in France in the same manner as it exists in the United States, at least as far as wine and beer are concerned. Wine is often present at the family dinner table. Children may drink wine that has been somewhat diluted with water at home and in school cafeterias. There are no laws prohibiting the sale of tobacco to children, but an intensive campaign against smoking has been going on for some time.

Permis de conduire (driver's license). Quel âge a cet homme?

PRÉPARATION 12

On n'est jamais content!

Simone est en train de montrer son album de photos à Mathieu.

Simone: Tiens, regarde cette photo. Elle est drôle, n'est-ce pas?

Mathieu: Oui, très drôle. Qui est le garçon qui dort? C'est ton frère?

Simone: Non, c'est mon cousin, malheureusement.

Mathieu: Malheureusement? Pourquoi?

Simone: Bof! J'ai une grande sœur, j'ai une petite sœur, mais je n'ai pas de frères.

Mathieu: Moi, j'ai des frères—quatre frères, mais pas de sœurs.

Simone: Oh là là! Quatre frères! Tu es l'aîné?

Mathieu: Oui. Heureusement, n'est-ce pas?

Simone: Oh oui, alors! Mais quatre petits frères, ce n'est pas marrant non plus!

Mathieu: Ah, on ne choisit pas . . . c'est la vie!

Some people are never satisfied!

Simone is showing her photo album to Mathieu.

Hey, look at this picture. It's funny, isn't it?

Yes, very funny. Who's the boy who's sleeping? Is it your brother?

No, it's my cousin, unfortunately.

Unfortunately? Why?

Oh, I have a big sister and I have a little sister, but I don't have any brothers.

I've got brothers—four brothers, but no sisters.

Wow! Four brothers! Are you the oldest?

Yes. Fortunately, right?

Oh, yes indeed! But four little brothers— That's not much fun either!

Ah, one has no choice... that's life!

Échange d'idées

1. Tell whether you have brothers and sisters, and how many; and indicate whether you consider yourself fortunate or unfortunate. Ask a classmate if he/she has brothers and sisters.
2. Tell about a brother or sister; invent one if you are a *fille unique* or *fils unique* (only child). Give the name, age, hair color. Say a little about his/her personality and what he/she likes or doesn't like to do.

les frères Jacques

1. Practice with *-re* verbs

1. The present-tense stem of *rendre* is _____. |

      rend- (The stem is the infinitive form minus the ending *-re.*)

2. Complete these phrases with the appropriate form of *rendre*.

   a. nous   c. je   e. tu
   b. on   d. ils f. vous |

      a. nous rendons b. on rend c. je rends d. ils rendent e. tu rends f. vous rendez

3. Complete the French equivalents, using these verbs: *perdre, répondre à, entendre, descendre.*

   a. Doris always loses her books. Doris _____ toujours ses livres. | a. perd

   b. Do you hear the radio? Vous _____ la radio? | b. entendez

   c. The campers are coming down from the mountain. Les campeurs _____ de la montagne. | c. descendent

   d. I answer the question. Je _____ la question. | d. réponds à

   e. That woman is getting out of the taxi. Cette femme _____ du taxi. | e. descend

Form new sentences by substituting new subjects as indicated.

   Modèle: Ils entendent le disque.
         Elle |

      Elle entend le disque.

4. Tu entends le téléphone.

   a. Vous
   b. Je |

      a. Vous entendez le téléphone. b. J'entends le téléphone.

5. Claudette rend le livre à Jacques.

   a. Mes amis
   b. Nous |

      a. Mes amis rendent le livre à Jacques. b. Nous rendons le livre à Jacques.

6. Write French equivalents. (See key.)

   a. I'm waiting for Marianne.
   b. Jean-François is answering the professor.
   c. Jacques and Anne are giving the radio back to Sophie.

2. Review of verbs in questions

1. In English, verbs in questions in the present tense often have two parts.

     Do you *speak* French?   *Are* you *watching* TV?
     Does she *live* in Paris?   *Is* he *listening* to the radio?

To express these questions in French, you use a single verb form only.

Vous *parlez* français?   Tu *regardes* la télé?

Elle *habite* à Paris?   Il *écoute* la radio?

2. Express the following questions in French. (See key.)
   a. Do they *(ils)* speak German?
   b. Is he waiting?
   c. Does he hear the telephone?
   d. Does Robert live in New York?
   e. Do Pierre and Jean like to skate?
   f. Is the car working now?
   g. Do they admire the president?
   h. Is she listening to the radio?

3. Vocabulary review

1. Write complete sentences to say what you are doing during the coming week. (See key.)

   Modèle: lundi/nager/avec Paul

   Lundi, je nage avec Paul.

   a. mardi/écouter/radio/avec Gabrielle
   b. jeudi/regarder/télévision avec Jean-François
   c. dimanche/patiner avec Daniel et Sylvie

2. Write sentences to say that you don't do these things: *danser, patiner, tricoter.* (See key.)

3. Complete the following dialogues with the correct name of an occupation. (See key.)
   a. —M. Leroi est médecin?
      —Non, il est d_nt_st_.
   b. —Mme Colbert est secrétaire?
      —Non, elle est c_mpt_b_e.
   c. —Roger est journaliste?
      —Non, il est p_ot_g__phe.
   d. —Denise est architecte?
      —Non, elle est ing_n___r.
   e. Et vous, vous êtes acteur à la télévision, Monsieur?
      —Non, je suis _criv__n.

4. Describe the girl in the picture by using the feminine form of the adjectives listed. (See key.)

   martiniquais, grand, mince, élégant, intelligent

   Cette jeune fille est _____. Elle est _____, _____, _____ et elle est _____.

5. Describe the boy in the picture by using the masculine form of the adjectives listed. (See key.)

anglaise, petite, rousse, belle, gentille

Ce garçon est _____. Il est _____, _____, _____ et il est _____.

6. Write the feminine forms of each occupation below. (See key.)

infirmier   musicien   ouvrier
acteur   chanteur   danseur

7. Look at the feminine adjectives below and write their masculine forms. (See key.)

canadienne   italienne   anglaise
belge   suisse

4. Review practice: reading comprehension

For each frame below, read the French sentences that describe a person. Then write the letter of the English phrase that describes the person most accurately. (See key.)

1. Chantal est danseuse. Elle est jeune et maigre, et elle habite à Montréal.

   Chantal is . . .
   a. a young singer from Montréal.
   b. a thin young dancer from Montréal.
   c. an intelligent young dancer from Montréal.

2. Jean-Pierre est suisse; il est journaliste et photographe. Il est assez vieux.

   Jean-Pierre is . . .
   a. a rather old Swiss reporter and photographer.
   b. a rather old Swiss lady who dislikes photographers and reporters.
   c. a young Swiss reporter and photographer.

3. Mme Lascala est musicienne. Elle est italienne et habite à Rome. Elle n'aime pas la vie à la campagne.

   Mme Lascala is . . .
   a. an Italian architect who lives in the capital of Italy.
   b. an Italian musician who doesn't like to live in the country.
   c. an Italian musician who likes to live in the country.

Note Culturelle
Administrative France

Administratively, mainland France is divided into 96 departments, including two in Corsica. In addition, France has five overseas departments (DOM = *Départements d'Outre-Mer*): Guadeloupe, Martinique, French Guyana, Saint-Pierre-et-Miquelon, and Réunion. Each department is headed by a *Commissaire de la République,* replacing the former *Préfet.*

A bill passed in July 1972 created 22 *régions* in France; each *région* encompasses several departments.

Both *régions* and departments are experiencing greater autonomy as a result of the decentralization policy pursued by the socialist government of M. François Mitterrand, elected President of France in May 1981.

La population: 53.400.000 Français

L'exécutif: Le Président de la
République
Le Premier Ministre
Le Conseil des Ministres

Le législatif: L'Assemblée Nationale
(le Parlement) Le Sénat

Le judiciare

22 Régions, divisées en:
96 Départements métropolitains
5 DOM
324 arrondissements
3509 cantons
36.394 communes

À Paris. Quelles sont les questions dont on s'occupe *(that people deal with)* dans ce ministère?

A la découverte de la France

What is this billboard advertising?

Vocabulaire

Noms

l'album de photos *m.*   *photo album*
le campeur/la campeuse   *camper*
la montagne   *mountain*
la photographie
  (photo)   *photograph; photography*
le téléphone   *telephone*

Les membres de la famille

l'aîné/e   *oldest child*
la fille unique   *only daughter*
le fils unique   *only son*
le frère   *brother*
la sœur   *sister*

Adjectifs

content/e   *happy, satisfied*
drôle   *funny, strange*
marrant   *fun, funny*
martiniquais/e   *from Martinique*
élégant/e   *elegant*

Verbes

comprendre   *to understand*
montrer (à)   *to show (someone)*

Autres mots et expressions

bof!   *(shows resigned indifference)*
c'est la vie!   *that's life!*
heureusement   *fortunately*
je voudrais être   *I would like to be*
malheureusement   *unfortunately*
ne... pas de   *not any*
ne... jamais   *never*

PRÉPARATION 13

1. The present tense of *-ir* verbs

1. One group of *-ir* verbs is regular: they all follow a predictable pattern. The verb *finir* (to finish) can be used as a model. Give an English equivalent of this sentence: *Je finis le livre maintenant.* |
   I'm finishing the book now.
2. Study the present tense forms of *finir*. Notice the change in stem in the plural forms.

je	**fini**	**s**	nous	**finiss**	**ons**
tu	fini	**s**	vous	finiss	**ez**
on/il/elle	fini	**t**	ils/elles	finiss	**ent**

   a. What is the stem for the singular forms of *finir*? |
      fini- (the infinitive minus *-r*)
   b. The plural stem of *finir* is the singular stem plus _____. |
      -ss (finiss-)
   c. Say all the forms aloud. How many *spoken* forms are there? |
      four (*Finis, finis,* and *finit* sound the same.)
3. Other regular *-ir* verbs are like *finir*.
   a. Write the singular stem for *choisir* (to choose) and *obéir à* (to obey). |
      choisi-, obéi-
   b. Write the plural stem for each verb. |
      choisiss-, obéiss-
4. Study the forms of *finir* for a moment, then say that everyone is finishing the newspaper now. Check your verb forms against the chart.
   Modèle: moi |
      Je finis le journal maintenant.

   a. Jacques   c. nous
   b. toi   d. Sylvie et Luc

5. Tell what each person is choosing as a present for Julie's birthday. (See key.)
   Modèle: Henri/cette cassette |
      Henri choisit cette cassette comme cadeau.

a. Georges et François/ce disque
b. Marc et moi, nous/ce livre
c. Marie et toi, vous/ce stylo
d. Alain/cette radio

Who would subscribe to this magazine?

6. Quite a few -ir verbs do not follow the pattern of *finir*. They are considered irregular, but most follow a specific pattern. Look at the forms of *partir* (to leave, to go away).

je	**par**	**s**	nous	**part**	**ons**
tu	par	s	vous	part	**ez**
on/il/elle	par	**t**	ils/elles	part	**ent**

a. Are the endings the same as those of *finir*?
> yes
b. What is the singular stem?
> par- (For verbs like *partir*, the singular stem ends with -r-.)
c. What is the plural stem?
> part- (The plural stem is the same as the infinitive stem. It has a consonant sound that doesn't exist in the singular stem.)

7. The verbs *sortir* (to go out) and *dormir* (to sleep) follow the same pattern as *partir*.

je sors, nous sortons
je dors, nous dormons

a. Write the stems of *sortir*.
> sor-, sort-
b. Write the stems of *dormir*.
> dor-, dorm-

8. Complete these sentences with a present tense form of the verb in parentheses.
a. Je _____ maintenant. *(sortir)*
b. Vous _____ demain? *(sortir)*
c. Tu _____ quand? *(partir)*
d. Nous _____ à midi *(at noon)*. *(partir)*
e. Il _____ en classe. *(dormir)*
f. Hélène et moi, nous ne _____ pas très bien en avion. *(dormir)*

> a. sors
> b. sortez
> c. pars
> d. partons
> e. dort
> f. dormons

9. *Sortir* means to go out of a building or out on a date. *Partir* means to go away on a trip. Complete these equivalents. (See key.)
   a. I go out a lot with Marc.   _____ souvent avec Marc.
   b. I'm leaving (the building) soon.   _____ bientôt.
   c. I leave for Tokyo soon.   _____ bientôt pour Tokyo.
   d. I'm leaving (for my trip) on   _____ samedi.
      Saturday.

À Propos!   Ask a classmate if he/she sleeps late on Saturdays: _____ *tard le samedi?*

2. Practice with adjectives

1. Look at the adjectives of nationality listed below.

A	B	C
italien	belge	français
canadien	suisse	anglais
		allemand
		espagnol
		américain

   a. In which group does the written feminine form consist of the masculine form + *-e?*   Group A, B, or C? |
      C (français, française; anglais, anglaise, etc.)
   b. In which group are the masculine and feminine forms identical? |
      B
   c. In group A, in the feminine forms the final consonant is doubled and an *-e* is added. Write the feminine forms of *italien* and *canadien.* |
      italienne, canadienne
2. At a conference, Philippe is identifying various students by their nationality. Write his statements, and remember to make the adjective agree with the gender of the subject.
   Modèle: Klaus *(allemand)* |
      Klaus est allemand.
   a. Nathalie *(suisse)* |
      Nathalie est suisse.
   b. Anna *(italien)* |
      Anna est italienne.

c. David *(canadien)* |
    David est canadien.

d. María *(espagnol)* |
    María est espagnole.

e. Linda *(anglais)* |
    Linda est anglaise.

3. Here are the adjectives you have been using in class to describe the way people look according to their hair color: *blond/blonde, brun/brune, roux/rousse. Très brun* is used for black hair. State that the girl in each pair of sentences has the same hair color as the boy.

    a. Alain est brun. Béatrice est ____. |
    b. Jean-Pierre est blond. Véronique est ____. |
    c. Michel est roux. Caroline est ____. |
    d. Bernard est très brun. Sarah est ____. |

    a. brune
    b. blonde
    c. rousse
    d. très brune

4. a. Read this sentence and complete the English equivalent: *Ce garçon brun est américain.* This ____ is American. |
        brown-haired boy

    b. In the English phrase *brown-haired boy,* the adjective comes before the noun. Where does the adjective occur in the French phrase *garçon brun*—before or after the noun? |
        after (Like many other French adjectives, adjectives of color always occur after the noun.)

5. Chantal wants a friend to identify some students for her. Write her questions by using the demonstrative adjective and the correct form of the other adjectives.

    Modèle: fille/blond/être/anglais |
        Cette fille blonde est anglaise?

    a. fille/roux/être/suisse |
        Cette fille rousse est suisse?
    b. garçon/roux/être/allemand |
        Ce garçon roux est allemand?
    c. garçon/brun/être/canadien |
        Ce garçon brun est canadien?
    d. fille/brun/être/italien |
        Cette fille brune est italienne? (Did you double the *n?*)

6. Give Chantal some additional information by telling what each person likes or doesn't like. Put the adjective after the noun. (See key.)

    Modèle: fille anglais/aimer chanter |
        La fille anglaise aime chanter.

    a. fille suisse/ne pas aimer les maths
    b. garçon allemand/aimer patiner

3. Writing practice

Tell about a performer whose music you like. For the time being, limit yourself to words and grammatical structures you have learned and practiced. Refer to the dialogues and vocabulary lists in Phases 1 and 2.

Tell who it is whose music you like. Tell his/her age (approximate age: 30 *ans environ*), nationality, and which city he/she lives in (or say you don't know). Tell whether he/she is tall or short, heavy or thin; describe his/her hair color, and personality. Tell how many records or cassettes of this performer you have.

Note Culturelle
Statesman and poet: Aimé Césaire

Aimé Césaire is a poet, playwright, and statesman who has represented the Caribbean island of Martinique in the French Assembly, and has served as mayor of Fort-de-France, the capital. Born in 1913, Césaire was one of many black students who explored their heritage while they were enrolled in universities in France. Césaire used the word *négritude* to characterize the cultural values of black African and Caribbean people. Césaire's literary work reflects a quest for an authentic culture, and a reaction against the experience of colonialism.

Cahier d'un retour au pays natal ("Return to my native land"), one of Césaire's early works, is an angry rejection of the colonial policy that belittled African and Caribbean culture. His plays include *Le Roi Christophe*, based on the life of a black king who ruled Haiti in the 1800s, and *Une Saison au Congo*, which deals with the struggle of Patrice Lumumba, the leader of the Congolese independence movement in the 1960s.

Vocabulaire

Noms

la personne   *person*

Adjectifs

raisonnable   *reasonable*
rapide   *fast quick*
silencieux/silencieuse   *silent, quiet*

Verbes

choisir (choisi-, choisiss-)   *to choose*
dormir (dor-, dorm-)   *to sleep*
finir (fini-, finiss-)   *to finish, complete;*   ~de faire   *to stop doing*
obéir à (obéi-, obéiss-)   *to obey*
partir (par-, part-)   *to depart, leave*
sortir (sor-, sort-)   *to go out*

Autres mots et expressions

bientôt   *soon*
en avion   *by plane*
environ   *approximately, around (+ quantity)*
ici   *here*
là   *there*
tard   *late*

Phase 3

Pas d'accord !

Qu'est-ce que vous allez apprendre?

By the end of this Phase you will be able to comment on the usefulness (or lack thereof) of a particular profession, on the pros and cons of the study of a particular subject, and on the philosopher Pascal's view of human nature. You will expand your vocabulary referring to family members, practice describing people and will become familiar with idiomatic expressions indicating surprise, bafflement, and delight.

Communication

In order to accomplish the above objectives, you will study:
Plural nouns, adjectives, and articles.
Irregular verbs: *faire* (to do), *connaître* (to know), *aller* (to go), *prendre* (to take), *voir* (to see).
A way to express possession.
How to refer to people or things using direct object pronouns *le, la, l', les.*
You will improve your command of *-er* and *-ir* verbs, the verb *avoir,* the plural, question formation, demonstrative adjectives, and French pronunciation.

Culture

Family size, relations between parents and children, friends and acquaintances, family meals, and education.

PRÉPARATION 14

Le Recensement

M. Moraud répond aux questions du recenseur, qui est un peu sourd.

Le recenseur Alors, Monsieur, il y a combien de personnes chez vous?

M. Moraud Eh bien, ma femme et moi et deux enfants.

Le recenseur Douze enfants.

M. Moraud Non, non, non, pas douze, *deux!*

Le recenseur Pourquoi deux? Vous dites douze . . .

M. Moraud Mais non, Monsieur, je dis DEUX . . . Deux enfants, une fille et un garçon.

The Census

Mr. Moraud answers the questions of the census-taker, who is a little hard of hearing.

Well, sir, how many people are there in your household?
Well, my wife and myself and two children.

Twelve children.
No, no, no, not twelve, *two!*
Why two? You said (say) twelve . . .

No, sir, I said (say) TWO. Two children, a girl and a boy.

114

Le recenseur Oh là là! Quelle histoire! Douze . . . deux . . . Décidez-vous. Alors, ça fait quatre personnes en tout?	My goodness! Such confusion! Twelve . . . two . . . Make up your mind. So that makes four people all together?
M. Moraud Oui, c'est ça, quatre . . . Ah, mais non, il y a aussi ma belle-mère.	Yes, that's right, four . . . Oh, no, there's also my mother-in-law.
Le recenseur Quoi? Qu'est-ce que vous dites? Je n'entends pas très bien.	What? What are you saying? I don't hear very well.
M. Moraud (criant) Je dis qu'il y a aussi ma BELLE-MÈRE!	(Shouting): I'm saying that there's also my MOTHER-IN-LAW!
Le recenseur Alors, ça fait cinq! Vous ne savez pas compter, Monsieur?	Then that makes five. Don't you know how to count, sir?
M. Moraud Et vous, Monsieur, vous ne savez pas être poli?	And you, sir, don't you know how to be polite?

Échange d'idées

1. S1: Ask your partner to list the people who live in his/her home (use *chez vous*).
   S2: List the people (make up a few if you like, include pets, etc.).
   S1: Add them up and ask if that's all.
   S2: Say no, add one (or a few) more.
   S1: Express your frustration.
   S2: Express *your* frustration.

2. S1: Show a picture of family or friends.
   S2: Find out something about the people you see: who they are, where they live, whether they are relatives of your partner.
   S1: Answer your partner's questions, and volunteer some information or opinions about each person in the picture.

1. Plural nouns and the plural definite article *les*

1. The simplest definition of *plural* is *more than one.* Consider how the plural works in English.

Singular:	egg	book	box	child
Plural:	eggs	books	boxes	children

   a. In written English, what are the endings of *most* plural nouns? |

   -s or *-es* (*Children* is irregular.)

   b. Are these endings pronounced in speech? |

   yes

2. Compare singular and plural forms of these French nouns.

   un garçon, deux garçons   un crayon, deux crayons
   une fille, deux filles   une table, deux tables

a. What ending is added to the noun to form the plural? |
s (But in spoken French, the plural *-s* is not pronounced.)

b. Rewrite these phrases with *deux: une élève, un cousin.* |
deux élèves, deux cousins

Definite articles

| Singular: | **le** garçon | **la** fille | **l'**homme | **le** livre |
| Plural: | **les** garçons | **les** filles | **les** hommes | **les** livres |

3. a. Which definite articles are used with singular nouns? |
le, la, l'

b. Which definite article is used with plural nouns? |
les

c. Is *les* used with both masculine and feminine nouns? |
yes (There is only one plural form of the definite article: *les.*)

4. Compare *the boys* and *les garçons.*
a. In English, what tells you the phrase is plural—*the* or the *-s?* |
the plural ending *-s*

b. In *written* French, how can you tell that *les garçons* is plural? |
by the article *les* and by the *-s* ending of *garçons*

c. In *spoken* French, how can you tell that *les garçons* is plural? |
by the article *les* (The plural noun ending *-s* is not usually pronounced.)

5. When *les* precedes a noun beginning with a vowel sound, there is a linking /z/ sound.
Read aloud: *les garçons, les enfants, les mathématiques, les étagères.*
In which phrases is there a linking /z/? |
les enfants, les étagères

6. Copy the phrases in which a linking /z/ will occur, and put a link mark (⌣) between the article and the noun.
les éléphants   les crocodiles   les girafes   les antilopes |
les éléphants, les antilopes

7. To indicate to whom a single item belongs, you would say, for example, *C'est la cassette de Pierre.* Write an English equivalent. |
This is Pierre's cassette; It's Pierre's cassette.

8. To talk about several items, you would say *These are Pierre's cassettes* or *They are Pierre's cassettes.* The French equivalent of *these are/they are* is *ce sont.*
Tell to whom the items below belong. Begin each sentence with *Ce sont* and *les.* Write the English equivalent of frames *a* and *b.*
Modèle: cahier/Pierre |
Ce sont les cahiers de Pierre. They (These) are Pierre's notebooks.

a. frère/Marie-Hélène |
Ce sont les frères de Marie-Hélène. They (These) are Marie-Hélène's brothers.

b. affiche/Agnès |

Ce sont les affiches d'Agnès. *They (These) are Agnès's posters.*

c. chaise/Mme Rimbaud |

Ce sont les chaises de Mme Rimbaud.

9. Correct the questioner's impression, using the cues provided. Write complete sentences. (See key.)

Modèle: Ce sont les disques d'Annette? |

Non, ce sont les cassettes d'Annette.

a. Ce sont les tables de M. Roger?

b. Ce sont les frères d'Henri? |

2. *Voilà* and *il y a*

1. The French expression *voilà* means *here is/here are* or *there is/there are.* You're in a friend's back yard looking for escaped pets. Point out what you see.

a. le serpent |

Voilà le serpent.

b. les souris |

Voilà les souris.

c. True or false? *Voilà* is used only with a singular noun. |

False. *Voilà* is used with a singular or a plural noun.

2. Use *voilà* and the following terms to write French equivalents.
l'oncle   la tante   les parents   les grands-parents

a. Here are Charles's grandparents. |

Voilà les grands-parents de Charles.

b. There's Paul's aunt. |

Voilà la tante de Paul.

c. There are Véronique's parents. |

Voilà les parents de Véronique.

d. Here's Yvonne's uncle. |

Voilà l'oncle d'Yvonne.

3. In English, you can use *there is/there are* to point to and call attention to a person or thing, and also to report the existence of a person or thing that may not be visible. The French equivalent for this second meaning of *there is/there are* is *il y a*.

   a. You are in a restaurant, and your companion informs you *Il y a une souris sous la table!* Write the equivalent. |
         There's a mouse under the table!

   b. *Il y a* can be used with singular or plural nouns. Write the equivalent for *There are two mice under the table!* |
         Il y a deux souris sous la table!

4. To point out something or someone visible, the expression _____ is used in French. To report the existence of something or someone, the expression _____ is used in French. |
         Voilà, il y a

5. Report to someone that there are two cassettes on the chair. |
         Il y a deux cassettes sur la chaise.

6. Point out this animal to someone: *un lion.* |
         Voilà un lion.

À Propos!

As an item of information, report the names of two people in your class. _____ *un garçon qui s'appelle* _____. _____ *une fille qui s'appelle* _____.

3. Practice with *finir* and similar verbs

1. As you learned in Préparation 13, regular *-ir* verbs have two stems in the present tense.
Je finis mon travail aujourd'hui, et mes amis finissent demain.

   a. The singular stem is _____. |
         fini- (the infinitive minus *r*).

   b. The plural stem is _____ . |
         finiss- (the singular stem plus *ss*).

2. One verb whose forms follow the same pattern is *choisir* (to choose). Using *finir* as a model, complete the sentences with the appropriate forms of *choisir*.

   a. Je _____ un stylo rouge. |
         choisis

   b. Si vous _____ la médecine, c'est que vous êtes intelligent. |
         choisissez

   c. Le professeur _____ Jacques pour expliquer ce problème. |
         choisit

                                        Phase trois

3. Fill the blanks with the correct forms of the verbs in the model sentences. (See key.)
   a. *Vous finissez le livre?* Ils ___ le voyage. Margot et moi, nous ___ la conversation.
   b. *Il choisit une bonne profession.* Moi aussi, je ___ une bonne profession. Vous ___ une bonne place au cinéma. Tu ___ un cadeau.
   c. *Cette dame vieillit* (grows old) *avec charme.* Ève ne ___ pas. Nous ___ avec regret.
      Roger maigrit (loses weight, gets thinner) *quand il est jaloux.* Je ne ___ pas quand je suis en voyage. Les hommes ___ quand ils sont amoureux.
   d. *Vous grossissez* (put on weight, get fat) *quand vous mangez trop.* Je ___ quand je mange trop. Nous ___ quand nous mangeons trop.
   e. *Mathieu réussit à* (succeeds in) *parler avec Dominique.* Monsieur Lebrun ___ à perdre 5 kilos. Vous ___ à communiquer en français.
   f. *Jean obéit à* (obeys) *la voix* (voice) *de la conscience.* Nous ___ à la directrice. On ___ à l'agent de police.

À Propos!

Quel livre finissez-vous cette semaine? Quand est-ce que vous maigrissez? Quelle profession choisissez-vous?

4. The plural indefinite article *des*

1. a. Suppose you are buying school supplies. You don't know how many pencils and erasers you want, but you need more than one. What word could you use to complete this? I'd like ___ pencils and ___ erasers. |

   some (*Some* is the plural indefinite article in English.)

   b. Could you say *I'd like pencils and erasers,* with no article? |

   yes

2. French, like English, has an indefinite article for use with plural nouns. In French, though, you must include the article.

Indefinite articles

Singular: Je voudrais **un** crayon et **une** gomme.
Plural: Je voudrais **des** crayons et **des** gommes.

3. *Des* is pronounced as /de/ before nouns beginning with a consonant. Read aloud: *des crayons.*

When *des* comes before a noun beginning with a vowel sound, there is a linking /z/ between *des* and the noun, as with the plural article *les.* Read aloud: *des affiches.*

Read the following phrases aloud. Write those in which a linking /z/ is heard and add a link mark ‿ .

des écrans   des livres   des hommes   des professeurs |

des écrans, des hommes

4. Say that you have more than one of these items.

Modèle: cassette |

J'ai des cassettes.

a. chaise |

J'ai des chaises.

b. étagère |

J'ai des étagères.

5. A new student who has just come into your class asks for certain supplies. Tell this person that there are some in the office *(au bureau).* (See key.)

Modèle: Je voudrais un crayon. |

Il y a des crayons au bureau.

a. Je voudrais un cahier.
b. Je voudrais une gomme.

5. *Ne pas...de* + noun

1. Read the following sentences, and look closely at the articles.

Nous avons un frère, mais nous n'avons pas de sœur.
Serge a une sœur, mais il n'a pas de frère.
Chantal et Anne ont des cousins, mais elles n'ont pas de cousines.

a. What are the English equivalents of all three sentences? |

We have a brother, but we don't have a sister. Serge has a sister, but he doesn't have a brother. Chantal and Anne have (some) male cousins, but they don't have (any) female cousins.

b. In the negative phrases *pas de sœur, pas de frère,* and *pas de cousines,* which article replaces *un, une,* and *des?* |

de (The articles *un, une, des* are replaced by *de* in most negative sentences. The major exception occurs with *être: C'est un stylo? Non, ce n'est pas un stylo.*)

c. Expressions of quantity also use *de* before a noun: *beaucoup de personnes.* Use *trop* to write the equivalent of *too many people.* |

trop de personnes

d. Like *ne, je, le, la,* and *ce, de* is elided before a word beginning with a vowel sound. Complete this sentence: M. Dufour
_ a pas _ enfants. |
n', d'

2. There are many things Martine doesn't have. Write negative answers to these questions, and write English equivalents of your
answers for *a* and *b*.

   Modèle: Martine a des stylos? |
   Non, elle n'a pas de stylos. No, she doesn't have any pens.

   a. Martine a une caméra? |
   Non, elle n'a pas de caméra. *No, she doesn't have a movie camera.*

   b. Elle a une voiture, n'est-ce pas? |
   Non, elle n'a pas de voiture.

   c. Elle a des affiches? |
   Non, elle n'a pas d'affiches.

   d. Elle a des cousines? (oui, beaucoup!) |
   Oui, elle a beaucoup de cousines!

3. The negative of *il y a* is *il n'y a pas de*. Complete the answer to the
following question.

   —Il y a un zèbre dans la classe?

   —Non, _____ zèbre dans la classe. |
   Il n'y a pas de

4. Imagine you have a little brother who is scared of finding strange
animals in the house. Tell him that there aren't any. (See key.)

   Modèle: Il y a un tigre sous la table? |
   Non, il n'y a pas de tigre sous la table!

   a. Il y a des crocodiles dans le tiroir?

   b. Il y a un lion sous la chaise?

Vocabulaire

Noms

l'activité *f. activity*
l'agent de police *m. police officer*
l'antilope *f. antelope*
l'appartement *m. apartment*
le charme *charm*
le/la comptable *accountant*
la conscience *conscience*
la conversation *conversation*
le crocodile *crocodile*
le démocrate *democrat*
le dictionnaire *dictionary*
l'éléphant *m. elephant*
le lion *lion*
la machine à calculer *calculator*

la place *seat*
la pratique *practice*
le problème *problem*
le recenseur *census taker*
le réfrigérateur *refrigerator*
le regret *regret*
le républicain *republican*
le serpent *snake*
la souris *mouse*
la théorie *theory*
le tigre *tiger*
le travail *work, job*
la voix *voice*
le voyage *trip*
le zèbre *zebra*

Note Culturelle
Family size

The size of the average French family has varied over the centuries. In the past when most people made their living from farming, families tended to be large (six members or more). Many hands were needed to work the land and the land ably supplied the foodstuffs to meet the needs of a large family.

In the 19th century, middle-class families living in the cities tended to keep the number of children small to insure them with a better education and the means for a better start in life.

In this century, in addition to the economic depression of the thirties, France suffered staggering losses of people during World War I, World War II, and the war in Indochina and Algeria. Families, as a result, had little faith in the future. Instead of growing, the population declined dramatically. To encourage families to have more children, an alarmed government took special steps, such as: instituting monthly income supplements *(allocations familiales)*, providing a special card allowing discounts on train and bus tickets to families with three or more children *(carte familiale)*, and establishing a national award each year for the mother with the most children *(la Médaille du Mérite familial)*.

À Paris. Une jeune famille.

La famille

le beau-père/frère *father/brother-in-law*

la belle-mère/soeur *mother/sister-in-law*

les beaux-parents *parents-in-law*

le cadet/la cadette *the second child in the family*

le cousin/la cousine *cousin*

la femme *wife*

la fille *daughter*

le fils *son*

la grand-mère *grandmother*

le grand-père *grandfather*

les grands-parents *grandparents*

le mari *husband*

la mère *mother*

le neveu *nephew*

la nièce *niece*

l'oncle *m.* *uncle*

les parents *parents*

le père *father*

la tante *aunt*

Adjectifs

amoureux/amoureuse *in love*

malade *sick, ill*

poli/e *polite*

sourd/e *deaf*

Verbes

communiquer *to communicate*

compter *to count*

crier *to shout*

dire *to say*

expliquer *to explain*

grossir (grossiss-) *to put on weight*

maigrir (maigriss-) *to lose weight*

réussir (réussiss-) *to succeed in*

savoir *to know*

vieillir (vieilliss-) *to grow old*

Autres mots et expressions

beaucoup (de) *a lot (of), very much*

ça fait... en tout? *that makes... all together?*

c'est ça *that's right*

c'est que . . . *it means that . . .*

c'est, ce sont (+ noms) *it's, they are*

chez *at someone's home*

combien de *how many, how much*

décidez-vous *make up your mind*

des *some*

eh bien . . . *well . . . (To initiate or hesitate)*

en tout *in all*

en voyage *on a trip*

faire du sport *to participate in sports*

il y a *there is/are;* il n'y a pas de *there is no/are no*

les *the (plural)*

ne pas... de (+ nom) *not... any; no... (+noun)*

pourquoi *why*

quel, quelle *which*

trop *too much*

voilà *here is/here are; there is/there are*

PRÉPARATION 15

Professions

Solange demande à Yvette, sa nouvelle camarade de chambre, ce que font ses parents.

Solange Que fait ton père?
Yvette Il travaille à IBM et il voyage énormément.
Solange Et ta mère, elle travaille?
Yvette Oui, à mi-temps; comme mon père n'est jamais là, elle s'ennuie.
Solange Ma mère est avocate. Elle pense que les femmes doivent être utiles à la société, comme les hommes.
Yvette Utiles à la société? Les avocats? Utiles à eux-mêmes, tu veux dire!
Solange Oh, écoute, tu exagères. Ils ne sont pas tous comme ça.

Professions

Solange asks Yvette, her new roommate, what her parents do.

What does your father do?
He works at IBM and he travels a great deal.
And your mother, does she work?
Yes, part-time; since my father is never home, she gets bored.
My mother is a lawyer. She thinks that women should be useful to society, like men.
Useful to society? Lawyers? Useful to themselves, you mean!
Oh, listen, you're exaggerating. They're not all like that.

Échange d'idées

1. S1: Ask what your partner's mother or father does for a living.
   S2: Reply; indicate how much your parent travels (*pas du tout, rarement, très peu, beaucoup, énormément*).
   S1: Ask if he/she works part-time or full-time (*à plein temps*). Ask if he/she likes his/her work. (*Il aime être comptable?*)
   S2: Reply, and ask about your partner's parents' work.

2. *Opinions:* In French, list 8 professions and occupations. Then put them into two lists—*Pour le bien de la société* and *Pas pour le bien de la société*—according to whether you think these people work more for the benefit of society or more for their own benefit.
   Compare your list with a classmate's.

1. *La Famille*

1. Here is the family tree of Henri Dupont. Take a moment to see how the other people are related to him, then answer the questions below.

LA FAMILLE DUPONT

Pierre Dupont   Hélène Dupont

Richard Larue   Yvonne (Dupont) Larue   Georges Dupont   Alice (Prévot) Dupont

Monique (20 ans)   Charles (18 ans)   Henri (17 ans)   Jacqueline (15 ans)   Édouard (12 ans)

a. Henri et Édouard Dupont sont les _____ de Georges et d'Alice Dupont. |

a. fils

b. Jacqueline Dupont est la _____ d'Henri et d'Édouard. |

b. sœur

c. Édouard Dupont est le _____ de Jacqueline et d'Henri. |

c. frère

d. Alice Dupont est la _____ d'Henri, de Jacqueline et d'Édouard, et la _____ de Georges Dupont. |

d. mère, femme

e. Georges Dupont est le _____ d'Henri, de Jacqueline et d'Édouard, et le _____ d'Alice Dupont. |

e. père, mari

f. Henri a une _____, Monique Larue, et un _____, Charles La-
rue. |

g. M. et Mme Larue sont l'_____ et la _____ d'Henri. |

h. Monique et Charles Larue sont la _____ et le _____ de M. et
Mme Dupont. |

i. Qui sont les parents de Monique et de Charles? |

j. Et les grands-parents? |

f. cousine, cousin

g. oncle, tante

h. nièce, neveu

i. Yvonne Dupont Larue
et Richard Larue

j. Hélène et Pierre Du-
pont

2. The irregular verb *faire*

1. In *Professions,* you saw one form of *faire* in *Que fait ton père?* Com-
plete the English equivalent: What does your father _____? |
   do

2. Here are the present tense forms of *faire (to do, to make).* Study
them for a few moments, then complete the phrases below; write
both subject and verb, and check your answers against the chart.

je	**fais**	nous	**faisons**
tu	**fais**	vous	**faites**
il/elle	**fait**	ils/elles	**font**

a. tu _____

b. elle _____

c. nous _____

d. je _____

e. ils _____

f. vous _____

3. Ask what the people below are doing. Say your answers aloud
before you write.

   Modèle: vous |
   Qu'est-ce que vous faites?

a. toi

b. la petite

c. Jean-Paul et Sylvie

d. toi e moi |

a. Qu'est-ce que tu fais?   b. Qu'est-ce qu'elle fait?
c. Qu'est-ce qu'ils font?   d. Qu'est-ce que nous faisons?

3. The plural of adjectives of nationality

1. The chart below shows the plural forms of adjectives of nationality. Other descriptive adjectives form the plural in the same
way. Read the sentences aloud.

	Singular	Plural
Masculine:	Jack est **américain.**	Jack et Bob sont **américains.**
Feminine:	Lois est **américaine.**	Lois et Mary sont **américaines.**

a. What ending is added to *américain* and *américaine* to indicate plurality? |

s (The written plural of most adjectives is formed by adding -s to the singular form. This -s is not pronounced.)

b. How many written forms of the adjective *américain* are there? |

four

c. How many spoken forms of *américain* are there? |

two (*Américain* and *américains* sound alike; *américaine* and *américaines* sound alike.)

d. In *Jack et Lois sont américains,* is *américains* masculine or feminine? |

masculine (When an adjective describes nouns of both genders at once, it is always in the masculine form.)

2. Now compare the following sentences.

Il est français.   Ils sont français.

a. If the masculine singular adjective already ends in *s,* does the masculine plural form change? |

no (The masculine singular and masculine plural forms are identical.)

3. Rewrite these sentences with the information in parentheses.
a. Tom est anglais. (William et James) |

William et James sont anglais.

b. Harriet est canadienne. (Sue et Betty) |

Sue et Betty sont canadiennes.

4. *Il est américain* is like an equation with *être* as the equals sign.
The initials MS stand for masculine singular.

Il   est   américain.
MS   =   MS

a. One side of the equation must balance on the other side. When the subject is masculine singular, the adjective must also be _____. |

masculine singular (MS = MS)

b. Write the subject pronoun whose gender and number will balance this equation. _____ *sont canadiennes.* |

Elles (FP = FP)

5. The people mentioned below are from various countries. What are their nationalities?

   Modèle: Mes grands-parents sont nés *(were born)* en Italie. |

   Ils sont italiens.

   a. M. et Mme Rocher sont nés en Belgique. |

   Ils sont belges.

   b. Les sœurs de mon ami sont nées en France. |

   Elles sont françaises.

   c. Heinz et Werther sont nés en Allemagne. |

   Ils sont allemands.

   d. W. Watanabe est né au Japon; M. et Mme Hu sont nés en Chine. |

   Il est japonais; ils sont chinois.

4. Practice with *avoir*

1. Write complete sentences with the following cues. (See key.)
   a. Mme Perrier/avoir/un grand bureau.
   b. Je/avoir/des soeurs.
   c. M. et Mme Victor/avoir/deux enfants.
   d. Vous/avoir/quel âge?
2. Some students are trying to put off taking a test by saying that they don't have any supplies. Use *ne... pas de* to write what they say. (See key.)

   Modèle: des stylos |

   Mais nous n'avons pas de stylos!

   a. des feuilles de papier
   b. des crayons
   c. une gomme
3. Tell what relatives or pets these people have or don't have. (See key.)

   Modèle: Elles/ne pas avoir/tantes |

   Elles n'ont pas de tantes.

   a. nous/avoir/grands-parents
   b. tu/avoir/chien
   c. Guy et Henri/ne pas avoir/sœur
   d. je/ne pas avoir/chat

À Propos!

Vous avez des tantes en France?
Vous avez des enfants?
Vous avez quel âge?

Phase trois

Note Culturelle

Relations between parents and children

French families tend to be close-knit. In many families, keeping in touch with grandparents, cousins, aunts and uncles, is considered to be important. In smaller cities and towns, the members of the extended family may gather for dinner on Sundays or holidays. As older children move away from home, they continue to maintain close contact with the family by telephone or mail when visits are impractical.

French parents tend to expect more restrained behavior from their children than Americans do. Particularly when the children are with a group of adults, parents expect them to be polite and unobtrusive.

There are varying degrees of permissiveness regarding the use of the TV set, the telephone, and the family car. The French are TV enthusiasts, and the conflict between watching TV and doing homework exists as it does in the United States. French children, however, are expected to do all their homework *before* they may watch TV. There is pressure to earn good grades in school, and great pressure to pass the *baccalauréat*—the difficult comprehensive examination at the end of high school that enables a person to go to the university or apply for a good job.

Telephones are more difficult to obtain in France than in the United States. Children don't have their own phones, and even teenagers tend to keep their calls short so as not to monopolize the phone and because each (even local) communication is added to the monthly bill.

The use of the family automobile by a teenager poses less of a problem than in the U.S. because the French cannot obtain an automobile driver's license (*permis de conduire*) before the age of eighteen.

Un mariage. On mange, on danse, on s'amuse (have a good time).

Vocabulaire

Noms

l'âge *m.*   *age*
le bien   *good, benefit*
le chat   *cat*
le chien   *dog*
le coiffeur/la coiffeuse   *hairdresser*
le joueur/la joueuse   *player*
la société   *society*

Adjectifs

nouveau/nouvelle   *new*
utile (à)   *useful*
chinois/e   *Chinese*

Verbes

aller (+ inf.)   *to be going to (+ inf.)*
compter   *to count*
devoir   *must*
exagérer   *to exaggerate*
faire   *to do, to make*
penser   *to think*
voyager   *to travel*

Autres mots et expressions

à mi-temps   *part time (work)*
à plein temps   *full time*
ce que   *what (indefinite pron.)*
elle s'ennuie   *she is bored*
énormément   *enormously, a lot*
environ   *approximately*
eux-mêmes   *themselves*
quel âge as-tu?   *how old are you?*
rarement   *rarely, not often*
tous   *all*
tu veux dire   *you mean*

PRÉPARATION 16

1. Plurals of descriptive adjectives

1. Compare the following sentences.

> Il est grand.   Ils sont grands
> Elle est grande.   Elles sont grandes.

a. In written French, what is added to *grand* and *grande* to indicate plurality? |

    s (Most adjectives form the plural by adding *-s* to the singular.)

b. How many spoken forms of *grand* are there? |

    two (Remember that the *-s* ending is not usually pronounced.)

2. Now read the following sentences aloud.

> Il est riche.   Ils sont riches.
> Elle est riche.   Elles sont riches.

a. In spoken French, do all the singular and plural forms of *riche* sound alike or different? |

    alike

Est-ce que vous connaissez cette pièce (play) de Cocteau?

3. Say that the relatives mentioned are like other members of their families.

    Modèle: Georges est riche. Et les sœurs de Georges? |

        Elles sont riches aussi.

a. Marie est maigre. Et les frères de Marie? |

        Ils sont maigres aussi.

b. Le fils des Dupont est intelligent. Et les filles? |

        Elles sont intelligentes aussi.

c. L'oncle de Charles est gentil. Et les cousins et les cousines de Charles? |

    Ils sont gentils aussi.

d. M. Ménard est impatient. Et les nièces de M. Ménard? |

    Elles sont impatientes aussi.

e. M. Ménard est optimiste. Et le neveu? |

    Il est optimiste aussi.

4. Like *français*, the following adjectives do not add -*s* in the masculine plural: *gros, roux, jaloux, vieux.*
An adjective ending in the letter _____ or _____ does not add -*s* in the masculine plural. |

    s, x (The *x* here is an old form of *s* that has been kept in some modern French words. As with a final *s*, a final *x* is not usually pronounced, but can be linked to a vowel with a /z/ sound.)

5. Explain that these people do *not* resemble each other. (See key.)
    Modèle: Marie est grosse, mais les frères de Marie _____. |

    ne sont pas gros

a. La tante d'André est vieille, mais les oncles d'André _____.
b. Guy est jaloux, mais Yvette et Lise _____.
c. Le gérant est ambitieux, mais les employés _____.
d. Je suis sérieuse, mais Georges et Margot _____ |

6. You have seen that when *s* and *x* occur at the end of a masculine singular adjective, they occur at the end of the plural form also. Now compare the adjectives in the sentences below.

        Étienne et Paul sont grands et beaux.
        Barbara et Thérèse sont grandes et belles.

a. The masculine plural form of *beau* is _____. |

    beaux (All adjectives and nouns ending in -*eau* and nouns in -*eu* are made plural by adding the letter -*x*.)

b. The feminine plural of *belle* is _____. |

    belles

7. Describe these things with the correct form of *beau*. (See key.)
a. Les chansons de Schubert
b. Cette radio et ce magnétophone
c. Les deux neveux de M. et Mme Larue

8. Compare the adjectives in these sentences.
C'est un enfant normal.   *Ce sont des enfants normaux.*
a. What happens when *normal* agrees with a masculine plural noun? |

    -*al* changes to -*aux*

b. Rewrite in the plural: *C'est un livre médical.* |

    Ce sont des livres médicaux.

c. Ce pays d'Afrique est tropical. |

    Ces pays d'Afrique sont tropicaux.

2. The present tense of *connaître*

1. In *Une rencontre* Philippe asks Jean *Tu connais ces deux filles?* What is the English equivalent? |

   Do you know those two girls?

2. *Connaître* means *to know, to be acquainted with,* or *to be familiar with* a person, place, or idea.

   —Tu connais Paris?   —Oui, très bien.

   Write a good English equivalent of *Tu connais Paris?* |

   Do you know Paris? (Are you familiar with Paris?)

3. Study the chart of the present tense forms of *connaître*. Refer to it as you answer items a–d.

je	**connai**	**s**	nous	**connaiss**	**ons**
tu	connai	**s**	vous	connaiss	**ez**
on/il/elle	**connaî**	**t**	ils/elles	connaiss	**ent**

   a. What are the two stems of *connaître?* |

   connai- (spelled connaî- in the il/elle-form) and connaiss-)

   b. Does the stem *connaiss-* appear in the singular or plural forms of *connaître?* |

   plural

   c. What are the written endings of *connaître?* |

   -s, -s, -t, -ons, -ez, -ent

   d. Write the three verb forms in which the letter combination *ss* appears. |

   connaissons, connaissez, connaissent

4. Spend a few minutes studying the chart. Then recall and write the forms of *connaître* that match these pronouns. Check your answers against the chart.

   a. je, tu   d. nous
   b. on, il, elle   e. vous |
   c. ils, elles

5. Say that the persons indicated are well acquainted with the city in which they live.

   Modèle: J'habite à Paris. |

   Je connais bien Paris.

   a. Tu habites à Bruxelles. |

   Tu connais bien Bruxelles.

   b. Il habite à Montréal. |

   Il connaît bien Montréal.

c. Mon ami Birago et moi, nous habitons à Dakar. |
Nous connaissons bien Dakar.
d. Vous habitez à Port-au-Prince. |
Vous connaissez bien Port-au-Prince.

6. Write an English equivalent.
Vous ne connaissez pas les États-Unis? |
You don't know (You aren't familiar with) the United States?

3. The possessive adjectives *mon, ma, ton, ta*

You are familiar with several kinds of determiners: the definite article *(le garçon)*, the indefinite article *(un garçon)*, and the demonstrative adjective *(ce garçon)*. In this Préparation you learn a few forms of another determiner: the possessive adjective.

1. A possessive adjective indicates possession of a thing, or close relationship to a person, thing, or idea.

In English, a speaker must use different possessive adjectives according to who the possessor is. Compare these sentences.

Charles: Is that your brother?
Paul: Yes, that's my brother.
Charles: And is that your sister?
Paul: Yes, that's my sister.

Write the two possessive adjectives. |
your, my

2. Read the French equivalent.

Charles: C'est ton frère?
Paul: Oui, c'est mon frère.
Charles: Et c'est ta sœur?
Paul: Oui, c'est ma sœur.

a. Write the four possessive adjectives. |
ton, mon, ta, ma
b. Which two forms mean *your?* |
ton, ta
c. Which two forms mean *my?* |
mon, ma
d. True or false? In French, a possessive adjective changes according to the gender of the noun it accompanies. |
true (*Mon* and *ma* mean *my*; *ton* and *ta* mean *your*.)

3. Look at the dialogue in frame 2 once more.
a. Which two forms match *frère—mon* and *ton* or *ma* and *ta?* |
mon, ton

b. Which two forms match *sœur*—*mon* and *ton* or *ma* and *ta*? |
    ma, ta

4. Express the idea of *my* and *your* by rewriting these noun phrases with the appropriate possessive adjectives—*mon* and *ton* or *ma* and *ta*.

    Modèle: cette cousine |
        ma cousine, ta cousine

    a. un crayon | a. mon crayon, ton crayon
    b. ce cousin | b. mon cousin, ton cousin
    c. la boîte | c. ma boîte, ta boîte
    d. cette cassette | d. ma cassette, ta cassette

5. Compare the adjectives in these groups of sentences.

    C'est un écran.   C'est une affiche.
    C'est mon écran.   C'est mon affiche.

    Mon is used with a feminine noun, *affiche*. Does *affiche* begin with a consonant sound or a vowel sound? |
        with a vowel sound (*Mon* and *ton* are used before any singular noun beginning with a vowel sound, regardless of gender.)

6. Rewrite each noun phrase to express the idea of *my* and *your*. Use the correct possessive adjectives: *mon* and *ton* or *ma* and *ta*.
    Modèle: ce bureau |
        mon bureau, ton bureau

    a. cette règle |
        ma règle, ta règle

    b. cette étagère |
        mon étagère, ton étagère

    c. cet écran |
        mon écran, ton écran

    d. cette élève |
        mon élève, ton élève

4. The possessive adjectives *son* and *sa*

1. You and Paul see a tape recorder and a guitar on the table. You want to know if they belong to Robert.

    You: Is that his tape recorder?
    Paul: Yes, it is.
    You: And is that his guitar?
    Paul: Yes, that's his guitar, too.

    Write the possessive adjective used with *tape recorder* and *guitar*. |
        his

2. Suppose the tape recorder and guitar belong to Monique.

> *You:* Is that her tape recorder?
> *Paul:* Yes, it is.
> *You:* And is that her guitar?
> *Paul:* Yes, that's her guitar, too.

Write the possessive adjective used with *tape recorder* and *guitar*. |

her

3. Now read the French equivalent asking if the items belong to Robert.

> *Vous:* C'est son magnétophone?
> *Paul:* Oui.
> *Vous:* Et c'est sa guitare?
> *Paul:* Oui, c'est sa guitare aussi.

a. Write the possessive adjectives used with *magnétophone* and *guitare*. |

son (magnétophone), sa (guitare)

b. Is the owner of the items male or female? |

male (Robert)

c. What is the English equivalent of *son* and *sa*? |

his

4. Here is the conversation if the items belong to Monique.

> *Vous:* C'est son magnétophone?
> *Paul:* Oui.
> *Vous:* Et c'est sa guitare?
> *Paul:* Oui, c'est sa guitare aussi.

a. Write the possessive adjectives used with *magnétophone* and *guitare*. |

son (magnétophone), sa (guitare)

b. Is the owner of the items male or female? |

female (Monique)

c. What is the English equivalent of *son* or *sa* when the owner is female? |

her

5. a. Does the choice of *son* or *sa* depend on whether the owner is male or female? |

no

b. Does the choice of *son* or *sa* depend on whether the item owned is masculine or feminine? |

yes

c. *Son* and *sa* each have two English equivalents, depending on whether the owner is male or female. They both can mean ___ or ___. |

his, her

6. Rewrite the following sentences, using the correct possessive, *son* or *sa*.

    Modèle: C'est le piano de Paul. |

            C'est son piano.

    a. C'est la clarinette de Paul. |

            C'est sa clarinette.

    b. C'est la clarinette de Monique. |

            C'est sa clarinette.

    c. C'est le vélo de Monique. |

            C'est son vélo.

    d. C'est le vélo de Paul. |

            C'est son vélo.

7. What are the two English equivalents for *son vélo?* |

            her bicycle, his bicycle

8. *Mon* and *ton* are used instead of *ma* and *ta* before a feminine noun beginning with a vowel sound: *mon affiche, ton affiche.* In the same way, *son* is used before a feminine noun beginning with a vowel sound: *C'est son affiche.*

    Answer in the affirmative: *C'est l'amie de Suzanne?* |

            Oui, c'est son amie.

À Propos!   Name three things that you own, and say that each is yours: *J'ai un _____. C'est mon _____.* Name three things that a friend or relative owns, and say that each is his or hers.

5. *Il y a* and numbers

Write the answers to the arithmetic problems in frames 1–3. (See key.)

    Modèle: Il y a quinze livres sur le bureau et vingt livres sur la table. Il y a combien de livres en tout *(in all)?* |

            Il y a 35 livres en tout.

1. Il y a treize chiens devant la porte, dix-sept chiens derrière la porte, dix chiens dans une boîte, et quinze chiens sur les tables et les chaises. Il y a combien de chiens en tout? |

2. Il y a vingt-cinq petits lions et onze grands lions dans le zoo. Il y a combien de lions en tout? |

3. Il y a trente-sept hommes et trente-deux femmes là-bas. Il y a combien de personnes en tout? |

4. Dans mon petit orchestre il y a trois guitares, une flûte, une clarinette et un piano. Il y a combien d'instruments en tout? |

Note Culturelle

Friends and acquaintances

French-speaking people generally make more of a distinction between friends and acquaintances than most Americans do. A friend (*un ami* or *une amie*) is someone that you know well and for whom you have a real affection. A *camarade* is someone you know well because you go to school together or work together, but who does not inspire the same warmth as a friend does. Chums or pals are *copains* or *copines*, a fa- miliar term used to refer to companions ranking between *amis* and *camarades*. The French refer to a person they know only slightly as *une connaissance* (an acquaint- ance).

Deux jeunes amoureux (two young people in love).

Vocabulaire

Noms

le café   *coffee, café*
l'employé/e   *employee*
la fac (faculté)   *university, college*
le métro   *subway*

Noms utiles

un appareil-photo   *camera*
une auto   *car*
une clarinette   *clarinet*
un électrophone   *record player*
une guitare   *guitar*
un magnétophone   *tape recorder*
une motocyclette (moto)   *motorcycle*
un piano   *piano*
un saxophone   *saxophone*
un vélo   *bicycle*
un vélomoteur   *moped*

Adjectifs

ambitieux/ambitieuse   *ambitious*
normal/e, normaux   *normal*
sérieux/sérieuse   *serious*

Verbes

apprendre   *to learn*
connaître   *to know, to be acquainted with*

Autres mots et expressions

eux   *them*
là-bas   *over there*
mon, ma   *my*
sa   *her/his*
son   *her/his*
ton, ta   *your*

PRÉPARATION 17

La sociologie, à quoi ça sert?

Hélène demande à son amie, Brigitte, si elle connaît le garçon qui est en train de parler avec Paul.

Hélène Tu connais ce garçon qui parle avec Paul?

Brigitte Oui, bien sûr. C'est un copain de mon frère.

Hélène Qu'est-ce qu'il fait?

Brigitte Il finit sa licence de sociologie.

Hélène Allons bon! Encore quelqu'un qui veut changer le monde!

Brigitte Qu'est-ce que tu as contre la sociologie? C'est quelque chose d'important et d'utile.

Hélène Utile? Tu plaisantes! Qu'est-ce qu'ils font d'utile, les sociologues? Ce sont tous des révolutionnaires. Ils critiquent tout, mais ils ne proposent aucune solution.

Brigitte Mais si, voyons . . . Oh là là, regarde l'heure. Il ne faut pas manquer la manif.

Hélène (avec enthousiasme) Ah oui! Vite, en route! Je crois que ça va être formidable aujourd'hui!

What is sociology good for?

Hélène asks her friend Brigitte whether she knows the boy who is speaking with Paul.

Do you know that boy who's speaking with Paul?

Yes, of course. He's a buddy of my brother's.

What does he do?

He's finishing his B.A. degree in sociology.

Here we go again! Another one who wants to change the world!

What have you got against sociology? It's something important and useful.

Useful? You're joking! What do sociologists do that's useful? They're all revolutionaries. They criticize everything, but they don't propose any solution.

Oh come on, yes they do! Oh my, look at the time. We mustn't miss the demonstration.

(With enthusiasm): Oh, yes! Quick, let's get going! I think it's going to be great today!

Échange d'idées

1. S1: Pretend you're new to the class. Ask your partner if he/she knows a certain person in the class. Identify the person by location, by hair color, or by the person he/she is talking to.

   S2: Reply affirmatively. Give some additional information about the person. For example: tell whom he/she is a friend of, another course that you and he/she are in, something that he/she likes or doesn't like.

2. S1: Ask your partner to defend one of these topics by asking what use it is: *le droit, la médecine, la musique, la sculpture, le théâtre*. Question the usefulness of the people who work in these areas.

S2: Ask what your partner has against the topic. Defend the topic or the people who work in that field.

1. The plural demonstrative adjective *ces*

1. You learned about the singular demonstrative adjectives *ce, cet,* and *cette* in Préparation 9.
   a. How would you say in French *this woman? this boy?* |
      cette femme, ce garçon
   b. How would you say in French *that boy? that child (male)?* |
      ce garçon, cet enfant
2. Suppose you want to point out several people or several items. Compare the following French and English noun phrases.

ces garçons	*these boys, those boys*
ces filles	*these girls, those girls*
ces enfants	*these children, those children*

   The French equivalent for both *these* and *those* is _____. |
   ces
3. When *ces* occurs before a noun beginning with a vowel sound, there is liaison, just as with *les* and *des*.
   a. What linking sound occurs—/s/ or /z/? |
      /z/
   b. Say the following noun phrases aloud. Copy those in which a linking /z/ sound occurs, and put a link mark ⌣ between *ces* and the noun: *ces étudiants, ces guitares, ces élèves, ces hommes, ces affiches.* |
      ces étudiants, ces affiches, ces élèves, ces hommes
4. How would you say in French *these bicycles? these motorcycles?* |
   ces vélos, ces motos (motocyclettes)

5. How would you say in French *those friends? those university students?*

6. You are in a department store with a friend who dislikes every item. Write what your friend says. (See key.)

   Modèle: guitare

   a. magnétophone   b. électrophone

7. You are having no luck finding things in your room. Express your frustration. (See key.)

   Modèle: Mais où est donc la cassette de Pavarotti?

   a. Mais où est donc l'article *(m.)* sur les Rolling Stones?
   b. Mais où sont donc les photos de ma famille?
   c. Mais où sont donc mes notes sur la Révolution?

2. The verb *aller*

Like the verb *to go, aller* is used to say where you are going or what you will do in the near future.

je	**vais**	nous	**allons**
tu	**vas**	vous	**allez**
on/il/elle	**va**	ils/elles	**vont**

1. Is *aller* a regular *-er* verb?

2. Some forms of *aller* can be predicted from the infinitive, and others cannot. Which two forms use the infinitive stem?

3. The form of *aller* that matches *ils* and *elles* is ____.
4. What form of *aller* matches *je?*
5. What form matches *tu?*
6. What form matches *on, il, elle?*

7. a. *Aller* may be followed by a noun phrase or by an infinitive: *Je vais à l'université. Nous allons manger.* Write English equivalents.

   b. To say that someone is going to do something in the near future, *aller* is followed by an ____.

8. Fill the blanks with the correct form of *aller* and translate the sentences.
   a. Je ____ fermer la porte. |
   b. Marguerite et Jean-Claude ____ à la cafétéria à midi. |
   c. Margot et moi, nous ____ travailler samedi. |
   d. Est-ce que tu ____ aller à Dallas avec moi? |
   e. Vous ____ répondre à cette question. |

   a. *vais*   I'm going to close the door.
   b. *vont*   Marguerite and Jean-Claude are going to go to the cafeteria at noon.
   c. *allons*   Margot and I are going to work on Saturday.
   d. *vas*   Are you going to go to Dallas with me?
   e. *allez*   You are going to answer this question.

À Propos!

Tell a friend what you're going to do after you finish this assignment. Ask a friend where he/she is going on Saturday night. *(Où est-ce que...?)*

3. The possessive adjectives *mes, tes, ses*

1. Compare the possessive adjectives in the chart below.

Singular		Plural	
mon cousin	**ma** cousine	**mes** cousins	**mes** cousines
ton frère	**ta** sœur	**tes** frères	**tes** sœurs
son oncle	**sa** tante	**ses** oncles	**ses** tantes

   a. True or false? The possessive adjectives *mes, tes,* and *ses* may be used with plural masculine and plural feminine nouns. |
      true
   b. As in the case of *les, des,* and *ces,* there is a linking /z/ when *mes, tes,* or *ses* occurs before nouns beginning with a ____ sound. |
      vowel
2. Write French equivalents for the following noun phrases. Use the correct plural adjectives.
   a. my brothers, your photos |
      mes frères, tes photos
   b. his (male) friends, his (female) friends |
      ses amis, ses amies

c. What is the other English translation for *ses amis* and *ses amies?* |

her (male) friends, her (female) friends

3. Answer the questions, using possessive adjectives and the information in parentheses.

    Modèle: Que font tes frères? (regarder la télévision) |

Mes frères regardent la télévision.

a. Où sont mes cahiers? (dans ce tiroir) |

Tes cahiers sont dans ce tiroir.

b. Où est-ce que tes parents habitent? (dans un appartement) |

Mes parents habitent dans un appartement.

c. Qu'est-ce que les copines d'Anne aiment faire? (aller danser) |

Ses copines aiment aller danser.

4. Now answer in the negative.

a. Vous connaissez les fils de Mme Garnier? |

Non, je ne connais pas ses fils.

b. Tu as mes disques? |

Non, je n'ai pas tes disques.

c. Ce sont tes cousins là-bas? |

Non, ce ne sont pas mes cousins.

4. More verbs in *-er*

1. Here are four *-er* verbs that you don't know. The items in this frame will help you think about their meanings.

a. What is the cognate equivalent of *aider?* |

to aid (Another equivalent is *to help*.)

b. *Trouver* is the opposite of *perdre. Trouver* means _____. |

to find

c. *Porter* is related to the English noun *porter.* What does a porter in an airport do for you if you have a very heavy suitcase? |

puts it on a cart to carry it for you (One meaning of *porter* is *to carry*.)

d. You have heard *fermer* in class in the command *Fermez le livre. Fermer* means _____. |

to close

e. *Laver* is related to the word *lavatory. Laver* means _____. |

to wash

f. What are the stems of *aider, trouver, porter, fermer,* and *laver?* |

aid-, trouv-, port-, ferm-, lav-

2. Rewrite these sentences, using the pronouns or names in parentheses; then think of an English equivalent for each one. (See key.)

    Modèle: Pierre cherche un disque. (Jeanne et Henri) |
           Jeanne et Henri cherchent un disque.

  a. Vous trouvez le magnétophone. (tu)
  b. Jacques et Alice portent une grosse boîte. (je)
  c. Paul aide M. et Mme Peyre, qui sont très vieux. (nous)
  d. Gérard ferme la porte. (Hélène et Lucie)
  e. Je lave la voiture. (vous)

5. Verbs in -*érer*

1. Verbs in -*érer* undergo a spelling change in some forms. Look at the chart of *préférer* and read the forms aloud.

je	**préfèr**	e	nous	**préfér**	ons
tu	préfèr	es	vous	préfér	ez
on/il/elle	préfèr	e	ils/elles	**préfèr**	ent

  a. Which forms have the same stem as the infinitive stem *pré-fér-?* |
        nous préférons, vous préférez (the forms with pronounced endings)
  b. Write the stem of the *je, tu, il, ils* forms. |
        préfèr- (The *accent grave* reflects the shift of the stress onto the second syllable in these forms.)
  c. Change *nous préférons* to *je.* |
        je préfère
  d. Change *vous préférez* to *tu.* |
        tu préfères

2. Verbs in -*érer* are often cognates. Can you guess the meanings of these verbs? *préférer, suggérer, considérer, exagérer* |
        to prefer, to suggest, to consider, to exaggerate

3. Rewite these sentences, using the cues in parentheses.
  a. Vous exagérez l'importance de la sociologie. (tu) |
        Tu exagères l'importance de la sociologie.
  b. Qu'est-ce que tu suggères maintenant? (vous) |
        Qu'est-ce que vous suggérez maintenant?
  c. Hélène préfère la science à la sociologie. (Hélène et Paul) |
        Hélène et Paul préfèrent la science à la sociologie.
  d. Elle considère que le travail d'une avocate est utile. (nous) |
        Nous considérons que le travail d'une avocate est utile.

Note Culturelle

Education

Most French-speaking countries have a minimum requirement for attending school (in France, up to age 16). At the age of 14, or after the equivalent of our ninth grade, students either enter a vocational or business school or begin work as apprentices in a trade, or they attend a *lycée* (college prep high school).

Lycée students stay in school until age 18 or 19, preparing for the exam called the *baccalauréat*. A student who has the *baccalauréat* has the approximate equivalent of a junior college education, and is automatically entitled to register at the university. In France and most French-speaking countries, a smaller percentage of the population attends universities than in the United States. The university system in France is run by the state, and is free. There are branches in many cities. The oldest and most famous is the Sorbonne in Paris.

À Paris, au jardin du Luxembourg. Vous aimez travailler dehors (outside)?

Vocabulaire

Noms

l'article *m.*   *article*
le copain/la copine   *pal, friend, buddy*
l'enthousiasme   *enthusiasm*
la fac   *university; (slang)*
la licence   *bachelor's degree*
la manifestation (manif)   *demonstration*
le monde   *world*
la musique   *music*
la note   *note; grade (academic)*
le/la révolutionnaire   *revolutionary man/woman*
la sculpture   *sculpture*
la sociologie   *sociology*
le/la sociologue   *sociologist*
la solution   *solution*
l'université *f.*   *university*

Adjectifs

aucun/e   *no, not any*
bleu/e   *blue*
ces   *these, those*
mes   *my*
ses   *his, her*
sympathique   *nice, pleasant, likeable*
tes   *your*

Verbes

aider   *to help*
aller   *to go*
considérer   *to consider*
critiquer   *to criticize*

exagérer   *to exaggerate*
fermer   *to close*
laver   *to wash*
manquer   *to miss*
plaisanter   *to joke*
porter   *to carry*
préférer   *to prefer*
proposer   *to suggest, propose*
réfléchir (réfléchiss-)   *to think, to reflect*
remplir (rempliss-)   *to fill (up)*
suggérer   *to suggest*
trouver   *to find*

Autres mots et expressions

allons bon!   *oh, no! (resignation)*
à quoi ça sert?   *what good is it? what is it used for?*
avec enthousiasme   *enthusiastically*
contre   *against*
encore   *again*
en route!   *let's go!*
est-ce que...   *(begins a question) is...? do...?*
je crois (que)   *I think (that)*
quelque chose de (beau)   *something (beautiful)*
quelqu'un   *someone*
rien de (beau)   *nothing (beautiful)*
vite   *fast; (exclamation) quick!*
voyons   *let's see*

PRÉPARATION 18

Différence d'opinion

Jean-Pierre et Marcel discutent au Bar du Dôme leur cours sur Pascal.

Jean-Pierre Tu es vraiment d'accord avec Pascal quand il dit que la nature humaine est mauvaise?

Marcel Mais oui. Je la trouve corrompue. Nous ne valons rien, et nous savons que nous ne valons rien, mais nous cachons ce fait aux autres et à nous-mêmes . . . Dis, on prend une autre glace?

A difference of opinion

Jean-Pierre and Marcel discuss their course on Pascal at the Bar du Dôme.

Do you really agree with Pascal when he says that human nature is evil?

Yes, of course. I find it corrupt. We are worthless, and we know that we are worthless, but we hide that fact from others and from ourselves . . . Say, shall we have another ice cream?

Jean-Pierre D'accord. (Il appelle le garçon) Monsieur . . . encore deux glaces, s'il vous plaît . . . Tu sais, je trouve que vous avez tort, Pascal et toi. Les êtres humains sont capables de sentiments généreux.	Sure. (He calls the waiter.) Waiter . . . two more ice creams, please . . . You know, I think you're wrong, you and Pascal. Human beings are capable of generous feelings.
Marcel Peut-être. Mais alors, ces sentiments sont motivés par la vanité et donc sans valeur. C'est une réaction purement égoïste.	Perhaps. But then they're motivated by sheer vanity and hence not worth a thing. It's a purely selfish reaction.
Jean-Pierre Alors quelle est la solution à notre condition?	Then what is the solution to our condition?
Marcel Souffrir, mon vieux, souffrir.	To suffer, old pal, to suffer.
Jean-Pierre Oui, sur les bancs de l'université . . . Bon, en attendant, finis ta glace!	Sure, studying at the university . . . Well, meanwhile, finish your ice cream!

Échange d'idées

1. S1: Suggest to your partner that you both have an additional ice cream. Tell the waiter you want two more.
   S2: Protest a bit and say with a sigh that you're going to put on weight.

2. Vous êtes d'accord avec Pascal? Vous trouvez la nature humaine bonne ou mauvaise? Vous trouvez les êtres humains essentielle-ment généreux ou égoïstes?

1. Review of possessive adjectives

1. Compare the meanings of the adjectives in these two sentences.

   Paul cherche son oncle, sa tante et ses cousins.
   Monique cherche son oncle, sa tante et ses cousins.

   a. When the possessor is a male, what is the English meaning of *son, sa,* and *ses?* |
      his
   b. When the possessor is a female, the English meaning of *son, sa,* and *ses* is _____. |
      her
   c. Which adjective—*son, sa,* or *ses*—is used with any singular noun that begins with a vowel sound? |
      son (son ami, son amie)

2. Write French equivalents for the following dialogues.
   a. —Is that Paul's guitar?   —Yes, it's his guitar. |
      —C'est la guitare de Paul? —Oui, c'est sa guitare.

b. —Is that Marie's bicycle?   —Yes, it's her bicycle. |

3. Answer according to the cues.
   a. C'est la moto d'Henri? (non)
   b. Ce sont les disques d'Alice? (oui)
   c. C'est l'amie d'Édouard? (oui) |

4. Complete the second sentence in each pair so that it refers to the person named in the first sentence. (See key.)
   a. J'ai un transistor. C'est _____ transistor.
   b. Tu as une clarinette. C'est _____ clarinette.
   c. Marie a un oncle qui habite à Bâton Rouge. C'est _____ oncle.
   d. J'ai des disques de jazz. Ce sont _____ disques de jazz.
   e. Tu as un vélomoteur. C'est _____ vélomoteur.

5. Tell what you like about your friend Marc. Write the noun phrases with the correct possessive adjective. (See key.)

J'aime _____ humour, _____ intelligence, _____ qualités artistiques, _____ voiture et _____ parents.

À Propos!   Make statements about three of your possessions or three of your relatives.

J'ai une voiture, un chat et trois petits frères. Ma voiture est rouge, mon chat est intelligent et mes trois petits frères sont impossibles!

2. The possessive adjectives *notre, votre, leur*

1. Look at the following examples.

M. Dufour, où est votre fille? Où est votre fils?
Mr. Dufour, where is your daughter? Where is your son?

Jacques est notre cousin. Jacqueline est notre sœur.
Jacques is our cousin. Jacqueline is our sister.

—C'est la voiture de M. et Mme Lussac? —Oui, c'est leur voiture.
Is that the Lussac's car? Yes, it's their car.
Elle est dans leur garage. *It's in their garage.*

Do *notre, votre,* and *leur* change form when they accompany a feminine noun? |

Phase trois

Subject Pronouns	Possessive Adjectives
nous	notre
vous	votre
ils/elles	leur

2. Write each question with the possessive adjective that refers to the people indicated.

a. *(vous deux)* Est-ce _____ chien? |
   Est-ce votre chien?

b. *(Sylvie et Jacques)* _____ père est ingénieur, n'est-ce pas? |
   Leur père est ingénieur, n'est-ce pas?

c. *(toi et moi)* Mais où est _____ auto? |
   Mais où est notre auto?

3. Restate each of the following sentences according to the *modèle*.

Modèle: René et Julie ont une caméra. |
   C'est leur caméra.

a. Mireille et moi, nous avons un appareil-photo. |
   C'est notre appareil-photo.

b. Madame Marmont, vous avez une moto. |
   C'est votre moto.

c. Étienne et Patrick ont un électrophone. |
   C'est leur électrophone.

3. Practice with *connaître*

1. Two friends are looking at their class photograph and discussing some of the people they see. Complete each sentence with the correct form of *connaître*.

a. —Tu _____ Martine Dumont, n'est-ce pas?
b. —Non, mais je _____ sa sœur.
c. —Tes parents _____ le président de l'université?
d. —Non, mais ma mère _____ sa sœur.
e. —Pierre et moi, nous _____ ce garçon.
f. —Ah oui? Et vous _____ sa cousine aussi? |

   a. connais   b. connais   c. connaissent (Remember that the plural stem ends in *ss*.)   d. connaît (Did you remember the *accent circonflexe?*)   e. connaissons
   f. connaissez

2. Write complete sentences, using the correct form of *connaître* and the correct form of the demonstrative or possessive adjective also. (See key.)

Modèle: Paulette/ c _ journaliste |
   Paulette connaît ce journaliste.

a. Angélique et Jeanne/ c_ avocat.
b. Tu/ c_ ville?
c. Paul/ ne... pas/ m_ tante
d. Je/ c_ mécanicienne |

À Propos!   Vous connaissez des artistes de cinéma? Des chanteurs? Quels *(which)* artistes? Quels chanteurs?

4. Asking questions with *est-ce que*

1. One way of asking *oui-non* questions is to use rising intonation. Which question below would you ask with rising intonation?
   Ton grand-père est français? Il a quel âge? |
   Ton grand-père est français?

2. Another way is to use a tag phrase. Change the following statement to a question using *n'est-ce pas*, and give the English equivalent:
   Elle connaît M. Monet. |
   Elle connaît M. Monet, n'est-ce pas? She knows Mr. Monet, doesn't she? (N'est-ce pas is usually used when the speaker expects the listener to agree.)

3. A third way of asking *oui-non* questions in French is to use the expression *est-ce que* at the beginning of the sentence.

   Est-ce que Pierre a une guitare? *Does Pierre have a guitar?*

   Change these statements into questions by using *est-ce que*.
   a. Tu aimes le cours de français. |
   Est-ce que tu aimes le cours de français?
   b. Vous avez vingt ans. |
   Est-ce que vous avez vingt ans?

4. *Est-ce qu'elle aime Charles?* How do you write *est-ce que* when it is used before a subject pronoun that begins with a vowel sound? |
   est-ce qu'

5. Write questions with *est-ce que* that would bring about the following answers.
   a. Oui, il parle espagnol. |
   Est-ce qu'il parle espagnol?
   b. Non, elle ne connaît pas ce village.
   Est-ce qu'elle connaît ce village?

6. *Est-ce que* is also used with information questions, after the interrogative phrase. *Où est-ce qu'ils habitent?*
   Complete these questions by adding *est-ce que*.
   a. Pourquoi/tu es triste aujourd'hui? |
   Pourquoi est-ce que tu es triste aujourd'hui?

b. Quand/ils arrivent? |

c. Combien de sœurs/vous avez? |

5. The present tense of *voir*

1. In *Une belle voiture, c'est important,* you saw this sentence: *Jacques taquine Roger qui voit sa petite amie parler avec un jeune homme.* What is the equivalent of *voit sa petite amie?* |

sees his girl friend

2. Compare the present tense endings of *voir* and *connaître.*

je	**voi**	s	connai	s
tu	voi	s	connai	s
on/il/elle	voi	t	connaî	t
nous	**voy**	ons	connaiss	ons
vous	voy	ez	connaiss	ez
ils/elles	**voi**	ent	connaiss	ent

In written French, are the endings for *voir* the same as for *connaître?* |

yes

3. a. What are the two stems of *voir?* |

voi-, voy-

b. Which subject pronouns are used with the stem *voy-?* |

nous, vous

4. Take a few minutes to study the forms of *voir,* then test yourself by writing these subject pronouns and matching forms of *voir.* Check your answers against the chart.

a. nous   e. je

b. vous   f. on

c. tu   g. elles |

5. Tell how many of these objects the following people see: *un vélo, un piano, une souris, une voiture, un serpent, un saxophone.* (See key.)

Modèle: Robert . . . |

Robert voit deux éléphants.

a. je . . .

b. Marc et Robert . . .

c. Georges et moi, nous . . .

d. Ils . . .

e. M. Lafayette . . .

f. Les enfants . . .

6. Writing practice

Below is a dialogue with no punctuation. Read the entire dialogue
first, then write each sentence with appropriate capitalization, punctuation, and accent marks. (See key.)

Hélène: tu connais ce garcon la bas
René: bien sur c'est mon cousin jean pierre
Hélène: il est medecin n'est ce pas
René: mais non il est ingenieur
Hélène: ah oui ou est ce qu'il travaille
René: chez renault

Vocabulaire

Noms

le banc   *bench*
la condition   *condition*
la différence   *difference*
l' être humain *m.*   *human being*
le fait   *fact*
la glace   *ice cream*
l' humour *m.*   *humor*
l' intelligence *f.*   *intelligence*
la nature humaine   *human nature*
l' opinion *f.*   *opinion*
la qualité   *quality*
la réaction   *reaction*
le sentiment   *feeling*
la solution   *solution*
la valeur   *value*
la vanité   *vanity*

Adjectifs

artistique   *artistic*
corrompu/e   *corrupted*
généreux/généreuse
   generous
humain/e   *human*
mauvais/e   *bad, evil*

Adjectifs possessifs

notre   *our*
votre   *your*
leur   *their*

Verbes

acheter   *to buy*
appeler   *to call*
avoir tort   *to be wrong*
cacher   *to hide*
discuter (de quelque
   chose)   *to discuss
   (something)*
être capable de
   to be able to
être d'accord   *to agree*

être motivé par   *to be motivated by*
souffrir (souffr-)   *to suffer*
valoir (vau-, val-)   *to be worth*
voir (voi-, voy-)   *to see*

Autres mots et expressions

bien   *well*
encore   *more*
mon vieux   *old buddy, old friend*
ne... rien   *nothing*
nous-mêmes   *ourselves*
pas bien   *not well*
peut-être   *maybe*
purement   *sheerly, purely*
sans   *without*
vraiment   *really*

*À Paris. Elle prépare
le dîner.*

PRÉPARATION 19

1. Direct object pronouns: *le, la, l', les*

This section will explain what a direct object is and show you how to use some direct object pronouns.

1. Read this sentence: *Robert aide Marie.*
   a. Who is doing the helping? Robert or Marie?
   > Robert (Robert is the subject of the verb. He is the doer of the action.)
   b. Who is being helped? Robert or Marie?
   > Marie (Marie is the direct object of the verb. She is the one directly affected by the process of helping.)

2. Find the direct objects in each of these sentences and write them. Include the article or other determiner with the noun.
   a. Ma cousine aime l'algèbre.
   > l'algèbre
   b. Mlle Duval a une grande voiture et aussi un petit vélomoteur.
   > une grande voiture, un petit vélomoteur
   c. Jean-Pierre déteste son cousin, mais il aime bien sa cousine.
   > son cousin, sa cousine
   d. Tu voudrais ces deux disques?
   > ces deux disques

3. Read the following exchange concerning a boy.

   > —Tu connais ce garçon?
   > —Oui, je le connais.

   a. What is the direct object of *Tu connais?*
   > ce garçon
   b. What word replaces *ce garçon* in the answer?
   > Le (*Le* is a direct object pronoun. It replaces a masculine singular noun or noun phrase.)

4. Compare the word order in the French sentence and its English equivalent.

   > Je le connais. *I know him.*

   a. In the English sentence, does the direct object pronoun *him* precede or follow the verb?
   > it follows the verb

b. In the French sentence, does the direct object pronoun *le* precede or follow the verb? |

5. Now read the following exchange concerning a girl.

—Tu connais cette fille?
—Oui, je la connais.

a. Which direct object pronoun replaces *cette fille?* |

la (The direct object pronoun *la* replaces a feminine singular noun phrase.)

b. What is the English equivalent of *Je la connais?* |

I know her.

6. Compare the noun phrases in the following chart with the direct object pronouns that replace them.

Le garçon?	Oui, je **le** connais.
La fille?	Oui, je **la** connais.
Les enfants?	Oui, je **les** connais.

a. Which direct object pronouns replace the noun phrases at the left? |

Le replaces a masculine singular noun or noun phrase, *la* replaces a feminine singular noun or noun phrase, *les* replaces a plural noun or noun phrase.

b. Write English equivalents of *Je le connais, Je la connais,* and *Je les connais.* |

I know him. I know her. I know them.

7. Compare the noun phrases in the following chart with the direct object pronouns that replace them.

Le tableau?	Oui, je **le** vois.
La guitare?	Oui, je **la** vois.
Les chaises?	Oui, je **les** vois.

a. Do *le, la, les* refer to things as well as to people? |

yes

b. Write English equivalents of *Je le vois, Je la vois, Jes les vois.* |

I see it. I see it. I see them. (In English, "it" may replace any singular noun or noun phrase that refers to a thing.)

8. Replace the direct object phrases in the following sentences with the pronouns *le, la,* or *les.* Write complete sentences and give English equivalents of your answers to frames a and b.
   Modèle: Je vois mon copain David. |

Je le vois. *(I see him.)*

a. Je ferme les fenêtres de la voiture. |

> Je les ferme. *(I'm closing them. I close them.)*

b. Je connais ces écrivains anglais. |

> Je les connais. *(I know them.)*

c. Je cherche ma règle. |

> Je la cherche.

9. Now look at this chart.

Le professeur?	Oui, je **l'**écoute.	**Mon cahier?**	Oui, je **l'**ai.
La chanteuse?	Oui, je **l'**écoute.	**Ma caméra?**	Oui, je **l'**ai.
Les acteurs?	Oui, je **les** écoute.	**Mes stylos?**	Oui, je **les** ai.

a. When *le* or *la* precedes a verb beginning with a vowel, it becomes _____. |

> l'

b. When *les* precedes a verb beginning with a vowel, what linking sound occurs? |

> /z/

10. Rewrite these sentences with direct object pronouns. Say them aloud after you write them.

a. J'entends la guitare. |

> Je l'entends.

b. Robert attend Guy. |

> Robert l'attend.

c. Tu aimes les films français, n'est-ce pas? |

> Tu les aimes, n'est-ce pas?

11. Compare the sentences below.

> J'écoute *l'*acteur.   Je *l'*écoute.
> J'aime *les* films français.   Je *les* aime.

a. When *le, la, l',* and *les* occur *before a noun,* they are definite _____. |

> articles

b. When they occur *before a verb,* they are _____. |

> direct object pronouns

12. Expand the answers to the following questions by adding the information in parentheses. Use an object pronoun in the answers.

Modèle: Où est-ce que Marc trouve son crayon? (sous la table) |

> Il le trouve sous la table.

a. Où est-ce que Nicolas trouve son stylo? (derrière la télé) |

> Il le trouve derrière la télé.

b. Vous deux, vous connaissez cette chanson? (oui, bien) |
> Oui, nous la connaissons bien.

c. Tu as ton cahier de physique, n'est-ce pas? (oui) |
> Oui, je l'ai.

d. Est-ce que Catherine aime ce disque de jazz? (oui, beaucoup) |
> Oui, elle l'aime beaucoup.

e. Votre famille et vous, vous voyez souvent vos amis canadiens? (oui, assez souvent) |
> Oui, nous les voyons assez souvent.

2. The verb *prendre*

1. In *Différence d'opinion* you saw the sentence *Dis, on prend une autre glace?* What is the English equivalent? |
> Say, shall we have another ice cream?

2. *Prendre* (to take) is an irregular *-re* verb. It is commonly used in three ways, illustrated by the following sentences. Read each one, write the form of *prendre* with its subject, and say the English equivalent of the sentence.

a. Après le dîner nous prenons le dessert. |
> Nous prenons *(After dinner we have/take dessert.)*

b. Pour aller à Montmartre, tu prends le métro. |
> Tu prends *(To go to Montmartre, you take the subway.)*

c. Les élèves prennent leurs livres et leurs cahiers. |
> Les élèves prennent *(The students take their books and their notebooks.)*

3. Compare the forms of *prendre* and *répondre*.

je	**prend**	s	**répond**	s
tu	prend	s	répond	s
on/il/elle	prend		répond	
nous	**pren**	ons	répond	ons
vous	pren	ez	répond	ez
ils/elles	**prenn**	ent	répond	ent

a. Are the endings of *prendre* the same as for the regular *-re* verb *répondre*? |
> yes

b. *Prendre* has regular endings, but it has three stems. Write them. |
> prend-, pren-, prenn- (Note the differences in sound: /pʀɑ̃/, /pʀən/, /pʀɛn/)

4. Say aloud and write the subject pronouns and forms of *prendre*. Check your answers against the chart.

    a. je, tu   c. nous, vous

    b. elle   d. ils

5. Answer the following questions, using the information in parentheses.

    a. —Qu'est-ce que je prends? (le métro) —Tu . . .

                     Tu prends le métro.

    b. —Quel train prenez-vous? *(Le Mistral)* —Nous . . .

                     Nous prenons *Le Mistral.*

    c. —Est-ce que tu prends le livre de Sylvie? (non)

       —Non, je . . .

                     Non, je ne prends pas le livre de Sylvie.

    d. —Est-ce qu'elles prennent la voiture? (oui) —Oui, elles . . .

                     Oui, elles prennent la voiture. (Oui, elles la prennent.)

3. The possessive adjectives *nos, vos, leurs*

1. Compare the possessive adjectives in the chart.

Singular		Plural	
notre cousin	**notre** cousine	**nos** cousins	**nos** cousines
votre frère	**votre** sœur	**vos** frères	**vos** sœurs
leur oncle	**leur** tante	**leurs** oncles	**leurs** tantes

    a. The possessives *notre, votre,* and *leur* are used with singular nouns. The corresponding plural adjectives _____, _____, and _____ are used with plural nouns.

                     nos, vos, leurs

    b. Can *nos, vos,* and *leurs* be used with both masculine and feminine nouns?

                     yes

    c. When *nos, vos,* and *leurs* occur before a noun that begins with a vowel (like *oncles*), is there a linking /z/ sound?

                     yes

2. Complete each sentence below to say what the people are looking for. Use *nos, vos,* and *leurs*.

    Modèle: Vous cherchez _____? (crayons)

                 vos crayons

    a. Elles cherchent _____ . (copains)

                 leurs copains

    b. Nous cherchons _____. (cahiers)

                 nos cahiers

c. Jean-Pierre et toi, vous cherchez _____? (disques)

d. Les Daumur cherchent _____. (enfants)

4. Round-up of possessive adjectives

The chart may be a useful reference for the following frames.

Possessive adjectives

The owner	Singular item		Plural items
je	mon	ma	mes
tu	ton	ta	tes
on/il/elle	son	sa	ses
nous	notre	notre	nos
vous	votre	votre	vos
ils/elles	leur	leur	leurs

1. A possessive adjective gives you information about who owns an item. Which subject pronouns represent the owners of the following items?
   a. ton magnétophone
   b. votre saxophone
   c. sa guitare
   d. ses bandes
   e. nos cassettes
   f. leur clarinette

   a. tu   b. vous   c. on, il, *or* elle   d. on, il, *or* elle
   e. nous   f. ils *or* elles

2. Complete the French equivalents of the sentences below with *notre, votre,* or *leur* + noun. (See key.)
   a. *Is your dentist nice?* Est-ce que _____ gentil?
   b. *Our doctor is French.* _____ est français.
   c. *Their teacher is intelligent.* _____ est intelligent.

3. Complete the second sentence in each pair with *son, sa,* or *leur,* or *leurs.* Remember that *leurs* refers to more than one item; *son, sa,* and *leur* refer to one item. (See key.)
   a. Nous connaissons la tante de Marcel et de Denise. Nous connaissons _____ tante.
   b. Mme Leduc trouve une guitare. C'est la guitare de _____ nièce Marie.
   c. Ces jeunes filles aiment beaucoup le rock. Elles écoutent _____ disques de rock.
   d. Michel trouve un cahier. C'est le cahier de _____ sœur.

4. Complete the second sentence in each pair with the appropriate possessive adjective.

    Modèle: Il a un neveu. C'est _____ neveu. |
              son

  a. Tu as des cousins. Ce sont _____ cousins.
  b. Ils ont une tante. C'est _____ tante.
  c. Il a une tante. C'est _____ tante.
  d. Elles ont des oncles. Ce sont _____ oncles. |
         a. tes b. leur c. sa d. leurs

5. Practice with *faire*

M. Pince-Nez, a strict and proper *professeur d'anglais* at *Lycée Louis-le-Bête,* dreams one night that he can fly. He flies to the homes of his students, and inquires about what they are doing. Each time, his unbelieving ears hear that they are doing their homework.

    Write the answers to M. Pince-Nez's questions; remember that the possessive adjectives will change.

    Modèle: Madame, que font vos fils? |
            Ils font leurs devoirs, Monsieur.

1. Madame, que font votre fils et votre fille? |
        Ils font leurs devoirs, Monsieur.

2. Monsieur, que fait votre fille? |
        Elle fait ses devoirs, Monsieur.

3. Marcel et Madeleine Morbleu, qu'est-ce que vous faites? |
        Nous faisons nos devoirs, Monsieur.

4. Charles Champignon, qu'est-ce que vous faites? |
        Je fais mes devoirs, Monsieur.

Vocabulaire

Noms

le dessert *dessert*
les devoirs *homework*
le dîner *dinner*
le docteur *doctor*
le film *movie*
le magasin *store*
le mistral *fierce cold wind in Southern France; name of a train*
le western *western movie*

Adjectifs possessifs

nos *our*
vos *your*
leurs *their*

Verbes

prendre (prend-, pren-, prenn-)
  to take
répondre *to answer*

Pronoms

la/l' *her, it*
le/l' *him, it*
les *them*

Autres mots et expressions

après *after*
au (à + le) *to the*
quel/s, quelle/s *what (is...)?*
  which (is...)?

Note Culturelle
Family meals

Traditionally, French families have eaten a large meal together, between noon and 2 P.M. This tradition is disappearing, however, as business establishments adopt the *journée continue* (workday with a short lunch break). The evening meal usually begins around 7:30 or 8 P.M.

The French generally would not serve all the parts of a meal on one plate. A sit-down meal usually consists of a series of courses, and often the plates are changed with each course. Cheese is almost always served before dessert, which often consists of fresh fruit. Ice cream and pastries are saved for special occasions. Adults usually finish their meal with a small cup of strong black coffee.

Dans un appartement à Paris: repas (meal) familial. Bon appétit! (Enjoy your meal!)

PRÉPARATION 20

1. Writing practice: Describing someone you know

First, think of a friend or relative you know well enough to describe. Then write a paragraph of at least ten sentences. Let the questions below suggest information you should include. If you write about a girl or woman, make adjectives and pronouns agree. *Faites un bon portrait!*

1. Qui est-ce? (C'est votre ami Robert? votre cousin?)
2. Quel âge a-t-il?
3. Il est américain?
4. Où est-ce qu'il habite? (Dans quelle ville?)
5. Il a combien de frères et de sœurs?
6. Il est blond? brun?
7. Est-ce qu'il est grand ou petit?
   Est-ce qu'il est gros? maigre?
8. À votre avis *(in your opinion)*, est-ce qu'il est intelligent ou stupide?
   Vous le trouvez beau? pas très beau?
   Vous le trouvez gentil? très gentil? sympathique?
9. Est-ce qu'il exagère souvent?
10. Est-ce qu'il critique tout ou est-ce qu'il critique très peu?
11. Qu'est-ce que vous faites ensemble *(together)* de temps en temps?
12. Que fait son père?
13. Est-ce que sa mère travaille?
    Qu'est-ce qu'elle fait?
14. Qu'est-ce qu'il voudrait *(would like)* être?
15. Est-ce qu'il a un transistor? un vélo? un chien?
16. Qu'est-ce qu'il n'a pas? un piano? une girafe? etc.
17. Qu'est-ce qu'il voudrait avoir? une moto? une caméra? etc.
18. Qu'est-ce qu'il aime? les maths? les voitures?
    Il aime danser? chanter? manger? patiner? écouter la radio?
19. À votre avis, pourquoi est-ce que vous êtes amis ou vous n'êtes pas amis?

Be prepared to hand in what you write and to talk about it in class.

2. Practice with articles in negative sentences

1. *Je n'ai pas de vélomoteur.* In a negative sentence, the articles *un,*
   une, and *des* become _____. |
       de

2. Now read this statement: *Je n'ai pas le livre de Patricia.* Do the
   articles *le, la, les* become *de* in a negative sentence? |
       no

3. Answer the following questions in the negative.
   a. Est-ce que Marc a une moto? |
       Non, il n'a pas de moto.
   b. Est-ce que tu as des sœurs? |
       Non, je n'ai pas de sœurs.
   c. Est-ce que ces deux jeunes filles ont quatorze ans? |
       Non, elles n'ont pas quatorze ans.
   d. Vous et Laure, vous avez les disques de Rémi? |
       Non, nous n'avons pas les disques de Rémi.

3. *Voilà* with direct object pronouns

1. You have used *le voilà* and *la voilà* to point out things.
   a. What is the equivalent of *la voilà* in this exchange?

   —Voilà l'actrice Brigitte Labelle.
   —Ah oui, la voilà. |
       there she is

   b. Suppose someone called your attention to some circus per-
   formers. What might you reply?
   —Voilà les acrobates!
   —Ah oui, _____. |
       les voilà (The direct object pronouns *le, la,* and *les* precede *voilà,* just as they do verbs.
       The word *voilà* is a verbal expression, from *vois là,* meaning *see there.*)

2. Your friend Charles is amusing the guests at a party with a mind-
   reading act. You are his assistant. The two of you have hidden
   pictures of people and objects around the room. When he an-
   nounces the location of an item you "find" it.
   Modèle: Charles: Il y a trois zèbres derrière la porte.
           Vous: C'est vrai! _____ |
           Les voilà.

   a. Charles: Il y a une vieille femme dans le tiroir.
           Vous: C'est vrai! _____ |
           La voilà.

b. Charles: Il y a trois pianos sous le bureau.
   Vous: C'est vrai! _____ |
   Les voilà.

c. Charles: Il y a un tigre derrière la porte.
   Vous: C'est vrai! _____ |
   Le voilà.

4. Review practice: direct object pronouns

1. For each picture write the French for *I see him, her, it, them*. Use the correct object pronoun. (See key.)
   Modèle: |
   Je la vois.

a.    b.    c.   d.

2. Use the cues to write a question using a demonstrative adjective. Then answer in the affirmative with a direct object pronoun. (See key.)
   Modèle: **Michèle et Georges/regarder** |
   Michèle et Georges regardent cette affiche? Oui, ils la regardent.

a. vous/connaître

c. Madeleine/voir

d. son père/aimer

b. M. et Mme Vincent/chercher

e. vous/écouter

5. Review practice: possessive adjectives

1. There are more forms for possessive adjectives in French than in English, and it takes practice to use them correctly. Complete the second sentence in each pair with the appropriate possessive adjective. (See key.)

   Modèle: J'ai une cousine. Voilà _____ cousine. |
                 ma

   a. Ma sœur et moi, nous avons quarante disques. Le dimanche nous écoutons _____ disques.
   b. Vous avez un appareil-photo. C'est _____ appareil-photo.
   c. J'ai un saxophone. Voilà _____ saxophone.
   d. Anne et Jean ont des sœurs? _____ sœurs sont sportives?
   e. Les parents de Luc ont une voiture. _____ voiture est anglaise.
   f. J'ai une moto. J'aime _____ moto.
   g. Mon frère a une moto aussi. Il préfère _____moto à _____moto.
   h. Tu as un transistor? Tu écoutes souvent _____ transistor?

6. Review practice: *voir, aller*

1. These people are in a museum that has all kinds of old things. Say what each person sees, using the correct form of *voir* and of *vieux*. (See key.)

   Modèle: tu/un téléphone |
                Tu vois un vieux téléphone.

   a. vous/une moto
   b. Jean-Paul/une chaise
   c. nous/une voiture
   d. mes parents/un piano
   e. moi/un vélo

2. Tell whom these people are going to see when they go visiting. (See key.)

   Modèle: Gérard/ses beaux-parents |
                Gérard va voir ses beaux-parents.

   a. moi/mon petit ami
   b. Jacques et toi/les Depardieu à Rome
   c. Charlotte et Yves/le cousin d'Yves
   d. toi/tous tes amis
   e. mon mari et moi/notre avocate

Vocabulaire

Noms

l'acrobate *m./f.*   acrobat
la banque   *bank*
la bibliothèque   *library*
la vitamine   *vitamin*
le soir   *evening*

Autres mots et expressions

à votre avis   *in your opinion*
ensemble   *together*
prendre un verre   *to have a drink*

Phase 4

Loisirs

Qu'est-ce que vous allez apprendre?

In this Phase you will talk about sports, games, and musical instruments. You will learn expressions useful for talking on the telephone, idiomatic expressions to indicate distaste and displeasure. You will learn vocabulary for leisure-time and cultural activities and for the weather, telling time, the days of the week, months and seasons.

Communication

By the end of the Phase you will have studied:
  The present tense of *vouloir* (to want) and *pouvoir* (to be able).
  Various idiomatic expressions with *faire*.
  The frequently-used subject pronoun *on* (they, you, one, we).
  The prepositions *à* and *de* + the definite article.
  How to talk about past events or actions using the *passé composé*.
  The difference between *savoir* and *connaître* (both translate as *to know*).
  Stressed pronouns (*moi*, etc.) and some of their uses.
  The verb *lire* (to read).
  How to talk about the near future: *aller* + infinitive.
  To beware of false cognates.

Culture

The popular game of *boules,* vacations, skiing and salt-water recreation, *le football* (i.e. soccer) and interesting customs and holidays in France.

PRÉPARATION 21

Un Coup de téléphone

Pierre téléphone à son ami André pour lui rappeler un match de basket. Le téléphone sonne quatre fois. C'est Mme Verlaine, la mère d'André, qui répond.

Mme Verlaine Allô.

Pierre Allô, Mme Verlaine? C'est Pierre. Je voudrais parler à André, s'il vous plaît.

Mme Verlaine D'accord, une minute. Ne quittez pas, s'il vous plaît.

Pierre Merci, Madame.

André Allô, Pierre? Ça va?

Pierre Oui, pas mal. Et toi?

André Bof! Plus ou moins.

Pierre Pourquoi? Qu'est-ce qu'il y a?

André Je planche depuis ce matin. On a un test de maths demain.

Pierre Mais on joue quand même au basket cet après-midi, n'est-ce pas?

André Ah oui, c'est vrai, j'avais oublié. Quelle barbe, cette trigo!

Pierre Écoute, laisse tomber ton travail un moment et viens au Club.

André Oui, tu as raison. À quelle heure?

Pierre À deux heures, si tu veux.

André Bon, d'accord. À tout à l'heure.

A telephone call

Pierre calls his friend André to remind him of a basketball game. The telephone rings four times. Mrs. Verlaine, André's mother, answers.

Hello?

Hello? Mrs. Verlaine? It's Pierre. I would like to speak to André, please.

Certainly, just a minute. Hold on, please.

Thank you.

Hello, Pierre? How are things?

Not bad. And you?

Oh well, O.K., more or less.

Why? What's the matter?

I've been working hard since this morning. We have a math test tomorrow.

But we're still playing basketball this afternoon, aren't we?

Oh, right. I had forgotten. What a drag this trig is!

Listen, leave your work for a while and come to the sports club.

Yes, you're right. At what time?

At two, if you like.

O.K., fine. See you later.

Échange d'idées

1. You are calling a friend of yours who is not home. Instead, you talk with his mother/father who tells you where he/she is. Leave a message *(message)*, and say good-by.

2. S1: Remind your partner of what you planned to do on Saturday (use *n'est-ce pas?*).

   S2: You have forgotten about the plans and have made others instead. Express annoyance and be apologetic.

1. Expressions with *faire*

1. In Phase 3 you had practice with the verb *faire*.
   a. Write the English equivalent of *Tu fais des devoirs de maths ce soir?* |

   Are you doing math homework tonight?

   b. What is the equivalent of *Que fait ton père?* |

   What does your father do (for a living)?

2. Compare the French and English verb forms.

Tu aimes le jazz?	*Do you like* jazz?
Que fait ta mère?	*What does* your mother *do?*

   In English, *do* and *does* are often used to signal the beginning of a question. Does French use an equivalent of *do* or *does* to begin a question? |

   no

3. Write French equivalents.
   a. Do you like to skate? |

   Tu aimes patiner?

   b. What does your buddy do? |

   Que fait ton copain?

4. *Faire* has many English meanings besides *to do*.
   a. See if you can write the English equivalent of *Ces artisans font des chaises.* |

   These artisans/craftspeople are making chairs.

   b. *Faire* can mean *to do* or _____. |

   to make

5. *Faire* is often used with other words in fixed expressions or idioms where it may not mean *to do* or *to make*. For example:
   a. *Je fais une promenade à la campagne* means _____. |

   I'm taking a walk in the country. (*Promenade* is the term used in square dancing to mean *to walk*.)

   b. *Je fais une promenade à vélo* means _____. |

   I'm taking a bike ride.

   Now write an English equivalent of *Nous faisons du ski dans les Alpes.* |

   We're skiing in the Alps. / We ski in the Alps.

6. Write a French equivalent of each English sentence.
   a. *(Are you doing your French exercises/homework?)* Tu/tes exercices de français?
   b. *(What are they doing?/What are they making?)* Qu'est-ce qu'ils/? |

   a. Tu fais tes exercices de français?   b. Qu'est-ce qu'ils font?

   c. *(Are you taking a walk today?)* Tu/aujourd'hui?

d. *(Are we skiing on Sunday?)* Est-ce que nous/dimanche? |

2. The present tense of *vouloir*

The verb *vouloir* (to want) helps you discuss what you and others want to have or want to do. You have already used *je voudrais,* a polite form of *vouloir* meaning *I would like.*

1. Study the chart for a few minutes. Notice that the present tense of *vouloir* has three stems.

je	**veu**	**x**	nous	**voul**	**ons**
tu	veu	**x**	vous	voul	**ez**
on/il/elle	veu	**t**	ils/elles	**veul**	**ent**

a. Which stem matches *je, tu, on, il,* and *elle?* |

veu-

b. What are the endings of the *je* and *tu* forms? |

-x, -x (The *x* is an old form of the *s* that appears in *je* and *tu* forms of many verbs.)

c. Which stem matches *nous* and *vous?* |

voul-

d. The *nous* and *vous* forms of *vouloir* have endings that are pronounced. Write the *nous* and *vous* forms. |

nous voulons, vous voulez

e. Which stem matches *ils* and *elles?* |

veul-

2. First say, then write each subject with the matching form of *vouloir.* Refer to the chart to check your work.
   a. Paul et moi, nous . . .   d. toi, tu . . .
   b. je . . .   e. vous . . .
   c. mes cousins . . .   f. les étudiants . . .

3. Tell what these people want.
   a. David et moi, nous/une affiche de Notre Dame |
   b. Yvonne et André/une motocyclette |
   c. Jacqueline/un disque de musique classique |

a. David et moi, nous voulons une affiche de Notre Dame.   b. Yvonne et André veulent une motocyclette.   c. Jacqueline veut un disque de musique classique.

4. So far you have used *vouloir* with a noun, as in *Je veux un disque.*
   Vouloir can also be followed by an infinitive phrase, just like *aimer* and *aller.*

Phase quatre

J'aime jouer au basket.	*I like to play basketball.*
Je vais jouer au basket.	*I'm going to play basketball.*
Je veux jouer au basket.	*I want to play basketball.*

5. When *vouloir* is followed by a second verb, that verb is always an infinitive. Write an equivalent for *We want to watch television.* |

    Nous voulons regarder la télévision.

6. What do the following people want or want to do? Answer with the information in parentheses. Say your French sentence aloud, then think of the English equivalent.

    a. Qu'est-ce qu'il veut? (un magnétophone) |

    Il veut un magnétophone. *(He wants a tape recorder.)*

    b. Qu'est-ce que tu veux faire? (écouter des disques) |

    Je veux écouter des disques. *(I want to listen to records.)*

    c. Qu'est-ce qu'ils veulent? (une photo de leurs amis) |

    Ils veulent une photo de leurs amis. *(They want a photograph of their friends.)*

    d. Qu'est-ce qu'elles veulent faire? (jouer au basket) |

    Elles veulent jouer au basket. *(They want to play basketball.)*

À Propos!

Et vous, qu'est-ce que vous voulez?

3. À + definite articles

This section will give you further practice using *parler* to say that someone is talking to someone else. It will also show you how to talk about playing various sports.

1. At the party after the opening of Mimi Fontinelle's new play, critic Marcel Duchamp observed the playwright talking to different people. Read the notes he took.

    La chanteuse américaine Barbara Sellers arrive; Mimi parle à la chanteuse. L'écrivain Paul Poirot arrive; Mimi parle à l'écrivain. Le photographe Albert Matignon arrive; Mimi parle au photographe.

    a. Write an English equivalent of the third note. |

    The photographer Albert Matignon arrives. Mimi talks with the photographer.

    b. Look again at the third note. The preposition before the word *photographe* is _____. |

    au (The preposition *à* contracts (combines) with *le* to form *au.*)

    c. Does *à* contract with *la?* |

    no (The preposition *à* never contracts with *la.*)

d. Does *à* contract with *l'*? |
no

2. Here are some more of Duchamp's notes.

   Voilà les musiciens; Mimi parle aux musiciens. Et voilà les danseuses italiennes; Mimi parle aux danseuses italiennes.

   The preposition *à* contracts with *les* and forms the word _____. |
   aux

À + Definite articles

à + la = **à la**   à + le = **au**
à + l' = **à l'**   à + les = **aux**

3. In spoken French there is a linking sound when *aux* is followed by a noun beginning with a vowel sound, just as there is with *les* and *des*. In which of these phrases is there a linking /z/?
   aux écrivains   aux danseuses   aux hommes |
   aux écrivains, aux hommes (Remember that the first sound in *hommes* is a vowel sound. See Note Linguistique p. 176.)

4. Write the French equivalent of *Mimi is talking to the reporters.* |
   Mimi parle aux journalistes (aux reporters).

5. The critic decides to stop working and talk to people. Write sentences to tell whom he talks to.
   Modèle: le journaliste |
   Il parle au journaliste.

   a. l'actrice anglaise |
   Il parle à l'actrice anglaise.

   b. les chanteurs francais |
   Il parle aux chanteurs français.

   c. les danseuses américaines |
   Il parle aux danseuses américaines

6. *Jouer à* is used to talk about playing games and sports. Write the English equivalent of *Philippe joue au tennis.* |
   Philippe is playing tennis. (The English equivalent has no preposition.)

7. Take a moment to look at the names of sports and games on p. 176. Then rewrite these sentences with the new information.
   Modèle: J'aime jouer au tennis. (les cartes) |
   J'aime jouer aux cartes.

   a. Tu veux jouer aux boules cet après-midi? (le volley-ball)
   Tu veux jouer au volley-ball cet après-midi?

   b. Renée et Raoul jouent aux échecs. (le hockey) |
   Renée et Raoul jouent au hockey. (See Note Linguistique p. 176.)

   c. Patrick veut jouer au basket. (les boules) |
   Patrick veut jouer aux boules.

4. Telling time

1. Philippe has forgotten to turn his clock ahead to daylight-saving time, and he is an hour late. As he arrives for his eight o'clock class, he glances at the hall clock and says: *Zut! Il est neuf heures!*
   a. What is the English equivalent of *Il est neuf heures?*
      It is nine o'clock. (Literally, "It is nine hours.")
   b. Does *il* in *Il est neuf heures* mean *he* or *it?*
      it
   c. *Il est _____ heure(s)* is a fixed expression used in telling time. Say that it is four o'clock.
      Il est quatre heures.

2. Complete this to ask what time it is:
   Quelle heure _____-il?
      est (When a question begins with a form of *quel?*, the verb can *precede* the subject.)

3. What is the linking sound in these phrases—*deux heures, dix heures*—/s/ as in *si* or /z/ as in *zut?*
      /z/ (deux heures, dix heures)

4. For each clock, ask in French *What time is it?* and then write the correct time.
   a.   b.

      Quelle heure est-il? Il est cinq heures. (Remember the hyphen between *est* and *il* in the question. Did you make *heures* plural in the answer?)
      Quelle heure est-il? Il est sept heures.

5. Tell what the following people are doing at a certain time.
   Modèle: Qu'est-ce que tu fais à une heure? (manger au restaurant universitaire)
      À une heure, je mange au restaurant universitaire.
   a. Qu'est-ce qu'elle fait à deux heures? (une promenade avec son grand-père)
   b. Qu'est-ce que tu fais à cinq heures? (jouer au basket)
   c. Qu'est-ce qu'ils font à six heures? (leurs devoirs de maths)
      a. À deux heures, elle fait une promenade avec son grand-père.   b. À cinq heures, je joue au basket.   c. À six heures ils font leurs devoirs de maths.

6. If you were to see *3h* on a train schedule, you could guess that it stands for _____.
      3 heures. (The abbreviation *h* is used on most timetables and listings of public events.)

À Propos!

Et maintenant, il est quatre heures, n'est-ce pas? Non? Alors quelle heure est-il environ *(approximately)*?

Note linguistique

The consonant *h*

In English, the consonant *h* is usually pronounced, as in *heart* or *hot*. Sometimes it is silent as in *honor, honorable, an honor.* In French, *h* is always silent. In most words it is totally ignored. The articles *l'* and *les* (with linking) are used, as with words beginning with a vowel: *l'homme, les hommes; l'humour,* *l'honneur.* In some words, however, though *h* is silent it is treated like a consonant. The article *le* or *la* is used, and there is no linking with *les: le héros, les héros, le hockey, la hâte* (haste), *Le Havre.* In dictionaries, a word like *hockey* is often indicated like this: **hockey (m.).*

Vocabulaire

Noms

l'après-midi *m.   afternoon*
le concert   *concert*
le doigt   *finger*
la fois   *time*
le matin   *morning*
la minute   *minute*
le moment   *moment*
le poster   *poster*
la promenade   *walk*
le reporter   *reporter*
le soir   *evening*
le téléphone   *telephone*
la trigonométrie (trigo)   *trigonometry*

Verbes

avoir raison   *to be right*
faire   *to make, do;* ~une
   promenade   *to take a walk;* ~des
   projets   *to make plans;* ~du
   ski   *to ski, go skiing*
laisser   *to leave;* ~tomber   *to drop*
oublier   *to forget*
plancher   *to work hard (slang)*
rappeler   *to remind*
sonner   *to ring*
téléphoner à   *to call (someone)*
je voudrais   *I would like*
vouloir (veu-, voul-, veul-)   *to want*

Autres mots et expressions

à quelle heure   *at what time? when?*
à tout à l'heure   *see you later*
allô   *hello (on telephone)*
bof   *oh, well . . . (resignation,*
   indifference)
bon   *O.K.*
demain   *tomorrow;* ~matin/
   soir   *~morning/evening*
depuis   *since*
il est neuf heures   *it is nine o'clock*
ne quittez pas   *hold on*
plus ou moins   *more or less*
quand même   *still, anyway*
quelle barbe   *what a drag*
quelle heure est-il?   *what time is it?*
viens   *come*

Les saisons

le printemps   *spring*
l'été *m.   summer*
l'automne *m.   fall, autumn*
l'hiver *m.   winter*
la saison   *season*

Les sports et les jeux

jouer   *to play;* ~aux boules
   ~*boules;* ~aux cartes;
   ~*cards;* ~aux échecs   ~*chess*
le base-ball   *baseball*
le basket-ball   *basketball*
le hockey   *hockey*
le ping-pong   *ping-pong*
le tennis   *tennis*
le volley-ball   *volleyball*
le sport   *sport*
le jeu   *game*

Note Culturelle
Les Boules

Les boules (or *la pétanque*) is a game played mostly in smaller towns *dans le Midi* (in southern France). The rules are simple, but the opportunities for heated discussion are endless. One player tosses *le cochonnet* (a small wooden ball that serves as the target). Each player then tries to toss a heavy metal ball to get close to the target or knock away the ball of the closest competitor. The game of *boules* is played by men and women, young and old. You may be familiar with the Italian version of the game, which is called *bocci.*

Le jeu de boules exige (requires) de l'adresse (skill) et de la concentration.

PRÉPARATION 22

Quel sale temps!

C'est samedi. Il pleut. Bernard arrive chez
Suzanne.

Bernard Dis donc, quel sale temps!
Suzanne Oui, on ne peut sûrement pas
   jouer au tennis aujourd'hui.
Bernard Non, bien sûr . . . On pourrait
   aller au musée des Beaux-Arts; il y a une
   nouvelle exposition d'art africain. Ou bien
   au cinéma, si tu veux. Il y a un film de
   science-fiction au Palace, je crois.

What awful weather!

It's Saturday. It is raining. Bernard arrives
at Suzanne's house.

Hey, what awful weather!
Yes, we certainly can't play tennis today.

No, that's for sure. We could go to the
Museum of Fine Arts; there's a new
exhibit of African art. Or (we could go) to
the movies if you like. There's a science
fiction film at the Palace, I think.

Suzanne Non, attends. Je viens de lire dans le journal qu'on joue l'*Apollon de Bellac* de Giraudoux en matinée. J'adore Giraudoux.	No, wait. I just read in the paper that there's a matinee of Giraudoux's *Apollo of Bellac*. I adore Giraudoux.
Bernard Moi aussi. C'est une bonne idée. Allons-y. À propos, c'est où? Au théâtre Marigny?	Me, too. That's a good idea. Let's go. By the way, where is it? At the Marigny theater?
Suzanne Non, à la Maison de la Culture.	No, at the Maison de la Culture.

*Échange
d'idées*

1. Because of weather conditions you and a classmate decide not to carry out your plans outdoors (pick any activity that you know).

   S1: Ask your partner if he/she wants to go to the movies. Tell where two different types of movies are playing.

   S2: Say "No, wait", or say what you prefer to do, or express agreement and set a day and time.

2. S1: Ask a classmate if there's a certain kind of film at a particular theater.

   S2: Reply either that you think so, or that you don't know. Ask your classmate if he/she likes that kind of film.

   S1: Answer yes, a lot; or yes, a little; or no, not much.

   S2: Ask if your classmate wants to go see a film that you name.

1. The direct object pronouns *me, te, nous, vous*

You have practiced using *le, la, l',* and *les* as equivalents for the direct object pronouns *him, her, it,* and *them*. This section presents the equivalents for *me, you,* and *us*.

1. Chantal is almost hidden by a tree. She asks Marie:

   —Marie, tu me vois? Je suis ici. —*Marie, do you see me? I'm here.*

   a. What is the subject in the phrase *tu me vois?* |

   tu

   b. What is the direct-object pronoun in *tu me vois?* |

   me (Although French *me* and English *me* are spelled the same way, they are pronounced differently. French *me* rhymes with *le*.)

2. Look at the chart and examples below.

me/m'	Tu **me** vois?	Tu **m'**attends?
te/t'	Je **te** vois.	Je **t'**attends.
nous	Ils **nous** voient.	Ils **nous** attendent.
vous	Nous **vous** voyons.	Nous **vous** attendons.

a. Read aloud, then write the English equivalents of: *Je te vois. Ils nous voient. Nous vous voyons.*

I see you. They see us. We see you. (If you hesitated, remember than nous cannot be the subject of voient and vous cannot be the subject of voyons.)

b. Where do *me, te, nous,* and *vous* occur—before or after the verb?

before the verb

3. Write the equivalents for these sentences.

a. Catherine and Michel, we see you.

Catherine et Michel, nous vous voyons.

b. Marc is looking for you, Peter.

Març te cherche, Pierre. (Remember that chercher, like many French verbs, uses no preposition, while the English verb does: to look for.)

c. That man knows me.

Cet homme me connaît.

d. Patricia is looking at us.

Patricia nous regarde. (Regarder uses no preposition.)

4. Look at the chart again, and write equivalents for these: *I'm waiting for you. They're waiting for us. Are you waiting for me?*

Je t'attends. (Je vous attends.) Ils nous attendent. Tu m'attends? (Vous m'attendez?)

5. Why do *me* and *te* change to *m'* and *t'* before *attendre?* Is there linking between *nous* and *vous* before *attendre?*

because attendre begins with a vowel sound; yes, there is linking.

6. Write equivalents for these sentences, then read them aloud.

a. They *(Ils)* are waiting for me.

Ils m'attendent.

b. She likes us, doesn't she?

Elle nous aime, n'est-ce pas?

c. I'm listening to you *(toi).*

Je t'écoute.

7. a. In the sentence *Vous nous écoutez?* which word does *écoutez* agree with?

With vous, the subject—not with the object nous.

b. Write the equivalent of *We like you (vous).*

Nous vous aimons. (Aimons agrees with the subject nous.)

8. Answer these questions with the appropriate pronoun.

Modèle: Est-ce que tu connais les sœurs de Paul?

Oui, je les connais.

a. Est-ce que Christian nous cherche, Monsieur?

Oui, il vous cherche.

b. Tu invites l'amie de Paul au match de foot *(soccer)?*

Oui, je l'invite.

c. Est-ce que tu m'entends bien?

Oui, je t'entends bien.

d. Tout le monde, vous m'écoutez?

Oui, nous vous écoutons./nous t'écoutons.

Est-ce que vous avez un frère, une sœur ou un copain qui vous admire?

2. Practice with *à* + definite articles

1. Complete the equations below, remembering that *à* contracts with two of the articles.

à + la = ____   à + le = ____

à + l' = ____   à + les = ____ |

à la; à l'; au; aux

2. a. To talk about playing a game or a sport, you use the expression ____. |

jouer à

b. To say that someone is talking to somebody else, you can use the expression ____. |

parler à

3. Write sentences to say what the following people are doing.
    a. Colette/jouer/le tennis
    b. Marc et Delphine/jouer/les échecs
    c. Laurent/parler/l'agent de police
    d. Chantal/parler/la directrice |

a. Colette joue au tennis.   b. Marc et Delphine jouent aux échecs.   c. Laurent parle à l'agent de police.   d. Chantal parle à la directrice.

4. The preposition *à* is also used in *être à*, or *aller à* meaning *to be at,* or *to go to,* a particular place.
    a. Jeanne is going to be late getting home, so she telephones her parents to let them know where she is. She says: *Je suis à la bibliothèque.* Write the English equivalent. |

I'm at the library.

b. An hour later, Jeanne calls to say that she's with friends at the *café (le café).* Complete her sentence. *Je ____ café.* |

suis au (Remember that à + le = au.)

5. It's another typical day in the lives of the people below. Say that they are in their usual places of work or play, and write the English equivalent of where they are. If you can't remember, look at the *vocabulaire* on p. 184.

    Modèle: Marc Lepied: le stade |

Marc Lepied est au stade. *At the stadium.*

a. L'ouvrière et l'ouvrier: l'usine |

L'ouvrière et l'ouvrier sont à l'usine. *At the factory.*

b. Le professeur et moi, nous: la bibliothèque |

Le professeur et moi, nous sommes à la bibliothèque. *At the library.*

c. Tu: le cinéma |

Tu es au cinéma. *At the movies.*

3. The subject pronoun *on*

1. Camille and François have just finished a game of chess on a rainy day, and Camille doesn't know what to do next. Use *on* to write the equivalent of her question: *What do we do now?* |

   Qu'est-ce qu'on fait maintenant?

2. Complete this sentence to say that in Canada, people play hockey. *Au Canada, _____ au hockey.* |

   on joue

3. Suppose you are a camp counselor, and one of your campers wants to know what the group is doing today. Answer using *on* and the information in parentheses.

   Modèle: Qu'est-ce qu'on fait cet après-midi? (jouer aux cartes) |

   Cet après-midi, on joue aux cartes.

   a. Qu'est-ce qu'on fait à quatre heures? (nager) |

   À quatre heures, on nage.

   b. Qu'est-ce qu'on fait à six heures? (aller manger) |

   À six heures, on va manger.

   c. Qu'est-ce qu'on fait à neuf heures? (jouer au ping-pong) |

   À neuf heures, on joue au ping-pong.

4. Practice with *vouloir*

1. Write the correct form of *vouloir.* (See key.)
   a. Tu _____ jouer aux cartes avec nous?
   b. Ils ne _____ pas manger maintenant.
   c. Qu'est-ce que vous _____ faire maintenant?

2. Write complete sentences with the cues below. (See key.)
   a. Qui/vouloir/faire une promenade
   b. Est-ce que/Paul et Marie/vouloir/jouer au volley-ball/demain
   c. Nous/ne . . . pas/vouloir/habiter à New York

5. Review of *aller*

1. The people below have had to cancel their plans. Use *aller* to tell where they are *not* going.

   Modèle: Pascal et moi/stade |

   Pascal et moi, nous n'allons pas au stade.

   a. Colette/usine |

   Colette ne va pas à l'usine.

Phase quatre

b. Mes copains/discothèque |

> Mes copains ne vont pas à la discothèque.

c. Vous/parc |

> Vous n'allez pas au parc.

2. Complete these sentences to say where various members of your imaginary family are going today, and write English equivalents.

a. Mon frère _____ au zoo.
b. Mes sœurs _____ à la plage.
c. À six heures, nous _____ à l'aéroport.
d. Et toi, maman, tu _____ au musée, n'est-ce pas? |

> a. va (My brother is going to the zoo.)   b. vont (My sisters are going to the beach.)
> c. allons (At 6:00, we're going to the airport.)   d. vas (And Mother, you're going to the museum, aren't you?)

Note Culturelle
Les grandes vacances

Traditionally, people have taken their summer vacation *(les grandes vacances)* in July or August. Most people are entitled to a five-week vacation with pay called *les congés payés.*

At the beginning of July and August, railroad stations are mobbed with travelers, and huge traffic jams develop as people take to the roads. For the many French people who drive to Spain, for instance, there is a wait of many hours at the border.

During August, Paris seems to be peopled only by tourists from other countries. Most Parisians have abandoned the city for the beaches and countryside, or for travels to Spain, England, Germany, and other lands. Most theaters and some museums close for a time. Neighborhood bakeries, butcher shops, grocery stores, and drug stores, as well as many restaurants and cafés, close on a rotating basis for the *fermeture annuelle* (yearly closing). Life returns to normal as people come home in September in time for *la rentrée* (the beginning of the school year.)

Cabourg

Deauville

Boulogne-Sur-Mer

"Forbidden to fish from the sea wall."

Vocabulaire

Noms

l'art *m.* *art*
l'exposition *f.* *exhibit*
le film d'épouvante *horror movie*
l'idée *f.* *idea*
la matinée *afternoon show*
la science fiction *science fiction*
le temps *weather; time*

Des noms de lieux

l'aéroport *m.* *airport*
la bibliothèque *library*
le café *cafe*
le cinéma *movie theater*
la discothèque *discotheque*
l'hôpital *m.* *hospital*
le parc *park*
la plage *beach*
le stade *stadium*
l'usine *f.* *factory*
le zoo *zoo*

Adjectifs

africain/e *African*
sale *dirty*

Pronoms objet

me *me*
te/vous *you*
nous *us*

Verbes

admirer *to admire*
allons-y *let's go*
je crois *I think*
écouter *to listen to*
inviter *to invite*
on pourrait *we could*
si tu veux *if you want*
je viens de lire *I just read*

Autres mots et expressions

ou bien *or*
sûrement *surely*

PRÉPARATION 23

1. Weather and seasons

Quel temps fait-il?

Il fait beau.

Il fait chaud.

Il pleut.

Il fait du vent.

Il fait frais: il ne fait pas chaud, mais il ne fait pas très froid.

Il fait mauvais.

Il fait froid.

Il neige.

1. What is the English meaning of —*Quel temps fait-il?* —*Il fait beau?* |

  —What's the weather like? —It's (it is) nice.

2. a. Which verb is generally used in English to talk about the weather? |

  is (a form of *to be*)

  b. Which is generally used in French—a form of *faire* or *être?* |

  faire

  c. Some weather expressions don't use the verb *faire*. How would you say *It's snowing* in French? |

  Il neige.

3. Here are the names of the seasons: *le printemps, l'été, l'automne, l'hiver.*

  a. Which is the equivalent of *summer—l'automne* or *l'été?* |

  l'été

b. Which is the equivalent of *spring—le printemps* or *l'automne?* |

      le printemps (from the Latin for *first season*)

c. Which is the equivalent of *winter—l'été* or *l'hiver?* |

      l'hiver (It's related to English *hibernate*.)

d. And how do you say *fall* in French? It's a cognate of *autumn*. |

      l'automne (The *m* in *automne* is not pronounced, but the *n* is.)

À Propos!

Et dans votre région, quel temps fait-il maintenant?

2. Practice with direct object pronouns

1. Denis is having a party. Say that he is introducing the first person or people to the second, and use the verb *présenter* (to introduce) with an object pronoun.

   Modèle: toi et moi à sa sœur |

      Denis nous présente à sa sœur.

a. moi/à Sylvie Lemaître |

      Denis me présente à Sylvie Lemaître.

b. Sylvie/à François Charpentier |

      Denis la présente à François Charpentier.

c. toi/à François aussi |

      Denis te présente à François aussi.

d. Sylvie et François/à son père |

      Denis les présente à son père.

2. Answer these questions with *Oui* and a direct object pronoun.

a. Vos grands-parents vous invitent souvent au théâtre? |

      Oui, ils nous invitent souvent au théâtre.

b. Ton professeur d'anglais te connaît bien, n'est-ce pas? |

      Oui, il me connaît bien.

3. Imagine that you are thinking about some of your friends, and say what it is that you like especially about each one. Make sure the adjective matches the gender of the direct object pronoun.

   Mòdele: Chantal/gentil |

      Je la trouve gentille. *I think she's nice. (I find her nice.)*

a. Henri/beau |

      Je le trouve beau.

b. Jean-Yves et ses parents/sympathique |

      Je les trouve sympathiques. (Add *-s* to *sympathiques* to make it match *les*.)

c. Marguerite/joli |

      Je la trouve jolie. (Add *-e* to *joli* to make it match *la*.)

4. Write the French equivalent for *I think they're nice./I find them nice.* |

      Je les trouve sympathiques.

Phase quatre

3. *Le, la, les* in negative sentences

1. So far you have used direct object pronouns only in affirmative sentences. Look at the chart and read the sentences aloud.

Le disque?	Je **ne le** vois **pas.**	Je **ne l'**ai **pas.**
La cassette?	Je **ne la** vois **pas.**	Je **ne l'**ai **pas.**
Les autres cadeaux?	Je **ne les** vois **pas.**	Je **ne les** ai **pas.**

Note that in speech, *ne* often drops its mute *e: Je n'le vois pas. Je n'l'ai pas.*

a. Does the negative particle *ne* occur just before the object pronoun or just before the verb? |
> just before the object pronoun

b. Where does *pas* occur? |
> just after the verb (The object pronoun and the verb make a unit that is surrounded by *ne... pas.*)

2. M. Rochambeau wants to make sure the older children are not making threats at their little brother. Write the denials using an object pronoun, then say them aloud.

a. Tu menaces ton petit frère? (Mais non . . .) |
> Mais non, je ne le menace pas.

b. Et les filles là, vous menacez le petit? (Mais non . . .) |
> Mais non, nous ne le menaçons pas. (Remember the *cédille?*)

c. Et tes copains, ils ne le menacent pas non plus? (Mais non . . .) |
> Mais non, ils ne le menacent pas non plus.

3. Write a complete negative answer to each question, and use the correct direct object pronoun. After you have written your answers, read them aloud.

a. Vous aimez ce musicien, Madame? (Non . . .) |
> Non, je ne l'aime pas.

b. L'agent de police cherche le directeur de la banque? (Non, l'agent . . .) |
> Non, l'agent ne le cherche pas.

c. Vous voulez ces vieux disques? (Non, nous . . .) |
> Non, nous ne les voulons pas.

4. The present tense of *pouvoir*

You have learned to use *vouloir* (to want to). You won't succeed at something you *want* to do unless you *can* do it. *Pouvoir* (akin to the English word *power*) is the equivalent of *can, to be able to,* or *may.*

1. Compare the forms of *pouvoir* with those of *vouloir*.

je	**peu**	**x**	**veu**	x
tu	peu	**x**	veu	x
on/il/elle	peu	**t**	veu	t
nous	**pouv**	**ons**	**voul**	ons
vous	pouv	**ez**	voul	ez
ils/elles	**peuv**	**ent**	**veul**	ent

   a. Are the endings of *vouloir* and *pouvoir* the same? |
       yes

   b. What are the three stems of *vouloir?* |
       veu-, voul-, veul-

   c. What are the three stems of *pouvoir?* |
       peu-, pouv-, peuv- (Both verbs have the same -*eu* and -*ou* vowel sounds in their stems.)

2. Say the forms of *pouvoir* to yourself, then write the forms that match the pronouns below. Check your answers against the chart.
   a. nous   d. je
   b. vous   e. on/il/elle
   c. ils/elles   f. tu

3. Nicolas keeps asking friends to do things with him. Everyone wants to, but unfortunately, nobody can. Write the answers to all his questions, and say the English equivalents.
   Modèle: Marc, tu veux jouer au basket? |
       Oui, mais malheureusement je ne peux pas. *(Yes, but unfortunately I can't.)*

   a. Jean-Paul et Solange, vous voulez aller au cinéma? |
       Oui, mais malheureusement nous ne pouvons pas. *(Yes, but unfortunately we can't.)*

   b. Est-ce que Sara et Eric veulent aller au café avec moi? |
       Oui, mais malheureusement ils ne peuvent pas. *(Yes, but unfortunately they can't.)*

   c. Est-ce que Christine veut jouer aux cartes avec moi? |
       Oui, mais malheureusement elle ne peut pas. *(Yes, but unfortunately she can't.)*

4. Here is a French proverb that uses both *vouloir* and *pouvoir.* Can you guess the equivalent English proverb? *Vouloir, c'est pouvoir.* |
       Where there's a will, there's a way. (To want to is to be able to.)

5. Vocabulary practice: logical responses

In English there are phrases that express emotions and attitudes: among others, *You're kidding!* (skepticism) and *Darn it!* (annoyance).

  Below is a list of such expressions you have seen in French. Some have more than one meaning, depending on the context. If you don't remember them, check the dialogues or the vocabulary.

Surprise, astonishment	Skepticism	Agreement
Oh là là!	Tu plaisantes!	Bien sûr!
Pas possible!	C'est vrai?	Bon.
Ça alors!	Pas possible!	D'accord!
Tiens!	Sans blague?	Oh oui, alors!
Sans blague!		
Dis donc!	*Annoyance*	*Disagreement*
C'est vrai!	Zut!	Mais non!
Tu plaisantes!	Ça alors!	Ah non, alors!
	Oh ça va, ça va!	
Indifference	Oh, là là!	*Contradiction of a negative*
Bof . . .		Mais si!
	Stalling for time	
	Alors . . .	
	Eh bien . . .	
	Bon . . .	

1. Which of the following phrases would you use to express the feelings listed?

surprise a) Ah non, alors!   b) Sans blague!   c) Alors . . .
annoyance a) Tiens!   b) Bof . . .   c) Zut!
agreement a) Pas possible!   b) Ça alors!   c) Bien sûr! |

Sans blague! Zut! Bien sûr!

2. Read the following sentences. Say which emotion or attitude each one expresses.

  a. Il part en Australie aujourd'hui? Tu plaisantes!
  b. Oh oui, alors! Je voudrais bien aller au cinéma ce soir.
  c. Mais non! Je te dis qu'elle est chez elle.
  d. Le concert d'hier? Bof . . .
  e. Tiens! Il est déjà midi!
  f. Oh ça va, ça va! Regarde la télévision, si tu veux! |

a. surprise/skepticism   b. agreement   c. disagreement   d. indifference
e. surprise   f. annoyance

6. The *passé composé* of -er verbs

1. In French, the *passé composé* is the tense commonly used in conversation to express action in the past. It is called *passé composé* (compound past) because the verb forms of this tense consist of more than one part. The *passé composé* of most verbs is made up of the present tense forms of *avoir* + a past participle.

2. Yesterday M. Martin and his boss worked late. He tells his wife about it.

  —Hier, j'ai travaillé tard.

—Oui, tu as travaillé tard. Et ton patron?
—Il a travaillé tard aussi. Nous avons travaillé très tard.

Which phrase is the French equivalent of *I worked late?*
j'ai travaillé tard (Notice that the equivalent verb in English is only one word.)

The *passé composé* expresses three English meanings.	**j'ai travaillé**	**I worked** **I have worked** **I did work**

4. a. Which word in *j'ai travaillé* is related to *travailler?*
   travaillé (*Travaillé* is the past participle of *travailler.*)

   b. In a compound tense, the past participle is used in combination with another verb form. Above, the *passé composé* verbs contain present tense forms of _____ plus the past participle _____.
   avoir; travaillé (*Avoir* is often called the auxiliary or helping verb. It "helps" by telling who did the action—*je, nous,* etc.—while the past participle gives the action.)

   c. In the phrases *j'ai travaillé* and *tu as travaillé*, do the forms of *avoir* change according to the subject?
   yes

   d. Does the past participle change form?
   no

5. Write the *passé composé* form of *travailler* for each item below.
   a. toi et moi, nous _____
   b. Jacques et Denis _____
   c. tu _____
   d. Brigitte _____
   e. vous _____
   f. j' _____

   a. avons travaillé
   b. ont travaillé
   c. as travaillé
   d. a travaillé
   e. avez travaillé
   f. ai travaillé

6. a. The past participle of an *-er* verb is formed with the infinitive stem (*travaill-*, for example) and the ending _____.
   é

   b. Write the past participles of *parler, écouter, chercher, visiter.*
   parlé, écouté, cherché, regardé, visité

7. Say that these people did yesterday what they are doing now. Add the words *Hier aussi* and rewrite in the *passé composé.*
   Modèle: Je visite des monuments historiques.
   Hier aussi, j'ai visité des monuments historiques.

   a. Serge et Cécile regardent la télévision.
   b. Alain danse avec Mireille.
   c. Tu dînes chez moi.
   a. Hier aussi, Serge et Cécile ont regardé la télévision.   b. Hier aussi, Alain a dansé avec Mireille.   c. Hier aussi, tu as dîné chez moi.

8. Write the French equivalent of *Yesterday I played volleyball.*
   Hier j'ai joué au volley-ball.

Phase quatre

Note Culturelle
Les Français et le ski

In France an active winter vacation consists of skiing—usually in the *Alpes* or *Pyrénées.* School children by the thousands go with their teachers for a month of *classes de neige,* with schoolwork in the morning and skiing in the afternoon. Some French people who don't ski themselves enjoy following the progress of French competitors in the international ski trials and in the Olympics. Skiing is one of the events in which French competitors often rank at the top.

Station de sports d'hiver dans les Alpes (Alpe d'Huez)

Vocabulaire

Noms

l' agent de police *m. policeman/ policewoman*
le champion/la championne *champion*
le jour de congé *day off*
le monument *monument*
le patron/la patronne *boss*

Adjectifs

autre *other*
historique *historical*

Verbes

dîner *to have dinner*
menacer *to threaten*
pouvoir (peu-, pouv-, peuv-) *can, may, to be able to*
présenter *to present, introduce*
visiter *to visit (places)*

Les instruments de musique

l' accordéon *m. accordion*
la batterie *drums*
les cymbales *cymbals*
la flûte *flute*
la trompette *trumpet*
le violon *violin*

Le temps

il fait beau/chaud/frais/froid/ mauvais *the weather is nice (beautiful)/hot/cool/cold/bad*
il fait du vent *it's windy*
il neige *it's snowing*
il pleut *it's raining*
quel temps fait-il? *what's the weather like?*

PRÉPARATION 24

Projets d'anniversaire

Gabrielle parle avec Florence. Georges arrive.

Gabrielle Tu sais, Florence, c'est bientôt l'anniversaire de Georges.
Florence Oui, je sais. On va faire une boum.

Gabrielle Ah oui? Où ça?
Florence Chez moi. Mes parents ne sont pas là.
Gabrielle Formidable! Super! *(Georges arrive.)* Euh . . . salut, Georges.
Georges Salut! Ça va?
Gabrielle et Florence (Silence embarrassé) Oui, oui, pas mal.

Birthday party plans

Gabrielle is talking with Florence. George arrives.

You know, Florence, it'll soon be George's birthday.
Yes, I know. We're going to have a little party!

Oh, really? Where?
At my house. My parents aren't there.

Great! Super! *(George arrives.)* Uh . . . Oh, hi, George.
Hi! How are things?
(An awkward silence) O.K., not bad.

Gabrielle Dis donc, Florence, ce truc dont tu m'as parlé, c'est quel jour?	Oh, Florence, this thing you mentioned, what day is it?
Georges Quel truc?	What thing?
Florence Oh, rien, rien, c'est personnel. Dis-moi, Georges, tu peux venir chez moi dimanche prochain pour faire les révisions de philo?	Oh, nothing, nothing. It's personal. Tell me, George, can you come to my house next Sunday to do some reviewing in philosophy?
Georges Oui, bien sûr. À dimanche, vers quatre heures alors? Oh là là, il est tard. Il faut que je me sauve. Salut, tout le monde. *(Il sort.)*	Yes, sure. Sunday, around four o'clock then? My goodness, it's late! I've got to run. Goodby, everybody. *(He leaves.)*
Florence (Avec animation) Bon alors, tout est arrangé. Dimanche après-midi à quatre heures. On va être douze.	*(Excitedly)* Well, everything is settled. Sunday afternoon at four. There'll be twelve of us.
Gabrielle Georges va être drôlement surpris!	George will really be surprised.

Échange d'idées

1. S1: Remind a classmate of a common friend's birthday party next week.
   S2: Ask the exact date and where it is taking place.
   S1: Reply that it is taking place at your house because your parents are leaving for the week-end. Give more information about the party. (How many people . . .)
   S2: Give suggestions about the food, the activities (dancing, charades . . .)
   S1: Confirm that everything is arranged. Take leave of each other.

2. S1: Ask a classmate if he/she feels a little sad today.
   S2: Reply affirmatively.
   S1: Ask what's wrong.
   S2: Be embarrassed and avoid telling your partner by saying "It's nothing, it's personal." Change the subject abruptly by asking a question about a different subject, or say, it's late, you're in a hurry and you have to leave very soon.

1. Practice with direct object pronouns

1. Answer this question using the object pronoun. *Est-ce que tu cherches les disques de François? (Non . . .)*

> Non, je ne les cherche pas. (Remember that the object pronoun *les* and the verb *cherche* form a unit that is surrounded by *ne . . . pas*.)

2. The same rule of placement exists for the other object pronouns.

Paul **ne**	**me** cherche **te** cherche **la** cherche **le** cherche **nous** cherche **vous** cherche **les** cherche	**pas**	

Rewrite these sentences in the negative. Then read them aloud.

a. Robert me connaît bien.

Robert ne me connaît pas bien.

b. Nos professeurs nous aiment.

Nos professeurs ne nous aiment pas.

c. Annie et moi, nous vous invitons au concert.

Nous ne vous invitons pas au concert.

3. The actions and feelings of the people below are not mutual. Complete each sentence to show that.

  Modèle: Tu aimes Michèle Daumier, mais elle . . .

. . . elle ne t'aime pas.

a. J'écoute mes parents, mais ils . . .

b. Nous vous écoutons toujours, mais vous . . .

c. Tu aimes Alain, mais il . . .

a. ... ne m'écoutent pas.   b. ... ne nous écoutez pas toujours.   c. ... ne t'aime pas.

2. *De* + the definite article

1. *Jouer à* is used to talk about playing a sport or game. *J'aime jouer au tennis et aux cartes.*

  When *jouer* is used to talk about playing a musical instrument, however, a different preposition is used. Find it in *J'aime jouer de la guitare.*

de

2. Compare the charts below. Note that both *à* and *de* contract with *le* and *les*.

De + definite articles	**À** + definite articles
de + la = **de la**	à + la = **à la**
de + l' = **de l'**	à + l' = **à l'**
de + le = **du**	à + le = **au**
de + les = **des**	à + les = **aux**

Complete the sentences with *de* and noun phrase, and write English equivalents for *a* and *b*.

a. Vous jouez _____? (le violon)

du violon *(Do you play the violin?)*

b. Ma mère aime jouer _____ (la trompette)

de la trompette *(My mother likes to play the trumpet.)*

c. Tu connais M. Ferrier, qui joue _____? (les cymbales)

des cymbales

d. Tu sais qui va jouer _____ ce soir? (l'accordéon)

de l'accordéon

3. Imagine that you are introducing your fellow musicians to a friend. Say what instrument each person plays.
   a. Chantal: le piano
   b. Jean-Claude: la flûte
   c. Bernadette: la batterie

a. Chantal joue du piano.   b. Jean-Claude joue de la flûte.   c. Bernadette joue de la batterie.

4. *De* is also used to show possession or close relationship.
   a. Write the English equivalent of *C'est le chien de Jean.*

It's John's dog.

   b. Instead of saying *It's John's dog,* you might say *It's the boy's dog.* Complete the French equivalent: *C'est le chien _____ .*

du garçon (de + le = du) |)

   c. Now complete the French equivalent of *It's the children's dog. C'est le chien _____.*

des enfants (de + les = des)

5. Write the English equivalent of these phrases: *le stylo du médecin, l'enfant de la femme.*

the doctor's pen, the woman's child

6. Now write French equivalents for the phrases below. (See vocabulary p. 191.)
   a. the student's cymbals

les cymbales de l'étudiant/e

   b. the (female) musician's flute

la flûte de la musicienne

   c. the (male) musician's trumpet

la trompette du musicien

À Propos!   Et vous, est-ce que vous jouez d'un instrument? Lequel? *(Which one?)*

3. The *passé composé:* negation

1. Write an English equivalent: *Ils ont écouté le président à la radio.*

They listened (have listened) to the president on the radio.

2. a. The past participle of every -er verb ends in the letter _____.
   é

   b. The auxiliary verb in most cases is a present tense form of *avoir*. How do you know which verb form to use?
   The auxiliary verb must agree with the subject.

3. The people below don't want to do certain things today because they did them yesterday. Use the *passé composé* to say what they did yesterday.
   Modèle: Pierre ne veut pas jouer aux cartes aujourd'hui.
   Il a joué aux cartes hier.

   a. Nous ne voulons pas montrer nos photos aujourd'hui.
   Nous avons montré nos photos hier.

   b. Tu ne veux pas visiter le musée aujourd'hui.
   Tu as visité le musée hier.

4. Read this sentence, paying attention to the word order: *Hier, Joël n'a pas regardé la télévision.*
   a. What is the English equivalent?
   Yesterday, Joël didn't watch television.

   b. Where are *ne* and *pas* placed?
   around a (*Ne* and *pas* surround the auxiliary verb.)

   c. Read the examples in the chart aloud.

je **n'ai pas** regardé	nous **n'avons pas** regardé
tu **n'as pas** regardé	vous **n'avez pas** regardé
il **n'a pas** regardé	ils **n'ont pas** regardé

5. Make the following sentences negative, and say the English equivalents.
   a. Carole a aidé sa mère.
   Carole n'a pas aidé sa mère. *Carol hasn't helped (didn't help) her mother.*

   b. Les étudiants ont acheté leurs livres.
   Les étudiants n'ont pas acheté leurs livres. *The students haven't bought (didn't buy) their books.*

   c. Nous avons aimé vos cassettes.
   Nous n'avons pas aimé vos cassettes. *We didn't like your cassettes.*

4. Practice with *aller*

1. Using the forms of *aller* plus an infinitive, complete the sentences to say what certain people are going to do. (See key.)
   Modèle: Louis/faire ses devoirs
   Louis va faire ses devoirs.

   a. vous/passer l'après-midi chez Jean

Phase quatre

b. elle/sortir avec ses amis dimanche
c. les ouvriers/travailler à l'usine
d. je/regarder un vieux film à la télé

2. The verb *aller* has another common use in French. In the expression *aller chez* it means *to visit someone*.

> Je vais aller chez Annick ce soir.
> *I'm going to visit Annick this evening.*

But the verb *visiter* is used for *to visit* a monument or a place.

> Ils veulent visiter New York.
> *They want to visit New York.*
> Je veux visiter le musée des Beaux-Arts.
> *I want to visit the Fine Arts Museum.*

Write the verb form that correctly completes each sentence below.
a. Tu (vas chez/visites) Marc ce soir?

vas chez

b. Mon professeur veut (aller chez/visiter) le musée Rodin.

visiter

À Propos!

Et vous, qu'est-ce que vous allez faire ce soir?

Vocabulaire

Noms

l'animation *f.*   *liveliness*
l'anniversaire *m.*   *birthday*
la boum   *party (young people)*
la petite fête   *small party*
le galet   *pebble*
tout le monde   *everybody*
le musée   *museum*
la philosophie (philo)   *philosophy*
la planche à voile   *windsurfing*
le/la président/e   *president*
le projet   *plan*
les révisions *f. pl.*   *review*
le silence   *silence*
la station-service   *gas station*
le supermarché   *supermarket*
le truc   *thing, gadget*

Adjectifs

embarrassé/e   *awkward, embarrassed*
formidable!   *great! wonderful!*
personnel/le   *personal*
prochain/e   *next*
super   *super (slang)*
surpris/e   *surprised*

Verbes

aller voir   *to visit (people, places)*
arranger   *to arrange*
jouer   *to play;* ~de la flûte   *~the flute;* ~du piano   *~the piano;* ~des cymbales   *~cymbals*
montrer   *to show*
savoir   *to know*

Autres mots et expressions

bientôt   *soon*
dont   *of which/whose*
drôlement   *really/very/quite*
il faut que je me sauve   *I've got to run*
rien   *nothing*

Note Culturelle

Saltwater recreation

The sea coast, which makes up at least two-thirds of France's boundaries, is a focal point for many leisure activities. The character of the French coast is quite varied. *La Bretagne,* in the north, has a coast of rugged granite, with few sandy beaches. *La Normandie* in the north and *la Côte d'Azur* on the Mediterranean have a mix of beaches covered with sand, and beaches covered with *galets* (large flat pebbles). Camping, picnicking, fishing, sailing, and swimming are all popular seaside activities. *La planche à voile* (windsurfing) is becoming as prevalent a sport as it is in the U.S.

In France, sailing is a professional competitive sport as well as a hobby. Those who design and sail a ship that can weather the dangers of a transatlantic crossing quickly become popular heroes.

Point Rouge, à Marseille. La planche à voile est un sport très populaire sûr les côtes de la Méditerranée.

PRÉPARATION 25

1. Vocabulary practice: instruments, weather

1. Pretend that you are interpreting the weather map for a visitor from France. (See key.)

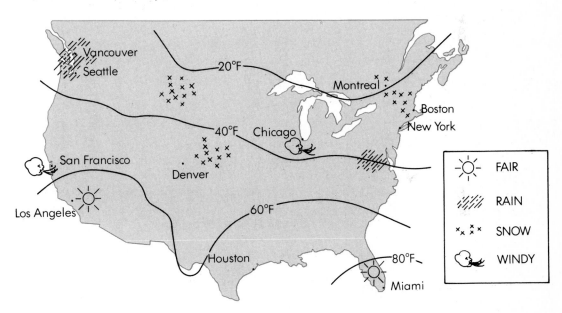

a. Quel temps fait-il à Montréal?
b. Quel temps fait-il à Miami?
c. Et à Chicago?
d. Quel temps fait-il à Vancouver?
e. Est-ce qu'il fait beau à Denver?
f. Est-ce qu'il fait frais ou chaud à Los Angeles?

2. Identify each instrument, with its definite article. (See key.)

a.

b.

c.

d.    e.    f.

2. *Savoir* vs. *connaître*

The verb *savoir* has the meaning *to know* but is used in different situations from the verb *connaître*. (See *connaître* p. 133).

1. Compare the meanings of these sentences.

> Je connais Patrick. *I know Patrick.*
> Je sais que Patrick *I know that Patrick is French.*
> est français.

a. Does the first sentence indicate that you know Patrick personally, or that you have particular information about him? |

> know him personally (*Connaître* expresses acquaintance with a person or familiarity with a place.)

b. The second sentence indicates that you know something factual about Patrick, although you may never have met him. What is it that you know about him? |

> that he is French (In French, to say that you know factual information, you use the verb *savoir*.)

2. Decide which verb you would use for each of the sentences below, *savoir* or *connaître*.

a. Does he know the people next door? |

> connaître

b. Do you know when the next train arrives? |

> savoir

c. I know what time it is. |

> savoir

d. They don't know Quebec very well. |

> connaître

e. We know where the best apples are sold. |

> savoir

3. Here is a chart of the present tense forms of *savoir*. Study them for a few moments, noting the stems and endings.

je	**sai**	s	nous	**sav**	**ons**
tu	sai	s	vous	sav	**ez**
on/il/elle	sai	t	ils/elles	sav	**ent**

a. Are the present tense endings of *savoir* the same as those of regular *-er* verbs or those of *connaître*? |
  those of *connaître*

b. What is the stem for the singular forms? |
  sai-

c. What is the stem for the plural forms? |
  sav-

4. a. Another meaning of *savoir* is *to know how to do something*. Write the English equivalent of *Je sais patiner*. |
  I know how to ice-skate.

b. There are two verb forms in the sentence: *sais* and *patiner*. Which verb is in its infinitive form? |
  patiner (As it is for *aimer, vouloir, pouvoir,* and *aller,* when a form of *savoir* is followed by a second verb, that verb is in the infinitive form.)

5. Use these phrases to give French equivalents for what these people know or know how to do. (See key.)

leurs leçons   faire du ski
où est l'aéroport   compter de zéro à cent
ton numéro de téléphone   jouer de la batterie

a. You *(tu)* know how to count from zero to a hundred.
b. You *(vous)* know how to ski.
c. These children know their lessons.
d. We don't know where the airport is.
e. I know how to play drums.
f. They *(elles)* know your telephone number.

6. In these sentences, first decide which verb to use, *savoir* or *connaître,* then write the correct forms.

a. Je _____ le médecin qui habite dans ton village. Je _____ qu'il n'est pas à l'hôpital aujourd'hui. |
  connais, sais

b. Ah, tu _____ cette jeune fille? Est-ce que tu _____ si elle joue au tennis? |
  connais, sais

3. More expressions with *faire*

1. You already know some of the following expressions; others you should be able to guess. Write the English equivalent of each.

a. faire une promenade   d. faire une petite fête
b. faire des projets   e. faire du camping
c. faire du ski   f. faire beau |
  a. to take a walk   b. to make plans   c. to ski/to go skiing   d. to have a small party   e. to go camping/to camp   f. to be nice weather

Partie de football au Bois de Boulogne, à Paris.

2. Write French equivalents.

    Modèle: We go skiing in March. _____ *en mars.* |
        Nous faisons du ski

  a. You go camping in the springtime, don't you? _____ *au printemps, n'est-ce pas?* |
        Tu fais du camping/Vous faites du camping

  b. She's going to have a party for her sister. _____ *pour sa sœur.* |
        Elle va faire une petite fête

  c. They're making plans for next week. _____ *pour la semaine prochaine.* |
        Ils font des projets

4. The *passé composé:* -re and -ir verbs

1. The following sentence is in the *passé composé: J'ai entendu un concert à la radio.*
  a. What is the past participle? |
        entendu
  b. The past participle of *entendre* is the infinitive stem plus the letter _____. |
        u

2. The past participle of most *-re* verbs is formed by adding *-u* to the infinitive stem.

    On the next page are descriptions of what some people are doing today. Say that they did similar things yesterday, using the cues in parentheses.

Modèle: Aujourd'hui nous entendons un discours *(speech)* à la
radio. (un concert) |
> Hier nous avons entendu un concert a la radio.

a. Aujourd'hui il perd son crayon. (son stylo) |
> Hier il a perdu son stylo.

b. Aujourd'hui tu réponds à une lettre de ton cousin. (une lettre
de ta grand-mère) |
> Hier tu as répondu à une lettre de ta grand-mère.

c. Aujourd'hui je vends des livres. (des cassettes) |
> Hier j'ai vendu des cassettes.

3. Read this sentence: *J'ai fini mon exposé* (report) *à 11h.*
a. What is the past participle? |
> fini

b. What is the infinitive stem of the verb? |
> fin- (Regularly conjugated *-ir* verbs form their past participle by adding *-i* to the infinitive stem.)

4. For each sentence in the present, state that the action happened
at the past time indicated.
> *Modèle:* Vous ne finissez pas votre dessert aujourd'hui?
> Hier . . . |
>> Lundi vous avez fini votre dessert.

a. Cette année Frédéric ne maigrit pas.
L'année dernière . . . |
> L'année dernière, il a maigri.

b. Aujourd'hui nous choisissons un cadeau pour papa.
Hier . . . pour Bruno. |
> Hier nous avons choisi un cadeau pour Bruno.

5. Rewrite each sentence in the negative. Say your answers aloud.
a. J'ai grossi.   c. Elles ont réussi.
b. Nous avons perdu.   d. Tu as répondu. |

> a. Je n'ai pas grossi.   b. Nous n'avons pas perdu.   c. Elles n'ont pas réussi.
> d. Tu n'as pas répondu.

À Propos!   Vous avez grossi depuis septembre?

5. Irregular verbs in the *passé composé*

You have learned that the *passé composé* of most verbs is composed
of the present tense of *avoir* plus the past participle of the main verb.
It's easy to know the past participle of regular verbs, but some verbs
have irregular past participles. Study the chart on the next page.

Verbs with irregular past participles

avoir	**eu**
connaître	**connu**
être	**été**
faire	**fait**
pouvoir	**pu**
savoir	**su**
voir	**vu**
vouloir	**voulu**

1. a. What letter do most of the participles end with? |

   -u

   b. Write the past participles of *être* and *faire*. |

   été, fait

2. Write personal answers to these questions, using the *passé composé* in the affirmative or negative. (No answers given.)

   a. Est-ce que vous avez été à l'heure *(on time)* au cours de français?

   b. Est-ce que vous avez connu une personne célèbre? Qui?

   c. L'été dernier est-ce que vous avez pu aller en vacances?

   d. Vous avez su la réponse à la question 1 b?

   e. Vous avez vu un bon film à la télé hier?

   f. Vous avez eu combien d'heures de cours hier?

   g. Est-ce que vous avez fait du camping la semaine dernière?

6. Practice: *à* and *de*

1. Where would you go to buy the items or do the things mentioned below? Write the location in French using *à* + the definite article.

   a. a can of peas and some sardines |

   b. some books |

   c. gasoline and oil for your car |

   d. to see a car being made |

   e. to see a play |

   f. to borrow some books |

   a. au supermarché
   b. à la librairie
   c. à la station-service
   d. à l'usine
   e. au théâtre
   f. à la bibliothèque

2. Complete each sentence with the correct form of *à* or *de* + definite article.

   a. —Danielle, tu vas jouer _____ piano maintenant?

   —Non, je préfère jouer _____ échecs ou _____ ping-pong.

   b. —Jacques et toi, vous allez jouer _____ hockey aujourd'hui?

   —Non, nous allons chez Max; il va jouer _____ accordéon. |

   a. du; aux, au   b. au; de l'

LE STADIUM CENTRE DE LOISIRS

PATINOIRE
BOWLING
PISCINE
RESTAURANT

Golf
Boxe
Education Physique
Arts Martiaux
Danses

LES OLYMPIADES 66 Avenue d'IVRY   75013 PARIS
Tel : 583 11 00   Métro : Porte d'Ivry

Quels sports peut-on faire au Stadium?

3. Say that the items these people have actually do belong to them, using *de* to express possession.

   Modèle: L'étudiant a un vélomoteur.
   C'est le vélomoteur de l'étudiant.

   a. Les frères Grandet ont une moto.
   b. Le garçon a un piano.
   c. Mme Grandet a une caméra.
   d. La directrice du lycée a un magnétophone.

   a. C'est la moto des frères Grandet.   b. C'est le piano du garçon.   c. C'est la caméra de Mme Grandet.   d. C'est le magnétophone de la directrice du lycée.

Vocabulaire

Noms

le discours   *speech*
l'exposé *m.*   *report*
la fête   *party*
le groupe   *group*
la lettre   *letter*
le numéro de téléphone   *telephone number*

Expressions avec faire

faire du bateau   *to go boating*
faire du camping   *to go camping*
faire des courses   *to go shopping, do errands*

faire des crêpes   *to make crêpes*
faire une petite fête   *to organize a small party*
faire du latin   *to study Latin*
faire le marché   *to go the market, grocery store*
faire du sport   *to practice sports*
faire du tennis   *to play tennis*
faire un voyage   *to go on a trip*

Autres mots et expressions

à l'heure   *on time*

PRÉPARATION 26

1. The *passé composé* with *être*

1. This sentence contains two verbs in the *passé composé: Hier, André est allé dans un magasin de musique et il a acheté un disque.*
   a. Give the English equivalent. |
      Yesterday André went into a music store and bought a record.
   b. In *il a acheté*, the past participle is *acheté;* the auxiliary verb is
      _____. |
         a (*Avoir* is the auxiliary used to form the *passé composé* of most verbs.)
   c. In *André est allé*, the auxiliary verb is _____. |
         être
   d. *Allé* is the past participle of the verb _____. |
         aller

2. *Aller* is one of a group of verbs that take *être* as the auxiliary verb in the *passé composé*. When the auxiliary verb is *être,* the form of the past participle is variable.

   Pierre est allé à la bibliothèque. Sa mère est allée au bureau. Ses frères sont allés au stade, et ses sœurs sont allées à la plage.

   a. Write the four forms of the past participle that occur in the paragraph. |
         allé, allée, allés, allées
   b. Like adjectives, these forms show gender (masculine or feminine) and number (singular or plural). When the auxiliary is *être,* the participle agrees with the _____. |
         subject

Agreement of past participles in verbs with *être*

	Singular	Plural
Masculine	Il est all**é**.	Ils sont all**és**.
Feminine	Elle est all**ée**.	Elles sont all**ées**.

When the auxiliary verb is *être,* the past participle must agree with the subject in gender and number.

3. Write the correct forms of the *passé composé* of *aller*.
   a. Il _____ à Paris. |
   b. Elle _____ à Paris. |
   c. Ils _____ à Paris. |
   d. Elles _____ à Paris. |

   a. est allé
   b. est allée
   c. sont allés
   d. sont allées

4. Most of the verbs that take *être* in the *passé composé* are verbs that indicate motion—to or from, up or down. They are usually intransitive (are not used with a direct object). Look at the "house of *être*" below. Some verbs you know already. Guess the meanings of as many others as you can, then write the infinitives that match the meanings below.

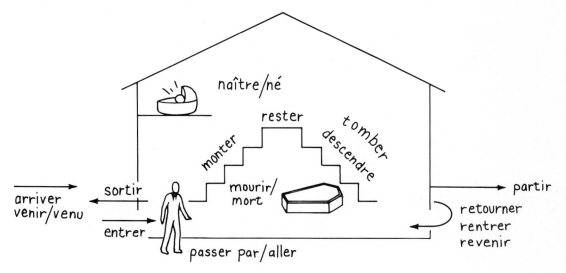

   a. to be born   d. to depart
   b. to die   e. to go
   c. to arrive   f. to come |

   a. naître (p.p. né/e)   b. mourir (p.p. mort/e)   c. arriver (à)   d. partir   e. aller
   f. venir (p.p. venu)

   g. to climb; to get in a vehi-   j. to go into; to enter
      cle; to go up   k. to remain; to stay
   h. to come down; to get out   l. to fall |
   i. to go out

   g. monter   h. descendre   i. sortir   j. entrer (dans)   k. rester   l. tomber

5. Write the French equivalents in the *passé composé* with *ils*.
   a. They arrived.
   b. They went in (entered). |

   a. Ils sont arrivés.   b. Ils sont entrés.

   c. They went up (climbed).
   d. They came down. |

   c. Ils sont montés.   d. Ils sont descendus.

e. They left. They came back home *(rentrer)*. |

f. They were born in '13.

g. They died in '73. |

6. The negative form of the *passé composé* with *être* is similar to the negative form with *avoir*. Compare:

> Je *n'ai pas pu* préparer ma dissertation parce que
> *je ne suis pas allé* à la bibliothèque.

In both verbs, *ne... pas* surrounds _____. |

7. Rewrite each verb phrase in the negative, then say it aloud. Normally there is liaison between *pas* and *allé* as well as in the places indicated below.

a. Vous êtes allé

b. Nous sommes allés

c. Elles sont allées

d. Je suis allé |

2. Stressed pronouns

1. Consider the sentence *Moi, j'ai quatre frères.* Which word has the same meaning as the subject *je?* |

2. The stressed pronoun can be used in another way. Give an English equivalent for: *Qui joue du piano? —Moi.* |

3. Stressed pronouns can also be used after *être.*
Mme Thévenard hasn't seen her cousin's children for years. On a visit, she points to one teenager and asks if that's Pierre.

> —Qui est-ce? C'est Pierre? —Oui, c'est lui.

Write the English equivalent of the answer. |

4. The stressed pronoun is also used in a fourth way. In *Paul est derrière moi*, the word that *moi* follows is not a noun, not a verb, but a _____. |

5. There are stressed pronoun forms for all subject pronouns. Use the chart on the next page to compare them.

Subject Pronouns		Stressed Pronouns	
je	nous	**moi**	**nous**
tu	vous	**toi**	**vous**
il/elle	ils/elles	**lui/elle**	**eux/elles**

The subject pronoun *elle* and the stressed pronoun *elle* are identical in form. Which other stressed pronouns are the same as their subject pronouns? |

nous, vous, elles

6. Write the correct stressed pronouns to emphasize each subject.
   a. _____, tu vas au café? |
   b. _____, ils vont faire du bateau. |
   c. _____, il va faire un voyage à Rome. |

   a. Toi
   b. Eux
   c. Lui

7. Véronique and Robert are planning a party with some friends. Use stressed pronouns to answer the questions.
   Modèle: Qui a un électrophone et des disques? *(Robert indicates Marc.)* |

   Lui

   a. Qui peut jouer de la guitare pour nous? *(Robert indicates Alice.)* |
   b. Qui va faire les crêpes pour la fête? *(Robert indicates Danielle and Jérôme.)* |
   c. Qui veut faire les courses avec moi? *(Yvette and Sophie volunteer.)* |

   a. Elle
   b. Eux
   c. Nous

8. Use the chart to answer the questions below.

Singular		Plural	
C'est moi.	C'est lui.	**C'est nous.**	**Ce sont eux.**
C'est toi.	C'est elle.	C'est vous.	Ce sont elles.

   a. *C'est* is used with what singular stressed pronouns? |
   b. *C'est* is used with two plural stressed pronouns: _____ and _____. |
   c. *Ce sont* is used with the plural pronouns _____ and _____. |

   a. all *(moi, toi, lui, elle)*
   b. nous, vous
   c. eux, elles

9. Mme Thévenard continues asking her cousin who's who. Write all the answers using *c'est* or *ce sont*.
   Modèle: C'est Martine? |

   Oui, c'est elle.

   a. Ce sont Christophe et Rémi? |
   b. Ce sont Béatrice et Catherine? |
   c. C'est Jean-Claude? |
   d. *(She's talking to the twins.)* Jean et Jeanne, c'est vous? |

   a. Oui, ce sont eux.
   b. Oui, ce sont elles.
   c. Oui, c'est lui.
   d. Oui, c'est nous.

10. Say that the following people are going home, using a stressed pronoun after the preposition *chez*. (See key.)

> *Modèle:* Paul va _____. |
>
>   chez lui

  a. Christine, Eric et Jean vont _____.

  b. Nous allons _____.

  c. Le médecin va chez _____.

  d. Ces trois jeunes filles vont _____.

3. Writing practice: *Loisirs*

From the list of questions below, choose five from *Sports, loisirs, projets*, two from *Musique*, and three from *Temps*, and write out your answers. Some of the questions have inverted verb forms like *Préférez-vous?*. Inversion is common in French.

Sports, loisirs, projets

1. Quels sports aimez-vous regarder à la télévision?
2. Préférez-vous jouer vous-même ou bien regarder les joueurs à la télévision?
3. Quel est votre sport préféré *(favorite)*?
4. Qui est votre joueur/joueuse préferé(e)?
5. Est-ce que vous faites du ski? Où?
6. Est-ce que vous aimez camper? En quelle saison? Avec qui? Où peut-on faire du camping dans votre région?
7. Est-ce que vous jouez aux cartes? aux échecs? au ping-pong? Avec qui jouez-vous en général?
8. Est-ce que vous invitez souvent des amis chez vous? À quelles occasions?
9. Qu'est-ce que vous faites pour les anniversaires? Est-ce que vous organisez des petites fêtes?
10. Est-ce qu'il y a un jour de la semaine que vous préférez? Quel jour? Pourquoi? Qu'est-ce que vous faites?

Musique

1. Vous préférez la musique classique, le rock, ou le jazz?
2. Où est-ce que vous allez pour écouter de la musique?
3. Vous écoutez souvent de la musique à la radio ou sur cassette?
4. Vous avez des camarades qui sont musiciens? De quels instruments jouent-ils?
5. Vous jouez avec un groupe de musiciens?

Temps

1. Quel temps fait-il aujourd'hui?
2. Quelle saison préférez-vous? Pourquoi?
3. Qu'est-ce que vous aimez faire quand il pleut? quand il neige? quand il fait beau?

Note Culturelle
Vélomoteurs

A *vélomoteur* is a lightweight motor bike (with a motor between 50 and 125 cc). It is a very popular form of inexpensive transportation in France and other European countries. A French speaker will often refer to the vehicle as *une Mobylette* or *un Solex* (one of the popular brand names) rather than calling it *un vélomoteur*.

Un vélomoteur, c'est très pratique (convenient)!

Vocabulaire

Noms
le bureau   *office*
le magasin de musique   *music store*

Verbes
arriver   *to arrive; to happen*
descendre   *to go down; get out of (a vehicle)*
entrer   *to go in, to come in*
monter   *to go up, climb*
mourir (*p.p.* mort)   *to die*
naître (*p.p.* né)   *to be born*
passer (par)   *to pass (by), to go by*
rentrer   *to go home, come home; come back*

rester   *to stay, to remain*
retourner   *to return, to go back*
revenir   *to come back*
tomber   *to fall down*
venir (*p.p.* venu)   *to come*

Pronoms emphatiques
moi   *me*
toi   *you*
elle/lui   *her/him*
nous   *us*
vous   *you*
elles/eux   *them*

PRÉPARATION 27

1. Review practice: direct object pronouns

1. Answer with a direct object pronoun.
   a. Vous voyez cette belle voiture là-bas? Oui . . .
   b. Tu m'aimes, n'est ce pas? Oui . . .
   c. Alain et Marie, vous nous attendez? Oui . . .
   d. Tu invites tes amis au concert? Oui . . .

   a. Oui, je la vois.   b. Oui, je t'aime.   c. Oui, nous vous attendons.   d. Oui, je les invite.

2. Use *on* and *trouver* to describe how others see these people. (See key.)

   Modèle: moi: égoïste

   On me trouve égoïste. *(People think I'm selfish.)*

   a. toi: généreux
   b. moi: sympathique
   c. nous: pas du tout sérieux
   d. Luc et Marc: pas timides

2. False cognates

By now you know that quite a few French words look like English words, but that some have entirely different meanings. These words are called false cognates or *faux amis* (false friends). *Faux amis* are tricky; they seem to be helpful but they'll let you down. If you see a French word that looks like an English word, but the English meaning doesn't seem to make sense, you may have *un faux ami*. Check a dictionary for the meaning of the word.

1. You are familiar with all of the false cognates below. Write the correct English equivalents.
   a. anniversaire
   b. librairie
   c. football
   d. en retard

   a. birthday   b. bookstore   c. soccer   d. late

2. Each sentence below has a cognate you've never seen in this book. Write what you think the English equivalent of the cognate is. Then write *faux ami* if you think it's a false cognate.
   a. J'ai fait une <u>expérience</u> au laboratoire.

   experiment—*faux ami* (In this context, it does not mean experience.)

b. Mon père va être <u>furieux</u>. |
  furious

c. Pour jouer au football, il faut un <u>ballon</u>. |
  ball—*faux ami* (It isn't a balloon.)

d. Jouer aux échecs, c'est un bon <u>passe-temps</u>. |
  pastime

3. Review practice: *savoir*

This part will give you a chance to test yourself. If you make mistakes, take some time to review.

1. Use *savoir* and other expressions you know to write French equivalents. (See key.)
   a. Do you know where that man lives? *Vous . . .?*
   b. Albert wants to know if you have a present for him. *Albert . . .*
   c. I know that it doesn't snow in Martinique. *Je . . .*
   d. Do you know what time it is? *Tu . . .?*
   e. My aunt and my mother know how to skate. *Elles . . .*

4. The verb *lire* (to read)

1. Study the chart for a few minutes.

Présent:	je **li** **s**		nous **lis** **ons**
	tu **li** **s**		vous **lis** **ez**
	on/il/elle **li** **s**		ils/elles **lis** **ent**
Passé composé:	**j'ai lu**		

2. a. Are the endings of *lire* like those of *partir* or of an *-er* verb? |
  like those of *partir*

b. What is the stem for the singular forms? for the plural forms? |
  li-; lis-

3. Which form of *lire* matches each subject pronoun below?
   a. on   d. nous
   b. elles   e. tu
   c. vous   f. il |
  a. lit   b. lisent   c. lisez   d. lisons   e. lis   f. lit

4. Write the French equivalents for the following sentences.
   a. Marguerite reads a good book. |
  Marguerite lit un bon livre.

b. Are you going to read the newspaper now?

    Tu vas lire/Vous allez lire le journal maintenant?

c. My parents read the newspaper at the office.

    Mes parents lisent le journal au bureau.

d. In class we are reading a novel *(roman)* by Sartre.

    En classe nous lisons un roman de Sartre.

5. Write sentences a and c above in the *passé composé*. (See key.)

5. *Passé composé* with *être:* practice

Refer to the chart on p. 207 to complete the French equivalents of the sentences below. Be sure to make the past participle agree with the subject.

    a. Jacques left this morning. _____ *ce matin.* |

    b. My mother arrived yesterday. _____ *hier.* |

    c. Robert and Paul came to France from the United States. _____ *en France des États-Unis.* |

    d. Bernadette went out with friends last night. _____ *avec des amis hier soir.* |

    e. My brother and I went up to his office on the fifth floor. *Mon frère et moi,* _____ *à son bureau au cinquième étage.* |

    f. I was not born in France. _____ *en France.* |

    g. He died in 1821. _____ *en 1821.* |

    h. I went by the market this morning. _____ *le marché ce matin.*

a. Jacques est parti

b. Ma mère est arrivée

c. Robert et Paul sont venus

d. Bernadette est sortie

e. nous sommes montés

f. Je ne suis pas né (née)

g. Il est mort

h. Je suis passé/e par

6. More on time and the 24-hour clock

1. In French, time is expressed by *il est* + number + *heure(s)*.
Look at this clock and the French sentence.

    Il est dix heures et demie.

In English, what time is it by the clock? |

    It's half-past ten./It's ten-thirty.

2. *Demi* means half, and *demie* is the feminine form, which agrees with *heure*. Write in French what time it is on these clocks.

a.

b.

c.

a. Il est quatre heures et demie.

b. Il est huit heures et demie.

c. Il est une heure et demie.

3. Look at the phrases used in French to distinguish different times of day.

10h00 du matin	*10:00 in the morning*
midi	*12:00 noon*
4h de l'après-midi	*4:00 in the afternoon*
8h du soir	*8:00 in the evening*
minuit	*12:00 midnight*

Say, then write French equivalents for these times.

a. 9 a.m.

b. 12 noon

c. 3:30 p.m.

d. 12 midnight

a. 9h du matin   b. midi   c. 3h et demie de l'après-midi   d. minuit

4. If you checked the newspaper for the performance time of the play *L'Apollon de Bellac,* you would see 20h. What time do you think that is?

8 p.m. (8h du soir)

5. In Europe, time on transportation schedules and listings of public events (plays, movies, sports events, etc.) is given on a 24-hour basis.

24-hour clock	*Regular clock*
1h → midi	1h du matin → midi 12h *(noon)*
13h → 24h	1h de l'après-midi → minuit 12h *(midnight)*

Write the equivalent time in French for these events. Use the terms in 5 above to establish the time of day. (For numbers over 12, subtract 12.)

a. Le train part pour Grenoble à 14h.

b. Le film *Le Blob* est à 20h30.

c. Nous partons pour la Chine à 23h.

d. Le président va faire un discours à 11h.

a. 2h de l'après-midi

b. 8h30 du soir

c. 11h du soir

d. 11h du matin

Vocabulaire

Noms

le laboratoire   *laboratory*

l'expérience *f.*   *(scientific context)*
   experiment; experience

le passe-temps   *pastime, hobby*

le ballon   *ball*

le roman   *novel*

la chaîne   *T.V. channel*

le programme   *program*

le documentaire   *documentary*

la comédie   *comedy*

le spectacle de variétés   *variety show*

Verbe

lire   *to read*

Adjectifs

furieux/se   *furious*

timide   *shy, timid*

Autres mots et expressions

en classe   *in class*

dix heures et demie   *half past ten*

minuit   *midnight*

(huit heures) du matin/du
   soir   *(eight o'clock) in the morning/
   in the evening*

(quatre heures) de l'après-
   midi   *(four o'clock) in the afternoon*

Note Culturelle

Customs and holidays in France

Le Jour de l'An: New Year's Day may be celebrated with phone calls or visits to older members of the family. *Le premier janvier* is also the day when one may give *étrennes* (small money gifts) to the *gardien/gardienne d'immeuble* or *concierge* (custodian), *le facteur* (mail carrier), and other household help and municipal employees. The equivalent for "Happy New Year" is *Bonne année.*

La Fête des rois: This holiday, also known as *la fête de l'Épiphanie,* is named for the three wise men who brought gifts to the infant Jesus. On January 6th *(le six janvier)* the tradition is to share *la galette des rois,* a flat round cake with a flaky crust and the texture and mild sweetness of a breakfast pastry. Hidden inside is a dried bean or a tiny plaster figurine. The person who receives the piece with the hidden object becomes king or queen, wins a paper crown, and is toasted by everyone.

Mardi Gras, Pâques: Mardi Gras means "fat Tuesday" and signifies the last great feast before Lent *(le Carême).* This period of feasting is ushered in with costume parades, dances, and parties.

The name *Pâques* (Easter) comes from *la Pâque* (Passover), the Jewish holiday which is also celebrated at this time of year. According to tradition, the church bells leave France for Rome and thus are silent between *le vendredi saint* (Good Friday) and *Pâques.* They return to ring joyously on *le dimanche de Pâques,* and leave chocolate chicks and eggs for children. *Le lundi de Pâques* is a national holiday and, weather permitting, people go for picnics and walks in the country. Depending on whether *Pâques*

is early or late, *les vacances de printemps,* a two-week break from school, may occur around this time.

Le 14 juillet: La Fête Nationale (Bastille Day) marks the day the Bastille prison was stormed in 1789 to set off the French Revolution. There are military parades, fireworks, and dancing in the streets in all towns, big and small. The dancing and other festivities continue into the wee hours of the morning.

14 juillet. Feu d'artifice (fireworks) à la Place de la Concorde, à Paris.

PRÉPARATION 28

1. Review practice: *passé composé*

1. The *passé composé* is a compound tense made up of the auxiliary *avoir* or *être* in the present tense + _____ of the main verb. |

the past participle

2. The past participles of *-er* verbs end in _____, of *-ir* verbs like *finir* and *partir* in _____, and of regular *-re* verbs in _____. |

-er verbs, é; -ir verbs, i; -re verbs, u

3. Write the past participles of *faire, être, naître,* and *mourir*. |

fait, été, né, mort

4. Write the past participles of *avoir, connaître, pouvoir, vouloir*. |

eu, connu, pu, voulu

5. Write what the following people did last night, using the cues indicated. (See key.)

Modèle: mes grands-parents: écouter la radio |

Mes grands-parents ont écouté la radio.
   a. nous: faire une promenade
   b. elles: parler avec leurs copains
   c. il: lire son magazine préféré
   d. vous: voir un film à la télévision
   e. je: dîner à neuf heures

6. On the day before an important exam, who went to the library and who didn't go?

Modèle: moi (Jeanne): non |

Je ne suis pas allée à la bibliothèque.
   a. toi (Alain): oui |

Tu es allé à la bibliothèque.
   b. ma sœur et moi (Anne): oui |

Nous sommes allées à la bibliothèque.
   c. moi (Béatrice): non |

Je ne suis pas allée à la bibliothèque.
   d. vous (Patricia et Antoine): non |

Vous n'êtes pas allés à la bibliothèque.

À Propos!   Pick an important character in history and tell in French when the person was born and when he/she died.

2. Review practice: *savoir* vs. *connaître*

1. Look at each English sentence below. Decide whether *savoir* or *connaître* would be the correct verb to use if you were writing in French, then write the infinitive of the verb. (See key.)
   a. Do you know how far it is from Orléans to Rouen?
   b. Do you know the city of Rouen?
   c. Do you know where the cathedral is?
   d. My friend Émile Monnier lives near the cathedral. Do you know him?
   e. The *Musée des Beaux Arts* in Rouen has some early Monet paintings I want to see. Do you know what days it's open?
   f. We always drive from Rouen to Paris. Do you know how to drive a car?

2. For each sentence below, decide whether to use *savoir* or *connaître*, then write the correct form of the verb. (See key.)
   a. Ils ne _____ pas où est leur voiture.
   b. Tu _____ quels sont les programmes ce soir à la télévision?
   c. Est-ce que vous _____ Montréal?
   d. Cette actrice est célèbre en France, mais aux États-Unis, on ne la _____ pas.
   e. Est-ce que vous _____ s'il va faire beau demain?

3. Review practice: *de* + definite article

1. You and some of your friends have formed an orchestra. Tell what instrument each person plays. (See key.)
   Modèle: Gaston/flûte |
   Il joue de la flûte.
   a. Nicole et Martine/piano   d. Le petit Maurice/violon
   b. Je/accordéon   e. Vous/trompette
   c. Tu/cymbales et/batterie   f. Françoise/saxophone

2. Make observations about the cars belonging to various people. (See key.)
   Modèle: le professeur: ne pas marcher bien |
   L'auto du professeur ne marche pas bien.
   a. ingénieur: marcher bien
   b. étudiante: être rouge
   c. médecin: ne pas être très grande
   d. la famille Gérard: est grande et vieille

À Propos!   Say something about your family's car.

Note Culturelle

Customs and holidays in France

La Toussaint: Le premier novembre is, in France, a somber holiday when families visit the cemetery to pay respect to the dead and leave flowers on the graves and tombs.

L'Armistice: Le 11 novembre commemorates the end of World War I, in which France lost nearly one quarter of its male population. In Paris, the torch that burns on the tomb of the unknown soldier *(le tombeau du Soldat inconnu)* is rekindled with great ceremony.

Noël: Christmas is a time of great festivity in France, with the same hustle and bustle of preparation as in the U.S. Children write letters to *le Père Noël* (Santa Claus), and people shop in gaily decorated stores. French families may decorate a tree or set up a *crèche* (nativity scene). Some crèches are peopled with *santons,* painted terra cotta figures that are made in Provence in the South of France. They include the people one would see in an old-fashioned village—the mayor, the baker, a lady with a basket of eggs, and so forth. French people also send cards saying *Joyeux Noël!* (Merry Christmas) and *Meilleurs Vœux!* (Best Wishes).

For church-going Catholics, the high point of Christmas is the midnight mass *(la messe de minuit).* All the churches are decorated and have a *crèche* on display. Following the

mass, *on réveillonne:* everyone sits down to a feast. Delicacies may often include oysters, turkey or goose, suckling pig, and champagne. A special dessert is *la bûche de Noël,* a rich cake roll in the shape of a Yule log. In some families, the feast and the exchange of gifts may occur on Christmas Day.

Joyeux Noël! Bonne et Heureuse Année!

Vocabulaire

Noms
le garage *garage*
le magazine *magazine*

Autres mots et expressions
en (juin) *in (June)*

Phase 5

À Table !

Qu'est-ce que vous allez apprendre?

The theme of this Phase is food. You will talk about your likes and dislikes concerning food, put together a menu in French, discuss dieting and (perhaps appropriately for the subject) learn to express regret.

Communication

To help you attain these goals, you will study:
  The partitive article and its uses.
  How to describe past events using the *imparfait.*
  The contrastive use of the *imparfait* and the *passé composé.*
  How to express the concept "to have to do something" using *il faut* + infinitive.
  Question formation with inverted word order.
  How to ask *which* or *what,* using the interrogative adjective *quel.*
  The verb *venir* (to come).
  More idiomatic expressions with *avoir.*
  How to say *to wash oneself, to comb one's hair,* etc. using reflexive verbs.

Culture

French breakfasts and French bread; Lunch and dinner in France; Eating in a French restaurant; and the recipe for a delicious *croque-monsieur* and for *crêpes.*

PRÉPARATION 29

Les Résolutions de Marie-Christine

Marie-Christine était une jolie étudiante de 18 ans. Elle n'était pas très grande (elle mesurait 1m52) et elle pensait qu'elle était trop grosse (elle pesait 52 kilos). Son grand problème était qu'elle adorait manger! Alors, elle prenait régulièrement de bonnes résolutions . . .

Scène 1: Le réveil
C'est le matin. Mme Bertrand entre dans la chambre de sa fille Marie-Christine et la réveille.

Marie-Christine's Resolutions

Marie-Christine was a pretty 18-year-old student. She was not very tall (1m52) and she thought that she was too fat (she weighed 52 kilos). Her big problem was that she loved to eat. So she regularly made resolutions . . .

Scene 1: Waking up
It's morning. Mrs. Bertrand goes in her daughter Marie-Christine's room and wakes her up.

Mme Bertrand Debout, Marie-Christine! Il est sept heures moins le quart. Le petit déjeuner est prêt.	Get up, Marie-Christine! It's a quarter to seven. Breakfast is ready.
Marie-Christine Je peux dormir encore un peu. Je ne veux pas de petit déjeuner.	I can sleep a little longer. I don't want any breakfast.
Mme Bertrand Ah? Et pourquoi?	Oh? And why not?
Marie-Christine Parce que je suis au régime.	Because I'm on a diet.
Mme Bertrand Tu es folle! Tu ne peux pas aller à la fac sans manger.	You're crazy! You can't go to your classes without eating.
Marie-Christine Mais si, je peux. Je n'ai pas faim.	Yes, I can. I'm not hungry.
Mme Bertrand Vraiment? Il y a du chocolat tout chaud, des croissants, de la confiture . . .	Really? There is nice hot chocolate, crescent rolls, jam . . .
Marie-Christine Oh non, arrête, arrête . . .	No, stop it, stop it . . .
Mme Bertrand Écoute, il faut manger le matin. Tu peux commencer ton régime à midi.	Listen, you must eat in the morning. You can start your diet at noon.
Marie-Christine Bon, d'accord. À midi, sans faute.	All right. At noon, for sure *(without fail)*.

Échange d'idées

1. Tell your classmate(s) what you usually have for breakfast in the morning. Ask a classmate what he/she has and what her/his favorite meal is: *le petit déjeuner, le déjeuner, le dîner.*

2. Work in a small group.
   S1: You are a camp counselor and you have to wake up kids you are in charge of, have them get up and go to breakfast.
   S2: Express that you are tired and you want to sleep some more.
   S3: Express that you don't like the food which is served at breakfast time and that you want to get up later.
   S4: You feel very hungry this morning (or you are always hungry in the morning) and you express your enthusiasm in getting up.
   S1: Reply to everybody's comments expressing surprise, irritation, annoyance, patience or any feeling of your choice, and renew your call for the few that are still asleep.

1. Another past tense: *l'imparfait*

In both French and English, when you talk about something that has happened, often you also describe something else that was going on at the same time. You use verbs in the past tense for both. But you may use two different past tenses: one for the event that you want to focus on, and another for describing the situation or circumstances surrounding that event.

1. The choice of past tense may depend on the event that the speaker wants to focus on.

   Suppose you're talking about your football team's latest misfortune:

   > We lost the football game yesterday. It was raining.

   a. Which sentence indicates the event on which you want to focus? |

   > We lost the football game yesterday.

   b. Which sentence describes the situation or circumstances at the time this event took place? |

   > It was raining.

2. Now suppose Harry sprained his ankle during the football game. Here's what you might say if you were talking about the accident.

   > Harry sprained his ankle. He was playing football.

   a. Which sentence indicates the event on which you want to focus? |

   > Harry sprained his ankle.

   b. Which sentence describes the situation or circumstances at the time this event took place? |

   > He was playing football.

3. Consider the sentences in 1b and 2b. In English, a verb used to describe the circumstances of a past event often takes the form illustrated in these sentences: it consists of *was* or *were* plus the verb with the ending _____. |

   > -ing

   In French, the *passé composé* is the tense used to focus on a key event that has been completed or that the speaker views as completed. Another past tense, *l'imparfait* (the imperfect), is used to describe the situation that existed at the time of the main event. Often, the appropriate English equivalent of a verb in the *imparfait* is *was/were . . . -ing*.

4. This sentence contains the *imparfait* form of *c'est: Aujourd'hui, c'est lundi. Hier, c'était dimanche.* The *imparfait* form of *c'est* is _____. |

   > c'était

5. A verb in the *passé composé* often occurs in combination with a verb in the *imparfait*. The *imparfait* sets the scene, and the *passé composé* tells the event. Give the English equivalent of this: *C'était dimanche quand Roméo a lu la lettre de Juliette.* |

   > It was Sunday when Romeo read Juliet's letter.

6. In the sentence above, the focus is on the fact that Romeo read a letter. In the sentences below, a phone call becomes the center of attention. Romeo's reading becomes part of the situation.

> C'était dimanche. Roméo lisait une lettre quand
> Juliette lui a téléphoné.

a. Give the English equivalent. |

It was Sunday. Romeo was reading a letter when Juliet called him.

b. *Romeo was reading a letter* is in the *imparfait*. The French equivalent is *Roméo* _____ *une lettre*. |

lisait

7. Compare *était* and *lisait*. What is alike about the structure of the two words? |

Both have the ending *-ait*.

8. If *-ait* is the ending of *lisait*, what is the stem? |

lis-

The *imparfait* stem of a verb is the same as the *nous* stem of the present tense. The only exception is *être*, whose stem is *ét*. All verbs have the same *imparfait* endings.

This chart shows the *imparfait* of *lire*. It can serve as a model for the formation of the *imparfait*.

Présent: **nous lisons**
Imparfait stem: ***lis-***

je	**lis**	**ais**	nous	lis	**ions**
tu	lis	**ais**	vous	lis	**iez**
on/il/elle	lis	**ait**	ils/elles	lis	**aient**

---

9. Say the *imparfait* forms of *lire* aloud. Four of them sound exactly alike. Write these four with their subject pronouns. |

Je lisais, tu lisais, il lisait, ils lisaient

10. Here is some practice with *lire* in the *imparfait*. One day a gorilla escaped from the zoo and walked into the library. Say what these people were reading when they saw the gorilla.

Modèle: Toi (une lettre) |

Tu lisais une lettre quand tu as vu le gorille.

a. Nous (le journal) |

Nous lisions le journal quand nous avons vu le gorille.

b. Éric et Paul (des livres de science-fiction) |

Éric et Paul lisaient des livres de science-fiction quand ils ont vu le gorille.

c. Sheila (un roman de Balzac) |

Sheila lisait un roman de Balzac quand elle a vu le gorille.

d. Vous (un livre de poèmes) |

Vous lisiez un livre de poèmes quand vous avez vu le gorille.

e. Moi (l'encyclopédie) |

Je lisais l'encyclopédie quand j'ai vu le gorille.

11. Try recognizing some other verbs in the *imparfait*. After reading each of these sentences, write the *imparfait* verb with its subject. Then say the English equivalent.

a. Anne jouait du piano quand Marcel est venu la voir. |

Anne jouait (Anne was playing the piano when Marcel came to see her.)

b. Quand le président a parlé, nous ne regardions pas la télévision. |

nous ne regardions pas (When the president spoke, we weren't watching television.)

c. Quand je suis arrivé tu étudiais tes leçons. |

tu étudiais (When I arrived, you were studying your homework.)

d. Ils écoutaient un concert à la radio quand le téléphone a sonné. |

Ils écoutaient (They were listening to a concert on the radio when the phone rang.)

12. Rewrite the following sentences in the *imparfait*. Remember that the *imparfait* stem is the same as the *nous*-stem of the present.

a. Nous ne pensons pas à notre travail. |

Nous ne pensions pas à notre travail.

b. Je visite Paris. |

Je visitais Paris.

c. Elle ne travaille pas à New York. |

Elle ne travaillait pas à New York.

d. Ils écrivent des lettres. |

Ils écrivaient des lettres.

2. Count nouns and measure nouns

In both English and French, some items are usually counted and others are measured. In order to talk about food in French, you need to recognize the two categories.

1. Apples are easy to count, and so are oranges. Things that can be counted are called *count nouns*. Which of the following are count nouns? *sugar   salt   tomatoes   pickles* |

tomatoes, pickles

2. Sugar and salt are more easily measured than counted: *a pound of sugar, a teaspoon of salt*. They are called *measure nouns*. Which of the following nouns would you be more likely to measure than count? *peaches   cherries   water   tea   onions* |

water, tea

3. Count nouns may occur in the singular or in the plural: *one pickle, ten pickles*. Measure nouns usually occur only in the singular. Which of the following nouns usually occur only in the singular?

potato   banana   milk   bean   juice |

milk, juice (You don't normally say "three milks" or "three juices" unless perhaps you're a waiter/waitress in a restaurant.)

4. Spend a few moments reviewing the names of foods in the *Vocabulaire*, p. 229. Match the names of the foods below with the drawings, and say whether each item is a count noun or a measure noun. Check your spelling carefully.

café   pomme   haricot vert   eau   lait

a.    b.    c.    d.    e.

a. eau: *measure noun*   b. haricot vert: *count noun*   c. café: *measure noun*   d. lait: *measure noun*   e. pomme: *count noun*

3. *Articles* with count and measure nouns

1. Read this sentence: *Je voudrais une pomme, un croissant et des fraises.*
   a. What type of article is used? |

   an indefinite article (Count nouns can be singular or plural, and are used with indefinite articles.)

   b. Give the English equivalent of the sentence. |

   I would like an apple, a croissant, and (some) strawberries.

2. Say that you would like the items below. Use je *voudrais* and *un, une,* or *des*. Write the English equivalents of a. and b.

   a.   b.

   a. Je voudrais une pomme de terre. *(I would like a potato.)*
   b. Je voudrais des poires. *(I would like some pears.)*

   c.   d.

   c. Je voudrais une pomme.   d. Je voudrais des haricots verts.

3. Which of these nouns are measure nouns? *poire, chocolat chaud, fraise, soupe, viande* |

   chocolat chaud, soupe, viande

4. Compare the French and English sentences below. |

Il y a de la soupe pour le déjeuner. *There's some soup for lunch.*

a. Which words are used before *soupe?* |

de la (*De la* is a *partitive* article. In French, partitive articles are used with measure nouns to mean *some.*)

b. Is *soupe* singular or plural? |

singular (Measure nouns are always used in the singular.)

c. Instead of saying *There's some soup for lunch,* could you say *There's soup for lunch?* |

yes (In English, you don't have to use the word *some.* In French, however, you must always use the partitive article.)

Partitive articles

Feminine	**de la** viande	*(la viande)*
Masculine	**du** fromage	*(le fromage)*
Elision	**de l'**eau	*(l'eau)*

5. Complete the sentences below with partitive articles and write an English equivalent for each sentence.

a. Je voudrais _____ confiture. |

de la (*I would like [some] jam.*)

b. Il y a _____ lait sur la table. |

du (*There's [some] milk on the table.*)

c. Elle veut _____ poisson. |

du (*She wants [some] fish.*)

d. Vous voulez _____ eau? |

de l' (*Do you want [some] water?*)

6. Identify the drawings below, using *c'est* or *ce sont.* Remember to use indefinite articles with count nouns, and partitive articles with measure nouns.

Modèle: |

C'est de l'eau.

a.

c.

e

b.

d.

f.

a. C'est un croissant.   b. Ce sont des laitues.   c. C'est du lait.   d. Ce sont des fraises.   e. C'est du poulet.   f. C'est du fromage.

Negation and Quantity

Indefinite	**des** pommes		**des** oranges
	pas de pommes		**pas d'**oranges
	beaucoup de pommes		**beaucoup d'**oranges

Partitive	**du** café	**de la** soupe	**de l'**eau
	pas de café	**pas de** soupe	**pas d'**eau
	beaucoup de café	**beaucoup de** soupe	**beaucoup d'**eau

7. Refer to the chart. Following *pas* or an expression of quantity, all indefinite and partitive articles become _____. |

de (or *d'* before a vowel)

8. Answer the questions below to say that Jean-Paul doesn't want any of the food he's offered.
   a. Est-ce que Jean-Paul veut des légumes? |

   Non, il ne veut pas de légumes.

   b. Est-ce qu'il veut du poisson? |

   Non, il ne veut pas de poisson.

   c. Est-ce qu'il veut de l'eau? |

   Non, il ne veut pas d'eau.

Vocabulaire

Noms

la chambre *bedroom*
l'encyclopédie *f.* *encyclopedia*
le gorille *gorilla*
le poème *poem*
le problème *problem*
le régime *diet*
le rendez-vous *appointment*
la résolution *resolution*
le restaurant universitaire *university cafeteria*
le réveil *awakening; alarm-clock*

Les aliments

les aliments *m.* *food*
le chocolat *chocolate*
la confiture *jam*
le croissant *crescent roll*
l'eau *water;* ~ minérale *mineral water*
la fraise *strawberry*
le fromage *cheese*
les haricots verts *green beans*
le lait *milk*

la laitue *lettuce*
les légumes *vegetables*
la poire *pear*
le poisson *fish*
la pomme *apple*
la pomme de terre *potato*
le poulet *chicken*
la soupe *soup*
la viande *meat*

Adjectifs

fou/folle *crazy, mad*
prêt/e *ready*

Verbes

arrêter *to stop*
avoir faim *to be hungry*
boire (boi-, buv-, boiv-, *pp* bu) *to drink*
commencer *to start, to begin*
discuter *to discuss*
être au régime *to be on a diet*
étudier *to study*

Note Culturelle
Lunch and Dinner in France

For a full-course meal at lunch time (*au déjeuner*), French people like to start with an *hors d'œuvre*—sliced tomatoes, grated carrots, *pâté*, or an assortment of fresh vegetables (*crudités*). The appetizer is followed by meat and a vegetable, a salad of green lettuce with a delicate oil and vinegar dressing, some cheese, and fruit. On Sundays, when people have more time to enjoy a good meal, the menu is usually a little more elaborate. Instead of a *steak-frites* (steak and french fries), for example, they might have some *poulet rôti* (roast chicken) or some meat or game marinated and cooked in wine, served with parslied potatoes and peas or green beans.

As a fancier dessert, there might be *une crème caramel* (molded egg custard), an open fruit pie, or a layer cake, baked at home or bought at *la pâtisserie*.

If lunch is a full-course meal, dinner tends to be lighter. It may begin with a *soupe*, followed by *une omelette au fromage* or *une omelette aux champignons* (a cheese or mushroom omelette), with a tossed salad. To end the meal, there is *du fromage et des fruits*.

Une belle charcuterie (delicatessen) à Paris. Cet homme est pressé et il a faim.

mesurer *to measure; to be... tall*
penser *to think*
peser *to weigh*
préparer *to prepare*
réveiller; se ~ *to wake up s.o; to wake up*
sonner *to ring*

Autres mots et expressions

avoir rendez-vous avec qqn; *to have a date with s.o;* ~ chez le dentiste *to have an appointment with the dentist*

prendre rendez-vous avec *to make an appointment with*
debout! *get up! stand up!*
encore un peu *a little more*
et quart *quarter past (the hour)*
moins le quart *quarter to (the hour)*
parce que *because*
régulièrement *regularly*
sans faute *without fail*

PRÉPARATION 30

1. Practice with *prendre* and food

1. The verb *prendre* (to take) is often used with foods and beverages to mean *to have, to eat,* or *to drink.* Review the verb forms in the chart below.

Présent:	je **prend** s	nous **pren** ons
	tu prend s	vous pren ez
	on/il/elle prend	ils/elles **prenn** ent

Imparfait: **je prenais**
Passé composé: **j'ai pris**

2. Say that all these people are having chicken. Use the present tense, and check your spelling against the chart.

   Modèle: Marc |

   Marc prend du poulet.

   a. moi, je
   b. tu
   c. ces jeunes filles
   d. nous
   e. vous
   f. Maman

3. Remember that indefinite articles—*un, une des*—are used with count nouns: *un poulet, des pommes;* and the partitive articles—*du, de la, de l'*—are used with measure nouns: *du vin, de la bière.*

   Say what the following people are having for lunch or dinner. Use the appropriate indefinite or partitive article.

   Modèle: Philippe: soupe, fromage |

   Philippe prend de la soupe et du fromage.

   a. Nathalie: poisson, pomme de terre |

   Nathalie prend du poisson et une pomme de terre.

   b. Je: viande, haricots vert, lait |

   Je prends de la viande, des haricots vert, et du lait.

   c. Bertrand: fromage |

   Bertrand prend du fromage.

   d. Vous: poisson, légumes, poire, café |

   Vous prenez du poisson, des légumes, une poire, et du café.

4. In a negative sentence, which word is used? *Je ne prends pas* _____
   lait. |

   de (d')

5. Say that these people aren't having any of what is offered.
   a. Vous prenez de la viande? (Non, je . . .) |

   a. Non, je ne prends pas de viande.

   b. Les enfants prennent des légumes? |

   b. Non, ils ne prennent pas de légumes.

6. Use the *passé composé* to explain that these people don't usually
   take certain foods, but today they did. Read your answers aloud.
   Modèle: moi: d'habitude pas de fruits / aujourd'hui une
   pêche |

   D'habitude je ne prends pas de fruits, mais aujourd'hui j'ai pris une pêche.

   a. Éric et Jeanne: d'habitude pas de café / aujourd'hui du café
   avec du sucre |

   b. vous: d'habitude pas de gâteau / aujourd'hui une tartelette aux
   fraises |

   a. D'habitude Éric et Jeanne ne prennent pas de café, mais aujourd'hui ils ont pris du
   café avec du sucre.   b. D'habitude vous ne prenez pas de gâteau mais aujourd'hui
   vous avez pris une tartelette aux fraises.

7. Use the *imparfait* of *prendre* and *a sonné* to write the equivalent of
   this sentence: *The girls were having strawberries and I was having some
   cheese when the phone rang.* |

   Les filles prenaient des fraises et moi, je prenais du fromage quand le téléphone a
   sonné.

2. The *imparfait:* repeated actions

1. To review the formation of the *imparfait,* for each verb below
   give the present tense *nous* form, then the *imparfait je* form. Say
   your answers first, then write.
   Modèle: partir |

   nous partons, je partais

   a. rendre   d. pouvoir
   b. choisir   e. oublier
   c. connaître   f. faire |

   a. nous rendons, je rendais   b. nous choisissons, je choisissais   c. nous connaissons, je connaissais   d. nous pouvons, je pouvais   e. nous oublions, j'oubliais
   f. nous faisons, je faisais

2. You have learned that the *imparfait* is used to describe the situation or circumstances that were going on when a past event took
   place. This part will show you another use of this tense: to express what used to happen regularly over a period of time.

   Pendant les vacances, David allait au cinéma tous les soirs.

a. Write the English equivalent of the sentence. |

> During vacation, David used to (would) go to the movies every night. (In English we add the phrase *used to* or *would* to the verb.)

b. What part of the French sentence tells what period of time is involved? |

> Pendant les vacances *(during vacation)*

c. What part of the sentence tells what happened regularly during that time? |

> David allait au cinéma.

3. Here, the *imparfait* describes a time in the past by telling something that used to happen. Give the English equivalents.

   a. L'année dernière, j'allais à Québec tous les mois. |

   > Last year, I went (used to go / would go) to Quebec every month.

   b. Généralement nous déjeunons à une heure, mais pendant les vacances nous déjeunions à midi et demi. |

   > Generally we eat lunch at one o'clock, but during vacation we used to (would) eat lunch at twelve-thirty.

   c. Pendant les vacances les enfants allaient à la plage tous les après-midi. |

   > During vacation, the children used to go (went) to the beach every afternoon.

4. The following sentences state that people now do certain things. Say that formerly they used to do the things indicated in parentheses. Begin with *autrefois* (formerly) and use the *imparfait*.

   Modèle: Maintenant, je joue au bridge. (les échecs) |

   > Autrefois, je jouais aux échecs.

   a. Maintenant, vous allez à l'université. (le lycée) |

   > Autrefois, vous alliez au lycée.

   b. Maintenant, nous aimons la musique classique. (le jazz) |

   > Autrefois, nous aimions le jazz.

   c. Maintenant, Jacques prend sa voiture pour aller voir ses grands-parents. (le train) |

   > Autrefois, Jacques prenait le train pour aller voir ses grands-parents.

5. This paragraph describes a time in the present. Rewrite it in the *imparfait* to describe the circumstances as they were in the past.

   Tous les week-ends, Philippe va chez des amis, à la campagne. Il quitte son bureau à Paris le vendredi à cinq heures, et il prend le train pour Saint-Lô. Le dimanche soir, il rentre à Paris par le train. Le weekend passe vite! |

   > Tous les week-ends, Philippe allait chez des amis, à la campagne. Il quittait son bureau à Paris le vendredi à cinq heures, et il prenait le train pour Saint-Lô. Le dimanche soir, il rentrait à Paris par le train. Le weekend passait vite!

À Propos!   Qu'est-ce que vous faisiez régulièrement l'année dernière? Vous le faites toujours *(still)*?

3. More about telling time

In Phase 4 you learned how to tell time on the hour and on the half hour. Now you'll learn how to tell time "in between."

1. Look at the clock and its caption.
   Il est cinq heures et quart.
   a. Write in English the time shown. |
      It's (a) quarter past five.
   b. Which two French words correspond to *quarter past*? |
      et quart
   c. Write the French equivalent of *It's (a) quarter past six.* |
      Il est six heures et quart.

2. A radio announcer is likely to give the time with the exact number of minutes after the hour: It's 10:22.
   French speakers write 10:22 nearly the way they say it. It is written 10h22. (Notice that there's no period after *h*.)
   a. Read aloud: 10h22. |
      dix heures vingt-deux
   b. Write the time for *dix heures vingt-cinq.* |
      10h25

3. Say aloud the times shown on the clocks below. Then write them out as in the model.
   Modèle: |
      Il est trois heures cinq. (3h05)

a.

b.

c.

a. Il est une heure vingt. (1h20)   b. Il est quatre heures dix. (4h10)   c. Il est neuf heures cinq. (9h05)

4. Now look at this clock and its caption.
   Il est cinq heures moins le quart.
   a. Which three French words correspond to *quarter to?* |
      moins le quart (This is the only time phrase in French that uses a definite article.)
   b. Write the French equivalent of *It's quarter to six.* |
      Il est six heures moins le quart.

5. As you just saw, French uses *moins* to express time *before* the hour. Now look at the clock.
   Il est deux heures moins dix.
   a. Is a definite article used in the French sentence? |
      no (A definite article is only used in the expression *moins le quart.*)
   b. Complete this sentence to say that it's five minutes to two:
      Il est deux heures _____. |
      moins cinq

6. Say what time it is according to each watch.

a.    b.    c.

a. Il est deux heures moins vingt.   b. Il est six heures moins le quart. (Did you remember to use *le*?)   c. Il est cinq heures moins vingt. (With the appearance of digital clocks, French people might also say: *Il est quatre heures quarante.*)

7. Say that the movie (film) starts at ten to eight. |

Le film commence à huit heures moins dix.

8. To express that a clock is fast or slow, French people will say:

Ma montre avance.   *My watch is fast.*
Ma montre retarde.   *My watch is slow.*

If your watch reads 5:25 and it is actually 5:20, what can you say? |

Ma montre avance.

À Propos!   À quelle heure partez-vous de chez vous le lundi matin?

4. Practice with *vouloir* and *pouvoir*

1. a. What is the French equivalent of this sentence? *We want to go to the beach but today we can't.* |

Nous voulons aller à la plage, mais aujourd'hui nous ne pouvons pas.

   b. Is the verb that directly follows *voulons* in a present tense form or in the infinitive form? |

in the infinitive (When one verb follows another directly, the second verb is always in the infinitive form.)

2. Say that these people want to do the activity indicated, but that today they can't.

   Modèle: Sylvie: écouter des disques |

Sylvie veut écouter des disques, mais aujourd'hui elle ne peut pas.

   a. Jacques: faire une promenade
   b. Nous: dormir
   c. Elles: travailler |

a. Jacques veut faire une promenade, mais aujourd'hui il ne peut pas.   b. Nous voulons dormir, mais aujourd'hui nous ne pouvons pas.   c. Elles veulent travailler, mais aujourd'hui elles ne peuvent pas.

3. If you made any mistakes in frame 2, review *vouloir* and *pouvoir* before doing this frame.

Do these people want to do these things? Are they able to? Choose affirmative or negative answers and write the correct forms of *vouloir* and *pouvoir*. (See key.)

Modèle: Je (être astronaute) |

Je veux être astronaute, mais je ne peux pas. / Je ne veux pas et je ne peux pas être astronaute. / Je veux et je peux être astronaute.

a. Nous (habiter en France)
b. Tu (chanter à l'opéra)
c. Elles (visiter Hawaii)

À Propos!   Et vous, désirez-vous visiter Hawaii? Ou l'avez-vous déjà fait?

5. More about food: all vs. some

This section explains which article to use in order to talk about a whole category of food as opposed to just a portion of it.

1. Read these sentences: *Je veux une poire et des pommes. Je veux du pain et de la confiture.*
   a. Give the English equivalents. |

   I want a pear and some apples. I want (some) bread and (some) jam.

   b. Does the speaker want all the pears, apples, bread and jam that exist, or just a portion of them? |

   a portion

   c. Are *poire* and *pomme* count or measure nouns? |

   count

   d. What type of article is used with count nouns (*poire* and *pommes*)—definite or indefinite? |

   indefinite

   e. What type of article is used with measure nouns (*pain* and *confiture*)—definite or partitive? |

   partitive

2. Now read these sentences: J'aime les pêches. *I like peaches.*
   a. Does the speaker like the whole category *peaches*, or just some portion of the category? |

   the whole category (The speaker likes all peaches in general.)

   b. Is *pêches* a count noun or a measure noun? |

   a count noun

   c. Which article is used—definite or indefinite? |

   definite

3. And now read these French and English sentences.

   J'aime le fromage.   *I like cheese.*

Note Culturelle
French breakfasts and French bread

For breakfast a French family usually has *café au lait* (hot coffee with hot milk) or *chocolat chaud* (hot chocolate) and toast or fresh bread with butter and jam. *Croissants* are usually reserved for Sundays or festive occasions. Fresh *croissants* or *brioches* (very light, round rolls, sweet and buttery) are bought at the *boulangerie-pâtisserie* (bakery-pastry shop).

Bread is an essential part of any French meal. "French" bread with a crunchy crust and a chewy center is bought fresh every day. It is sold, unsliced, in a variety of shapes and sizes, ranging from long and thin *(une baguette)* to round, thick, and often a foot in diameter *(une miche)*.

Rye bread *(pain de seigle)* and whole wheat bread *(pain complet)* are also available. *Pain complet* is generally sold in health food stores or specialty departments of large department stores.

Ah, du pain frais et croustillant (crunchy)!

J'adore la viande.   *I love meat.*
Je déteste l'eau.   *I hate water.*

a. To make a general statement about a category of food, the definite articles ____, ____, ____, ____ are used with both count nouns and measure nouns. |

     le, la, l', les (Notice that no article is used in the English sentences.)

b. Look at the sentences below:

J'aime beaucoup les pêches mais je n'aime pas les pommes.
J'aime beaucoup le café mais je n'aime pas le thé.

Does an expression of quantity or a negation bring any change to the definite article? |

     no

4. Write the French equivalent for each sentence.
   a. I love strawberries. |
   J'adore les fraises.
   b. I don't like jam. |
   Je n'aime pas la confiture.
   c. I hate coffee. |
   Je déteste le café.
5. Complete the sentences below to say that you like each food and that you're going to have some. Remember to use *le, la, l'* or *les* in making a general statement about the food you like, and *un, une, des* or *du, de la, de l'* to refer to some portion of food.
   Modèle: J'aime _____ riz. Je vais prendre _____ riz. |
   le; du
   a. J'aime _____ viande. Je vais prendre _____ viande. |
   a. la; de la
   b. J'aime _____ haricots verts et j'aime _____ beurre. Je vais prendre _____ haricots verts avec _____ beurre. |
   b. les, le; des, du
   c. J'aime _____ thé. Je vais prendre _____ thé. |
   c. le; du
   d. J'aime bien _____ eau minérale. Je vais prendre _____ eau minerale. |
   d. l'; de l'
   e. J'adore _____ poires. Je vais prendre _____ poire. |
   e. les; une
   f. J'aime _____ fruits. Je vais prendre _____ fruit. |
   f. les; un (For speakers of French, *fruit* is a count noun.)

Vocabulaire

Noms

l'autocar *m.*   *bus*
la gare   *station*
l'opéra *m.*   *opera*

Autres aliments

le beurre   *butter*
la cerise   *cherry*
le fruit   *fruit*
le gâteau   *cake*
la glace   *ice cream*
la jambon   *ham*
le jus de fruit   *fruit juice*
l'œuf *m.*   *egg*
la pêche   *peach*
les petits pois *m. pl.*   *peas*
le poivre   *pepper*
le riz   *rice*
le sandwich   *sandwich*
le sel   *salt*
le sucre   *sugar*
la tarte   *pie*
le thé   *tea*

Adjectifs

dernier/dernière   *last*

Verbes

avancer: ma montre avance
   my watch is fast
déjeuner   *to have lunch*
prendre   *to take;* ~un verre
   to have a drink
retarder: ma montre retarde
   my watch is slow

Autres mots et expressions

autrefois   *formerly, in the past*
d'habitude   *usually*
généralement   *generally*
ni . . . ni   *neither . . . nor*
pendant   *during*
toujours   *still*

PRÉPARATION 31

Les Résolutions de Marie-Christine

Marie-Christine's Resolutions

Scène 2: Un Message publicitaire
Marie-Christine est en train de manger son petit déjeuner avec grand plaisir. En même temps, elle écoute distraitement la radio: musique, informations, météo . . . Soudain un message publicitaire attire son attention.

"Êtes-vous jeune, jolie et solitaire? Vos amies vont au cinéma, à la plage, à la discothèque avec des jeunes gens beaux et

Scene 2: A Commercial
Marie-Christine is eating her breakfast with great pleasure. At the same time she listens inattentively to the radio: music, news, weather report . . . Suddenly, a commercial catches her attention.

"Are you young, pretty, and lonely? Your friends go to the movies, to the beach, to discotheques with handsome and elegant

élégants. Mais vous, on ne vous invite pas. Pourquoi? Vous savez la réponse. Vous n'êtes pas mince, vous n'êtes pas élégante. Vite, commencez votre régime AUJOUR-D'HUI—avec SILHOUETTE, le yaourt diététique et nourrissant. SILHOUETTE, le yaourt naturel. SILHOUETTE, le dessert idéal des personnes minces, élégantes et raffinées."

Marie-Christine arrête la radio . . . C'est décidé: elle va manger du yaourt et seulement du yaourt . . . !

young men. But you are not invited. Why not? You know the answer. You're not slim, you're not elegant. Quick, start your diet TODAY—with SILHOUETTE, the low-calorie, nourishing yogurt. SILHOUETTE, the natural yogurt. SILHOUETTE, the ideal dessert for slender, elegant, refined people."

Marie-Christine turns the radio off . . . It's decided: she is going to eat yogurt and only yogurt . . . !

Échange d'idées

Tell a classmate about a commercial you have heard on the radio or seen on T.V. and which caught your attention. What did it advertise? What was the "plot"? Were there adults or children in it? Did you like it or dislike it?

1. *Imparfait* or *passé composé?*

This part will give you practice deciding which past tense to use in French. Remember that context is important.

1. Tell which tense—*imparfait* or *passé composé*—is used for these functions.
   a. To describe a past situation that was happening while another event took place: *We were playing cards at the time.*
   b. To focus on a specific event that took place at a particular time: *The Red Sox won the pennant that year.*
   c. To talk about events that took place repeatedly, over an unspecified period of time: *I used to eat a lot of ice cream.* |

   a. imparfait   b. passé composé   c. imparfait

In frames 2 and 3, read each pair of French sentences. Then choose the French sentence that fits each situation described in English.

   Modèle: J'ai joué au base-ball. Je jouais au base-ball.
   a. The speaker is saying what he did yesterday. |

   J'ai joué au base-ball.
   b. The speaker is saying that he used to play a lot of baseball when he was young. |

   Je jouais au base-ball.

2. Nous sommes allés à la campagne. Nous allions à la campagne.
   a. The speaker is telling about getting a flat tire when he and his family were going to the country. |

   Nous allions à la campagne.

b. The speaker is saying that they went to the country last week-end. |

3. Elle a pris le train. Elle prenait le train.

a. The speaker is talking about a train trip to Marseilles taken last August by her sister. |

b. The speaker is talking about a commuter who traveled frequently by train. |

4. To do this frame, you must make choices between the *passé composé* and the *imparfait*. In the paragraph below, Pierre is writing to his family about his evening. Think about the situation as you read.

After you have read the paragraph once, go back to choose the appropriate verb form for each sentence. Ask yourself whether the verb describes the background circumstances *(imparfait)*, whether it focuses on a particular event that took place at a particular time *(passé composé)*, or whether it describes repeated events *(imparfait)*. Write the verbs you choose.

Hier soir j'étais au Jardin du Luxembourg. Il *(a fait, faisait)* très beau. *(J'ai lu, Je lisais)* le journal et de temps en temps *(j'ai regardé, je regardais)* aussi les gens qui *(sont passés, passaient)*, quand soudain *(j'ai vu, je voyais)* mon ami André. Il *(m'a dit, me disait)* qu'il allait dîner dans un restaurant, et il m' *(a invité, invitait)* à venir avec lui. Nous *(sommes allés, allions)* au restaurant où *(j'ai pris, je prenais)* mes repas quand j'étais étudiant. Nous *(avons mangé, mangions)* un excellent dîner. |

À Propos! Tell about something you did today or yesterday. Tell about something you used to do last summer.

2. Expressions with *avoir*

1. You already know at least one French expression that uses the verb *avoir*. Give the French equivalent of *I'm fifteen years old*. |

2. Read the following exchanges carefully. All the responses contain expressions with the verb *avoir*.

—Il fait beau, n'est-ce pas?   —Oui, mais *j'ai chaud.*
—Tu n'as pas bien dormi la nuit dernière?   —Non, et *j'ai sommeil.*
—Oh là là, il neige beaucoup!   —Oui, et *j'ai très froid.*
—Tu veux de l'eau?   —Oh oui, *j'ai soif.*
—Tu veux du pain et du beurre?   —Non, merci, *je n'ai pas faim.*
—Tu vois, il fait beau.   —Ah oui, *tu as raison.*
—Deux et deux font cinq, n'est-ce pas?   —Non, *tu as tort.*

Now give English equivalents. Try to guess the meaning of the expressions from the contexts illustrated above.

a. J'ai chaud. |
b. J'ai très froid. |
c. J'ai soif. |
d. Je n'ai pas faim. |
e. Tu as raison. |
f. Tu as tort. |
g. J'ai sommeil. |

a. I'm hot.
b. I'm very cold.
c. I'm thirsty.
d. I'm not hungry.
e. You're right.
f. You're wrong.
g. I'm sleepy.

3. *Je n'ai pas faim* means *I'm not hungry.* How would you say *I'm not thirsty?* |

Je n'ai pas soif.

4. *J'ai très froid* means *I'm very cold.* How would you say *I'm very hot?* |

J'ai très chaud. (While *très* is not usually used after forms of *avoir*, it is used to give emphasis to *avoir faim/soif/chaud/froid* and a few other *avoir* expressions.)

5. Write the French equivalents of the following sentences.
   a. Are you thirsty? (Use *vous*)
   b. I'm very hot.
   c. They (elles) aren't hungry. |

a. Vous avez soif? / Est-ce que vous avez soif?   b. J'ai très chaud.   c. Elles n'ont pas faim.

   d. He is eighty-five years old.
   e. We're not cold.
   f. Of course, he's right. |

d. Il a quatre-vingt-cinq ans.   e. Nous n'avons pas froid.   f. Bien sûr, il a raison.

   g. No, he is wrong, as always!
   h. Oh my, it's midnight. I'm sleepy! |

g. Non, il a tort, comme toujours!   h. Oh là là, il est minuit. J'ai sommeil!

3. More practice with food vocabulary

1. Say that you love the first category of food but don't like the second one.
   a. Beurre/confiture   b. Légumes/viande |

a. J'aime le beurre, mais je n'aime pas la confiture.   b. J'aime les légumes, mais je n'aime pas la viande.

2. Three friends are in the cafeteria discussing what they're going to have. Complete the sentences with the appropriate articles. Keep in mind whether the statement refers to a whole category or only to some portion, and whether the nouns are count or measure.

Modèle: Moi, j'aime _____ pain. Je vais prendre _____ pain.
le, du

a. Tu aimes _____ pommes de terre, n'est-ce pas? Tu vas prendre _____ pommes de terre?

a. les, des

b. Tiens, tu prends _____ haricots! Tu aimes _____ haricots, toi aussi.

b. des, les

c. Je vais prendre _____ poisson. Et toi, tu aimes _____ poisson?

c. du, le

3. Nicolas is a very finicky eater. Say that he doesn't want any of the foods he is offered because he doesn't like them.

Modèle: petits pois

Il ne veut pas de petits pois. Il n'aime pas les petits pois.

a. poulet

Il ne veut pas de poulet. Il n'aime pas le poulet.

b. œufs

Il ne veut pas d'œufs. Il n'aime pas les œufs.

c. fromage

Il ne veut pas de fromage. Il n'aime pas le fromage.

4. Poor Nathalie. Her father's telling her what's for dinner, and it sounds as if she isn't going to enjoy it much. Complete the sentences with the appropriate article.

a. —Pour le dîner, il y a _____ soupe. —Oh, je déteste _____ soupe.

b. —Il y a aussi _____ poulet, _____ haricots verts et _____ pommes de terre.
—Tu sais que je n'aime pas _____ poulet, et je déteste _____ haricots verts et _____ pommes de terre.

c. —Comme dessert, il y a _____ fromage, _____ glace aux fraises et _____ fruits.
—Alors, je vais prendre _____ fruits. Je déteste _____ glace aux fraises et _____ fromage.

a. de la; la   b. du, des, des; le, les, les   c. du, de la, des; des, la, le

4. The expression *il faut* + infinitive

1. In *Les Résolutions de Marie-Christine*, Mme Bertrand says to Marie-Christine: *Il faut manger le matin.* What must Marie-Christine do in the morning, according to her mother?

eat

2. In the sentence *Il faut manger le matin,* what verb form follows *il faut*—a present tense form or an infinitive? |

> an infinitive *(manger)*

3. In the expression *il faut,* does *il* refer to a male? |

> no (*Il faut* is an impersonal expression, and *il* does not refer to a specific person.)

4. The meaning of *il faut* may be expressed in English in several ways according to the context: *you have to, you must; we have to, we must; people have to, it is necessary to; one must.*
Give two English equivalents of *Il faut dormir.* |

> You must sleep. / You have to sleep. / It is necessary to sleep. / One must sleep.

5. Give the English equivalent of each French sentence.
   Modèle: Pour aller à la montagne, il faut avoir une voiture. |

   > In order to go to the mountains, it's necessary to have a car.

   a. Si vous voulez voir la Tour Eiffel, il faut aller à Paris. |

   > If you want to see the Eiffel Tower, you must go to Paris.

   b. Si on veut être riche, il faut travailler. |

   > If one wants to be rich, one must work.

6. Pretend you are a parent whose children sometimes refuse to do certain things. Each time one of your children refuses to do something, tell him or her that it's necessary to do it.
   Modèle: Je ne veux pas aller chez le dentiste. |

   > Il faut aller chez le dentiste.

   a. Nous n'aimons pas aller à l'école.
   b. Je ne vais pas manger à midi.
   c. Je ne veux pas jouer aux cartes ce soir. |

   > a. Il faut aller à l'école.   b. Il faut manger à midi.   c. Il faut jouer aux cartes ce soir.

À Propos!   Qu'est-ce qu'il faut faire pour être en bonne santé *(in good health)*?

5. Reading comprehension

This is an illustrated, step-by-step recipe. It contains some new vocabulary, but with the aid of the pictures you should be able to figure out most of the steps. Try to understand the French by using the pictures. There is a glossary after step 6. After finishing this Préparation, you could try out the recipe.

Un Croque-monsieur

—Comment fait-on un croque-monsieur?
—C'est facile!

1. Prenez deux tranches de pain.
2. Mettez du beurre sur les deux tranches.

244

3. Mettez une tranche de jambon et du fromage sur une des deux tranches de pain et couvrez le tout avec la deuxième tranche. Maintenant, vous avez un sandwich, n'est ce pas?
4. Bon. Mettez du beurre sur les deux côtés extérieurs du sandwich.
5. Mettez le sandwich dans un four chaud.
6. Huit ou dix minutes après, votre croque-monsieur est prêt! Bon appétit!

Glossary

une tranche	*slice*	facile	*easy*
le jambon	*ham*	première	*first*
le four	*oven*	deuxième	*second*
le côté	*side*	prêt	*ready*
mettez	*put* (from *mettre,* to put)	bon appétit!	*See note below.*

What is the nearest English equivalent of *un croque-monsieur?*

a grilled ham-and-cheese sandwich

Bon appétit! means much more than simply *good appetite!* It is closer to *Enjoy your meal,* a wish that the whole occasion be enjoyable: the food, the wine, the people, the atmosphere, and the conversation.

Vocabulaire

Noms
le côté *side*
le four *oven*
les informations *news*
les jeunes gens *young people*
le message publicitaire *commercial*
le pain *bread*
la réponse *answer*
la tranche *slice*
le yaourt *yogurt*

Adjectifs
deuxième *second*
diététique *dietetic, low-calorie*
élégant/e *elegant*
facile *easy*
idéal/e *ideal*
merveilleux/merveilleuse *marvelous, wonderful*
naturel/le *natural*
nourrissant/e *nourishing*
premier/première *first*
raffiné/e *refined*
solitaire *lonely*

Verbes
attirer l'attention de qqn *to catch somebody's attention*
avoir *to have;* ~ chaud; ~ faim; *to be hot; to be hungry*
~ froid; ~ raison; *to be cold; to be right;*
~ soif; ~ sommeil; *to be thirsty; to be sleepy;*
~ tort *to be wrong*
décider *to decide*
il faut (+ inf.) *it is necessary, you/ one must*
mettre *to put*

Autres mots et expressions
avec grand plaisir *with great pleasure*
bon appétit! *enjoy your meal!*
distraitement *inattentively*
en bonne santé *in good health*
même *same;* en ~ temps *at the same time*
soudain *suddenly*

PRÉPARATION 32

Les Résolutions de Marie-Christine

Scène 3: Midi

Il est midi, l'heure du déjeuner. Marie-Christine et son amie Yvonne sont dans la rue devant le restaurant universitaire.

Yvonne Tu viens déjeuner, Marie-Christine?
Marie-Christine Non, je ne déjeune pas aujourd'hui.
Yvonne Pourquoi? Tu n'as pas faim?
Marie-Christine Si, j'ai faim. Mais je suis au régime.
Yvonne Ah, oui? Je ne savais pas. Depuis quand?
Marie-Christine Depuis aujourd'hui.
Yvonne Quel dommage! J'ai vu qu'il y avait du bifteck haché et des frites.
Marie-Christine Oh non...! J'adore les frites.
Yvonne Alors viens. Tu peux commencer ton régime ce soir.
Marie-Christine Bon, ce soir, sans faute

Pauvre Marie-Christine, va-t-elle réussir un jour à suivre un régime?

Marie-Christine's resolutions

Scene 3: Noon

It is noon, the lunch hour. Marie-Christine and her friend Yvonne are on the street in front of the university cafeteria.

Are you coming to lunch, Marie-Christine?
No, I'm not having lunch today.

Why not? Aren't you hungry?
Of course I'm hungry. But I'm on a diet.

Oh, you are? I didn't know that. Since when?
Since today.
What a shame. I saw that there were hamburgers and french fries.
Oh no...! I love french fries.
Then come on. You can start your diet this evening.
OK, this evening, for sure *(without fail)!*

Poor Marie-Christine; is she going to succeed some day in going on a diet?

Échange d'idées

1. Work with a partner.
   S1: Ask your partner to go have lunch at the cafeteria.
   S2: Reply negatively. Find a reason.
   S1: Express your surprise and ask why not.
   S2: Explain your reason for refusing. Say you have to go.
   You both part from each other.

2. List a few good resolutions you have made once (or several times). Compare your list with a classmate's and ask each other if you have remained faithful to them.

1. Reflexive verbs: introduction

You know the expression *Je m'appelle* (my name is). The infinitive, *s'appeler,* is a reflexive verb. Reflexive constructions are quite common in French, much more so than in English. This section will begin to familiarize you with these important verbs.

1. Read this statement: *Quand ma voiture est sale, je la lave.*
   a. What gets washed when it is dirty? |
      the speaker's car
   b. In *je la lave,* the subject is _____ and the direct object is _____. |
      je; la
   c. Which word—*je* or *la*—represents the car? |
      la

2. Now look at this statement: *Le matin je me lave.*
   a. Who or what gets washed? |
      me (*Me* is the direct object.)
   b. What is the English equivalent of *je me lave?* |
      I wash (myself.)
   c. In *je me lave,* are the subject and the direct object the same person or two different people? |
      the same person

A reflexive construction is one in which the subject and the direct object represent the same person. The direct object "reflects" the subject.

3. Read aloud each sentence below. Write the direct object pronoun, and the English equivalent.
   Modèle: Je me lave. |
      me *(I wash myself.)*
   a. Tu te laves. |
      te *(You wash yourself.)*
   b. Nous nous lavons. |
      nous *(We wash ourselves.)*
   c. Vous vous lavez. |
      vous *(You wash yourself/yourselves.)*

4. Are the reflexive object pronouns the same as the direct object pronouns you have been using? |
      yes

5. For *on/il/elle* and *ils/elles,* the reflexive pronoun is different from the other direct object pronouns. Compare the pronouns in the sentences below.

Jacques a un an seulement. Sa mère *le* lave.

Frédéric a six ans. Il *se* lave.

Marie a un an. Son père *la* lave.

Lisa a cinq ans. Elle *se* lave.

Pierre et Hélène ont un an.   Monique et Charles ont
                             sept ans.

Leurs parents *les* lavent.   Ils *se* lavent.

The reflexive pronoun that is equivalent to *himself, herself,* and
themselves is _____. |
                         se

The direct object pronouns *me, te, nous, vous* are used both reflexively and nonreflexively. But for *on/il/elle* and *ils/elles* in a reflexive construction, the pronoun *se* is used instead of *le/la/les*.

6. Look at the meanings of these verbs.

   réveiller quelqu'un   *to wake someone up*
   coucher quelqu'un   *to put someone to bed*
   amuser quelqu'un   *to entertain, amuse someone*
   intéresser quelqu'un   *to interest someone in (doing)*
    à (faire) quelque chose   *something*
   fâcher quelqu'un   *to anger someone*

Now look at the verbs used reflexively. Say each sentence aloud
and write a good, idiomatic English equivalent.

a. Je me réveille à 7h. |
                         I wake up at 7 a.m.
b. Je me couche à 11h du soir. |
                                I go to bed at 11 p.m.
c. Je m'amuse bien quand je sors avec toi. |
                        I have a good time when I go out with you. (*S'amuser* and *to have a good time* illustrate
                        in what very different terms French and English sometimes express the same notion.)
d. Je m'intéresse beaucoup à la biologie. |
                        I am very interested in biology.
e. Je me fâche quand je perds mes gants *(gloves)*. |
                        I get angry when I lose my gloves.

7. Complete the following sentences describing the daily routine of
   several people, using *se réveiller, se laver,* and *se coucher.*
   Modèle: (Eric) _____ à sept heures. À sept heures et quart
   _____. À onze heures du soir _____. |
                        Il se réveille; il se lave; il se couche
   a. (toi) _____ à six heures et demie. À sept heures moins le quart
   _____. À dix heures du soir _____. |
                        Tu te réveilles; tu te laves; tu te couches
   b. (vous) _____ à huit heures. À huit heures dix _____. À minuit
   _____. |
                        Vous vous réveillez; vous vous lavez; vous vous couchez
   c. (moi) _____ à neuf heures. À neuf heures vingt-cinq _____. À
   minuit et demi _____. |
                        Je me réveille; je me lave; je me couche

d. (Sophie) _____ à sept heures. À sept heures et quart _____. À onze heures et quart _____. |

e. (Philippe et Anne) _____ à huit heures moins le quart. À huit heures _____. À onze heures et quart _____. |

f. (nous) _____ à sept heures et demie. À huit heures moins vingt _____. À dix heures moins le quart _____. |

À Propos!   Complete these sentences.
Je m'amuse quand...   Je me fâche quand...
Je m'intéresse à...

2. Equivalents of *to be: être, avoir, aller, faire*

1. Read the sentences below, and notice the verbs that are used.

Elle est très grande.   Je vais bien.
Il a dix-neuf ans.   Il fait froid.

Think of the English equivalent for the sentences. What verb is used in English? |

2. Which verb do you use in French to talk about age? to talk about health? to talk about weather? |

3. Complete these dialogues with appropriate equivalents of *to be* according to the context.
   a. —Bonjour, Christope, tu _____ bien?
      —Oui, merci, ça _____ très bien. |
   b. —Marie-Christine _____ dix-huit ans aujourd'hui.
      —Elle _____ contente? |
   c. —J' _____ très froid ce matin.
      —Oui, il _____ froid dehors (*outside*). |

4. Besides being used to refer to age, *avoir* is used in several idiomatic expressions where English uses *to be*. Give French equivalents for these sentences. (See key.)
   a. We're hungry.   c. Patricia's right.
   b. I'm not thirsty.   d. They're very cold.

À Propos!   Fait-il froid dehors aujourd'hui? Avez-vous froid dans votre chambre? Avez-vous sommeil maintenant?

3. The *imparfait:* practice with *être* and *avoir*

Because *être* and *avoir* are used more often than any other French verbs, it is worthwhile to practice them in the *imparfait*.

1. Read this sentence: *Quand il était petit, il aimait jouer avec ses cousins.* What is the *imparfait* stem of *être*? |

   ét-

2. From which verb form do you derive the *imparfait* stem for all other verbs? |

   nous form, present tense

3. Write the *imparfait* stem of *avoir*. |

   av- (from *nous avons*)

Imparfait of être and avoir

j'**étais**	**avais**
tu **étais**	**avais**
on/il/elle **était**	**avait**
nous **étions**	**avions**
vous **étiez**	**aviez**
ils/elles **étaient**	**avaient**

4. The following people are classmates conversing at their 25th college reunion. Use *avoir* and *être* to complete the sentences below that say what used to make each subject happy.

   Modèle: André/un bon livre |

   Quand André avait un bon livre, il était content.

   a. Monique/une bonne note |

   Quand Monique avait une bonne note, elle était contente.

   b. nous/le temps de bavarder *(to chat)* |

   Quand nous avions le temps de bavarder, nous étions content/e/s.

   c. Albert et Lucie/un examen facile |

   Quand Albert et Lucie avaient un examen facile, ils étaient contents.

   d. tu/vingt francs |

   Quand tu avais vingt francs, tu étais content/e.

   e. vous/des cours intéressants |

   Quand vous aviez des cours intéressants, vous étiez content/e/s.

   f. je/un professeur sympathique |

   Quand j'avais un professeur sympathique, j'étais content/e.

5. You can also use the expressions *c'est* and *il y a* in the *imparfait*. Rewrite the following sentences in the past.

   a. C'est janvier et il y a beaucoup de neige. |

   C'était janvier et il y avait beaucoup de neige.

   b. Quand il y a du soleil, c'est très agréable. |

   Quand il y avait du soleil, c'était très agréable.

À Propos!   *Complete these sentences.*
Quand j'avais dix ans, j'aimais...
Quand j'avais quinze ans, j'étais triste quand...

4. More on possessive adjectives

1. This section will give you a quick review of how to say *his, her,* and *their* in French. Read these two sentences.

> Robert aime son frère, sa sœur et ses amis.
> Marie-Jeanne aime son frère, sa sœur et ses amis.

a. Are *son, sa, ses* used with one possessor or with more than one? |
        one

b. What is the equivalent of *son, sa,* and *ses* in the sentence about Robert? |
        his

c. And in the sentence about Marie-Jeanne? |
        her

d. In French, does the possessive adjective agree in gender and number with the item possessed or with the possessor? |
        with the item possessed

2. Read these sentences: *Voilà leur frère. Voilà leurs frères. Voilà ses frères.*

a. Which sentences indicate that there is more than one possessor? |
        Voilà leur frère. Voilà leurs frères.

b. Which ones indicate that there is more than one brother? |
        Voilà ses frères. (Here are his brothers.) *Voilà leurs frères.* (Here are their brothers.)

3. Complete the French equivalents of these sentences.

a. *They love their dog.* Ils aiment _____ chien.

b. *They also love their cats.* Ils aiment aussi _____ chats.

c. *They always have their animals with them.* Ils ont toujours _____ animaux avex eux. |
        a. leur   b. leurs   c. leurs

4. English-speaking people sometimes need extra practice in distinguishing between *son, sa, ses,* and *leur, leurs.* Use these adjectives to complete the second sentence in each pair below. (See key.)

> *Modèle:* Christine et Gérard ont une voiture. _____. |
>   C'est leur voiture

a. Monique a une maison. _____.

b. Marie-Jeanne a un vélomoteur. _____.

Mangez-vous souvent des grillades (broiled meat)?

c. Monsieur et Madame Dupont ont des enfants. _____.

d. Michel a une guitare. _____.

e. Mon ami Vincent avaient des disques. _____.

f. Le petit garçon avait une trompette. _____.

g. Mon père et mon oncle avaient un restaurant. _____.

5. Practice with telling time

1. Write complete sentences to say where the following people are going and at what time, using the 24-hour clock. (See key.)
   Modèle: le pilote
       5:30

Le pilote va à l'aéroport à cinq heures et demie/cinq heures trente.

a. les étudiants
19:30

b. le médecin
10:55

c. nous
17:00

d. les ouvrières
5:45

e. l'acteur
18:15

f. le comptable
8:20

Quelle est l'heure exacte maintenant?
Que faites-vous en général à 7h du matin? à midi? à minuit?

6. Articles with food: practice

1. Sylvie's father is telling her what's available for dessert. Read this exchange between them.

>—Il y a une pomme, une pêche et des cerises.
> Qu'est-ce que tu veux?
>—Je voudrais la pêche, s'il te plaît.

a. Which French article is used to focus attention on the peach? |

une (an indefinite article)

b. Which French article is used once the focus has been established? |

la (a definite article)

2. When Mathieu and Louis are looking in the refrigerator for something to eat, they discover a plain yogurt and a strawberry yogurt. Write what the boys say to each other, using *un* or *le*.

Louis: Il y a _____ yaourt nature et _____ yaourt aux fraises.
Mathieu: Je vais prendre _____ yaourt aux fraises. |

—Il y a un yaourt nature et un yaourt aux fraises.
—Je vais prendre le yaourt aux fraises.

3. Now compare these sentences.

>—Il y a du jus d'orange sur la table.
>—Passe-moi le jus d'orange, s'il te plaît.

a. Which French article is used to focus attention on the juice? |

the partitive article *du*

b. Which French article is used to refer to the juice after attention has been focused on it? |

the definite article *le*

4. Marie-Christine just sat down at the table. As soon as she spots something she wants, she asks someone to pass it to her. Complete the sentences below, then read your answers aloud. (See key.)

Modèle: fromage |

il y a du fromage! Passez-moi le fromage, s'il vous plaît.

a. petits pois
b. jambon
c. glace

5. To summarize what you have just learned, complete these sentences.

a. The articles ____, ____, ____, or ____, ____, ____ are used to focus attention on a kind of food. |

un, une, des, du, de la, de l'

b. The articles ____, ____, ____ may be used after a particular item of food has been mentioned. |

le, la, les

Note Culturelle
Eating out in a French restaurant

The excellence of French *cuisine* (cooking) is famous the world over. Even small restaurants can usually provide a typical example of good French cooking. You can consult the menu which must (according to law) be posted outside the restaurant, on the door or window, and compare the various choices and prices. If you choose a *menu à prix fixe,* you can have a comlete meal for a set price. You might be served an *hors d'oeuvre* followed by *le plat du jour* (main course)—for example, *une grillade* (grilled steak or shops) with French fries, or *un sauté d'agneau* (lamb stewed with various vegetables, sometimes in a wine sauce). After the main course you would be offered a salad to refresh the appetite. You would finish with *un plateau de fromage* (cheese platter) or a dessert such as pastry *(une pâtisserie)* or fruit. Sometimes a beverage *(du vin, de l'eau minérale)* is included in the price, too *(boisson comprise).*

If you prefer, you can eat *à la carte* and choose only one or two dishes. Most menus say *service compris,* meaning that a tip of 10% to 15% has already been included in the price of the meal. When you wish to pay the bill, say *s'il vous plaît* to the *serveur* or *serveuse* and ask for *l'addition.*

À Marseille. Elle prend de la bouillabaisse (hearty seafood soup with fish and shellfish)— une spécialité du sud de la France.

Vocabulaire

Noms

l'escalier *m.*   *stairs*
la note   *grade*
la rue   *street*

Autres aliments

la banane   *banana*
le bifteck haché   *hamburger*
le bœuf   *beef*
le bonbon   *candy, sweets*
la carotte   *carrot*
les frites   *French fries*
le gâteau   *cake*
l'orange *f.*   *orange*
le pain grillé   *toasted bread*
le pamplemousse   *grapefruit*
le petit pain   *small bread roll*
le porc   *pork*
la salade   *salad*
la saucisse   *sausage*
la tomate   *tomato*

Adjectifs

affreux/affreuse   *terrible*
heureux/heureuse   *happy*
malheureux/malheureuse   *unhappy*

Autres mots et expressions

avant   *before*
dehors   *outside*
depuis   *since*
en bas   *downstairs*
en haut   *upstairs*
faire de la voile   *to go sailing*
lentement   *slowly*
mal   *bad*
quel dommage!   *what a pity!*
tôt   *early*

Verbes

s'amuser   *to have fun, to have a good time*
s'appeler   *to be called, to be named*
bavarder   *to chat*
se coucher   *to go to bed*
se fâcher   *to get angry*
s'intéresser   *to be interested*
se laver   *to wash oneself*
terminer   *to finish, to end*

Aimez-vous la cuisine simple et naturelle ou la cuisine riche et compliquée?

PRÉPARATION 33

1. Reflexive verbs: affirmative and negative

1. Which of the following sentences are reflexive?

> Jacques lave sa voiture.   Nous nous réveillons.
> Marie se lave.   Vous nous réveillez. |

Marie se lave. Nous nous réveillons.

2. A verb is reflexive if its object is the same person as the _____. |

subject

3. Like other object pronouns, reflexive pronouns occur right before the verb, in both affirmative and negative sentences. Rewrite this sentence in the negative.

> Je me réveille tôt. |

Je ne me réveille pas tôt.

Affirmative and Negative Reflexive Verbs

je me	couche	je ne me	couche **pas**
tu te	couches	tu ne te	couches **pas**
on/il/elle se	couche	on/il/elle ne se	couche **pas**
nous nous	couchons	nous ne nous	couchons **pas**
vous vous	couchez	vous ne vous	couchez **pas**
ils/elles se	couchent	ils/elles ne se	couchent **pas**

---

4. Read aloud the negative forms in the chart. Then complete these sentences in the negative. Say, then write your answers.

  a. Paulette s'habille. Paul _____. |

Paul ne s'habille pas. (As with other object pronouns, the reflexive pronouns drop the -e before a verb beginning with a vowel sound.)

  b. Elles s'amusent. Nous _____. |

Nous ne nous amusons pas.

  c. Bernadette se prépare. Son frère _____. |

Son frère ne se prépare pas.

5. The following verbs are illustrated by the drawings. Respond to each question as shown in the model.

se réveiller   se coiffer *(to fix one's hair)*
se coucher / se lever   se laver
s'habiller / se déshabiller   se peigner *(to comb one's hair)*

Modèle: Est-ce qu'elle se peigne? |

Non, elle ne se peigne pas. Elle se lave.

a. Est-ce qu'il se lave? |

Non, il ne se lave pas. Il se réveille.

b. Est-ce qu'il se couche? |

Non, il ne se couche pas. Il se lève.

c. Est-ce qu'elle se déshabille? |

Non, elle ne se déshabille pas. Elle se coiffe.

d. Est-ce qu'elles s'habillent? |

Non, elles ne s'habillent pas. Elles se lavent.

e. Est-ce qu'ils se peignent? |

Non, ils ne se peignent pas. Ils s'habillent.

À Propos!

Est-ce que vous vous lavez avant de vous lever? Est-ce que vous vous coiffez avant de vous coucher?

2. Forms of the adjective *quel*

You have seen and heard *quel* in questions and exclamations.
1. Compare the forms of *quel* in these two questions.

Quel temps fait-il? Quelle heure est-il?

a. Which form of *quel* goes with *temps?* |
quel (This is the masculine singular form.)

b. Which form of *quel* goes with *heure?* |
quelle (This is the feminine singular form.)

2. Look at the chart for a moment.

	Singular	Plural
Masculine	**quel** disque!	**quels** disques?
Feminine	**quelle** chanson!	**quelles** chansons?

a. Write English equivalents for *quelle chanson!* and *quelles chansons?* |

> What a song! (Such a song!) / What songs? (Which songs?)

b. How many spoken forms of *quel* are represented in the chart? |

> one (There is a second spoken form. *Quels* and *quelles* link with a following vowel, as in *Quelles objections?*)

3. Complete each question with the correct form of *quel* and write English equivalents of *a* and *b*.
   a. _____ sports faites-vous en hiver?
   b. _____ boissons aimez-vous?
   c. _____ chanteurs aimez-vous?
   d. _____ actrices préférez-vous? |

> a. Quels; *Which sports do you do in the winter?*   b. Quelles; *Which beverages do you like?*   c. Quels   d. Quelles

3. Questions with inverted word order

You have seen and heard inverted word order in questions. Now you will have a chance to practice using inversion—a common way of asking questions in French.

1. Look at this question: —*Quelle heure est-il?*
   a. Which comes first: the subject *il* or the verb *est?* |

> the verb *est* (When the positions of the subject and the verb are reversed, it is called inversion.)

   b. When *il* and *est* are inverted (reversed), what punctuation mark comes between them? |

> a hyphen (A hyphen is used every time a subject pronoun and a verb are inverted.)

   c. The English equivalent of the question is *What time is it?* Are the subject and the verb inverted? |

> yes (Inversion takes place in English as well as in French.)

3. The adjective *quel* is called an interrogative word when it is used to ask questions. Sentences that begin with interrogatives usually have inverted word order. Complete this question: *Quel temps _____?* |

> *fait-il* (Did you remember the hyphen?)

4. Below are some answers. Using the cues provided, write the questions you would ask in order to get those answers; use inversion.

Modèle: C'est ma cousine Marie-Louise. *(Qui...)* |
            Qui est-ce?

  a. Il est midi. *(Quelle...)* |
            Quelle heure est-il? (Did you remember the hyphen?)

  b. Il fait beau. *(Quel...)* |
            Quel temps fait-il?

  c. Nous allons au cinéma. *(Où...)* |
            Où allez-vous? (Où allons-nous?)

5. You can use inversion without interrogatives to ask questions. Write the English equivalent of *Aimez-vous le jazz?* |
            Do you like jazz? (Again, English uses inversion, too.)

6. Rewrite these questions, using inversion. Remember the hyphen.

  a. Vous prenez du chocolat pour le petit déjeuner? |
            Prenez-vous du chocolat pour le petit déjeuner?

  b. Nous allons à la campagne ce week-end? |
            Allons-nous à la campagne ce week-end?

7. Now read this question with inverted word order: *Quel âge a-t-elle?*

  a. What is added between the verb *a* and the subject *elle?* |
            -t-

  b. Does the *-t-* occur between two consonants or two vowels? |
            two vowels

8. The *-t-* is used with the *on/il/elle*-form of *avoir, aller,* and all regular *-er* verbs because these forms end with a written vowel. (The /t/ sound was present in the old Latin verb forms and was retained as modern French developed.)

  a. Write the inverted form of *elle habite.* |
            habite-t-elle

  b. Give the French equivalent of *Where does she live?* |
            Où habite-t-elle? (Did you remember the hyphens?)

  c. Give the French equivalent of *Where are we going?* Use *on.* |
            Où va-t-on?

9. Rewrite these questions using inversion, then read them aloud.

  a. Il nage en été? |
            Nage-t-il en été?

  b. Tu vas à la montagne cet hiver? |
            Vas-tu à la montagne cet hiver?

  c. Où est-ce que tu habites? |
            Où habites-tu? (*Est-ce que* is not used in an inverted question.)

À Propos!

Use inversion: 1) to ask your teacher whether he or she likes a particular musical performer, 2) to ask a classmate if he or she knows some songs in French.

4. The verb *venir* and the recent past

Study the chart of *venir* (to come) and say the verb forms aloud.

Présent:	je	**vien**	s	nous	**ven**	ons
	tu	vien	s	vous	ven	ez
	on/il/elle	vien	t	ils/elles	**vienn**	ent

Imparfait: **je venais**
Passé composé **je suis venu/e**

1. The present tense stem of *venir* has three forms. Write them on your worksheet. |

    vien-, ven-, vienn-

2. Say aloud, then write the subject pronouns and the corresponding verb forms.
   a. on, elles, vous
   b. nous, tu, je |

    a. on vient, elles viennent, vous venez   b. nous venons, tu viens, je viens

3. The preposition *de* can mean *of* or *from*. Give an English equivalent of this sentence: *Jean vient de la bibliothèque.* |

    Jean is coming from the library.

4. Say aloud, then write sentences to say where people are coming from.
   Modèle: Caroline/la librairie |

    Caroline vient de la librairie.

   a. Nous/la cantine   c. Je/l'aéroport
   b. Elles/le théâtre   d. Marc/le lycé |

    a. Nous venons de la cantine.   b. Elles viennent du théâtre.   c. Je viens de l'aéroport.   d. Marc vient du lycée.

5. Use the *imparfait* to give the French equivalent of this sentence: I used to come here often in the summer. |

    Je venais souvent ici en été.

6. Tell whether these people came to the party on time or not. Use the *passé composé*.
   a. Nous: à l'heure   c. Sonia et Gilberte: à l'heure
   b. Richard: pas à l'heure   d. Toi: pas à l'heure. |

    a. Nous sommes venus à l'heure.   b. Richard n'est pas venu à l'heure.   c. Sonia et Gilbert sont venues à l'heure.   d. Tu n'es pas venu/e à l'heure.

7. Read the following sentence taken from the dialogue *Qu'est-ce que c'est?* in Phase 1: *Martine ouvre un cadeau que Pierre vient de lui offrir.*
   a. Give the English equivalent of the sentence. |

    Martine is opening a present that Pierre has just given her.

b. The French equivalent for *to have just done something* is
_____.

venir de

c. *Venir de* is followed by what verb form?

an infinitive (The structure *venir de* + *infinitive* is called the *recent past*, because it is used to talk about things that have just happened recently.)

8. Make sentences out of the cues provided, using *venir de*. Write the English equivalents of frames *a* and *b*.

Modèle: le président/parler

Le président vient de parler. *The president just spoke.*

a. Nous/manger

Nous venons de manger. *We just ate.*

b. Le cours de français/commencer

Le cours de français vient de commencer. *The French class just started.*

c. Tu/téléphoner/à Marie

Tu viens de téléphoner à Marie.

d. Vous/finir/vos devoirs

Vous venez de finir vos devoirs.

9. Now look at this sentence: *Il vient écouter des disques chez moi.*

a. Here, *venir* is followed by the infinitive _____.

écouter (Remember that the second verb is always in the infinitive.)

b. Write the English equivalent of the sentence.

He's coming to listen to some records at my place.

Vocabulaire

Noms

la figure *face*
les mains *hands*
le week-end *weekend*

Verbes

se brosser (les dents/les cheveux) *to brush (one's teeth/one's hair)*
se coiffer *to fix one's hair*
se déshabiller *to get undressed*
s'habiller *to get dressed*
se lever (lèv-, lev-) *to get up*
se peigner *to comb one's hair*
se préparer *to get ready*
refuser *to refuse*
venir; ~ de *to come; to have just (done something)*

Autres mots et expressions

ma chérie *my darling*
quel/le *which*

Préférez-vous le poisson ou la viande? Est-ce qu'on trouve facilement des fruits-de-mer (shellfish) là où vous habitez?

PRÉPARATION 34

1. Some tips on taking a *dictée*

The following frames will help you connect the way a word sounds with the way it looks. Be sure to say all the French sentences aloud.

1. You learned that the letter *g* may have a hard sound as in *gomme* or a soft sound as in *manger*.

   a. Is the *g* soft or hard if it precedes an *o*? |

   hard

   b. Write the *nous* form of *manger*. |

   nous mangeons (You need an *e* between the *g* and *o* so that the stem of the *nous* form sounds the same as the stem of the other forms.)

2. Write the subject and corresponding form of *manger* for the following sentences.

   a. Ils _____ du gâteau au chocolat.

   b. Nous _____ de la glace à la vanille.

   c. *(imparfait)* Luc _____ beaucoup. |

   a. Ils mangent   b. Nous mangeons   c. Luc mangeait (add *e* before the *a*)

3. The letter *c* can have a hard sound before *a* or *o*. What mark can make a *c* soft even when it precedes an *a* or an *o*? |

   a cedilla *(français, garçon)*

4. Write the subject and corresponding form of *commencer* for each sentence.

   a. Tu _____ tes devoirs à 6 heures.

   b. Nous _____ nos devoirs à 8 heures.

   c. *(imparfait)* Je _____ mon travail.

   d. *(imparfait)* Vous _____ toujours tôt. |

   a. Tu commences
   b. Nous commençons
   c. Je commençais
   d. Vous commenciez

5. Several forms of *venir* sound alike, but are spelled differently, depending on the subject. Write both the subject pronoun and the correct verb form.

   a. Il _____ au bureau à 6 heures.

   b. Tu _____ chez moi.

   c. Je _____ souvent chez vous. |

   a. Il vient
   b. Tu viens
   c. Je viens

6. The word *ses* and the phrase *c'est* also sound alike. Complete these sentences with the appropriate word or phrase.

   a. _____ très beau.

   b. _____ cousins sont très beaux. |

   a. *C'est* (Can be followed by an adjective or a noun phrase.)
   b. *Ses* (Must be followed by a noun plural.)

7. The plural and singular forms of many nouns sound identical. Articles, adjectives, and verbs will tell you whether the nouns are singular or plural. For items *a – c*, insert the correct noun.

   a. C'est son _____. (frères, frère)
   b. Voilà ses _____. (sœurs, sœur)
   c. Sa _____ a un beau chien. (cousine, cousin) |

   a. frère   b. sœurs   c. cousine

2. Making up a menu

In this part you will make up three sample meals: breakfast, lunch, and dinner. The following frames will help you remember the French for certain words. Write the complete noun phrase in each answer.

1. a. The French word for *lunch* is *le _____.* |

   le déjeuner

   b. In French, the phrase for *breakfast* is the equivalent of *little lunch.* It is le _____. |

   le petit déjeuner

   c. The French word for dinner is a cognate, but the spelling is different. Write the complete word: *le _____.* |

   le dîner

2. a. *Un sandwich au jambon* is a _____. |

   ham sandwich

   b. What is a *cheese sandwich* in French? |

   un sandwich au fromage

3. a. *An apple pie* is _____. |

   une tarte aux pommes

   b. A *strawberry pie* is _____ *aux* _____. |

   une tarte aux fraises

   c. A *small individual fruit pie* is _____. |

   une tartelette

Viennoiserie

St Honoré

Saint Honoré. Les croissants comme on les aime.

5. a. *Vanilla ice cream is* _____ *à la vanille.* |
   de la glace à la vanille
   b. *Chocolate ice cream is* _____ *au* _____. |
   de la glace au chocolat
   c. *Strawberry ice cream is* _____ *à la* _____. |
   de la glace à la fraise

6. Now write the French headings for *breakfast*, *lunch*, and *dinner*, and write your menu for each of these meals. List at least 4 items for breakfast, 4 items for lunch, and 6 items for dinner. With each food, use a partitive article, an indefinite article, or a number (for example, *deux œufs*). You'll have a chance to compare menus with your classmates.

Soupe, viande, etc.
le bœuf
le poisson
le porc
le poulet
le sandwich (au jambon, etc.)
la saucisse
la soupe
le steak
le bifteck haché

Œufs et produits laitiers
le beurre
le fromage
la glace
le lait
l'œuf *(m.)*
le yaourt

Boissons
le café
le chocolat au lait
l'eau *(f.)* minérale
le jus d'orange
le lait
le thé

Fruit et légumes
la banane
la fraise
l'orange (f.)
le pamplemousse
la poire
la pomme
la carotte
les frites
les haricots verts
la laitue
les pommes de terre
la salade
la tomate

Desserts
le fromage
le gâteau (au chocolat)
la glace
la tarte (aux pommes)
le yaourt

Pain, etc.
le croissant
le pain
le petit pain
le pain grillé
la confiture

3. The *passé composé:* review and *pas de*

This section will remind you of much that you have learned about the *passé composé.*

1. The past participles of most *-ir* verbs end in *-i*. Past participles of most *-re* verbs end in *-u*. A number of frequently-used verbs have unpredictable past participles. Write the participles for these verbs.
   a. avoir, lire, vouloir |
      eu, lu, voulu
   b. voir, connaître, venir, boire |
      vu, connu, venu, bu
   c. faire, être, prendre |
      fait, été, pris

2. Some verbs use *être* as an auxiliary. Say aloud, then write the *passé composé je* form (masculine) for each verb.
   a. aller, venir, rentrer |
      je suis allé, je suis venu, je suis rentré
   b. monter, descendre, tomber |
      je suis monté, je suis descendu, je suis tombé
   c. arriver, rester |
      je suis arrivé, je suis resté
   d. naître, mourir |
      je suis né, je suis mort

3. Ask your friend Marie whether she did the following things last night. (See key.)
   Modèle: écouter la radio |
      Tu as écouté la radio hier soir?
   a. téléphoner à Jeanne
   b. faire tes devoirs
   c. aller au cinéma
   d. partir avant la fin *(end)* du film

4. In a negative sentence in the *passé composé*, where do *ne* and *pas* occur—around the auxiliary *(avoir* or *être)* or around the past participle? |
      around the auxiliary: Je n'ai pas dormi; Je ne suis pas allé

5. These people had a terrible day because they didn't accomplish what they wanted to. (See key.)
   Modèle: Georges/terminer ses devoirs |
      Georges n'a pas terminé ses devoirs.
   a. Anne/jouer du violon
   b. je/aller voir mes amis
   c. ma mère/lire le journal

6. Look at the chart.

Pas de in the *passé composé*

J'ai fait **des** courses.	Je n'ai **pas** fait **de** courses.
J'ai pris **du** jus d'orange.	Je n'ai **pas** pris **de** jus d'orange.

The indefinite and partitive articles become *de* or *(d')* in the *passé composé*, *pas* and *de* do not occur next to each other. What word comes in between? |

the past participle

7. Answer these questions in the negative, with *ne...pas...de*.
   a. As-tu fait des courses aujourd'hui? (non, je...) |

Non, je n'ai pas fait de courses.

   b. Ont-ils vu des légumes frais *(fresh)* au marché? |

Non, ils n'ont pas vu de légumes frais.

   c. Avez-vous pris un dessert? (non, je...) |

Non, je n'ai pas pris de dessert.

4. Practice with inversion

1. Beatrice has just run into her friend Philippe, who's holding a child by the hand. Below are Philippe's answers; write Beatrice's questions. Use the question words *qui, quel, (quelle), comment* or *où* and inversion.
   a. —_____?
      —Je vais bien, merci. |

Comment vas-tu? (Did you remember the hyphen?)

   b. —_____?
      —C'est ma cousine Hélène. |

Qui est-ce?

   c. —_____?
      —Elle a trois ans. |

Quel âge a-t-elle? (Did you remember to insert -t- between the verb and pronoun?)

   d. —_____?
      —Nous allons au parc. |

Où allez-vous?

   e. —_____?
      —Il est trois heures et demie. |

Quelle heure est-il?

2. Inversion occurs in the *passé composé* as well.

   Nous avons mangé à 7 heures. Et vous, avez-vous mangé?

   a. Write the English equivalent. |

We ate at 7. What about you, have you eaten? (Did you eat?)

   b. In the *passé composé*, inversion occurs between the subject and the _____ verb. |

auxiliary

3. Read aloud the forms in the chart.

Inversion in the *passé composé*

(est-ce que) j'ai	oublié?		je suis	allé/e?
as-tu	oublié?		**es-tu**	all**é/e**?
a-t-il/-on/-elle	oublié?		**est-il/-on/-elle**	all**é/e**?
avons-nous	oublié?		**sommes-nous**	all**é/e/s**?
avez-vous	oublié?		**êtes-vous**	all**é/e/s**?
ont-ils/-elles	oublié?		**sont-ils/-elles**	all**é/e/s**?

4. Complete these sentences with questions, using inversion.

Modèle: Marie-Christine a refusé de manger. Et vous,...?

avez-vous refusé de manger?

a. Elle est allée à la fac sans déjeuner. Et son amie...?

est-elle allée à la fac sans déjeuner?

b. Elle est arrivée au restaurant universitaire à midi. Et son amie Yvonne...?

est-elle arrivée à midi?

c. Yvonne a aidé Marie-Christine à abandonner ses résolutions. Et sa mère...?

a-t-elle aidé Marie-Christine à abandonner ses résolutions?

d. Marie-Christine a bien mangé à midi. Et vous...?

avez-vous bien mangé à midi?

Le Champignon de Paris.
Un légume tout rond, tout bon.

Faites-vous la cuisine chez vous? Employez-vous souvent des champignons?

Vocabulaire

Noms
le déjeuner *lunch*
le dîner *dinner*
le lit *bed*
le petit déjeuner *breakfast*
le pilote, la femme pilote *pilot*
la tartelette *small fruit pie*
la vanille *vanilla*

Adjectifs
célèbre *famous*
curieux/curieuse *curious*
frais/fraîche *fresh*
intellectuel/le *intellectual*

Verbes
abandonner *to give up, to abandon*

Autres mots & expressions
passe-moi le sel, s'il te plaît *pass the salt, please*

Note Culturelle

Le Fromage

There is a saying that illustrates the important role of cheese in a French meal: *Un repas sans fromage n'est pas un repas* ("A meal without cheese is not a meal.") More than three hundred types of cheese are produced and eaten in France. A few of the more common ones are *camembert* (a round, semi-soft cheese with a crust), *gruyère* (a Swiss cheese), *fromage de chèvre* (sharp-flavored), made from goat's milk, and *roquefort* (a sharp, blue-veined cheese.)

Pour les amateurs de fromage (those who love cheese), la France, c'est le paradis.

PRÉPARATION 35

1. Reading comprehension

The following dialogue will give you an idea of what a customer and a waiter in a restaurant might say.

First, read the dialogue once straight through. Keep the words in the margin covered and use them only after you've tried to guess the general meaning of the new words in context. As you read, look for the answers to the following questions:

> Does M. Grandet order chicken, meat, or fish?
> What does he have to drink with his meal?
> He is offered ice cream, pastry, fruit, and
> cheese to end the meal—what does he have?

La Truite d'Or

Maître d'hôtel° Bonsoir, Monsieur.

M. Grandet Bonsoir, Pierre. Ça va?

Maître d'hôtel Très bien, merci, Monsieur. Vous voulez cette table, n'est-ce pas?

M. Grandet: Oui, comme d'habitude.° *(Il s'assied.)°*

Maître d'hôtel Vous désirez regarder le menu, Monsieur?

M. Grandet Oui, s'il vous plaît.

Maître d'hôtel (Il lui donne° le menu.) Voilà, Monsieur. Bon appétit!

(M. Grandet regarde le menu, puis fait signe° à la serveuse.°)

Serveuse Bonsoir, Monsieur. Vous voulez commander°?

M. Grandet Oui. Voyons°... *(Il regarde le menu.)* comme hors d'œuvre... du pâté°... du saucisson°... Non... Qu'est-ce que vous avez comme soupe?

Serveuse Ce soir, nous avons de la soupe à l'oignon.° Elle est très bonne.

M. Grandet: D'accord, je vais prendre la soupe à l'oignon. Comme plat°... *(Il regarde le menu.)* Voyons... Poulet aux champignons,° gigot d'agneau°, truite°... Je vais prendre le gigot d'agneau.

Serveuse Bien, Monsieur. Qu'est-ce que vous voulez comme légumes? Nous avons des haricots verts, des carottes, des petits pois et des oignons à la crème.°

	The Golden Trout
	headwaiter
	as usual / he sits down
	gives him
	signals / waitress
	to order
	let's see
	meat spread / salami
	onion soup
	main dish / mushrooms
	leg of lamb / trout
	creamed onions

Préparation 35

M. Grandet Je voudrais des haricots verts. Vous avez des pommes de terre?

Serveuse Oui, Monsieur. Des pommes au gratin,° des frites... | potatoes with grated cheese and bread crumbs

M. Grandet Des pommes au gratin...

Serveuse Bien, Monsieur. Vous désirez une salade?

M. Grandet Oui, s'il vous plaît. Maintenant, comme boisson...

Serveuse Du vin rosé? rouge?

M. Grandet Non, pas de vin aujourd'hui. Une demi-bouteille° d'eau minérale | half-bottle

Serveuse Bien, Monsieur.

(Plus tard°...) | later

Serveuse Vous avez terminé° avec le gigot, Monsieur? On peut débarrasser°? | are you finished? clear the table

M. Grandet Oui, c'était délicieux. Qu'est-ce que vous avez comme dessert?

Serveuse Nous avons de la glace, des fruits, des pâtisseries°... | pastries

M. Grandet Euh... Quels fruits avez-vous?

Serveuse Des poires et des pêches.

M. Grandet Bon, alors je vais prendre une pêche.

Serveuse Du fromage avant le dessert, Monsieur?

M. Grandet Non, pas de fromage, merci.

Serveuse Bien, Monsieur.

M. Grandet Et donnez-moi° l'addition° avec le dessert, s'il vous plaît. Je suis un peu pressé ce soir. | give me / bill

Serveuse Très bien, Monsieur.

1. Now go back and read again, then answer the following questions with a word or phrase.

   a. M. Grandet mange-t-il souvent au restaurant *La Truite d'Or*? |
      Oui (You can tell because he knows the *Maître d'hôtel*, and he sits at his usual table.)

   b. Comment dit-on *to order* en français? |
      commander

   c. Qui est-ce qui commande? la serveuse? M. Grandet? |
      M. Grandet

2. a. Qu'est-ce que M. Grandet commande comme soupe? |
      de la soupe à l'oignon

   b. Est-ce que la truite est un dessert ou un poisson? |
      un poisson

3. a. Qu'est-ce que M. Grandet prend avec le gigot d'agneau? |
      des haricots verts et des pommes au gratin

   b. Est-ce que M. Grandet prend de la salade? |
      Oui

4. a. Qu'est-ce qu'il prend comme boisson? |
      une demi-bouteille d'eau minérale

   b. Qu'est-ce qu'il y a comme dessert à la Truite d'Or? |
      de la glace, des fruits et des pâtisseries

2. Equivalents of *to be*

1. Write the infinitive forms of the verbs used in certain French expressions:
   a. To talk about the weather *Il _____ beau.* |
   b. To talk about age *Elle _____ 45 ans.* |
   c. To talk about being cold, hot, hungry, thirsty *Nous _____ très faim.* |
   d. To talk about health *Vous _____ bien?* |

   a. faire (Il fait beau.)
   b. avoir (Elle a 45 ans.)
   c. avoir (Nous avons très faim.)
   d. aller (Vous allez bien?)

2. Two neighbors have just met in the street. Complete their dialogues with the correct forms of *être, avoir, aller,* or *faire.*
   —Bonjour, Monsieur, comment __a.__-vous?
   —Bien, merci. Quel beau temps, n'est-ce pas?

   —Oui. Mais il __b.__ frais.
   —Ah oui? Vous __c.__ froid?

   —Oui, un peu.
   —Venez prendre un café avec moi. Vous n' __d.__ pas pressé?
   —Si, malheureusement. Je __e.__ en retard. |

   a. allez
   b. fait
   c. avez
   d. êtes
   e. suis

3. Practice with food vocabulary

1. Say that you like these foods in general: *viande, haricots verts, jambon.* |

   J'aime la viande, les haricots verts et le jambon.

2. Say that you don't like these foods:
   a. riz   b. carottes |

   a. Je n'aime pas le riz.   b. Je n'aime pas les carottes.

3. Say that you want some of the following: *salade, eau minérale, tomates.* |

   Je veux de la salade, de l'eau minérale et des tomates.

4. Say that Paul is having a portion of each food listed. Use *prendre.*
   a. carottes   c. bœuf
   b. salade   d. banane |

   a. Paul prend des carottes.   b. Paul prend de la salade.   c. Paul prend du boeuf.
   d. Paul prend une banane.

5. Say that you aren't going to have any of the foods listed below.
   Modèle: frites |

   Je ne vais pas prendre de frites.

   a. eau minérale   c. bœuf
   b. croissants   d. fruits |

   a. Je ne vais pas prendre d'eau minérale.   b. Je ne vais pas prendre de croissants.
   c. Je ne vais pas prendre de bœuf.   d. Je ne vais pas prendre de fruits.

6. All these items are on the dinner table. Ask your neighbors to pass each of them to you. Use *Passe-moi..., s'il te plaît.*
    a. eau
    b. poulet
    c. tomates
    d. beurre |

    a. Passe-moi l'eau, s'il te plaît.   b. Passe-moi le poulet, s'il te plaît.   c. Passe-moi les tomates, s'il te plaît.   d. Passe-moi le beurre, s'il te plaît.

7. You have learned that nouns are usually either count nouns or measure nouns. Certain nouns, however, can be count nouns in one context, and measure nouns in another.

8. If Nathalie says in French *I've caught some fish: a bass and a perch,* will she say *du poisson* or *des poissons?* |

    des poissons (Here *fish* are whole animals that can be counted.)

9. a. You are at a café with some friends. The waiter comes over to take your order and you say *Nous voulons un thé et un jus d'orange.* Are tea and orange juice treated as count nouns or measure nouns? |

    count nouns (In restaurant orders, food is often a count noun.)

    b. Tell the waiter you also want one ice cream, two coffees, and one *tartelette* (small pie). |

    Nous voulons aussi une glace, deux cafés et une tertelette.

4. Review practice: rejoinders

For each item below choose the response that is most logical. (See key.)

1. Vous aimez les fruits?
    a. Oui, je les vois.
    b. Oui, beaucoup.
    c. Bon, ce soir, sans faute.

2. Voulez-vous voir ce film de science-fiction?
    a. Formidable! C'est mon sport préféré.
    b. Oui, mais je n'ai pas soif.
    c. Non, merci. J'ai trop de devoirs.

3. Y a-t-il des sandwichs au jambon?
    a. Mais oui! Je mange bien à midi.
    b. Non, mais il a des croque-monsieur.
    c. Bonne idée! Nous allons au restaurant

4. On va à la plage?
    a. D'accord! Je viens avec toi!
    b. Je vais bien, merci.
    c. Bof! Je ne sais pas patiner.

Vocabulaire

Noms

la bouteille   *bottle*
la crème   *cream*
le pâté   *meat spread, pâté*
le saucisson   *dry sausage, salami*
la soupe à l'oignon   *onion soup*
la truite   *trout*
le vin rouge/blanc   *red/white wine*

Verbes

faire la cuisine   *to cook*

PRÉPARATION 36

1. Review practice: *venir*

1. Tell which season comes after winter and which month comes after March. |

> Le printemps vient après l'hiver. Avril vient après mars.

2. Ask Mme Grandet if she comes from Marseille. |

> Vous venez de Marseille, Madame?   (There are, as you know, other ways of asking questions.)

3. Say that Anne and Georges come from Lille. |

> Anne et Georges viennent de Lille.

4. Ask your friend Susan what she just ate and Marguerite and Paul what they just drank. |

> Susanne, qu'est-ce que tu viens de manger? Marguerite et Paul, qu'est-ce que vous venez de boire?

2. General review

1. Below you see a series of paired sentences. Complete the second sentence in each pair with the appropriate indefinite or partitive article. (See key.)
   a. —J'aime beaucoup le thé.
      —Veux-tu prendre _____ thé maintenant?
   b. Ma mère aime les légumes.
      Elle achète _____ petits pois.
   c. —Il aime les fruits comme dessert?
      —Oui, il va prendre _____ pomme.
   d. Noëlle aime le sucre, mais elle est au régime.
      Alors, elle ne prend pas _____ sucre avec son café.
2. Complete the sentences to say that people are going home. Use the appropriate stressed pronoun. (See key.)
   a. Je vais chez _____.   c. Elles vont chez _____.
   b. Il va chez _____.   d. Ils vont chez _____.
3. Answer the following questions with complete sentences.
   a. Qu'est-ce que vous préférez comme petit déjeuner?
   b. Qu'est-ce que vous allez manger ce soir pour le dîner?

4. Read the narrative, then answer the questions. (See key.)

Les Guilbert vont toujours au supermarché le vendredi. Il faut acheter de la viande, des légumes et des fruits pour le week-end. Mais ce samedi, des amis viennent dîner. Alors, il faut trouver un dessert spécial—une grande tarte aux fraises, peut-être?

a. Les Guilbert vont toujours au supermarché...
   A quand il fait beau.   B le vendredi.   C le samedi.
b. Ils veulent trouver une tarte aux fraises...
   A parce qu'ils aiment la glace.
   B parce que c'est vendredi.
   C parce que des amis viennent dîner chez eux.

5. a. Transpose the following paragraph into the past. (See key.) When it describes Nadine and does not relate events of a specific date, which tense should be used? |

the imparfait

b. When it lists the events of a particular day, which tense should be used? |

the passé composé

Nadine a 18 ans. C'est une étudiante intelligente et sympathique. Mais son gros problème, c'est qu'elle est maigre. Elle n'aime pas manger et par exemple, elle ne prend jamais de petit déjeuner. Samedi dernier, Nadine *(1) décide* de se peser. Elle *(2) monte* sur la balance et, oh là là! elle *(3) pèse* seulement 45 kilos! Il *(4) faut* faire quelque chose! Après quelques minutes de réflexion, elle *(5) prend* une décision: à partir d'aujourd'hui, elle *(6) va* se forcer à manger le matin et à midi—et le soir, elle *(7) va* prendre un repas copieux. Pour commencer, elle *(8) prend* un bon petit déjeuner. À midi elle *(9) mange* du bifteck haché, des frites, des haricots verts, de la salade, du fromage et une pomme. À quatre heures elle *(10) prend* un petit pain au chocolat et du café au lait. Puis, elle *(11) monte* vite sur la balance: fantastique! Elle *(12) pèse* maintenant 46 kilos! Mais à 7 heures, hélas, elle *(13) est* très malheureuse: elle ne *(14) peut* pas dîner, elle n' *(15) a* pas faim!

Vocabulaire

Noms
le bateau à voile   *sailboat*

Adjectifs
parfait   *perfect*

Les couleurs
bleu/e   *blue*
blanc/blanche   *white*
brun/e (cheveux, yeux)   *brown*

gris/e   *grey*
jaune   *yellow*
marron (inv.)   *brown*
noir/e   *black*
orange (inv.)   *orange*
rose   *pink*
rouge   *red*
vert/e   *green*
violet/te   *purple*

Note Culturelle

Crêpes

In the United States we serve pancakes for a hearty breakfast. The French serve *crêpes* for snacks or parties, lunch or dinner. *Crêpes* are very thin pancakes fried to a golden brown on the griddle. When served as *entrées,* the *crêpes* are filled with such delicacies as shrimp, lobster, or melted cheese. Dessert *crêpes* can be prepared in many ways. Sometimes they are sprinkled with orange liqueur; sometimes they are topped with jelly, and then folded and served. Tourists in France can sample *crêpes* without splurging on *haute cuisine.* Vendors sell "dessert" *crêpes* on beaches and street corners for the price of an ice cream cone.

Des crêpes toutes chaudes, quel délice (delight)!

Recette (recipe)

one egg
one cup of flour
one cup of milk
one teaspoon of oil
a pinch of salt

butter for the pan
confectioners sugar

Optional
jam
ice cream

Combine the egg and the flour. Add the milk, the oil, and the salt. It is a good idea to put this through a blender. Let the *pâte* (the batter) sit, covered, for a few hours in the refrigerator. Heat a frying pan and melt a teaspoon of butter. Pour in a small amount of batter to cover the pan with a thin coating. (You may have to tilt and turn the pan to help spread the batter.) After a few moments, turn the *crêpe* to brown it on both sides. Slide it on to a plate. Add some sugar, perhaps ice cream and/or jam. Then, roll it. *Bon appétit!*

Phase 6

Modes

Qu'est-ce que vous allez apprendre?

By the end of this Phase you will be able to talk about different kinds of clothing, discuss what one wears for various occasions, comment on people's attitudes toward clothes, and negotiate the purchase of a pair of shoes. You will be able to express impatience and annoyed surprise, and berate someone for being stubborn.

Communication

You will:
- Use word sets referring to clothing and colors.
- Use amusing animal metaphors for human characteristics.
- Use the verbs *dire* (to say) and *devoir* (to owe, to have to, to be supposed to).
- Tell people to do things, using *tu* and *vous* commands.
- Make suggestions, using *nous* commands.
- Use *ne...rien, ne...jamais,* and *ne...personne* to express the ideas of *nothing, never,* and *no one.*
- Use *porter* (to wear) and *mettre* (to put, to put on).
- Report what others say, using indirect discourse.
- Refer to the person to whom or for whom something is done, using indirect object pronouns.

Culture

French sizes for clothing and shoes; Marie-Antoinette and the French Revolution; regional costumes.

PRÉPARATION 37

Histoire de chaussures

La scène se passe dans un grand magasin parisien, les Galeries Lafayette. Nous sommes au rayon des chaussures. Nous voyons une jeune vendeuse avec une cliente qui essaie des chaussures. Oh là là... toutes ces boîtes! Une, deux, trois, cinq, dix boîtes de chaussures... Et la cliente n'est pas contente.

Cliente Non, non, non, Mademoiselle! Ces chaussures sont trop grandes, je vous dis.
Vendeuse Mais madame, c'est votre pointure... 38 environ.

A question of shoes

The scene takes place in a Parisian department store, the Galeries Lafayette. We're in the shoe department. We see a young saleslady with a customer trying on shoes. Oh, my, all those boxes! One, two, three, five, ten boxes of shoes . . . And the customer is still not happy.

No, no, no! These shoes are too large, I tell you.
But, that's your size . . . You take about a 38.

Cliente Trente-huit! Jamais de la vie! Je chausse du 37 au maximum, vous entendez, Mademoiselle, MA-XI-MUM!	Thirty-eight! Never (Not on your life)! I take a 37, maximum, do you hear me, Miss, MAX-I-MUM!
Vendeuse Bien, Madame. Voilà un 37. Donnez-moi votre pied droit, s'il vous plaît.	Very well, madam, here is a 37. Give me your right foot, please.
Cliente Aïe! Mais c'est trop petit, voyons!	Ouch! But that's too small, for heaven's sake!
Vendeuse Vous voyez, Madame, vous devez prendre un 38, au moins.	As you see, madam, you take at least a 38.
Cliente Un 38! Au moins! Ça alors, c'est trop fort! Eh bien, gardez-les, vos chaussures, Mademoiselle!	At least a 38! That's going too far! You can keep your shoes, miss.
Vendeuse Je regrette, Madame. Au revoir, Madame.	I'm sorry, madam. Goodby, madam.
Cliente (*en sortant*) Oh là là, ces vendeuses! Qu'elles sont stupides!	(*Leaving*) Oh, these salespeople! They're so stupid!
Vendeuse (*à mi-voix*) Oh là là, ces clientes! J'en ai marre!	(*To herself*) Oh, these customers! I've had it with them!

Échange d'idées

1. Demandez à un/une camarade de classe s'il/si elle achète souvent des chaussures.
   Demandez-lui s'il/si elle aime les chaussures chères (*expensive*).
   Demandez-lui s'il/si elle préfère les bottes (*boots*).

2. Work in a pair. The setting is a department store; one of you is a customer, one of you is a sales clerk. The customer tries on a particular item of clothing, and keeps asking for a different size or a different color. The clerk tries to remain polite but eventually expresses frustration. The customer replies with frustration also.

1. Position of adjectives with nouns

In this section, you will practice using some adjectives that follow the noun in French.

1. Notice the position of the adjectives in these sentences.

Je voudrais acheter une chemise *bleue*.	Vous connaissez cette dame *italienne?*
Ma sœur a une jupe *rouge*.	Roger est un étudiant *américain*.

a. Do adjectives of color, like *bleu* and *rouge*, precede or follow the noun? |

follow

b. Adjectives of nationality, like *italien* and *américain*, also _____ the noun. |

follow

2. Write French equivalents for the sentences below.

Modèle: Roger is an American student. |

Roger est un étudiant américain.

a. Marie-France is a Canadian student. |

Marie-France est une étudiante canadienne.

b. Jean-Pierre is a student from Martinique. |

Jean-Pierre est un étudiant martiniquais.

c. Marianne is a Belgian student. |

Marianne est une étudiante belge.

3. Write the French equivalent for each phrase below.

a. a red skirt, a white blouse |

une jupe rouge, un chemisier blanc

b. black shoes, gray socks |

des chaussures noires, des chaussettes grises (Remember that even though *des* nned not be said in English, it must be used in French.)

4. The majority of French adjectives follow the noun. Here are some other adjectives you know which also follow the noun: *affreux, célèbre, intelligent, maigre.* Use them to write French equivalents for the phrases below.

a. an awful film   c. some famous actors

b. an intelligent secretary   d. two skinny dogs |

a. un film affreux   b. un/e secrétaire intelligent/e   c. des acteurs célèbres   d. deux chiens maigres

5. Although the majority of French adjectives usually follow the noun they describe, there are a few that usually precede the noun. They are adjectives that are used very frequently. Here is a list of the ones you have learned so far.

autre	gros, grosse	mauvais, mauvaise
beau, belle	jeune	petit, petite
bon, bonne	joli, jolie	vieux, vieille

In items *a-d,* add the correct form of the adjective to each sentence.

Modèle: (gros) C'est un éléphant. |

C'est un gros éléphant.

a. (bon) C'est une idée. |

C'est une bonne idée.

b. (vieux) J'ai un pantalon. |

J'ai un vieux pantalon.

c. (joli) Il n'y a pas de manteaux dans ce magasin. |

Il n'y a pas de jolis manteaux dans ce magasin.

d. (autre) J'ai besoin d'un stylo rouge. |

J'ai besoin d'un autre stylo rouge.

2. Practice with paired words

1. Look at each pair of opposites below, and say the English equivalents. Go through the whole list once before you check the answers.

a. pourquoi/parce que

b. heureux/malheureux

c. commencer/terminer

d. merveilleux/affreux

e. vite/lentement

f. bon/mauvais

g. bien/mal

h. avant/après

i. minuit/midi

a. why/because   b. happy/unhappy   c. begin/end   d. marvelous/awful
e. quickly/slowly   f. good/bad   g. well/badly   h. before/after   i. midnight/noon

2. Answer each question below by using a word that is opposite in meaning to the italicized word. Keep your answer short.

   Modèle: Ils vont arriver à *midi?*

   Non, à minuit.

a. Tu *termines* tes devoirs?

   Non, je les commence.

b. Tu vas jouer au football *après* le déjeuner?

   Non, avant le déjeuner.

c. Le chocolat est *bon* pour les enfants?

   Non, il est mauvais.

d. Comme ces musiciens jouent *mal,* n'est-ce pas?

   Mais non, ils jouent bien!

3. Which of the following do not belong in each group? Answers follow *d.*

a. maison, appartement, manteau, hôtel

b. croissant, viande, poisson, soir

c. jouer des cymbales, jouer au football, jouer du violon, jouer de la guitare

d. petits pois, pêches, pommes de terre, carottes

a. manteau

b. soir

c. jouer au football

d. pêches

À Propos!   Prenez-vous de la salade avant ou après le plat principal?

3. Practice with -*ir* verbs

1. As you learned in Préparation 13, regular -*ir* verbs have two stems in the present tense.

   Je finis mon travail à 6h, et mes amis finissent à 6h30.

a. The singular stem of *finir* is _____.

   fini- (the infinitive minus -*r*)

b. The plural stem is _____. |

finiss- (the singular stem plus -ss)

2. Write forms of *choisir* to complete these sentences:
   a. Je _____ une table dans un restaurant. |
   b. Quand vous _____ une bouteille de vin, il faut bien regarder l'étiquette *(label).* |
   c. Georges _____ une pomme comme dessert. |

a. choisis

b. choisissez

c. choisit

3. Say that everyone is really filling up their plates.

   Modèle: Les enfants/leurs assiettes |

   Les enfants remplissent bien leurs assiettes.

   a. moi/mon assiette
   b. toi/ton assiette
   c. vous/vos assiettes |

   a. Je remplis bien mon assiette.   b. Tu remplis bien ton assiette.   c. Vous remplissez bien vos assiettes.

4. Since you know how to find the *imparfait* stem of a verb (Préparation 29) and you know the endings, you can form the *imparfait* of regular *-ir* verbs. Complete these sentences with the *imparfait.*
   a. *(finir)* L'année dernière, je ne _____ jamais mes devoirs avant minuit. |
   b. *(choisir)* Quand nous _____ le plat principal, nous commandions toujours du bifteck haché. |
   c. *(obéir)* Elles n' _____ pas toujours à leurs professeurs. |

a. finissais

b. choisissions

c. obéissaient

5. The past participle of *-ir* verbs is the infinitive minus *r.* Give the English equivalent of this sentence: *As-tu fini tes devoirs, Jacques?* |

   Did you finish your homework, Jacques?

6. Say that yesterday these people did not do what they usually do.
   a. François choisit toujours les programmes de sports à la télévision. |

   Hier, il n'a pas choisi les programmes de sport.

   b. M. Parfait obéit toujours à sa conscience. |

   Hier, M. Parfait n'a pas obéi à sa conscience.

   c. Elles finissent toujours leur dessert. |

   Hier, elles n'ont pas fini leur dessert.

7. The past participles of *sortir* and *partir* are formed the same way as that of *finir.* What are they? |

   sorti, parti

8. Both *partir* and *sortir*, like *aller*, take the auxiliary *être* in the *passé composé.* Rewrite these sentences in the *passé composé.* Don't forget to make the participle agree with the subject.
   a. Elles _____ avec leurs copains. (partir)
   b. Ils _____ à neuf heures. (sortir)
   c. Et vous, Mme Pierrot, vous _____ avec eux? (sortir) |

a. sont parties

b. sont sortis

c. êtes sortie

Vocabulaire

Noms

l'anorak *m.* *windbreaker, ski jacket*
l'assiette *f.* *plate*
la chaussure *shoe*
la chemise *man's shirt*
la chemise de nuit *nightgown*
le chemisier *woman's blouse or shirt*
le/la client/e *customer*
la conscience *conscience*
la dissertation *academic paper, essay*
l'étiquette *f.* *label*
le grand magasin *department store*
le jean *jeans*
la langue étrangère *foreign
   language*
le pied *foot*
le plat principal *main dish, entrée*
la pointure *(shoe, glove) size*
le pyjama *pajamas*
le pull/pyl/ *pullover*
le rayon *department*
le sac *bag*
la serviette *briefcase, attaché-case*
le T-shirt/ti ʃœʀt/ *tee shirt*
le vendeur/la vendeuse *salesman/
   saleswoman*
les vêtements *clothes*

Adjectifs

actif/active *active*
complet/complète *complete*
cruel/le *cruel*
droit/e *right (direction)*
sportif/sportive *athletic*

Verbes

avoir besoin de *to need to*
fumer *to smoke*
remplir *to fill up*

Autres mots et expressions

au moins *at least*
c'est trop fort! *that's going too far!*
j'en ai marre! *I've had it!*
jamais de la vie! *never! (not on your
   life!)*

À Paris. Des acheteurs sous la pluie.

PRÉPARATION 38

1. The verb *devoir*

Devoir can mean *to owe,* or can express obligation or probability. Like *venir* and *prendre,* it has three stems in the present tense. Study the forms in the chart.

Présent:		je	**doi**	s		nous	**dev**	ons
		tu	doi	s		vous	**dev**	ez
		on/il/elle	doi	t		ils/elles	**doiv**	ent

Imparfait: **je devais**
Passé composé: **j'ai dû**

1. Write the three present tense stems of *devoir*. |
     doi-, dev-, doiv-

2. Which of these words is the past participle of *devoir—dû* or *du?* |
     dû (*Du* is the contraction of the preposition *de* + *le*.)

3. Give the English equivalent of *Tu me dois toujours 10 francs.* |
     You still owe me ten francs.

4. Ask for confirmation that these people owe Claire 8 francs.
     Modèle: toi |
          Tu dois 8F à Claire, n'est-ce pas?

   a. moi   b. Louise et Paul   c. nous |
          a. Je dois 8F à Claire, n'est-ce pas?
          b. Louise et Paul doivent 8F à Claire, n'est-ce pas?
          c. Nous devons 8F à Claire, n'est-ce pas?

5. Victor can't play tennis today.

          Michel: Dis, Victor, tu veux jouer au tennis?
          Victor: Non, je ne peux pas.
          Michel: Pourquoi pas?
          Victor: Je dois faire des courses.

   a. Why can't Victor play tennis? |
          Because he has to do some errands.

   b. One English equivalent of *Je dois faire des courses* is *I have to do some errands.* What are some other equivalents that mean just about the same thing as *I have to?*

I must/I should/I'm supposed to/I've got to

  c. In *Je dois faire des courses,* what verb form follows *je dois?*

an infinitive

6. Write the French equivalent: *I've got to work Saturday.*

Je dois travailler samedi.

7. Compare the equivalents below.

Present Obligation:	Je dois partir.	*I have to leave.*
Unfulfilled or habitual obligation:	Nous devions partir à 9h.	*We were supposed to (had to) leave at 9:00.*
Fulfilled obligation:	Ils ont dû partir.	*They had to leave.*
Probability or supposition in the present:	Tiens! Je dois être à l'heure!	*Well! I must be (I suppose I'm) on time!*
in the past:	Il a dû oublier notre rendez-vous.	*He must have forgotten (he probably forgot) our appointment.*

8. Write the appropriate tense and form of *devoir* to tell what these people have to or had to do.
  a. Les enfants Dulac _____ aller chez le dentiste aujourd'hui.   a. doivent
  b. L'année passée vous _____ dîner à huit heures tous les soirs. *(every evening)*   b. deviez
  c. Tu _____ trouver ton imperméable tout de suite!   c. dois
  d. Dans ce cours on _____ parler français.   d. doit
  e. Nous _____ finir nos devoirs avant 5h quand nous étions petits.   e. devions
  f. Hier soir j'_____ me coucher très tard.   f. ai dû

9. Draw the conclusion that each of these people must be late.
  Modèle: Tu marches vite.

Tu dois être en retard.

  a. Georges marche vite.
  b. Les clientes marchent vite.
  c. Vous marchez vite.

a. Il doit être en retard.   b. Elles doivent être en retard.   c. Vous devez être en retard.

À Propos!

Qu'est-ce que vous devez faire avant de vous coucher le soir?

2. Practice with clothing vocabulary

Choose the items of clothing that complete each situation below. Here, the verb *mettre* means *to put on* and *porter* means *to wear*. Notice that to refer to parts of the body, *la* or *à la, le* or *au, les* or *aux* are used rather than a possessive adjective.

> *Modèle:* Sur la tête *(head)* vous mettez un *(chapeau, collant, jupe).* |
>
> un chapeau

1. Quand il pleut, on met un *(chemisier, gant, imperméable).* |
2. Si vous avez froid aux pieds *(feet),* vous mettez des *(chapeaux, chaussures, chaussettes).* |
3. En général, les hommes portent des *(chemisiers, chemises)* et les femmes portent des *(chemisiers, chemises).* |
4. Pour nager, il faut porter un *(maillot de bain, gilet, tailleur).* |
5. En général, les hommes portent *(un sac, une jupe, un pantalon).* |
6. Thérèse ne peut pas trouver *(la veste, le short, les chaussettes)* de son tailleur. |
7. Vous emportez vos papiers et vos livres à la bibliothèque dans *(une serviette, une chaussette, un short).* |

1. un imperméable
2. des chaussettes, des chaussures
3. des chemises, des chemisiers
4. un maillot de bain
5. un pantalon
6. la veste
7. une serviette

3. Spelling-changing verbs in *-érer, -eter, -ever, -eler*

1. a. In an earlier Phase you worked with the verbs *préférer, suggérer, exagérer.* Write the *tu* and *vous* forms of *exagérer.* |

   tu exagères, vous exagérez

   b. Which other present tense form matches the stem *exagér-* (accent aigu)? |

   nous exagérons (The *je, tu, il/elle, ils/elles* forms all use the stem *exagèr-* [accent grave].)

Like verbs in *-érer,* some other verbs have a similar spelling change in their stems. Look at the chart of *acheter.*

Présent:				
	j' **achèt** e		nous **achet** ons
	tu achèt es		vous achet ez
	on/il/elle achèt e		ils/elles **achèt** ent
Imparfait:	**j'achetais**			
Passé composé:	**j'ai acheté**			

2. a. What present tense stem matches the *nous* and *vous* forms? |

   achet- (the regular infinitive stem)

b. What present tense stem matches the other forms? |

achèt- (accent grave)

c. Does the stem *achèt-* occur with endings that are pronounced or silent? |

with endings that are silent

3. Say aloud the present tense of *acheter*—When the letter *e* of the 2nd syllable has an accent grave (è), it bears the stress; the accent is dropped when the *e* is followed by a pronounced ending:

achète → /a ʃɛt/   **achetons** → /a ʃtɔ̃/

In most instances when a verb stem differs from the infinitive stem, the variant stem occurs when the endings are silent, in the syllable before that silent ending. Write each of these verb phrases and supply its missing accent marks: *j'achete, je prefere, ils achetent, nous preferons.* |

j'achète, je préfère, ils achètent, nous préférons

4. Some friends happen to meet in the *rayon de disques* of a large department store. Complete the sentences below with forms of *acheter*. To get used to the sounds of the stem, read each sentence aloud.

a. Qu'est-ce que vous ＿＿＿? |
b. Nous ＿＿＿ des disques pour Sylvie. |
c. Jean-Luc! Nous devons ＿＿＿ ce disque de Brahms pour Marc. |
d. Est-ce que Pierre et son frère ＿＿＿ souvent des disques? |
e. Moi, je ne suis pas riche cette semaine. Je n'＿＿＿ pas de disques. |

a. achetez
b. achetons
c. acheter
d. achètent
e. achète

5. Write the French equivalents. (See key.)

a. For dessert, you prefer coffee ice cream *(glace au café),* don't you?
b. We have to buy this beautiful sweater for Marc!

The following verbs, like *acheter,* change *e* to *è* in the present tense *je, tu, il/elle, ils/elles* forms.

lever *to raise*
se lever *to get up (from lying down)*
enlever *to take off (a lid, clothing, etc.)*

emmener *to take (someone) along*
se promener *to take a walk*
amener *to bring (someone)*

And the following verbs, like *préférer,* change the *é* to *è.*

répéter *to repeat*   espérer *to hope*
considérer *to consider*

6. Use the above verbs to write French equivalents.

a. Tomorrow you *(tu)* get up at 7:00, don't you?

b. When I go for a walk, I always take along my dog.
c. Hélène and Gisèle hope to travel in Europe this summer.
d. The professor and I (we) are considering that question.
e. Repeat, please!
f. He's taking off his windbreaker. |

7. Some verbs double a consonant instead of using an *accent grave*. Two are *jeter* (to throw) and *s'appeler* (to be named).

Présent:			
	je	**jette**	**m'appelle**
	tu	jettes	t'appelles
	on/il/elle	jette	s'appelle
	nous	**jetons**	**nous appelons**
	vous	jetez	vous appelez
	ils/elles	jettent	s'appellent
Imparfait:	je **jetais**, je **m'appelais**		
Passé composé:	j'ai **jeté**, je me suis **appelé**		

Write French equivalents.
a. And your name is...? *(formal)*
b. The dog's name is Cyrano.
c. You *(familiar)* always throw your clothes on the floor! *(par terre)* |

8. Look back at the charts. Are the *imparfait* and *passé composé* forms based on the infinitive stem or the stem with the spelling change? |

9. Use the *imparfait* to give equivalents for these sentences.
a. She used to get up very early.
b. Papa always used to bring friends home. |

10. Now use the *passé composé*.
a. The baby has thrown the carrots on the floor.
b. The children took off their shoes. |

4. More on placement of adjectives

1. Adjectives usually follow the nouns they describe. Here are some you have learned:

affreux/-euse	laid/e	moche
intelligent/-e	merveilleux/-euse	riche
heureux/-euse	célèbre	stupide
jaloux/-se	maigre	

Complete the following sentences with a noun phrase using an appropriate adjective from the list.
a. Cet homme n'est pas intelligent, c'est _____. | un homme stupide
b. Cette chanson n'est pas merveilleuse, c'est _____. | une chanson affreuse
c. Cet enfant n'est pas heureux, c'est _____. | un enfant malheureux

2. While having coffee together, Anne tells Guy who some of the people in the café are. Rewrite each sentence, using the adjective provided.
   Modèle: Cet homme est musicien. (roux) |
   Cet homme roux est musicien.
a. Cette femme est journaliste. (maigre)
b. Ces gens sont architectes. (curieux)
c. Cet homme est un écrivain célèbre. (laid) |

a. Cette femme maigre est journaliste.   b. Ces gens curieux sont architectes.
c. Cet homme laid est un écrivain célèbre.

4. Adjectives of color usually follow the noun. Remember that *marron* and *orange* have only one form; and note that *marron* refers to clothing and objects, while *brun* refers to hair and complexion. Tell what Anne-Marie is packing for her weekend trip. Recall the color (*Vocabulaire* p. 275), then write the noun phrase that completes each sentence.
   Modèle: Elle prend une jupe *(brown)*. |
   une jupe marron
a. Elle prend une robe *(white)* et sa veste *(violet)*. |
   une robe blanche, sa veste violette
b. Elle a un imperméable *(green)* et des chaussures *(black)*. |
   un imperméable vert, des chaussures noires

5. Write the complete sentence, placing the adjective. (See key.)
a. Le directeur est un _____ homme _____. (sympathique)
b. Mon frère a une _____ voiture _____. (vieux)
c. Tu porte des _____ chaussures _____. (élégant)
d. M. Delisle habite dans un _____ appartement _____. (petit)

À Propos!   *Tell the color of items of clothing you like a lot.* J'aime beaucoup mon/ ma....

5. The partitive and adjectives in the plural

1. Although most French adjectives follow the noun, some of the most often-used adjectives usually precede the noun (*bon, beau, gros, petit, mauvais, vieux,* etc.) When they are used in the plural, something happens to the partitive article. Read these sentences:

C'est un film intéressant.   Ce sont des films intéressants.
C'est un bon film.   Ce sont de bons films.

In the sentences above, the marker *des* becomes _____ when it is used with an ajective that comes before the noun. |

> de (This use of *de* before a plural adjective is changing. The rule is often violated, especially in informal speech and in adjective-noun groups of great frequency, such as *des petits pois.*)

2. Rewrite each sentence below to start with *C'est* or *Ce sont.* Then read each sentence aloud.

   Modèle: Ce restaurant est petit. |
   > C'est un petit restaurant.

   a. Ce gâteau est bon.
   b. Ces tables sont vieilles.
   c. Cette fille est jolie.
   d. Ces musiciens sont mauvais.
   e. Cet éléphant est vieux.
   f. Cet appartement est beau. |

   > a. C'est un bon gâteau.   b. Ce sont de vieilles tables.   c. C'est une jolie fille.
   > d. Ce sont de mauvais musiciens.   e. C'est un vieil éléphant.   f. C'est un bel appartement.

6. The imperative

In this part you will learn how to give commands in French, using the *vous* form and the *nous* form of the imperative.

1. Here's a command addressed to *vous: Prenez une feuille de papier.* Which word expresses the action of the command? |
   > Prenez

2. a. Even though no subject pronoun appears in *Prenez une feuille de papier,* a subject is implied or understood. What is it? |
   > vous

   b. Compare *Prenez une feuille de papier* and *Vous prenez une feuille de papier.* Is the imperative of the verb the same as, or different from, the form that is used with *vous?* |
   > the same as (The imperative of all but a few verbs is identical to the present tense.)

3. Complete each sentence with the imperative of the verb given.
   a. *(donner)* _____ vingt francs à la vendeuse. |
   > a. Donnez

   b. *(téléphoner à)* _____ vos parents à huit heures. |
   > b. Téléphonez à

   c. *(venir)* _____ chez moi demain soir. |
   > c. Venez

d. *(prendre)* _____ vos affaires, s'il vous plaît. | d. Prenez
e. *(faire)* _____ une bonne soupe pour ce soir. | e. Faites

4. As in English, the imperative may be used more as a suggestion than as a command. Read this ad for a resort on the *Côte d'Azur* (the French Riviera).

Pour des vacances parfaites°...   perfect

Vous êtes fatigué°? Vous voulez prendre des vacances? Alors, pour des vacances parfaites, venez à l'Auberge° de la Couronne d'Or°. Laissez° vos problèmes chez vous! Passez vos journées à la plage, jouez au tennis, au golf, aux boules. Faites de la voile° ou allez à la pêche.° Le soir, prenez votre dîner dans notre restaurant quatre étoiles.° La Couronne d'Or, c'est le paradis sur terre°!

tired
Inn / Golden Crown
leave
go sailing
go fishing
four stars (very high quality) / on earth

a. Write English equivalents for *Venez à l'Auberge de la Couronne d'Or!* and *Laissez vos problèmes chez vous!* |
Come to the Gold Crown Inn! Leave your problems at home!

b. Write the French equivalent of *Play tennis* and *Go sailing.* |
Jouez au tennis. Faites de la voile.

5. Here, someone makes a suggestion. See if you can find it.

Georges: Allons au cinéma. Il y a un bon film ce soir.
Marianne: D'accord, je veux bien.

a. The suggestion is _____. |
Allons au cinéma.

b. *Allons* is another form of the imperative. Is it different from the *nous* form of the present tense? |
no (Most French verbs use identical forms for the present tense and the imperative.)

6. What is the English equivalent of *Allons au cinéma?* |
Let's go to the movies. (The English equivalent of the *nous* form of the imperative begins with *let us* or *let's.* The speaker is then including himself or herself in the group.)

7. Say that you want to do the things suggested below, and write a *nous* command to express the idea of *let us/let's.*
Modèle: Tu veux aller au cinéma? |
Bon, allons au cinéma.

a. Vous voulez jouer au ping-pong? |
Bon, jouons au ping-pong.

b. Il voudrait faire de la voile. |
Bon, faisons de la voile.

c. Tu voudrais faire une promenade? |
Bon, faisons une promenade.

À Propos!   Think of two things you'd like to do soon, and suggest to friends that you all do them.

Dans un magasin parisien. Quoi acheté? Une veste? Une jupe? Les deux?

Vocabulaire

Noms

Les vêtements
le chapeau   *hat*
la chemise   *shirt*
le collant   *pantyhose*
le costume   *man's suit*
les gants   *gloves*
le gilet   *vest*
l'imperméable *m.*   *raincoat*
le maillot de bain   *bathing suit*
le pull   *sweater*
la robe   *dress*
le short   *shorts*
le tailleur   *woman's suit*
le tricot   *sweater*
la veste   *jacket*

Autres mots et expressions

par terre   *on the floor, on the ground*

Verbes

amener   *to bring (someone)*
considérer   *to consider*
devoir (doi-, dev-, doiv-; pp. dû)
   to owe; to have to, must, should,
   ought to
emmener   *to take (someone) along*
enlever   *to take off (something)*
espérer   *to hope*
exagérer   *to exaggerate*
jeter   *to throw*
laisser   *to let, to leave*
mettre (un vêtement)   *to put on*
porter   *to wear*
se promener   *to take a walk*
répéter   *to repeat*
suggérer   *to suggest*

PRÉPARATION 39

Têtu comme une mule!

Stubborn as a mule!

Aux Galeries Lafayette, au rayon des vêtements pour hommes. Une femme et son mari regardent des costumes, des imperméables, des vestes de sport. La femme voit une veste. Elle l'aime beaucoup, mais son mari ne l'aime pas du tout.

At the Galeries Lafayette, in the men's clothing department. A wife and her husband are looking at suits, raincoats, sports jackets. The wife sees a jacket. She likes it very much but her husband doesn't like it at all.

Mari Non, je n'aime pas cette veste, je te dis! Regarde toutes ces couleurs, elles sont horribles.

No, I don't like this jacket, I tell you! Look at all those colors, they're horrible.

Femme Au contraire, elles sont à la mode maintenant.

On the contrary, they're in style now.

Mari À la mode? Pour des étudiants comme Jean-Louis, mais pas pour moi.	In style! For students like Jean-Louis, but not for me.
Femme Mais si, pour toi! Regarde, elle est parfaite avec ton pantalon marron.	But of course, for you; look, it goes perfectly with your brown slacks.
Mari Jamais de la vie! Elle est parfaite pour Jean-Louis. Achetons-lui cette veste pour son anniversaire.	Not on your life! It's perfect for Jean-Louis. Let's buy him this jacket for his birthday.
Femme Jean-Louis! Tu plaisantes. Il porte seulement des jeans et des pulls.	Jean-Louis? You're kidding! He wears only blue jeans and sweaters.
Mari Et cette veste, à mon âge? Tu plaisantes toi aussi!	And that jacket, at *my* age? You must be kidding, too!
Femme Mais, voyons, on doit changer de temps en temps.	But don't you see, one has to change from time to time.
Mari Pourquoi «on doit»? Moi, je ne veux pas changer.	What do you mean "one *has* to"? I don't want to change.
Femme Oh toi! Tu es têtu comme une mule.	Oh, you! You're as stubborn as a mule.

Échange d'idées

1. Demandez à un/une camarade s'il/si elle aime porter des vetements à la mode, et pourquoi.
   Demandez-lui quel style et quelles couleurs de vêtements il/elle préfère.

2. You are shopping together.
   S1: Try on a piece of clothing and express your opinion of it.
   S2: Express the opposite opinion and give a reason for it.
   S1: Persist with your opinion (insist on buying the clothing or not buying it).
   S2: Comment on your partner's stubbornness.

Y a-t-il dans votre région des magasins qui ressemblent aux Galeries Lafayette?

1. More about the imperative

1. Are subject pronouns used in French commands?
   no (Invitons Paul.)
2. Write *nous* or *vous* commands, using the cues.
   a. nous: aller aux Galeries Lafayette
      Allons aux Galeries Lafayette!

b. vous: acheter une veste pour Louis |

Achetez une veste pour Louis!

3. Now compare these present tense *tu* forms with their *tu* forms of the imperative.

Tu viens?   Viens vite!
Tu prends ton gros pull?   Prends ton gros pull!

Are the *tu* command forms of *venir* and *prendre* identical to the present tense *tu* forms? |

yes (This is true for most -ir and -re verbs. The -er verbs and a few irregular verbs are different.)

4. Use these verbs to write equivalents for the following sentences: *rendre, attendre, faire, lire, finir.* Then read them aloud.
   a. Wait!
   b. Finish your soup.
   c. Do your homework.
   d. Read the paragraph *(le paragraphe)* that talks about the elections.
   e. Give the guitar back to Sophie. |

a. Attends!   b. Finis ta soupe.   c. Fais tes devoirs.   d. Lis le paragraphe qui parle des élections.   e. Rends la guitare à Sophie.

5. Now compare the verb forms in these sentences:

Tu cherches ton pull.   Cherche ton pull!
Tu vas chez Julie.   Va chez Julie!

   a. What are the *tu* forms of the imperative for *chercher* and *aller?* |

cherche; va

   b. How is the *tu* command of an *-er* verb different from the present tense *tu* form? |

The tu command form drops the final -s: Tu cherches. Cherche!/ Tu vas. Va!

6. Claire is having a dinner for two friends who have just returned from South America. For each sentence below write what she would say in speaking to one friend only.

   Modèle: Prenez du fromage, si vous voulez. |

Prends du fromage, si tu veux.

   a. Passez le pain, s'il vous plaît. |

Passe le pain, s'il te plaît.

   b. Parlez de votre voyage. |

Parle de ton voyage.

   c. Montrez vos photos. |

Montre tes photos.

   d. Si vous savez jouer de la guitare, prenez cette guitare. |

Si tu sais jouer de la guitare, prends cette guitare.

   e. Si vous voulez, chantez une chanson brésilienne! |

Si tu veux, chante une chanson brésilienne!

2. Practice with *devoir* and *il faut*

1. Paul and some friends are going to make a strawberry tart. Say what the following people have to buy.

   Modèle: Paul: des œufs |
   > Paul doit acheter des œufs.

   a. Jeanne: du beurre |
   > Jeanne doit acheter du beurre.

   b. nous: des fraises |
   > Nous devons acheter des fraises.

   c. toi: du sucre |
   > Tu dois acheter du sucre.

   d. vous: du lait |
   > Vous devez acheter du lait.

   e. moi: de la farine *(flour)* |
   > Je dois acheter de la farine.

   f. Raoul et Marc: de la confiture |
   > Raoul et Marc doivent acheter de la confiture.

2. The impersonal expression *il faut* is often used to make a general statement. *Devoir* is used to make a statement directed toward specific persons. Both *devoir* and *il faut* can express many shades of obligation in French, depending on the context and the tone of voice of the speaker. Read the following examples.

   a. A soccer coach is talking to several members of the soccer team: *Pour bien jouer au football, il faut jouer souvent.* Write an English equivalent. |
   > In order to play soccer well, it's necessary to (you must, should) play often.

   b. The next day the coach says to one of the team members: *Pour bien jouer au football, tu dois jouer souvent.* What is the English equivalent? |
   > To play soccer well, you must (you have to, you've got to) play often.

3. In expressing obligation, the forms of *devoir* and the expression *il faut* are followed by a verb in the _____ form. |
   > infinitive

4. When you use the verb *devoir*, you must use the form of the verb that matches the _____. |
   > subject (For example, you use *dois* to match *tu*. *Il faut* never refers to a specific person.)

5. Use *il faut* to say that it's necessary to go to the dentist. |
   > Il faut aller chez le dentiste.

6. Use *devoir* to say that Marc and Alain have to go to the dentist tomorrow. |
   > Demain Marc et Alain doivent aller chez le dentiste.

7. Restate with *devoir*: *Viens avant midi.* |
   > Tu dois venir avant midi.

3. Practice with some irregular verbs

This section gives you practice expressing the ideas of *doing, wanting, being able to,* and *knowing* using *faire, vouloir, pouvoir, savoir* and *connaître.*

1. Complete these sentences with present tense forms of *faire.*
   a. Tu _____ un gâteau au chocolat pour l'anniversaire de Jacqueline?
   b. Nous _____ des courses cet après-midi.
   c. Qu'est-ce que vous _____ ce soir?
   d. Mes cousins _____ du camping en Suisse.

   a. fais b. faisons c. faites d. font

2. Now complete the following sentences with *imparfait* forms of *faire.*
   a. Tous les hivers, Marianne et moi, nous _____ du ski avec ma famille.
   b. Heureusement il _____ toujours beau.
   c. Qu'est-ce que vous _____ à midi?
   d. Tous les soirs ma sœur et mon frère _____ leurs devoirs.

   a. faisions b. faisait c. faisiez d. faisaient

3. Madeleine and Barbara decide to do errands. Say what they want to do and can do. Write appropriate forms of *vouloir* and *pouvoir* for each sentence.

   Modèle: Barbara, tu p_____ venir á Monoprix avec moi? Je v_____ acheter une jupe.

   peux, veux

   a. —Bon, d'accord! Ma cousine v_____ un livre comme cadeau d'anniversaire. Je p_____ l'acheter là-bas.

   veut, peux

   b. —Je v_____ aussi aller au rayon de disques. On p_____ toujours trouver de bons disques de jazz dans ce magasin.

   veux, peut

   c. —Et ensuite nous p_____ aller au café pour prendre quelque chose, d'accord?

   pouvons

4. When Alain and Pierre return from shopping, they discover that they forgot to buy a certain number of items. Complete these sentences with the correct form of the *imparfait* of *vouloir*.

   a. Zut! Je _____ acheter du savon et j'ai oublié.

   b. Ma mère _____ aussi du sucre et du café.

   c. Nous _____ du café hier soir et il n'y en avait pas. |

a. voulais   b. voulait   c. voulions

5. Read these sentences and compare the meanings of the verbs.

Je sais que Lyon est une jolie ville, mais je ne la connais pas. Je voudrais tricoter un pull pour ma mère, mais je ne sais pas tricoter!

   a. Which verb above means *to know something* or *to know factual information*? |

sais (from *savoir*)

   b. Which verb above means *being acquainted with a person* or *being familiar with a place?* |

connais (from *connaître*)

6. Complete these sentences with the appropriate forms of *connaître* or *savoir*.

   Modèle: Vous _____ Paris? Vous _____ où est l'Opéra? |

connaissez, savez

   a. Vous _____ les Fournier? Ma mère les _____ bien. |

connaissez, connaît

   b. Ten years ago Paul and Gisèle spent several years in Europe. Now they are reminiscing. Use the *imparfait*.
Nous _____ bien l'Italie et nous _____ parler italien. |

connaissions, savions

   c. Their friends talk about Paul and Gisèle. Use the *imparfait*.
Ils _____ l'histoire de France, et ils _____ les noms de tous les rois *(kings)*. |

connaissaient, savaient

À Propos!

La dernière fois que vous avez fait des courses, où êtes-vous allé? Qu'est-ce que vous vouliez acheter? Qu'est-ce que vous avez acheté finalement?

4. Negative expressions

1. Transport yourself back to the time of the French Revolution in 1789. Imagine that you are a revolutionary leader in Paris. To stir up the people against the ruling class, in a speech you cry out:

Eux, ils ont du pain! Et nous, nous n'avons pas de pain.
Eux, ils ont de la viande! Et nous, nous n'avons pas de viande.
Eux, ils ont tout! *Et nous, nous n'avons rien!*

a. What does the last line of your speech mean in English? |

   They have everything! And *we* have nothing.

b. In the negative expression *ne...rien, ne* precedes the verb and
   _____ follows it. |

   rien

2. Answer the questions below, using *ne...rien.*
   Modèle: Qu'est-ce qu'il y a sur la table? |

   Il n'y a rien sur la table.

   a. Qu'est-ce que tu manges à midi? |

      Je ne mange rien à midi.

   b. Qu'est-ce que Philippe cherche? |

      Il ne cherche rien.

3. The expression *ne...personne* is used when you are talking about
   people. For example:

   Où sont les étudiants et le professeur? Je ne vois personne.

   a. Write an English equivalent of *Je ne vois personne.* |

      I don't see anyone./I see no one.

   b. Does *ne* precede the verb and *personne* follow the verb, as in
      the case of *ne...pas* and *ne...rien?* |

      yes

   c. Compare the place of *pas, rien, personne* in the *passé composé.*

   Je n'ai pas vu la voiture.   Je n'ai rien vu.
   Je n'ai pas vu le conducteur *(driver).*   Je n'ai vu personne.

   Which ones are placed right after the auxiliary? |

   pas and *rien* (*Personne* is the exception; it follows the past participle instead of preceding it.)

4. Contradict each statement below with *ne...personne* or *ne...rien,* according to the context.
   Modèle: Ce matin il y a beaucoup de monde sur la plage. |

   Mais non, ce matin il n'y a personne sur la plage.

   a. Paul connaît quelqu'un ici. |

      Mais non, Paul ne connaît personne ici.

   b. Tu as regardé un film à la télévision. |

      Mais non, je n'ai rien regardé à la télévision.

   c. Ils ont vu leurs amis au stade. |

      Mais non, ils n'ont vu personne au stade. (Did you remember that *personne* follows the
      past participle?)

5. Write equivalents: *Ils n'ont parlé à personne. Je n'ai rien vu.* |

   They haven't talked to anyone./They didn't talk to anyone.
   I didn't see anything./I haven't seen anything.

6. These sentences contrast the meanings of *sometimes* and *never*.

—Tu manges quelquefois dans ce restaurant?

—Non, je ne mange jamais dans ce restaurant.

a. Write an English equivalent for *Non, je ne mange jamais dans ce restaurant.* |

> I never eat in this restaurant.

b. In the *passé composé*, you would say *Je n'ai jamais mangé dans ce restaurant.* Is *jamais* placed like *rien* or like *personne*? |

> like *rien* (between the auxiliary and the past participle)

7. The Ledoux children have become very unruly. Use *ne...jamais* to say that they never do what they are supposed to.

Modèle: Ils doivent téléphoner à leurs grands-parents. |

> Ils ne téléphonent jamais à leurs grands-parents.

a. Robert doit aider sa petite sœur. |

> Robert n'aide jamais sa petite sœur.

b. Julie doit préparer la salade. |

> Julie ne prépare jamais la salade.

8. *Jamais* can be used with *de* + a noun to mean *never any*.

Cet homme est végétarien, donc il ne mange pas de viande et il n'achète jamais de viande.

Write an English equivalent of *Il n'achète jamais de viande.* |

> He never buys any meat. (Like *pas de*, *jamais de* may be used with either count or measure nouns in a negative sentence.)

9. Use *prendre* and *ne... jamais de* to answer these questions about what people eat and drink.

a. Tu vas prendre du thé? |

> Non, je ne prends jamais de thé.

b. Est-ce que Marc veut un dessert? |

> Non, il ne prend jamais de dessert.

c. Est-ce que Lise va prendre de l'eau minérale? |

> Non, elle ne prend jamais d'eau minérale.

5. Practice with direct object pronouns

1. Write a complete sentence to answer each question below. Follow the cues and use a direct-object pronoun in each answer.

Modèle: Tu me vois? (non) |

> Non, je ne te vois pas.

a. Il fait froid. Veux-tu mon cardigan rose? (oui) |

> Oui, je le voudrais. (Oui, je le veux.)

b. Donnes-tu ta guitare à Sophie? (oui) |

> Oui, je la donne a Sophie.

c. Robert et Jean-Pierre, vous cherchez Michèle? (non)

   Non, nous ne la cherchons pas.

2. Answer each question below, using a direct object pronoun and the additional information in parentheses.

   Modèle: Vous invitez les Depardieu pour quel week-end? (le week-end du 27)

   Nous les invitons pour le week-end du 27.

   a. À qui est-ce que tu donnes ta guitare? (à Sophie)
   b. Comment trouvez-vous cette suggestion? (utile)
   c. Est-ce que Laurent t'emmène à la boum? (non, malheureusement)
   d. Est-ce que Laurent considère les conséquences de sa décision? (oui, bien sûr)
   e. Vous trouvez Laurent têtu? (oui, comme une mule!)

   a. Je la donne à Sophie.   b. Je la trouve (nous la trouvons) utile.   c. Non, malheureusement, il ne m'emmène pas à la boum.   d. Oui, bien sûr, il les considère.   e. Oui, je le trouve têtu comme une mule!

Vocabulaire

Noms

la mule *mule*
le clown *clown*
le mariage *wedding*
le/la photographe *photographer*
la danse classique *ballet dancing*
le paragraphe *paragraph*
la farine *flour*
le savon *soap*
la ville *city, town*
le champagne *champagne*

Adjectifs

têtu/e *stubborn*
horrible *horrible*
brésilien/ne *Brazilian*
fort/e (en qqch) *strong; good (in something)*

Expressions de négation

ne...rien *nothing, not...anything*
ne...personne *nobody, not...anybody*
ne...jamais *never*
ne...jamais de *never any*

Autres mots et expressions

à la mode *in fashion, fashionable*
après-demain *the day after tomorrow*
au contraire *on the contrary*
de temps en temps *from time to time*
donc *thus*
encore *again; some more*
maintenant *now*
pour *in order to*
quelqu'un *someone*
quelque chose *something*
quelquefois *sometimes*
qui (pronom relatif) *who, which*
récemment *recently*
seulement *only*
toute l'année *all year*
toute la journée *all day*

Note Culturelle

French clothing and shoe sizes

If you went to a French department store, you might at first have some difficulty finding clothes in your size. French *tailles* (clothing sizes) and *pointures* (shoe sizes) differ considerably from American sizes. However, airlines and some large department stores try to help American tourists by publishing conversion charts for sizes. Some of the ranges are given here.

		French	*American*
Men	Suits:	34–52	34–46
	Sweaters:	46–59	36–46
	Shoes:	41–46	9–13

Women	Dresses:	40–48	10–16
	Sweaters:	40–48	32–40
	Shoes:	36–43	6–10

Of course, the size you take will depend on the cut of the dress or suit, and may vary from store to store, just as it often does in the United States.

Mannequins dans une vitrine (display window) de grand magasin.

PRÉPARATION 40

1. Practice with *devoir*, clothing, and colors

The Larose family is going to the wedding of a close friend. Say what clothes they have to buy, using the verb *devoir*.

Modèle: Je/acheter/ /vert |

Je dois acheter une robe verte.

1. Patrice et Marc/acheter/ /noir

Patrice et Marc doivent acheter des chaussures noires.

2. M. Larose/acheter/ /gris |

M. Larose doit acheter une veste grise.

3. tu/acheter/ /gris

Tu dois acheter des chaussettes grises.

4. Mme Larose/acheter/ /bleu |

Mme Larose doit acheter un chemisier bleu.

5. nous/acheter/ /blanc |

Nous devons acheter des gants blancs.

2. The verb *mettre*

1. Compare the meaning of *mettre* in these sentences:

Julie met son imperméable.   *Julie is putting on her raincoat.*
Qu'est-ce que vous mettez dans   *What are you putting in your*
votre sac?   *pocketbook?*

When *mettre* is used with articles of clothing, it usually means
_____. In another context *mettre* can mean _____. |

to put on; to put something somewhere

2. *Mettre,* like many of the slightly irregular verbs in French, has
one stem in the singular and a second stem in the plural.

Présent:		je	**mets**	nous	**mett**ons
		tu	mets	vous	mettez
	on/il/elle	met		ils/elles	mettent

Passé composé: **j'ai mis**
Imparfait: **je mettais**

The plural stem *mett-* is the same as the infinitive stem *mett-*.
Which stem is used in the singular forms of the verb? |

met-

3. The following people decide to put on what they have just bought
at the *marché aux puces* (flea market). Complete the sentences with
mettre.

   Modèle: Philippe _____ sa cravate de soie *(silk)*. |

   met

   a. Nous _____ nos chapeaux rouges. |
   b. Tu _____ ton grand manteau noir. |
   c. Anne et Nathalie _____ de vieux gants violets. |
   d. Jules _____ son pantalon de clown. |

   a. mettons
   b. mets
   c. mettent
   d. met

4. Tell what clothing each person is putting on or did put on for
the occasion stated. Use *mettre* in the present, the *imparfait,* or the
passé composé. (See key.)

   Modèle: Marianne va jouer au tennis. (short, manteau, col-
   lant) |

   Elle met un short.

   a. Tous les matins M. Legrand allait au bureau. (maillot de bain,
   costume, jean)
   b. Nous allons à la plage. (chaussettes, maillot de bain, veste)
   c. Vous aviez toujours froid aux pieds. (chaussettes, gants, chapeau)
   d. Rosalie et Charles voient qu'il pleut. (imperméable, jupe, gilet)
   e. Hier tu as joué au basket. (maillot de bain, gilet, short et chemise)

À *Propos!*

Est-ce que vous avez mis du sucre dans votre café ou votre thé au
petit déjeuner?

3. Adverbs of time

This section will give you practice with the meanings of some common adverbial expressions of time.

après	quelquefois	tard	tout de suite
avant	rarement	tôt	toute l'année
encore	souvent	toujours	toute la journée
jamais			tout à l'heure

1. Choose the correct English equivalent for the French phrase.
   Modèle: Françoise travaille *toute la journée* dans une banque. *(all day, all the while)*
   all day

   a. *Quelquefois* je vais au café des Artistes avec elle. *(every time, sometimes)*
   b. Là, on trouve *toujours* des amis. *(always, all day)*
   c. Nous jouons *souvent* aux échecs. *(never, often)*
   d. Françoise va passer *toute l'année* à Toulouse. *(all week, all year)*
   e. Elle doit prendre le train très *tôt* demain. *(early, late)*
   f. Elle va arriver *tard* à Toulouse. *(tomorrow, late)*
   g. Je dois lui téléphoner *tout de suit!* *(early, right away)*

   a. sometimes
   b. always
   c. often
   d. all year
   e. early
   f. late
   g. right away

2. Max is going to spend a year in the United States and has many questions about the climate in some parts of the country. Write the word or phrase that best answers his questions. (See key.)
   a. Est-ce qu'il neige à Miami en juillet?
      oui, souvent   oui, quelquefois   non, jamais
   b. Est-ce qu'il pleut dans le Nevada en été?
      oui, toujours   rarement   oui, souvent
   c. Est-ce qu'il neige dans le Vermont en mars?
      oui, quelquefois   rarement   non, jamais

4. Telling what other people say

In direct quotations, someone reports the exact words of a speaker.

   Paul says, *"I'm going to the movies."*
In indirect quotations, someone reports that a speaker says something.

   Paul says *that* he's going to the movies.
Notice that we change Paul's words *"I'm going . . ."* to our words *"He's going . . ."*.

In this section you'll learn how to express indirect quotations similarly in French.

1. Who reports what someone else says—Monique or Edouard? Write the sentence.

Monique: Tu veux aller au cinéma?

Edouard: Non. Mon frère dit que le film n'est pas bon. |

Edouard: Mon frère dit que le film n'est pas bon.

Jeune couple devant une boutique du Quartier latin.

2. Does Edouard report the exact words used by his brother?

   not necessarily (His brother might have said *"Le film est affreux," "C'est un mauvais film,"* etc.)

3. In *Il dit que le film n'est pas bon,* which word links *il dit* with *le film n'est pas bon?*

   que

4. What does *que* mean? *My brother says _____ the film isn't good.*

   that

5. In English, the linking word *that* is not necessary in order for the sentence to make sense. In French the linking word *que* is always necessary in indirect quotations. Rewrite the following statement to report what the speaker says. Be sure to use *que.* Jeanne dit: Cette chemise est jolie.

   Jeanne dit que cette chemise est jolie.

7. Write French equivalents for these sentences: *Alain says: "I'm hungry." Alain says (that) he's hungry.*

   Alain dit: J'ai faim. Alain dit qu'il a faim.

8. In frame 7 the indirect quotation beginning with *je* is reported using the subject pronoun _____.

   il (A direct quote beginning with *je* or *nous* is reported with the *il/elle* or *ils/elles* subject pronouns and verb forms, and corresponding changes in possessive markers.)

9. Report what each person is saying by writing an indirect quotation.
   a. Jean-Luc dit: Je vais au stade avec Jean-Paul.

      Jean-Luc dit qu'il va au stade avec Jean-Paul.

   b. Anne dit: Ma robe n'est pas jolie.

      Anne dit que sa robe n'est pas jolie.

10. Rewrite as indirect quotations. (See key.)
    a. Marie dit: Ma voiture est belle.
    b. Marcel dit: Je dois travailler.
    c. Jacques dit: Pierre et moi, nous pouvons aller à la plage.

Vocabulaire

Noms

le costume   *costume*
le métro   *subway*
la perruque   *wig*
le prêt-à-porter   *ready-to-wear*
le transistor   *portable radio*
la valise   *suitcase*
le velours   *velvet*

Adjectifs

indien/indienne   *Indian*
médiocre   *mediocre*

Verbes

mettre (met-, mett-; pp. mis)   *to put; to put on*
porter   *to wear*

Autres mots et expressions

d'où...?   *where...from?*
près d'ici   *nearby*
que   *that (conjunction)*

PRÉPARATION 41

La fête du Mardi Gras

Bertrand Tu viens à la fête du Mardi Gras?

Isabelle Bien sûr! J'ai déjà mon costume.

Bertrand Ah oui? Qu'est-ce que tu vas être?

Isabelle Devine! Je vais porter une veste de velours et un pantalon de soie.

Bertrand Ça ne veut rien dire! Tu peux être un homme ou une femme!

Isabelle Tu as raison. Alors, je vais être un homme, avec une magnifique perruque blanche.

Bertrand Un homme? Avec une perruque? Je n'y comprends absolument rien.

Isabelle Écoute. Tu vas comprendre tout de suite. Je suis très important et très célèbre. J'ai une femme très belle, qui adore les fêtes et les bals.

Bertrand Je ne connais personne comme ça.

Isabelle Mais si, tu connais, je te dis. Écoute. Qui a dit: "S'ils n'ont pas de pain, qu'ils mangent de la brioche?"

Bertrand Ah, Marie-Antoinette, bien sûr! Alors, tu vas être Louis XVI?

Isabelle C'est ça! Tu peux être Marie-Antoinette, si tu veux!

Bertrand Non, merci! Je préfère être la guillotine!

Mardi Gras party

Are you going to the Mardi Gras party?

Of course! I already have my costume.

Oh you have? What are you going as?

Guess! I'm going to wear a velvet jacket and silk trousers.

That doesn't mean anything. You could be a man or a woman.

You're right. Well, I'm going as a man with a magnificent white wig.

A man! With a wig! I don't get it at all.

Listen. You'll understand right away. I'm very important and very famous. I have a very beautiful wife, who loves parties and balls.

I don't know anyone like that.

Of course, you do, I tell you! Listen. Who said: "If they don't have any bread, let them eat cake?" (*Brioche* is a rich sweet roll.)

Oh, Marie-Antoinette, naturally. So you're going as Louis XVI?

That's it! You can be Marie-Antoinette, if you like!

No, thanks, I prefer to be the guillotine!

Échange d'idées

1. Demandez à un/une camarade de classe s'il/si elle a vécu (*has lived*) dans un pays gouverné par un roi ou une reine (*king or queen*). Demandez-lui comment était l'expérience.

   Demandez-lui ce qu'il/elle pense des monarques absolues. Est-ce qu'il en existe (*are there any*) de nos jours?

2. S1: You are going to a *bal masqué* next week. Pick a historical or fictional character you want to be. Give your partner one or two clues about your costume.

S2: Say, "You must be kidding!" or otherwise express your sense of confusion.

S1: Give more clues about your character, such as: man, woman, when you lived, what it is you're famous for.

S2: If you've guessed, express triumph; if you can't guess, express your regret and exasperation.

1. Reading comprehension

This reading gives you some background information about *le Mardi Gras*.

Read the questions that precede each paragraph. Read the paragraph, then write brief answers in French to the questions. No answers are given in the book. Some words are given in the margin. Cognates are not given.

1. À Nice et à Cannes fait-il beau ou mauvais en général?
2. Est-ce que le Carnaval d'aujourd'hui est une fête religieuse ou une fête folklorique?

Le Carnaval sur la Côte d'Azur

Nice et Cannes sont deux villes sur la Côte d'Azur, dans le Midi de la France. La région est renommée° pour son climat tempéré°, ses fleurs° et ses parfums. Les deux villes sont célèbres aussi pour leurs fêtes du Carnaval. Ces fêtes durent° une semaine au début du printemps. Le Carnaval, une grande fête d'origine religieuse, est aujourd'hui une fête folklorique et populaire.

famous / temperate

flowers

last

Now that you've read the paragraph, look back at questions 1 and 2, and write brief answers in French.

3. Que font les gens pour le Mardi Gras?
4. Quelles sortes de personnages y a-t-il dans les chars?

Le Mardi Gras est le dernier° jour du Carnaval. L'atmosphère est gaie. Les gens° sont joyeux.° Ils dansent, ils chantent, ils s'amusent° beaucoup! À Nice il y a des défilés° qui passent sur la Promenade des Anglais (la plus grande° avenue de Nice). On voit des chars° avec beaucoup de jolies fleurs. Sur les chars il y a des personnages en costume. Ce sont des personnages historiques, ou bien° des personnages de légende. Les spectateurs regardent le défilé, mais ils sont là aussi pour les batailles° de fleurs et de confettis.

last

people / merry / enjoy
themselves / parades

the longest / floats

or else

battles

Now write brief answers to questions 3 and 4. Then continue reading.

5. Que portent les danseurs le soir du Mardi Gras? À votre avis, c'est amusant *(fun)* de porter un costume de Carnaval?
6. Aux États-Unis, quand voit-on des feux d'artifice, le 25 décembre ou le 4 juillet?

Le soir du Mardi Gras, il y a souvent des fêtes et des bals. On les appelle° des bals masqués parce que les danseurs portent des costumes et des masques. À Nice, ce soir-là, Sa Majesté° Carnaval (le mannequin grotesque° qui représente l'esprit du Carnaval) est jeté° dans la mer°. Il y a des feux d'artifice° merveilleux.

they are called
king, his majesty
giant doll or puppet /
thrown / sea / fireworks

Answer questions 5 and 6 briefly. Then read the last section.

7. La fête du Carnaval est célébrée dans deux îles *(islands)* de notre hémisphère. Quelles sont ces îles?
8. Quelle est la ville américaine où on célèbre la fête du Mardi Gras? Cette grande fête est célébrée également° en Martinique et en Guadeloupe, à Quebec, à la Nouvelle Orléans, et dans d'autres pays° où cette tradition continue.

also
other countries

Write answers for questions 7 and 8.

À Propos! Avez-vous jamais *(ever)* aidé à construire un char? Quelle est la dernière fois que vous avez mis un costume de carnaval?

2. Indirect object pronouns

1. Read this conversation, and see if you can give the meaning of *lui*.

—Tu parles à Henri? —Oui, je lui parle.

a. Write an English equivalent for *Je lui parle.* |
b. Write the phrase that *lui* replaces. |
c. Does *lui* precede or follow the verb? |

a. I'm talking to him. b. à Henri c. precede

2. Now look carefully at this conversation.

—Tu parles à Marie? —Oui, je lui parle.

a. Write an English equivalent for *Je lui parle.* |

I'm talking to her.

b. What phrase does *lui* replace? |

à Marie

3. The indirect-object pronoun *lui* can refer to either a _____ or a _____. |

   man, woman (male, female)

4. Here is another conversational exchange.

   —Tu parles à Henri et à Marie?   —Oui, je leur parle.

   The English equivalent of *Je leur parle* is *I'm talking to* _____. |

   them

5. A direct object noun usually answers the question *whom?* or *what?* An indirect object noun usually answers the question *to whom?* or *for whom?* Read this sentence, which contains both a direct object and an indirect object: *Je donne un livre à Paul.*
   a. What is the speaker giving? |
   b. To whom is the speaker giving the book? |
   c. The direct object noun phrase is _____. |
   d. The indirect object noun phrase is _____. |
   e. In the indirect object noun phrase, *Paul* is preceded by the preposition _____. |

   a. un livre
   b. à Paul
   c. un livre
   d. à Paul
   e. à

6. In French, the indirect object pronouns *lui* and *leur* usually replace the preposition *à* + a noun or noun phrase. Read the pairs of sentences below. Write the phrase from the first sentence that is replaced by *lui* or *leur* in the second.
   a. Je téléphone à Louise et à Hélène. Je leur téléphone. |

      à Louise et à Hélène

   b. Elle parle à son copain et à sa copine. Elle leur parle. |

      à son copain et à sa copine

   c. Vous donnez un disque à la cousine de Claire? Vous lui donnez un disque? |

      à la cousine de Claire

Here are some common verbs that take an indirect object pronoun. *Qqch* and *qqn* are abbreviations for *quelque chose* (something) and *quelqu'un* (someone).

acheter qqch à qqn	*to buy something for someone*
demander qqch à qqn	*to ask someone for something*
demander à qqn de faire qqch	*to ask someone to do something*
dire qqch à qqn	*to tell something to someone*
donner qqch à qqn	*to give someone something*
montrer qqch à qqn	*to show someone something*
parler à qqn	*to speak to someone*
téléphoner à qqn	*to call someone (on the phone)*

With most of these English verbs, both things and persons can be direct objects (i.e. without a preposition). With these French verbs, the *thing* is always the direct object, and the *person* is always the indirect object.

7. Answer each question below with *Oui* and *lui* or *leur*. Read your answers aloud.
  a. Est-ce que tu téléphones à Brigitte? |
     Oui, je lui téléphone.
  b. Est-ce que tu donnes un livre à Robert et à Jean? |
     Oui, je leur donne un livre.
  c. Vous parlez à cet homme? |
     Oui, je lui parle.
  d. Vous donnez des stylos à vos copains? |
     Oui, je leur donne des stylos.

8. Answer the questions by saying that you are showing pictures of your trip *(les photos de mon voyage)*. Say, then write your answers.
  a. Qu'est-ce que tu montres à ta cousine? |
     Je lui montre les photos de mon voyage.
  b. Qu'est-ce que tu montres au professeur? |
     Je lui montre les photos de mon voyage.
  c. Qu'est-ce que tu montres aux parents de ton camarade? |
     Je leur montre les photos de mon voyage.

9. There are four other indirect object pronouns besides *lui* and *leur*.

Mélanie me donne son adresse.	*Mélanie gives her address to me.*
Je vais te téléphoner demain.	*I'm going to call you tomorrow.*
Il nous montre les photos.	*He shows the photographs to us.*
Pierre va vous parler de son voyage.	*Pierre is going to talk to you about his trip.*

10. Compare all the indirect object pronouns with the direct object pronouns.

Direct and indirect object pronouns

Direct:	me	te	nous	vous	**le, la, l', les**
Indirect:	me	te	nous	vous	**lui, leur**

The indirect object pronouns are identical in form to the direct object pronouns except for _____ and _____. |
    lui, leur

11. Write a French equivalent for each sentence below.
  a. I'm talking to you. (Use the *vous* form.) |
     Je vous parle.
  b. He's talking to me. |
     Il me parle.
  c. They're talking to us. |
     Ils/Elles nous parlent.

d. She's talking to you. (Use the object form of *tu*.)
> Elle te parle.

12. You know that an indirect object pronoun usually answers the question *to whom?*
    a. Use *to* to write the English equivalent of *Elle me chante une chanson.*
    > She is singing a song to me.
    b. Write a second English equivalent, without using *to*.
    > She is singing me a song. (The preposition *to* is implied.)

13. Write two English equivalents for *Il nous donne de l'eau.*
> He's giving some water to us./He's giving us some water.

14. As you saw when you learned the direct object pronouns, in a negative sentence, *ne* precedes both the indirect object pronoun and the verb form, and *pas* follows them. For practice, rewrite *Il me parle* in the negative.
> Il ne me parle pas.

15. Pretend there's a lot of noise and you can't figure out who's talking to whom. Answer the questions in the negative.
    Modèle: Louis, est-ce que vous me parlez?
    > Mais non, je ne vous parle pas.
    a. Est-ce qu'il me parle?
    > Mais non, il ne te parle pas (ne vous parle pas).
    b. Est-ce qu'elle nous parle?
    > Mais non, elle ne vous parle pas (ne nous parle pas).
    c. Est-ce que tu me parles?
    > Mais non, je ne te parle pas.

3. Writing a dialogue

Write a dialogue based on *Têtu comme une mule* (p. 293). Be prepared to hand in a copy of it in your next class. Use humor in the situation, but check carefully for word order, spelling, and accents.

Qui s'habille bien vit bien

TED LAPIDUS
PARIS   DIFFUSION

Que pensez-vous de cette devise? ("One who dresses well, lives well.")
D'accord ou non? Et pourquoi?

4. Practice with indirect quotations

1. Compare the following sentences about what Paul says. *Paul dit: J'ai faim. Paul dit qu'il a faim.*
   a. When you report what someone else says, it's often necessary to change the subject pronoun and verb form. In the sentences above, *J'ai* changes to _____. |

   il a

Note Culturelle
Marie-Antoinette and the French Revolution

Marie-Antoinette, daughter of the Austrian emperor Francis I and Queen Maria-Theresa, was married to the French crown prince Louis in 1770 to strengthen the alliance between Austria and France. They were not a well-matched couple: Marie-Antoinette was impulsive and fun-loving; Louis XVI was serious-minded and indecisive.

When Louis XVI came to the throne in 1774, France's rising middle class (the *bourgeoisie*) was clamoring for reform. Marie-Antoinette's court and its childish and extravagant way of life angered the bourgeoisie, who suffered under heavy taxation while the nobility and clergy paid no taxes at all. Inspired by liberal ideas from England (such as the English constitutional system, which guaranteed representation of all the people), the French people were becoming more and more dissatisfied with their lot.

Marie-Antoinette's unpopularity increased as she became involved in court intrigues with the nobles who resisted reforms. Her name was linked to the courtly extravagance that was considered to be one cause of the disastrous financial situation in France. If the king had not hesitated to carry out the financial reforms presented by his minister Turgot, he might have saved the monarchy. His wife, however, had no conception of the need for reform and economy. History has recorded her complete lack of understanding of the starvation menacing her people, shown by this remark she allegedly made: *"S'ils n'ont pas de pain, qu'ils mangent de la brioche." Brioche,* a roll rich in eggs and butter, was something a poor person could not buy in the best of times, much less when bread was scarce.

The tide of history abruptly turned against Marie-Antoinette on July 14, 1789, when the Parisians stormed the Bastille prison, which had long been a symbol of the monarchy's authority. Several weeks later, the Parisian townspeople took over the Tuileries palace and imprisoned the royal family, who tried several times to escape, but without success. Louis XVI was executed in January 1793. After a brief trial on October 14, 1793, Marie-Antoinette was sentenced to death. She was guillotined on the *Place de la Révolution* (now *Place de la Concorde*) two days later. Eyewitnesses reported that she was calm and dignified as she went to her fate.

b. The linking word *que* becomes ____ before *il* or *elle*. |

> qu' (because of *élision*)

2. Suppose you report to a friend what color Jeanne says her bicycle is. You could say *Jeanne dit: Mon vélo est jaune* or *Jeanne dit que son vélo est jaune*. When you turn the direct quotation into an indirect quotation, the possessive *mon* becomes ____. |

> son (You have to remember to change the possessive so that the new sentence makes sense.)

3. Now report what the following people say:

   Modèle: Alain: Il fait très beau.

   Roger: Mais non, il fait mauvais. |

> Alain dit qu'il fait très beau. Roger dit qu'il fait mauvais.

   a. *Nanette:* Mes cousins viennent demain.

   Philippe: Ma tante Lucie vient ce soir. |

> Nanette dit que ses cousins viennent demain. Philippe dit que sa tante Lucie vient ce soir.

   b. *Barbara:* J'aime jouer au tennis.

   Robert: Je préfère jouer au basket. |

> Barbara dit qu'elle aime jouer au tennis. Robert dit qu'il préfère jouer au basket.

   c. *Pierre:* Ma couleur préférée est le vert.

   Renée: Moi, je déteste le vert. |

> Pierre dit que sa couleur préférée est le vert. Renée dit qu'elle déteste le vert.

Vocabulaire

Noms

le bal *ball, dance*
la brioche *sweet roll*
le château *castle*
les gens *people*
la guillotine *guillotine*
le membre *member*
la raquette de tennis *tennis racket*
la soie *silk*

Adjectifs

magnifique *magnificent*

Autres mots et expressions

absolument *absolutely*
bien sûr *naturally*
lui (indirect object pronoun) *to her/ him*
leur (indirect object pronoun) *to them*
rien du tout *nothing at all*

Verbes

Verbs taking an indirect object pronoun
acheter qqch à qqn *to buy something for someone*
demander qqch à qqn *to ask someone something*
dire qqch à qqn *to say something to someone*
donner qqch à qqn *to give something to someone*
montrer qqch à qqn *to show something to someone*
parler à qqn *to talk, speak to someone*
téléphoner à qqn *to telephone someone*

PRÉPARATION 42

1. More on object pronouns

This part will help you decide when to use the direct object pronouns *le, la, les* and when to use the indirect object pronouns *lui, leur.*

1. Read the following question and the two responses.

   —Tu donnes ce gilet à ton   —Oui, je le donne à mon
      frère?   frère.
                               —Oui, je lui donne ce gilet.

  a. Which noun phrase does *le* replace—*à ton frère* or *ce gilet?*
                    ce gilet

  b. Does *ce gilet* follow the verb directly or does it follow the preposition *à?*
                It follows the verb directly. (In French, direct object noun phrases usually follow the verb directly.)

  c. Which question does the direct object pronoun *le* answer—*what?* or *to whom?*
                what (*Qu'est-ce que* tu donnes à ton frère?)

2. Look at the example at the beginning of frame 1 again.
  a. Which noun phrase does *lui* replace—*ce gilet* or *à ton frère?*
                à ton frère

  b. Does *ton frère* follow the verb directly?
                no (In French, most indirect object noun phrases follow a form of the preposition *à.*)

  c. Which question does the indirect object pronoun *lui* answer—*what?* or *to whom?*
                to whom (*À qui* donnes-tu ce gilet? —À mon frère.)

3. Rewrite each of the following sentences, substituting the appropriate object pronoun—*le, la, les* or *lui, leur*—for the italicized noun phrase.
    Modèle: Ma mère parle *à son amie Michèle.*
          Ma mère lui parle.

  a. Je donne *ces trois disques* à mon ami Yves.
          Je les donne à mon ami Yves.

  b. Ils montrent le film *aux petits garçons.*
          Ils leur montrent le film.

  c. J'achète *cette chemise rouge.*
          Je l'achète.

d. Elizabeth chante une chanson *à son petit frère.*

        Elle lui chante une chanson.

4. Many English verbs contain a preposition as part of the verb; e.g., *to look at.* Prepositions do not always occur in the French equivalents, however; e.g., *regarder.*

5. Compare the French infinitive phrases below with their English equivalents.

écouter qqch/qqn	*to listen to something/to someone*
chercher qqch/qqn	*to look for something/for someone*
regarder qqch/qqn	*to look at something/at someone*

These French verbs take a direct object:

—Qu'est-ce que tu écoutes?   —J'écoute la radio./Je l'écoute.

Write French equivalents for each pair of sentences below.

a. I'm looking for Nancy's dog. I'm looking for it.

        Je cherche le chien de Nancy. Je le cherche.

b. We're listening to Jean's records. We're listening to them.

        Nous écoutons les disques de Jean. Nous les écoutons.

c. He's looking at that old bicycle. He's looking at it.

        Il regarde ce vieux vélo. Il le regarde.

6. Sometimes, on the other hand, French verbs use a preposition when their English equivalents do not. Some of them are listed in Préparation 41 (p. 311). English speakers often need extra practice in deciding when to use the preposition or the indirect object pronoun with these verbs. Use caution as you give the French equivalent of the sentences below.

a. Mme Prévot is calling her lawyer.

        Mme Prevot téléphone à son avocat.

b. Margot is showing him a book.

        Margot lui montre un livre.

c. Georges is giving them these shoes.

        Georges leur donne ces chaussures.

d. We call her often.

        Nous lui téléphonons souvent.

e. I asked them for their address.

        Je leur ai demandé leur adresse.

8. Now answer the following questions with the cue in parentheses and replace the italic phrases with the appropriate object pronouns.

a. Qu'est-ce que Jacques donne *à Mathieu?* (sa guitare)

b. Qu'est-ce que vous montrez *à vos grands-parents?* (un joli livre)

c. À qui est-ce qu'il montre *ses devoirs?* (au professeur)

d. À qui donnent-elles *cette jupe?* (à Mlle André)

        a. Il lui donne sa guitare.   b. Je leur montre un joli livre.   c. Il les montre au professeur.   d. Elles la donnent à Mlle André.

2. Articles with food and abstract nouns

1. The Lefranc family has gathered *chez tante Monique* for a Sunday dinner, and everyone is saying how good the food is. Write the exclamations.

   Modèle: cidre/bon |

   Que le cidre est bon!

   a. pommes de terres/bonnes
   b. poulet/bon
   c. tarte aux pommes/bonne |

   a. Que les pommes de terres sont bonnes!   b. Que le poulet est bon!   c. Que la tarte aux pommes est bonne!

2. Write a phrase to ask for some of each food below. Use the appropriate article—*un, une, des* or *du, de la, de l'.*

   Modèle: poire |

   Une poire, s'il vous plaît.

   a. bonbons   c. poisson
   b. thé   d. glace à la vanille |

   a. Des bonbons, s'il vous plaît.   b. Du thé, s'il vous plaît.   c. Du poisson, s'il vous plaît.   d. Une glace/De la glace à la vanille, s'il vous plaît.

3. Say that you don't want any of what is being offered.

   Modèle: des carottes |

   Pas de carottes, merci.

   a. du café   c. de l'eau
   b. des cerises   d. un fruit |

   a. Pas de café, merci.   b. Pas de cerises, merci.   c. Pas d'eau, merci.   d. Pas de fruit, merci.

4. Abstract nouns are considered to be measure nouns, and so partitive articles are used with them. Write an equivalent of this sentence:

   Il y a de l'humour dans les pièces *(plays)* de Thornton Wilder. |

   There is humor in Thornton Wilder's plays.

À Propos!

Write the name of a novel, play, or story you have read recently. Tell whether it has or has not any of these qualities.

Il y a du/de la/de l'... Il n'y a pas ...

le courage	le réalisme
l'amour *m. (love)*	la fantaisie
l'humour *f.*	la tristesse *(sadness)*
la passion	

3. The imperative and direct object pronouns

You learned in Phases 3 and 4 how to use direct object pronouns in affirmative and negative statements: *Je l'achète. Je ne l'achète pas.* In this section you'll learn how to use direct object pronouns with the imperative.

1. Compare these commands using the transitive verb *regarder*. (A transitive verb has a direct object answering the question *what?* or *whom?*)

Regarde le vélo!	Regarde-**le**!
Regarde la bicyclette!	Regarde-**la**!
Regarde les vélomoteurs!	Regarde-**les**!

   a. When you use a direct object pronoun with the imperative, does it precede or follow the verb? |

           it follows (just as it does in English: Look at him!)

   b. In writing, what mark of punctuation is used between the verb form and the direct object pronoun? |

           a hyphen

2. Suppose you're trying to convince a friend to buy a second-hand automobile your older brother wants to sell. *C'est une bonne petite voiture.*

   a. Tell your friend to buy it. | a. Achète-la!

   b. Try to convince two friends to buy it. | b. Achetez-la!

   c. Include yourself in the command. | c. Achetons-la!

Vocabulaire

Noms
le cidre   *cider*

Adjectifs
faux/fausse   *false, wrong*
ordinaire   *ordinary*

Verbes
il a dû (+ inf.)   *he must have*

PRÉPARATION 43

1. Practice with *devoir*

In doing this part of the Préparation, remember that *devoir* has various meanings (*to have to* or *must; to be supposed to; must be, must have been,* etc.), depending on the tone of voice and the situation.

1. Rewrite the following sentences, using *devoir* in the present or the imparfait.

> *Modèle:* Je vais chez le dentiste demain. |
>> Je dois aller chez le dentiste demain.

a. Est-ce que vous faisiez vous devoirs hier soir? |
>> Est-ce que vous deviez faire vos devoirs hier soir?

b. Paul et Philippe achetaient des vêtements. |
>> Paul et Philippe devaient acheter des vêtements.

c. Nous déjeunons avec tante Germaine. |
>> Nous devons déjeuner avec tante Germaine.

d. Ta mère travaille à mi-temps. |
>> Ta mère doit travailler à mi-temps.

2. Rewrite each sentence, and use the *a dû* + infinitive phrase to express the idea of *must have (probably)*.

> *Modèle:* Il a acheté son anorak aux États-Unis? |
>> Oui, il a dû l'acheter aux États-Unis.

a. Elle a trouvé son chien qui était perdu? |
>> Oui, elle a dû le trouver.

b. Il est parti sans nous? |
>> Oui, il a dû partir sans nous.

c. Il a téléphoné a Suzanne? |
>> Oui, il a dû lui téléphoner.

2. Writing practice

Tell what articles of clothing Sylvie, Michel, and their friends put on in order to do certain activities. Form complete sentences according to the numbered cues. Be sure to put the adjectives in column A before the noun, and the adjectives in column C after the noun.

A	B	C	D
1. joli	1. pantalon	1. blanc	1. aller au théâtre
2. petit	2. veste	2. jaune	2. faire de la voile
3. grand	3. maillot	3. marron	3. jouer au tennis
4. vieux	4. costume	4. noir	4. aller au restaurant
5. beau	5. chemise	5. rouge	5. faire une promenade
	6. chapeau	6. gris	6. aller au bureau
	7. pardessus	7. bleu	7. aller à la plage

Modèle: Raoul: 4 1 4 2 |
> Raoul met un vieux pantalon noir pour faire de la voile.

a. Serge: 5 7 6 1 |
> Serge met un beau pardessus gris pour aller au théâtre.

b. Michel et Jean: 5 4 4 6 |
> Michel et Jean mettent un beau costume noir pour aller au bureau.

c. Anne: 4 1 3 5 |
> Anne met un vieux pantalon marron pour faire une promenade.

d. Jeanne et Hélène: 2 6 1 3 |
> Jeanne et Hélène mettent un petit chapeau blanc pour jouer au tennis.

e. Pauline: 1 3 7 7 |
> Pauline met un joli maillot bleu pour aller à la plage.

f. Pierre: 5 2 5 4 |
> Pierre met une belle veste rouge pour aller au restaurant.

g. Georges: 4 5 1 2 |
> Georges met une vieille chemise blanche pour faire de la voile.

3. Review practice: spelling-changing verbs

1. a. Say, then write the present tense *je* and *nous* forms of *acheter.* |
   > j'achète, nous achetons

   b. Remember that the *passé composé* and the *imparfait* are regular. Say, then write the *je* form of each tense. |
   > j'ai acheté, j'achetais

2. Complete each sentence with the present tense of *acheter* and the nouns represented by the drawings.

   a. Ces hommes/_____ marron et _____ noirs.

> Ces hommes achètent des chaussures marron et des pantalons noirs.

b. Est-ce que vous/_____ ou _____?

Est-ce que vous achetez une auto ou un vélomoteur?

3. Complete with the *passé composé*.
   a. Hier Jeanne et moi, nous/trois _____ et une _____.

Jeanne et moi, nous avons acheté trois chemisiers et une jupe.

   b. Ma mère/_____ et _____.

Ma mère a acheté des pommes et des cerises.

See key.

4. The verb *manger* has only one spelling change in the present tense.
   a. That change occurs in the *nous* form, which is spelled _____.
   b. Write the *imparfait je* form of *manger*.
   c. Write down the *imparfait nous* and *vous* forms. Why is there no spelling change?

5. a. The verb *commencer* also has one spelling change in the present tense *nous* form. Write it.
   b. Write all the *imparfait* forms of *commencer* that have a spelling change. Why is there a change?

6. The verb *préférer* has accents on every present tense form, but they are not always the same ones. Write the forms that match *je, elle, nous,* and *ils.*

7. Write the present *je* and *nous* forms of *amener, se lever, espérer, exagérer.*

8. Write the present *je, nous,* and *ils* forms for *jeter* and *s'appeler.*

4. Practice with indirect quotations

See if you can write the correct answers to all frames in this section in less than three minutes. Remember to change the subject pronoun, verb form, and possessive adjectives if necessary.

322

1. Rewrite the direct quotations as indirect quotations.
   a. Jean: J'ai une grande sœur.
   b. Marianne: Je suis l'aînée de la famille.
   c. Gilles: Mes parents habitent à Grenoble. |

   a. Jean dit qu'il a une grande sœur.   b. Marianne dit qu'elle est l'aînée de la famille.
   c. Gilles dit que ses parents habitent à Grenoble.

2. Report what Alain, Jules, and Renée say they are going to do this afternoon.
   Alain: Je vais au cinéma avec mon cousin.
   Jules: Je vais jouer aux boules avec mon grand-père.
   Renée: Je vais faire du patin (go skating) avec mes copines.
   a. Que dit Alain?   b. Que dit Jules?   c. Que dit Renée? |

   a. Alain dit qu'il va au cinéma avec son cousin.   b. Jules dit qu'il va jouer aux boules
   avec son grand-père.   c. Renée dit qu'elle va faire du patin avec ses copines.

5. Review practice: negative expressions

1. Answer these questions with *ne...rien, ne...personne,* or *ne...jamais.*
   Say, then write, complete answers. (See key.)
   Modèle: Ils veulent quelque chose? |

   Non, ils ne veulent rien.

   a. M. et Mme Vincent, vous achetez quelque chose aujourd'hui?
   b. Est-ce qu'il y avait quelqu'un chez toi?
   c. Elle connaissait quelqu'un à Paris?
   d. Tu as vu les Bertrand là-bas?
   e. Il y a quelque chose dans cette boîte?
   f. Est-ce que Madeleine a acheté un pantalon?

2. Give one-word answers with *rien, personne,* or *jamais.* (See key.)
   a. Qu'est-ce que tu vois?
   b. Allez-vous souvent au théâtre?
   c. Qui est là?

À Propos!   Complete these sentences.
Je n'ai jamais (fait)... . Je ne connais rien de... .

Vocabulaire

Verbes
envoyer (à) *to send (to)*
répondre (à) *to answer*
vendre (à) *to sell (to)*

Noms
le mur *wall*

Note Culturelle
Regional costumes

In France, especially in small towns, and *dans les provinces* (regions outside of Paris), people may wear traditional folk costumes for patriotic holidays, folk festivals, and weddings.

Each region has its distinctive costumes—some ornate, and some plain. Women usually wear a long dress, or skirt and full-sleeved blouse, with a lace headdress called a *coiffe*. The dark skirts are often embroidered with bright colors. In some regions such as *Bretagne*, the tall, round, starched *coiffes* are intricate works of art that have cost the *dentellière* (lace maker) weeks of work.

Men usually wear dark pants with an embroidered vest, and sometimes a round felt hat. In many regions, *sabots* (wooden shoes) accompany the costumes.

En Bretagne, on porte les costumes traditionnels pour les fêtes religieuses.

PRÉPARATION 44

1. More reflexive verbs

1. Many verbs in French are used reflexively as well as non-reflexively. Give an equivalent for this sentence: *Tu te prends trop au sérieux.*

   You take yourself too seriously.

2. You can usually figure out the meaning by saying the English equivalent of the verb, plus *oneself*. For example, if you know that *préparer* means *to prepare, to get ready*, think of *se préparer* as *to prepare oneself, to get oneself ready*. If your meaning fits the context, you've made a good guess.

   a. Try this one. *Demander* means _____. *Se demander* probably means _____.

   to ask; to ask oneself

   b. Now let the context refine your guess. Give an equivalent for:
   Je me demande s'il va faire beau demain.

   I wonder if it's going to be nice tomorrow. *(Se demander* means both *to ask oneself* and *to wonder.)*

   c. Say, then write an equivalent for *I wonder if it's going to snow.*

   Je me demande s'il va neiger.

The following paragraph uses a number of reflexive verbs. As you read, write each reflexive verb and your guess at its meaning. Use resemblance to English plus the context of the story. You already know some of the verbs.

Une journée spéciale

Bernadette, une jeune fille de 22 ans, est en vacances au bord de° la mer. En général, quand elle est en vacances, elle se lève à 8h. Quand il fait très beau, elle se promène sur la plage pendant une demi-heure. Puis, après son petit déjeuner, elle va de nouveau° à la plage. Là, elle s'assied sur le sable° où elle ramasse° des coquillages°, et elle s'amuse à jeter des cailloux° dans l'eau. Quand elle a trop chaud elle se baigne. Après le déjeuner elle est un peu fatiguée et elle se repose généralement jusqu'à° 3h de l'après-midi.

    Aujourd'hui sa journée commence comme un jour de vacances ordinaire. Mais à 3h, trois amies arrivent chez elle. Toutes les jeunes

by (at the edge of)

again
sand / pick up / shells
stones

until

filles s'installent dans la chambre de Bernadette et elles s'habillent en robes longues très élégantes. Bernadette aussi se prépare avec beaucoup de soin°. Elle se maquille, se peigne, et met une très belle robe blanche. Elle se regarde dans la glace. Oui, elle est prête°...

care
ready

Pourquoi tous ces préparatifs extraordinaires? C'est parce que, cet après-midi, dans une petite église° de campagne, Bernadette va se marier avec Alain.

church

3. Now check to see if you found all the verbs. |

> elle se lève, elle se promène, elle s'assied, elle s'amuse, elle se baigne, elle se repose, (elles) s'installent, elles s'habillent, (elle) se prépare, elle se maquille, elle se peigne, elle se regarde, (elle) va se marier

4. See if you remembered the correct meanings for these verbs: *se lever, se promener, s'amuser, s'habiller, se préparer, se peigner.* |

> to get up, to take a walk, to have a good time (have fun), to get dressed, to get ready, to comb one's hair

5. The next verbs bear little resemblance to English. Check whether you guessed their meanings accurately.

   a. elle s'assied |

   > she sits down (The infinitive of this highly irregular verb is *s'asseoir*. It has two present tense stems; je m'*assieds,* nous nous *asseyons*; past participle *assis*.)

   b. elle se baigne |

   > she goes swimming

   c. elle se maquille |

   > she puts on makeup

The verbs in the final group have English cognates.

6. *Se reposer* means to rest. What related English noun means *rest*? |

> repose

7. a. The English cognate related to *installer* is _____ |

   > install

   b. *S'installer* doesn't really mean *to install oneself*. What's a good English equivalent? |

   > to get settled

8. a. *Se regarder* means _____. |

   > to look at oneself

   b. Let's see how wide awake your common sense is. What's the meaning of *la glace* in *Elle se regarde dans la glace?* |

   > mirror (not *ice cream!*)

9. a. *Se marier* means _____. |

   > to get married (*Marier* alone means to marry someone to someone else: *Le prêtre marie Alain et Bernadette.*)

   b. In English we say *to marry someone*. The French equivalent needs a preposition: *se marier* _____ *quelqu'un.* |

   > avec

10. Look at this exchange. What is the equivalent of the second sentence? *Tu me parles et je te parle. Donc, nous nous parlons.* |

        Thus, we are speaking to each other.

The *nous, vous,* and *se* forms of reflexive verbs can have a *reciprocal* meaning. That is, they indicate an exchange of action between or among people.

    Use *se connaître* to express this idea: *We know each other well.* |

        Nous nous connaissons bien./On se connaît bien.

11. At the end of the wedding ceremony, *Bernadette et Alain s'embrassent.* Write an equivalent. |

        They embrace each other./ They kiss each other./ They hug each other. (*S'embrasser* can mean all these things.)

À Propos!   Vous et votre camarade de chambre, est-ce que vous vous connaissez bien ou pas très bien?

2. The verb *dire*

Dire means *to say* or *to tell.* You have used it in expressions like *dis...* and *il/elle dit que....* Look now at the other forms.

Présent:		je	**dis**	nous	**dis**ons
		tu	dis	vous	**dites**
	on/il/elle		dit	ils/elles	disent
Imparfait:	**je disais**				
Passé composé:	**j'ai dit**				

1. **Dire** is called irregular because its present tense forms cannot be predicted from the infinitive. Which form of **dire** matches each pronoun or set of pronouns below?
   a. ils/elles   c. je, tu
   b. nous   d. vous
                      e. on/il/elle |

           a. disent   b. disons   c. dis   d. dites   e. dit

2. Say what these people have to say about a painting they are looking at, using the present tense of *dire.*
   Modèle: Marie-Hélène: laid |

           Marie-Hélène dit que c'est laid.

   a. nous: très intéressant |

           Nous disons que c'est très intéressant.

b. tu: un ballon *(ball)* |

Tu dis que c'est un ballon.

c. vous: une grosse tomate |

Vous dites que c'est une grosse tomate.

d. Philippe: une orange |

Philippe dit que c'est une orange.

e. ils: une blague *(joke)* |

Ils disent que c'est une blague.

f. je: amusant *(funny)* |

Je dis que c'est amusant.

3. Give English equivalents for the last three items in frame 2. |

Philippe says (that) it's an orange. They say (that) it's a joke. I say (that) it's amusing.

4. Write French equivalents for the following sentences. (See key.)
   a. I tell you that I don't like coffee.
   b. They *(on)* tell us that it's nice today.
5. When the group of people who looked at the painting comes to art class the following day they try to recall their impressions. Complete with the appropriate past tenses of *dire*.
   a. Georgette, tu ＿＿＿ que c'était un ballon. |

   as dit

   b. Ce n'est pas vrai, elle ＿＿＿ que c'était une grosse tomate. |

   a dit

   c. Le professeur et toi, vous ＿＿＿ que c'était intéressant. |

   avez dit

   d. Pendant que Philippe ＿＿＿ que c'était un orange, nous regardions déjà un autre tableau. |

   disait

3. Review practice: indirect object pronouns

1. Answer the following questions in the affirmative. Use an indirect object pronoun and the additional information. (See key.)

   Modèle: Qu'est-ce que tu donnes à Louis? *(un crayon)* |

   Je lui donne un crayon.

   a. Qu'est-ce qu'elle te donne? *(son appareil-photo)*
   b. Qu'est-ce qu'il donne à son fils? *(un cadeau)*
   c. Nous téléphonons à Roger ce soir? *(oui, à 7h.)*
2. Answer these questions in the negative, and use an indirect object pronoun in your responses. (See key.)

   Modèle: Vous parlez à Nathalie? |

   Non, je ne lui parle pas.

   a. Vous donnez des fraises aux enfants?
   b. Est-ce qu'elle me téléphone aujourd'hui?
   c. Ils vous montrent les photos de leurs vacances?

Est-ce que ces noms sont familiers aux États-Unis? Pourquoi?

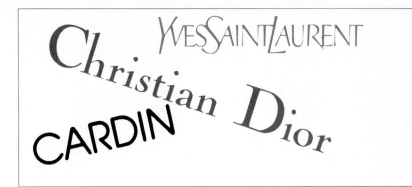

Vocabulaire

Noms
le défilé   *(military) parade, procession*
la glace   *mirror*
le prêtre   *priest*

Adjectifs
amusant/e   *funny*

Verbes
se demander (si)   *to wonder (if)*
se baigner   *to go swimming, to have a swim*
se reposer   *to rest*
s'installer   *to get settled*
se maquiller   *to put on makeup*
se regarder   *to look at oneself*
se marier (avec)   *to get married (to)*
se connaître   *to know one another*
s'embrasser   *to hug, kiss, embrace one another*
s'asseoir (assied- assey-; pp. assis)   *to sit down*
dire (di-, dis-, dites; pp. dit)   *to say*
se prendre trop au sérieux   *to take oneself too seriously*

Autres mots et expressions
jusqu'à   *until, up to (a certain time)*

Phase 7

Au Sénégal

Qu'est-ce que vous allez apprendre?

In this Phase you will hear about a young Frenchman who is going to live and work in Senegal with the *Service de la Coopération* (an alternative form of military service), and some of his impressions and experiences in this French-speaking West African nation. You will also discuss various means of transportation, geography, and use vocabulary referring to parts of the body.

Communication

You will:
- Express the notions of *who, which,* and *that* using the relative pronouns *qui* and *que.*
- Compare qualities of people and things.
- Express *how* things are done, using adverbs in *-ment.*
- Use the verbs *envoyer* (to send) and *écrire* (to write).
- Talk about travel to and from a number of cities and countries, using appropriate prepositions.
- Discuss quantities using expressions such as *assez de, beaucoup de, trop de.*

Culture

The history, food, climate and people of Senegal; Languages, ethnic groups; Urban-rural contrasts in Senegal; Léopold Sédar Senghor, Senegalese statesman and poet.

PRÉPARATION 45

Séjour au Sénégal

(Beginning in Phase 7, no translations of the dialogues are given.)

Le Service de la Coopération

Aujourd'hui est un jour mémorable pour Michel Bertrand. Après deux ans dans un institut technique et des examens difficiles... enfin°... il est caméraman! Il est très heureux. Maintenant il peut travailler dans une station de télévision. Mais d'abord°, il doit faire son service militaire...armée de terre°? armée de mer°? armée de l'air°? Pas très passionnant° pour un jeune homme qui veut faire de la photographie, de la télévision, des films.... Mais le service militaire est obligatoire,° alors....

Michel a une idée: on peut remplacer° le service militaire par le service national, dans la «Coopération»! On vous envoie° généralement pendant° seize mois dans un pays pour «coopérer°» avec ses habitants°. Là, vous travaillez avec eux dans des domaines° variés: médecine, éducation, technique, etc. Vous travaillez beaucoup mais vous participez à la vie économique et sociale des pays qui sont souvent exotiques et fascinants.

at last

first
army / navy / air force
exciting

compulsory
replace
send
for / cooperate
inhabitants / areas

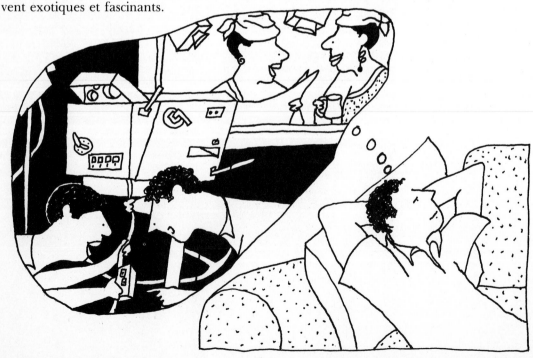

Préparez-vous à donner votre avis *(opinion)* sur une des trois questions posées:

1. Est-ce que le service militaire obligatoire est une bonne chose? Pourquoi?
2. Si le service militaire est acceptable pour les hommes, doit-il être obligatoire pour les femmes aussi?
3. Quel est l'âge préférable pour faire son service militaire? Pourquoi?

1. The relative pronouns *qui* and *que*

1. A relative pronoun combines information about a person, thing, or idea with information in another statement.

> Je connais cette femme. *Elle* travaille là-bas.
> Je connais la femme *qui* travaille là-bas.

a. Write the English equivalent of *Je connais la femme qui travaille là-bas.* |

> I know the woman who is working over there.

b. The relative pronoun *qui* replaces elle. Is *elle* the subject or the direct object of *travaille*? |

> subject (The relative pronoun *qui* replaces a noun or pronoun: the subject in the second statement.)

2. Write one sentence that combines both statements below.
   a. Voilà une voiture. Cette voiture est chère *(expensive)*. |

> Voilà une voiture qui est chère.

   b. Je ne connais pas le jeune homme. Ce jeune homme a parlé avec Mimi. |

> Je ne connais pas le jeune homme qui a parlé avec Mimi.

3. The example below shows the relative pronoun *que* connecting two statements.

> Dans ce magasin il y a *une belle moto.*
> Je voudrais acheter *cette moto.*
> Dans ce magasin il y a *une belle moto que* je voudrais acheter.

a. Give an English equivalent for *il y a une belle moto que je voudrais acheter.* |

> There's a beautiful motorcycle (that) I would like to buy.

b. The relative *que* replaces *cette moto.* Is *cette moto* the subject or the direct object of *je voudrais acheter*? |

> direct object (The relative pronoun *que* replaces a direct object noun phrase or pronoun: the object of the verb in the second sentence.)

4. a. Give an English equivalent for *Tu connais la jeune fille que François invite à la fête?*

    > Do you know the girl (whom) François is inviting to the party?

   b. Can the relative *que* refer to people as well as to things?

    > yes

   c. In English, are the direct object pronouns *whom, which,* or *that* always expressed?

    > no (In English one may omit the object relative pronoun when connecting two sentences. In French, the relative pronoun may not be omitted.)

   d. Now read this sentence. *Tu connais la jeune fille qu'Eric invite au cinéma?*

    What form does *que* take when it precedes a word beginning with a vowel sound, like Eric?

    > qu'

5. *Que* changes to *qu'* before a vowel sound. *Qui,* however, never changes form. Connect these two sentences with *qui: Thierry était un garçon. Thierry avait beaucoup d'amis.*

   > Thierry était un garçon qui avait beaucoup d'amis.

6. Use *que* or *qu'* to combine each pair of statements below.
   Modèle: C'est un vieil ami. J'aime beaucoup *ce vieil ami.*

   > C'est un vieil ami que j'aime beaucoup.

   a. C'est une jolie robe. Elle porte souvent *cette jolie robe.*

    > C'est une jolie robe qu'elle porte souvent.

   b. Il a deux frères. Je ne *les* connais pas.

    > Il a deux frères que je ne connais pas.

   c. C'était un chien très gentil. Toute ma famille aimait beaucoup *ce chien.*

    > C'était un chien très gentil que toute ma famille aimait beaucoup.

7. Write French equivalents with the appropriate pronoun, *qui* or *que.*
   Modèle: Georges sees a red vest that he wants to buy.
   Georges/voir/gilet rouge/il veut acheter

    > Georges voit un gilet rouge qu'il veut acheter.

   a. Adeline is a young Haitian woman who wants to work in the United States.
   Adeline/être/jeune Haïtienne/veut travailler aux États-Unis.

    > Adeline est une jeune Haïtienne qui veut travailler aux États-Unis.

   b. I know something you don't know.
   Je/savoir/quelque chose/tu ne sais pas.

    > Je sais quelque chose que tu ne sais pas.

À Propos!

Complétez ces phrases:
Une personne que j'admire beaucoup, c'est... .
Un pays qui me semble *(seems)* fascinant, c'est... .

2. Practice with direct and indirect object pronouns

1. Some French verbs use a preposition that the English equivalent doesn't use. Some English verbs use a preposition that the French equivalent doesn't use. Write each French phrase below, adding the preposition where needed.

   a. *to look at something:* regarder _____ qqch
   b. *to call someone:* téléphoner _____ qqn
   c. *to show someone something:* montrer _____ qqch _____ qqn
   d. *to ask someone for something:* demander _____ qqch _____ qqn
   e. *to listen to someone:* écouter _____ qqn
   f. *to look for something:* chercher _____ qqch
   g. *to give someone something:* donner _____ qqch _____ qqn
   h. *to tell someone something:* dire _____ qqch _____ qqn
   i. *to answer someone:* répondre _____ qqn
   j. *to ask someone a question:* poser _____ une question _____ qqn

   a. — b. à c. —, à d. —, à e. — f. — g. —, à h. —, à i. à
   j. —, à

2. a. In French, the pronouns that are used to mean *him, her, it,* or *them* are _____.

   a. le, la, les

   b. The pronoun that is used to mean *to him* or *to her* is _____.

   b. lui

   c. The pronoun that means *to them* is _____.

   c. leur

3. You are planning a slide show for some friends. Your cousin keeps asking you questions. Answer according to the cue, and use an object pronoun to replace each italicized phrase.

   Modèle: Tu invites *ta petite sœur et ses copines? (Non...)*

   Non, je ne les invite pas.

   a. Tu invites *la jeune Américaine* qui habite chez tante Marthe? *(Oui...)*
   b. Est-ce qu'elle a *notre adresse? (Non...)*
   c. Tu montres *les diapos de nos vacances en Bretagne? (Non...)*
   d. Alors, tu montres *à tes amis* nos diapos d'Espagne? *(Oui...)*
   e. Tu téléphones *à ton oncle* pour emprunter *(borrow)* son écran? *(Oui...)*
   f. Ta sœur et toi, vous mettez *les diapos* en ordre samedi? *(Non, nous... vendredi).*

   a. *Oui, je l'invite.*   b. *Non, elle ne l'a pas.*   c. *Non, je ne les montre pas.*   d. *Oui, je leur montre nos diapos d'Espagne.*   e. *Oui, je lui téléphone.*   f. *Non, nous les mettons en ordre vendredi.*

À Propos!

Donnez-vous des cadeaux de Noël à vos amis? Posez-vous souvent des questions au professeur du cours de français?

Note Culturelle
Military service

Military service is obligatory in France. All French males must, at the age of 18, go to their City Hall (*Hôtel de ville* or *Mairie*) where they are assigned to a recruiting office. They may be exempted (*exempté*) for various physical or mental reasons. They may also receive *un sursis* (deferment) up to the age of 25 (for example, if they are in the middle of their studies). Military service lasts twelve months.

Military service may be replaced by *Service National (la Coopération)*. The *Coopération* resembles the Peace Corps insofar as people are sent to a foreign country to work with the inhabitants on some specific projects. There is a limited number of posts available, mostly in Francophone countries (though some *coopérants* are sent to South America and Asia). *Coopérants* are assigned to a specific work area in accordance with their studies and professional training, for example: education, communication, equipment, health, economy, administration. Service in the *Coopération* lasts sixteen months instead of the twelve in the military service.

Vocabulaire

Noms

l'adresse *f.* *address*
l'armée *f.*; ~ de terre; ~ de l'air; ~ de mer *army; infantry; air force; navy*
l'aviation *f.* *air force, aviation*
le caméraman *cameraman*
le coopérant *participant in Le Service de la Coopération*
le domaine *field, area of interest*
l'éducation *f.* *education*
l'habitant *m.* *inhabitant*
l'institut *m.* *institute*
le marin *sailor*
la marine *navy*
l'ordre *m.* *order*
le pays *country*
le service militaire *military service*
le soldat *soldier*

Autres mots et expressions

à qui? *to whom?*
d'abord *first*
dans la vie *in life*
en ordre *in order*
enfin *at last*

Adjectifs

cher/chère *expensive*
difficile *difficult*
exotique *exotic*
mémorable *memorable*
national/e *national*
obligatoire *compulsory*
passionnant/e *fascinating, exciting*
technique *technical*
varié/e *varied*

Verbes

coopérer *to cooperate*
emprunter *to borrow*
faire son service militaire *serve time in the military*
participer *to participate*
sembler *to seem*

PRÉPARATION 46

1. Making comparisons with adjectives

In this section, you'll learn how to express comparisons in French; for example: *taller than, as tall as, less tall than.*

1. The following sentences contrast Jean and Guy.

> Jean est plus petit que Guy.   *Jean is shorter than Guy.*
> Jean est plus sportif que   *Jean is more athletic than*
>   Guy.   *Guy.*

In comparisons of superiority, French uses the word pattern
_____ + adjective + _____. |
     plus... que

2. Suppose you and a business partner are arguing about whether to hire David or Paul as a sales representative. Say that Paul is more qualified than David in some respects.

    Modèle: —David est gentil. |
         —Oui, mais Paul est plus gentil que David.

   a. —David est intelligent. |
         —Oui, mais Paul est plus intelligent que David.

   b. —David est sympathique. |
         —Oui, mais Paul est plus sympathique que David.

   c. —David est consciencieux. |
         —Oui, mais Paul est plus consciencieux que David.

3. Now look at this sentence, which contrasts Hélène and Monique.

> Hélène est moins sportive   *Hélène is less athletic*
>   que Monique.   *than Monique.*

In comparisons of inferiority, French uses the word pattern
_____ + adjective + _____. |
     moins... que

4. You and a friend are arguing about whether Yvette or Barbara should play center on the basketball team. Say that Yvette is less qualified in certain respects than Barbara.

    Modèle: —Yvette est rapide. |
         —Oui, mais elle est moins rapide que Barbara.

   a. —Yvette est forte *(strong).* |
         —Oui, mais elle est moins forte que Barbara.

b. —Yvette est consciencieuse. |

5. Now compare Henriette and Julie.

> Henriette est aussi adroite   *Henriette is as skillful*
> que Julie.   *as Julie.*

In comparisons of equality, French uses the word pattern _____
+ adjective + ____. |

aussi...que

6. You and your friend Alice are each making a film. When Alice
says that her film is better in certain respects than yours, reply
that yours is as good as hers.

   Modèle: —Mon film est plus intéressant que ton film. |

   —Mais non! Mon film est aussi intéressant que ton film.

   a. —Mon film est plus original que ton film. |

   —Mais non! Mon film est aussi original que ton film.

   b. —Mon film est plus émouvant *(moving)* que ton film. |

   —Mais non! Mon film est aussi émouvant que ton film.

   c. —Mon film est plus artistique que ton film. |

   —Mais non! Non film est aussi artistique que ton film.

7. Sometimes the people or things you want to compare are different in gender and number.

> Laure et Julie sont aussi gentilles que Léonard.
> Mon pantalon est plus élégant que ma jupe.

Does the adjective agree with the subject, or with the noun that
follows the word *que?* |

It agrees with the subject.

8. Complete each sentence below with the appropriate form of the
adjective.

   a. Ces femmes sont plus *(grand)* que M. Moraud. | a. grandes
   b. Cette photo est moins *(beau)* que les autres. | b. belle
   c. Ces jeunes filles sont aussi *(maigre)* que ce garçon. | c. maigres
   d. Les légumes sont aussi *(important)* que la viande. | d. importants

2. Practice with relative pronouns *qui* and *que*

Qui	Subject	**Cet homme** connaît Paul.
		C'est un homme **qui** connaît Paul.
Que	Object	Paul connaît **cet homme.**
		C'est un homme **que** Paul connaît.

1. Each time Jeanne makes a statement about someone they know, Albert disagrees and gives his own opinion. Complete Albert's statements with the relative pronoun *qui* or *que*.

   a. *Jeanne:* Tout le monde dit que tu aimes Monique. C'est vrai?

     Albert: Mais non, Monique est une fille _____ je ne trouve pas du tout sympathique! |

                                                    a. que

   b. *Jeanne:* Laurent me dit qu'il est au régime.

     Albert: Impossible! C'est un garçon _____ mange tout le temps. |

                                                      b. qui

2. Complete each sentence below with the information in the second sentence. Use *qui* to replace a subject, *que* to replace an object.

     Modèle: Voilà une jeune fille _____. (*Elle* joue au basket.) |

          Voilà une jeune fille qui joue au basket.

        Voilà une jeune fille. (Je *la* trouve sympathique.) |

          Voilà une jeune fille que je trouve sympathique.

   a. Voilà la jeune fille _____. (*Elle* a invité mon frère à une petite fête.)

     Voilà la jeune fille _____. (Mon frère *la* trouve sympathique.) |

          Voilà la jeune fille qui a invité mon frère à une petite fête.

          Voilà la jeune fille que mon frère trouve sympathique.

   b. J'aime bien les bonnes crêpes _____. (On fait *de bonnes crêpes* en Bretagne.)

     J'aime bien ces crêpes _____. (*Ces crêpes* ont beaucoup de confiture.) |

          J'aime bien les bonnes crêpes qu'on fait en Bretagne.

          J'aime bien ces crêpes qui ont beaucoup de confiture.

   c. Hélène a un cours de maths _____. (*Le cours* est difficile.)

     C'est un cours _____. (Elle *le* trouve passionnant.) |

          Hélène a un cours de maths qui est difficile. C'est un cours qu'elle trouve passionnant *(exciting).*

À Propos!

     Complétez la phrase:

     Un sportif / une sportive que je trouve excellent/e, c'est...

     Un film que j'ai trouvé émouvant, c'est...

3. Stressed pronouns

In this Préparation, you'll use stressed pronouns after prepositions, and to express possession.

1. Write the stressed pronouns for these subject pronouns: *je, te, il,* and *ils.* |

   moi, toi, lui, eux

2. Imagine that you are having a dream in which you are a soldier named Dupont, who is being sent on a dangerous mission. You can't quite believe it, and simply echo the end of each statement you hear. Respond by repeating the preposition and using the appropriate stressed pronoun. Note that officers usually address enlisted men and women as *tu.*

   Modèle: Dupont, tu dois parler avec le capitaine. |

   Avec lui?

   a. Oui. Nous avons une mission dangereuse pour toi. | a. Pour moi?
   b. Oui. C'est un message secret pour le Président. | b. Pour lui?
   c. Oui. Tu vas aller au palais avec Leduc et Poiret. | c. Avec eux?
   d. Oui. Tu vas aller au Palais avec eux mais tu vas délivrer le message sans Leduc et Poiret. | d. Sans eux?
   e. Oui. Ensuite tu dois revenir ici avec Mme X, la fameuse espionne. | e. Avec elle?
   f. Oui. Il y a grand danger pour elle et pour toi. | f. Pour nous?
   Oui. Bonne chance, Dupont!

3. Where is the dog in the drawings in relation to the persons shown —*devant, derrière,* or *entre?* Use stressed pronouns in your responses.

   Modèle: Le chien est devant la femme? |

   Non, il est derrière elle.

   a. Le chien est derrière l'homme? |

   Non, il est devant lui.

   b. Le chien est derrière la fille et le garçon? |

   Non, il est entre eux.

4. The prepositions *avant* and *après* describe relative position in time. In the sentences below, indicate who arrives *after* whom.

   Modèle: J'arrive avant lui. |

   Il arrive après moi.

   a. Elle arrive avant eux. | Ils arrivent après elle.
   b. Tu arrives avant elle. | Elle arrive après toi.
   c. Vous arrivez avant moi.   J'arrive après vous.

5. Stressed pronouns are often used after the expression *être à* to show ownership. The English equivalent is *to belong to.*

—Est-ce que cette voiture — *Does that car belong to*
    est à Roger? *Roger?*
—Non, elle est à moi. — *No, it belongs to me.*

a. Give the English for *Cet électrophone est à eux.* |
      That record player belongs to them.
b. Give the French for *That record belongs to me.* |
      Ce disque est à moi.

6. At the end of a party you and your roommate are handing the
following articles of clothing to your friends.
    Modèle: Ces gants sont à Leonard? |
      Oui, ils sont à lui.

a. Ces bottes sont à Barbara?
b. Ce chapeau est à Georges?
c. Ces manteaux sont à vous, Jacqueline et Marie?
d. Les vestes sont à Christian et à Roger? |

      a. Oui, elles sont à elle. b. Oui, il est à lui. c. Oui, ils sont a nous. d. Oui, elles
      sont à eux.

À Propos!   D'habitude, est-ce que vous arrivez au cours de français avant ou
après le professeur? Savez-vous qui a dit «L'état, c'est moi»?

4. Adverbs ending in *-ment*

You've been using adverbs since the beginning of the course. Adverbs usually answer the question *comment? quand?* or *où?* In this
section, you'll learn how to form a large group of adverbs that end
in *-ment;* they usually answer the question *comment?*

1. In English, many adverbs are formed by adding the ending *-ly* to
the base form of the adjective. For example: *careful, carefully.*

    Look at the adverbs below. What is the base form of the adjec-
tives to which the ending *-ly* is added? easily, actually, quickly |
      easy, actual, quick

2. In French, adverbs are generally formed by adding *-ment* to the
feminine singular form of the adjective.

Masculine	*Feminine*	*Adverb*
sérieux	série**use**	**sérieusement**
naturel	natur**elle**	**naturellement**
rare	rar**e**	**rarement**

3. It's easy to guess the meaning of most adverbs ending in -*ment,* because they usually have an English equivalent ending in -*ly.* Give equivalents of these sentences.

   a. Heureusement, je n'ai pas perdu mon portefeuille. |
       Fortunately, I didn't lose (haven't lost) my wallet.

   b. Naturellement, il a réussi à son examen de maths! |
       Naturally (of course), he passed his math exam!

   c. Ton candidat ne va pas nécessairement gagner *(win).* |
       Your candidate is not necessarily going to win.

4. Note that French does not always use an adverb, but may use an adverbial phrase.

   a. Give the English equivalent: *Elle a parlé de ses enfants avec joie.* |
       She spoke of her children with joy (joyfully).

   b. Use the noun *enthousiasme* to say that Nathalie spoke about her courses enthusiastically. |
       Nathalie a parlé de ses cours avec enthousiasme.

5. Now complete the second sentence in each pair with an adverb in -*ment* that corresponds to the adjective.

   Modèle: Dans le désert l'eau est *rare.* Il pleut _____. |
       rarement

   a. En *général,* nous passons nos vacances à la plage. _____ nos cousins viennent avec nous. | a. Généralement

   b. Mon frère est *sérieux.* Il travaille _____. | b. sérieusement

   c. Mon père trouve le français *difficile.* Il le parle _____. | c. difficilement

   d. Ma mère trouve le français *facile (easy).* Elle le parle _____. | d. facilement

6. Look at these sentences.

       C'est vrai. Cette veste est vraiment belle.

   a. *Vraiment (really)* ends in -*ment.* Is -*ment* added to the masculine or feminine form of the adjective? |
       masculine

   If the masculine adjective ends in the vowel, it is used to form the adverb. Other examples are: *joli, joliment; spontané, spontanément.*

   b. Write a sentence to say that Didier dances really well. |
       Didier danse vraiment bien.

   c. Laurence est polie. Elle parle _____. |
       poliment

À Propos!   Conduisez-vous *(do you drive)* calmement ou imprudemment?

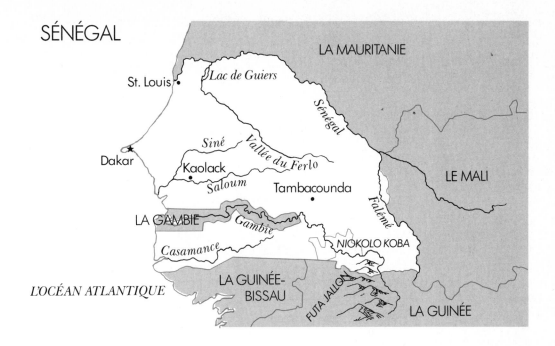

SÉNÉGAL

LA MAURITANIE

St. Louis
Lac de Guiers
Sénégal
Dakar
Siné
Vallée du Ferlo
Kaolack
Saloum
Tambacounda
Falémé
LE MALI
LA GAMBIE
Gambie
NIOKOLO KOBA
Casamance
L'OCÉAN ATLANTIQUE
LA GUINÉE-BISSAU
FUTA JALLON
LA GUINÉE

Vocabulaire

Noms

le capitaine *captain*
l'enthousiasme *m.* *enthusiasm*
l'espion/espionne *spy*
l'état *m.* *state*
la mission *mission*

Adjectifs

adroit/e *skillful*
artistique *artistic*
consciencieux/se *conscientious*
dangereux/se *dangerous*
émouvant/e *moving*
original/e *original*
secret/secrète *secret*

Verbes

délivrer *to deliver*

Adverbes

calmement *calmly*
difficilement *with difficulty*
facilement *easily*
généralement *generally*

gentiment *nicely*
heureusement *happily*
naturellement *naturally*
nécessairement *necessarily*
nerveusement *nervously*
nord *north;* au ~ *to the*
poliment *politely*
prudemment *cautiously*
puis *then*
rarement *rarely*
sérieusement *seriously*
vraiment *truly*

Autres mots et expressions

aussi (+ adj.) que *as... as*
bonne chance! *good luck*
ensuite *then*
loin de *far from*
moins (+ adj.) que *less... than*
plus (+ adj.) que *more... than*
près de *close to*
tout le temps *all the time*
tout à l'heure *later*

PRÉPARATION 47

Séjour au Sénégal

Où aller? (1)

C'est décidé, Michel voudrait° être «coopérant». Oui, mais où? Voilà la question. Son ami, Gérard Lemarchand, est coopérant au Canada, à Québec. Hier soir Michel à téléphoné à Mme Lemarchand, la mère de Gérard, pour lui poser quelques questions°. Voici une partie° de leur conversation.

Michel: Comment va Gérard? Il est content dans la «Coopération»?

Mme Lemarchand: Oui, très content. Vous aussi, vous voulez aller au Canada comme coopérant?

Michel: Oh, non! Moi, je déteste la neige et le froid! Je préfère les pays chauds.

Mme Lemarchand: L'Afrique alors?

Michel: Oui, peut-être°. La Côte d'Ivoire°, le Bénin, le Sénégal... Je ne sais pas.

would like

ask some questions / part

perhaps / Ivory Coast

À Dakar. Femmes au Marché Sandaga.

1. Imaginez que vous vous réveillez ce matin dans un pays extrêmement chaud/froid. Quelle est votre réaction?
2. Est-ce que le service de seize mois en coopération vous semble
préférable au service militaire d'un an? Pourquoi?

1. Making comparisons with adverbs

Having learned how to make comparisons with adjectives, you'll find
it easy to make comparisons with adverbs.

Henri a mangé plus vite que Guy.	*Henri ate faster than (more quickly than) Guy.*
Paulette voyage moins souvent que Claire.	*Paulette travels less often than Claire.*
Ma mère marche aussi rapidement que mon père.	*My mother walks as rapidly as my father.*

1. a. The French expressions above that express inequality are
    ——. |

    plus vite que, moins souvent que

   b. The French expression above that expresses equality is
    ——. |

    aussi rapidement que

In French (as in English) regular adjectives and adverbs are com-
pared in the same way.

Comparisons of regular adjectives and adverbs

plus	adjective		more (-er)...than
aussi +	or	+ **que**	as...as
moins	adverb		less...than

Adjective:	Thomas est **plus grand que** Paul.	Thomas is *taller than* Paul.
Adverb:	Paul nage **plus vite que** Thomas.	Paul swims *faster than* Thomas.

2. Now compare the activities of the people mentioned, using the
adverbs indicated.

    Modèle: Gertrude va à Paris en février, en mai, en septembre et
    en décembre. Monique va à Paris en juin. Monique va
    à Paris *(souvent).* |

    Monique va à Paris moins souvent que Gertrude.

a. Nanette est arrivée à 9h. Gauthier est arrivé à 10h. Gauthier est arrivé *(tard).* |

b. Marcel commence son déjeuner à 1h, et il le finit à 2h. André commence son déjeuner à 1h, et il le finit à 1h30. Marcel mange *(lentement).* |

c. Roger peut nager 100 mètres en une minute et trente secondes. Delphine peut nager 100 mètres en une minute et trente secondes. Delphine nage *(vite).* |

d. Les amis d'Yves prennent du vin tous les soirs. Les amis de Robert prennent du vin le dimanche seulement. Les amis de Robert prennent du vin *(souvent).* |

3. Read these comparative sentences below in which *bien* (well) is used.

Denise chante aussi bien qu'Angélique.	*Denise sings as well as Angélique.*
Bertrand chante moins bien que Laurent.	*Bertrand sings less well than Laurent.*

a. Are the *aussi... que* and *moins... que* forms of the comparative used with *bien* regular? |

b. Here is the French equivalent of *Laure sings better than Denise: Laure chante mieux que Denise.* What word expresses the meaning *better?* |

4. With the information below, say that the first person does something better than the second.

   Modèle: Tu/nager/ta sœur |

a. Nathalie/patiner/Eric
b. Paul/jouer du violon/son cousin
c. le jeune garçon/parler anglais/ses amis |

2. *Envoyer* and other *-yer* verbs

You have been introduced to the verb *envoyer (to send).* Take a moment to look at the chart, especially the stems.

Présent:		j'	**envoi**	e		nous	**envoy**	ons
		tu	envoi	es		vous	envoy	ez
		on/il/elle	envoi	e	ils/elles	envoi	ent

Passe composé: j'ai envoyé
Imparfait: j'envoyais

1. The endings of *envoyer* are those of any regular *-er* verb.
   a. The stem, however, has two forms. What are they? |
      envoi-, envoy-
   b. The stem *envoy-* occurs in the infinitive and where else? |
      nous envoyons, vous envoyez *(present);* j'envoyais *and the other imparfait forms;* j'ai
      envoyé (participe passé). (The stem *envoy-* occurs in the forms that have a pronounced
      ending.)
   c. Which form of the stem matches the *je, tu, on/il/elle,* and *ils/elles* forms? |
      envoi-

2. Write French equivalents for each sentence below. (*Envoyer* is used like *donner, dire,* and some other verbs: *envoyer quelque chose à quelqu'un.*)
   Modèle: You're sending them a card. |
      Vous leur envoyez une carte.
   a. We're sending them a card.
   b. She sent them a card.
   c. I'm not sending them a card.
   d. They *(ils)* aren't sending them a card. |
      a. Nous leur envoyons une carte.   b. Elle leur a envoyé une carte.   c. Je ne leur
      envoie pas de carte.   d. Ils ne leur envoient pas de carte.

3. Use these verbs to complete each sentence below.
   essayer *to try*   payer *to pay, pay for*   nettoyer *to clean*
   a. *(payer)* Qui _____ les boissons? |
      paie
   b. *(essayer)* J'ai _____, mais malheureusement je n'ai pas réussi. |
      essayé
   c. *(nettoyer)* Quand il était jeune, mon grand-père _____ tous les matins le magasin où il travaillait. |
      nettoyait
   d. *(nettoyer)* Je _____ ma chambre tous les samedis. |
      nettoie

À Propos!

Avez-vous jamais envoyé une lettre à l'étranger *(to a foreign country)?* Selon vous, qui doit payer pour nettoyer un fleuve *(river)* pollué, les compagnies industrielles ou le gouvernement?

3. Practice with the *imparfait*

Complete Michel Bertrand's remembrance of times past with the *imparfait*.

Quinze ans ont passé. Michel Bertrand pense maintenant á ses moments d'hésitation avant son départ pour le Sénégal. *(See key.)*

Quand je/j' *a. (être)* jeune, je/j' *b. (avoir)* une grande décision à prendre. Je *c. (vouloir)* devenir *(to become)* caméraman et travailler dans une station de télévision. Mais d'abord je *d. (devoir)* faire mon service militaire. Je *e. (savoir)* qu'on pouvait remplacer le service militaire par le service national, dans la "Coopération." Mes parents *f. (ne pas aimer)* cette idée. Ils *g. (penser)* que le Sénégal *h. (être)* trop loin d'eux et ma mère *i. (penser)* que je/j' *j. (être)* trop jeune pour aller vivre *(to live)* dans un pays où elle *k. (imaginer)* qu'il y *l. (avoir)* beaucoup de danger. Mon père *m. (espérer)* aussi que je/j' *n. (aller)* rester en France. Mes parents *o. (avoir)* ils raison?

4. Reflexives with parts of the body

In English, possessive adjectives are common with parts of the body: *my hands, your face, their arms*, etc. In French, the definite article is used in most cases. The reflexive construction tells you whose body is involved.

Je me lave les mains.	*I'm washing my hands.*
Elle se lave les mains.	*She's washing her hands.*

1. Everyone is getting cleaned up after a walk in the woods. Give French equivalents.
   a. Marc is washing his face. |
      Marc se lave la figure.
   b. Laurence is washing her feet. (foot = *le pied*) |
      Laurence se lave les pieds.
   c. Henri is washing his hands. |
      Henri se lave les mains.
   d. Guillaume is washing his hair. |
      Guillaume se lave les cheveux.
2. *Se brosser* (to brush) is also used with some parts of the body. Give French equivalents:
   a. Jacques is brushing his hair. |
      Jacques se brosse les cheveux.
   b. We're brushing our teeth. |
      Nous nous brossons les dents.

5. Reflexive verbs in the *passé composé*

Look at the *passé composé,* affirmative and negative. Read the forms aloud.

je **me suis**	couché/**e**	je **ne me suis pas**	couché/**e**
tu **t'es**	couché/**e**	tu **ne t'es pas**	couché/**e**
on/il/elle **s'est**	couché/**e**	on/il/elle **ne s'est pas**	couché/**e**
nous **nous sommes**	couché/**e/s**	nous **ne nous sommes pas**	couché/**e/s**
vous **vous êtes**	couché/**e/s**	vous **ne vous êtes pas**	couché/**e/s**
ils/elles **se sont**	couché/**e/s**	ils/elles **ne se sont pas**	couché/**e/s**

1. Ce soir Alain se couche tôt parce qu'il s'est couché à minuit et demi hier soir.
   a. The *passé composé* of *se coucher* is formed with the auxiliary _____ and the past participle _____. |
      être; couché
   b. Does the reflexive pronoun take the same position that other object pronouns take? |
      yes (The object pronoun always precedes the auxiliary verb.)
   c. Complete with the correct form of *se coucher.* Remember to make the participle agree with the subject. *Hier soir, Catherine _____ à onze heures.* |
      s'est couchée
   d. The negative of a reflexive verb in the *passé composé* is the same as the negative of any *passé composé* with an object pronoun. Make the following sentence negative: *Nous nous sommes levés à cinq heures.* |
      Nous ne nous sommes pas levés à cinq heures. (*Ne* precedes the pronoun; *pas* follows the auxiliary verb.)

2. Say what the following people did yesterday at eleven. Read the answers aloud.
   a. Sophie: se lever |
      Sophie s'est levée. (Did you remember to make the past participle agree with the subject?)
   b. Mes amis: se reposer |
      Mes amis se sont reposés.
   c. Toi (Bernard): s'habiller |
      Tu t'es habillé.
   d. Vous (Mme Labelle): se réveiller |
      Vous vous êtes réveillée.
   e. Françoise et Marie: se promener |
      Françoise et Marie se sont promenées.

3. Answer these questions in the negative; read the answers aloud.
   a. Bernadette, est-ce que tu t'es coiffée? |
   > Non, je ne me suis pas coiffée.

   b. Paulette et Simone, est-ce que vous vous êtes promenées hier? |
   > Non, nous ne nous sommes pas promenées hier.

4. Change the following sentences to the *passé composé*. Say each answer aloud, then write it.
   a. Etienne s'habille pour le mariage.
   b. Mme Robert ne se maquille pas.
   c. Mon frère se rase *(shaves)* avant de sortir. |
   > a. Étienne s'est habillé pour le mariage.   b. Mme Robert ne s'est pas maquillée.
   > c. Mon frère s'est rasé avant de sortir.

À Propos!

Pourquoi est-ce que vous vous êtes décidé/e à faire vos études à votre université?

Vocabulaire

Noms

la boisson   *drink*
la carte   *card*
la compagnie   *company, firm*
le conversation   *conversation*
le danger   *danger*
le gouvernement   *government*
la partie   *part*
l'hésitation *f.*   *hesitation*

Adjectifs

industriel/le   *industrial*

Autres mots et expressions

mieux   *better*

Verbes

devenir   *to become*
envoyer (envoi-, envoy-, *pp* envoyé)   *to send*
imaginer   *to imagine*
nager   *to swim*
nettoyer   *to clean*
payer   *to pay (for)*
se décider   *to decide*
se parler   *to speak (with)*
se raser   *to shave*
vivre (vi-, viv-, *pp* vécu)   *to live*

L'Afrique vous attend

Dans un village, les hommes bavardent à l'ombre (shade) du baobab (arbre africain au tronc énorme).

Note Culturelle

Languages, ethnic groups, and religion in Senegal

French is the official language of Senegal, providing a single language in which the affairs of the nation can be conducted. The people of Senegal comprise a number of ethnic groups, each with its own oral language—Ouolof, Serère, Peul, Toucouleur, Diola, Mandingue, Maure. Of these, the Ouolof group is the largest. Here are some phrases in Ouolof:

Bonjour: *Diam 'ngam* (literally, "Do you have peace?")
Bonsoir: *Diame nga yendou* ("Have you spent the day in peace?")
Au revoir: *Diam ac diam* ("Peace")

In addition to native Senegalese people and Europeans, there are a number of Syrian and Lebanese people living in Senegal.

The Islamic religion has been established in West Africa for several hundred years, and most Senegalese are Moslems (*musulmans*). Many men can read and recite verses in Arabic from the Koran, the Islamic holy book. The most impressive mosque is in Touba, a town in the interior, and once a year there is a great pilgrimage to Touba. There are many Catholics in Dakar and among the Serère people. In addition, many people in the interior of the country are animists. An animist believes that inanimate objects, like trees and rocks, and phenomena, like rain and wind, have souls.

Dakar. La Grande Mosquée.

PRÉPARATION 48

Séjour au Sénégal

Où aller? (2)

Mme Lemarchand: Un ami de Gérard est à Dakar. Il dit que c'est une
ville très agréable.

Michel: Oui, il paraît°. Je pense sérieusement à Dakar. Je vais peut-être faire une demande° pour le Sénégal.

Mme Lemarchand: Il faut la faire très vite, vous savez.

Michel: Oui, je suppose... Mais d'abord, je dois parler de cette question avec mes parents.

Mme Lemarchand: Oui, naturellement, c'est une décision importante.
Alors, bonne chance°!

Michel: Merci beaucoup, Madame.

so it seems

to make a request

good luck

*Échange
d'idées*

1. Avec qui parlez-vous quand vous avez une décision à prendre?
   Quelles sortes de problèmes discutez-vous avec vos parents ou
   avec vos amis?
2. Quelle a été une grande décision de votre vie?

1. Practice with the relative pronouns *qui* and *que*

1. The sentences in this frame tell you about Pierre. Combine each
   pair of ideas, using the relative pronoun *qui* as in the model.
   Modèle: Mon ami Pierre a dix-huit ans. Il est plus grand que
   moi. |

   Mon ami Pierre, qui est plus grand que moi, a dix-huit ans.

   a. Mon ami Pierre nous invite souvent pour le week-end. Il habite dans un petit village. |

   Mon ami Pierre, qui habite dans un petit village, nous invite souvent pour le week-end.

   b. Mon ami Pierre écrit des chansons. C'est un excellent musicien. |

   Mon ami Pierre, qui est un excellent musicien, écrit des chansons.

Note Culturelle
History of Senegal

The history of human beings in Africa is a long one, and prehistoric stone ruins throughout Senegal testify to long-time human habitation.

Before the first French explorers arrived in Senegal in the seventeenth century, there was a flourishing civilization in West Africa. In the cooperative life of the village, everyone had a vital part to play. Women planted and harvested rice, cooked, made pots and cloth, took care of the smallest children, and taught the older girls to do these things. Men tended other crops, hunted, and taught *(continued)*

Une femme occupée (busy) à préparer le repas familial.

the older boys, who were also responsible for tending the goats. Since Islam was already an established religion, some men could read and write a little Arabic, but the tribal languages had no written form. As in many cultures, the responsibility for maintaining the government and religion of the society belonged to the men alone.

Visitors to the village might have included the wide-ranging merchants from Mali, who brought cloth, gold, jewelry, and other materials from all over West Africa, or traveling wrestlers whose arrival was an occasion to stop work and celebrate. Everyone gathered to enjoy the music and gaiety that accompanied the wrestlers' skillful dance-like exhibition.

Perhaps the most important and most welcome visitor was the *griot,* the oral historian. Since the tribal language was not written, the history of the village and the tribe was passed on by word of mouth to each new generation. A *griot* was able to recount in detail the history of his region for a period of several hundred years. The *griot* travelled from village to village, learning news, and bringing other news or folk tales to tell. His vivid descriptions were accompanied by music on the *kora* (a kind of lute), the *bala-fon* (a kind of xylophone), and the *tam-tam* (drums). Many in the audience knew the songs that the *griot* wove through the narration, and young and old joined in singing the refrain. In modern-day Africa, the role of the *griot* is primarily that of a dramatic narrator of folktales.

The first Europeans arrived in Senegal around 1445, when Portuguese navigators landed at *le Cap vert* (Cape Verde)—the peninsula on which Dakar, the capital, is now situated. The French came nearly 200 years later, and built a trading post at the mouth of the Senegal River in 1638. They influenced Senegalese history to a greater extent than any other European people.

Like most of western Africa, the area that is now Senegal was heavily exploited as a source for slaves. Men and women were kidnapped and shipped across the Atlantic. Those who survived the nightmarish conditions of the voyage were sold in North America and in the Caribbean.

In the 1800s, the French governor Faidherbe established colonial authority more firmly, built roads, and made it possible for civilization in the French pattern to begin to develop in Senegal. During this period, French authorities encouraged the colonists to raise and export *cacahuètes* (peanuts), a valuable crop which plays an important role in the economy of Senegal today.

Many Senegalese riflemen *(les tirailleurs sénégalais)* fought for the Allies in both World Wars, and French citizenship was granted to all Senegalese. In 1960 Senegal became independent of France, and is today *la République de Sénégal.*

Senegal produces mostly peanuts, cotton, rice, and sugar cane. The commercial fishing industry is expanding. The mineral wealth of the country consists of phosphates, salt, copper, and iron. Dakar is the cultural center of the country. In addition to the university, the museum, and an institute of folk arts, there are the *Théâtre National Daniel Solano*—which promotes performances by Senegalese musicians and dancers, as well as actors—and two film societies.

2. Now use the relative pronoun *que* to say two things about Pierre's relatives. Write a complete sentence according to the model.

> *Modèle:* La tante de Pierre/j'aime bien/arrive bientôt chez lui |
>> La tante de Pierre, que j'aime bien, arrive bientôt chez lui.

a. son grand-père/il voit de temps en temps/vient de Montréal |
>> Son grand-père, qu'il voit de temps en temps, vient de Montréal. (Did you remember that *que* becomes *qu'* before a subject beginning with a vowel?)

b. son frère aîné / je ne connais pas très bien / est ingénieur |
>> Son frère aîné, que je ne connais pas très bien, est ingénieur.

3. Write the English equivalent of *Son frère aîné, que je ne connais pas très bien, est ingénieur.* |
>> His older brother, whom I don't know very well, is an engineer.

4. Notice that the word *que* has more than one meaning in French. As a relative pronoun, it means *which* or *whom,* as a conjunction it means *that,* and in a comparison it means *than.* Write the English equivalent of *Elle m'a dit que le voyage qu'elle va faire au Sénégal est plus intéressant qu'un voyage aux États-Unis.* |
>> She told me that the trip (which) she's going to take to Senegal is more interesting than a trip to the United States.

2. The verb *écrire*

1. Look at the chart showing the forms of *écrire* (to write).

Présent:						
	j'	écri	s	nous	écriv	ons
	tu	écri	s	vous	écriv	ez
	on/il/elle	écri	t	ils/elles	écriv	ent
Imparfait:	**j'écrivais**					
Passé composé:	**j'ai écrit**					

a. How many forms does the present tense stem have? |
>> two

b. One form of the stem ends with *v: écriv-*. Does this form occur with singular subjects or with plural subjects? |
>> plural subjects

2. Complete these sentences with the appropriate forms of *écrire*. Refer to the chart to check your answers.

a. Nous ——— des lettres à nos parents.

b. Il faut ——— «France» avec un F majuscule.

c. En février dernier M. Perrault _____ un article excellent pour un journal.

d. L'année dernière je lui _____ tous les samedis.

e. Avant de commencer votre examen, _____ votre nom sur votre feuille.

3. Answer these questions according to the cues.

a. Est-ce que j'écris aussi bien qu'un poète? *(non)* |

a. Non, tu n'écris pas (vous n'écrivez pas) aussi bien qu'un poète.

b. Tu as écrit des lettres à tes amis? *(non)* |

b. Non, je n'ai pas écrit de lettres à mes amis. Je ne leur ai pas écrit de lettres.

3. Practice with the *passé composé*

1. Hubert loves to talk about what he has read in the morning paper. He discusses the news with Vincent, a fellow worker.

a. Write the *passé composé* forms of the verbs in parentheses.

Vincent: Tu *(acheter)* le journal ce matin?

Hubert: Oui, et je *(regarder)* la page des sports tout de suite.
Notre équipe de football *(gagner)* le match hier soir.

Vincent: Ah oui! C'est formidable!

Hubert: Oui, je suis très content. |

tu as acheté, j'ai regardé, a gagné

2. Some participles end in the sound /i/ or /y/. Write past participles for these verbs.

a. mettre
b. sortir
c. écrire

d. connaître
e. pouvoir
f. boire |

a. mis   b. sorti   c. écrit   d. connu   e. pu   f. bu

3. Jeanne and Marie talk about Jeanne's latest trip.

a. Which *passé composé* forms are used?

Marie: Tu es partie de New York ou de Boston?

Jeanne: De Boston et je suis allée directement à Paris. |

tu es partie, je suis allée

b. Which auxiliary verb is used to form the *passé composé* of intransitive verbs? |

être

4. Restate in the *passé composé*.

Modèle: Je parle anglais avec M. Brown. |

J'ai parlé anglais avec M. Brown.

a. Mme Décibelle chante une aria italienne.

b. Nous voyons une opérette.

c. Ils ne font pas de ski nautique au Canada.

d. Elle lit un livre important.

e. M. Cassepied revient du bal avec Mlle Lapauvre.

f. Germaine choisit un cours de sciences politiques.

g. Paul et Philippe répondent «peut-être».

h. Michel, vous allez au Sénégal? |

a. Mme Décibelle a chanté une aria italienne.   b. Nous avons vu une opérette.
c. Ils n'ont pas fait de ski nautique au Canada.   d. Elle a lu un livre important   e. M.
Cassepied est revenu du bal avec Mlle Lapauvre.   f. Germaine a choisi un cours de
sciences politiques.   g. Paul et Philippe ont répondu «peut-être».   h. Michel, vous
êtes allé au Sénégal?

5. This frame will give you practice in using the *futur proche* or the *passé composé*. Use the cues indicated to say what you did, are doing, or are going to do.

> *Modèle:* Demain soir _____. (téléphoner à ma copine Simone) |
> Demain soir je vais téléphoner à ma copine Simone.
>
> Hier matin _____. (envoyer une lettre à Pierre) |
> Hier matin j'ai envoyé une lettre à Pierre.

a. Hier soir _____. (parler à mon oncle au téléphone)

b. Dans une demi-heure _____. (regarder la télévision)

c. Hier après-midi _____. (envoyer au cadeau d'anniversaire à un ami à Dakar)

d. La semaine prochaine _____. (chercher un appartement) |

a. Hier soir j'ai parlé à mon oncle au téléphone   b. Dans une demi-heure je vais regarder la télévision.   c. Hier après-midi j'ai envoyé un cadeau d'anniversaire à un ami
à Dakar.   d. La semaine prochaine je vais chercher un appartement.

À Propos!

Demandez à un/e camarade de classe...

... s'il/elle va faire du sport cet après-midi.

... s'il/elle est allé/e au cinéma la semaine dernière. Si oui, demandez s'il/elle a aimé le film et pourquoi.

... si ses parents vont souvent au cinéma.

4. Indirect object pronouns in the *passé composé*

1. Look at this exchange.

> —Est-ce que tes cousines t'ont écrit?
> —Oui, elles m'ont écrit.

Where are the object pronouns placed? |

before the auxiliary verb

2. Rewrite these sentences in the *passé composé*.
   a. Mélanie nous écrit une carte. |

Mélanie nous a écrit une carte. (Read your answers aloud. This word order is quite different from English, and you need to practice it until it becomes familiar.)

   b. Je t'écris. |

Je t'ai écrit.

   c. Je leur écris. |

Je leur ai écrit.

   d. Vous nous écrivez? |

Vous nous avez écrit.

3. Now look at a negative statement and read it aloud.

   Jules ne nous a pas écrit cette semaine.

   a. What words do *ne* and *pas* surround? |

nous a (the object pronou,. and the auxiliary verb; *pas* comes *before* the participle)

   b. Rewrite this sentence in the negative: *Nous leur avons ré-pondu.* |

Nous ne leur avons pas répondu.

4. Answer these questions in the negative, once with the noun object, then with the pronoun object. Say or read your answers aloud.
   a. As-tu écrit à tes amis? *(non)* |

Non, je n'ai pas écrit à mes amis. Non, je ne leur ai pas écrit.

   b. Est-ce que ton petit frère a obéi à tes parents? *(non)* |

Non, il n'a pas obéi à mes parents. Non, il ne leur a pas obéi.

   c. A-t-elle répondu à son professeur? *(nón)* |

Non, elle n'a pas répondu à son professeur. Non, elle ne lui a pas répondu.

5. Now answer the following questions with object pronouns and the information in parentheses.
   a. Dites, Francois et Christine, qu'est-ce que Michel vous a envoyé de Dakar? *(un beau livre de photos)* |

Il nous a envoyé un beau livre de photos.

   b. Qu'est-ce qu'il a envoyé à son professeur? *(le journal de Dakar)* |

Il lui a envoyé le journal de Dakar.

   c. Est-ce qu'il a écrit à ses parents tous les jours? *(non, pas tous les jours)* |

Non, il ne leur a pas écrit tous les jours.

   d. Est-ce qu'il a écrit à Thérèse? *(oui, souvent)*

Oui, il lui a écrit souvent.

   e. Qu'est-ce qu'il a envoyé à son chien? *(rien!)* |

Il ne lui a rien envoyé!

Note Culturelle
Le riz, le mil et le couscous

Three kinds of grain form an important part of the diet in Senegal: *le riz, le mil* (millet) and *le couscous* (tiny pellets of milled wheat). In rural areas, women prepare *le mil* for cooking by pounding it briskly in a wooden bowl. Often several women work together and sing to the rhythm made by the drumming of the wooden pestle in the bowl. These sounds may be just as much a part of life in an African village as the sound of a teakettle whistling or a coffeepot perking in towns and cities here.

Vocabulaire

Noms

l'argent *m.   money*
le chèque   *check*
la décision   *decision*
la demande   *request*
la facture   *bill*
la lettre ~ d'amour; ~ de condoléances; ~ de félicitations; ~ d'invitation   *letter; love letter; sympathy letter; congratulatory letter; invitation*
la montre   *watch*
l'objet *m.   object*
l'opérette *f.   operetta*
le pique-nique   *picnic*
le ski nautique   *water skiing*
le télégramme   *telegram*

Noms géographiques

le glacier   *glacier*
l'île *f.   island*
le lac   *lake*
la montagne   *mountain*
l'océan *m.   ocean*
la péninsule   *peninsula*
la plaine   *meadow*
le plateau   *plateau*
la rivière   *river*
la vallée   *valley*

Adjectifs

agréable   *pleasant*
excellent   *excellent*

Verbes

coûter   *to cost*
écrire (écri-, écriv-, *pp* écrit)   *to write*
gagner   *to win*
paraître (paraî-, paraiss-, *pp* paru)   *to seem*

Autres mots et expressions

aussi bien   *as well as*
il paraît   *so it seems*
penser à   *to think about*

PRÉPARATION 49

1. Prepositions with cities and countries

1. Look at the patterns below and note the different words French uses to express *in* and *to* with names of cities and countries.

Je vais/Je suis	**à Paris.**	**À:** with names of most cities
	en France.	**En:** with countries with feminine names;
	en Iran.	and with countries with masculine names beginning with a vowel
	au Canada.	**Au:** with countries with masculine singular names
	aux États-Unis.	**Aux:** with countries with plural names

The great majority of countries have feminine singular names. Thus, *en* is used much more frequently than *au* or *aux*. Here are some of the countries with masculine or plural names.

le Canada	le Japon	le Mexique
les États-Unis	le Luxembourg	le Portugal

1. Tell what languages people speak in these countries.
   Modèle: Mexique: espagnol |
   Au Mexique, on parle espagnol.
   a. Belgique: français et flamand
   b. Japon: japonais
   c. Chine: chinois
   d. États-Unis: anglais |

   a. En Belgique, on parle français et flamand.   b. Au Japon, on parle japonais.
   c. En Chine, on parle chinois.   d. Aux États-Unis, on parle anglais.

2. Now look at the following patterns and note the words used to express *from* with the names of cities and countries.

J'arrive	**de Paris.**	**De:** with names of most cities (*du* or *de la* if *le* or *la* are part of the name, e.g. Le Havre, La Havane
	de France. **d'Iran.**	**De** (without article) with countries with feminine names, and with masculine names beginning with a vowel
	du Canada.	**Du:** with countries with masculine singular names
	des États-Unis.	**Des:** with countries with plural names

Say that Bernard is arriving from *l'Italie* (f.) tomorrow.

    Bernard arrive d'Italie demain.

3. Imagine that you're on a film crew touring Sénégal. Tell which city the crew is going to visit on different days of the month. (See key.)

    Modèle: Où va-t-on le six? (Saint-Louis)

        Le six, on va à Saint-Louis.

   a. Où va-t-on le dix? (Thiès)
   b. Où va-t-on le quinze? (Dakar)

4. Tell which cities M. Santini's grandchildren are coming from to celebrate his seventieth birthday. (See key.)

    Modèle: Louise/Grenoble

        Louise vient de Grenoble.

   a. Janine/Montpellier   b. Hervé/Arles

5. Say where the second person in each pair is going. (See key.)
   a. M. Durand va en Suisse; sa femme _____. (Allemagne)
   b. Mme Lambert va aux îles Baléares; son mari _____. (États-Unis)
   c. Mme Cressier va au Maroc; son mari _____. (Canada)

6. Tell what time the following people are arriving at the airport from their country of departure. (See key.)
   a. Mme Joly arrive (Allemagne) à 17h 30.
   b. M. Clément arrive (États-Unis) à 15h.
   c. Michel Bertrand arrive (Sénégal) à midi.

À Propos!   Et vous, êtes-vous allé/e... en Suisse?... au Japon?

2. *La géographie de votre région*

Review the geography terms on p. 359. Then read the following questions aloud. Answer them in complete French sentences. Your answers will depend on where you live; the ones given are just possibilities.

1. Est-ce qu'il y a des montagnes dans l'état (le pays) où vous habitez?

    Oui, il y a des montagnes dans l'état (le pays) où j'habite.

2. Habitez-vous près de la côte? près de quel océan?

    Oui, j'habite près de la côte de l'Océan Atlantique (Pacifique).

3. Votre état (pays) est au nord (au sud, à l'est, à l'ouest) de quel autre état (pays)?

    Mon état est au nord de l'Iowa.

4. Quels grands fleuves y a-t-il dans votre région?

    Il y a le Missouri et le Kansas.

5. Y a-t-il des collines près de votre ville?

    Non, il n'y a pas de collines près de ma ville.

6. Y a-t-il des lacs dans votre état? Près de chez vous?

    Oui, il y a des lacs dans mon état, mais il n'y a pas de lac près de chez moi.

7. Est-ce que votre ville est sur un plateau? Dans une vallée? Près d'un fleuve?

    Ma ville n'est pas sur un plateau. Elle est près d'un fleuve.

3. More on comparisons

Using what you see in the pictures, compare the first person listed with the others listed.

1. a. Constantin/Alphonse *(fort)*

Constantin   Alphonse

Constantin est plus fort qu'Alphonse.

   b. Alphonse/Constantin *(fort)*

Alphonse est moins fort que Constantin.

2. a. Mme Bâton/M. Lepoids *(gros)*

M. Lepoids   M. Bâton   Mme Bâton

Mme Bâton est moins grosse que M. Lepoids.

b. M. et Mme Bâton/M. Lepoids *(maigre)* |

M. et Mme Bâton sont plus maigres que M. Lepoids.

c. Mme Bâton/M. Bâton *(maigre)* |

Mme Bâton est aussi maigre que M. Bâton.

3. a. Charles/Charlotte *(intelligent)* |

Charles   Charlotte

Charles est aussi intelligent que Charlotte.

b. Charlotte/Charles *(intelligent)* |

Charlotte est aussi intelligente que Charles.

4. Now look at these statements.

Cet imperméable n'a pas duré longtemps. Il n'était pas de bonne qualité. Je vais acheter un imperméable de meilleure qualité.

Which word expresses the idea of better? |

meilleure

5. Like the adverb *bien,* the adjective *bon/ne* has an irregular comparative form.

	Equality	*Comparative*
Adjective	aussi **bon**/bons bonne/ bonnes	**meilleur/s** *(superiority)* **meilleure/s** moins bon/s *(inferiority)* moins bonne/s
Adverb	aussi **bien**	**mieux** *(superiority)* moins bien *(inferiority)*

a. Does the adverb form *mieux* change to show gender and number agreement? |

no (Adverbs have only one form.)

b. Give the equivalent of *We have a better idea.* |

Nous avons une meilleure idée.

6. Denis and Claude have different tastes. Use *trouver* to write Denis's statements about what he thinks is better.

Modèle: Claude: J'aime ce disque.

Denis: Moi, je préfère ce disque-ci. |

Je trouve ce disque meilleur.

a. *Claude:* J'aime beaucoup les films de science fiction.

Denis: Moi, je préfère les films policiers. |

Je trouve les films policiers meilleurs.

b. *Claude:* J'aime la moto de Paul.
   Denis: Moi, je préfère ma moto. |

   Je trouve ma moto meilleure.

c. *Claude:* J'aime les tableaux de David et d'Ingres.
   Denis: Moi, je préfère les tableaux des impressionnistes. |

   Je trouve leurs tableaux meilleurs.

7. Read these statements.

   Luciano est applaudi quand il chante.
   Moi, quand je chante, mes amis me demandent d'arrêter.

   Complete these comparisons.
   Luciano chante _____ que moi. C'est un _____ chanteur. |

   mieux; meilleur

4. Stressed pronouns in comparisons

1. Look at these pairs of sentences.

   Charlotte est intelligente. Charles est aussi intelligent qu'elle.
   Charles est intelligent. Charlotte est aussi intelligente que lui.

   What words follow the comparative word *que/qu'*? |

   the pronouns *elle* and *lui*

2. Are these subject pronouns, stressed pronouns, or object pronouns? |

   stressed pronouns

3. Complete these comparisons using the cues with the correct forms of the stressed pronouns.
   a. tu/plus grand/je
   b. il/moins riche/tu
   c. nous/aussi heureux/vous
   d. elles/de meilleures musiciennes/ils |

   a. Tu es plus grand que moi.

   b. Il est moins riche que toi.

   c. Nous sommes aussi heureux que vous.

   d. Elles sont de meilleures musiciennes qu'eux.

À Propos!   Compare yourself to a member of your family.
                Compare two of your friends.
                Compare winter and summer.
                Compare dogs and cats.

5. Double verbs with direct object pronouns

1. You already know how to use direct object pronouns in French sentences that contain one verb, as in the following example.

>Je visite le musée.   *I'm visiting the museum.*
>Je le visite.   *I'm visiting it.*

In French, does the object pronoun precede or follow the verb of which it is an object? |

it precedes (The single exception is that of affirmative imperative: *Visite-le.*)

2. Now look at this example.

>*Jeanne invites Nicole to go to the museum.*
>—Il y a une belle exposition au musée, tu sais! Tu veux la voir aujourd'hui?

a. What is the English equivalent of *Tu veux la voir?* |

Do you want to see it?

b. What are the two verb forms in *Tu veux la voir?* |

veux, voir

c. Which verb is in the infinitive form? |

voir (*Veux* is a present tense form of *vouloir.*)

d. The pronoun *la* refers to *l'exposition.* Is *la* the object of *veux* or of *voir?* |

of *voir* (There's a difference between asking *Tu la veux?* Do you want it?—and *Tu veux la voir?*—Do you want to see it?)

e. In a double verb construction like *Tu veux la voir?* where does the object pronoun occur? |

it precedes the infinitive (because it is the object of the infinitive)

3. Answer this question with *Oui,* and use an object pronoun in your answer. *Tu veux voir le match de football samedi prochain?* |

Oui, je veux le voir.

4. Luc and Françoise like to listen to these records, but Lucie and Annick don't.

>Ils aiment les écouter. Elles n'aiment pas les écouter.

In the negative statement above, which verb is negated—the conjugated verb or the infinitive? |

the conjugated verb

5. Suppose that your little niece has asked you to finish some cookies so that she can ask her parents to buy a new box.

a. Say that you don't want to eat them. |

Je ne veux pas les manger.

b. Say that you can't eat them. |

Je ne peux pas les manger.

6. The verbs below are often used with a second verb that is in the infinitive form. Use them in the situation that follows.

aimer   aller   devoir   pouvoir   vouloir

Various people need to buy shoes and are looking in a store. Write what some of them are thinking as they examine the shoes.

Modèle: I want to buy them in this store. |
Je veux les acheter dans ce magasin.

a. I'm going to buy them in this store. |
Je vais les acheter dans ce magasin.

b. I don't like to buy them in this store.
Je n'aime pas les acheter dans ce magasin.

c. I can't buy them in this store. |
Je ne peux pas les acheter dans ce magasin.

LA COUSCOUSSERIE

Quelle est la spécialité de la maison? En France, il y a partout des restaurants où on peut manger du couscous.

Vocabulaire

Noms
l'arbre *m.   tree*
l'avenue *f.   avenue*
la chose   *thing*
la colline   *hill*
le contraste   *contrast*
la côte   *coast*
le flamand   *Flemish language*
le fleuve   *river*
l'immeuble *m.   building*
le jardin   *garden*
le jardin public   *public garden, park*
la profession   *profession*
le quartier   *neighborhood*
le tableau   *painting*
le technicien   *technician*

Adjectifs
meilleur/e   *better*

Verbes
s'échapper   *to escape*
se précipiter   *to rush*

Autres mots et expressions
déjà   *already*
plusieurs   *several*

PRÉPARATION 50

Séjour au Sénégal

Un An plus tard (1)

Michel est maintenant coopérant à Dakar. Il travaille à la station de
télévision avec des techniciens sénégalais°. Aujourd'hui, il écrit une
lettre à son amie Thérèse qui va avoir 18 ans bientôt.

Senegalese

Chère Thérèse, Joyeux anniversaire°! Dix-huit ans déjà°! Dis donc,
tu es vieille! J'espère que tu vas bien et que tu ne travailles pas trop
au lycée°!

birthday / already

high school

Moi, je travaille beaucoup mais je suis très heureux au Sénégal.
Dakar est une ville d'environ° 390.000 (trois cent quatre-vingt-dix
mille) habitants. Elle est européenne et africaine, et les contrastes
sont très intéressants. Il y a des immeubles° très modernes, de belles
avenues avec des arbres, des jardins publics, des cinémas, des stades
de sport, et une grande université. Mais il y a aussi des quartiers°
très vieux et très pauvres.

approximately

apartment buildings

sections

Échange d'idées

1. Est-ce que vous envoyez souvent des cartes d'anniversaire? À qui?
   Est-ce que vous aimez les cartes sentimentales? humoristiques?
2. Quelles ressemblances y a-t-il entre votre ville et Dakar? Quelles
   différences?

1. Review of some irregular verbs in the *passé composé*

1. Read the statements below made by a group of people who visited
   Senegal and are talking about what they saw.

   Nous avons vu l'université à Dakar.
   J'ai vu la Maison des Esclaves *(slaves)* à Gorée.
   Mes frères ont vu des villages de pêcheurs *(fishing villages)*
   et des pirogues *(small fishing boats, often brightly decorated)*.

   a. What is the English equivalent of the first sentence?
      We saw the university at Dakar.

b. *Vu* is the past participle of the verb _____.

voir

c. Write the French equivalent of *We saw some fishing villages.*

Nous avons vu des villages de pêcheurs.

2. The sentences below talk about what people are seeing at the moment. Rewrite the sentences to tell or ask what they saw in the past. Include the time phrase in your answer. (See key.)

   Modèle: Nous voyons la voiture que tu veux acheter. (hier soir)

Hier soir nous avons vu la voiture que tu veux acheter./Nous avons vu hier soir la voiture que tu veux acheter. (The time phrase may occur in more than one location.)

   a. Ma sœur et ses amis voient un très bon film. (hier soir)
   b. Tu vois les clowns? (hier)
   c. Vous voyez toutes les autos sur la route? (ce soir)

3. Other verbs have an irregular past participle which is a monosyllable with a /y/ sound.

   Do you remember what are the infinitives corresponding to: *dû? pu? lu? bu? eu?*

   devoir   pouvoir   lire   boire   avoir

4. Rewrite the sentences below in the *passé composé* to say that the same things took place before.

   Modèle: Je ne peux pas faire mes exercices.

Je n'ai pas pu faire mes exercices.

   a. Tu as vingt ans aujourd'hui.

Tu as eu vingt ans aujourd'hui.

   b. Nous lisons un excellent article dans le journal.

Nous avons lu un excellent article dans le journal.

   c. Elle ne boit jamais de vin.

Elle n'a jamais bu de vin.

   d. Vous devez être fatigués après votre long voyage.

Vous avez dû être fatigués après votre long voyage.

5. a. *J'ai fait* and *je suis venu(e)* are *passé composé* forms of the infinitives _____ and _____.

faire; venir

   b. Write the French equivalent of *This morning my sister did some errands and came to see me.*

Ce matin ma sœur a fait des courses et elle est venue me voir.

2. Adverbs of quantity

People use adverbs of quantity to measure how much or to count how many in an approximate fashion. You are already acquainted with a number of them. Study the list below and remember that they are all followed by *de* before any noun, singular or plural.

beaucoup de	*a lot of*	ne... pas de	*not any, no*
assez de	*enough*	un peu de	*a small amount of, a little*
ne... jamais de	*never any*		
tant de	*so many, so much*	peu de	*little, few*
trop de	*too much*	(ne) plus de	*(no) more*
		trop peu de	*too little, too few*

1. Henri is teaching his younger sister to make crêpes. Say, then write French equivalents for what he says.

   a. You need a lot of eggs. *Il faut...* |

       Il faut beaucoup d'œufs. (Remember, *de* becomes *d'* before a vowel sound.)

   b. There's not enough flour *(farine).* |

       Il n'y a pas assez de farine.

   c. Don't put in too much milk. *Ne mets pas...* |

       Ne mets pas trop de lait.

   d. Put in more sugar. *Mets...* |

       Mets plus de sucre.

   e. Drat! There's no more sugar! |

       Zut! Il n'y a plus de sucre!

2. You and a couple of friends are planning a backpacking trip. Here are some of the things you are taking.

      des pulls   de l'eau

      des chaussettes   du lait en poudre

      du chocolat   des pommes

As leader of the excursion you are checking the supplies. Give the French equivalents.

   a. We don't have enough water. *(On...)*   d. Do you *(tu)* have enough socks?

   b. We have too much chocolate.   e. I have too many sweaters.

   c. There's too little powdered milk.   f. There are so many apples! |

       a. On n'a pas assez d'eau.   b. On a trop de chocolat.   c. Il y a trop peu de lait en poudre.   d. Tu as assez de chaussettes?   e. J'ai trop de pulls.   f. Il y a tant de pommes!

À Propos!   Comment on two or three aspects of your university life, using adverbs of quantity. (Some topics: *les cours, l'argent, les activités, le temps qu'il fait.*)

3. Using *rien ne, personne ne*

1. *Rien* and *personne* are pronouns. They can be used alone or as objects of a sentence. But they can also function as the subject of a sentence. Read each dialogue, and write English equivalents.

a. —Qu'est-ce que tu veux voir à la télé ce soir?
   —Rien ne m'intéresse. |

b. —Qui va au cinéma avec toi?
   —Personne ne veut sortir ce soir. |

2. When *rien* and *personne* act as subjects, where does *ne* occur? |

3. Victor is feeling low. Write what his friend Alain says about him.
   a. He says that nothing interests him. |

   b. He thinks that no one understands him. |

4. Use *personne ne* and *rien ne* to answer these questions.
   a. Qu'est-ce qui s'est passé? |

   b. Qui a pris mon desert?! |

   c. Qu'est-ce qui te fait peur *(frightens you)*? |

   d. Quelqu'un a téléphoné? |

4. Review: commands with direct object pronouns

1. Tell Yves to do these things. Use a pronoun. (See key.)
   Modèle: Tu dois mettre tes gants. |

   a. Tu dois chercher ton cahier.
   b. Tu dois écrire ces cartes postales.
   c. Tu dois prendre cette salade.
2. Tell Maurice and Claire to do the following things. (See key.)
   Modèle: Vous devez aider vos grands-parents. |

   a. Vous devez envoyer cette carte.
   b. Vous devez manger votre dîner.
   c. Vous devez acheter ces chaussures marron.
3. Suggest to your friends that you do the following things all together. Use the *nous* form of the verb. (See key.)
   a. Il faut écouter ce disque.
   b. Il faut faire cet exercice.
   c. Il faut manger ces crêpes.

Note Culturelle

Urban-rural contrasts in Senegal

In Dakar, one can travel around by bus, by *vélomoteur,* by bicycle, or on foot. To cover a long distance, planes are frequently used. While there are railroad tracks to the interior, the trains tend to be old and unreliable. People going between a city and a nearby village often take a *taxi de brousse* (a large chauffeured station wagon). To travel by river there are ferries—whose schedules may be somewhat unpredictable.

In a city, people live in buildings like those in any European or American city, and an inhabitant isn't likely to know most of the other people in the neighborhood. In a village, houses are made of locally available building materials. In a coastal village, the paths are paved with crushed shells. In an interior village, houses are made of sticks and mud, with a thatched roof. Each house is called *une case,* and each family (consisting of several generations of people) has a number of *cases* gathered together in a group called *une concession.* The chickens, sheep, and goats of the village are not fenced in, but wander at random. Villagers live very close to nature and have great respect for the power of a drought, storm, or illness to influence their lives.

In most parts of a city there is running water and electricity. In a village, water is drawn from a well that the men have dug together, and kerosene lamps and candles provide illumination after dark.

In a city, people's lives run by the clock. In villages, where clocks are often rare, time is measured in more general units, like "tomorrow afternoon."

In a city, many people adopt industrialized values. They compete with each other for better-paying jobs. In a village, people fish or farm with very simple equipment. They cooperate in work in order to survive. They also value friends highly and treat conversation as a skill and as an important means of maintaining personal relationships.

Like many developing nations, Senegal is trying to reconcile the consequences of industrial development with the need to maintain stable cultural values.

À Dakar. Un grand carrefour (intersection).

5. Reading comprehension

Read the following paragraphs concerning the climate of Sénégal. Then answer the questions that follow.

Le Climat du Sénégal

Le Sénégal, sur la côte ouest de l'Afrique, est un pays qui a un climat chaud. Le température maximum est de 29 degrés° et la température minimum est de 18 degrés°.

84°F
64°F

    Il y a deux saisons principales: une saison pluvieuse° et une saison sèche°. En été, de mai à octobre, c'est la saison pluvieuse, qu'on appelle *l'hivernage*. La saison sèche dure de novembre à avril. Le climat n'est pas très bon pour l'agriculture parce qu'il y a trop de pluie° pendant l'hivernage, et pas assez de pluie pendant la saison sèche.

rainy
dry

rain

    Write answers to the questions below.
1. Est-ce que le Sénégal a un climat froid, chaud, ou modéré *(temperate)?*
2. Combien de saisons y a-t-il?
3. Quelle est la température minimum, maximum, et moyenne *(average)?*
4. Est-ce qu'il neige plus ou moins au Sénégal que chez vous?
5. Ce climat est-il bon ou mauvais pour l'agriculture?
6. En général, est-ce que vous jugez ce climat agréable? Pourquoi?

Vocabulaire

Noms

l'autobus   *municipal bus*
l'esclave *m.f.*   *slave*
le lait en poudre   *powdered milk*
la ressemblance   *resemblance*
la route   *road*
le village de pêcheurs   *fishing village*

Autres mots et expressions

à pied   *on foot*
faire peur à qqn   *to frighten someone*
passionnément   *passionately*
plus tard   *later*
toute la journée   *all day*
voyager en   *to travel by a means of transportation*

Verbes

s'habituér à   *to get used to*
se dépêcher   *to hurry*
se moquer de   *to make fun of*
se tromper   *to make a mistake*

Adverbes de quantité

à la folie   *immensely*
assez de   *enough of*
beaucoup de   *a lot of*
ne... jamais de   *never any*
ne... pas de   *not any, no, none*
(ne) plus de   *(no) more of*
(un) peu de   *(a) little bit of*
tant de   *so many*
trop de   *too much of*
trop peu de   *too little of*

PRÉPARATION 51

Séjour au Sénégal

Un an plus tard (2)

J'habite avec un autre coopérant français dans un appartement agréable, avec eau courante° et électricité. Nous avons beaucoup d'amis ⟶ running water
sénégalais. Ils sont gentils, accueillants°, et ils parlent le français aussi ⟶ hospitable
bien que nous. Plusieurs pays d'Afrique ont des dialectes différents
et le français est la seule langue de communication entre eux.

    Je t'envoie une photo de la station de télévision. Devant la porte,
c'est moi avec mon vélo! Ici les autos, même les petites deux che-
vaux°, sont très chères. Et moi, je ne suis pas riche! Alors, je circule° ⟶ with very low horsepower / get around
en vélo, comme tout le monde.

    Je te quitte° maintenant, ma chère Thérèse. Le vélo et le boulot° ⟶ leave / job
m'attendent! Donne le bonjour° de ma part° à tout le monde°. Et ⟶ say hello / for me / everyone / again
encore°, bon anniversaire!

Affectueusement°, ⟶ love
Michel

Préparez un bref message à un/une ami/e pour accompagner une photo que vous envoyez.

There are several ways of ending a letter in French, depending on whom the letter is addressed to. To members of the family or close friends, one could say:

Affectueusement   Bons baisers   Je t'(vous) embrasse (bien fort)

Friends could also say:

En toute amitié   Avec toute mon amitié   (Avec) mes meilleures amitiés   (Avec) mes sincères amitiés   Cordialement.

Formal endings would be:

Je vous prie d'agréer l'assurance de mes sentiments les meilleurs.
Veuillez agréer l'expression de mes sentiments distingués.

1. Review of the *passé composé: prendre, mettre, dire, écrire*

1. Rewrite each verb phrase in the *passé composé.*
   Modèle: Nous prenons du café. |
   Nous avons pris

   a. Je mets mon pull. | a. J'ai mis
   b. Louise et Claude prennent de la glace. | b. Louise et Claude ont pris
   c. Il dit au revoir à sa copine. | c. Il a dit
   d. Vous écrivez une lettre à votre ami? | d. Vous avez écrit

2. Answer these questions according to the cues, and use pronouns when possible.
   Modèle: Qu'est-ce qu'elle t'a dit? *(où elle habite)* |
   Elle m'a dit où elle habite.

   a. Est-ce que Serge a mis son imperméable? *(non)* |
      Non, il ne l'a pas mis.

   b. Ton père et toi, qu'est-ce que vous avez pris au petit déjeuner?
      (des croissants) |
      Nous avons pris des croissants.

   c. Est-ce que les élèves ont dit bonjour au professeur? *(non)* |
      Non, ils ne lui ont pas dit bonjour.

   d. Tu n'as pas écrit à ta cousine? (mais si) |
      Mais si, je lui ai écrit.

3. Write the French equivalent of each sentence.
   a. I put on my gloves.
   b. Brigitte wrote a letter to her aunt.
   c. You did not say good-by to Pierre.

d. We had eggs for breakfast.

> a. J'ai mis mes gants.   b. Brigitte a écrit une lettre à sa tante.   c. Tu n'as pas dit / vous n'avez pas dit au revoir à Pierre.   d. Nous avons pris des œufs pour le petit déjeuner.

4. Do these past participles end in the vowel sound /e/ or /i/ ? |

> in the vowel sound / i / (The final consonants *s* and *t* are not pronounced in the masculine forms.)

À Propos!

Qu'est-ce que vous avez mis la dernière fois que vous êtes allé/e à un match de football? à un mariage?

2. Practice with reflexive verbs in the *passé composé*

You have seen that, like the intransitive verbs (*aller, venir,* etc.) the reflexive verbs use *être* to form the *passé composé,* and their past participles agree with the subject. Read the following sentences:

> Elle se lève à 8h et elle va déjeuner.
> *She gets up at 8 and she goes to have breakfast.*

> Elle s'est levée à 8h et elle est allée déjeuner.
> *She got up at 8 and she went to have breakfast.*

Most of the reflexive verbs you have used so far express physical actions done to oneself (*se peigner, s'habiller, se coucher,* etc.). Many useful reflexive verbs have a more abstract meaning:

se dépêcher (de)	*to hurry to (do something)*
se fâcher (contre)	*to get upset or angry at*
s'habituer (à)	*to get used to*
se tromper (de)	*to make a mistake*

1. Use these verbs to complete the following statements, using the *passé composé,* and write the English equivalents.

> *Modèle:* Ils _____ quand je leur ai dit qu'ils étaient stupides. (se fâcher) |

> Ils se sont fâchés *(They got upset when I told them they were stupid.)*

a. Vous _____! Vous avez tourné à droite et vous deviez tourner à gauche. (se tromper) |

> Vous vous êtes trompé *(You made a mistake! You turned right when you were supposed to turn left.)*

b. Nous _____ à cette ville, mais au commencement nous ne l'ai-
mions pas. (s'habituer) |

> Nous nous sommes habitués *(We got accustomed to this city, but at first we did not like it.)*

c. Ils _____ pour arriver plus tôt que nous. (se dépêcher) |

> Ils se sont dépêchés *(They hurried to arrive earlier than we did.)*

3. More on double verbs with object pronouns

In Préparation 49, you practiced using direct object pronouns in double-verb constructions, as in *Je vais le voir.* (I'm going to see him.)
Indirect object pronouns will be used in the same way.
Complete the French equivalent of each sentence.

a. He's going to write me tomorrow. Il va _____ demain. |

> m'écrire

b. You have to call him. Tu dois _____. |

> lui téléphoner

c. In the French sentence, does the object pronoun precede the
main verb or the infinitive? |

> it precedes the infinitive (Object pronouns in a double-verb construction precede the verb of which they are an object—the *second* verb.)

Placement of object pronouns

One verb	*Verb + infinitive*
Subject + object pronoun + verb	Subject + verb + object pronoun + infinitive
Je **l'**achète.	Je vais **l'**acheter.
Je **ne l'**achète **pas.**	Je **ne** vais **pas l'**acheter.

2. Say aloud, then write that Mireille wants to speak to the following
people. Use the appropriate indirect object pronoun.

> *Modèle:* à sa tante |
> Elle veut lui parler.

a. à son grand-père | Elle veut lui parler.
b. à ses amies | Elle veut leur parler.
c. à toi | Elle veut te parler.
d. à vous et à moi | Elle veut nous parler.

3. Say that it's necessary to buy or do the following things right
away. Use *il faut* and the appropriate object pronoun in your responses.

> *Modèle:* acheter ce chapeau |
> Il faut l'acheter tout de suite.

a. écrire à votre père   c. inviter tes cousins
b. téléphoner à tes parents   d. mettre ce manteau |

a. Il faut lui écrire tout de suite.   b. Il faut leur téléphoner tout de suite.   c. Il faut les inviter tout de suite.   d. Il faut le mettre tout de suite.

4. Tell a friend that he or she should do the following things. Use an indirect object pronoun in your answers. (See key.)

    Modèle: envoyer une carte à Jean et à Marguerite |

        Tu dois leur envoyer une carte.

a. écrire à ton amie Françoise
b. répondre tout de suite à ton professeur
c. donner ton adresse à tes amis

Que voyez-vous sur ce dessin?

4. The recent past and object pronouns

1. Look at the questions and answers below.

    —Tu as regardé la photo de la station de télévision?
    —Oui, je viens de la regarder.

    —Tu as dit au revoir à tes grands-parents?
    —Oui, je viens de leur dire au revoir.

2. In sentences using the recent past, are direct and indirect object pronouns placed before *venir de* or before the infinitive? |

    before the infinitive (Note that the *pronouns le* and *les* never contract with *de*.)

3. Answer using *venir de* and an object pronoun.

    Modèle: Tu as vu mon vélo? |

        Oui, je viens de le voir.

a. Vous avez acheté cette "deux-chevaux" *(small Citroën car)*? |

        Oui, je viens de l'acheter.

b. Est-ce que vous avez envoyé la photo de Michel? |

        Oui, je viens de l'envoyer.

c. Thérèse lui a répondu? |

        Oui, Thérèse vient de lui répondre.

d. Leurs parents leur ont téléphoné au Sénégal? |

        Oui, ils viennent de leur téléphoner.

5. Reading comprehension

Each frame in this section is a riddle about one kind of transportation. English equivalents are given for new words you might not be able to guess.

French speakers use *ça (it or that)* in riddles because *ça* doesn't give away the gender of the unnamed thing, as *il* or *elle* would. (See key.)

Moyens de transports	*(Means of transportation)*
l'autobus *m.*	le train
l'autocar *m.*	le vélo (la bicyclette)
l'avion *m.*	le vélomoteur
le bateau	la voiture (l'auto) *f.*
la moto	

Moyens de transport

1. Ça a deux roues° comme une bicyclette, mais ça a aussi un petit moteur. Quand il pleut ou quand il fait froid, ça n'est pas très agréable. Qu'est-ce que c'est? — wheels

2. Ça contient° des places pour deux, quatre, et même° six personnes. Ça a une grande variété de styles et de modèles. Mais en ville, il y a souvent un problème difficile—on ne sait pas où la mettre. Qu'est-ce que c'est? — contains / even

3. Vous prenez le petit déjeuner à New York, et vous voulez être à San Francisco pour le déjeuner? Oui, c'est possible avec ça. Qu'est-ce que c'est?

4. Ça n'a pas de moteur. Ça a une place pour une personne seulement. C'est moins rapide que les autres moyens de transport, mais c'est moins cher aussi. Qu'est-ce que c'est?

5. Ça a deux roues comme une bicyclette ou un vélomoteur. Ça a aussi un moteur puissant° et bruyant°. Est-ce que c'est dangereux? Ça dépend du chauffeur. Qu'est-ce que c'est? — powerful / noisy

6. Ça peut naviguer sur les océans, les lacs, ou les rivières. Parfois°, ça a un moteur; parfois ça a des voiles°. Ça n'est pas très rapide, mais si vous n'êtes pas pressé, c'est la manière idéale de voyager. Qu'est-ce que c'est? — sometimes / sails

7. Si vous voulez voyager d'une ville à une autre, vous pouvez utiliser ce mode de locomotion. Ça a un gros moteur. Ça a assez de places pour un grand nombre de passagers. Ça roule° rapidement sur les autoroutes. Qu'est-ce que c'est? — travels, "rolls"

8. Ça n'est pas aussi rapide qu'un avion, mais c'est plus rapide qu'une voiture. Vous faites un long voyage? Pas de problème, parce qu'il y a un restaurant et même des wagons-lits°. Qu'est-ce que c'est? — sleeping cars

6. *Imparfait* vs. *passé composé*

Fill the blanks in the following text with the correct form of either the *imparfait* or the *passé composé* of the verb in parentheses. Decide whether the verb expresses a one-time action or event *(passé composé),* or describes the situation that existed when the action or event took place *(imparfait).*

Michel Bertrand se rappelle son arrivée au Sénégal. Le jour où je/j' *(1. arriver)* au Sénégal, il *(2. faire)* un temps splendide. Ce/C' *(3. être)* un dimanche matin et les oiseaux tropicaux *(4. chanter).* Je/J' *(5. décider)* de faire le tour de la ville tout de suite, parce qu'il y *(6. avoir)* beaucoup de choses que je/j' *(7. vouloir)* voir. Je/J' *(8. prendre)* une vieille rue et bientôt je/j' *(9. voir)* des hommes qui *(10. porter)* des tuniques longues et flottantes, des femmes avec des jupes de couleurs vives et brillantes. Il y *(11. avoir)* aussi beaucoup d'enfants qui *(12. être)* très gentils et qui *(13. dire bonjour)* poliment. Je/J' *(14. acheter)* quelques fruits exotiques qui *(15. être)* délicieux. Dakar me *(16. paraître)* une jolie ville et je *(17. être)* heureux. |

1. je suis arrivé 2. il faisait 3. c'était 4. chantaient 5. j'ai decidé 6. il y avait 7. je voulais 8. j'ai pris 9. j'ai vu 10. portaient 11. il y avait 12. étaient 13. disaient 14. j'ai acheté 15. étaient 16. m'a paru / me paraissait 17. j'étais

À Dakar. Longues robes bariolées (many-colored), démarche (bearing) noble et gracieuse: les femmes traversent la rue, le marché fini.

Note Culturelle
A statesman's poetry

Léopold Sédar Senghor, the first president of Senegal, is also well known as a poet and essayist in French. In his writings, he celebrates the warmth and humanity of African societies—qualities which he feels have been lost in many industrial cultures. His poetry combines both French and African artistic traditions. Some of his works are intended to be read aloud to the accompaniment of traditional African music played on the kora, balafon, and tam-tam. Here is part of the poem *"Nuit de Sine"* (excerpted from *Chants d'ombre,* copyright Editions du Seuil, 1945) and an English translation.

... Là-haut, les palmes balancées qui bruissent dans la haute brise nocturne
À peine. Pas même la chanson de nourrice.
Qu'il nous berce, le silence rythmé.
Écoutons son chant, écoutons battre notre sang sombre, écoutons
Battre le pouls profond de l'Afrique dans la brume des villages perdus...

... Above, swaying palms that rustle in the high night breeze
Almost not at all. Not even a lullaby.
Let the rhythmic silence cradle us.
Let us listen to its song, let us listen to the drumming of our dark blood,
Let us listen
To the deep pulse of Africa, beating in the mist of villages forgotten...

Vocabulaire

Noms

l'arme *f.* *arm*
le boulot *work*
le cheval/chevaux *horse(es)*
le climat *climate*
la communication *communication*
le coureur *runner*
le correspondant *pen pal*
la deux-chevaux *low horsepower car*
le dialecte *dialect*
l'expert *m.* *expert*
la langue *language*
le nom *name*
l'oiseau *m.* *bird*
le prisonnier *prisoner*
la situation *situation*

Adjectifs

accueillant/e *welcoming*
tropical/e *tropical*

Verbes

circuler *to get around*
courir *to run*
sauter *to jump*
quitter *to leave*

Autres mots et expressions

donner le bonjour *say hello*
tout de suite *right away*
de ma part *from/for me*

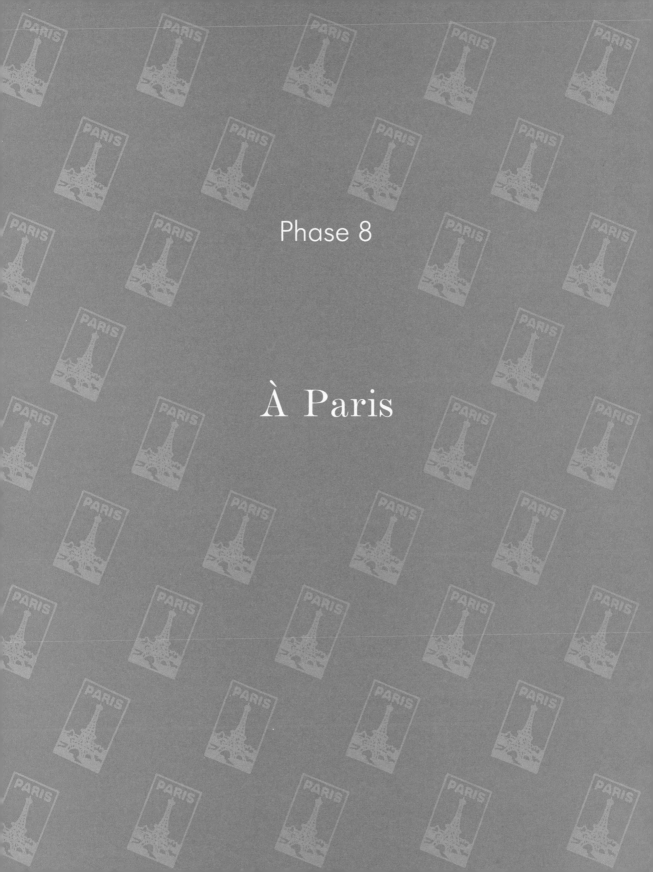

Phase 8

À Paris

Qu'est-ce que vous allez apprendre?

In this Phase you will hear about Michel Bertrand's return from his stay as a *coopérant* in Senegal and his impressions of Paris after his long absence from home.

Communication

By the end of this Phase you will be able to:
  Use interrogative pronouns for expressing *who* or *what*.
  Express duration with *journée, matinée, soirée, année.*
  Distinguish three expressions: *le temps, la fois, l'heure,* all of which can translate as *time.*
  Replace locative expressions with the pronoun *y* and partitive phrases with the pronoun *en.*
  Use the appropriate prepositions after certain verbs.
  Express the notions of *all, every, whole,* and *entire* using the adjective *tout.*
  Express various possible results of a situation by using conditional verb forms.

Culture

Paris as a modern city, as a center for intellectual and artistic activities (*Quartier latin, le Marais, Beaubourg*) and as a city where one can enjoy a leisurely stroll down a tree-lined boulevard or a boat trip on the Seine.

PRÉPARATION 52

Retour à Paris

Scène 1 Sur les Champs-Elysées

Michel et Thérèse sont sur les Champs-Elysées, près de la Place de
la Concorde.

Thérèse Alors, comment trouves-tu Paris après ta longue absence?
Michel Merveilleux! Et grand!
Thérèse Comment, grand? Mais Paris a toujours été grand!
Michel Oui, mais quand on est loin, on oublie... Maintenant, après
    Dakar, je trouve Paris immense.
Thérèse Tu as pensé à Paris pendant ton séjour au Sénégal?
Michel Oui, bien sûr! Dans mon esprit°, j'ai souvent revu° les   mind / seen again
    Champs-Elysées, par exemple, mais jamais tellement° beaux, telle-   so
    ment impressionnants°.   impressive
Thérèse Dis donc, tu parles comme un poète! Tu as oublié les as-
    pects désagréables de Paris...
Michel Quoi? Tu veux dire° toute cette circulation°...   you mean / traffic
Thérèse Oui, la circulation difficile, les gens qui courent toujours, et
    aussi la pollution, les prix astronomiques...

Échange d'idées

1. Work in pairs.
   A friend of yours just came back from abroad where he/she spent
   his/her junior year. You first ask a few questions about what he/
   she did... etc. and then:
   S1: Ask your partner how he/she feels being back at the college.
   S2: Reply.
   S1: Ask for precision. *Qu'est-ce que tu veux dire?*
   S2: Try to explain.
   S1: Ask if S2 has thought of friends back in the states a lot?
   S2: Reply either «Oui, bien sûr; Quelquefois...; Non pas du
   tout,... (oublier)»
   S1: Express satisfaction, annoyance, surprise, depending on the
   previous answer.
2. Tell a classmate about your reactions to your last visit to a big
   city. Express your likes and dislikes of big cities and the lifestyle
   of city people. (Use the verb *trouver.*) Are you a city person?

Les toits de Paris et la Tour Eiffel.

1. Practice with relative pronouns

1. The relative pronoun _____ is the subject of a relative clause. |

   qui

2. The relative pronoun _____ is the direct object of the verb in a relative clause. |

   que

3. Complete the sentences with a *qui*- or a *que*-clause based on the information given in parentheses. (See key.)

   Modèle: La petite fille _____ est ma sœur. *(Tu vois la petite fille.)* |

   La petite fille que tu vois est ma sœur.

   a. Les pays d'Afrique _____ sont fascinants. *(Tu viens de visiter ces pays.)*

   b. Cette jeune fille _____ est professeur à Paris. *(Elle va venir nous voir.)*

c. Les diapos _____ sont excellentes. (*Vous montrez les diapos aux étudiants.*)

d. Mon père _____ aime faire des promenades en auto. (*Il est assez vieux.*)

e. Ma tante Lucie _____ ne m'écrit pas souvent. (*Elle habite à Marseille.*)

2. Practice with comparisons

Write the retort of somebody who feels superior to everyone else.

Modèle: Mon cousin est très riche. |

Je suis plus riche que lui.

Il nage très vite. |

Je nage plus vite que lui.

a. Sa voiture marche vite.

b. Il a une maison très confortable.

c. Il a beaucoup d'amis.

d. Il voyage souvent. |

a. Ma voiture marche plus vite que sa voiture. b. J'ai une maison plus confortable que sa maison. c. J'ai plus d'amis que lui. d. Je voyage plus souvent que lui.

3. Double verbs with object pronouns: practice

1. Direct and indirect object pronouns usually precede a conjugated verb form, for example, *Je lui écris.* When there is a double-verb construction, however, as in *Je vais lui écrire,* where is the object pronoun? |

before the infinitive (the second verb)

2. Answer the following questions in the affirmative. Replace the italic words with the appropriate object pronouns. (See key.)

Modèle: Tu aimes écouter *la musique moderne?* |

Oui, j'aime l'écouter.

a. Vous allez donner ce disque *à votre frère?*

b. Ton père veut dire bonjour *aux voisins?*

c. Est-ce que Jeanine va voir *ses amis sénégalais* au restaurant?

d. Vous voulez acheter *ce maillot de bain?*

3. Say that you can't do these things now. (See key.)

Modèle: Parle aux enfants! |

Non, je ne peux pas leur parler maintenant.

a. Écris à ton oncle!

b. Envoie ces cadeaux à Gilliane et à Catherine.

c. Donne ce transistor au professeur.

4. Practice with *ne... rien, ne... personne*

1. Remember that in the *passé composé, rien* occupies the same place in a sentence as *pas* and *jamais. Personne,* however, occupies a different place.

    a. Insert *rien: Je n'ai _____ vu _____.* |

    Je n'ai rien vu. *(I didn't see anything.)*

    b. Insert *personne: Je n'ai _____ vu _____.* |

    Je n'ai vu personne. *(I didn't see anyone.)*

2. Two witnesses to a break-in contradict each other. Write what the second one says.

    Modèle: Quand nous sommes arrivés, j'ai entendu un bruit. |

    Je n'ai rien entendu.

    J'ai vu un homme qui entrait. |

    Je n'ai vu personne qui entrait.

    a. —J'ai appelé M. Durand. —Je n'_____.

    b. —M. Durand a dit qu'il allait téléphoner à la police.
    —M. Durand n'_____.

    c. —L'homme a pris plusieurs objets. —L'homme n'_____.

    d. —La police a attrapé *(caught)* l'homme. —La police n'_____. |

    a. Je n'ai appelé personne.   b. M. Durand n'a téléphoné à personne.   c. L'homme n'a rien pris.   d. La police n'a attrapé personne.

Vocabulaire

Noms

l'absence *f.*   *absence*
l'aspect *m.*   *aspect, characteristic*
le bruit   *noise*
la carte postale   *post card*
la circulation   *traffic*
l'esprit *m.*   *mind*
la nourriture   *food*
le poète   *poet*
la pollution   *pollution*
le prix   *price*
le séjour   *stay*

Adjectifs

astronomique   *astronomical*
bête   *stupid, silly*
bon marché *(inv.)*   *inexpensive*
confortable   *comfortable*
désagréable   *unpleasant*
immense   *immense*
impressionnant/e   *impressive*
long/ue   *long*

Verbes

attraper   *to catch*
fabriquer   *to build*
permettre   *to allow*
revoir   *to see again*

Autres mots et expressions

comment?   *what do you mean?*
par exemple   *for example*
quoi?   *what?*

PRÉPARATION 53

1. Verbs followed directly by the infinitive

1. Look at the following sentence and give the English equivalent:
   a. La semaine prochaine nous allons partir en voyage. |
      Next week we are going to leave on a trip.
   b. In the *futur proche* construction, the conjugated verb *aller* is followed directly by the _____. |
      infinitive
   c. Two more verbs followed directly by the infinitive mean *to want to* and *can, to be able to:* _____ and _____. |
      vouloir, pouvoir

Here are a number of other verbs that are followed directly by an infinitive.

aimer mieux	*to prefer to*	**espérer**	*to hope to*
adorer	*to like very much to*	**devoir**	*to have to, must*
préférer	*to prefer to*	**savoir**	*to know how to*
il vaut mieux	*it is better to*	**sembler**	*to seem to*

Les Invalides.

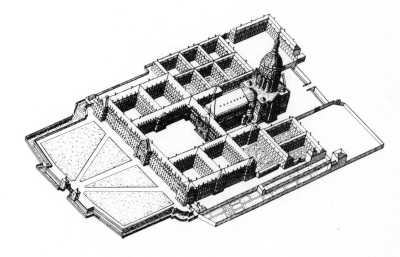

2. Make eight logical sentences, using possible combinations of the elements below. Make four of them affirmative, two negative, and two interrogative.

> Modèle: 6–2–2 |
>
> Je dois me lever à sept heures.

1 vous	1 vouloir	1 manger de la glace
2 Suzanne	2 devoir	2 se lever à sept heures
3 les étudiants	3 espérer	3 jouer aux échecs
4 nous	4 adorer	4 s'habiller pour sortir
5 tu	5 pouvoir	5 composer un poème
6 je	6 aller	6 se promener à pied

2. Practice with negation in the *passé composé*

1. Read these sentences:

> Pour le petit déjeuner, Pierre prend du thé. Il ne prend pas de café.
> Anne a pris de la viande mais elle n'a pas pris de légumes.

a. In a sentence with the *passé composé*, are *ne* and *pas* placed around the auxiliary verb or the past participle? |

the auxiliary verb

b. After a negative verb, the markers *du, de la, de l', un, une,* and *des* usually become _____. |

de

2. Answer the following questions with a negative sentence.

> Modèle: Tu as envoyé des lettres à ta famille? |
>
> Non, je n'ai pas envoyé de lettres à ma famille.

a. Vous avez fait un gâteau pour son anniversaire? |

Non, nous n'avons pas fait de gâteau pour son anniversaire.

b. Philippe a donné des fleurs (*flowers*) à Marie-Hélène? |

Non, il n'a pas donné de fleurs à Marie-Hélène.

c. Gérard et Guy ont pris un taxi pour venir? |

Non, ils n'ont pas pris de taxi pour venir.

d. Tu as donné ton numéro de téléphone à Philippe? |

Non, je n'ai pas donné mon numéro de téléphone à Philippe.

e. Il a invité ses amis pour vendredi soir? |

Non, il n'a pas invité ses amis pour vendredi soir.

3. Georges is going to be in a circus and is putting together a clown costume. Say that he has never bought the following clothes before. (See key.)

> Modèle: acheter un pantalon de velours |
>
> Il n'a jamais acheté de pantalon de velours.

a. un chapeau jaune

b. des chaussures rouges

c. une chemise rose

d. des gants gris

À Propos!   Prepare a question asking your classmate if she/he has ever bought velvet pants; if he/she has given flowers to someone recently. Be prepared to answer for yourself.

3. Interrogative pronouns

In this section you will learn ways of phrasing questions that ask *who? what?* or *whom?,* alone or with a preposition. There are two ways to form such questions in French—a short form and a long form.

Look at the chart of the short forms.

	Person *(Who? Whom?)*	Thing *(what?)*
Subject of a verb	**Qui a fait** ce bruit?	*(no short form)*
Direct object of a verb	**Qui voyez-vous?**	**Que voyez-vous?**
Indirect object (with a preposition)	**De qui as-tu parlé?**	**De quoi as-tu parlé?**

1. a. What is the meaning of *Qui a fait ce bruit?* |

   Who made that noise?

   b. Is the word order the same in French and in English? |

   yes

2. a. What are the meanings of *Qui voyez-vous?* and *Que voyez-vous?* |

   Whom (who) do you see? What do you see? (*Qui* asks about people, *que* asks about things. When *qui* and *que* function as direct objects, the subject and verb are inverted to form the question, while in English we use the auxiliary *do.*)

3. a. Write the equivalents of *De qui as-tu parlé?* and *De quoi as-tu parlé?* |

   Whom did you talk about? What did you talk about? (With a preposition, *qui* is used to ask about people, *quoi*—a stressed form of *que*—about things.)

   b. Do the prepositions occur in the same place in French as in English? |

   no (In English, *Of what did you speak?* sounds stilted. In French, a preposition cannot be placed at the end of a sentence.)

   c. In French, what is the order of the subject and verb? |

   inverted

4. Refer to the chart in order to write French equivalents.
   a. Who is living in France?
   b. Whom do you *(vous)* love?
   c. What do you *(vous)* like?
   d. Whom does she go out with?
   e. What do they write with? |

5. Read the answers aloud to become familiar with the word order. Now look at the chart of long interrogative forms.

	People	*Things*
Subject of a verb	**Qui est-ce qui** a fait ce bruit?	**Qu'est-ce qui** a fait ce bruit?
Direct object of a verb	**Qui est-ce que** vous voyez?	**Qu'est-ce que** vous voyez?
Indirect object of a verb (with a preposition)	**De qui est-ce que** tu as parlé?	**De quoi est-ce que** tu as parlé?

The sentences used as examples for the long form have *exactly* the same meaning as the sentences used for the short form:

Who made that noise? What made that noise?
Whom do you see? What do you see?
Whom did you talk about? What did you talk about?

6. Look at the subject interrogative forms. What is the only difference between the form for people and the form for things? |

The first word—*qui* or *qu'*—tells whether the pronoun refers to people or things. The phrase *est-ce qui* indicates the function of the phrase as a subject.

7. Look at the four object interrogative forms. What phrase follows *qui* and *qu'*, *de qui* and *de quoi*? |

8. Even though the long forms may seem unwieldy, most of them are used more frequently in informal speech than the short forms. Write equivalents using the long forms.
   a. Who is living in France?
   b. What happened *(est arrivé)*?
   c. Whom do you love?
   d. What do you like?
   e. Whom does she go out with?
   f. What do they write with? |

Phase huit

4. Expressions of duration: *jour, journée,* etc.

While English has only one word for year, day, morning, and evening, French has two: *un an, une année; un jour, une journée; un matin, une matinée; un soir, une soirée.*

1. The short word is used to express a basic division of time: *un an* = 365 days, *un jour* = 24 hours. *Le matin* is roughly the period from dawn to noon, *le soir* is roughly from the evening meal to bedtime.

   The longer word expresses time as felt and experienced rather than clock time or calendar time. It refers to the passage of a period of time, and its contents, activities, and events.

   Read the following to compare the long and short forms.

   Mon oncle a passé trois *ans* au Japon. La première *année* a été difficile parce qu'il ne connaissait personne.

   Mes parents sont allés en Floride pour quinze *jours* de vacances. Ils ont bien profité *(took advantage of)* des merveilleuses *journées* ensoleillées *(sunny).*

2. Decide whether to use *le jour* or *la journée.*
   a. Il pleut et il fait froid. Quel(le) _____ désagréable!
   b. J'ai beaucoup de cours aujourd'hui. Le (La) _____ va être long(ue).
   c. Il y a sept _____ dans une semaine.
   d. Il pleuvait le (la) _____ où il a rencontré Suzie.
   e. Le (La) _____ de son mariage, elle est tombée malade.
   f. Je ne regarde jamais la télévision pendant le (la) _____. |

   a. journée   b. journée   c. jours   d. jour   e. jour   f. journée

5. Three words for time: *temps, fois, heure*

1. Compare these English and French sentences.

Time is money.	Le temps, c'est de l'argent.
What time is it?	Quelle heure est-il?
He called three times this week.	Il a téléphoné trois fois cette semaine.

   a. Which sentence refers to clock time? |

   Quelle heure est-il? (*Heure* can mean *time* as in clock time, or *hour.*)

   b. Which sentence refers to a specific number of occurrences? |

   Il a téléphoné trois fois *(three times)* cette semaine.

   c. Which sentence refers to time as a general, abstract idea—not to a specific time? |

   Le temps, c'est de l'argent.

2. Complete with *Combien de fois* or *Combien de temps*.
   a. _____ faut-il pour aller d'ici à Paris? |
      Combien de temps (*How much* time?)
   b. _____ par an allez-vous à Paris? |
      Combien de fois (*How many* times?)

3. Which term completes each sentence—*le temps, la fois,* or *l'heure*?
   a. _____ passe vite quand on s'amuse. |
   b. Il arrive toujours à six _____. |
   c. Une _____ j'ai oublié mon stylo et j'avais un examen. |
   d. Tu passes trop de _____ à te regarder dans la glace. |
   e. Vous avez beaucoup de _____ aujourd'hui, vous pouvez nettoyer l'appartement. Je l'ai nettoyé deux _____ le mois dernier. |
   f. Le professeur va à la fac trois _____ par semaine.

a. Le temps
b. heures
c. fois
d. temps

e. temps/fois
f. fois

6. Writing practice: *votre région*

1. Read the following paragraph about Geneva, which may help you write about your country or region.

Genève est une ville importante dans la partie francophone de la Suisse. On appelle cette région «la Suisse romande». Genève est une jolie ville située au bord du lac Léman. Elle est connue pour toutes les organisations internationales qui y° sont installées, la Croix° Rouge, l'ancienne Société des Nations, etc. Dans un de ses squares°, au face du lac, s'élève° la statue de Jean-Jacques Rousseau, un grand philosophe et écrivain, né dans cette ville en 1712.

there / cross
public square
rises

   Le premier août est une grande fête. C'est la fête de l'indépendance suisse. Ce jour-là, il y a beaucoup de monde° dans les rues° et, le soir, on tire° de beaux feux d'artifice° sur le lac.

people / streets
they shoot / fireworks

   Ce jour-là aussi, certains groupes régionaux portent des costumes folkloriques. Les autres jours, bien sûr, les Suisses portent des vêtements ordinaires et la mode° à Genève n'est pas différente de la mode des grandes villes européennes.

fashion

1. Décrivez une ville ou région importante de votre pays, de votre état ou de votre région.
   a. Quelles langues ou quels dialectes est-ce qu'on y parle?
   b. Cette ville ou région est connue pour quelles choses?
   c. Quelle sorte de nourriture mange-t-on le plus souvent?
   d. Quels sont les sports populaires?
2. Écrivez quelques phrases sur un des sujets suivants:
   a. un monument ou personnage (*character*) célèbre, important, ou historique de votre pays.
   b. un écrivain, un musicien, ou un peintre de votre pays.
   c. une des grandes fêtes (*holidays, festivals*) de votre pays.

Phase huit

Up to now, the *Notes Culturelles* have been written in English. They
will be in French from now on because you have learned enough to
understand them easily, and this practice in reading will reinforce
what you know.

Note Culturelle
L'économie de la France

La France est un pays où l'agriculture est
très importante. La culture du blé *(wheat)*
est importante dans la Beauce, une grande
plaine au sud de Paris. En Normandie, on
élève[1] des vaches[2] pour avoir du lait, de la
crème, du beurre et du fromage. Le vin est
un produit qui a une importance énorme en
France. Les Français exportent beaucoup
de vin.

Mais il y a aussi beaucoup de régions
industrielles en France. À Billancourt, près
de Paris, il y a une usine d'automobiles
Renault. On fabrique[3] des vélos Peugeot
dans une usine à Valentigney, près de la
Suisse. La ville de Lyon, par exemple, est
renommée[4] pour l'industrie de la soie[5] et du
pétrole.

1 raise 2 cows 3 manufacture 4 famous 5 silk

Vocabulaire

Noms

l'avant-garde *f.* *avant garde*
la fleur *flower*
l'hôtel *m.* *hotel*
le peintre *painter*
le personnage *character*
la poche *pocket*
la région *region*
le taxi *taxi*

Adjectifs

ensoleillé/e *sunny*
rafraîchissant/e *refreshing*

Verbes

arriver (with impersonal subject) *to happen*
composer *to compose, to write*
occuper *to fill (time)*
passer *to spend (time)*
profiter de *to take advantage of*
tirer *to shoot*

Autres mots et expressions

de qui, de quoi *about whom?, about what?*
il vaut mieux *it's better*
qu'est-ce que *what (object)*
qu'est-ce qui *what (subject)*
qui est-ce que *whom (object)*
qui est-ce qui *who (subject)*

Expressions de durée

un soir, une soirée *an evening*
par (an) *per (year), in a (year)*
un an, une année *a year*
un jour, une journée *a day*
un matin, une matinée *a morning*

PRÉPARATION 54

Retour à Paris

Scène 2 À la Place de la Concorde

Michel et Thérèse sont maintenant à la Place de la Concorde. Il y a beaucoup de voitures, beaucoup de monde°...   many people

Michel Oh là là! Qu'est-ce que c'est, toute cette foule°? Et tous ces agents de police°?   crowd / policemen

Thérèse Je ne sais pas! Encore° un accident, sans doute.   another

Femme 1 Oui, un taxi a écrasé° une femme et deux enfants.   run over

Homme 1 Mais non, un chauffeur de taxi a kidnappé deux enfants.

Femme 2 Pas du tout°! Il y a eu un hold-up dans un taxi. Une femme armée d'un revolver a pris l'argent du chauffeur.   not at all

Agent Allons, allons, circulez°, circulez!   move on, drive on

Homme 2 On a arrêté° les gangsters?   did they arrest

Agent Quels gangsters? Il n'y a pas eu de gangsters. Un taxi a ren-
versé° un motocycliste, c'est tout... Allez, allez, circulez, s'il vous   knocked down
plaît.

Thérèse Alors°, Michel, comment trouves-tu Paris maintenant?   well

Michel Quoi? Paris a des problèmes? Bien sûr, comme toutes les
grandes villes!

Échange
d'idées

1. Avez-vous vu ou eu un accident d'auto? Racontez-le: Quand, où
   et dans quelles circonstances? Quels étaient vos sentiments?
   Quelles ont été les conséquences de l'accident?
2. Imagine that you and a classmate are standing on the sidewalk
   near the scene of an accident. Passers-by ask you what happened.
   Carry out a short conversation between all of you.

1. The pronoun *y*

The pronoun *y* (there) can replace locative expressions introduced
by a preposition such as *à, chez, dans, devant,* etc. In this section
you'll learn how to use *y* in affirmative and negative sentences.

1. Read the following pairs of sentences. Write the prepositional
   phrases that *y* replaces.
   a. —Tu vas à Lyon?
      —Oui, j'y vais la semaine prochaine. | a. à Lyon
   b. —Le cahier est dans le tiroir?
      —Oui, il y est. | b. dans le tiroir
   c. —Tu manges au restaurant universitaire?
      —Non, je n'y mange pas. | c. au restaurant
      universitaire
2. Look back at frame 1. In affirmative and negative statements,
   does *y* precede or follow the verb? |
       it precedes
3. In English, if someone asks you *Are you going to the stadium?*, you
   can respond simply with *Yes* or with complete sentences: *Yes, I'm
   going there,* or *Yes, I'm going,* or *Yes, I am.* You don't need to
   include the word "there." In French, if someone asks *Tu vas au
   stade?* you may answer with just *Oui.* In a complete answer, however, you must always include the word *y.*
   Answer these questions with a complete sentence.
   a. Tu vas en Suisse? |
          Oui, j'y vais. *(Yes, I'm going (there)/Yes, I am.)*
   b. Roger va à l'aéroport? |
          Oui, il y va. *(Yes, he's going (there)./Yes, he is.)*
4. Answer these questions according to the cues, using *y.*
   Modèle: Jean va au supermarché? (oui, à deux heures) |
          Oui, il y va à deux heures.

a. Vos parents vont en Europe? (oui, en août) |

 Oui, ils y vont en août.

b. Tu travailles à Bordeaux? (non) |

 Non, je n'y travaille pas.

c. On va au match avec Paul? (non, avec Gilles) |

 Non, on y va avec Gilles.

d. Tu es allé/e à New York pendant les vacances? (oui) |

 Oui, j'y suis allé/e.

e. Est-ce que l'avion est arrivé à Londres? (non, pas encore) |

 Non, il n'y est pas encore arrivé.

5. Write this dialogue in French.

—Does Alice go to her classes by subway?

—No, she goes on foot. |

 —Alice va en classe en métro? —Non, elle y va à pied.

6. Write the French equivalent of this exchange.

—Is he going to the airport?

—Yes, he is. |

 —Va-t-il à l'aéroport? —Oui, il y va.

À Propos!

Ask a classmate if he/she goes to a certain local place. Then ask if he/she goes there often.

une semaine de paris
pariscop

À Paris, on ne s'ennuie pas! (You don't get bored!)

Phase huit

2. Verbs followed by *à* or *de* plus infinitive

1. You have learned many verbs that can be followed directly by an infinitive. *(aimer, aller, pouvoir,* etc.)
2. Other verbs are followed by the preposition *à* or *de* before an infinitive. Look at the following sentence: *J'ai invité Jeanne à sortir avec nous, mais elle a refusé de venir.*
   a. Which verb is followed by *à* before an infinitive? |
      J'ai invité (Jeanne) à sortir.
   b. Which verb is followed by *de?* |
      Elle a refusé de venir.

Here is a list of frequently used verbs which take either *à* or *de* before an infinitive construction. There is no logic or rule concerning the use of *à* or *de* after a verb. You should memorize these verbs as whole verb phrases.

Verb + *à* + infinitive	Verb + *de* + infinitive
aider qqn **à** faire qqch *(to help)*	**accepter de** faire qqch *(to accept)*
apprendre à qqn **à** faire qqch *(to teach)*	**décider de** faire qqch *(to decide)*
commencer à faire qqch *(to begin)*	**demander** à qqn **de** faire qqch *(to ask)*
continuer à faire qqch *(to continue)*	**dire** à qqn **de** faire qqch *(to tell)*
encourager qqn **à** faire qqch *(to encourage)*	**essayer de** faire qqch *(to try)*
hésiter à faire qqch *(to hesitate)*	**empêcher** qqn **de** faire qqch *(to prevent)*
s'intéresser à faire qqch *(to be interested in)*	**oublier de** faire qqch *(to forget)*
inviter qqn **à** faire qqch *(to invite)*	**permettre** à qqn **de** faire qqch *(to allow)*
réussir à faire qqch *(to succeed)*	**refuser de** faire qqch *(to refuse)*
	regretter de faire qqch *(to regret, to be sorry about)*

3. Replace the italic noun phrases with *à* + the infinitive phrase indicated.

   Modèle: L'étudiant apprend *le français.* (faire ses devoirs soigneusement) |

   L'étudiant apprend à faire ses devoirs soigneusement.

   a. Thérèse a invité Michel *chez elle.* (faire un tour en bateau) |
      Thérèse a invité Michel à faire un tour en bateau.
   b. Ils s'intéressent *aux aspects pittoresques de la ville.* (regarder les monuments de Paris) |
      Ils s'intéressent à regarder les monuments de Paris.
   c. Thérèse n'hésite pas *devant les problèmes difficiles.* (parler des aspects désagréables de la ville) |
      Thérèse n'hésite pas à parler des aspects désagréables de la ville.
4. Now use *de* + the infinitive phrase.

a. Le soir Thérèse accepte *une invitation.* (aller au théâtre avec Michel) |

    Le soir Thérèse accepte d'aller au théâtre avec Michel.

b. Elle essaie *une nouvelle robe.* (coudre [*sew*] une nouvelle robe) |

    Elle essaie de coudre une nouvelle robe.

c. Est-ce qu'elle regrette *sa décision?* (avoir accepté l'invitation) |

    Est-ce qu'elle regrette d'avoir accepté l'invitation?

d. Michel a oublié *son imperméable dans l'autobus.* (prendre son parapluie [*umbrella*]) |

    Jacques a oublié de prendre son parapluie.

5. You will have to repeat and use these patterns for a while before they become as automatic for you as they are for French speakers. Study these two lists and practice by filling in the blanks with *à* or *de,* using your memory as much as possible. (See key.)

Michel a invité Thérèse *1.* _____ se promener dans Paris. Elle n'a pas hésité *2.* _____ accepter son invitation et ils ont décidé *3.* _____ aller à la Place de la Concorde. Là, une grande foule les a empêchés *4.* _____ continuer leur promenade. Les gens refusaient *5.* _____ les laisser passer quand ils essayaient *6.* _____ avancer. Ils ont réussi *7.* _____ traverser quand un agent de police a dit à la foule *8.* _____ se disperser. |

3. Direct object pronouns in the *passé composé*

1. You have learned that in the *passé composé* with *être,* the past participle agrees with the subject.

   Elles se sont réveillées à 7 heures et elles sont parties à 9 heures.

2. But the past participle does not agree with the subject when the auxiliary is *avoir.*

                   Elles ont appelé un taxi.

3. Now look at the sentences below:

        1. J'ai acheté une robe bleue.
        2. Je l'ai achetée ce matin.
        3. Quelle robe as-tu achetée?
        4. La robe que j'ai achetée est bleue.

   a. *Acheté* has changed in sentences 2, 3, and 4. What was added? |

       the letter e

   b. Since *acheté* cannot agree with the subject (because *avoir* is the auxiliary), what other word could it be agreeing with? |

       the word *robe*

Note Culturelle

Le Quartier latin

Le Quartier latin est le domaine de la jeunesse. Une grande animation y règne[1] toujours grâce aux[2] nombreux étudiants français et étrangers qui suivent des cours dans les divers établissements de l'Université de Paris. Le Boulevard Saint-Michel (ou «Boul' Mich'») qui est une des rues principales, est un centre d'activité pendant le jour et pendant la nuit. Là, et dans les petites rues aux alentours[3], on trouve de nombreux cafés, des cinémas, des magasins exotiques et des librairies. Chaque petite rue a aussi plusieurs restaurants, quelques-uns très chers, d'autres très bon marché. Il y a aussi des «caves» (c'étaient de vraies caves[4] autrefois) où l'on peut écouter du jazz. De nombreux cafés-théâtres attirent[5] toujours beaucoup de monde. Dans ces minuscules cafés-théâtres on peut manger et boire quelque chose et voir en même temps[6] un petit spectacle[7].

Un des charmes de ce quartier est le contraste entre l'ambiance jeune et animée[8] et les vieux bâtiments dans les petites rues étroites et anciennes. Un de ces vieux bâtiments est la Sorbonne, le coeur de l'Université de Paris. Au 13ème siècle[9] les étudiants y venaient de partout. On a appelé ce quartier le Quartier latin parce que, à cette époque, le latin était la langue de communication entre les étudiants de tous les pays.

1 prevails 2 thanks to 3 in the vicinity 4 cellars 5 attract 6 at the same time 7 show 8 animated 9 century

Au Quartier latin. Le Boul' Mich'.

4. *Robe* is the direct object in sentence 1 (#3), where it follows the verb.
   a. Write the direct objects from sentences 2, 3, and 4. |
      l' (elided form of *la*), *quelle robe,* and *que*
   b. Where do they occur—before or after the verb? |
      before
   c. What gender are they? |
      Each is feminine.

In the *passé composé* with *avoir,* when the direct object precedes the verb (whether in a statement or a question), the past participle shows agreement with the direct object.

> J'ai pris *la pomme.* Je *l'ai prise.*
> J'ai vu *mes amis.* Je *les* ai *vus.*

5. Answer the questions below using a direct object pronoun. Be sure to add *e* for feminine and *s* for plural as appropriate.
   a. Tu as choisi ces roses? |
      Oui, je les ai choisies.
   b. Il a perdu ton numéro de téléphone? |
      Oui, il l'a perdu. (no change here because the object is masculine singular)
   c. Avez-vous tricoté ces pulls? (oui, nous) |
      Oui, nous les avons tricotés.
   d. Ont-ils oublié leurs valises? (oui) |
      Oui, ils les ont oubliées.

À Propos!

L'année dernière, avez-vous écrit toutes vos cartes de Noël ou de Nouvel An *(New Year)* avant le 15 décembre?

Vocabulaire

Noms

l'accident *m.* *accident*
l'agent de police *m.* *policeman/woman*
la boîte aux lettres *mailbox*
la carte *map*
le chauffeur de taxi *cab driver*
la circonstance *circumstance*
le courrier *mailman/woman*
la foule *crowd*
le gangster *gangster*
le hold-up *hold-up*
les lunettes *f. pl.* *(eye) glasses*
le parapluie *umbrella*
le révolver *gun*

Verbes

arrêter *to stop*

avancer *to go ahead*
coudre (coud-, cous-, *pp* cousu) *to sew*
disperser *to scatter*
écraser *to run over*
kidnapper *to kidnap*
raconter *to tell*
renverser *to upset (physically)*
traverser *to cross*

Autres mots et expressions

appartenir à *to belong to*
faire la vaisselle *to wash dishes*
sans doute *probably*
soigneusement *carefully*
y *there; (replaces prep. + n. phrase referring to a place, thing, or idea)*

PRÉPARATION 55

1. Practice with the pronoun *y*

As with other pronouns, the pronoun *y* precedes the verb form in affirmative and negative sentences. Remember also that in French, you *must* include *y* when you answer in a complete sentence.

1. Look at the following sentences.

   Nous chantons *la Marseillaise.*   Je parle *à Michel.*   Roland va *à l'école.*

   Which italicized phrase could you refer to with the pronoun *y*? |
   > à l'école (*Y* can be used to refer to a location.)

2. Rewrite these sentences, using the adverbial pronoun *y*. Say your answers aloud to practice the word order.

   Modèle: Roger va chez le médecin à deux heures. |
   > Roger y va à deux heures.

   a. Nous allons à la montagne pour faire du camping. |
   > Nous y allons pour faire du camping.

   b. Je ne vais pas au club ce soir. |
   > Je n'y vais pas ce soir.

   c. Mes grands-parents vont au Canada cet été. |
   > Mes grands-parents y vont cet été.

   d. Vous n'allez pas à la campagne en hiver. |
   > Vous n'y allez pas en hiver.

   e. On va à Chamonix pour faire du ski. |
   > On y va pour faire du ski.

3. Answer according to the cue. (See key.)

   Modèle: Tu vas à Québec? (oui) |
   > Oui, j'y vais.

   a. Tu vas au cinéma? (non)
   b. Est-ce que Véronique va au match de football? (oui)
   c. Elles ne vont pas au supermarché, n'est-ce pas? (si)
   d. Ton camarade de chambre est chez le dentiste? (oui)

À Propos!   Combien de fois par an doit-on aller chez le dentiste? Vous y allez plus ou moins souvent?

2. Practice with *dire*

1. Write the present tense form of *dire* that matches each pronoun.
   (See chart p. 327.)
   a. je   c. ils   e. tu
   b. elle   d. nous   f. vous |
   a. dis   b. dit   c. disent   d. disons   e. dis   f. dites

2. Béatrice wants to know what the following people have to say about Paris. Use the correct form of *dire* and the cues indicated. (See answer key.)
   Modèle: son père/la circulation est très difficile |
   Son père dit que la circulation est très difficile.

   a. Vous/les gens courent toujours à Paris
   b. sa mère et sa tante/les prix sont astronomiques
   c. tu/il y a beaucoup de musées
   d. nous/c'est une belle ville
   e. je/c'est une ville moderne

3. The pronoun *en*

Pronouns are very useful; they keep sentences from becoming cumbersome. Here's one more useful French pronoun: *en* (some, any). It is often used to replace a partitive noun phrase.

1. Read these questions and answers.

   —Ton amie veut du chocolat?   —Ton amie veut de la glace?
   —Oui, elle en veut.   —Non, elle n'en veut pas.

   a. Which phrases does *en* replace? |
   du chocolat, de la glace
   b. Does *en* precede or follow the verb? |
   it precedes (*En* precedes a verb in an affirmative or negative statement.)
   c. Write equivalents for *Elle en veut* and *Elle n'en veut pas.* |
   She wants some (of it). She doesn't want any (of it).

4. Write the words that *en* refers to in these pairs of sentences.
   a. —Je veux des haricots   c. —Avez-vous de l'eau
      verts.   minérale?
      —Moi aussi, j'en veux.   —Oui, nous en avons.
   b. —Vous prenez de la   d. —Tu ne prends pas de
      salade?   dessert?
      —Oui, j'en prends.   —Non, je n'en prends pas. |
   a. des haricots verts   b. de la salade   c. de l'eau minérale   d. de dessert

5. Answer the following questions according to the cues.
   Modèle: Est-ce que ta sœur a des disques? (oui) |
   Oui, elle en a.

a. Tu voudrais du poisson? (oui)

b. Isabelle prend de la viande? (non)

c. Vous deux, vous achetez des fruits? (non)

d. Tu ne manges pas de pain? (si)

6. In French, the pronoun *en* is used in a response, if the speaker repeats the verb but not the noun. In English, neither the verb nor the noun need to be repeated; an auxiliary verb is enough.

—Tu veux des bananes?   —*Do you want some bananas?*

—Oui, j'en veux.   —*Yes, I do. (Yes, I want some.)*

—Il prend du thé?   —*Is he having tea?*

—Non, il n'en prend pas.   —*No, he isn't. (No, he's not having any.)*

Write French equivalents for these dialogues.

a. —Is your buddy (male) having coffee?

—No, he isn't.

b. —Does your brother want dessert?

—Yes, he does.

7. Write French equivalents, using *tu*. (See key.)

a. —Would you like some   b. —Aren't you having tea?

chicken?   —No, I'm not.

—Yes, I would.

4. The adjective *tout*

The adjective *tout* is used in many expressions in French, sometimes with the meaning *all* or *the whole,* sometimes with the meaning *every* or *each.* In this part, you'll practice *tout* meaning *all* or *the whole.*

1. Read the following passage about Mother Hubbard, and notice especially the forms of the adjective *tout.*

Mme Hubbard arrive chez elle un jour et voit que le réfrigérateur est vide *(empty).* Pourquoi? Parce que M. Hubbard, son mari, a mangé tout le gigot *(leg of lamb).* Yvette, sa fille, a mangé tous les fruits. François, son fils, a mangé toutes les pommes de terre. Socrate, le chien, a mangé toute la glace.

Write the form of *tout* that is used with each noun.

a. le gigot

b. la glace

c. les fruits

d. les pommes de terre

2. The adjective *tout* is usually followed by a definite article, a possessive or a demonstrative adjective, and a noun phrase.
   a. Write the articles and adjectives that follow forms of *tout* in these noun phrases: *toutes ces voitures, tous mes amis, tout le gâteau, toute la classe.* |
      ces, mes, le, la
   b. Write an English equivalent for each phrase. |
      all these (those) cars; all my friends; the whole cake; the whole class

	Masculine	Feminine
Singular	**tout le** gâteau	**toute la** journée
Plural	**tous les** jours	**toutes les** circonstances

3. Complete the following sentences with a form of *tout,* and give an English equivalent for each sentence.
   Modèle: _____ les petites villes de France sont jolies. |
      Toutes (All the small towns in France are pretty.)
   a. Je connais bien la France; _____ le pays est intéressant et agréable. |
      tout (I know France well; the whole country is interesting and pleasant.)
   b. Mais Paris est vraiment spécial; _____ la ville est magnifique. |
      toute (But Paris is truly special; the whole city is magnificent.)
   c. Bien sûr, _____ les maisons et _____ les immeubles ne sont pas beaux. |
      toutes, tous (Of course, all the houses and all the buildings aren't beautiful.)

5. Review of interrogative pronouns

Refer to the chart on p. 389–390.
1. Which French interrogative expressions are used when *who* is subject of the sentence? |
   qui? qui est-ce qui?
2. Which interrogative expressions are used when *who/whom* is the object of the sentence? |
   qui? qui est-ce que?
3. a. When the question refers to things rather than persons, the French interrogative pronouns are _____. |
      qu'est-ce qui? que? qu'est-ce que?
   b. If the pronoun referring to a thing is the subject of the verb, only one form can be used: _____. |
      Qu'est-ce qui?

c. How does the subject form *qu'est-ce qui* compare with the subject form *qui est-ce qui*, used for people? |

The first *qui* in *qui est-ce qui* refers to people, and the first word *que (qu')* in *qu'est-ce qui* refers to things. *Qui*, the last word in both expressions, identifies each one as a subject form.

4. a. After a preposition the interrogative pronoun used to refer to things is _____. |

quoi (or prep. + *quoi* + *est-ce que*)

b. To refer to persons, what form follows a preposition? |

qui (or prep. + *qui* + *est-ce que*)

5. To ask questions in French, there are short forms of interrogative pronouns, and long forms. Which form is used with inverted subject and verb—short or long? |

short

6. Write questions asking about the italic portion of the sentence which could elicit the answers below. Use the short form for the first five questions and long forms for the last five.

Modèle: Le moteur fait du bruit. |

Qu'est-ce qui fait du bruit?

a. Guillaume pense *à Marie*.
b. Marie pense *à l'argent*.
c. *Le petite fille* joue du violon.
d. Il y a *du pain* sur la table.
e. On fait le cidre *avec des pommes*.
f. Elle a acheté *les billets*.
g. Elle a acheté des billets *pour le concert*.
h. *Une symphonie de Berlioz* est au programme.
i. *La musique classique* ne nous intéresse pas.
j. Cette table est faite *en bois*. |

a. À qui Guillaume pense-t-il?   b. À quoi Marie pense-t-elle?   c. Qui joue du violon?   d. Qu'y a-t-il sur la table?   e. Avec quoi fait-on le cidre?   f. Qu'est-ce qu'elle a acheté?   g. Pour quoi est-ce qu'elle a acheté des billets?   h. Qu'est-ce qu'il y a au programme?   i. Qu'est-ce qui ne vous intéresse pas?   j. En quoi est-ce que cette table est faite?

Vocabulaire

Noms

le billet   *ticket*
l'exercice *m.*   *exercise*
le gigot   *leg of lamb*
le moteur   *motor*
l'obscurité *f.*   *darkness*
la symphonie   *symphony*

Adjectifs

spécial/e   *special*
tout/e   *all*

Autres mots et expressions

c'est tout   *that's all*
en   *some; (replaces de + n. phrase referring to a thing or a place)*
en bois   *made of wood*
tous les jours   *everyday*
toute la journée   *all day*
toutes les fois   *every time*

PRÉPARATION 56

1. The *passé composé* with indirect object pronouns

1. Hélène and Guy are talking about a friend on vacation.

> —Ta copine t'a écrit?
> —Oui, elle m'a écrit et m'a envoyé des photos.

a. Which indirect object pronouns are used in the question and answer? |

  t', m', m'

b. What is the English equivalent of the question? |

  Has your friend written (to) you?

c. In the French sentences, do the indirect object pronouns occur before or after the *passé composé* verb forms? |

  before

2. Answer the following commands by saying that you have already (*déjà*) done what you are being asked to do. Use indirect object pronouns. Say your answer aloud before you write it.

  Modèle: Demande de l'argent à ton père. |

  Je lui ai déjà demandé de l'argent.

a. Montre tes dessins (*drawings*) à tes professeurs.
b. Envoie une lettre à ta tante.
c. Parle-nous de ton travail.
d. Envoie des cartes à tes amis américains. |

  a. Je leur ai déjà montré mes dessins.   b. Je lui ai déjà envoyé une lettre.   c. Je vous ai déjà parlé de mon travail.   d. Je leur ai déjà envoyé des cartes.

2. Reading comprehension

Do large cities have anything in common? How would you describe Paris as a city? What are Paris's most famous parks like? If you are fond of shopping, where would you go? Read the selection below for the answers to these and other questions.

Toutes les grandes villes ont des problèmes, mais toutes les grandes villes ne sont pas belles! Paris est une ville très belle et très intéressante.

Par exemple, si on veut faire une promenade à pied, on peut aller aux Tuileries ou au Luxembourg. Là, on peut admirer° les fleurs°, les arbres, les bassins°, les grandes allées° avec leurs statues magnifiques. Si on veut voir des magasins élégants, on peut aller à pied ou en autobus aux Champs-Elysées ou sur les grands boulevards.

admire / flowers
fountains / wide paths

1. Complete the following sentences based on the passage above.
   a. Une grande ville n'est jamais sans _____.
   b. Le contraire de *laide* est _____.
   c. On peut dire que _____ est une ville très belle et très intéressante.

   a. problèmes
   b. belle
   c. Paris

2. Complete each statement below with the appropriate phrase chosen from those in parentheses.
   a. Les Tuileries et le Luxembourg sont _____. (deux parcs, deux musées, deux grands magasins)
   b. Aux Tuileries et au Luxembourg il y a des _____ splendides. (des magasins et des livres, des arbres et des fleurs)
   c. Aux Champs-Elysées on peut _____. (acheter de belles choses, nager)
   d. On peut aller sur les grands boulevards _____. (en autobus, en bateau)

   a. deux parcs
   b. des arbres et des fleurs
   c. acheter de belles choses
   d. en autobus

Would you like to see artists at work? Would you like to meet students from many other countries? Read below to see where art lovers, students, writers, and artists like to spend their time in Paris.

Si on aime la peinture°, on peut visiter plusieurs musées célèbres ou, simplement, faire une promenade à Montmartre. Là, dans toutes les rues, on peut voir des artistes plus ou moins bons en train de peindre° des tableaux° plus ou moins bons. Si on veut parler avec des étudiants de tous les pays, on peut aller au Quartier latin. Là, il y a aussi des restaurants et des cafés très connus° où viennent des écrivains et des artistes de tous les pays.

Oui, bien sûr... la circulation, la pollution, l'inflation...: Paris a tous ces problèmes. Mais, malgré° tout, Paris est une ville intéressante, merveilleuse, unique.

painting
painting / pictures
known
in spite of

1. Answer these questions based on the passage above.
   a. How do you say in French *if one loves painting...?*
      si on aime la peinture
   b. Write a good English equivalent of *des artistes plus ou moins bons.*
      artists—some good, some less so
   c. How would you say in French: *paintings—some good, some less so?*
      des tableaux plus ou moins bons

2. Write a brief answer in French to each question below. (See key.)
   a. Que peut-on visiter pour voir des objets d'art?

b. Où peut-on aller à Paris pour voir des artistes en train de peindre des tableaux? |
c. Qui aime aller dans les restaurants et les cafés du Quartier latin? |
d. Comme toutes les grandes villes, Paris a des problèmes. Quels sont ces problèmes? |

À Propos!

Avez-vous de beaux jardins publics dans votre ville?
Y allez-vous souvent?
Allez-vous de temps en temps dans les musées? Pourquoi ou pourquoi pas?

3. The conditional

1. Since the beginning of your French course, you have used the expression *Je voudrais* as a polite way of saying what you want. *Je voudrais* is the verb *vouloir* in the form called the conditional. The conditional corresponds to the English verb construction with *would*.

Je voudrais sortir.   *I would like to go out.*

2. Study the conditional forms of *vouloir* and see whether you can recognize the endings.

je	voudr	**ais**	nous	voudr	**ions**
tu	voudr	**ais**	vous	voudr	**iez**
on/il/elle	voudr	**ait**	ils/elles	voudr	**aient**

a. *Vouloir* has only one conditional stem. What is it? |
   voudr-
b. The conditional endings are the same as the endings of another tense you already know. What tense is that? |
   l'imparfait (Every verb has only one conditional stem. All verbs have the same conditional endings, which are the same as the endings of the *imparfait*.)
3. A group of students from Quebec is planning a trip to Paris. Use the conditional of *vouloir* to say what attractions different people would like to visit.
   Modèle: Moi: les musées |
      Je voudrais visiter les musées.
a. Rémi et Dominique: Montmartre |
   Rémi et Dominique voudraient visiter Montmartre.

b. Toi: Notre-Dame de Paris |

Tu voudrais visiter Notre-Dame de Paris.

c. Serge: le Quartier latin |

Serge voudrait visiter le Quartier latin.

d. Nous: la Sorbonne |

Nous voudrions visiter la Sorbonne.

e. Vous: le Louvre |

Vous voudriez visiter le Louvre.

4. In this sentence, *aimer* is in the conditional.

Demain, j'aimerais aller à la piscine.

a. Copy the conditional verb with its subject. |

j'aimerais

b. What is the ending of *j'aimerais?* |

-ais

c. Remember that verbs have only one conditional stem. What is the conditional stem of *aimer?* |

aimer- (This is the same as the *infinitive* of the verb.)

d. Give the English equivalent of the sentence above. |

Tomorrow, I would like to go to the swimming pool.

5. Say in French: *We would like to go to the swimming pool also.* |

Nous aimerions aller à la piscine aussi.

6. Below you are told some things that people used to like to do. Say that they would like to do them again, completing the statements with the conditional of *aimer*. Remember, the endings are the same as the ones for the *imparfait*. (See key.)

Modéle: Nous aimions faire du camping.

Nous aimerions faire du camping de nouveau.

a. Jean-Marc aimait étudier le latin. |
b. Les Bouvier aimaient aller à la plage. |
c. Tu aimais collectionner des timbres *(to collect stamps)*. |
d. Vous aimiez écrire des chansons. |

À Propos! Aimeriez-vous passer un an au Sénégal ou à Paris? Qu'est-ce qui vous y attire *(to attract)?*

4. Practice with the pronoun *en*

1. Compare these pairs of sentences.

Je prends du lait.	Elle achète des	Il n'a pas voulu de
J'en prends.	haricots.	poisson.
	Elle en achète.	Il n'en a pas voulu.

a. Which words does the pronoun *en* replace? |
    du lait, des haricots, de poisson

b. Give equivalents of *J'en prends, Elle en achète, Il n'en a pas voulu.* |
    I'm having some (of it). She buys some (of them). He didn't want any (of it).

c. In negative and affirmative sentences, in the past and in the present, does *en* immediately precede or follow the verb? |
    precede

2. Rewrite each sentence, using *en* to replace the noun phrase. Write English equivalents.

a. Nous avons acheté des poires. |
    Nous en avons acheté. (We bought some.)

b. Tu as du fromage? |
    Tu en as? (Do you have any/some?) |

c. Ils n'ont pas voulu de dessert. |
    Ils n'en ont pas voulu. (They didn't want any.)

3. The pronoun *en* is often used with the expression *il y a* or *il y avait.*

—Il y a des chaises dans la classe?   —*Are there any chairs in the classroom?*

—Oui, il y en a.   —*Yes, there are.*

—Il y a des bancs?   —*Are there some benches?*
—Non, il n'y en a pas.   —*No, there aren't.*

—Il y avait des tables?   —*Were there any tables?*
—Non, il n'y en avait pas.   —*No, there weren't any.*

4. Answer these questions with *il y en a,* or *il n'y en a pas,* according to the cues.

    Modèle: Est-ce qu'il y a des montagnes en Floride? (non) |
        Non, il n'y en a pas.

a. Est-ce qu'il y a de grandes villes en France? (oui) | a. Oui, il y en a.
b. Est-ce qu'il y a de la neige en hiver chez vous? (non) | b. Non, il n'y en a pas.
c. Il n'y a pas de pluie en été chez vous, n'est-ce pas? (si) | c. Si, il y en a.
d. Est-ce qu'il y avait des fruits dans le réfrigérateur? (non)   d. Non, il n'y en avait pas.

5. Compare the following questions and answers.

Combien de filles y a-t-il dans la classe?   *How many girls are there in the classroom?*

Il y en a treize.   *There are thirteen (of them).*

In statements of quantity, the pronoun *en* must be used to refer to the item being counted. In English, the reference is often understood without being stated.

Tell how many of the following items you have, according to the cues. Say each answer aloud before you write it, and look up from the page as you speak.

a. Combien de manteaux avez-vous? (1)
b. Combien de crayons avez-vous? (13)
c. Combien de livres avez-vous lus? (22)
d. Combien de frères avez-vous? (3) │

a. J'en ai un.   b. J'en ai treize.   c. J'en ai lu vingt-deux. (The pronoun *en* does not require agreement of the past participle.)   d. J'en ai trois.

À Propos!

Combien de tasses de thé avez-vous bues aujourd'hui?
Avez-vous lu des poèmes aujourd'hui?

Vocabulaire

Noms
l'allée *f.   alley*
le bassin   *pond, fountain*
le boulevard   *boulevard*
le dessin   *drawing*
la piscine   *swimming pool*
le réfrigérateur   *refrigerator*
la statue   *statue*
la tasse   *cup*
le timbre   *stamp*

Verbes
collectionner   *to collect*
peindre (pein-, peign-, *pp* peint)   *to paint*

Adjectifs
méchant/e   *nasty*

Autres mots et expressions
de nouveau   *again*
j'aimerais   *I would like*
personnellement   *personally*

DEUX CONCERTS EXCEPTIONNELS   •   15 ET 16 JUIN   A 21 H
AU PROFIT DES CHANTIERS DU CARDINAL
NOTRE-DAME DE PARIS

Note Culturelle

Le Marais

Le Marais est un très vieux quartier[1] de Paris. Son nom date de l'époque romaine, quand justement c'était un endroit couvert[2] de marais et de marécages[3]. Petit à petit, on y a construit[4] de belles maisons. Les rois[5] de France ont habité ce quartier jusqu'au 17ème siècle.

Au début de ce siècle, le roi Henri IV a fait construire la Place Royale (maintenant appelée Place des Vosges). C'était le centre de la vie élégante. À cette époque aussi, on a construit de grandes maisons de style classique, avec une cour[6] et un jardin, appelées hôtels particuliers[7]. Ces maisons appartenaient à de riches particuliers.[8]

Pendant la Révolution française, beaucoup de ces hôtels particuliers ont été détruits[9]. Mais maintenant, plusieurs ont été restaurés, et on peut visiter ces belles maisons qui ont d'énormes pièces, de beaux et grands escaliers, des portes de bois sculpté[10] et des statues dans les cours et le long des murs.[11]

Une grande animation culturelle règne[12] chaque été au Marais où est présenté un festival de musique et de théâtre. Les concerts et représentations ont lieu[13] dehors, dans les cours de différents hôtels particuliers. Ce festival dure[14] à peu près un mois.

1 area 2 covered with 3 marshes and bogs 4 built
5 kings 6 courtyard 7 private residences 8 individuals
9 were destroyed 10 sculpted wood 11 along the walls
12 reigns 13 take place 14 lasts

À Paris. Des enfants jouent à la Place des Vosges.

PRÉPARATION 57

Retour à Paris

Scène 3 Une Promenade en bateau-mouche

Michel Une promenade en bateau-mouche°, c'est toujours sensationnel!

Thérèse Oui, tu as raison... Le Louvre, Notre Dame, tous les monuments sont vraiment très impressionnants°.

Michel Et la Seine est toujours belle!

Thérèse Oh, Michel! Tu veux voir seulement les beaux aspects de
Paris. Tu as oublié qu'il y a des rues sales° et tristes°...

Michel Et des appartements où le soleil° n'entre jamais? Non, je n'ai
pas oublié. Mon appartement est sombre°, microscopique°, et dans
un quartier plutôt° pauvre.

Thérèse Comment? Tu n'habites pas chez tes parents, dans leur bel
appartement?

° type of boat for
sightseeing

° impressive

° dirty streets / sad

° sun
° dark / tiny
° rather

Michel Mais non, j'ai préféré être indépendant. Ce n'est pas facile° **easy**
sans travail et sans beaucoup d'argent.

Thérèse Alors, Paris n'est pas tellement beau, après tout!

Michel Mais si, c'est beau; c'est très, très beau. Tu sais, après une
longue absence, on l'apprécie!

*Échange
d'idées*

1. Y a-t-il de belles rues et des rues sales et tristes dans votre ville?
   Quelles sont-elles?
2. Choisissez les adjectifs du texte qui peuvent caractériser votre
   logement *(dwelling)*.

1. Object pronouns in double-verb constructions

	Affirmative	Negative
Présent	Je veux **lui parler.**	Je ne veux **pas lui parler.**
Passé composé	J'ai pu **le trouver.**	Je n'ai **pas** pu **le trouver.**

1. a. In the present, when the first verb *(veux)* is followed by a sec-
   ond verb *(parler),* where is the object pronoun placed? |
   before the second verb
2. In the *passé composé,* does the object pronoun fall before the aux-
   iliary verb, before the *participle,* or before the *infinitive?* |
   before the infinitive—the verb of which it is the object
3. Answer in the affirmative, and use an object pronoun.
   a. Est-ce que vous voudriez visiter les grandes villes d'Europe? |
   Oui, je voudrais les visiter.
   a. As-tu aimé regarder les matchs de basket à la télé? |
   Oui, j'ai aimé les regarder.
   c. Est-ce que vous devez téléphoner à votre copain ce soir? |
   Oui, je dois lui téléphoner ce soir.
4. Now answer the following questions in the negative, and use an
   object pronoun in each response. You can increase your fluency
   in speech by saying your answers aloud before you write them.
   Modèle: Tu aimes parler à tes professeurs? |
   Non, je n'aime pas leur parler.
   a. Est-ce que vous voulez voir le Musée du Louvre? |
   Non, je ne veux pas le voir.
   b. Avez-vous pu aider vos parents? |
   Non, je n'ai pas pu les aider.
   c. Est-ce qu'on va montrer les diapos du voyage en Afrique? |
   Non, on ne va pas les montrer.

5. Answer the following questions in the affirmative or negative, according to the cues. (See key.)

> *Modèle:* Doit-elle vous écrire, Paul? (oui) |
>
> Oui, elle doit m'écrire.

a. Maman, papa va me donner de l'argent? (non)
b. Veut-elle vous voir demain? (non)
c. Sont-ils venus dire au revoir aux enfants? (oui)

2. Review practice: the pronouns *y* and *en*

1. Answer each question with the pronoun *y*. (See key.)
   a. —Tu vas à Lyon? (Oui, la semaine prochaine)
   b. —M. Nadeau est allé au bureau? (oui, comme toujours)
   c. —Tu manges au restaurant universitaire? (non, jamais)
2. Write French equivalents for the pairs of questions and answers below. (See key.)
   a. —Is Anne going to class today?
      —No, she's not going today.
   b. —How do we go to this museum?
      —We go by bus.
   c. —Are you going to the movies with Gisèle?
      —No, she can't go.
3. Replace the direct object nouns with *en*. (See key.)

> *Modèle:* Ils ont pris de la salade. |
>
> Ils en ont pris.

a. Roger a du lait.
b. Nous n'avons pas de pain.
c. Je veux de la glace.
d. Vous n'avez pas pris de poulet?
e. Tu n'a pas acheté de légumes?

3. Review of the *passé composé*

1. Write sentences in the *passé composé,* using the items that correspond to the numbers you are given. Make your sentences affirmative or negative as indicated. (See key.)

Subjects	*Verbs*	*Objects*
1. Je	1. manger	1. trop de frites
2. Vous	2. acheter	2. assez de sandwichs
3. Nous	3. répondre à	3. les devoirs
4. Mme Drouin	4. vendre	4. des chaussures
	5. choisir	5. la jupe
	6. finir	6. l'agent de police

Modèle: 4–2–4 (negative) |

Mme Drouin n'a pas acheté de chaussures.

  a. 1–1–1 (affirmative)   d. 3–5–4 (affirmative)
  b. 2–2–2 (negative)   e. 4–4–5 (negative)
  c. 1–6–3 (affirmative)   f. 2–3–6 (affirmative)

2. You are familiar with a number of irregular verbs and their past participles. Use the phrases in parentheses to write complete French equivalents for each English sentence. (See key.)

  a. Paul and Gérard went camping. *(faire du camping)*
  b. We said good-by to the neighbors. *(dire au revoir aux voisins)*
  c. Julie saw M. Lille this morning. *(voir M. Lille ce matin)*
  d. They *(on)* didn't put any salt in the soup. *(mettre du sel dans la soupe)*

3. Mme Drouin finds her kitchen in complete disorder and asks her children if they are responsible for the mess. Respond to her questions in the negative, using the *passé composé.* (See key.)

  Modèle: Bernard, tu as mis du beurre sur la chaise? |

Non, je n'ai pas mis de beurre sur la chaise.

  a. Anne-Marie et Julie, vous avez pris des petits gâteaux?
  b. Julie, tu as mangé de la glace?
  c. Alain, tu as pris du jus d'orange?
  d. Alain, tu as fait une omelette?

4. You and your friends are asked to do certain things. Say that you did do them, according to the cues. Replace the words in italics with direct or indirect object pronouns. (See key.)

  Modèle: Tu n'as pas téléphoné *à tes parents?* (si) |

Si, je leur ai téléphoné.

  a. Tu as écrit à *Jeanne et à Guy?* (oui)
  b. Marie a donné un cadeau *à Chantal?* (oui)
  c. Vous n'avez pas envoyé *le livre* aux Drouin? (si)

4. Practice with comparisons

1. How are comparisons expressed in French, whether one uses an adjective or an adverb? |

plus, moins, or *aussi* + adjective or adverb + *que*
(more...than, less...than, as...as)

2. Express your opinion in answer to the following questions. (See key.)

  Modèle: Qu'est-ce qui est plus désirable, la paix ou la guerre? |

La paix est plus désirable que la guerre.

  a. Qu'est-ce qui est plus confortable, une chaise ou un sofa?
  b. Qu'est-ce qui est moins riche en calories, le chocolat ou le céleri?

c. Est-ce qu'un train et un avion sont aussi rapides?

d. Croyez-vous *(do you think)* que Roméo était aussi amoureux que Juliette?

e. Qu'est-ce qui calcule plus rapidement, un ordinateur *(computer)* ou une personne?

f. Comment voyage-t-on plus confortablement, en première classe ou en classe touriste?

g. Où vit-on plus agréablement, à la campagne ou à la ville?

h. Qu'est-ce qui est plus peuplé, le Sahara ou le Canada?

i. Qu'est-ce qui est moins cher, une auto ou un vélo?

j. Quand le temps paraît-il plus long, quand on est en vacances ou quand on travaille?

Vocabulaire

Noms

le bateau-mouche *sightseeing boat*
la calorie *calorie*
la chanson *song*
la première classe; ~ touriste *first class; tourist class*
le crocodile *crocodile*
la guerre *war*
l'ordinateur *m.* *computer*
la paix *peace*
le/la pianiste *pianist*
le sofa *sofa*
le/la touriste *tourist*

Adjectifs

connu/e *well-known*
désirable *desirable*
haut/e *tall*
indépendant/e *independent*
microscopique *microscopic*
peuplé/e *populated*
sensationnel/le *fantastic*
sombre *dark*

Verbes

apprécier *to appreciate*
calculer *to calculate*
peupler *to populate*

Autres mots et expressions

après tout *after all*
plutôt *rather*
rapidement *quickly*

Les films américains sont populaires en France.

PRÉPARATION 58

1. Review of infinitive constructions

Review the lists of verbs + infinitives on pp. 387, 397. Then copy the following paragraph, adding *à* or *de* where necessary. (See key.)

Le roi Louis XIV n'aimait pas _____ vivre à Paris. Il a décidé _____ transporter sa cour° à Versailles. Il a demandé aux meilleurs artistes de son temps _____ collaborer à la construction du nouveau palais°. Le Vau, Mansard, Le Nôtre, ont accepté avec joie _____ travailler pour le roi Soleil°. Mais ils devaient _____ consulter le roi sur chaque° détail. Ils n'étaient pas toujours sûrs° _____ lui plaire. Il ne pouvaient pas refuser _____ choisir le style qu'il aimait. Ils ont encouragé le roi _____ adopter le style classique. Les ouvriers ont commencé _____ construire° le palais en 1661. Le roi a dû _____ lever° beaucoup d'impôts° pour finir la construction. Le peuple° n'a pas essayé _____ se révolter contre les lourdes charges°. Mais il regrettait peut-être _____ payer si cher un palais si beau.

- court
- palace
- the Sun King / every
- sure
- build / raise
- taxes / population
- heavy burden

2. Review of interrogative pronouns

Express in French, once with the short interrogative form, once with the long form.

1. *Who* caused the accident?
   Qui a causé l'accident? Qui est-ce qui a causé l'accident?
2. *What* caused the accident? *(Long form only)*
   Qu'est-ce qui a causé l'accident?
3. *Whom* do you know here?
   Qui connaissez-vous ici? Qui est-ce que vous connaissez ici?
4. *What* do you know?
   Que savez-vous? Qu'est-ce que vous savez?
5. *With whom* does he work?
   Avec qui travaille-t-il? Avec qui est-ce qu'il travaille?
6. *With what* does he work?
   Avec quoi travaille-t-il? Avec quoi est-ce qu'il travaille?

3. The interrogative pronoun *lequel*

The pronoun *lequel* is made of the definite article *le/la/les* and the interrogative *quel/quels/quelle/quelles*, made into one word; it has four forms, to agree in gender and number with the noun it stands for.

Masc. sing.	*Quel manteau* préfères-tu?	**Lequel** préfères-tu?
	Which coat do you prefer?	*Which one do you prefer?*
Fem. sing.	*Quelle robe* préfères-tu?	**Laquelle** préfères-tu?
Masc. pl.	*Quels pantalons* préfères-tu?	**Lesquels** préfères-tu?
Fem. pl.	*Quelles jupes* préfères-tu?	**Lesquelles** préfères-tu?

1. Now look at the following examples.

—J'ai parlé à un des employés.   —*Auquel* as-tu parlé?
—Il m'a parlé de ses amis.   —*Desquels* est-ce qu'il a parlé?

Write English equivalents of the two questions in the example. |

Which one did you speak to? Which ones did he talk about?

Lequel, when used with *à* and *de,* uses contracted forms.

	À	**De**
Masc. sing.	**au**quel	**du**quel
Masc. pl.	**aux**quels	**des**quels
Fem. sing.	**à la**quelle	**de la**quelle
Fem. pl.	**aux**quelles	**des**quelles

2. Fill in the blanks with the appropriate forms of the interrogative pronoun *lequel.*

a. J'ai écrit à une de mes amies. _____ as-tu écrit?
b. J'ai choisi deux livres. _____ as-tu choisis?
c. J'ai répondu à trois questions. _____ as-tu répondu?

a. À laquelle
b. Lesquels
c. Auxquelles

4. More about the conditional

1. Read the following sentences and their equivalents. For each, write the subject-verb phrase that is in the conditional, and write the infinitive of the conditional verb.

a. Est-ce que vous voyageriez, si vous aviez assez d'argent? *(Would you travel if you had enough money?)* |

vous voyageriez; voyager

b. Si j'avais le temps, je finirais cette lettre. *(If I had time, I would finish this letter.)*

    je finirais; finir

c. Is the stem for each verb the same as the infinitive?

    yes (Most *-er* and *-ir* verbs use the infinitive as the stem for the conditional.)

2. Now write the conditional subject-verb phrase, and its infinitive.
    a. Si j'allais à Seattle, je prendrais l'avion.

        je prendrais; prendre

    b. How is the conditional stem different from the infinitive?

        The conditional stem drops the *-e* of the infinitive. (Most *-re* verbs use the infinitive minus *-e* as the conditional stem.)

Regular Formation of the Conditional

	Stem	+ *imparfait* endings
-er verbs	**parler-**	je **parlerais**
-ir verbs	**finir-**	je **finirais**
	sortir-	je **sortirais**
-re verbs	**entendr-**	j'**entendrais**
	dir-	je **dirais**

3. The following people, looking back, say what they would (or wouldn't) do if they could go back to school. Form sentences in the conditional, and say the English equivalents.

    Modèle: Moi/ne...pas/sortir tous les soirs

        Je ne sortirais pas tous les soirs. *(I wouldn't go out every night.)*

    a. Albert/étudier l'histoire de l'art

        Albert étudierait l'histoire de l'art. *(Albert would study art history.)*

    b. Nous/apprendre le russe

        Nous apprendrions le russe. *(We would learn Russian.)*

    c. Vous/ne...pas/jouer aux cartes à la bibliothèque

        Vous ne joueriez pas aux cartes à la bibliothèque. *(You wouldn't play cards in the library.)*

    d. Tu/ne...pas/perdre tes livres

        Tu ne perdrais pas tes livres. *(You wouldn't lose your books.)*

    e. Émile et Marc/finir toujours leurs devoirs

        Émile et Marc finiraient toujours leurs devoirs. *(Émile and Mark would always finish their homework.)*

4. *-Er* verbs with spelling changes in the present tense use the spelling-changing stem in the conditional. Write the conditional forms from these sentences.
    a. Si nous étions riches, nous achèterions une villa au bord de la mer.

        nous achèterions

b. S'il y avait un hold-up dans un magasin, nous appellerions la police.

nous appellerions

Conditional Stems of Spelling-changing -er Verbs

Spelling-changing stem		Conditional
j'achète:	**achèt-**	j'**achèterais**
j'appelle:	**appell-**	j'**appellerais**
je me promène:	**promèn-** + -er	je me **promènerais**
je jette:	**jett-**	je **jetterais**

5. Some people don't like their names. Form sentences with *s'appeler* in the conditional to say what the following people would be called if it were up to them.
   a. Lancelot: Muggsy

   Lancelot s'appellerait Muggsy.

   b. M. et Mme Lefaible, vous: M. et Mme Bonaparte

   Vous vous appelleriez M. et Mme Bonaparte.

6. Most people's schedules are different when they are on vacation. Complete the following statements with the conditional of *se lever*.
   a. Nous nous levons à six heures pour aller au bureau. Si nous étions en vacances, _____ à onze heures.

   nous nous lèverions

   b. Tu te lèves a sept heures pour aller en classe. Si tu étais en vacances, _____ à midi.

   tu te lèverais

7. Complete these sentences with the conditional. (See key.)
   a. Si je pouvais changer mon nom, je _____ Chantal. (s'appeler)
   b. Si vous aviez de l'argent, vous _____ une voiture. (acheter)
   c. Si Pierre habitait en Italie, il _____ italien. (parler)
   d. Si j'étais français, je _____ habiter à Paris. (aimer)
   e. Si je gagnais à la Loterie Nationale, je _____ de l'argent à tous mes amis. (donner)

Vocabulaire

Noms
le chimpanzé   *chimpanzee*
la lune   *moon*

Verbes
accuser   *to accuse*
attirer   *to attract*
causer   *to cause*
ressembler   *to look like*

Adjectifs
marocain/e   *Moroccan*
seul/e   *alone*

Autres mots et expressions
être sûr/e (de)   *to be sure (of)*
le plus   *the most*

Note Culturelle
Les Halles et Beaubourg

Il y a quelques années[1], il y avait un quartier[2] de Paris, appelé les Halles, où les restaurateurs et les commerçants[3] venaient dans la nuit pour acheter leur provisions. A la place des Halles, on a construit[6] le «Forum des Halles», avec des magasins, des cafés, etc., autour d'un beau jardin.

Pas très loin, un immense édifice nouveau a été inauguré[7] en 1977. C'est Beaubourg.

Beaubourg, aussi appelé le Centre Georges-Pompidou, est un musée créé par l'ancien président de la République française, Georges Pompidou. Monsieur Pompidou voulait créer un centre culturel, un centre pour tous les arts. Il voulait que ce centre attire[8] tout le monde, et spécialement les personnes qui n'allaient pas normalement dans les musées.

Beaubourg attire en effet[9] beaucoup de monde. L'architecture est ultra-moderne. Le bâtiment[10] est en verre et en acier[11] et est peint[12] en rouge, bleu et jaune vifs[13]. Et tout ceci est au milieu d'un des plus vieux quartiers de Paris, avec de toutes petites rues et de belles maisons anciennes. Certaines personnes comparent Beaubourg à une raffinerie[14], d'autres à un gigantesque[15] jeu de construction, ou même à un véhicule spatial.

Ce musée rassemble toutes les formes d'art. On peut voir des tableaux d'artistes célèbres de même que[16] des sculptures faites avec des morceaux de carrosserie de voiture et de vieux pneus[17]. Il y a une énorme bibliothèque de trois étages où on prend

ses livres soi-même. Il y a un endroit où on peut écouter les disques de son choix[18]. Il y a des films contemporains et des expositions de toutes sortes[19]. Il y a un centre de recherche[20] de musique et d'acoustique. Et il y a même un café-restaurant sur une très belle terrasse d'où on a une vue magnifique sur Paris.

1 A few years ago 2 area 3 restaurant owners and shop owners 4 market 5 part 6 built 7 was recently inaugurated 8 attract 9 indeed 10 the building 11 steel 12 painted 13 bright 14 refinery 15 gigantic 16 as well as 17 car bodies and old tires 18 of one's choice 19 of all kinds 20 research center

Extérieur du Centre Pompidou: un musée pas comme les autres.

Phase 9

Journal parlé

Qu'est-ce que vous allez apprendre?

This Phase will introduce you to vocabulary and expressions related to radio and television broadcasting (the news, weather, advertising) and French currency.

Communication

At the end of the Phase you will be able to:

Speak of future events using the future tense.

Indicate possession using possessive pronouns.

Express the pronominal notion of *all, everything* using *tout*.

Derive adjectives from past participles.

Indicate periods of time with the expression *il y a* (ago), *depuis* (since), and *pendant* (for, during).

You will also enhance your ability to use actively: comparisons, the conditional, the *passé composé* with object pronouns, possessive adjectives, infinitive constructions, interrogative pronouns, and the verbs *savoir* and *connaître*.

Culture

French radio, advertising, labor unions and strikes, the French and monetary system.

PRÉPARATION 59

Journal parlé

Faits divers

Jean-Paul Collet: Mesdames, messieurs, bonsoir. Au micro, Jean-Paul
  Collet. Voici nos informations°.   news
  Accident de circulation ce matin à l'angle de l'avenue des
Champs-Elysées et de la Place de la Concorde. Un taxi qui tour-
nait à droite a renversé un motocycliste imprudent° qui voulait le   careless
dépasser°. Les agents de police accourus° sur les lieux° ont dis-   pass / rushed / scene
persé la foule rassemblée° et l'ambulance a transporté le motocy-   gathered
cliste blessé à l'hôpital le plus proche°.   near
  Forte° explosion cet après-midi dans un garage de l'avenue des   powerful
Lilas. Les dégâts° ont été importants°, mais, heureusement, il n'y a damage / heavy
pas eu de victimes. On ne sait pas encore la cause de cette explosion. La police est allée au garage immédiatement et continue son
enquête° cet après-midi.   investigation

Échange d'idées

1. Quelles peuvent être les causes d'explosion dans un garage?
2. S1: Ask your classmate if he/she heard about the accident.
   Tu as entendu parler de...?

   S2: Say no. Ask questions about it: Where was it? What happened (*Qu'est-ce qui s'est passé*)? Were there many people hurt
   (*des blessés*)?

   S1, S2: Make a comment that expresses your opinion: it's too
   bad, motorcycles are dangerous, you hate to drive in the
   city, etc.

1. The *passé composé* with indirect object pronouns

Certain French verbs that take indirect objects have English equivalents that do not. Therefore, it's helpful to learn these French verbs
plus some others that usually take direct objects.
1. Look at this sentence: *Je vais écrire une lettre aux enfants.*
   a. What is the indirect object? |

   enfants (The indirect object, usually a person, is introduced by the preposition *à*.)

b. What is the direct object? |

        une lettre

2. Write the infinitive. Then write *qqn, à qqn,* or *qqch à qqn* to tell whether the verb refers to people as direct or indirect objects.

  Modèle: aider |

              aider qqn (direct object)

      donner |

              donner qqch à qqn (person is indirect object)

aider	dire	envoyer	regarder
aimer	donner	montrer	répondre
chercher	écouter	parler	téléphoner
demander	écrire	quitter	vendre	

    aider qqn; aimer qqn; chercher qqn; demander qqch à qqn; dire qqch à qqn; donner qqch à qqn; écouter qqn; écrire qqch à qqn; envoyer qqch à qqn; montrer qqch à qqn; parler à qqn; quitter qqn; regarder qqn; répondre à qqn; téléphoner à qqn; vendre qqch à qqn

3. Write the indirect object pronouns used in these sentences.
   a. Nos grands-parents nous ont donné une radio. | a. nous
   b. Quand Guy a téléphoné à ses amis, il leur a donné son a-dresse. | b. leur
   c. La vendeuse lui a vendu une belle guitare. | c. lui
   d. Est-ce que vous m'avez envoyé une carte de New York? | d. me (m')

4. a. In the *passé composé,* where is the object pronoun placed—right after the auxiliary verb, right before the auxiliary verb, right before the past participle? |

      right before the auxiliary verb

   b. Does the participle show gender and number agreement when an *indirect* object precedes the verb? |

      no (only when a direct object precedes)

5. Put the following sentences in the *passé composé.*
   a. Ils nous vendent leur appartement. |

      Ils nous ont vendu leur appartement.

   b. Est-ce que vous lui envoyez un cadeau? |

      Est-ce que vous lui avez envoyé un cadeau?

   c. Je vous donne mon numéro de téléphone. |

      Je vous ai donné mon numéro de téléphone.

6. Write sentences in the *passé composé* with a pronoun object.

SUBJECT	VERB PHRASE	INDIRECT OBJECT
1. vous	1. répondre	1. à moi
2. on	2. téléphoner ce matin	2. à toi
3. Bernard	3. donner des livres	3. à ce garçon
4. Paul et Guy	4. présenter une amie	4. à cette femme
5. tu	5. parler des vacances	5. aux élèves
6. le professeur	6. vendre des disques	6. à nous
7. je	7. envoyer les photos	7. à vous

Modèle: 3–7–1 |

Bernard m'a envoyé les photos.

a. 6–1–5 |

a. Le professeur leur a répondu.

b. 3–4–1 |

b. Bernard m'a présenté une amie.

c. 1–6–6 |

c. Vous nous avez vendu des disques.

d. 4–7–2 |

d. Paul et Guy t'ont envoyé les photos.

e. 7–3–3 |

e. Je lui ai donné des livres.

f. 2–2–7 |

f. On vous a téléphoné ce matin.

g. 5–5–4 |

g. Tu lui as parlé des vacances.

7. Answer these questions by adding the information in parentheses. Use an object pronoun in your answers. (See key.)
   a. Qu'est-ce que vous avez dit à Bernard? (que je voudrais bien aller voir ce film de science-fiction)
   b. Avez-vous parlé à Annick? (oui, de mes expériences de chimie)
   c. Qu'est-ce que Lucie t'a rendu? (mon dictionnaire français-anglais)

2. More practice with the conditional

1. Here are verbs whose conditional stems are irregular.

aller	**ir-**	pouvoir	**pourr-**
avoir	**aur-**	venir	**viendr-**
être	**ser-**	voir	**verr-**
faire	**fer-**	vouloir	**voudr-**

   a. Look at each stem and notice which sounds are like those of the verb's infinitive.
   b. What is the final letter in each stem? |

r (The sound /r/ ends every conditional stem, regular or irregular.)

   c. Endings for the conditional are the same as those for what tense? |

imparfait: -ais, -ais, -ait, -ions, -iez, -aient

2. The sentences below describe what people *would* do and how they *would* feel if they suddenly received a little extra money. For each

sentence, first say the English equivalent. Then write the subject, the conditional verb, and its infinitive.

a. Nous aurions beaucoup de chance. |

(We would be very lucky.) Nous aurions; avoir

b. Nous serions très heureux. |

(We would be very happy.) Nous serions; être

c. Je ferais un petit voyage. |

(I would take a short trip.) Je ferais; faire

d. Nous irions au concert tous les week-ends. |

(We would go to concerts every weekend.) Nous irions; aller

e. Nous verrions tous les films récents. |

(We would see all the recent movies.) Nous verrions; voir

f. Mes amis viendraient dîner chez moi tous les samedis. |

(My friends would come to dinner at my house every Saturday.) Mes amis viendraient; venir

g. Tu pourrais acheter un nouveau vélo. |

(You would be able to buy a new bike.) Tu pourrais; pouvoir

3. Tell what these people would choose as a profession/occupation or identity if they could be anything they wanted. Say your answers before you write them.

Modèle: Anne: pilote |

Anne serait pilote.

a. Jean: caméraman
b. Georges et moi: musiciens
c. toi: garagiste?
d. Béatrice et David: commerçants *(shopkeepers)*
e. Sylvie et Luc, vous: écrivains?
f. moi: millionnaire |

a. Jean serait caméraman.   b. Georges et moi serions musiciens.   c. Tu serais garagiste?   d. Béatrice et David seraient commerçants.   e. Sylvie et Luc, vous seriez écrivains?   f. Moi, je serais millionnaire.

4. Most *-re* verbs with some irregular forms in the present tense or with irregular past participles have a regular conditional stem:

prendre	je prendrais
dire	je dirais
connaître	je connaîtrais
écrire	j'écrirais
mettre	je mettrais

5. Each of the sentences below begins with a supposition. Tell what the result would be by using the conditional to complete the sentence.

a. Si je pouvais avoir un chien,... (un cocker)
b. S'il revenait aux États-Unis,... (en septembre ou en octobre)
c. Si vous pouviez venir au cours régulièrement,... (apprendre beaucoup plus de choses)

428

d. Si elles allaient en Afrique,... (au Sénégal)
e. Si nous étions malades,... (à l'hôpital)
f. S'il décidait de faire un gâteau,... (un gâteau au chocolat)
g. Si tu voyais ce film,... (une actrice extraordinaire)
h. Si je prenais une glace,... (une glace à la fraises) |

a. j'aurais un cocker.   b. il reviendrait en septembre ou en octobre. (*Revenir* is a compound of *venir,* so its stem is the same except for the prefix *re-*.)   c. vous apprendriez beaucoup plus de choses.   d. elles iraient au Sénégal.   e. nous serions à l'hôpital.   f. il ferait un gâteau au chocolat.   g. tu verrais une actrice extraordinaire.   h. je prendrais une glace à la fraises.

À Propos!

What kind of car would you like to have?
Si j'avais une voiture,....
Pourquoi? Parce que c'est une voiture... (puissante/confortable/jolie/économique/luxueuse).

3. *Il y a* with time expressions

1. *Il y a* can be used to express a time relationship. Can you guess the English equivalent? *Mes parents ont acheté notre maison il y a cinq ans.* |

My parents bought our house five years ago.

> il y a + expression of time = ago
>
> **il y a cinq ans**   = five years ago
> **il y a longtemps**   = a long time ago

2. Notice that *il y a* precedes the expression of time, while *ago* follows it. Give the French equivalents of these sentences.
   a. We went to France two years ago. |

Nous sommes allés en France il y a deux ans.

   b. A month ago, she won the skating prize (*le prix de patinage*). |

Il y a un mois, elle a gagné le prix de patinage.

À Propos!

Remember a specific thing you were doing at these times.
Que faisiez-vous il y a dix ans? |

Il y a dix ans, j'allais à l'école.

   a. Que faisiez-vous il y a cinq ans?
   b. ... il y a deux ans?   f. ... il y a une semaine?
   c. ... il y a un an?   g. ... il y a deux jours?
   d. ... il y a six mois?   h. ... il y a vingt minutes?
   e. ... il y a un mois?

Note Culturelle
La radio

À la radio en France, on a le même choix[1] de programmes qu'aux États-Unis. On peut écouter des informations[2], des jeux, des interviews, et bien sûr, de la musique. Il y a plusieurs postes: France-Musique, France-Culture, Europe 1, France-Inter, Radio Monte-Carlo, R.T.L. (Luxembourg), ainsi que[3] les stations locales et régionales.

France-Musique présente des programmes de musique classique et des commentaires sur cette musique. France-Culture offre des émissions[4] culturelles: discussions, interviews, tables rondes[5] avec des personnalités du monde des lettres et des arts.

Les autres stations ont surtout de la musique moderne: rock, jazz, etc. Pour certaines émissions, il y a souvent deux animateurs[7] (ou un animateur et une animatrice). Ils échangent des commentaires entre eux en même temps[8] qu'ils parlent aux auditeurs. Ainsi, l'atmosphère à la radio est généralement amicale et détendue.[9]

Souvent les «tubes»[10] qu'on entend à la radio sont des chansons américaines ou anglaises. Certaines sont traduites[11] et chantées par des chanteurs français.

Beaucoup de chanteurs, populaires depuis très longtemps, Yves Montand, Edith Piaf, Jacques Brel par exemple, continuent à être appréciés de nos jours.

1 choice 2 the news 3 as well as 4 broadcasts 5 panel discussions 6 mainly 7 emcees 8 at the same time as 9 relaxed 10 ''hits'' 11 translated

À Paris. La Maison de la Radio.

Vocabulaire

Noms

l'ambulance f.   *ambulance*
l'angle m.   *corner*
la cause   *cause*
le/la commerçant/e   *shopkeeper*
les dégâts m.   *damages*
l'enquête f.   *investigation*
l'explosion f.   *explosion*
les faits divers m.   *local news in brief*
le fauteuil   *armchair*
le garage   *garage*
le/la garagiste   *garage mechanic or owner*
les informations f.   *news*
le journal parlé   *newscast*
les lieux m.   *scene*
le micro   *microphone*
le/la millionnaire   *millionaire*
la vérité   *truth*
la victime   *victim*

Adjectifs

antipathique   *unpleasant, disagreeable*
blessé/e   *wounded*
économique   *economical*
habillé/e   *dressed*
imprudent/e   *careless*
légal/e   *legal*
luxueux/se   *luxurious*
proche   *near, close*
puissant/e   *powerful*
vulgaire   *vulgar*

Verbes

accourir   *to rush, to run to*
dépasser   *to pass*
rencontrer   *to meet*
se rassembler   *to gather*
tourner   *to turn*

Autres mots et expressions

à la radio   *on the radio*
avoir de la chance   *to be lucky*
avoir lieu   *to take place*
entendre parler de   *to hear about*
extrêmement   *extremely*
il y a; ~ eu; ~ 5 ans   *there was, there has been; 5 years ago*
immédiatement   *immediately*
si seulement   *if only*

Sur un boulevard parisien, une colonne Morris (parfois appelé aussi un kiosque.)

PRÉPARATION 60

Journal parlé

Un Message publicitaire

Jérôme Dorin Et maintenant, nous vous demandons d'écouter Brigitte
Labelle, la charmante vedette° de cinéma, qui nous présente un   star
message publicitaire.

Brigitte Labelle Connaissez-vous les jeans Vély? Les jeans Vély sont
mes meilleurs amis. Ils vont avec moi partout°: au jardin, dans la   everywhere
maison, à la plage, à la campagne, à la montagne... Les jeans Vély
ne me quittent jamais... Les jeans Vély, je les adore...

Jérôme Dorin Nous continuons avec un autre message, présenté par
Robert Lafont, le célèbre champion cycliste.

Robert Lafont Les jeans Vély... formidables! Pour le vélo, pour l'auto,
pour le bateau, pour les vacances, pour les sports, je porte seulement les jeans Vély...

Jérôme Dorin Merci, Brigitte Labelle, merci, Robert Lafont... Pour le
confort et l'élégance, faites comme toutes les grandes vedettes,
portez les jeans Vély... N'oubliez pas... Jeans Vély... La marque° de   brand
qualité... En vente° dans tous les grands magasins...   for sale

1. Est-ce que vous portez souvent des jeans? Quand? Quand et où n'est-il pas recommandé de porter des jeans?
2. Écrivez un message publicitaire pour un nouveau produit. Dites ce qu'il faut pour bien le vendre.
3. Pensez à une ou deux réclames américaines, à la radio, à la télévision ou dans un magazine, qui utilisent des personnalités célèbres pour vendre le produit. Qu'en pensez-vous?

1. Past participles used as adjectives

In both English and French, many past participles are used as descriptive adjectives. In fact, most French adjectives with the ending -*é* come from an -*er* verb.

1. You are working in this phase with news features from something called a *journal parlé*.
   a. What is the -*er* verb that gives the adjective *parlé*? |
      parler
   b. A literal translation of *journal parlé* is _____ *newspaper*. |
      spoken

2. This sentence occurs in the *journal parlé*:

   Les agents de police ont dispersé la foule rassemblée.

   a. What is the past participle adjective in the sentence? |
      rassemblée (*Dispersé* is part of the verb form *ont dispersé*.)
   b. What does *rassemblée* describe? |
      foule
   c. Why is *rassemblée* written with an -*e*? |
      It agrees with the feminine singular noun *foule*.

3. Complete each sentence with the correct form of *apprécié*.
   a. C'est un musicien très _____. | a. apprécié
   b. C'est une musicienne très _____. | b. appréciée
   c. Ce sont des musiciens très _____. | c. appréciés
   d. Ce sont des musiciennes très _____. | d. appréciées

   To decide whether a past participle is used as an adjective or as a verb in the *passé composé*, ask yourself:

   —Does the word describe a noun, or does it indicate an action?
   —Is it preceded by a noun, or by an auxiliary verb form (*avoir* or *être*)?

4. In each pair of sentences, complete the second sentence with the past participle adjective from the verb used in the first sentence.
   Modèle: La station de télévision télévise le match de football.
         C'est un match _____. |
         télévisé (It's a televised game.)

a. Tout le monde déteste cet homme. C'est un homme _____. |
   détesté (He's a hated man.)

b. Hier, deux personnes ont kidnappé un enfant. La police a re-
   trouvé l'enfant _____. |
   kidnappé (The police have found the kidnapped child.)

c. Quand je vais dans un restaurant, je réserve toujours une ta-
   ble. Je préfère avoir une table _____. |
   réservée (I prefer to have a reserved table.)

d. Notre professeur organise une visite au Louvre pour toute la
   classe. C'est une visite _____. |
   organisée (It's an organized visit.)

e. Tout le monde connaît cet écrivain. C'est un écrivain _____. |
   connu (a [well-] known writer)

2. More expressions with *faire*

1. Here are a few more expressions with *faire*. Match each with its
   English equivalent.

   faire ses devoirs   faire un discours
   faire des économies   faire la grève
   faire le ménage   faire du sport
                              faire la vaisselle

   a. to go on strike | a. faire la grève
   b. to participate in sports | b. faire du sport
   c. to do one's homework | c. faire ses devoirs
   d. to do the dishes | d. faire la vaisselle
   e. to save money | e. faire des économies
   f. to give a speech | f. faire un discours
   g. to do the housework | g. faire le ménage

2. Complete the sentences that follow with the correct tense of *faire*.
   a. Hier je _____ mes devoirs quand Gertrude est arrivée. | a. faisais
   b. Tu _____ ton travail demain? (immediate future) | b. vas faire
   c. L'hiver dernier on _____ du ski à la montagne. | c. a fait /faisait
   d. Maintenant on _____ du camping en Suisse. | d. fait
   e. Nous _____ des courses le samedi. | e. faisons
   f. Qu'est-ce que vous _____ maintenant? | f. faites

3. Say what everyone's doing, using the cues provided. (See key.)
   a. Elle _____.   b. Nous _____.   c. Ils _____.   d. Vous _____. |

À Propos!

a. Est-ce que le sport est bon pour la santé *(for your health)*?
   Est-ce que vous faites du sport? Quel sport?
b. Quand on est étudiant, est-ce qu'on peut faire des économies?
   Connaissez-vous des étudiants qui font la cuisine/la vaisselle au restaurant universitaire pour gagner un peu d'argent?

3. Practice with possessive adjectives

Below are names of people and drawings of their "possessions." Pretend that you are pointing out the possessions to a friend. (See key.)

   Modèle: Caroline: un chat
   Voilà son chat.

1. Roger: une vache   un chien   des poissons

2. Mme Jolie: une robe   un bateau   des admirateurs

3. mes amis et moi: une université   une piscine   des copains

4. les élèves: une salle de classe un professeur   des stylos

4. Possessive pronouns

In English, you may say:

> This is my book; it's *mine*.
> This is my chair; it's *mine*.
>
> These are my records; they are *mine*.
> These are my cassettes; they are *mine*.

Look at the equivalent sentences in French:

> C'est mon livre; c'est *le mien*.
> C'est ma chaise; c'est *la mienne*.
>
> Ce sont mes disques; ce sont *les miens*.
> Ce sont mes cassettes; ce sont *les miennes*.

1. a. What phrase replaces *mon livre?* |
      le mien (masculine singular)
   b. What phrase replaces *ma chaise?* |
      la mienne (feminine singular)
   c. What phrase replaces *mes disques?* |
      les miens (masculine plural)
   d. What phrase replaces *mes cassettes?* |
      les miennes (feminine plural)
2. In French, the possessive pronoun has two parts: a form of the
   _____ + a pronoun form. |
      definite article (*le, la,* or *les*)

Possessive Pronouns

| Singular | | Plural | | English |
Masculine	*Feminine*	*Masculine*	*Feminine*	equivalent
le mien	**la mienne**	les miens	les miennes	*mine*
le tien	**la tienne**	les tiens	les tiennes	*yours*
le sien	**la sienne**	les siens	les siennes	*his, hers, its*
	le/la nôtre	les nôtres		*ours*
	le/la vôtre	les vôtres		*yours*
	le/la leur	les leurs		*theirs*

3. Read aloud each form or repeat after the recording.
4. Replace each noun phrase with the appropriate pronoun.
   Modèle: mon manteau |
      le mien

a. ton anorak   f. mes stylos   a. le tien   f. les miens
b. son pantalon   g. tes cousins   b. le sien   g. les tiens
c. notre voiture   h. les chaussures de Louis   c. la nôtre   h. les siennes
d. votre maison   i. nos vestes   d. la vôtre   i. les nôtres
e. leur motocyclette   j. leurs gants   e. la leur   j. les leurs

5. You are at a meeting on a rainy day. You've offered to get everybody's umbrella, but you're not having much luck. Ask questions
   according to the model.

   Modèle: Est-ce le parapluie de Rodolphe?
             Non, ce n'est pas le sien.

   a. C'est ton parapluie?
   b. Ce sont les parapluies de Solange et de Marianne?
   c. C'est votre parapluie, monsieur?
   d. Marc et Robert, ce sont vos parapluies?
   e. C'est le parapluie de Mme Vincent?

   a. Non, ce n'est pas le mien.   b. Non, ce ne sont pas les leurs.   c. Non, ce n'est
   pas le mien.   d. Non, ce ne sont pas les nôtres.   e. Non, ce n'est pas le sien.

Vocabulaire

Noms

la caisse *cash register*
le confort *comfort*
le cycliste *cyclist*
l'élégance *f.* *elegance*
l'entracte *m.* *intermission*
l'impatience *f.* *impatience*
la joie *joy*
la marque *brand*
le message *message*
le public *public, audience*
la publicité *advertising*
la qualité *quality*
la santé *health*
le sourire *smile*
la vente *sale*
l'étoile *f.* *star*

Adjectifs

apprécié/e *appreciated*
charmant/e *charming*
distingué/e *distinguished*
groupé/e *grouped*
organisé/e *organised*
préféré/e *preferred, favorite*
réservé/e *reserved*
réussi/e *successful*
télévisé/e *televised*

Verbes

apparaître *to appear*
faire un discours; ~ la grève; *to
   make a speech; to go on strike;*
   ~ des devoirs; *to do homework;*
   ~ des économies *to save money*
offrir *to offer*
ouvrir *to open*
réapparaître *to reappear*
rechercher *to look for*

Autres mots et expressions

en vente *on sale*
exercer de l'influence sur *to exert
   influence on*
partout *everywhere*

Note Culturelle
La publicité

En France, comme aux États-Unis, on trouve de la publicité dans les journaux, à la radio, à la télévision, sur les affiches. Mais la publicité française est souvent présentée d'une manière différente[1]. Par exemple, à la télévision, plusieurs messages publicitaires sont groupés avant les informations de 13 heures ou de 20 heures. Ainsi, on peut voir un film à la télévision sans interruption.

Au cinéma aussi, il y a de la publicité. Au début de chaque séance[2], il y a des films publicitaires pour des grands magasins, des eaux minérales, des appareils électroménagers[3], etc. Il y a toujours également[4] des réclames[5] pour les bonbons et les glaces que les spectateurs peuvent acheter pendant l'entracte dans la salle de cinéma.

Le métro a d'énormes affiches dans ses longs couloirs et sur les murs[6] des stations. Il y en a aussi dans les wagons. On trouve aussi cette publicité aux arrêts d'autobus et dans les autobus.

À Paris, il y a des endroits réservés aux affiches de concerts et de théâtres. Ce sont des colonnes[7] d'environ 4 mètres de hauteur et 2 mètres de diamètre qui ressemblent à de petites maisons rondes. On les appelle des «colonnes Morris».

1 in a different way 2 show 3 household appliances 4 also 5 advertisements 6 walls 7 columns

À Paris. Une station de métro.

PRÉPARATION 61

Journal parlé

Informations

Jean-Paul Collet Nous vous présentons maintenant la suite° de nos informations. Le président de la République va faire un discours ce soir à la télévision à Paris. Il va parler de la situation économique, de l'augmentation° des prix et des grèves récentes.

the next part

increase

Aujourd'hui, dans plusieurs° villes, les femmes boycottent les supermarchés et les magasins d'alimentation°. Elles refusent d'acheter de la viande, du beurre, des œufs, du fromage, des légumes ou des fruits.

a number of
food

Notre reporter, Françoise Guilloux, est allée dans un supermarché pour poser des questions. Françoise, à vous... (Silence)... Françoise... Françoise Guilloux... Oh là là, qu'est-ce qui se passe? On ne vous entend pas! Excusez-nous, mesdames et messieurs, nous avons un petit problème technique.

Échange d'idées

1. Work in pairs.
   Listen to or read the news today. Then, imagine that your partner hasn't been able to do the same because of too much work and asks you to provide her/him with the information you know.
   S1: Ask what's happening in the world.
   Qu'est-ce qui se passe dans le monde aujourd'hui?
   S2: Oh là là! Beaucoup de mauvaises nouvelles... (Continuez la conversation.)
2. Que pensez-vous des prix et des produits chers? Si vous aviez beaucoup d'argent, est-ce que vous achèteriez tout ce qui vous plaît (everything you like)? oui? non? pourquoi?

1. Infinitive constructions: review

Look at the lists of verbs and prepositions on p. 397.
1. Write sentences according to the model, using *à* or *de* before the infinitive as necessary. (See key.)

Modèle: Nos amis nous offrent leur aide. (devoir) |
           Nos amis doivent nous offrir leur aide.

   a. (décider)   c. (continuer)   e. (commencer)
   b. (hésiter)   d. (refuser)

2.   *Modèle:* Il n'a pas fini son travail hier soir. (pouvoir) |
           Il peut le finir ce matin.

   a. (vouloir)   c. (oublier)   e. (réussir)
   b. (espérer)   d. (essayer)

À Propos!

Qu'est-ce que vous avez oublié de faire récemment?
Qu'est-ce que vous avez réussi à faire?
Qu'est-ce que vous espérez faire dimanche?
Qu'est-ce que vous avez décidé de faire pendant les vacances?

2. Interrogative pronouns: review

1. Choose a logical answer to the questions below, after deciding whether the question applies to a person or a thing.
   a. Avec quoi avez-vous fait ce gâteau?
   b. Qu'est-ce que vous avez acheté pour le faire?
   c. Qui est-ce qui est allé au marché avec vous?
   d. Il y a le supermarché de M. Dupont et le marché du coin. Auquel êtes-vous allé?
2. Refer to the chart on p. 389 or 390. Use an appropriate interrogative pronoun to get additional information. (See key.)
   a. Oh, ce gâteau est délicieux! *(What did you make the cake with?)*
   b. Quel beau costume, Jacques! *(Where did you buy it?)*
   c. Quel match extraordinaire! *(With whom did you go?)*
   d. Vous avez vu les photos dans le journal? *(Which one was the criminal?)*

3. Third person possessive pronouns: practice

1. Restate the sentences, using forms of *le sien* or *le leur*. Refer to the chart on p. 436. (See key.)
   Modèle: Ce livre est à Marie. |
              C'est le sien.

   a. Cette auto est à mes parents.   e. Ce sont les amies de Paul.
   b. Cette bicyclette est à mon frère.   f. Ce sont les amies de Suzanne.
   c. Ce vélo est à ma sœur.   g. Ces trois jeans sont à ma sœur.
   d. Ce sont les amis de Paul et de Suzanne.   h. Ces trois chemises sont à mon frère.

2. Answer the questions, following the pattern indicated in the model. (See key.)

    Modèle: Vois-tu ce vélo là-bas? |

        Oui, je le vois, c'est le mien.

          Voyez-vous ces motocyclettes là-bas? |

        Oui, nous les voyons, ce sont les nôtres.

  a. Est-ce que je vois mon disque? (Oui, tu...)
  b. Voyons-nous notre bateau? (Oui, vous...)
  c. Vois-tu cette auto? (Oui, je...)
  d. Vois-tu ces journaux? (Oui, je...)
  e. Vois-tu ces affiches? (Oui, je...)
  f. Voyez-vous ce tableau? (Oui, nous...)
  g. Voyez-vous ces dessins? (Oui, je...)
  h. Est-ce que je vois votre maison, là-bas? (Oui, vous...)

4. More on the adjective *tout*

1. Write the proper form of *tout* for the following phrases.

  _____ le concert   _____ les nouvelles   _____ les auditeurs
  _____ la chanson |

    tout, toutes, tous, toute

2. a. Give English equivalents for these sentences.
    J'ai écouté attentivement pendant tout le concert.
    Tous les concerts cet été ont été bons. |

    I listened attentively during the whole concert. All (of) the concerts this summer have been good.

  b. Compare *pendant tout le concert* and *tous les concerts*. Which phrase measures an amount of time? |

    pendant tout le concert

  c. Which phrase refers to a quantity of concerts? |

    tous les concerts

  d. When does *tout* have the meaning *the whole*—when it measures an amount or when it counts a quantity? |

    when it measures an amount

3. In English you may say *I like all the programs* or *I like them all.* In which sentence is *all* a pronoun, replacing a noun phrase?

    in the second sentence; in the first sentence, all is an adjective.

4. In French, *tout* can be used as a pronoun also. When *tous* acts as a pronoun, the *s* is pronounced: /tus/.

  a. J'aime tous les programmes de
    variétés.   Je *les* aime *tous.*
  b. J'écoute toutes les nouvelles.   Je *les* écoute *toutes.*

c. Il connaît toute la chanson.   Il *la* connaît *toute*.

d. Nous comprenons tout le poème.   Nous *le* comprenons *tout*.

Give the English equivalents of the sentences in the right-hand column above. |

    a. I like all of them. I like them all.

    b. I listen to all of them. I listen to them all.

    c. He knows all of it (the whole thing). He knows it all (the whole song).

    d. We understand all of it. We understand it all.

5. Answer the following questions with *oui* or *non*, using the appropriate pronoun form of *tout*. (See key.)

    a. Aimez-vous tous les fruits?

    b. Avez-vous visité toutes les expositions de peinture cette année?

    c. Connais-tu toutes les filles de la classe?

    d. Connais-tu toutes les paroles de la Marseillaise?

6. The adverbial phrase *du tout* is added to strengthen the negative value of: *rien, pas, point, sans rien.*

      Il n'aura rien du tout.   *He will have nothing at all.*

What is the English equivalent of the following sentences?

    a. Je n'en veux pas du tout.

    b. Sans étudier du tout, il veut réussir. |

    a. I don't want any of it at all.   b. Without studying at all, he wants to succeed.

7. Other adverbial expressions with *tout:*

tout le monde	everybody
tout à coup	suddenly
tout à l'heure	just now (past) or presently (future)
tout de suite	immediately
tout à fait	quite, entirely
tout au plus	at the most
voilà tout	that is all

Write a paragraph about a party you attended recently, using as many adverbial expressions with *tout* as possible.

Vocabulaire

Noms

l'alimentation *f. food*

l'augmentation *f. increase*

le/la caissier/caissière *cashier*

le/la criminel/criminelle *criminal*

l'établissement *m. institution, building*

la gendarmerie *state police*

la grève *strike*

la parole *word*

le résultat *result*

la situation *situation*

la suite *continuation, following part, rest*

le syndicat *union*

Note Culturelle

Les grèves

La France peut être parfois complètement paralysée par des grèves[1].

Les grèves dans les industries sont fréquentes et sont généralement encouragées par les syndicats[2] ouvriers. Les syndicats les plus connus[3] sont la C.G.T. (Confédération générale du travail) et la C.F.D.T. (Confédération française démocratique du travail).

Il arrive[4] que les compagnies d'électricité, de gaz et de transports (autobus et métro) fassent la grève[5] toutes en même temps. La vie devient[6] alors très difficile.

Lorsqu'il[7] y a une grève des transports, les camions[8] militaires remplacent souvent les autobus. De même[9], si les éboueurs[10] sont en grève, l'armée fait le ramassage des poubelles[11].

En mai et juin 1968, la France a été paralysée par des grèves très sérieuses auxquelles[12] les étudiants ont pris une part importante[13]. Les revendications[14] des grévistes[15] ont donné naissance à de nouvelles lois[16] sur le travail aussi bien que sur l'enseignement.

1 strikes 2 unions 3 best-known 4 it happens 5 go on strike 6 becomes 7 when 8 trucks 9 similarly 10 trash collectors 11 garbage cans 12 in which 13 played an important part 14 demands 15 strikers 16 gave rise to new laws

Employés en grève.

Autres mots et expressions

plusieurs *several*

tout: pas du ~; sans rien du ~; ~ à fait; ~ au plus; voilà ~ *not at all; without anything at all; exactly, entirely; at the most; that's all*

Verbes

abattre *to knock out, shoot down*
boycotter *to boycott*
forcer *to force*
hésiter *to hesitate*

PRÉPARATION 62

Journal parlé

Informations (suite)

Françoise Guilloux Jean-Paul Collet?... Ah, voilà... Mon micro° marche   microphone
maintenant... Excusez-moi... Mesdames, messieurs, nous sommes
devant le Supermarché Sibon. Il y a à côté de moi plusieurs
femmes qui portent des pancartes°. On peut lire: LA VIANDE   placards, posters
EST TROP CHÈRE—LE BEURRE EST TROP CHER—LE LAIT
EST TROP CHER—À BAS° LA VIE CHÈRE!... Oh, voilà une   down with
pancarte différente... Madame, vous voulez nous lire votre pancarte?

La Femme Bien sûr, mademoiselle. Sur ma pancarte, j'ai écrit: NOS
ENFANTS ONT FAIM. NOS MARIS ONT FAIM. NOUS
AVONS FAIM... NOUS VOULONS DES PRIX RAISONNA-
BLES!

Phase neuf

Françoise Guilloux Alors, madame, qu'est-ce que vous allez faire si cette situation continue?

La Femme C'est très simple, mademoiselle: la grève de la faim. Nous, nos maris, nos enfants, nous allons faire la grève de la faim.

Françoise Guilloux Bien. Merci, madame. Vous avez entendu cette réponse? La situation est grave. Et maintenant, à vous, Jean-Paul Collet.

Jean-Paul Collet Merci, Françoise Guilloux... Cette affaire de boycottage est vraiment sérieuse. On espère que le gouvernement va prendre des mesures immédiates.

Échange d'idées

1. Avez-vous déjà participé à une manifestation? Laquelle?
2. Vous rappelez-vous un exemple récent de grève, de boycottage ou de manifestation dans votre région ou même à l'échelon national (*national level*)? Racontez-le.

1. Indirect object pronouns; negative *passé composé*

1. Unscramble these groups of words to form statements in the *passé composé*.
   a. leur/avons/téléphoné/nous |
      Nous leur avons téléphoné. (We telephoned them.)
   b. a/elle/répondu/vous |
      Elle vous a répondu. (She answered you.)
   c. parlé/m'/ils/ont |
      Ils m'ont parlé. (They talked to me.)
2. The pronoun *y*, takes the same position as all indirect object pronouns. Rewrite the sentences with *y*.
   a. Elle est allée à la banque. |
   b. Nous avons travaillé à la bibliothèque. |
   c. Tu as répondu aux questions. |

   a. Elle y est allée.
   b. Nous y avons travaillé.
   c. Tu y as répondu.

3. The following sentence illustrates the word order of a negative statement with an indirect object pronoun in the *passé composé*. *Vous ne m'avez pas téléphoné hier.*
   a. Say the English equivalent. |
      You didn't telephone me yesterday.
   b. Unscramble these elements to give the word order of a negative statement in the *passé composé*. Use the above sentence as a model.

   pas / past participle / auxiliary verb / *ne* / object pronoun / subject |

      subject/*ne*/object pronoun/auxiliary verb/*pas*/past participle

4. Say that these things did not happen.
   a. Vous lui avez parlé hier soir. |
      Vous ne lui avez pas parlé hier soir.
   b. Elles t'ont répondu tout de suite. |
      Elles ne t'ont pas répondu tout de suite.

5. Say that Louis did not do yesterday what he is doing today. Use an indirect object pronoun in each sentence.
   Modèle: Aujourd'hui Louis parle à son professeur d'anglais. |
      Il ne lui a pas parlé hier.
   a. Aujourd'hui Louis téléphone à sa tante. |
      Il ne lui a pas téléphoné hier.
   b. Aujourd'hui Louis me donne mes disques. |
      Il ne m'a pas donné mes disques hier.
   c. Aujourd'hui Louis vous montre ses devoirs. |
      Il ne vous a pas montré ses devoirs hier.

6. Marie-Claire also puts things off. Say that she didn't do these things yesterday. Replace the italicized phrases with *lui, leur,* or *y.*
   a. Elle va *à la poste.*
   b. Elle téléphone *à ses grands-parents.*
   c. Elle donne le cadeau *à sa sœur.*
   d. Elle répond *à la lettre de son copain.* |

   a. Elle n'y est pas allée hier.   b. Elle ne leur a pas téléphoné hier.   c. Elle ne lui a pas donné le cadeau hier.   d. Elle n'y a pas répondu hier.

À Propos!

Find out from a classmate:
Tu as réussi à ton dernier examen?
Tu as téléphoné au président de l'université?

2. Review of pronoun *tout*

1. Read the following sentences and give the English equivalents.
   a. *Tous* sont arrivés.
   b. *Toutes* sont arrivées.
   c. *Tout* est là sur la table.
   d. J'aime la viande, le poisson, les légumes,—en un mot, j'aime *tout.* |

   a. Everybody (Everyone) has arrived.

   b. Everybody (Everyone, *feminine*) has arrived.

   c. Everything is there on the table.

   d. I like meat, fish, vegetables,—in a word I like everything. (*Note: Toute* (feminine singular) is never used alone as a subject. *Tout* (masculine singular) has the general meaning of "everything.")

2. Agree with the opinions suggested below. Use the pronoun *tout*, as in the model. (See key.)

   Modèle: Vous trouvez que, dans ce supermarché, les fruits sont chers? (Oui) |
   Oui, tous sont chers.

   a. Vous trouvez que les boissons sont chères aussi? (Oui)
   b. Vous trouvez que les produits laitiers sont très chers? (Oui)
   c. Vous trouvez que les fruits, les légumes, la viande—que tout est de bonne qualité? (Oui)
   d. Vous achetez toutes vos provisions ici? (Oui, je les achète _____ ici)

À Propos!   Est-ce que vous aimez tous vos cours ce semestre? (Oui ou non)

3. The conditional: stating conditions and results

1. Usually, sentences that contain the conditional have two parts: one part tells what would happen under certain conditions; the other explains what those conditions are. For example:

   Si Jean avait de l'argent, il achèterait un vélo.

   a. Give the English equivalent. |
   If Jean had some money, he would buy a bike.
   b. Which part expresses the condition, and what is the tense of the verb? |
   Si Jean avait de l'argent; l'imparfait
   c. Which part tells what would happen if the right condition existed, and what verb form is used here? |
   il achèterait un vélo; the conditional

Si-clauses + conditional

Si + imparfait expresses the condition
   Si Jean avait de l'argent...

The conditional expresses the result of that condition
   ... il voyagerait.

2. The *si*-clause can occur at the beginning or the end of the sentence. Write the English equivalent: *Nicole achèterait un nouveau costume de ski si elle avait de l'argent.* |
   Nicole would buy a new ski outfit if she had the money.

3. Martine is sick in bed and is daydreaming about the things she could do if she had more money. She has decided it's time to get a job *(un emploi)*. For each pair of phrases below, decide which expresses a condition, and which the result. Write a complete sentence using *si* + the *imparfait,* and the conditional.

Modèle: Martine (être) contente/elle (avoir) un emploi |
Martine serait contente si elle avait un emploi. *(Martine would be happy if she had a job.)*

a. elle (avoir) un emploi/elle (avoir) de l'argent |
Si elle avait un emploi, elle aurait de l'argent.

b. elle (pouvoir) acheter une voiture/elle (avoir) assez d'argent |
Elle pourrait acheter une voiture si elle avait assez d'argent.

c. elle (avoir) une voiture/elle (aller) en Suisse |
Si elle avait une voiture, elle irait en Suisse.

d. elle (aller) en Suisse/elle (faire) du ski |
Si elle allait en Suisse, elle ferait du ski.

Invitation au voyage!

Phase neuf

e. elle (voir) son cousin François/elle (aller) à Lausanne |

        Elle verrait son cousin François si elle allait à Lausanne.

f. elle (faire) du ski en Suisse/elle (revenir) en France sans argent |

        Si elle faisait du ski en Suisse, elle reviendrait en France sans argent.

4. Here are some additional irregular conditional stems:

devoir	**devr-**	pleuvoir *(to rain)*	**il pleuvr-**
falloir (il faut)	**il faudr-**	savoir	**saur-**
mourir	**mourr-**	valoir (il vaut)	**il vaudr-**

For each pair of phrases below, decide which expresses a condition, and which the result. Write a complete sentence using *si* + the *imparfait,* and the conditional. (See key.)

a. Si j' (acheter) ce tableau aujourd'hui, il (valoir) peut-être deux fois plus dans dix ans.

b. Si vous (venir) régulièrement en classe, vous (savoir) que nous avons un test au laboratoire aujourd'hui.

c. Si tu (vouloir) savoir comment vont tes parents, tu (devoir) leur téléphoner plus souvent.

d. Si nous ne leur (donner) pas à manger, ils (mourir) de faim.

À *Propos!*

Qu'est-ce que vous feriez si vous étiez témoin d'un accident d'auto? si vous ne saviez pas un mot d'anglais?

4. *Savoir* and *connaître:* practice

1. Indicate which verb—*savoir* or *connaître*—expresses each meaning.

a. to know a fact (*Je voudrais* _____ *où elle habite.*) |

        savoir (I would like to know where she lives.)

b. to be familiar or acquainted with (*Je voudrais* _____ *Paris.*) |

        connaître (I would like to know Paris.)

c. to know how to do something (*Pour faire de la voile, il faut* _____ *nager.*) |

        savoir (To go sailing, you have to know how to swim.)

2. Complete the following conversation with the appropriate forms of *savoir* or *connaître.* (See key.)

Une jeune fille qui porte une petite valise voit un agent de police. Elle va vers (toward) lui.

Jeune Fille Pardon, monsieur l'agent. Je ne *a.* _____ pas très bien Paris. Est-ce que vous pouvez m'aider?

Agent Mais bien sûr. Où voulez-vous aller?

Jeune Fille Rue de la Villette. Je vais chez ma tante; je *b.* _____ son adresse mais je ne *c.* _____ pas toutes ces petites rues.

Agent C'est facile: c'est cette rue-là, à droite. Mais vous parlez très bien français, mademoiselle! D'où venez-vous?

Jeune Fille Oh, merci!... Je suis américaine. J'apprends le français à l'université et je vais souvent au cinéma voir des films français. Mes amis et moi, nous *d.* _____ tous les films de François Truffaut.

Agent Ah, oui? Alors, vous devez aussi *e.* _____ beaucoup d'acteurs français?

Jeune Fille Bien sûr! Une «fana» de cinéma *(movie fan)* comme moi *f.* _____ tous les acteurs célèbres et tous leurs films.

Agent Mais... Et moi, vous ne *g.* _____ pas qui je suis?

Jeune Fille Vous? Ah... non... Je ne *h.* _____ pas... Pourquoi?

Agent i. _____ -vous Claude Lelouch, le réalisateur *(director)*? Eh bien, je suis acteur, et j'ai joué dans beaucoup de ses films. Je ne suis pas un véritable agent de police!

Jeune Fille Pas possible! Ça alors!

Vocabulaire

Noms

l'affaire *f.* *business*
l'arc-en-ciel *m.* *rainbow*
le boycottage *boycotting*
l'emploi *m.* *job*
la faim *hunger*
la mesure *measure*
la pancarte *placard*
la pièce *play*
la poste *post office*
les produits laitiers *m.* *dairy products*
le semestre *semester*

Adjectifs

immédiat/e *quick, immediate*
raisonnable *reasonable*

Verbes

mélanger *to mix*
obtenir *to get, to obtain*
participer *to participate*
valoir *to be worth*

Autres mots et expressions

à (+ personal pronoun) *my (your/ her/his/our/their) turn*
à bas...! *down with...!*
à côté de *near*
absolument *absolutely*

PRÉPARATION 63

1. The future tense

1. Both French and English frequently use the present tense to talk about actions that are expected to take place in the future.

Je pars en vacances samedi.   *I'm leaving for vacation Saturday.*
Je vais voyager pendant un   *I'm going to travel for a month.*
  mois.

Both French and English also have a "true" future tense. Compare these French and English sentences.

Si tu me donnes ton numéro,   *If you give me your number,*
  je te téléphonerai.   *I will call you.*

  a. In English, the future is a compound tense: the auxiliary verb
     ____ + the main verb. |
           will or shall (People often say I'll call.)
  b. The French future tense, unlike English, has no auxiliary verb.
    The equivalent of I will call is ____. |
          je téléphonerai

2. The future stem is the same as the conditional stem. Look again at *je te téléphonerai.*
  a. What is the future stem of *téléphoner?* |
         téléphoner- (The future ending is -ai.)
  b. What are the future/conditional stems of these verbs: *parler, finir, prendre?* |
         parler-, finir-, prendr- (Remember that for -re verbs, the -e is dropped.)
  c. The future/conditional stem always ends in the letter ____. |
      -r

3. Here are the future forms of *parler.*

je	**parler ai**	nous	parler **ons**
tu	parler **as**	vous	parler **ez**
on/il/elle	parler **a**	ils/elles	parler **ont**

  a. Read each form aloud, then write the future endings.
      -ai, -as, -a, -ons, -ez, -ont

b. The stems of the future and conditional are the same. Are their endings the same also?

no (conditional: -ais, -ais, -ait, -ions, -iez, -aient)

4. The people below have been invited to a party. Use the future of *prendre* to say what means of transportation they will be using.

Modèle: Alain _____ le train.

prendra

a. Annie et Marguerite _____ l'autobus.
b. Catherine _____ le métro.
c. Jean-Paul et toi, vous _____ l'autobus.
d. Moi, je _____ un taxi.
e. Véronique, tu _____ ton vélo.
f. Nous _____ le métro.

a. prendront
b. prendra
c. prendrez
d. prendrai
e. prendras
f. prendrons

5. Write the infinitive and the future of the main verb used in the sentences below.

a. Ils lisent le journal.
b. Elle apprend le français.

c. Il réussit à tous ses examens.
d. Nous connaissons les amis de Jean.

e. Je sais son adresse.
f. Nous pouvons acheter ces chaussures.
g. Ils attendent l'arrivée du train.
h. Je finis mes devoirs ce soir.

a. lire; ils liront
b. apprendre; elle apprendra

c. réussir; il réussira
d. connaître; nous connaîtrons

e. savoir; je saurai
f. pouvoir; nous pourrons
g. attendre; ils attendront
h. finir; je finirai

6. Generally, the future is used for the same situations in French and English. But there is one type of phrase in which the uses are different.

Quand j'arriverai à l'aéroport, je vous téléphonerai.

a. What is the English equivalent?

When I arrive at the airport, I'll call you.

b. What part of the sentence is expressed by the present in English but by the future in French?

When I arrive... (Quand j'arriverai...)

In French, the future must be used after *quand* when the action is to take place in the future.

7. Say what will happen in the future after the parade is over.

Modèle: quand vous/lire le journal/vous/apprendre quelques détails sur le défilé *(parade)* d'hier

Quand vous lirez le journal, vous apprendrez quelques détails sur le défilé d'hier.

a. quand l'agent / donner le signal / les automobilistes / s'arrêter

Quand l'agent donnera le signal, les automobilistes s'arrêteront.

b. quand le président / passer / je / prendre une photo

Quand le président passera, je prendrai une photo.

Phase neuf

c. quand je / écrire à mes amis / je leur raconter ma conversation
avec le reporter |

2. Review of possessive pronouns

Jean-Paul Collet is trying to clear up a few points off the air during
the radio broadcast of his colleague, Françoise Guilloux. Complete
her answers to his questions, using possessive pronouns. (See key.)

    Modèle: C'est mon micro qui ne marche pas? —Non, ce n'est
       pas... |

1. —C'est votre micro qui ne marche pas? —Oui, c'est...
2. —C'est notre situation économique qui est difficile? —Oui,
   c'est...
3. —Ce sont les pancartes des manifestants? —Oui, ce sont...
4. —C'est le slogan de la première femme? —Oui, c'est...
5. —C'est sa voix que nous entendons? —Oui, c'est...
6. —Ce sont ses protestations que nous écoutons? —Non, ce ne
   sont pas...
7. —Ce sont les protestations des clientes? —Oui, ce sont...
8. —La grève de la faim est la réponse des consommateurs? —Oui,
   c'est...
9. —C'est votre réponse à vous aussi? —Non, ce n'est pas...
10. —C'est le discours du président qui va suivre? —Oui, c'est...

3. *Il y a* vs. *pendant* with time expressions

1. Compare the meaning of *il y a* + a time expression with that of
pendant + a time expression.

Il y a cinq minutes, je lisais.	*Five minutes ago, I was reading.*
J'ai lu *la Guerre et la Paix* il y a deux ans.	*I read War and Peace two years ago.*
J'ai lu pendant deux heures hier soir.	*I read for two hours last night.*

   a. Which expression—*il y a* or *pendant*—tells how long ago some-
      thing occurred? |

   b. Which expression tells *for* how long (over how long a time)
      something happened? |

3. Give the French equivalent of this sentence:
   They lived in Europe for ten years and they came to the United States two years ago. |

   > Ils ont habité en Europe pendant dix ans et ils sont venus aux États-Unis il y a deux ans.

4. Decide whether each time expression describes *how long ago* something occurred or *for how long* it occurred. Complete the sentence with *il y a* or *pendant,* accordingly.
   a. J'ai acheté ce manteau... quinze jours. |
                                                  4a. il y a
   b. J'ai cherché dans les magasins... un mois avant de le trouver. |
                                                  b. pendant
   c. Il a habité à New York.... un an avant de déménager (*to move*). |
                                                  c. pendant
   d. Il a déménagé... trois semaines. |
                                                d. il y a

5. Answer each question with a phrase. Use *il y a* or *pendant* plus the time expression in parentheses.
   a. Pendant combien de temps avez-vous voyagé en Europe? (... un mois)
   b. Quand avez-vous quitté l'Europe? (... deux jours)
   c. Pendant combien de temps avez-vous nettoyé la maison? (... tout le week-end)
   d. Quand avez-vous fini? (... une heure) |

   > a. pendant un mois   b. il y a deux jours   c. pendant tout le week-end   d. il y a une heure

À Propos!

Pendant combien de temps avez-vous travaillé à ces exercices?

Vocabulaire

Noms

l'admirateur/admiratrice *m./f.*
  admirer
l'arrivée *f.* *arrival*
l'automobiliste *m.* *driver*
le billet *bill*
la cage *cage*
la conférence; ~ de presse *lecture;*
  press conference
le hold-up *hold-up*
le/la manifestant/e *demonstrator*
le miroir *mirror*
la pièce *coin*
le plancher *floor*
le porte-feuille *wallet*
la protestation *protest*
le reportage *report*
le slogan *slogan*

Adjectifs

grave *serious, dangerous*
typique *typical*

Verbes

pleurer *to cry*
suivre (sui-, suiv-, p.p. suivi) *to follow*

Autres mots et expressions

c'est trop cher! *It's too expensive!*

Note Culturelle

L'argent français

En France, comme en Belgique et en Suisse, l'unité de monnaie[1] s'appelle le franc. Cent centimes font un franc. Sur les pièces[2], il est écrit «Liberté, Égalité, Fraternité». C'est, depuis la révolution de 1789, la devise[3] de la République Française. Ces trois mots sont aussi inscrits[4] sur les écoles et sur les édifices publics.

Il existe neuf pièces de monnaie françaises: les pièces de 10 francs, 5 francs, 1 franc, 50 centimes, 20 centimes, 10 centimes, 5 centimes et 1 centime.

Les billets[5] français ne ressemblent pas du tout aux billets américains. Ils sont en général plus grands et, en plus[6], ils ne sont pas tous de la même taille. C'est pourquoi les portefeuilles[7] français, qui doivent contenir[8] des billets de grandeurs différentes, ne ressemblent pas aux portefeuilles américains.

1 monetary unit 2 coins 3 motto 4 inscribed 5 bills 6 furthermore 7 wallets 8 hold 9 famous person 10 writer 11 century 12 composer

Contrairement aux billets américains, les billets français sont très colorés. Sur chaque billet français, comme sur les billets américains, il y a le portrait d'un personnage célèbre[9]. Le billet de 500 francs, par exemple, a le portrait de Pascal, grand écrivain[10] et mathématicien du XVIIème siècle[11]. On trouve Corneille sur le billet de 100 francs et Racine sur le billet de 50 francs. Corneille et Racine sont deux écrivains célèbres du XVIIème siècle. Le billet de 10 francs a le portrait d'Hector Berlioz, grand compositeur[12] du XIXème siècle.

PRÉPARATION 64

Journal parlé

La météo°

Nous terminons nos informations avec quelques mots° sur le temps d'aujourd'hui. Le temps a été splendide dans notre région avec des températures de 22 à 24 degrés. Il a fait beau presque partout en France excepté sur la côte Atlantique. Là il pleut encore en ce moment, mais on annonce que la pluie va cesser° plus tard. Demain, il fera beau partout et les températures seront modérées et très agréables.

    Eh bien, voilà° pour aujourd'hui. Restez à l'écoute pour le discours du président qui suit immédiatement. Je vous dis bonsoir et à demain. Au micro, Jean-Paul Collet.

weather report

words

stop

that's all

Échange d'idées

1. Work in pairs. Your parents are coming to visit you at your university. Tell them what the weather is like on the phone and what it will be like in the next few days. Carry on a conversation.
   S1: Allô Maman?
   S2: Bonjour,...
2. Imagine you are a French-speaking radio reporter in Quebec. Check the newspaper to get your information, then prepare a general report for Canada similar to that of Jean-Paul Collet.
3. Est-ce que vous aimeriez travailler à la télévision ou à la radio? Donnez vos raisons.

1. Comparing people and things

1. a. In an English comparison, the adjective is followed by *than* or *as.* These are both expressed in French by _____. |
      que
   b. The French equivalent of *more . . . than* is _____. |
      plus... que (English also uses the pattern *-er + than: he is richer than....*)
   c. The French equivalent of *less . . . than* is _____. |
      moins... que
   d. The French equivalent of *as . . . as* is _____. |
      aussi... que

                                            Phase neuf

2. Look at the drawings, then give the English equivalents of the descriptions given in French.

Mme Labelle

M. Lepauvre

M. Lebeau

a. Mme Labelle is richer than M. Lepauvre. |
    Mme Labelle est plus riche que M. Lepauvre.

b. M. Lepauvre is less rich than Mme Labelle. |
    M. Lepauvre est moins riche que Mme Labelle.

c. M. Lebeau is as rich as Mme Labelle. |
    M. Lebeau est aussi riche que Mme Labelle.

3. Frames *a-c* describe the drawings below. For each sentence, say which noun(s) the adjective describes.

   Modèle: La mouche *(fly)* est plus forte que le singe. |
       forte describes *mouche*

La mouche

Le chien

Le singe

a. La mouche est plus forte que le chien. |
    forte describes *mouche*

b. Le singe est moins fort que le chien et la mouche. |
    fort describes *singe* (The part of the comparison that follows *que* doesn't affect the form of the adjective.)

c. Le singe et le chien sont moins forts que la mouche. |
    forts describes *singe et chien*

4. Look at the illustrations below and the adjectives that accompany them. Form comparisons based on the illustrations, using *plus... que* or *aussi... que* with the adjectives, and say the English equivalents.

a. Anne   Jeannette   fatigué |
    Anne est plus fatiguée que Jeannette. (Anne is more tired than Jeannette.)

b.   mon oncle   ton oncle   pauvre |

Mon oncle est aussi pauvre que ton oncle. (My uncle is as poor as your uncle.)

c.   vos chats   leurs chats   maigre |

Vos chats sont plus maigres que leurs chats. (*Your* cats are skinnier/thinner than *their* cats.)

5. Now make comparisons based on the following illustrations, using *aussi... que* or *moins... que*.

a.   ma maison   ta maison   moderne |

Ma maison est moins moderne que ta maison.

b. le jeune sorcière   le vieille sorcière   laid |

La jeune sorcière est aussi laide que la vieille sorcière.

c. notre voiture   leur voiture   rapide |

Notre voiture est moins rapide que leur voiture.

2. Practice with the future

The first frames of this section will help you check yourself on what you learned.

1. The future endings are the same as the last syllable of the corresponding present tense forms of *avoir*. Write the endings. |

    -ai, -as, -a, -ons, -ez, -ont

2. The future stem is the same as the _____ stem. |

    conditional

3. For most verbs the conditional/future stem is the same as the _____ of the verb. |

    infinitive (If the infinitive stem ends in -*re*, the *e* is dropped.)

4. All conditional/future stems end in the letter _____. |

    -r

5. By now, you should know the conditional/future stem of these verbs. Write them. If you make any mistakes, stop and memorize the stems.

    a. être   c. aller   e. faire
    b. avoir   d. venir   f. pouvoir |

    a. ser-   c. ir-   e. fer-
    b. aur-   d. viendr-   f. pourr

6. Say what the following people will be doing at 9:30 a.m. tomorrow.

    a. moi: me lever |

    Je me lèverai. (Lever has a stem change in some forms of the present: e becomes è. Remember that this change also occurs in all forms of the future/conditional stem.)

    b. toi: être au bureau |

    Tu seras au bureau.

    c. nous: aller au supermarché |

    Nous irons au supermarché.

    d. vous: prendre votre petit déjeuner |

    Vous prendrez votre petit déjeuner.

    e. Pierre: faire son lit |

    Pierre fera son lit.

    f. Bernadette et Laure: écrire des lettres |

    Bernadette et Laure écriront des lettres.

7. Use the "true" future forms to tell what will take place in the country. (See key.)

    Modèle: Demain, nous allons passer toute la journée à la campagne. |

    Demain, nous passerons toute la journée à la campagne.

    a. Nous allons prendre la voiture de mon père.
    b. À midi, nous allons faire un pique-nique.
    c. Jeannette va acheter des provisions.

d. Je vais emporter un poulet froid.

e. Vous allez préparer un gâteau au chocolat.

À Propos! Est-ce que vous ferez un pique-nique demain? Si oui, où? avec qui? Si non, pourquoi pas?

3. Review of infinitive constructions

In this section, you will review infinitive constructions combined with interrogative pronouns. (Chart of pronouns, pp. 389, 390, chart of verbs, pp. 387 and 397.)

Formulate questions about the element of the sentence which has been underlined, and fill the blanks with *à* or *de* if necessary.

Modèle: <u>Jean-Paul Collet</u> continue ____ présenter les informations. |

Qui continue à présenter les informations?

1. <u>Le Président</u> va ____ faire un discours ce soir.
2. Il veut ____ parler <u>de la situation économique</u>.
3. Les femmes ont décidé ____ boycotter <u>les supermarchés</u>.
4. Elles refusent ____ acheter <u>la nourriture trop chère</u>.
5. <u>Françoise Guilloux</u> essaie ____ obtenir une interview. |

1. Qui va faire un discours ce soir? 2. De quoi veut-il parler? 3. Qu'est-ce que les femmes ont décidé de boycotter? 4. Que refusent-elles d'acheter? 5. Qui essaie d'obtenir une interview?

6. <u>Son micro</u> refuse ____ marcher.
7. Jean-Paul Collet demande <u>aux auditeurs</u> ____ être patients.
8. Françoise Guilloux invite <u>une manifestante</u> ____ parler au micro.
9. La manifestante accepte ____ lire <u>sa pancarte</u>.
10. <u>Elle</u> espère ____ obtenir des résultats en faisant la grève de la faim.
11. Il faut ____ souhaiter <u>le succès des mesures gouvernementales</u>. |

6. Qu'est-ce qui refuse de marcher? 7. À qui Jean-Paul Collet demande-t-il d'être patients? 8. Qui Françoise Guilloux invite-t-elle à parler au micro? 9. Qu'est-ce que la manifestante accepte de lire? 10. Qui espère obtenir des résultats en faisant la grève de la faim? 11. Que faut-il souhaiter?

À Propos! Parlez-vous souvent de la situation économique? Avec qui? Quels sont vos points de vue?

Phase neuf

4. Reading comprehension

Read the rather fanciful passage below. Then answer the questions that follow.

Bizarre! Très bizarre!

Une conversation dans une salle° du musée du Louvre...　　　　　　room

Un visiteur Excusez-moi...
Le gardien° Oui, monsieur?　　　　　　guard
Visiteur Cette statue là-bas m'a parlé tout à l'heure.

(Le gardien tourne le dos° à la statue en question.)　　　　　　back

Gardien (Sarcastique) Ah oui, vraiment? Et qu'est-ce qu'elle vous
　a dit?
Visiteur Elle m'a demandé une cigarette.
Gardien (Toujours° sarcastique) Pas possible! Et alors, vous lui avez　　　still
　donné une cigarette?
Visiteur Mais, monsieur, je lui ai dit qu'il est interdit° de fumer° au　　forbidden / to smoke
　Louvre.
Gardien Monsieur, vous avez beaucoup d'imagination, mais je peux
　vous assurer que nos statues ne parlent pas. Au Musée d'Art mo-
　derne, peut-être, mais ici, jamais.

(Le visiteur continue à parler.)

Visiteur Et puis elle m'a dit, «Je vais faire une petite promenade. Je veux voir les autres salles.»

Gardien Mais monsieur, vous êtes fou! Je vous dis que cette statue...

(Le gardien tourne la tête° et voit que la statue n'est pas là.)   head

    Mais où est-elle? Elle n'est pas là! Au voleur°! Au voleur!   Stop, thief!

Visiteur Mais monsieur, je vous ai dit qu'elle faisait une promenade. Elle ne va pas aller trop loin.

Gardien Quelqu'un a kidnappé notre magnifique statue italienne. Au voleur! Au voleur!

Visiteur Italienne? Ah, ça explique° son accent. Mais magnifique? Ah   that explains
non, alors! Moi, je la trouve plutôt° laide.   rather

Un Des Portraits Peut-être, monsieur. Mais elle est très gentille, vous savez.

Now answer the following questions in French, in complete sentences. Answers are in the answer key.

    Modèle: Que dit le visiteur au gardien? |

        Il dit qu'une statue lui a parlé.

1. Qu'est-ce que la statue a demandé au visiteur? Et qu'est-ce que le visiteur lui a répondu *(answered)*?
2. Est-ce que le gardien croit *(croire: to believe)* le visiteur?
3. Le gardien assure le visiteur qu'au Louvre les statues ne parlent pas. Quel endroit a, peut-être, des statues qui parlent?
4. Pourquoi la statue a-t-elle quitté la salle? Qu'est-ce qu'elle a voulu faire?
5. Quand le gardien voit que la statue n'est pas là, que pense-t-il?
6. La statue vient de quel pays?
7. Qui pense que la statue est très gentille?

Vocabulaire

Noms

la côte Atlantique   *the Atlantic coast*
le degré   *degree*
l'endroit *m.*   *place*
l'interview *f.*   *interview*
la météo   *weather forecast*
la mouche   *fly*
la pluie   *rain*
le point de vue   *point of view*
les provisions *f.*   *food supplies*
le reste   *remaining part*
la sorcière   *witch*
le succès   *success*
la température   *temperature*

Deux amoureux au jardin des Tuileries.

Adjectifs
modéré/e *moderate*
gouvernemental/e *governmental*
splendide *beautiful, splendid*

Verbes
annoncer *to announce, to foresee*
cesser *to stop, to cease*
pleuvoir *to rain*
souhaiter *to wish*

Autres mots et expressions
à l'écoute; rester ~ *tuned in; to keep listening*
en ce moment *right now*
excepté *except*
par rapport à *in relation to*
quelques *several*

PRÉPARATION 65

1. Review of the *passé composé*

This part will give you a chance to review the forms of the *passé composé* and remember which verbs are used with *avoir*, which with *être*.

1. Many past participles have endings that follow a predictable pattern.

   a. For an *-er* verb, you add _____ to the infinitive stem. |
      -é

   b. For a regular *-re* verb, you add _____ to the infinitive stem. |
      -u

   c. Most *-ir* verbs add _____ to the infinitive stem. |
      -i

   d. *Venir* has an irregular past participle. What is it? |
      venu

2. Which of the verbs listed below take the auxiliary verb *être* in the *passé composé*?

   demander   venir   répondre
   arriver   aller   descendre
   regarder   téléphoner   partir
   entendre   sortir   monter |

   arriver, venir, aller, sortir, descendre, partir, monter (all verbs of motion)

3. The participle agrees . . .

   a. with the _____ of a verb conjugated with *être*. |
      subject (ils sont venus; je suis tombée)

   b. with a preceding _____ (always a verb conjugated with *avoir*. |
      direct object (les roses qu'ils m'ont offertes; je les ai emportées)

4. Put the following sentences in the *passé composé*. In doing so, consider three things: is *avoir* or *être* used? what is the past participle? should the past participle agree with the subject? (See key.)

   a. La famille Calvet perd son chien.
   b. Ma tante arrive à la gare.
   c. Tu refuses de manger des épinards.
   d. Ils descendent pour le petit déjeuner.
   e. Les gangsters terrorisent les clients.
   f. Mes copains viennent chez moi cet après-midi.

5. a. Make this sentence negative: *Il est allé au cinéma.* |
   Il n'est pas allé au cinéma.
   b. When a verb in the *passé composé* is negative, where are *ne... pas* placed? |
   around the auxiliary verb (*être* or *avoir*)
6. Say the following things did not happen yesterday. (See key.)
   a. Suzanne/écouter ses disques
   b. Votre copine/aller à la poste
   c. Ils/vendre leur maison
   d. Nous/manger

2. Review practice: object pronouns

This section summarizes the word order of different kinds of sentences with indirect object pronouns and *y*.
1. Complete the sentences with indirect object pronouns or the pronoun *y*.
   a. Charles parle à son singe. Charles _____ parle. | 1a. lui
   b. Elle habite à Genève. Elle _____ habite. | b. y
   c. Elle pense aux examens. Elle _____ pense. | c. y
2. In the present tense, indirect object pronouns and *y* are placed _____. | 2. right before the verb
3. a. Make this sentence negative: *Elle nous parle.* | 3a. Elle ne nous parle pas.
   b. In a negative sentence containing an indirect object pronoun or *y*, *ne... pas* are placed around _____. | b. the pronoun and the verb
4. Rewrite each sentence with an indirect object pronoun or *y*. (See key.)
   a. Robert téléphone à ses amis.
   b. Il pense à ses problèmes.
   c. Il ne donne pas le cadeau à son amie.
   d. Nous ne répondons pas aux questions.
5. a. Rewrite this sentence with *lui: Paul a donné le poisson au chat.* |
   Paul lui a donné le poisson.
   b. Is the indirect object pronoun placed before the auxiliary verb or the past participle? |
   before the auxiliary verb (The same is true of *y*.)
6. Say you have done everything yesterday. Use the *passé composé* and an indirect object pronoun or *y* in your answers. (See key.)
   Modèle: Tu vas écrire à ton oncle? |
   Je lui ai écrit hier.
   a. Tu vas répondre à ces lettres?
   b. Tu vas aller à la poste?

c. Tu vas nous raconter ce film, à Pauline et à moi?

d. Tu vas dire au revoir à tes amis suisses?

7. a. Make this sentence negative: *Elle m'a téléphoné.* |

Elle ne m'a pas téléphoné.

b. *Ne... pas* is placed around _____. |

the pronoun and the auxiliary verb

8. Put the following sentences in the *passé composé,* and use an object pronoun or *y* in each sentence. (See key.)

a. Elles arrivent à Marseille.

b. Nous demandons à Paul et à vous de chanter.

c. Ils ne vont pas au cinéma.

d. Je ne réponds pas à Marie.

3. *Depuis* vs. *pendant*

1. Read the following sentence:

Il a habité à Boston *pendant* deux ans.

You know that this sentence means that he lived in Boston for two years, and the past tense used in both French and English implies that he is no longer living here. Now read this sentence:

Il habite à Boston *depuis* deux ans.

What has been changed? |

The verb is in the present. The preposition is *depuis* instead of *pendant.*

Depuis means *since.* Use that meaning to help you figure out the meaning of the sentence. Then write a *good* English equivalent. |

He lives in Boston since two years is a literal word-by-word translation. *He has been living in Boston for two years* is a good translation.

When *depuis* + a time measure is used in a sentence, the verb in French is often in the present, while in English a progressive past is used. The two languages look at the action from different points of view: English considers the action as having started in the past, French considers it still going on in the present.

Decide whether to use *pendant* + *passé composé* or *depuis* + present in these sentences. Give English equivalents. (See key.)

Modèle: J'ai étudié mon piano _____ deux heures hier soir. |

pendant (I practiced the piano for two hours last night.)

J'étudie le piano _____ deux mois. |

depuis (I've been studying piano for two months.)

a. Quelle longue conférence! Le professeur parle _____ deux heures.

b. Il a parlé _____ 45 minutes hier.

c. Il a fait du soleil ____ toute la journée d'hier.

d. Il pleut ____ ce matin.

e. Quand nous étions en vacances, il a fait du vent ____ trois jours.

f. Samedi, les clientes du supermarché ont manifesté ____ tout l'après-midi.

g. Elles font la grève de la faim ____ deux jours.

h. Après l'explosion, le garage a brûlé ____ plusieurs heures.

i. La police cherche la cause de l'accident ____ quelques jours.

Vous préférez les vêtements classiques ou les vêtements à la dernière mode?

QUINZAINE DE L'IMPERMEABLE

style-30 ans-classique

4. Conditional vs. future

This section will help you understand the differences between the conditional and the future with *si*-clauses.

1. Below are two similar sentences. One contains a verb in the future and the other a verb in the conditional.

> Si tu allais à Chartres, tu verrais la cathédrale.
> Si tu vas à Chartres, tu verras la cathédrale.

a. Give English equivalents.

> If you went to Chartres, you would see the cathedral.
> If you go to Chartres, you will see the cathedral.

b. When the *si*-clause is in the present, what is the tense of the other verb? |

future (just as in English)

c. When the *si*-clause is in the past, what is the tense of the other verb? |

conditional (just as in English)

> **Si + present → future**
> **Si j'ai** assez d'argent, **je voyagerai** cet été.
>
> **Si + imparfait → conditional**
> **Si j'avais** assez d'argent, **je voyagerais** cet été.

2. Choose the verb form, either conditional or future, that is right for each sentence in this conversation about a trip to France. Write the English equivalents.

    a. —Si vous allez en France, qu'est-ce que vous (feriez, ferez), Albert et toi? |

        ferez (If you go to France, what will you do, you and Albert?)

    b. —Nous (visiterions, visiterons) la Bretagne et la Normandie si nous allons en France. |

        visiterons (We will visit Brittany and Normandy if we go to France.)

    c. —Moi, si j'étais en France, j'(irais, irai) en Provence. |

        irais (If I was (were) in France, I would go to Provence.)

    d. —Oui, nous (voyagerions, voyagerons) aussi dans tout le Midi si nous avions plus de temps. |

        voyagerions (Yes, we would also travel throughout the Midi if we had more time.)

    e. —Si tu prends des photos tu me les (montrerais, montreras), n'est-ce pas? |

        montreras (If you take pictures you will show them to me, won't you?)

3. A group of friends who live in Toulouse are discussing what they would do if they lived in Paris. Write the appropriate conditional forms of the verbs in parentheses, with subject pronouns.

    a. Si Paul et Dominique allaient habiter à Paris, ils (chercher) un appartement au Quartier latin. | ils chercheraient

    b. Si vous habitiez à Paris, vous (avoir) besoin de beaucoup d'argent, n'est-ce pas? | vous auriez

    c. Si Alain habitait à Paris, il (sortir) souvent. | il sortirait

    d. Si j'habitais à Paris, je (vendre) ma voiture et je (prendre) toujours le métro. | je vendrais, je prendrais

    e. Si nous habitions à Paris, nous (aller) au théâtre ou à l'opéra tous les samedis. | nous irions

4. Several French students hope to spend the summer in the United States. They are discussing some of the things they will do if their plans work out. Write the appropriate forms of the future, with subject pronouns.

    a. Si je vais aux États-Unis, je (parler) anglais tout le temps. | je parlerai

    b. Si tu vas aux États-Unis, est-ce que tu (écrire) souvent à ta famille? | tu écriras

    c. Si Philippe va aux États-Unis, il nous (dire) si la télévision américaine est intéressante. | il dira

    d. Si vous allez aux États-Unis, vous (visiter) certainement Washington. | vous visiterez

    e. Si on va aux États-Unis, on (pouvoir) aller voir un match de baseball. | on pourra

    f. Si Anne et Monique vont aux États-Unis, elles (aller) voir la Maison blanche. | elles iront

5. Writing activity

1. After you leave the campus or class today, notice what you see and hear for the next hour. Prepare a brief *compte-rendu* (account) in the style of Jean-Paul Collet's reports. Even if what you saw was uneventful, dress up your report of it with Collet's vigorous adjectives and verbs *(imprudent, disperser,* etc.).
2. Write a weather report for a day six months from now.

Vocabulaire

Noms

la cathédrale *cathedral*
le dictateur *dictator*
la dictature *dictatorship*
les épinards *m.* *spinach*
la police *police*
le thermomètre *thermometer*

Les animaux

l'âne *m.* *donkey*
le canard *duck*
le cheval *horse*
la chèvre *goat*
le coq *rooster*
le coucou *cuckoo*
le hibou *owl*
le mouton *sheep*
la poule *hen*

Verbes

brûler *to burn*
terroriser *terrorize*

Autres mots et expressions

au-dessous *below*
pendant *during, for*

Est-ce que ce restaurant est ouvert toute la semaine?

Phase 10

Chez soi

Qu'est-ce que vous allez apprendre?

This Phase will acquaint you with vocabulary and expressions useful for purchasing or renting a house or apartment, and for deciphering newspaper ads for living accommodations or furniture. At the end of the Phase you will write about your ideal living situation.

Communication

You will:

   Express strong opinions about quality and value, using superlatives.

   Expand your knowledge and active use of adjectives.

   Learn noun formation with the help of word families and cognates in English.

   Learn to understand French telephone numbers.

You will improve and refine your ability to use adjectives, the pronouns *y* and *en* and indirect object pronouns, the imperative with pronouns, vocabulary for parts of the body, the conditional and the *passé composé*.

Culture

French preferences and habits regarding living accommodations, French television, contrasts between small neighborhood shops and large shopping centers, and the telephone in France.

PRÉPARATION 66

Un conte°: «Boucles d'Or°»

story / Goldilocks

Monsieur et Madame Collinet sont une famille parisienne typique.
Ils ont toujours habité à Paris. Les voici aujourd'hui chez eux, dans
leur appartement à Montparnasse.

    Toute la famille est réunie° dans la salle à manger, sauf° la petite
Caroline qui a cinq ans. C'est l'heure de son programme favori,
«l'Heure des petits». Elle est dans la salle de séjour°, devant la télévision, et elle écoute la belle histoire que raconte le narrateur°. Le
conte d'aujourd'hui s'appelle «Boucles d'Or.» Si vous avez de jeunes
enfants chez vous, mesdames et messieurs, ils écoutent peut-être eux
aussi ce joli conte...

gathered / except for

living room
which the narrator tells

Il était une fois° une jolie petite fille avec des cheveux blonds. Son
nom était Boucles d'Or. Un jour, elle faisait une promenade dans la
forêt quand elle a vu une jolie petite maison blanche. C'était la mai-

Once upon a time there
  was

son de la famille Ours°. Boucles d'Or a pensé: «Tiens!° Qui habite ici?» Elle a frappé° à la porte: «Toc, toc, toc! Il y a quelqu'un?°» Pas de réponse. Boucles d'Or a ouvert la porte... Il n'y avait personne dans la maison. Dans la salle, elle a vu une table et trois chaises. Sur la table, il y avait trois bols° de tailles° différentes: un grand bol, un deuxième bol moins grand, et un troisième° bol très petit. Dans les bols, il y avait de la bouillie°. Boucles d'Or avait faim. Elle a goûté° la bouillie du premier° bol, puis la bouillie du deuxième bol, et elle a mangé toute la bouillie qui était dans le petit bol.

Ensuite° elle a vu une chambre à coucher°. Dans cette chambre, il y avait trois lits°: un très grand lit, un deuxième lit moins grand, et un troisième lit assez petit. Boucles d'Or était fatiguée et elle avait sommeil°. Elle a décidé de dormir un peu. Elle a essayé le premier lit: il était trop grand. Elle a essayé le deuxième lit: il était trop grand aussi. Elle a essayé le troisième lit: il était parfait pour elle. Elle a fermé les yeux°. Quelques minutes plus tard, elle dormait.

Dans l'après-midi, la famille Ours est revenue à la maison. Le papa Ours a regardé son bol et a dit: «Ah, ah! quelqu'un a goûté ma bouillie.» La maman Ours a regardé son bol et a dit: «Ah, ah! quelqu'un a goûté ma bouillie.» Et le petit Ours a regardé son bol et a dit: «Ah, ah! quelqu'un a mangé toute ma bouillie! Quelle chance°! Je déteste la bouillie!»

Ensuite la famille Ours est entrée dans la chambre à coucher. Le papa Ours a dit: «Ah, ah! quelqu'un a dormi dans mon lit!» La maman Ours a dit: «Ah, Ah! quelqu'un a dormi dans mon lit!» Et le petit Ours a regardé son lit et a dit: «Ah, ah! quelqu'un dort dans mon lit! Papa, maman, regardez la jolie petite fille avec les cheveux blonds!»

Boucles d'Or a ouvert les yeux et elle a vu les trois Ours qui la regardaient. Elle a dit: «Oh, bonjour, mes amis. Je suis contente de vous voir. Je m'appelle Boucles d'Or. Excusez-moi, j'avais faim et j'avais sommeil. Alors j'ai mangé votre bouillie qui était très bonne, et j'ai dormi.»

Et le papa Ours a répondu: «Nous sommes très contents de votre visite, Mlle Boucles d'Or.» Et la maman Ours a dit: «Oui, nous sommes très contents de votre visite, Mlle Boucles d'Or.» Et le petit Ours a dit: «Oui, nous sommes très contents de ta visite. Reste° avec nous, toujours! Si tu veux, tu peux manger toute ma bouillie...»

Mais Boucles d'Or a répondu qu'elle ne pouvait pas rester, parce qu'elle avait des parents, des frères et des sœurs qui l'aimaient beaucoup. Alors, ils ont décidé d'accompagner Boucles d'Or chez elle pour dire bonjour à toute la famille. Le papa Ours a mis son beau pardessus et son chapeau, la maman Ours a mis son beau chapeau et ses gants, et le petit Ours a mis un pantalon et une chemise propres°.

Bear / Well
knocked / Is somebody there?

bowls / sizes
third
porridge / tasted
first

next/bedroom
beds

was sleepy

closed her eyes

luck

remain

clean

Mme Ours a demandé: «On y va à pied°?» Et M. Ours a répondu: on foot
«Jamais de la vie! Nous allons prendre la nouvelle voiture.»
   Et tout le monde était très content.

Échange d'idées

1. With a few classmates, act out the story. Change some of the details if you like. Substitute different food, have Boucles d'Or make use of different pieces of furniture, have the characters express other attitudes: amusement, fear, etc.
2. Quel conte avez-vous beaucoup aimé quand vous étiez petit(e)? Donnez quelques détails sur les personnages et sur l'intrigue (*plot*).

1. Word set: parts of a house

In this phase, you will read and hear about a French family, the Collinets. Their best friends live in a suburb in a house with two floors and a basement. Identify the rooms in the diagrams on p. 475.

le rez-de-chaussée *ground floor*	les W.C. *toilet*	l'escalier *staircase*
le 1er étage *2nd floor*	la chambre à coucher *bedroom*	l'entrée *entrance hall*
le 2ème étage *3rd floor*	la salle de séjour *living room*	le sous-sol *basement*
le grenier *attic*	la salle à manger *dining room*	la terrasse *terrace*
la cuisine *kitchen*	le bureau *den*	le balcon *balcony*
la salle de bains *bath*	le hall *hallway*	le placard *closet*

À Propos!

Où est-ce que vous passez le plus de temps chez vous? Dans la salle de séjour, dans votre chambre, dans la cuisine?

2. French telephone numbers

1. Mr. Roberts has both French- and English-speaking friends. Compare what he says in the two languages when he gives his telephone number: 723-4165.

Mon numéro de téléphone est le sept cent vingt-trois, quarante et un, soixante-cinq.
My phone number is seven-two-three, four-one-six-five.

  a. In French, Mr. Roberts groups the digits. How does he say the numbers? (Write the groups.) |
       He says three numbers: 723, 41, and 65.

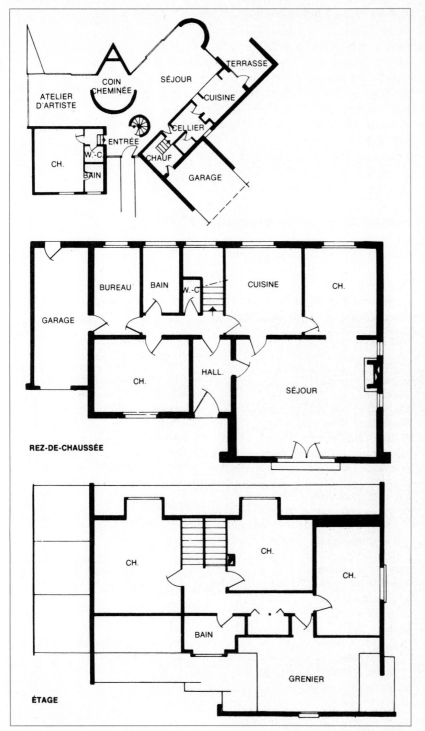

Un bel appartement

Une maison spacieuse

Dans la figure :

- Un bel appartement : ATELIER D'ARTISTE, COIN CHEMINÉE, SÉJOUR, TERRASSE, CUISINE, CELLIER, ENTRÉE, W.-C., CHAUF, GARAGE, CH., BAIN
- Une maison spacieuse
  - REZ-DE-CHAUSSÉE : GARAGE, BUREAU, BAIN, W.-C., CUISINE, CH., CH., HALL, SÉJOUR
  - ÉTAGE : CH., CH., CH., BAIN, GRENIER

b. In Paris and its suburbs, telephone numbers have seven digits and are given in three parts: the number formed by the first three digits, and two numbers of two digits each: 342.01.06. The groups of digits are separated by periods. Write Mr. Roberts' telephone number as a French person would. |

    723.41.65

2. How would these numbers appear in a Paris phone book?
   a. neuf cent quarante et un, vingt-deux, quatre-vingt-treize |

      941.22.93

   b. deux cent soixante seize, douze, zéro-quatre |

      276.12.04

3. Say the following telephone numbers aloud in French.
   a. 438.65.21 |

      quatre cent trente-huit, soixante-cinq, vingt-et-un

   b. 729.26.09 |

      sept cent vingt-neuf, vingt-six, zéro-neuf

À Propos!

Write and say your own or someone else's telephone number as it would appear in the Paris directory.

Vocabulaire

Noms

le balcon   *balcony*
le bol   *bowl*
la bouillie   *porridge*
le bureau   *office; den*
la cave   *cellar*
la chambre à coucher   *bedroom*
la chance   *luck*
le conte   *story*
la cuisine   *kitchen*
l'étage *m.*; premier ~ ; deuxième ~
    floor; first floor (American second floor); second floor (American third floor)
l'entrée *f.*   *entrance*
l'escalier *m.*   *staircase, stairs*
le garage   *garage*
le grenier   *attic*
le hall   *hall*
la maman   *mother*
Montparnasse   *(a section of Paris on the left bank of the Seine)*
le narrateur   *narrator*
le papa   *father*
le pardessus   *man's overcoat*
le placard   *cabinet, closet*

le rez-de-chaussée   *ground floor*
la salle à manger   *dining room*
la salle de bain   *bathroom*
la salle de séjour   *living room*
la série   *series*
le sous-sol   *basement*
la taille   *size*
la terrasse   *terrace*
les w.c.   *toilet*

Adjectifs

propre   *clean*

Verbes

accompagner   *to accompany, to go with*
frapper   *to knock*
goûter   *to taste*
réunir   *to gather*

Autres mots et expressions

le plus de   *most of*
sauf   *except for*
chez soi   *at home*

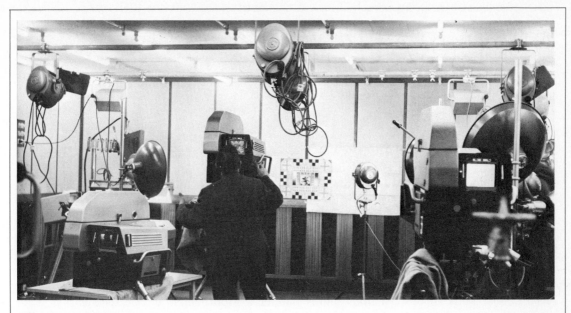

Note Culturelle
La télévision

Il y a beaucoup de différences entre la télévision française et la télévision américaine. En France, par exemple, il y a seulement trois chaînes: TF 1 (Télévision Française 1), A 2 (Antenne 2) et FR 3 (France Régions 3). Il y a aussi beaucoup moins de programmes qu'aux États-Unis. Enfin, il y a une présentatrice[1] qui est une sorte d'hôtesse et qui, après les informations de 20 heures, annonce tous les programmes du soir. Elle réapparaît plus tard entre certaines émissions.

La télévision française ne fonctionne pas le matin sauf[2] le dimanche où il y a des émissions[3] religieuses ou philosophiques. À midi, il y a les informations et quelques[4] jeux ou interviews. L'après-midi il y a quelquefois un programme pour les femmes, et le mercredi il y a des programmes pour les enfants. (Le mercredi est jour de congé pour les écoliers.)

La majorité des programmes sont entre 6 heures et 11 heures du soir. Leur durée[5] n'est pas toujours exactement d'une heure ou d'une demi-heure. Comme aux États-Unis, il y a une grande variété de programmes: films, jeux, feuilletons[6], sports, et informations. Si on passe le samedi soir devant le petit écran[7], on a très souvent le choix entre un programme de variétés (danses et chansons populaires), un feuilleton policier[8] ou un film.

Il y a beaucoup de programmes américains doublés[9] en français, en particulier les séries, ou histoires qui continuent en plusieurs épisodes. Ces programmes passent sur les ondes[10] françaises quelques années après leur succès aux États-Unis.

1 announcer 2 except 3 telecasts 4 a few 5 duration 6 serials 7 TV screen 8 detective 9 dubbed 10 airways

Studio au centre universitaire de Vincennes.

PRÉPARATION 67

À la recherche d'un logement

Pendant que Caroline regarde la télévision les autres membres de la famille Collinet attendent l'heure du dîner.

Marc Maman, il est sept heures et demie. On mange bientôt?

Mme Collinet Pas tout de suite°. Le dîner n'est pas tout à fait° prêt.   right away / quite

M. Collinet Maman a oublié l'heure. Elle lisait le journal!

Mme Collinet Oui, le journal de Montpellier. Je lisais les annonces°.   classified ads

Laurence Oh, les annonces! Encore!

Mme Collinet Mais voyons°, si nous allons habiter à Montpellier, il   Oh, come on
faut absolument trouver un logement° là-bas°.   a place to live / over there

Laurence Oh, on peut toujours installer° une tente sur la plage°!   set up / beach

Marc Oui, bonne idée!

Mme Collinet Vous deux, taisez-vous et écoutez.   keep quiet

> ÉBLOUISSANT—Villa bord de mer, ultra-moderne, gd
> terrain, gd séjour double, 4 ch., terrasse 1er étage,
> grande cheminée extérieure. Vue sur mer exceptionnelle.
> S'adresser agence Beauséjour 41.45.67°.   outside Paris, phone numbers are 6 digits.

M. Collinet Mais voyons, Colette, c'est sûrement trop grand et trop
cher pour nous.

Mme Collinet Oui, je sais. Tu as raison... Tiens, et ça?°   how about that?

> Banlieue résidentielle 6 km OUEST—Très beau pavillon
> récent, ensoleillé, ss sol, gar. 2 voit., gde entrée, séjour,
> salon, balcon, cuisine, 3 ch., s.bs., w.c., pelouse, jardin,
> allée privée. Téléphoner au 63.76.54.

Marc Mais pourquoi habiter dans une maison en banlieue°, loin° de   suburbs / far
tout?

Laurence Oui, c'est vrai, un appartement, c'est mieux. C'est près du
centre°, des cinémas, des magasins. Laisse-moi regarder le jour-   downtown
nal... Là... j'ai trouvé!

> Immeuble impeccable, centre ville, 8e étage plein sud,
> vue sur parc, double living avec gd balcon plus 3 ch.,
> cuisine équipée, bains, douche, asc. desc. Visite de 13 h
> à 17 h., 38, avenue de la République.

Mme Collinet Mais ça aussi, c'est trop cher pour nous!

Marc Non, non, non! Écoutez! J'ai trouvé le logement idéal.

> Résidence St. Clément, près CES, autobus, gd centre commercial, appart. tt confort, gd. séjour, 3 ch., s.bs. et cab. toil., gde entrée, cuisine avec lave-vaisselle, téléphone, 3e étage sans asc. Téléphoner au propriétaire pour visiter. 41.18.61

M. Collinet Mais pourquoi toutes ces discussions maintenant? Il vaut mieux attendre, voyons! On va bientôt visiter Montpellier. On peut prendre une décision° après.   make up one's mind

Échange d'idées

Work with a partner. One of you take the role of someone calling to rent one of the homes described in *À la recherche d'un logement*. The other take the role of the rental agent.

Choose your attitudes:

a. The renter *(locataire)* really wants the place but can't afford it. The agent doesn't want to rent it to you, and tries to dissuade you.

b. The renter is not very interested. The agent is trying to persuade you to take it.

1. Direct object pronouns with negative imperatives

1. In affirmative commands, direct object pronouns are placed right *after* the verb. A hyphen connects the verb and the object pronoun.

    Tu dois me regarder. Regarde-moi!

    The pronoun *me* becomes _____ in the affirmative imperative. |

    moi (and *te* changes to *toi*)

2. There are times when you want to tell someone *not* to do something.

    a. Give the English equivalent of *Ne réveille pas ta mère.* |

    Don't wake up your mother.

    b. If you replace *ta mère* with a pronoun, the sentence becomes *Ne la réveille pas.* Where is the direct object pronoun? |

    right before the verb (as in all other tenses)

    In the negative imperative, the direct object pronoun is placed right before the verb. Object pronouns follow the verb only in *affirmative* use of the imperative.

3. Write negative commands based on these statements.

    Modèle: Nous ne devons pas oublier la caméra. |

    Ne l'oublions pas.

a. Vous ne devez pas lire ces romans. |
b. Tu ne dois pas acheter cette revue. |
c. Tu ne dois pas me regarder. |

a. Ne les lisez pas.
b. Ne l'achète pas.
c. Ne me regarde pas.

2. Nouns ending in *-ment*

You have seen that French adverbs are formed by adding the suffix *-ment* to an adjective: *rapide → rapidement.* In the core material you have just read, you saw the noun *un logement* (a place to live; lodgings). The suffix *-ment* is added to the verb *loger,* which means to live at or to lodge. Many nouns are formed in this manner, and they are all masculine. A few of them are listed below. Give the infinitive of the verb from which they are derived, and guess the meaning of the noun.

> *Modèle:* le commencement |
> commencer (the beginning)

1. l'avancement |
avancer (advancement)

2. le remplacement |
remplacer (replacement)

3. le déménagement |
déménager (the act of moving from one house to another)

4. le changement |
changer (change)

5. le gouvernement |
gouverner (government)

Vocabulaire

Noms

l'allée privée   *private driveway*
l'annonce   *newspaper ad*
le centre; ~ ville   *center; center of town*
l'ascenseur   *elevator*
le balcon   *balcony*
la banlieue   *suburbs*
le bord de mer   *seaside*
le cabinet de toilette   *half-bath*
la cheminée   *chimney; fireplace*
la cigarette   *cigarette*
la discussion   *discussion*
la douche   *shower*
le lave-vaisselle   *dishwasher*
le logement   *habitation*
le pavillon   *small house (single)*

la pelouse   *lawn*
le/la propriétaire   *owner, landlord/ lady*
la résidence   *dwelling*
la réunion   *reunion*
le sous-sol   *basement*
la tente   *tent*
le terrain   *piece of land*
la villa   *country house*
la vue   *view*

Note Culturelle
L'habitat

Dans les grandes villes les gens habitent généralement des appartements dans des immeubles. Ils peuvent louer[1] ou être propriétaires de leur appartement. Dans les banlieues on trouve beaucoup de pavillons[2] ou de villas avec parfois[3] un petit jardin devant ou derrière la maison. Une villa est d'habitude une maison de plaisance[4] à la campagne. Un pavillon était, à l'origine[5], une petite maison séparée par des jardins d'une maison principale. Aujourd'hui le terme pavillon s'emploie couramment[6] dans le sens de petite villa.

Le rez-de-chaussée est la partie d'un immeuble ou d'une maison qui se trouve au niveau[7] de la rue ou du *sol*. Ceci correspond aux États-Unis au «first floor». Le premier étage est donc le «second floor» américain, et ainsi de suite.

L'entrée des immeubles français n'est pas éclairée[8] en permanence. Il y a seulement un bouton illuminé. C'est la minuterie. Quand on appuie[9] sur la minuterie, l'entrée et l'escalier sont éclairés pendant deux ou trois minutes. Ainsi le locataire[10] a juste le temps de monter l'escalier (ou de prendre l'ascenseur) et d'ouvrir sa porte.

Dans beaucoup d'immeubles anciens il y a un ou une «concierge». La/le concierge (appelé aussi gardienne/gardien d'immeuble) nettoie[11] l'immeuble, distribue le courrier[12] et peut donner des renseignements[13] aux visiteurs. Dans les vieux immeubles, au

dernier[14] étage, il y a souvent des «chambres de bonnes[15]». Ces chambres ne sont plus utilisées comme telles[16] et sont souvent louées à des étudiants. Elles ne coûtent pas cher, mais elles n'ont pas de salle de bains; il y a seulement des toilettes et un petit évier[17] souvent sur le palier.[18]

1 rent 2 single house 3 sometimes 4 pleasure 5 originally 6 is used normally 7 at the ground level 8 lighted 9 presses 10 tenant 11 cleans 12 mail 13 information 14 top 15 maids 16 for that purpose 17 sink 18 landing

Jolie petite cour d'entrée d'un immeuble parisien.

TABLES BASSES

RIONEL 89, Avenue Paul Doumer – 75016 PARIS
(a la Muette)   (1) 527-87-59

Noms se terminant par -ment
l'avancement *m.* *advancement, promotion*
le changement *change*
le commencement *beginning*
le déménagement *moving out*
le gouvernement *government*
le logement *habitation, lodgings*
le remplacement *replacement*

Nombres ordinaux
premier/première (1er/1ère) *first*
deuxième (2e/2ème) *second*
troisième *third*
quatrième *fourth*
cinquième *fifth*
sixième *sixth*
septième *seventh*
huitième *eighth*
neuvième *ninth*
dixième *tenth*
vingt-et-unième *twenty-first*

Adjectifs
éblouissant/e *dazzling*
équipé/e *equipped, furnished*
extérieur/e *outside*
impeccable *impeccable*
privé/e *private*
résidentiel/le *residential*

Verbes
louer *to rent*
prendre une décision *to make a decision*
préoccuper *to preoccupy*

Autres mots et expressions
il vaut mieux *it is better*
taisez-vous! *be quiet!*
ultra- *ultra*

PRÉPARATION 68

La famille Collinet (première partie)

The passage you see below is about the Collinet family, who are preparing to move away from Paris. The narrative explains why they are leaving the capital. Read the entire passage carefully. Remember to read in terms of thoughts, or sentences, not of individual words. The questions that follow the text will help you to check your comprehension and to understand some of the new words and phrases.

Monsieur et Madame Collinet ont toujours adoré Paris, mais maintenant la famille se prépare à un grand changement. M. Collinet a quitté son travail et bientôt la famille va quitter Paris pour aller habiter dans le sud de la France, à Montpellier. Pourquoi ce changement?

M. Collinet n'aimait pas son travail. Il le trouvait monotone et sans avenir. Il travaillait comme comptable dans une importante entreprise alimentaire: un homme parmi des centaines d'hommes... Souvent, il pensait: «Suis-je vraiment un homme, ou simplement une machine?» À 40 ans, métro-boulot-dodo?... Non, il ne pouvait pas continuer ainsi.

Heureusement, il y a quelque temps, un ami lui a proposé de travailler avec lui à Montpellier, dans une grande surface de la chaîne Mammouth. On avait justement besoin d'un chef-comptable, capable de prendre des responsabilités... Et il y avait des possibilités d'avancement rapide. L'offre était tentante.

Échange d'idées

1. Connaissez-vous quelqu'un qui a changé de travail? Était-ce pour avoir plus d'argent ou un travail plus intéressant?
2. Quelles sont pour vous les professions monotones et sans avenir?

1. Reading comprehension

1. Consider each of the following statements. If it is true, write *C'est vrai*. If not, write *C'est faux* and correct the false statement.
   a. Les Collinet quittent Paris parce qu'ils ne l'aiment pas. |
      C'est faux. Les Collinet adorent Paris.
   b. À Paris les Collinet habitent dans un appartement. |
      C'est vrai.
   c. Les Collinet vont bientôt habiter dans le nord de la France. |
      C'est faux. Ils vont bientôt habiter dans le sud de la France.
   d. M. Collinet trouvait que son travail à Paris n'était pas très agréable. |
      C'est vrai.
   e. M. Collinet n'est pas intéressé par l'offre de son ami à Montpellier. |
      C'est faux. M. Collinet est très intéressé par cette offre.

Now, use logic, your knowledge of the context, and the clues supplied to figure out the English equivalent of each sentence below.

2. *Mais maintenant la famille se prépare à un grand changement.*
   How would you say the sentence in English? |
      But now the family is preparing itself (is getting ready) for a big change.

3. *Il le trouvait monotone et sans avenir.*
   Monotone is a cognate. *Sans* is the opposite of *avec*. The noun *avenir* is made up of *à* + *venir*, or *that which is to come*. Can you guess the English equivalent of the sentence? |
      He found it (his job) monotonous and without a future. (*l'avenir* = the future)

4. *Il travaillait comme comptable dans une importante entreprise alimentaire.*

Alimentaire is a cognate you won't have trouble with if you remember the boycott of *les magasins d'alimentation.* In English, what was M. Collinet's job in Paris? |

He was working as an accountant in a large food firm.

5. *... un homme parmi des centaines d'hommes.*

Look for a number within *des centaines. Parmi* is a preposition that is also new, but if you understand *des centaines* and M. Collinet's situation, you can probably guess it. |

... a man among hundreds of men.

6. *À 40 ans, métro-boulot-dodo?...*

The only new word here is *dodo.* This is actually "baby-talk" that comes from *dormir.* You should know *métro,* and you may remember that *boulot* is a word for *le travail.* There's no real equivalent in English for the expression, but what is the general idea? |

At age 40, subway-work-sleep? (Like *nine-to-five grind,* the expression describes an unrewarding job that leaves little time for enjoyment of life.)

7. *Non, il ne pouvait pas continuer ainsi.*

The only new item is *ainsi.* The context alone gives you a good idea of the meaning. Make a logical guess. |

No, he couldn't continue that way (in that manner).

8. *Heureusement, il y a quelque temps, un ami lui a proposé de travailler avec lui...*

a. You know that *quelque chose* means *something.* What do you think *quelque temps* means? |

some time (*Temps* also means *weather,* but that meaning wouldn't fit here.)

b. What is the English equivalent of the French sentence? |

Fortunately, some time ago, a friend proposed that he work with him...

9. *L'offre était tentante.*

Tentante describes M. Collinet's new job offer, and the context suggests the meaning. The word resembles its English equivalent fairly closely. Change the first *-n-* to *-m-*, substitute *-ing* for *-ante,* and you almost have the word. What does the sentence mean? |

The offer was tempting.

2. Practice with the pronoun *en*

1. In this frame, decide when to use *en* and when to use other direct object pronouns. Answer according to the cues.

a. Est-ce que ton frère aime les westerns? (oui) |

Oui, il les aime.

b. Ton frère voit souvent des westerns? (oui) |

Oui, il en voit souvent.

c. Ton cousin Charles met son pantalon marron? (oui) |
     Oui, il le met.

2. Now use *il y en a* in the negative.

   —Est-ce qu'il y a des œufs sur la table?   —Non, _____. |
     il n'y en a pas

3. Answer according to the cues, using *en*. (See key.)
   a. Est-ce qu'il y a de la neige dans les Alpes? (oui)
   b. Est-ce qu'il y a de l'eau dans le désert? (non)
   c. Est-ce qu'il y a des éléphants en Afrique? (oui)

4. Answer by telling how many of each item you see.
   Modèle: Est-ce que tu vois des cerises? |
     Oui, j'en vois trois.

   a. Est-ce que tu vois un chat? |
     Oui, j'en vois un.

   b. Est-ce que tu vois des chiens? |
     Oui, j'en vois cinq.

   c. Est-ce que tu vois des éléphants? |

     Oui, j'en vois deux.

À Propos!

Answer with *en*.
Combien de cours avez-vous aujourd'hui?
Est-ce que vous cherchez du travail?
Combien de filles y a-t-il dans votre classe?
Et combien de garçons?

3. Review: parts of the body and some silly rhymes

Frames 1–6 consist of rhyming couplets, with the last word missing
from each couplet. Each one can be completed with a word from the
list below. If you do this correctly, the couplets will rhyme and they
will match the illustrations.

   Say all of the words from the list and read the verses aloud; it will
help you find the rhyme for your couplets. (In frame 4, the second
and third couplets don't rhyme exactly.)

la bouche	les dents *(f.)*	la main	la tête
le bras	le dos	le nez	le ventre
les cheveux *(m.)*	la figure	l'oreille *(f.)*	
le corps	la jambe	le pied	

1. Eric ne veut pas être médecin,
   Parce qu'il faut se laver les _____. |

   mains

2. Quand Anne mange de la confiture
   On en voit des traces sur sa _____. |

   figure

3. Les lunettes de Madame Musset
   Refusent de rester sur son _____. |

   nez

   Et quand elles glissent *(slip)*, de temps en temps,
   Elle les rattrape entre ses _____. |

   dents

4. (Note: *se casser* + part of the body = *to break a bone; il s'est cassé* is
   a form of the *passé composé*.)
   Jacques n'a pas aimé le Mardi Gras.
   C'est parce qu'il s'est cassé le _____. |

   bras

   Et un jour au mois de juillet
   Le pauvre Jacques s'est cassé le _____. |

   pied

   Mauvaise année! Le 10 septembre
   Notre ami s'est cassé la _____. |

   jambe

   Tout l'hiver notre héros dort
   Pour préserver son pauvre _____. |

   corps

5. «A la plage,» dit Monsieur Lecentre,
   «Les fourmis *(ants)* dansent sur mon _____. |

   ventre

   Quand je vais me baigner dans l'eau,
   Les poissons dansent sur mon _____.» |

   dos

6. Michel proteste quand les mouches *(flies)*
   S'invitent à entrer dans sa _____. |

   bouche

   Et il préfère que les abeilles *(bees)*
   Ne s'installent pas dans ses _____. |

   oreilles

7. Il se déclare très malheureux
   D'avoir des poux *(lice)* dans les _____. |

   cheveux

   Est-il méchant envers ces bêtes *(toward these creatures)*
   qui voudraient habiter sa _____? |

   tête

Note Culturelle
Les grandes surfaces

Les grands supermarchés français sont généralement appelés «grandes surfaces». Contrairement aux supermarchés américains, on y trouve non seulement des rayons[1] d'alimentation (viandes, poissons, fromages, légumes, vins, bières, etc.) mais aussi des rayons d'appareils ménagers[2], de vêtements, de chaussures, de jouets[3], de meubles[4], etc. On y trouve aussi une cafétéria où on peut déjeuner ou dîner.

Comme aux Etats-Unis, le client met ses achats dans un petit chariot et paie à l'une des nombreuses caisses. Là, la caissière lui donne quelques sacs en plastique ou en papier pour y mettre ses achats. Personne ne l'aide[5], il doit faire tout cela tout seul, et ce n'est pas toujours facile.

Parmi les grandes surfaces françaises, MAMMOUTH, CASINO et RECORD sont très connues et très populaires. Elles sont ouvertes toute la journée et tard dans la soirée. Pour beaucoup de jeunes familles françaises, faire les courses dans ces grandes surfaces est devenu la sortie[6] du samedi qui se termine par[7] un repas dans la cafétéria.

1 departments 2 household appliances 3 toys 4 furniture 5 no one helps 6 outing 7 ends with

---

Dans une grande surface: files de clients à la caisse (register).

CLUB
des amis de la revue
MAISON & JARDIN

Qui doit s'occuper de la maison, du jardin? La femme? Le mari?

Vocabulaire

Noms

les Alpes *f.*   *Alps*
l'avancement *m.*   *promotion*
l'avenir *m.*   *future*
la chaîne   *chain (of stores)*
le changement   *change*
le/la chef comptable   *head accountant*
la conclusion   *conclusion*
le désert   *desert*
l'entreprise d'alimentation   *food firm*
la grande surface   *supermarket, shopping mall*
l'offre *f.*   *offer*
la possibilité   *possibility*
la responsabilité   *responsibility*
la terrasse   *terrace*

La lecture

la lecture   *reading*
le magazine   *magazine*
le roman; ~ policier; ~ d'aventure; ~ historique; ~ d'amour; ~ de science fiction   *novel; detective story; adventure story; historical novel; love story; science fiction novel*

Adjectifs

alimentaire   *having to do with food*
monotone   *monotonous, dull*
pratique   *practical*
tentant/e   *tempting*

Verbes

proposer   *to offer, to propose*

Autres mots et expressions

dodo (*from* dormir)   *baby-talk for sleep*
justement   *actually, in fact*
métro-boulot-dodo   *nine-to-five grind (literally: subway, work, sleep)*
parmi   *among*
tout confort   *with all amenities*

PRÉPARATION 69

La famille Collinet (deuxième partie)

Cependant avant de prendre une décision, toute la famille a fait un petit voyage à Montpellier. Monsieur Collinet a trouvé le travail intéressant et tout le monde a trouvé la ville très agréable, les gens très gentils et la région très jolie, avec la mer à quelques kilomètres seulement. Les enfants étaient enchantés: pouvoir aller à la plage pendant toutes les grandes vacances, et même avant... Quelle chance! *À leur retour* à Paris, *la décision était prise:* d'accord pour quitter Paris!

Naturellement, tous les amis des Collinet ont été très surpris d'apprendre cette nouvelle. Les Parisiens pensent généralement que, *en dehors de* Paris, la France n'existe pas! *Selon eux,* Paris est la plus belle, la «seule» ville de France. Aller vivre en province? Quelle horreur!

Les Collinet n'ont pas essayé d'expliquer. Après tout, eux aussi *pensaient de la même manière* il y a quelque temps. Bien sûr, ils vont regretter Paris et leurs amis. Mais, d'autre part, le changement, le départ, c'est aussi la grande aventure. Bientôt ils pourront dire «Au revoir, Paris, salut Montpellier!»

Échange d'idées

Vous et votre camarade de chambre cherchez la ville idéale aux États-Unis ou au Canada où vous pourriez vous établir après la fin de vos études. Quelles seront les qualités de cette ville?

1. Reading comprehension

The narrative you just read continues the description of the Collinets' moving preparations and of their thoughts about the change. Use all of the techniques you know for increasing reading comprehension in order to understand as much of the passage as you can. Then try to answer the questions that follow. (Parts of the text are italicized. These parts are referred to in a later frame.)

1. Consider each of the following statements carefully. If the statement is true, write *C'est vrai.* If it isn't true, write *C'est faux* and correct it.

   a. Les Collinet ont décidé de vivre à Montpellier avant de visiter la région. |

   > C'est faux. Les Collinet ont visité Montpellier avant de prendre leur décision.

   b. Leurs amis ne comprennent pas pourquoi les Collinet veulent déménager *(to move)*. |

   > C'est vrai.

   c. Généralement, les Parisiens n'aiment pas habiter la capitale. |

   > C'est faux. En général, les Parisiens adorent Paris et ils sont très contents d'y habiter.

   d. Les Collinet quittent Paris sans regret. |

   > C'est faux. Les Collinet vont regretter Paris et leurs amis.

2. In each part of this frame you see the beginning of a statement, followed by four possible ways to complete the sentence. Three of the four choices would make the statement true; one of them would make the statement false. Write the *incorrect* one.

   a. Montpellier ...est dans une région très pittoresque.
   ...est loin de la mer.
   ...est moins grand que Paris. |

   > ...est loin de la mer.

   b. les Collinet ...n'ont jamais visité Montpellier.
   ...pensent que Paris n'est pas la seule ville intéressante de France.
   ...aiment aller à la plage. |

   > ...n'ont jamais visité Montpellier.

   c. M. Collinet ...est heureux de changer de travail.
   ...préfère rester à Paris.
   ...n'explique pas sa décision à ses amis. |

   > ...préfère rester à Paris.

3. Read the phrases below and write the equivalent phrase from the narrative.

   Modèle: quand ils sont retournés |

   > à leur retour

   a. c'était décidé   c. (ils) étaient d'accord
   b. à l'exception de   d. leur opinion est que |

   > a. la décision était prise   b. en dehors de   c. (ils) pensaient de la même manière
   > d. selon eux

Frames 4–6 refer to specific structures that occur in the narrative.

4. The French equivalent of *to make a decision* is _____ *une décision.* |

   > prendre

5. This phrase is in the text: *Paris est la plus belle ville de France.*

   a. The construction *le/la/les + plus +* adjective means *the most.*
   Give the English equivalent of *la plus belle ville de France.* |

   > the most beautiful city in France

b. How would you say *the biggest city in France?*

la plus grande ville de France

6. In the narrative, *quel* is used twice to form exclamations. Give the French equivalents for:
   a. What luck! (How lucky!)
   b. How horrible! (What a horror!)

a. Quelle chance!   b. Quelle horreur!

7. This frame will help you with some of the new vocabulary. Match the French words with their English equivalents: *however, news, in spite of, according to, in the same way.*

   a. cependant   b. une nouvelle
   c. selon   d. malgré
                               e. de la même manière

a. cependant—*however*   b. une nouvelle—*news*   c. selon—*according to*

d. malgré—*in spite of*   e. de la même manière—*in the same way*

2. Getting ready for a *dictée*

In class you will have a *dictée* that will focus on the *imparfait*. When you take a *dictée*, you must combine writing skills and listening skills. By now you may have figured out your own best technique for *dictées*, but the following few frames may give you some guidance toward improving your performance.

1. When you take a *dictée*, you first hear the entire passage without writing anything. Rather than worrying about the details of every word this first time, what should you try to do?

Try to understand the context of the passage: who or what is involved, and the basics of what is going on. (This will make it easier for you to figure out words you might not be sure of otherwise.)

2. The second time you hear the *dictée*, you write it. You can use your idea of the context to help you interpret logically what you hear. Learn to anticipate logically and to make good guesses based on the situation. Suppose in each sentence there's one word you don't quite catch—you get just the first sound. Using the context, supply the missing word.
   a. Nous jou _____ au football quand Serge est venu.

jouions (Because the verb describes what was happening when Serge arrived, the verb *jouer* must be in the *imparfait*.)

   b. Quand j'ai vu Roberta hier, elle por _____ une jolie robe verte.

portait

   c. Je regard _____ le journal quand tu as téléphoné.

regardais

3. Sometimes you may hear a word pretty well, but you aren't sure which of the similar sounding words to write. For example:

> Quand le professeur est arrivé, Alain (*lycée, lisait*).

a. Which word—*lycée* or *lisait*—is correct? |

> lisait

b. How do you know to write *lisait* and not *lycée*? |

> Following the subject *Alain*, you expect a verb. *Lisait* is a verb, and it fits. *Lycée* is a noun, and it wouldn't make any sense there.

Before writing a word, ask yourself: Does this word fit in this position in this sentence?

4. Choose the word that fits in each of the following sentences.
   a. Elles sont _____ ensemble dans le jardin. (allées, allaient)
   b. Nous habitions à la campagne pendant l' (été, était). |

> a. allées   b. été

5. Suppose you aren't sure which verb form was used:

> Quand je vous ai vu à Paris, vous (*parlez, parliez*) français.

6. Which verb form is correct? How can you tell, even if you don't hear the difference in sound? |

> The correct form is *parliez* (the *imparfait*). The *passé composé* in the first part of the sentence tells you that the action took place in the past. So the *imparfait,* a past tense, is appropriate. The present wouldn't fit the time of the action.

Be sure that the verb forms reflect the proper time of the action. The time of the action is often indicated by other verbs or by time words (*hier, l'année dernière, à 5 heures*). Always be sure the verb form matches its subject.

7. Complete the verbs below with *imparfait* or present-tense endings, according to the context. Write the complete verb.
   a. Quand je suis avec Pierre, nous parl_____ français. | a. parlons
   b. Quand je vous ai vu l'année dernière, vous travaill_____ dans un supermarché. | b. travailliez
   c. Nous ferm_____ juste le magasin quand il est arrivé. | c. fermions
   d. Quand nous quittons la maison, nous ferm_____ toujours les d. fermons
      portes et les fenêtres. |

8. In the *imparfait*, the *je-, tu-, il-,* and *ils-* forms sound the same. Below are four forms of the *imparfait* of *faire*. They sound exactly alike. Choose the correct forms to complete sentences a–d.

> *faisaient   faisais   faisait   faisais*

   a. Hier à midi, tu _____ une promenade. | a. faisais
   b. Robert _____ ses devoirs quand le téléphone a sonné. | b. faisait
   c. Mes amis _____ du ski quand je suis arrivée. | c. faisaient
   d. Quand le téléphone a sonné, je _____ la vaisselle. | d. faisais

3. Le superlatif

1. Write the superlative phrase from each pair of statements below.

   a. Le Texas est un grand état, mais l'Alaska est plus grand que le Texas. L'Alaska est l'état le plus grand des États-Unis. |

   l'état le plus grand des États-Unis

   b. Dans le Colorado il y a de hautes montagnes, mais les montagnes de l'Alaska sont plus hautes. C'est dans l'Alaska qu'on trouve les montagnes les plus hautes des États-Unis. |

   les montagnes les plus hautes des États-Unis

2. The above sentences show how to form the superlative.

   a. The comparative form of an adjective is *plus* (or *moins*) followed by the adjective. The superlative is formed by adding _____ before the comparative form. |

   le, la, or les (a definite article)

   b. What other part of a superlative (besides the adjective itself) agrees with the noun? |

   the definite article

   c. A superlative describes a noun as it compares to others in a similar area, group, time period, etc. For example: *Alaska is the biggest state* (compared to others) *in the United States* (the group of states being compared). In French, the area or the group you are talking about is introduced by the word _____. |

   de (Remember that *de* combines with *le* and *les* to form *du* and *des*.)

   d. In the examples in frame 1, are the superlatives placed before or after the nouns they describe? |

   after (Superlative adjective phrases are usually placed after the noun.)

3. All the superlative statements above indicate *the most* of something. Read this example to see how to say *the least*.

   La population du Nevada n'est pas grande, mais la population de l'Alaska est moins grande.
   L'Alaska a la population la moins grande des États-Unis.

   a. Write the superlative phrase. |

   la population la moins grande

   b. In this superlative statement the word _____ is used instead of *plus*. |

   moins

Formation of the Superlative

Noun + definite article + **plus/moins** + **de**-phrases
La montagne **la plus haute du monde**
Les magasins **les moins chers de la ville**

4. Use the cues below to make superlative statements about each place. Use *plus* or *moins* according to your knowledge of geography. Remember to make the adjective agree.

Modèle: L'Alaska/l'état/grand/les États-Unis |

L'Alaska est l'état le plus grand des États-Unis.

a. Tokyo/la ville/grande/le Japon |

Tokyo est la ville la plus grande du Japon.

b. les montagnes de l'Himalaya/haut/le monde |

Les montagnes de l'Himalaya sont les montagnes les plus hautes du monde.

c. les états du nord-ouest/aride/les États-Unis |

Les états du nord-ouest sont les états les moins arides des États-Unis.

d. le Rhode Island/l'état/petit/les États-Unis |

Le Rhode Island est l'état le plus petit des États-Unis.

e. l'Amazone/le fleuve/long/l'Amérique du Sud |

L'Amazone est le fleuve le plus long de l'Amérique du Sud.

5. Give the French equivalents. (See key.)
   a. Philippe is the tallest boy in the class.
   b. Jeanne is the most intelligent girl in the family.
   c. Dogs are the nicest animals in the world.

À Propos!

Quand vous votez, choisissez-vous le candidat le plus jeune ou le plus âgé? le plus sympathique ou le plus intelligent? Discutez avec un/une camarade et indiquez les qualités les plus importantes.

Vocabulaire

Noms
l'abeille *f.* *bee*
la bête *animal; creature*
la capitale *capital*
la fourmi *ant*
la nouvelle *news*
le pou/les poux *lice*
la province *province*
le retour *return*

Les parties du corps
la bouche *mouth*
le bras *arm*
les cheveux *m.* *hair*
le corps *body*
les dents *f.* *teeth*
le dos *back*
la figure *face*
la jambe *leg*
la main *hand*
le nez *nose*
l'oreille *f.* *ear*

le pied *foot*
la tête *head*
le ventre *stomach*

Adjectifs
aride *arid, dry*
enchanté/e *delighted*
honnête *honest*
pittoresque *picturesque*
ravissant/e *lovely, ravishing*

Autres mots et expressions
cependant *however*
d'une part...d'autre part *on the one hand...on the other hand*
des centaines de *hundreds of*
en dehors de *outside of*
envers *toward*
malgré *in spite of*
quelle chance! *what luck!*
quelle horreur! *how horrible!*
selon *according to*

Note Culturelle

Le métro

Dans Paris il est facile de ne pas utiliser de voiture, car[1] les autobus et le métro sont très pratiques. Des lignes[2] vont dans toutes les directions et il y a de nombreuses stations où plusieurs lignes se rencontrent. Ainsi[3] on peut changer de lignes facilement. Presque toutes les lignes de métro sont maintenant sur pneumatiques[4]. C'est plus confortable et moins bruyant[5] pour les voyageurs.

Beaucoup de lignes vont jusque dans[6] la banlieue. Une ligne récente est très populaire. C'est le R.E.R. (Réseau express régional) qui roule à 100 km (62 miles) à l'heure. Il traverse Paris en vingt minutes et s'arrête seulement à quatre stations. L'une d'elles[7] est la station «Châtelet-les Halles» au centre de Paris. C'est probablement la plus grande station de métro du monde. Là les voyageurs peuvent prendre des métros pour toutes les directions.

La ligne du R.E.R. va en dehors de[8] Paris aussi. Cela permet aux gens qui habitent la banlieue d'aller travailler à Paris très rapidement.

Tous les métros (sauf la ligne du R.E.R.) ont des wagons de première classe et des wagons de seconde classe. Les wagons de première classe sont plus confortables, mais ils sont plus chers.

Pour payer le métro, le voyageur achète des tickets individuels. Il peut aussi acheter un carnet[9] de dix tickets, ce qui revient moins cher[10]. Autrefois, les tickets étaient poinçonnés[11] par des hommes et des femmes (des poinçonneurs). Maintenant, tout est automatique. Il y a une bande magnétique sur les tickets. Avant de passer

dans le tourniquet[12] les voyageurs mettent leur ticket dans une machine électronique.

Depuis quelques années, les Parisiens peuvent acheter une carte orange mensuelle[13] qui leur permet de voyager dans les autobus et les métros autant[14] qu'ils le veulent. C'est très pratique et ce n'est pas cher si on utilise souvent les transports publics.

Des efforts constants sont faits pour rendre l'atmosphère du métro agréable. Dans certaines stations, comme celle du Louvre par exemple, les voyageurs peuvent admirer des reproductions de tableaux et de statues. Il y a aussi dans beaucoup de stations des petits magasins de vêtements, d'alimentation, de journaux, de fleurs, etc.

1 because 2 subway lines 3 thus 4 rubber tires 5 noisy
6 into 7 one of them 8 outside of 9 booklet 10 costs less
11 punched 12 turnstile 13 monthly 14 as much as

Le métro de Paris est efficace (efficient) et rapide.

PRÉPARATION 70

Question de meubles

Nous retrouvons° les Collinet quelque temps avant leur départ pour Montpellier. Ils préparent leur déménagement.° — we meet again / move

Laurence Mais maman, si tu ne veux pas emporter° notre vieille salle à manger et ta chambre à Montpellier, qu'est-ce que nous allons en° faire? — take along / with them

Mme Collinet Nous allons les vendre.

Marc Mais nous ne sommes pas marchands° de meubles! Comment vas-tu faire? — dealers

Mme Collinet Les petites annonces servent° aussi à vendre beaucoup de choses. Écoute, par exemple: — are used

> Cause départ, vends mobilier ancien, 50% valeur: salle à manger acajou, table ronde, six chaises, 6000 F, lit Louis XV complet et doubles rideaux, deux fauteuils Louis XVI 8000 F, secrétaire Empire. Tél. 924.36.41

Marc Oh, dis donc!° Ça ne ressemble° pas du tout à nos vieux meubles! — Hey! / look like

Mme Collinet Tu sais, toutes les annonces ne sont pas pour des articles de grande valeur°. Tiens, écoute: — value

> Particulier vend belle salle à manger rustique, paire chaises rustiques, fauteuil, chambre à coucher, lit deux places. Prix raisonnable. Tél. 725.06.03

Laurence Ah ça, ça ressemble tout à fait à nos meubles! Mets vite l'annonce, maman.

Marc Eh, attendez... Nous pouvons peut-être vendre encore d'autres choses, comme dans cette annonce. Écoutez:

> Cause départ, vends aspirateur, réfrigérateur, machine à laver, matelas état neuf, rideaux tergal blanc, canapé-lit convertible une place. Éléments de cuisine de toutes sortes, tables et chaises. Faire offre. Tél. 482.79.37

Mme Collinet Marc, n'exagère pas! Tous nos appareils ménagers° sont encore en excellent état° et les placards° de la cuisine restent dans l'appartement. — appliances / condition / cabinets

1. *Petites annonces:* Avec un camarade, écrivez une annonce pour l'auto que vous voulez vendre.
2. *Vendeur et acheteur:* Choisissez une chose que vous possédez et essayez de la vendre à votre camarade qui refuse.

1. Not-so-irregular adjectives

The more adjectives you know, the more precisely you can communicate. A lot of French adjectives are cognates that you can recognize easily, but in order for an adjective to be part of your active vocabulary, you must be able to use all of its forms.

1. The written forms of adjectives usually follow a simple pattern.
   a. The feminine singular is formed by adding _____ to the masculine singular. |

     e (except when the masculine singular already ends in -*e*)

   b. The plural is formed by adding _____ to the singular. |

     s (except when the singular ends in -*s* or -*x*)

Adjectives that don't fit this pattern fall into two categories: those that are truly irregular, and those whose forms follow some other pattern that is different but predictable.

Complete the noun phrases that follow by supplying the other forms of *beau* or *vieux*.

2. le beau garçon
   a. la _____ fille   c. le _____ homme
   b. les _____ livres   d. les _____ voitures |

     a. belle   b. beaux   c. bel   d. belles

3. la vieille maison
   a. le _____ vélo   c. les _____ femmes
   b. le _____ arbre   d. les _____ vêtements |

     a. vieux   b. vieil   c. vieilles   d. vieux

The remaining frames illustrate the patterns of other categories of adjectives. At the beginning of each frame, use the model to figure out the forms of the rest of the adjectives, which all follow the same pattern.

4. un homme heureux, une femme heureuse
   a. un élève studieux, une élève _____
   b. un vent dangereux, une situation _____
   c. une foule furieuse, un professeur _____
   d. Describe the pattern followed by these adjectives. |

     studieuse, dangereuse, furieux: When the masculine singular adjective ends in -*eux*,
     the feminine singular ends in -*euse*.

5. le climat méditerranéen, la côte méditerranéenne
   a. du vin italien, de la glace _____
   b. un meuble ancien, une table _____

c. une famille parisienne, un ami _____

d. Describe the pattern.

italienne, ancienne, parisien: Masculine singular in -en, feminine -enne.

6. un événement sportif, une compétition sportive

 a. un enfant actif, une classe _____

 b. une fille passive, un garçon _____

 c. un lion agressif, une lionne _____

 d. Describe the pattern.

active, passif, agressif: Masculine singular in -if, feminine in -ive.

7. un discours officiel, une réponse officielle

 a. un détail superficiel, une description _____

 b. une machine essentielle, un travail _____

 c. une pièce sensationnelle, un film _____

 d. Describe the pattern.

superficielle, essentiel, sensationnel: Masculine singular in -el, feminine in -elle.

8. un groupe social, des groupes sociaux

 a. un parc national, des parcs _____

 b. des repas normaux, un repas _____

 c. un instrument musical, des instruments _____

 d. Describe the pattern.

nationaux, normal, musicaux: Masculine singular in -al, masculine plural in -aux.

9. Give the appropriate forms of the following adjectives.

 a. Mon oncle est parisien. Ma tante est _____ aussi.

 b. Jean-Marc est très actif. Marianne est _____ aussi.

 c. Thérèse est amoureuse de Paul, mais il n'est pas _____ d'elle.

a. parisienne   b. active   c. amoureux

2. Vocabulary review: *les meubles*

1. Consider the following items of furniture. (Refer to list, p. 503.)

une armoire	une cheminée	une glace
un buffet	une commode	un lit ou un canapé
un bureau	un fauteuil	une table de nuit

Which piece of furniture from the list would you go to for each of the following things?

 a. to find a cup and saucer — a. un buffet

 b. to find a book you were reading in bed last night — b. une table de nuit

 c. to comb your hair and straighten your coat — c. une glace

 d. to hang up a suit — d. une armoire

 e. to write a letter — e. un bureau

 f. to get a pair of socks — f. une commode

 g. to make a fire — g. une cheminée

 h. to sit down — h. un fauteuil

 i. to lie down — i. un lit ou un canapé

3. *Les petites annonces*

Read the following *petites annonces*. Then answer frames 1–3.

Annonce A: Banlieue sud: belle maison bd. de mer, jard., gde. pelouse, gar. 2 voit. 8 pièces tt. conf., cheminée. Centre comm. à 5 km. Visite 18h–20h, wk-end 10h–17h. Tél. 63.12.91 après 19h30.

Annonce B: 47 rue Matisse: 1 gde. pièce, excellent état. Près métro, théâtre, ciné., centre comm. 5e étage sans asc. Visite 16h–23h. Tél. 95.36.24.

1. Which residences are preferable for the following people? Compare your reasoning with that given in parentheses.
   a. Un homme qui a soixante-deux ans et sa femme qui a soixante ans. Ils ont une petite voiture. |

      Annonce A. (These people don't need a lot of room. What they do need is convenience. In this residence they would have a parking space for their car, an elevator, a modern kitchen and bathroom, a telephone, and easy access to shops.)

   b. Une étudiante. |

      Annonce B. (This one sounds like a student's apartment—small, located near theaters and stores, and probably relatively cheap.)

Frames 2–3 are each based on one of the ads. Answer the questions in English. The last part of each frame involves rewriting the ad. Read aloud the "long version" of each *annonce*, and write the words that are abbreviated in the original.

2. These questions refer to *annonce A*.
   a. Where is this house located in relation to the city? |

      It is in a suburb south of the city, by the seashore.

   b. Describe the grounds. |

      There is a large garden and a large lawn.

   c. When can people visit the house? |

      from six o'clock to eight o'clock evenings, and on weekends from ten A.M. to five P.M.

   d. Is it possible to have wood fires in the house? |

      Yes. (There's a fireplace.)

   e. Cette belle maison dans la banlieue _____ est au _____ de la mer. Elle a un _____, une _____ pelouse, et un _____ pour deux _____. Il y a huit pièces avec _____, et une cheminée. C'est à cinq kilomètres d'un centre _____. |

      Sud; bord; jardin; grande; garage; voitures; tout le confort; commercial

3. These questions refer to *annonce B*.
   a. Give an English description of the apartment itself. |

      The apartment consists of one large room in excellent condition.

b. What advantages of the apartment are mentioned? |

c. Is there an elevator? |

no

d. How many flights of stairs must you climb in order to reach the apartment? |

five (cinquième étage = sixth floor)

e. Cet appartement, 47 rue Matisse, avec une pièce en _____ état est près du métro, d'un théâtre, d'un _____, et d'un centre _____. Il est au cinquième étage et il n'y a pas d'_____. |

excellent; cinéma; commercial; ascenseur

4. More on the conditional

1. Imagine that you are a presidential candidate. You are making the following promises:

Si vous votez pour moi,

je combattrai *(fight)* l'inflation;
je réduirai *(reduce)* le chômage *(unemployment)*;
j'augmenterai les salaires;
j'améliorerai *(improve)* les transports publics;
je donnerai des emplois aux femmes;
je fournirai *(provide)* des logements à bon marché *(inexpensive)* à
 tous les travailleurs;
j'augmenterai la pension des vieillards;
je limiterai les dépenses *(spending)* de l'État.

2. You were elected and are now a second-term candidate. Your constituents remind you of your promises. Transpose the above sentences.

   Modèle: Vous avez dit que vous combattriez l'inflation. |

   vous réduiriez le chômage;

   vous augmenteriez les salaires;

   vous amélioreriez les transports publics;

   vous donneriez des emplois aux femmes;

   vous fourniriez des logements à bon marché à tous les travailleurs;

   vous augmenteriez la pension des vieillards;

   vous limiteriez les dépenses de l'État.

À Propos!   Reproach a friend for not having done three things, beginning your sentence with *Tu m'avais dit que....*

Note Culturelle
Le téléphone en France

Depuis plusieurs années, on peut téléphoner directement de Paris aux États-Unis et dans plusieurs pays d'Europe, sans téléphoniste. Autrefois il fallait attendre souvent des années pour obtenir le téléphone. À l'heure actuelle[1], cela est devenu beaucoup plus facile, mais le branchement continue à coûter cher, beaucoup plus cher qu'aux États-Unis.

Si on n'a pas le téléphone, on peut téléphoner dans une cabine téléphonique. Il y en a dans les rues, dans les métros et dans les cafés. D'abord, on met une pièce de monnaie (ou un jeton[2]) dans l'appareil, et ensuite on compose[3] le numéro. Mais quand la personne répond, il faut appuyer[4] sur un bouton. Sinon[5], votre interlocuteur[6] ne peut pas vous entendre.

Il est très facile de trouver un numéro de téléphone en France. Il y a trois sortes d'annuaires[7]. Certains ont la liste alphabétique des noms. D'autres ont des listes par rues. Il y a aussi des listes par professions.

---

1 at the present time 2 token 3 dials 4 press 5 otherwise
6 the person you are calling 7 directories

Cabines téléphoniques sur une place publique.

Vocabulaire

Noms

l'acajou *m.* *mahogany*
l'annuaire *m.* *telephone book*
l'article *m.* *item*
la cabine (téléphonique) *phone booth*
le chômage *unemployment*
le déménagement *moving-out (of a house)*
le départ *departure*
les dépenses *f.* *expenses*
la description *description*
l'état *m.* *condition*
le marchand *dealer, merchant*
le particulier *private party (person)*
les petites annonces *f.* *classified ads*
la question *matter*
le salaire *salary*
le vieillard *old man*

Meubles

les appareils ménagers *m.* *appliances*
l'armoire *f.* *wardrobe, free-standing closet*
l'aspirateur *m.* *vacuum cleaner*
le buffet *buffet, china cupboard*
le canapé *couch*
la cheminée *fireplace*
la commode *chest of drawers*
la cuisinière *stove*
le divan *sofa*
l'évier *m.* *kitchen sink*
le fauteuil *armchair*

le lavabo *bathroom sink*
le lit à deux places *double bed*
la machine à laver *washing machine*
le meuble *piece of furniture*
le rideau *curtain*
le secrétaire *(furniture) secretary*
le sofa *sofa*
la table de nuit *bedside table*
le tapis *rug*

Adjectifs

ancien/ne *old; antique*
dangereux/dangereuse *dangerous*
mécontent/e *dissatisfied, discontented*
méditerranéen/ne *Mediterranean*
rond/e *round*
rustique *rustic, French Provincial*

Autres adjectifs (accord)

agressif/agressive *aggressive*
essentiel/le *essential*
officiel/le *official*
passif/passive *passive*
studieux/studieuse *studious*
superficiel/le *superficial*

Verbes

améliorer *to improve*
avoir mal *to be in pain, be sick*
combattre *to fight*
fournir *to provide*
réduire (rédui-, réduis-, réduit) *to reduce*
ressembler à *to look like*

Autres mots et expressions

quelque part *somewhere*

Préférez-vous les meubles modernes ou les meubles anciens?

La boutique écossaise

DES MEUBLES QUI VOUS VONT BIEN.

PRÉPARATION 71

1. Nouns in *-ation* and *-aine*

Like the suffix *-ment* (see p 480), the suffix *-ation* occurs often in both French and English. In many cases the French word is identical or almost identical to its English equivalent.

1. Think of some English words that end in *-ation,* such as *information* and *hesitation.* Are they formed by adding *-ation* to a noun, a verb, or an adjective? |

> a verb (A noun with the ending *-ation* means the *act of doing* whatever is expressed by the verb.)

2. Many French nouns are formed by adding *-ation* to the stem of an *-er* verb. All nouns in *-ation* are feminine. For example:

> Il veut *préparer* un bon dîner.
> Pour la *préparation* d'un bon dîner, il faut avoir de bons
> ingrédients.

The verbs below form nouns in the same way. Write the related noun with its article.
   a. Tu as *imaginé* cet accident. Tu as une _____ trop active! |
   b. Les Allemands ont *occupé* la France en 1940. Cette _____ a duré quatre ans. |
   c. Yvette *imite* la voix de ses amis. Elle fait une _____ amusante de Philippe. |

   a. une imagination

   b. Cette occupation

   c. une imitation

3. In verbs that end in *-quer,* *-qu-* changes to *-c-:*

> Un professeur doit *communiquer* avec ses élèves.
> La *communication* est essentielle.

Write the appropriate nouns to complete the following.
   a. Ce livre *explique* les principes de la relativité. Malheureusement, je ne comprends pas les _____. |
   b. Très souvent, la direction du vent *indique* le temps qu'il va faire. Faites attention à ces _____. |

   a. les explications

   b. ces indications

4. Verbs that end in *-ier* generally form nouns by adding *-cation* to the infinitive stem. For example:

> Dans ce guide, ce symbole *signifie* qu'il y a un téléphone public.
> Je ne sais pas quelle est la *signification* de cet autre symbole.

Write the appropriate nouns to complete the following sentences:

a. Comment *justifiez*-vous votre absence? Quelle _____ pouvez-vous donner? |

b. Ce roman *glorifie* la Révolution Française. Que pensez-vous de cette _____ de la guerre? |

5. There's also a group of feminine nouns that end in *-aine*.

| une douzaine de livres | une vingtaine d'élèves | une soixantaine de voitures |

Nouns like this express approximate amounts. Which phrase above is related to the English *dozen?* |

une douzaine (In phrases like *une douzaine d'œufs, d'oranges, une douzaine* means *exactly* twelve.)

6. Slight spelling changes occur in some numbers when they form nouns of this kind.

dix jours environ = une dizaine de jours
trente années environ = une trentaine d'années

When *-aine* is added to *dix,* the *-x* changes to _____. |

-z (Remember that when dix is followed by a word beginning with the vowel sound, the same change from /s/ to /z/ occurs in pronunciation.)

7. Give English equivalents for the following, and be sure to make appropriate spelling changes.

a. about forty men |

une quarantaine d'hommes

b. about 100 houses |

une centaine de maisons

c. about fifty women |

une cinquantaine de femmes

d. about fifteen apartments |

une quinzaine d'appartements

e. about ten rooms |

une dizaine de pièces

(The phrase *une quinzaine,* short for *une quinzaine de jours,* means *two weeks.*)

2. The passive voice

1. Write the English meaning of *Les magasins étaient fermés.* |

The stores were closed.

In English, when a form of *to be* is followed by a past participle, it is called the passive voice. For example:

Several people *were injured* in the accident.
Cream and sugar *are served* with coffee.

In French, the structure is the same as the English passive voice: *être* plus the past participle. All verbs that can take direct objects can also be used in the passive voice.

Le propriétaire *ferme* le magasin. *The owner closes the store.*
Le magasin *est fermé* par le propriétaire. *The store is closed by the owner.*

2. Give the English equivalent of the following sentences:

a. La souris est attrapée.| a. The mouse is caught.
b. La souris a été attrapée. | b. The mouse was caught.
c. La souris sera attrapée. | c. The mouse will be caught.
d. La souris serait attrapée. | d. The mouse would be caught.

3. Change each sentence to the passive. Use the present tense of *être* + the past participle of the verb.
    Modèle: Notre équipe gagne le match. |
        Le match est gagné par notre équipe.
a. Le chat attrape la souris. |
        La souris est attrapée par le chat. (Did you remember to make the past participle agree with the subject?)
b. Mes parents regardent régulièrement ce programme. |
        Ce programme est regardé régulièrement par mes parents.

4. Now change these to the passive. Use the *passé composé* of *être* + the past participle of the verb.
a. M. Collinet a annoncé la nouvelle hier. |
        La nouvelle a été annoncée par M. Collinet hier.
b. Les spectateurs ont apprécié le récital de ce pianiste. |
        Le récital de ce pianiste a été apprécié par les spectateurs.

Vocabulaire

Noms

l'agacement *m.*   *annoyance*
une douzaine   *a dozen*
la glace   *mirror*
l'incrédulité *f.*   *disbelief*
le matelas   *mattress*
une soixantaine   *about sixty*
une vingtaine   *about twenty*

Verbes

attraper   *to catch*
valoir   *to be worth*

Note Culturelle

Les petits magasins

En France, même dans les grandes villes, on trouve encore beaucoup de petits magasins. Chaque quartier[1] a son épicerie, sa boulangerie, sa boucherie, et aussi parfois, une quincaillerie[2] et une papèterie[3]. À l'épicerie, on peut acheter des produits laitiers[4], des légumes et des fruits, de la charcuterie[5], des conserves[6], des vins et des eaux minérales. Certaines épiceries vendent aussi du pain.

Dans ces petits magasins on ne fait généralement pas de très nombreux achats[7]. On achète seulement ce qui est nécessaire pour les repas de la journée. Les clients emportent ces achats dans un panier[8] ou dans un filet à provisions[9]. Les prix dans ces petits magasins sont parfois plus élevés[10] que dans les grandes surfaces[11].

1 Each neighborhood 2 hardware store 3 stationery 4 dairy products 5 pork products 6 canned goods 7 very many purchases 8 basket 9 net used for shopping 10 higher 11 very large supermarkets

Dans les grandes boulangeries, on achète non seulement du pain, mais aussi des gâteaux et des friandises (sweets) de toutes sortes.

PRÉPARATION 72

1. Writing practice: *Maison ou appartement?*

You are going to write a paragraph about your ideal living situation. Say whether you prefer an apartment or a house, and why; whether you prefer the city or the country, and why; whether you want a big house, etc . . . Then describe your ideal house or apartment. Below are some words and phrases you can use in your discussion.

Noms	*Prépositions*	*Adjectifs*	*Expressions*
la banlieue	à côté de	agréable	à mon avis...
le centre	au bord de	beau (bel), belle	en général...
une chambre	loin de	cher, chère	j'aime mieux...
l'entretien (m.)	près de	confortable	je crois que...
un étage		grand	je préfère...
un immeuble		petit	je trouve que...
un jardin		préférable	
une pelouse		spacieux, spacieuse	
une pièce			
un quartier			
un terrain			

Think about the question, then practice by completing the following sentences according to your opinions, which you may use in your final draft. Also, take a few minutes to review the vocabulary you have learned in this Phase.

1. En général, une maison est plus/moins ＿＿ qu'un appartement.
2. En général, un appartement est plus/moins ＿＿ qu'une maison.
3. Il est préférable d'habiter dans ＿＿ si on veut être près (de) ＿＿.
4. Il est préférable d'habiter dans ＿＿ si on veut être loin (de) ＿＿.
5. Je trouve qu'une maison est trop ＿＿.
6. À mon avis, un appartement est trop ＿＿.
7. Je préfère ＿＿ parce que ＿＿.

2. When the passive voice is impossible

Many verbs can have direct and indirect objects. For example:

I give a bird to the child.   I give the child a bird.

Because both objects may be used *directly* (without a preposition), both can be used as the subject of a passive form:

> *A bird is given to the child (by me).*
> *The child is given a bird (by me).*

French does not have such flexibility, and the sentence *Je donne un oiseau à l'enfant* has only one passive equivalent: *Un oiseau est donné à l'enfant.* However, an active sentence using *on* as a subject is very frequently used when no agent is mentioned: *On donne un oiseau à l'enfant.*

Write French equivalents of the following sentences, with *on*.

  a. The students are shown a film. |
        On montre un film aux étudiants.
  b. His parents were told the truth. |
        On a dit la vérité à ses parents.
  c. The children will be given presents. |
        On donnera des cadeaux aux enfants.

3. Practice with indirect object pronouns and *y*

1. *Lui, leur* and *y* are used in similar ways. Which one refers to:
   a. a place, a thing, or an idea? | a. y
   b. more than one person? | b. leur
   c. one person? | c. lui
2. Rewrite these sentences, using *lui* or *leur* to replace peoples' names, and *y* to replace things or places mentioned. (See key.)
   a. J'écris souvent à Léonard.
   b. Je vais à Montpellier demain.
   c. Nous parlons à Véronique et à Jérôme.
   d. Il téléphone à ses parents.
   e. Tu penses à tes vacances?
3. In negative statements, *ne* comes before the pronoun, which comes right before the verb. Rewrite these sentences, substituting *lui, leur,* or *y* for the italicized words. (See key.)
   a. Nous n'allons pas *à la bibliothèque.*
   b. Je ne demande pas *à mes amis* de m'aider.
   c. Tu ne donnes pas de bonbons *à cet enfant.*
   d. Albert a téléphoné *à Françoise.*

e. Nous n'avons pas pensé *à ce problème*.

f. Vous n'avez pas parlé *à vos amis?*

4. In affirmative commands, object pronouns come right after the verb. Rewrite the following, using *lui, leur,* or *y*.

a. Téléphone à tes parents.   c. Parle à ce petit garçon.

b. Allez à la poste.

5. The people in this frame live by the motto "variety is the spice of life." After each statement about one day (today or yesterday), say that the opposite is true of the other day. Use the *passé composé* or the present, and *lui, leur* or *y*.

> *Modèle:* Jacques a écrit un poème d'amour à sa petite amie aujourd'hui. |
>> Il ne lui a pas écrit de poème d'amour hier.

a. Jean-Michel joue aux cartes aujourd'hui.

b. Carole n'est pas allée à l'opéra hier.

c. Jean parle au président aujourd'hui.

d. Eric ne nage pas dans la rivière aujourd'hui. |

> a Jean-Michel n'y a pas joué hier.   b. Carole y va aujourd'hui.   c. Jean ne lui a pas parlé hier.   d Eric y a nagé hier.

Vocabulaire

Noms

l'entretien *m.*   *maintenance*

Adjectifs

préférable   *preferable*

spacieux/spacieuse   *spacious*

Adjectifs de couleurs

aubergine   *purple, eggplant color*

bleu roi   *royal blue*

bordeaux   *burgundy (color)*

coquille d'œuf   *eggshell color*

grenat   *garnet-red*

jaune citron   *lemon yellow*

or   *golden*

turquoise   *turquoise*

vert feuille   *leaf green*

vieux rose   *dusty rose*

Verbes

penser à   *to think about*

réfléchir   *to think, to reflect*

Autres mots et expressions

davantage   *more*

Phase 11

Troubadours

Qu'est-ce que vous allez apprendre?

This Phase introduces you to some contemporary French poetry. You will talk about the feelings that a poem gives you, and how metaphors, similes, and alliteration help convey those feelings. At the end of the Phase you will have a chance to use your own imagery as you compose a poem in French.

Communication

You will:
   Learn an important new structure that will allow you to express desires and preferences: the subjunctive.
   Use the expression *s'en aller* (to go away) and many idiomatic flavor words in situations in which native speakers of French would use them.
   Learn substitutes for the passive voice, which is relatively little-used in French.
   Learn to use the relative pronouns *dont* and *lequel* with prepositions.
You will improve your grasp of commands with reflexive verbs or with object pronouns, the passive voice, the *passé composé* and the *imparfait,* the conditional and the future, the relative pronouns *qui, que, où,* and the present participle.

Culture

The French dislike of constraint as embodied in Prévert's poetry, and a poem by Maurice Carême; French singers; the French institution of the sidewalk café; students' vacations; and the French postal service.

PRÉPARATION 73

1. *Le subjonctif: il faut que* + *-er* verbs

In this Phase, you will work intensively with a new verb form, the subjunctive mode. The subjunctive is used frequently in French after verbs and expressions that describe a speaker's attitude toward an action, idea, or fact.

1. Read and compare these two sentences:

> Il faut travailler. Il faut que je travaille.

a. In both sentences the expression that expresses necessity is
_____. |

il faut

b. Which sentence makes the general statement *It is necessary to work?* |

Il faut travailler.

c. Write the sentence that says that a specific person has to work, and write its English equivalent. |

Il faut que je travaille. *(I have to work/It is necessary that I work.)*

2. a. *Il faut travailler.* When *il faut* is used in a general statement, what is the form of the verb that tells what needs to be done? |

the infinitive (*travailler* in this example)

b. *Il faut que je travaille.* When a specific subject needs to do something, *il faut* introduces the subject and its verb. *Il faut* and this subject-verb phrase are linked by _____. |

que

Verbs following *il faut que* and other expressions to be presented later are in a form called the *subjunctive mode.* Mode, like tense, is a characteristic of all verb forms. You have already mastered three of the modes:

Modes of verbs

L'infinitif:	Tu vas **parler.**
L'impératif:	**Parle!**
L'indicatif:	Tu **parles** trop vite.
Le subjonctif:	Il faut **que tu parles** moins vite.

In English, the subjunctive mode has almost disappeared from use, except in a few situations in formal speech or writing. The second sentence in each pair below has a subjunctive verb form.

He is accused of stealing. He showed her the money lest
he be accused of stealing.
She follows the action in every game. It is necessary
that *she follow* the action in every game.
The king lives! Long *live the king*.
He acts as if he is happy. He acts as if *he were* happy.

3. For each sentence, write the subjunctive phrase: *que* + subject + verb.
   a. Il faut que je regarde ce livre. |
   b. Il faut que tu achètes un journal. |
   c. Il faut qu'il donne de l'argent à la vendeuse. |
   d. Il faut qu'elles aident leurs parents. |

   a. que je regarde
   b. que tu achètes
   c. qu'il donne
   d. qu'elles aident

4. This chart summarizes the present subjunctive of *écouter*. Study the different forms carefully, saying each one aloud a few times.

il faut	que	j'	écout	e
	que	tu	écout	es
	qu'	on/il/elle	écout	e
	que	nous	écout	ions
	que	vous	écout	iez
	qu'	ils/elles	écout	ent

   a. Is the present subjunctive stem the same as the present indicative stem? |

   yes *(écout-)*

   b. For which two subjects are the endings of the present subjunctive different from those of the present indicative? |

   nous (écoutions), vous (écoutiez)

For all -*er* verbs except *aller,* the subjunctive stem is the same as the indicative stem. For *all* verbs except *être* and *avoir,* the subjunctive endings are the same.

5. In the following sentences, use the cues to say what each person must do to realize his or her wish. Use *il faut que* + present subjunctive, as in the model.

   Modèle: John veut travailler à Paris. Pour travailler à Paris, il faut parler français. |

   Il faut que John parle français.

   a. Tu veux gagner de l'argent. Pour gagner de l'argent, il faut travailler. |

   Il faut que tu travailles.

b. Je veux connaître des pays différents. Pour connaître des pays différents, il faut voyager. |

Il faut que je voyage.

c. Louise et Béatrice veulent faire du camping. Pour faire du camping, il faut acheter une tente. |

Il faut que Louise et Béatrice achètent une tente.

3. The subjunctive after expressions of volition

The present subjunctive allows you not only to tell people what they must do, but also allows you to express your wishes and preferences.

1. a. Complete the French equivalent.
   I want to talk to the teacher. Je veux _____ au professeur. | a. parler
   b. Is the person who is going to talk to the teacher the same as the person who expresses the wish? | b. yes
   c. In this case, the verb that follows *je veux* is in the _____ form. | c. infinitive

2. a. Now write the English equivalent of *Je veux que vous parliez au professeur.* |

   I want you to talk to the teacher.

   b. In this case, is the person expressing the wish the same as the one who is to talk to the teacher? |

   no

   c. Write the subjunctive phrase from the French sentence. |

   que vous parliez (The subjunctive is almost always introduced by *que*.)

When the subject of *vouloir* wishes to do something, *vouloir* is followed by an infinitive. When the subject of *vouloir* expresses a wish for someone else to do something, *vouloir* is followed by a subjunctive verb phrase.

3. Write the second verb form in each sentence, and indicate *infinitif* or *subjonctif*.

   Modèle: Je veux que vous parliez au professeur. |

   que vous parliez; subjonctif

   a. Je veux que tu travailles aujourd'hui. | a. que tu travailles; subjonctif
   b. Je ne veux pas travailler. | b. travailler; infinitif
   c. Jacques veut jouer au base-ball. | c. jouer; infinitif
   d. Il veut que je joue aussi. | d. que je joue; subjonctif
   e. Francine veut que nous jouions avec elle. | e. que nous jouions; subjonctif

4. In this frame you see what certain people want to do, followed by what other people want them to do. Express these conflicts in pairs of sentences. Use *vouloir* + infinitive in the first, and *vouloir* + subjunctive in the second.

Modèle: nous (jouer au base-ball); notre mère (laver la voiture) |

> Nous voulons jouer au base-ball. Notre mère veut que nous lavions la voiture.

a. moi (regarder un western); mes parents (écouter un concert) |

> Je veux regarder un western. Mes parents veulent que j'écoute un concert. *(I want to watch a western. My parents want me to listen to a concert.)*

b. Henri (manger des bonbons); son père (manger des fruits) |

> Henri veut manger des bonbons. Son père veut qu'il mange des fruits.

c. les élèves (chanter); le professeur (travailler) |

> Les élèves veulent chanter. Le professeur veut qu'ils travaillent.

Here are other verbs that express volition and that are followed by the subjunctive.

j'aime mieux que *(prefer)*	**j'exige que** *(demand, require)*
je conseille que *(advise)*	**j'ordonne que** *(order)*
je défends que *(forbid)*	**je permets que** *(allow)*
je demande que *(ask)*	**je souhaite que** *(wish)*
je désire que *(desire)*	**je suggère que** *(advise, suggest)*

4. The imperative of reflexive verbs

1. As you saw in Phase 5 many verbs can be used either reflexively or non-reflexively. *Cacher* (to hide) is an example. Compare these two commands.

> Cache-toi!   Cache-le!

In which sentence is the verb *cacher* used reflexively? |

> the first sentence (In the first sentence the person is being told to hide himself/herself.
> In the second sentence the person is being told to hide something or someone else.)

2. Bernard is preparing a surprise party for a friend's birthday. Before the friend arrives, he tells everyone where to hide. Write what he says.

Modèle: Marc: sous un lit |

> Cache-toi sous un lit.

a. Michel: derrière les rideaux |

> Cache-toi derrière les rideaux.

b. Sylvie et Monique: derrière le canapé |

> Cachez-vous derrière le canapé.

c. Robert, Anne et moi: dans l'armoire |

> Cachons-nous dans l'armoire.

d. Béatrice: sous le bureau |

> Cache-toi sous le bureau.

3. Look at this command: *Ne te cache pas maintenant, Robert n'est pas encore là.*

    a. Is the word order the same for a negative command as for an affirmative command? |

    no

    b. Where does the object pronoun occur in a negative command? |

    before the verb, after *ne* (Remember also that although *me* and *te* become *moi* and *toi* in affirmative commands, they do not change form in negative commands.)

4. Imagine that you are teaching an unruly class. Tell your students to stop doing what they're doing.

    Modèle: Pierre Durand se peigne *(to comb one's hair)* en classe. |

    Ne vous peignez pas en classe!

    a. Monique Latour se lève pendant la discussion. |

    Ne vous levez pas pendant le discussion!

    b. André Prévost se promène pendant la dictée. |

    Ne vous promenez pas pendant le dictée!

    c. Catherine Renard se maquille en classe. |

    Ne vous maquillez pas en classe!

5. French children often say to each other: *Va-t'en!*

    a. What do you think is the English equivalent? |

    Go away! (Get out of here!)

    b. How would you tell two friends to go away? |

    Allez-vous-en! (There is a hyphen after *vous*, but not after *t'* in *va-t'en*.)

À Propos!

Use the imperative to state three things you wish your friends would or would not do.

Vocabulaire

Noms

le ciel *sky*
l'encre *f.* *ink*
la falaise *cliff (sometimes white)*
le maître *teacher (elementary school)*
l'oiseau-lyre *lyre-bird*
le passeport *passport*
le porte-plume *penholder*
le pupitre *pupil's desk*

Adverbes

également *also, equally*
tranquillement *calmly*

Verbes

s'en aller *to go away*

se cacher *to hide oneself*
crier *to cry out*
démonter *to take down, to disassemble*
s'écrouler *to collapse, to crumble*
se lever *to stand up, to get up*

Autres mots et expressions

à leur tour *in turn, one after the other*
allons-nous-en! *let's go!*
de toute façon *anyhow, at any rate*
ficher le camp (slang) *to go away, to "split"*
va-t-en! *go away!*

PRÉPARATION 74

In this Phase the texts that you will read and discuss are poems. Instead of listening to the text before class as you may have done in the previous Phases, you will discuss each poem in class before the *Préparation*.

Page d'écriture (1)

Deux et deux quatre
quatre et quatre huit
huit et huit font seize...
Répétez! dit le maître° the school teacher *(male)* /
Deux et deux quatre
quatre et quatre huit
huit et huit font seize.
Mais voilà l'oiseau-lyre° lyre-bird
qui passe dans le ciel

l'enfant le voit
l'enfant l'entend
l'enfant l'appelle:
Sauve-moi° save me
joue avec moi
oiseau!
Alors l'oiseau descend
et joue avec l'enfant
Deux et deux quatre...

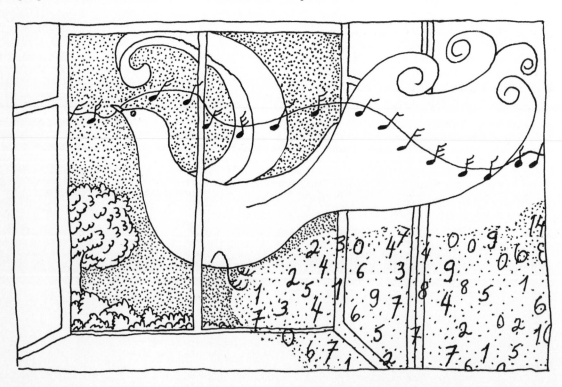

Répétez! dit le maître
et l'enfant joue
l'oiseau joue avec lui...
Quatre et quatre huit
huit et huit font seize
et seize et seize qu'est-ce qu'ils
  font?

Ils ne font rien seize et seize
et surtout pas trente-deux
de toute façon°   anyway
et ils s'en vont
... (à suivre)°   to be continued

Jacques Prévert
Paroles, © 1949 Éditions Gallimard

Échange
d'idées

Avez-vous aimé ce poème? Pourquoi?
Quelles phrases vous ont fait sourire *(made you smile)*?
Quelles phrases vous ont rendu triste *(made you sad)*?

1. Practice with the subjunctive

1. Give the French equivalents of these two sentences:
   a. I want to watch TV. |
      Je veux regarder la télé.
   b. I want you *(vous)* to watch TV with me. |
      Je veux que vous regardiez la télé avec moi.
2. When the subject expresses a wish or preference for himself or herself, the verb following the "wish" verb is in the _____. |
   infinitive
3. When the subject expresses a wish for someone else, the verb following the "wish" verb is in the _____. |
   subjunctive
4. Which of these verb phrases are often followed by the subjunctive? préférer, dire, voir, savoir, il faut. |
   préférer, il faut
5. Compare these two sentences.

   Je ne veux pas parler.   Je ne veux pas que tu parles.

   a. Does *ne... pas* surround the verb *vouloir* in both sentences? |
      yes (The verb *vouloir* is put in the negative, not *parler.*)
   b. Give the English equivalents of the two sentences. |
      I don't want to talk. I don't want you to talk.
6. Mlle Boudreau is a schoolteacher. Say what her students would like to do, as indicated by the cues, then say that Mlle Boudreau doesn't want them to do those things.
   Modèle: Victor (parler à sa camarade) |
      Victor veut parler à sa camarade. Mlle Boudreau ne veut pas qu'il parle à sa camarade.
   a. toi (écouter tes cassettes) |
      Tu veux écouter tes cassettes. Mlle Boudreau ne veut pas que tu écoutes tes cassettes.

b. nous (chanter) |

     Nous voulons chanter. Mlle Boudreau ne veut pas que nous chantions.

c. vous (regarder des magazines) |

     Vous voulez regarder des magazines. Mlle Boudreau ne veut pas que vous regardiez des magazines.

d. moi (me promener) |

     Je veux me promener. Mlle Boudreau ne veut pas que je me promène.

e. tous les élèves (jouer aux cartes) |

     Tous les élèves veulent jouer aux cartes. Mlle Boudreau ne veut pas qu'ils jouent aux cartes.

7. Give French equivalents of these sentences, and remember to choose between the infinitive and the subjunctive.

a. We want to look at the magazine. |

     Nous voulons regarder la revue.

b. They prefer to look at the newspaper. |

     Ils préfèrent regarder le journal.

c. She wants me to speak French. |

     Elle veut que je parle français.

d. You *(Tu)* want us to talk faster? |

     Tu veux que nous parlions plus vite?

e. He wants to listen to us. |

     Il veut nous écouter.

8. Using *je voudrais* instead of *je veux* is a polite way of expressing a wish. Rewrite the following using *je voudrais*. (See key.)

    Modèle: Lève-toi! |

     Je voudrais que tu te lèves.

a. Habillez-vous! b. Lavez-vous! c. Reposons-nous!

2. Substitutes for the passive voice

Look at the following sentence:

    French is spoken in France, Belgium, and Switzerland.

No agent is mentioned. The same meaning can be expressed in the active voice: *People speak French in France...* or *They speak French in France...* Words such as *people* or *they* are used as subjects when the identity of the subjects (or agents) is unimportant.

    As you know, *on* is the word often used to express an indefinite subject:

    On parle français en France, en Belgique et en Suisse.

The above sentence is equivalent in meaning to:

    Le français est parlé en France, en Belgique et en Suisse.

Of these two French sentences the *on* construction is more frequently used. Rephrase each passive construction in frames 1–5 with a sentence containing *on*.

1. En France, un repas léger est pris le soir. |

> En France, on prend un repas léger le soir.

2. Le grand repas est servi à midi. |

> On sert le grand repas à midi.

3. Généralement, le pain est consommé sans beurre. |

> On consomme le pain sans beurre.

4. La salade est mangée juste avant le dessert. |

> On mange la salade juste avant le dessert.

5. Le café est bu sans crème après les repas. |

> On boit le café sans crème après les repas.

There is another construction that is very often used in French instead of a passive form when no agent is mentioned or needed. Instead of saying *un repas léger est pris le soir*, one may use a pronominal form and say: *Un repas léger se prend le soir.*

The sentences in frames 6–9 are the same as those in frames 2–5. Rephrase each statement, using a pronominal construction.

6. Le grand repas est servi à midi. |

> Le grand repas se sert à midi.

7. Généralement, le pain est consommé sans beurre. |

> Le pain se consomme sans beurre.

8. La salade est mangée juste avant le dessert. |

> La salade se mange juste avant le dessert.

9. Le café est bu sans crème. |

> Le café se boit sans crème.

Aimez-vous les bandes dessinées (comics)? Quelle est votre préférée? Pourquoi?

Vocabulaire

Verbes

compris *(p.p. of comprendre)*
revenir *to come back, to come*
surprendre *to surprise*

Autres mots et expressions

ça m'est égal *I don't care, it's all the same to me*
chut! *sh!*
faire l'idiot *to act silly*

Note Culturelle

Les cafés

Le café est un des lieux de rencontre[1] favori des Français. On y va après le travail ou après les cours, pour prendre un café ou un apéritif[2] avec ses amis et discuter[3] avec eux. Ou, le matin, si on n'a pas pris de petit déjeuner à la maison on peut aller au café pour prendre un croissant et un café-crème ou café au lait.

Le matin, l'après-midi ou le soir, on peut rester assis dans la salle ou à la terrasse pendant plusieurs heures avec simplement un café ou un jus de fruits. Personne ne vous oblige à consommer davantage[4]. On peut lire, discuter, ou regarder passer les gens dans la rue. Si on a faim, on peut prendre un repas léger: un sandwich, un croque-monsieur, une glace ou un gâteau.

Dans certains quartiers de Paris, comme Montmartre, Montparnasse et Saint-Germain, certains cafés sont devenus célèbres[5]. Au 19ème siècle[6] et au début du 20ème siècle, des écrivains, des artistes, des exilés politiques ont choisi «Les deux Magots», «La Coupole» et «La Rotonde» comme lieux de rencontre. Picasso, Hemingway, Sartre et Stravinsky, par exemple, avaient «leur» café favori.

Bien sûr, le café est un des endroits préférés des touristes. Ils peuvent se reposer entre deux visites de musées, manger quelque chose et regarder passer les Parisiens... et les autres touristes.

1 meeting place 2 before-dinner drink 3 discuss 4 forces you to have more 5 famous 6 century

PRÉPARATION 75

Page d'écriture (2)

Et l'enfant a caché l'oiseau
dans son pupitre°
et tous les enfants
entendent sa chanson
et tous les enfants
entendent la musique
et huit et huit à leur tour°
  s'en vont
et quatre et quatre
  et deux et deux
à leur tour fichent le camp°
et un et un ne font ni° une
  ni deux
un à un s'en vont également.°

Et l'oiseau-lyre joue
et l'enfant chante   desk
et le professeur crie:
Quand vous aurez fini de faire
  le pitre!°   to clown around
Mais tous les autres enfants
écoutent la musique   in turn
et les murs° de la classe   walls
s'écroulent° tranquillement°   tumble / quietly
Et les vitres° redeviennent° sable°   panes become sand again
l'encre° redevient eau   go away / ink
les pupitres redeviennent arbres°   neither...nor / trees
la craie redevient falaise°   cliff
le porte-plume° redevient oiseau.   also / quill pen holder

Jacques Prévert
Paroles, © 1949 Éditions Gallimard

Échange d'idées

Est-ce que les enfants aiment en général les animaux et en particulier les oiseaux? Pourquoi?

Est-ce que tous les écoliers *(school-children)* aiment rêver? À quoi rêviez-vous quand vous étiez écolier (écolière)?

1. Two object pronouns in statements and commands

1. You are used to replacing direct and indirect objects with pronouns. Look at the sentence below:

        Tu donnes tes bottes à Solange.

  a. Using a direct object pronoun, what would you say? |
        Tu les donnes à Solange.

  b. Using an indirect object pronoun, what would you say? |
        Tu lui donnes tes bottes.

c. Very often, especially in answering questions, one would replace all the objects with pronouns: *You give them to her*. French would use *les* and *lui* and both pronouns would precede the verb:

Tu les lui donnes.

In this sentence, which comes first, the direct or the indirect object pronoun? |

the direct object pronoun: *les*

2. Answer the following questions affirmatively, using two object pronouns: *le, la,* or *les* first, *lui* or *leur* second.

Modèle: Tu as raconté l'accident à ton amie? |

Oui, je le lui ai raconté.

a. Tu envoies l'adresse à tes parents? |

Oui, je la leur envoie.

b. Paul explique les exercices aux autres étudiants? |

Oui, il les leur explique.

c. Vous annoncez la bonne nouvelle à Suzanne? |

Oui, je la lui annonce.

3. If an affirmative command contains two object pronouns, the direct object comes first also. In other words: *le, la, les* before *lui, leur.*

1. It's dinner time for Sultan, the family dog. But there's no more dog food, so M. Lafleur scrounges around the kitchen looking for leftovers. When he finds something, he tells his son to give it to Sultan. Write M. Lafleur's commands, using two object pronouns.

Modèle: J'ai trouvé les petits pois d'hier. |

Alors, donne-les-lui.

a. Et voici les épinards de la semaine dernière. |
b. Tiens! Voilà la tranche de jambon que tu n'as pas voulue. |
c. Et aussi l'œuf qu'on a oublié. |

a. Alors, donne-les-lui.
b. Alors, donne-la-lui.
c. Alors, donne-le-lui.

2. The subjunctive of other verbs

The subjunctive forms of regular *-er* verbs are very close to the indicative. The subjunctive forms of other verbs don't resemble the indicative as closely. However, all verbs except *être* and *avoir* have the same subjunctive endings: *-e, -es, -e, -ions, -iez, -ent.* You just need to know how to find the stem to be able to use any verb in the subjunctive.

1. The subjunctive stem of most verbs is the same as the *ils/elles* stem of the present indicative. Consider the verb *finir.*

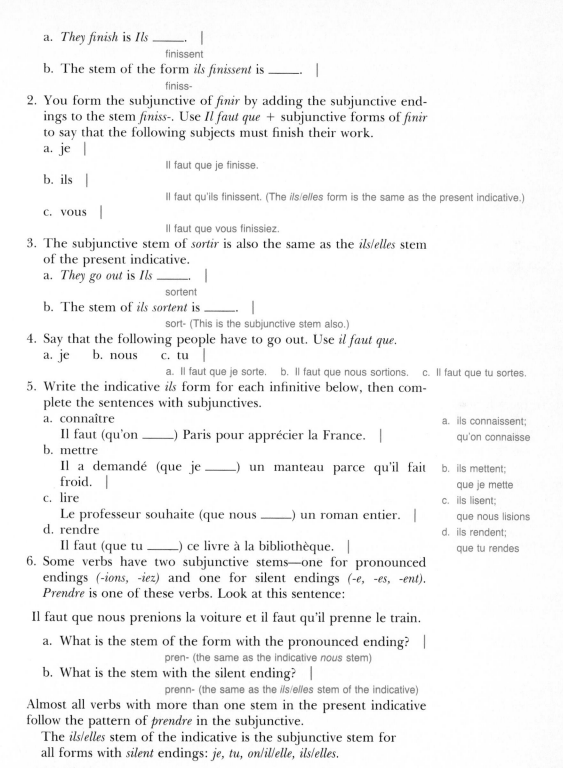

a. *They finish* is *Ils* _____.

finissent

b. The stem of the form *ils finissent* is _____.

finiss-

2. You form the subjunctive of *finir* by adding the subjunctive endings to the stem *finiss-*. Use *Il faut que* + subjunctive forms of *finir* to say that the following subjects must finish their work.

a. je

Il faut que je finisse.

b. ils

Il faut qu'ils finissent. (The *ils/elles* form is the same as the present indicative.)

c. vous

Il faut que vous finissiez.

3. The subjunctive stem of *sortir* is also the same as the *ils/elles* stem of the present indicative.

a. *They go out* is *Ils* _____.

sortent

b. The stem of *ils sortent* is _____.

sort- (This is the subjunctive stem also.)

4. Say that the following people have to go out. Use *il faut que*.

a. je   b. nous   c. tu

a. Il faut que je sorte.   b. Il faut que nous sortions.   c. Il faut que tu sortes.

5. Write the indicative *ils* form for each infinitive below, then complete the sentences with subjunctives.

a. connaître

Il faut (qu'on _____) Paris pour apprécier la France.

    a. ils connaissent;
       qu'on connaisse

b. mettre

Il a demandé (que je _____) un manteau parce qu'il fait froid.

    b. ils mettent;
       que je mette

c. lire

Le professeur souhaite (que nous _____) un roman entier.

    c. ils lisent;
       que nous lisions

d. rendre

Il faut (que tu _____) ce livre à la bibliothèque.

    d. ils rendent;
       que tu rendes

6. Some verbs have two subjunctive stems—one for pronounced endings *(-ions, -iez)* and one for silent endings *(-e, -es, -ent)*. *Prendre* is one of these verbs. Look at this sentence:

Il faut que nous prenions la voiture et il faut qu'il prenne le train.

a. What is the stem of the form with the pronounced ending?

pren- (the same as the indicative *nous* stem)

b. What is the stem with the silent ending?

prenn- (the same as the *ils/elles* stem of the indicative)

Almost all verbs with more than one stem in the present indicative follow the pattern of *prendre* in the subjunctive.

The *ils/elles* stem of the indicative is the subjunctive stem for all forms with *silent* endings: *je, tu, on/il/elle, ils/elles.*

The *nous* form stem of the indicative is the subjunctive stem for the two forms with *pronounced* endings: *nous, vous.*

Formation of the subjunctive of irregular verbs

All verbs but *être* and *avoir* use the regular subjunctive endings:

-e, -es, -e, -ions, -iez, -ent

Present indicative	*Present subjunctive*	
ils **prenn**ent	que je	**prenne**
	que tu	**prennes**
	qu'on/il/elle	**prenne**
	qu'ils/elles	**prennent**
nous **pren**ons	que nous	**prenions**
	que vous	**preniez**

Elles **prennent** l'autobus. Il faut **que je prenne** l'autobus aussi.

Nous **prenons** l'avion. Il **faut que vous preniez** l'avion aussi.

7. a. (finir) Mes enfants, je veux (que vous _____) vos légumes. |
   que vous finissiez

   b. (prendre) Et je ne veux pas (que vous _____) trop de dessert. |
   que vous preniez

   c. (sortir) Je ne veux pas (que vous _____) après le dîner. |
   que vous sortiez

8. a. (sortir) Il faut (que je _____) cet après-midi. |
   que je sorte

   b. (prendre) Tu préfères (que je _____) la voiture ou l'autobus? |
   que je prenne

   c. (finir) Je voudrais (que nous _____) notre travail avant le week-end. |
   que nous finissions

9. a. (finir) Quel mauvais week-end! Le professeur de maths veut (que je _____) tous mes problèmes. |
   que je finisse

   b. (prendre) Tes parents ne veulent pas (que tu _____) la voiture. |
   que tu prennes

   c. (sortir) Et les parents de Pierre et de Jean-Claude ne veulent pas (qu'ils _____). |
   qu'ils sortent

Note Culturelle

Les chanteurs français

Déjà au Moyen-Age[1] (12ème et 13ème siècles[2]) la chanson tenait une place importante en France: les troubadours allaient de château en château chanter leurs poèmes et ballades. Durant[3] la Révolution, on chantait beaucoup de chansons politiques et patriotiques.

Au 19ème siècle, le folklore régional s'était beaucoup développé. Notre siècle a vu le music-hall, influencé par le jazz américain, devenir populaire.

Il y a certains chanteurs qui restent pendant des années[4] des favoris parmi[5] les Français. Même après leur mort, Edith Piaf, Maurice Chevalier, Jacques Brel et Georges Brassens sont encore très appréciés. D'autres chanteurs comme Georges Moustaki, Yves Montand, Catherine Lara et Nana Mouscouri continuent de plaire.[6] Ils savent allier poésie et mélodie et peuvent raconter toute une histoire ou présenter une «tranche de vie»[7] dans une chanson.

La poésie tient une place importante dans la chanson française qu'elle[8] vienne de France, de Belgique, du Canada ou d'autres pays francophones. Certains poèmes très connus[9] ont été mis en musique[10] et demeurent des favoris du public. Certains poètes écrivent des poèmes spécialement pour des chanteurs.

1 Middle Ages 2 centuries 3 during 4 for 5 among 6 to please 7 slice of life 8 whether 9 well-known 10 put to music

Petit spectacle musical dans la rue.

PRÉPARATION 76

1. Subjunctive forms: *aller, pouvoir, savoir, vouloir*

1. *Aller* is irregular in the subjunctive. Say all the forms aloud.

que	j'	aill	e
que	tu	aill	es
qu'	on/il/elle	aill	e
que	**nous**	**all**	**ions**
que	vous	all	iez
qu'	ils/elles	aill	ent

2. The subjunctive endings of *aller* are regular. There are two stems.
   a. What is the stem when the ending is silent? |
      aill- /aj/
   b. What is the stem when the ending is pronounced? |
      all- /al/ (This stem is actually regular.)

3. The students in this frame have habits of which their teachers don't approve. Complete the sentences that express the teachers' feelings. Say the sentences aloud.

   Modèle: Tu vas souvent au stade. Tes professeurs aiment mieux _____ à la bibliothèque. |
   que tu ailles

   a. Henri va souvent au café. Ses professeurs aiment mieux _____ au théâtre. |
      a. qu'il aille
   b. Je vais souvent au magasin de disques. Mes professeurs préfèrent _____ à la librairie. |
      b. que j'aille
   c. Nous allons souvent dans des discothèques. Nos professeurs aiment mieux _____ au concert. |
      c. que nous allions
   d. Jean-Richard et Dominique vont souvent à des concerts de rock. Leurs professeurs souhaitent _____ à l'opéra. |
      d. qu'ils aillent
   e. Vous allez souvent au cinéma. Vos professeurs préfèrent _____ au musée. |
      e. que vous alliez
   f. Tu vas souvent au stade. Tes professeurs désirent _____ au laboratoire de chimie. |
      f. que tu ailles

4. *Venir* is irregular in the indicative, but it forms the subjunctive according to a normal pattern.

a. The stem for the forms with silent endings is the same as the *ils/elles* stem for the indicative. Write this stem. |

        vienn-

5. The subjunctive stems of these verbs are not predictable: *savoir (sach-), vouloir (veuill-, voul-),* and *pouvoir (puiss-).*

Write equivalents of these sentences:

a. I don't want him to know (it). |

        Je ne veux pas qu'il le sache.

b. I'm surprised that he wants to accompany *(accompagner)* us. |

        Je suis surpris/e qu'il veuille nous accompagner.

c. I'm sorry that you *(tu)* can't go (there). |

        Je regrette que tu ne puisses pas y aller.

2. Practice with subjunctive forms

Many verbs that have two present indicative stems, like *finir (fini-, finiss-)* have a regular subjunctive stem and all use regular endings.

1. For each verb, write the present indicative *ils* form, then the subjunctive phrase *que je....*

a. choisir   b. partir |

        a. ils choisissent; que je choisisse   b. ils partent; que je parte

c. paraître   d. attendre   e. dire |

        c. ils paraissent; que je paraisse   d. ils attendent; que j'attende   e. ils disent; que je dise

2. Give the appropriate subjunctive forms of these verbs.

   Modèle: je: vendre |

        que je vende

a. je: finir   c. il: partir   e. nous: descendre

b. tu: sortir   d. elles: lire   f. vous: réfléchir |

        a. que je finisse   b. que tu sortes   c. qu'il parte   d. qu'elles lisent   e. que nous descendions   f. que vous réfléchissiez

3. Verbs with two subjunctive stems form the subjunctive in a predictable way. Write the indicative *ils* and *nous* stems for these verbs:

a. prendre   b. venir | a. prenn-, pren- b. vienn-, ven-

c. envoyer   d. boire | c. envoi-, envoy- d. boiv-, buv-

4. Now use those stems to write the *je* and *nous* subjunctive forms of the verbs above. |

        a. que je prenne, que nous prenions   b. que je vienne, que nous venions   c. que j'envoie, que nous envoyions   d. que je boive, que nous buvions

5. An international agency based in Paris has representatives all over the world. Because of important developments, everyone must return. Say where each person must come back from.

Modèle: Paul Faillot (Tokyo) |

Il faut que Paul Faillot revienne de Tokyo.

a. nous (Casablanca) |

Il faut que nous revenions de Casablanca.

b. toi (Rio de Janeiro) |

Il faut que tu reviennes de Rio de Janeiro.

c. Sonia Spiegel (Bangkok) |

Il faut que Sonia Spiegel revienne de Bangkok.

d. vous (Hong-Kong) |

Il faut que vous reveniez de Hong-Kong.

e. moi (Londres) |

Il faut que je revienne de Londres.

f. Henri et Françoise Dumas (Moscou) |

Il faut qu'Henri et Françoise Dumas reviennent de Moscou.

6. Georges is having a hard time. One little voice *(la voix de la tentation)* tells him to do one thing, while his conscience *(la voix de la conscience)* tells him to do the opposite. Complete what *la voix de la conscience* says.

Modèle: La tentation: «Regarde la télé.» La conscience: «Il ne faut pas _____ la télé.» |

que tu regardes

a. La tentation: «Ne finis pas ton travail.» La conscience: «Il faut _____ ton travail.»

b. La tentation: «Vends ton livre de français.» La conscience: «Il ne faut pas _____ ton livre de français.»

c. La tentation: «N'apprends pas cette leçon.» La conscience: «Il faut _____ cette leçon.»

d. La tentation: «Sors avec tes amis.» La conscience: «Il ne faut pas _____ avec tes amis.»

e. La tentation: «Ne réponds pas à cette lettre.» La conscience: «Il faut _____ à cette lettre.»

f. La tentation: «Lis cette bande dessinée.» La conscience: «Il ne faut pas _____ cette bande dessinée.»

g. La tentation: «Ne prends pas ton petit déjeuner.» La conscience: «Il faut que _____ ton petit déjeuner.» |

a. que tu finisses   b. que tu vendes   c. que tu apprennes   d. que tu sortes
e. que tu répondes   f. que tu lises   g. que tu prennes

3. Subjunctive: Impersonal expressions of opinion

Like *il faut,* other impersonal expressions that represent a speaker's opinion are also followed by *que* + a subjunctive phrase.

Say the expressions aloud, notice how many are cognates.

Now choose expressions from the list to substitute below for *il faut* (positive advice) and *il ne faut pas* (negative advice). Rewrite these admonitions to Georges' conscience. (See key.)

a. Il ne faut pas que tu regardes la télé
b. Il faut que tu finisses ton travail
c. Il ne faut pas que tu vendes ton livre de français
d. Il faut que tu apprennes cette leçon
e. Il ne faut pas que tu sortes avec tes amis
f. Il faut que tu répondes à cette lettre
g. Il ne faut pas que tu lises cette bande dessinée
h. Il faut que tu prennes ton petit déjeuner

À Propos!

Make a statement of your opinions of a current news event by completing these statements: *Il est bon que... Il est préférable que... Il est regrettable que...*

4. Practice with the conditional and the future

1. As you know, both the conditional and the future are often used in conjunction with *si* (if) clauses.

a. The conditional is used with the *imparfait* to express what would happen if certain hypothetical conditions were met. Give the English equivalent of *Si j'avais assez d'argent, je voyagerais.* |

> If I had enough money, I would travel.

b. In a similar way, the future is used with the present to say what will definitely happen at a particular time in the future, if certain conditions are met. Give the English equivalent of *Si j'ai assez d'argent, je voyagerai.* |

> If I have enough money, I will travel.

2. Guy is going to spend the summer in either New York or California. He's telling his friends about his plans. They are saying what they would do if they were going instead. Complete each sentence with the future or the conditional of the phrase in parentheses.

    Modèle: Si je vais en Californie, j'... (aller à San Francisco) |
          j'irai à San Francisco

a. Si nous allions en Californie, nous... (aller à Los Angeles) |
      nous irions à Los Angeles

b. Si je vais à New York, je... (visiter tous les musées) |
      je visiterai tous les musées

c. Si nous allions à New York, nous... (visiter les différents quartiers de la ville) |
      nous visiterions les différents quartiers de la ville

d. Si je vais en Californie, je... (prendre le train) |
      je prendrai le train

e. Si nous allions en Californie, nous... (prendre l'avion) |
      nous prendrions l'avion

                                                          Phase onze

PRÉPARATION 77

1. Reading poetry: *Déjeuner du matin*

When you read *«Page d'écriture»*, you saw how Jacques Prévert used simple, straightforward language and vocabulary to create a scene that reveals a person's feelings and emotions. Now, read *«Déjeuner du matin»* for another example of Prévert's poetic art.

Déjeuner du matin

Il a mis le café
Dans la tasse
Il a mis le lait
Dans la tasse de café
5   Il a mis le sucre
Dans le café au lait
Avec la petite cuiller
Il a tourné
Il a bu le café au lait
10   Et il a reposé la tasse
Sans me parler
Il a allumé
Une cigarette
Il a fait des ronds
15   Avec la fumée
Il a mis les cendres

Dans le cendrier
Sans me parler
Sans me regarder
20   Il s'est levé
Il a mis
Son chapeau sur sa tête
Il a mis
Son manteau de pluie
25   Parce qu'il pleuvait
Et il est parti
Sous la pluie
Sans une parole
Sans me regarder
30   Et moi j'ai pris
Ma tête dans ma main
Et j'ai pleuré.

Jacques Prévert
Paroles, © 1949 Éditions Gallimard

1. If you think about what is being described in lines 1–10, you should have no trouble figuring out any of the vocabulary.
   a. If *la tasse* is where the man puts his coffee, what is its English equivalent? |
      > the cup
   b. *Il a tourné* expresses what the man does to the coffee, milk, and sugar. How would you say it in English? |
      > he stirred (*Tourner* and *to turn* are cognates, although *turn* isn't used with the meaning *stir.*)

c. To stir his coffee, the man uses *une cuiller*—in English, a
_____. |

        spoon

d. *Poser une question* could be translated as *to put a question to some-one*. With this meaning in mind, give an equivalent for *Il y a reposé la tasse.* |

        He put down the cup.

2. Lines 12–17 also present a clear context.

a. *La fumée* is the result of burning tobacco (or anything else). Give the English cognate and the equivalent. |

        fume, smoke (The French verb meaning *to smoke* is *fumer*.)

b. With the smoke, the man makes *des ronds. Rond* is an adjective used here as a noun. What is the English cognate of the adjective *rond*? What are *des ronds de fumée* in English? |

        rond—round; smoke rings

c. Besides *la fumée*, another product of burning is *les cendres*. Give the cognate and the more common word for *les cendres*. |

        cinders, ashes

d. The man places *les cendres* in *le cendrier*—the _____. |

        ashtray

3. The words *pluie* (1. 24, 1. 27) and *pleuvait* (1. 25) are related.

a. *Il pleuvait* is the *imparfait* of a familiar weather expression. Write the expression in the present tense. |

        il pleut (The infinitive is *pleuvoir*.)

b. *La pluie* comes from *pleuvoir*. What is the English equivalent? |

        rain

c. *Un manteau de pluie* is an article of clothing. What is another name for it in French? |

        un imperméable (*Manteau de pluie* is an old-fashioned, poetic expression.)

4. a. Look at the phrases that start with *sans*. What verb form can complete a phrase that begins with *sans*? |

        an infinitive

b. Give the English equivalent of *sans me parler* (1. 11). |

        without speaking to me

5. A phrase with *sans* can also be completed with a noun. The noun *la parole* comes from the same Latin root as the verb *parler*. How would you say *sans une parole* (1. 28) in English? |

        without a word, without speaking

6. The verb *pleurer* is an appropriate one to end this very sad poem. *Pleurer* is the opposite of *rire (to laugh)*. What is the English equivalent of *j'ai pleuré* (1. 32)? |

        I cried

In frames 7–9, no written answers are required, but you will be asked to discuss these questions in class.

7. The person telling the story clearly feels very sad and hurt. How are these feelings expressed? Consider not just the words themselves, but also the way the scene is described. For example, why is it significant that the speaker notices so many details? When two people sit together drinking coffee, is it "normal" for them not to speak?
8. How would you describe the rhythm of the poem? Do you think the feeling would be expressed as clearly if the lines and sentences were longer or more even? Why or why not?
9. Who are the people? *Il* is obviously a male. But is he a young man or an older man? Who is talking: a man, a boy, a woman, a girl? What is their relationship—parent/child, husband/wife? What has happened between them?

2. Indicative, subjunctive, or infinitive?

In this part, you must decide which form of the verb is appropriate—indicative, subjunctive, or infinitive. You will have to give subjunctive forms of verbs that you haven't yet used in the subjunctive; it won't be a problem if you remember how the subjunctive is formed. The first two frames will help you review.

1. Frames *a* and *b* apply to most verbs.
   a. For the subjunctive forms with silent endings, use the _____ stem of the present indicative. |
   b. For the subjunctive forms with pronounced endings, use the _____ stem of the present indicative. |
2. Frames *a* and *b* apply to *aller*.
   a. The present subjunctive stem of *aller* for all forms that have silent endings is _____. |
   b. The present subjunctive stem of *aller* for all forms that have pronounced endings is _____. |

   a. ils/elles

   b. nous

   a. aill-

   b. all-

3. The following conversation takes place at a travel agency in a small city near Paris. Write the correct form of the verb in parentheses and indicate whether it is in the indicative, subjunctive, or infinitive. (See key.)

   Agent Madame?
   Cliente Oui... C'est pour (a. *aller*) à Avignon, Monsieur.
   Agent Très bien. Que préférez-vous (b. *prendre*)? Le train de jour? Le train de nuit?
   Cliente J'aime mieux (c. *prendre*) le train de jour.
   Agent Bon... Quand est-ce que vous devez (d. *partir*)?
   Cliente Le 17 juillet, je pense. Et il faut que j' (e. *arriver*) à Avignon avant 9h du soir.

Agent	Bien. Un instant, s'il vous plaît; il faut que je (f. *regarder*) l'horaire... Bon. D'abord, il faut que vous (g. *aller*) à Paris. Voulez-vous que je vous (h. *dire*) les heures des trains pour Paris?
Cliente	Non, merci, je (i. *aller*) à Paris en voiture.
Agent	Bon; à Paris vous (j. *prendre*) «le TGV» qui (k. *quitter*) la gare de Lyon à 10h55. Et vous (l. *arriver*) à Avignon à 15h20.
Cliente	Bon. Et pour le retour? Il faut que je (m. *revenir*) le 22 ou le 23.
Agent	Vous pouvez (n. *revenir*) par le TGV aussi. Il (o. *partir*) d'Avignon à 15h30 et il (p. *arriver*) à Paris à 20h10.
Cliente	Une dernière question, s'il vous plaît. C'est combien, le billet aller-retour° en seconde classe?
Agent	500 F, Madame. Vous voulez que je vous (q. *préparer*) votre billet maintenant?
Cliente	Non merci. Il faut que je (r. *réfléchir*) un peu.
Agent	Très bien. Voulez-vous que je vous (s. *écrire*) vos heures de train sur ce papier?
Cliente	Oui, s'il vous plaît. Merci beaucoup, Monsieur.
Agent	De rien, Madame.

TGV = train à grande vitesse

round trip ticket

3. Subjunctive after expressions of feelings

In French, when the main clause of a sentence expresses any kind of feeling or emotion, the following *que* clause will be in the subjunctive.

Je *suis heureux* que tu *viennes* avec nous mais *je regrette* que ton frère ne *vienne* pas.

Here is a list of some frequently used expressions which are followed by the subjunctive. Study their meanings and say them aloud.

être content que *(glad)*	être ravi que *(delighted)*
être désolé que *(sorry)*	être surpris que *(surprised)*
être étonné que *(surprised, astonished)*	être triste que *(sad)*
	avoir peur que *(to be afraid that . . .)*
être fâché que *(upset)*	s'étonner que *(to be surprised that . . .)*
être fier que *(proud)*	regretter que *(to be sorry that . . .)*
être heureux que *(happy)*	

1. Madeleine is going to Africa for a year. Tell what various people's reactions are, as in the model.

> *Modèle:* (Her friend Alain is sorry.) |
>> Je suis désolé qu'elle y aille./Je regrette qu'elle y aille.

a. (Her sister is angry.) |
>> Je suis fâchée qu'elle y aille.

b. (Her mother is delighted.) |
>> Je suis ravie qu'elle y aille.

c. (Her best friend is sad.) |
>> Je suis triste qu'elle y aille.

d. (Her father is surprised.) |
>> Je suis étonné/surpris qu'elle y aille./Je m'étonne qu'elle y aille.

e. (Her professor is glad.) |
>> Je suis content/heureux qu'elle y aille.

f. (Her grandmother is not sorry.) |
>> Je ne regrette pas qu'elle y aille./Je ne suis pas désolée qu'elle y aille.

g. (Her friend Georges is proud.) |
>> Je suis fier /fjɛr/ qu'elle y aille.

4. The subjunctive of *être* and *avoir*

Être and *avoir* are the only verbs that do not have regular subjunctive endings.

1. Read the following sentences, with *être* in the subjunctive.

> Je souhaite que vous soyez toujours heureux.
> Le professeur voudrait que tous les élèves soient attentifs.
> Mme Ledoux est enchantée que sa fille soit musicienne.

a. Write the subjunctive clauses from the sentences above (*que* + subject + verb). |
>> que vous soyez, que tous les élèves soient, que sa fille soit

b. What are the two subjunctive stems of *être*? |
>> soi-, soy-

c. Give an English equivalent of the first sentence. |
>> I wish that you always be happy (that you will always be happy).

2. Study the subjunctive forms of *être*. Notice that the endings are irregular.

que je	**sois**	que nous	**soyons**
que tu	sois	que vous	soyez
qu'on/il/elle	soit	qu'ils/elles	soient

a. Which stem is used for forms with silent endings: *soi-* or *soy-*?

a. soi-

b. *Soy-* is the subjunctive stem for the _____ and _____ forms.

b. nous, vous

3. Parents always seem to transfer their ideals to their children. Complete the sentences below with the subjunctive of *être*. Write *que*, the subject, and the verb.

a. Mme Auriol a deux jeunes enfants. Elle veut qu'ils _____ toujours gentils.

a. qu'ils soient

b. Ton père est moniteur de ski. Il voudrait que tu _____ un excellent skieur.

b. que tu sois

c. Les enfants Boulet disent: «Nos parents sont médecins. Ils sont fiers que nous _____ toujours en bonne santé *(in good health)*.»

c. que nous soyons

d. Le gangster dit a ses fils: "Je suis désolé que vous _____ si *(so)* honnêtes."

d. que vous soyez

e. Jacqueline dit: «Mes parents sont tous les deux *(both)* avocats. Ils ne sont pas surpris que je _____ bavarde *(talkative)*.»

e. que je sois

f. Le père de Michel est professeur. Il désire que Michel _____ un bon élève.

f. que Michel soit

4. The following sentence contains *avoir* in the subjunctive.

Faut-il que les jeunes aient le droit *(right)* de participer aux décisions familiales?

a. What is the subjunctive form?

aient

b. Write the English equivalent.

Is it necessary that (should) young people have the right to participate in family decisions?

5. Study the chart of *avoir* in the subjunctive.

que j'**aie**	que nous **ayons**
que tu aies	que vous ayez
qu'on/il/elle ait	qu'ils/elles aient

a. Which stem is used with silent endings?

ai- (Note that *on/il/elle ait* has an irregular ending.)

b. Which stem is used with the *nous/vous* forms?

ay-

6. Complete the sentences that follow. Write *que*, the subject, and the verb.

a. Il ne veut pas que ses animaux _____ faim.

a. ue ses animaux aient

b. Nos parents sont contents que nous _____ beaucoup d'amis.

b. que nous ayons

c. Elle est surprise que j'_____ peur *(fear)* de l'orage *(storm)*.

c. que j'aie

d. Nous sommes heureux que vous _____ ces disques. |
e. Il faut que tu _____ de bonnes notes en classe. |
f. Je suis furieux qu'il _____ oublié *(forgotten)* notre rendez-vous. |

d. que vous ayez

e. que tu aies

f. qu'il ait

5. The present participle

When two actions are closely related to each other, a verb form called the present participle *(le participe présent)* may be used to show the relationship.

1. One common use of the present participle is to say that an action takes place at the same time as another.

> Pierre chante en travaillant.   *Pierre sings while working.*

a. Write the French phrase that expresses the meaning *while working.* |

en travaillant

b. What is the infinitive that *travaillant* comes from? |

travailler

2. The form *travaillant* is the present participle of *travailler*. Write the present participle from each of the following sentences, and say the English equivalent of the sentence.

a. Nous faisons nos devoirs en écoutant la radio. |

écoutant (We do our homework while listening to the radio.)

b. Elle regarde la télévision en faisant la vaisselle. |

faisant (She watches television while doing the dishes.)

c. Ils lisent le journal en prenant leur déjeuner. |

prenant (They read the newspaper while having lunch.)

3. a. What ending do the present participles all have? |

-ant

b. This ending is added to a stem. Is it the infinitive stem, the present indicative *nous* stem, or the present indicative *ils* stem? |

the present indicative *nous* stem.

4. What word introduces the participle in all of the examples? |

en (The present participle is often introduced by *en*, but it may also be used alone.)

5. Complete the French equivalent of each sentence below by writing *en* plus the appropriate present participle.

a. *Do you sing while taking your bath?* Est-ce que tu chantes _____ ton bain? |

en prenant

b. *Brigitte called her mother upon arriving.* Brigitte a téléphoné à sa mère _____. |

en arrivant

c. *Jacqueline always comes in singing.* Jacqueline arrive toujours _____. |

en chantant

d. *You can't play the trumpet while eating.* Vous ne pouvez pas jouer de la trompette _____. |

en mangeant

e. *He discovered this painting while visiting an old farm.* Il a découvert ce tableau _____ une vieille ferme. |

en visitant

f. *Charles plays with his dog while doing his homework.* Charles joue avec son chien _____ ses devoirs. |

en faisant

Vocabulaire

Noms

l'agent *m.   agent*
l'atelier *m.   studio, workshop*
le billet aller-retour   *round-trip ticket*
le bois   *woods*
l'endroit *m.   location, place*
l'horaire *m.   timetable*
la route   *road, highway*

Verbes

caresser   *to caress, to stroke*
se jeter   *to throw oneself*
mordu   *(p.p. of mordre, to bite)*
mort   *(p.p. of mourir, to die)*
refermer   *to close again*

Autres mots et expressions

de rien   *it's nothing, you're welcome*
en danger   *in danger*
en général   *generally, usually*
F *(abbr.)   franc(s)*

PRÉPARATION 78

Le Message

La porte que quelqu'un a ouverte
La porte que quelqu'un a refermée
La chaise où quelqu'un s'est assis
Le chat que quelqu'un a caressé
Le fruit que quelqu'un a mordu
La lettre que quelqu'un a lue

La chaise que quelqu'un a renversée
La porte que quelqu'un a ouverte
La route où quelqu'un court encore
Le bois que quelqu'un traverse
La rivière où quelqu'un se jette
L'hôpital où quelqu'un est mort.

Jacques Prévert
Paroles, © 1949 Éditions Gallimard

Échange d'idées

1. Aimez-vous les poèmes tristes? Oui? Non? Pourquoi?
2. Selon vous, qui est la personne qui s'est jetée dans la rivière? un homme? une femme? un enfant? Pour quelle(s) raison(s) cette personne a-t-elle fait cela?

1. The relative pronouns *qui, que, où*

The poem *Le Message* is composed mainly of relative clauses. A relative clause contains a subject and a verb and, like an adjective, describes a noun.

1. *Qui* in a relative clause is always the subject. It can refer to things or to people. Give the English equivalents of these sentences.
   a. J'ai une amie qui voyage beaucoup. |
      I have a friend who travels a lot.
   b. Nous avons vu des bateaux qui étaient en danger. |
      We saw some boats that (which) were in danger.
2. In a relative clause, *que* is always the direct object. Like *qui*, it follows the noun that it refers to, and, like *qui*, it can refer to things or to people. Give English equivalents for these examples.
   a. L'homme que j'ai rencontré hier était très intéressant. |
      The man (whom) I met yesterday was very interesting.
   b. Les photos que tu as prises sont excellentes. |
      The pictures (that) you took are excellent. (Remember, if the relative clause is in the *passé composé,* the past participle agrees with the noun *que* refers to.)

3. In a relative clause, *où* follows the noun that names the place or the time of the action. Give English equivalents.
   a. Nous avons vu l'université où vous avez fait vos études. |
      We saw the university where you studied.
   b. C'est le jour où nous nous sommes mariés. |
      It's the day (when) we got married. (*Où* is the French equivalent of *when* in such an adverbial clause.)
4. Complete each sentence with *qui, que,* or *où*.
   a. Tu aimes le chapeau ____ j'ai acheté hier? | a. que
   b. C'est le chapeau ____ est sur la commode. | b. qui
   c. Tu connais le magasin ____ je l'ai acheté? | c. où

2. Writing practice: interpreting «Le Message»

Now that you have read Jacques Prévert's poem «Le Message», give an interpretation of the events described in the poem. In 10–15 sentences, write the letter that is referred to in the poem. Before you start, think about these questions:

> Qui a écrit la lettre? À qui?
> Pour donner quel message?
> Est-ce que la lettre était longue ou courte?
> Est-ce qu'elle était adressée à la personne qui l'a lue?

3. Sentences with two object pronouns

1. This frame will show you how to give negative commands with two object pronouns.
   Sylvie and Bernard are arguing over whether Anne should show her boyfriend's picture to her brother.

> Sylvie: Montre-la-lui.
> Bernard: Non, ne la lui montre pas.

   a. In an *affirmative* command, the object pronouns ____ the verb. |
      follow
   b. In a *negative* command, the object pronouns ____ the verb. |
      precede
   c. In the examples above, are the object pronouns in the same order for both the affirmative and the negative commands? |
      yes

2. Médor, the new puppy, keeps a collection of odds and ends that he finds in the neighborhood and exhibits in the front yard. M. Liautet, his owner, wants Médor to return *(rapporter)* the objects to their owners, but the Liautet children want to keep all the things. Write the conflicting commands that poor Médor hears.

Modèle: Voilà la radio de Pierre. |

—Rapporte-la-lui. —Non, ne la lui rapporte pas.

a. Voilà les bottes de Mme Hugo. |

—Rapporte-les-lui. —Non, ne les lui rapporte pas.

b. Voilà les chapeaux de Mlle Labelle et de sa sœur. |

—Rapporte-les-leur. —Non, ne les leur rapporte pas.

c. Voilà la souris du chat. |

—Rapporte-la-lui. —Non, ne la lui rapporte pas.

d. Voilà le cahier du professeur Lafrance. |

—Rapporte-le-lui. —Non, ne le lui rapporte pas.

e. Voilà le *Napoléon* des Verley. |

—Rapporte-le-leur. —Non, ne le leur rapporte pas.

3. When a statement contains two object pronouns, both of them come before the verb. Now consider the word order in such a statement. Read this exchange about showing a new radio to a little boy.

> Marie: Ne la lui montre pas.
> Alain: D'accord, je ne la lui montre pas.

Is the order of the object pronouns the same in the statement as in the negative command? |

yes

Third person object pronouns in statements

Affirmative				*Negative*				
	le					**le**		
		lui					**lui**	
Je	**la**		montre.		Je **ne**	**la**		montre **pas.**
		leur					**leur**	
	les					**les**		

4. A young child is very proud of the things he collected during the day. Say that he shows the items below to the people indicated. Say your answers, then write them. (See key.)

Modèle: Il montre le jouet *(toy)* à son frère. |

Il le lui montre.

a. Il montre ses crayons à sa sœur.

b. Il montre la vieille revue à sa mère.

c. Il montre sa grenouille *(frog)* à sa grand-mère.

d. Il montre ses timbres *(stamps)* à son père.

e. Il montre ses dessins à ses parents.

5. You need to know how to use pronouns referring to the first and second persons as well. You have used them before:

Il me montre ses photos.

See what happens when the pronoun *les* replaces *ses photos*.

Il me les montre.   *He is showing them to me.*

Which comes first in French, the direct object or the indirect object pronoun? |

the indirect object pronoun: *me*

6. Suppose an artist is showing his paintings to various people. The following statements are based on this situation. Read each sentence aloud and write the two object pronouns in the order in which they occur. Then write the English equivalent of the sentence.

a. Il me les montre. |

me les; He shows them to me.

b. Il te les montre. |

te les; He shows them to you.

c. Il nous les montre. |

nous les; He shows them to us.

d. Il vous les montre. |

vous les; He shows them to you.

7. Refer to the answers of frame 6 to answer these questions.

a. True or false: In statements with two object pronouns, the direct object always precedes the indirect object. |

false

b. Which indirect object pronouns come before the direct objects *le, la,* or *les?* |

me, te, nous, vous

In statements containing two object pronouns, the pronouns *me, te, nous, vous* always come first.

8. Rewrite these statements using two object pronouns.

a. Il me montre la photo. |

Il me la montre. (If *me* has to come in first place, *la* has to come in second.)

b. Il nous donne le disque. |

Il nous le donne.

The word order of a statement with two object pronouns depends on the pronouns involved.

—*Me, te, nous, vous* always come first.

—*Lui* and *leur* always come second.

—*Le, la,* and *les* come either first or second, depending on which indirect object is used.

This little graph may help you remember this word order. Only the combinations within either circle A or circle B are possible.

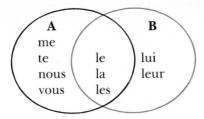

9. Roland is giving out his telephone number. Using two object pronouns in each sentence, say that he gives it to the following people. Remember that *numéro de téléphone* is masculine.

   Modèle: moi |

   Il me le donne.

   a. nous   b. vous   c. toi |

   a. Il nous le donne.   b. Il vous le donne.   c. Il te le donne.

10. Sylvie is showing off her new house. Say that she shows it to the following people. Remember that *maison* is feminine.

   Modèle: moi |

   Elle me la montre.

   a. toi   b. vous   c. nous |

   a Elle te la montre.   b Elle vous la montre.   c Elle nous la montre.

11. Jacques and Philippe are putting together a photo album. They are asking friends for the pictures they took together. Say that they ask the following people.

   Modèle: toi |

   Ils te les demandent.

   a. moi   b. nous |

   a Ils me les demandent.   b Ils nous les demandent.

4. Practice with the subjunctive of *être* and *avoir*

1. See if you remember all the subjunctive forms of *être*. Write *que*, the subject, and the verb.
   a. Il faut que je _____ courageux. | a. que je sois
   b. Il faut que tu _____ calme. | b. que tu sois
   c. Il faut qu'elle _____ travailleuse. | c. qu'elle soit
   d. Il faut qu'ils _____ sportifs. | d. qu'ils soient
   e. Il faut que nous _____ polis. | e. que nous soyons
   f. Il faut que vous _____ aimables. | f. que vous soyez

2. Complete the following sentences with the subjunctive forms of *avoir*. Write *que*, the subject, and the verb.
   a. Il est surpris que j'_____ peur du chien. | a. que j'aie

b. Il ne faut pas que tu _____ froid. |

c. Vous ne voulez pas qu'il _____ une nouvelle moto? |

d. Nous aimerions qu'elles _____ confiance en nous. |

e. Ma femme aimerait que nous _____ beaucoup d'argent. |

f. Nous souhaitons que vous _____ beaucoup de bonheur. |

b. que tu aies

c. qu'il ait

d. qu'elles aient

e. que nous ayons

f. que vous ayez

Note Culturelle

Le bureau de poste

Aux États-Unis, le téléphone et le télégraphe appartiennent à[1] des compagnies privées[2]. Mais en France ils appartiennent à l'État[3]. Dans les bureaux de poste, on peut acheter des timbres[4] et envoyer des lettres, et on peut aussi téléphoner et envoyer des télégrammes.

1 belong to 2 private 3 the State 4 stamps 5 thanks to 6 letters in cylinders sent by air pressure through an underground network of tubes 7 addressees

En France beaucoup de gens n'ont pas le téléphone. À Paris, on peut communiquer rapidement, même sans téléphone, grâce à[5] un service de pneumatiques[6]. Ces pneumatiques sont envoyés d'un bureau de poste à un autre et apportés aux destinataires[7] en deux ou trois heures. C'est donc très pratique et beaucoup plus rapide qu'une lettre.

Bureau de poste typique («les P.T.T.»)

Vocabulaire

Noms

les cendres *f. pl.* *ashes*
le cendrier *ashtray*
la cuiller *spoon*
la défense *defense*
le dictionnaire *dictionary*
la difficulté *difficulty, trouble*
l'encyclopédie *f.* *encyclopedia*
la fumée *smoke*
le glacier *glacier*
la grenouille *frog*
la lune *moon*
le manteau de pluie *raincoat*
la note *evaluation of performance;*
    bonnes notes *good grades;*
    mauvaises notes *bad grades*
la parole *word*
la référence *reference*
le rond *round, circle*

Adjectifs

bizarre *strange, odd*
désolé, -e *sorry*
fâché, -e *upset*
ravi, -e *delighted*

Verbes

assurer *to assure*
allumer *to light, to set fire to*
avoir honte *to be ashamed*
s'étonner *to be surprised*
exister *to be, to exist*
parcourir *to travel over*
se plaindre *to complain*
rapporter *to bring back, to return*
se réjouir *to rejoice*
reposer *to set down, to put*

Autres mots et expressions

à bout *at the end of one's rope*
à cheval *on horseback*
en forme *in form, in (good) shape*
je vous en prie *you're welcome*
mille *thousand*

Le merveilleux et le ‹théâtre du silence›

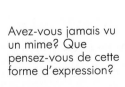

Avez-vous jamais vu un mime? Que pensez-vous de cette forme d'expression?

PRÉPARATION 79

Liberté

Prenez du soleil°
Dans le creux des mains,°
Un peu de soleil
Et partez au loin!

Partez dans le vent,
Suivez° votre rêve°;
Partez à l'instant°,
La jeunesse est brève°!

Il est des chemins°
Inconnus° des hommes
Il est des chemins
Si aériens°!

Ne regrettez pas
Ce que vous quittez
Regardez, là-bas,
L'horizon briller°.

Loin, toujours plus loin,
Partez en chantant°!
Le monde appartient°
À ceux° qui n'ont rien.

Maurice Carême
La Lanterne magique
© 1947 Maurice Carême

sun
the palm of your hands

shine

follow / dream / singing
immediately / belongs
brief / those

roads, lanes
unknown

ethereal

Échange d'idées

Quel est le rêve que vous voudriez poursuivre?
Est-ce que vous êtes d'accord que le monde appartient aux pauvres?
Expliquez.

1. More on the present participle

1. Read these sentences and their English equivalents.

Françoise a rencontré Frank en
faisant des courses.

Françoise met Frank while she was shopping.

Françoise a rencontré Frank
faisant des courses.

Françoise met Frank while he was shopping.

   a. Which French sentence says *Françoise* was shopping? |

      Françoise a rencontré Frank en faisant des courses.

   b. In the other sentence, who's doing the shopping? |

      Frank

   c. Is *en* used when the present participle refers to the *subject* of the sentence or when it refers to *someone else*? |

      When it refers to the subject of the sentence.

When a present participle is preceded by *en*, it always refers to the subject of the sentence.

When a present participle is used *without* the preposition *en*, it may refer to someone other than the subject. In that case, *qui* + verb can be substituted for the present participle.

2. Write the English equivalents of these sentences.

   a. Elle aime écouter la radio en conduisant sa voiture. |

      She likes to listen to the radio while she drives her car.

   b. Nous connaissons plusieurs ouvriers travaillant dans cette usine.

      We know many workers working in this factory.

   c. Les voyageurs partant à 9h arrivent à Montréal à 10h. |

      Passengers leaving at nine (will) arrive in Montreal at ten.

3. Rewrite each sentence with a present participle.

   a. J'ai rencontré des spectateurs qui faisaient des paris. |

      J'ai rencontré des spectateurs faisant des paris.

   b. Il y a une foule énorme qui applaudit les coureurs à l'arrivée. |

      Il y a une foule énorme applaudissant les coureurs à l'arrivée.

4. *En* is the only preposition which can introduce a present participle. Its meaning can be *while* (doing) or *by (doing)*. *All* English prepositions must be followed by the *-ing* form of the verb: *after* (doing), *before* (doing), *without* (doing), etc. The only exception is the preposition *to*.

In French, all prepositions except *en* are followed by the infinitive.

5. Give the French equivalent of the following phrases:

   a. before watching TV

   b. without having eaten

   c. instead of singing the "Marseillaise"

   d. while listening to the president |

      a. avant de regarder la télévision   b. sans avoir mangé   c. au lieu de chanter la «Marseillaise»   d. en écoutant le président

Tell about one thing you do while doing something else.

2. Sentences with two object pronouns: *passé composé*

Frame 1 is for review.

1. A friend of yours warns you not to repeat what she has been telling you to other people. Rewrite her commands, using two object pronouns.
   a. Ne dis pas ce secret à ton frère.
   b. Ne raconte pas cette histoire à tes parents.
   c. Ne décris *(describe)* pas la scène à Michel.
   d. N'explique pas mes idées à tes copains.
   e. N'annonce pas la nouvelle à Béatrice.
   f. Ne répète pas mes opinions à tes amis. |

   a. Ne le lui dis pas. b. Ne la leur raconte pas. c. Ne la lui décris pas. d. Ne les leur explique pas. e. Ne la lui annonce pas. f. Ne les leur répète pas.

2. Now look at these sentences in the *passé composé*.

   > Richard a montré sa nouvelle moto à Thérèse.
   > Richard la lui a montrée.

   a. Do the object pronouns come before the auxiliary *avoir (a)*, or before the past participle? |

   before *avoir* (Object pronouns always precede the auxiliary verb.)

   b. When a verb in the *passé composé* is preceded by its direct object, what must agree with the direct object? |

   the past participle

   c. *Montrée* above agrees with the pronoun _____, which refers to the noun phrase _____. |

   la; sa nouvelle moto

3. In the following sentences, M. Radar's boss asks him to do several things. M. Radar replies that he did them yesterday. Write his answers to the requests, using object pronouns wherever possible. Remember to make the necessary agreements between the direct object and the participle. Check your spelling carefully.

   Modèle: Je voudrais que vous montriez ces chiffres à M. Mauriac. |

   Je les lui ai montrés hier.

   a. Je voudrais que vous envoyiez la carte d'anniversaire à Mme Valérie. |
   b. Donnez les cassettes à M. Juillard, s'il vous plaît. |
   c. Je voudrais que vous montriez ce cahier à Mlle Diaz et à Mme Houle. |
   d. Je voudrais que vous demandiez les livres à M. Nadeau. |
   e. Donnez ma réponse à M. Montreuil, s'il vous plaît. |

   a. Je la lui ai envoyée hier.
   b. Je les lui ai données hier.

   c. Je le leur ai montré hier.
   d. Je les lui ai demandés hier.
   e. Je la lui ai donnée hier.

4. Rewrite the sentences below using direct and indirect object pronouns. Remember that the past participle agrees with the direct object pronoun that precedes it. (See key.)

 a. Jean a montré sa voiture à sa sœur.
 b. Le boulanger a vendu les croissants à Eloïse.
 c. Henri et Catherine ont donné le cadeau aux enfants.
 d. J'ai rendu le dictionnaire au prof.

À Propos! Make a statement about something you wanted to give or show to someone. Then explain under what circumstances you did it, or tell why you didn't. Use object pronouns.

3. Review practice: the subjunctive

1. The whole Duval family has come down with a mysterious disease. Dr. Duval prescribes the treatment for himself and the rest of the family. Complete his orders, using the verbs in parentheses. (See key.)

 a. Tout le monde, je défends qu'on _____ (regarder) constamment la télévision.
 b. Henriette, il est essentiel que tu _____. (se reposer)
 c. Il est nécessaire que nous _____ des jus de fruits. (prendre)
 d. Je souhaite que les enfants _____ leurs médicaments (*medicine*). (prendre)
 e. Je désire qu'on _____ au bord de la mer. (aller)
 f. Il est important que je _____ mon journal. (lire)
 g. Françoise, il impossible que tu _____ au bureau aujourd'hui. (aller)
 h. Anne, je ne veux pas que tu _____ avec ton ami ce soir. (sortir)

2. Complete the sentences with the infinitive or subjunctive form, as appropriate. (See key.)

 a. Nous aimons mieux _____ au cinéma qu'au théâtre. (aller)
    Mais il faut que nous _____ au supermarché. (aller)
 b. Nous voulons qu'il _____ au théâtre avec nous. (aller)
    Mais il est important qu'il _____ ce poème. (finir)
 c. Elles veulent _____ avec nous. (venir)
    Mais nous ne désirons pas qu'elles _____ avec nous. (venir)
 d. Nous souhaitons _____ l'auto. (prendre)
    Mais il faut que nous _____ nos vélos. (prendre)
    Et nous préférons qu'ils _____ leurs vélos aussi. (prendre)

3. Pierre is talking to an old salt who tells him about life at sea. Write the old sailor's statements with the correct form of the verb in parentheses. You must decide whether to use the infinitive, the indicative, or the subjunctive. (See key.)

a. Bon, tu veux / marin. (devenir)
b. Tu veux que je te / la vie d'un marin? (décrire)
c. D'abord, il faut que tu / à naviguer *(to navigate)*. (apprendre)
d. Il faut que tu / loin. (partir)
e. Quelquefois, le capitaine veut que les marins / toute la nuit. (travailler)
f. Quelquefois il faut / des tempêtes. (braver)
g. Il ne faut pas / le danger. (craindre)
h. Est-ce que tu / le poisson? Un marin en mange beaucoup. (aimer)

À Propos!   Connaissez-vous des marins? Aimeriez-vous être marin? Pourquoi?

Vocabulaire

Noms

l'antiquaire *m.* *antique dealer*
l'article *m.* *article*
le capitaine *captain*
la collection *collection*
le creux *hollow, cavity*
l'horizon *m.* *horizon*
la jeunesse *youth*
les jumeaux *pl.* *twins;* le jumeau
 m.s.; la jumelle *f.s.*
le perroquet *parrot*
la poétesse *(woman) poet*
le rêve *dream, daydream*
le vers *line of poetry;* les vers *pl.*
 verses, poetry

Adjectifs

aérien, -ne *airy, ethereal*
bref, brève *brief*
inconnu, -e *unknown*
précis, -e *precise*
sensible *sensitive*

Verbes

briller *to shine*
découvrir *discover*
se demander *to wonder*
entretenir *to take care of*
inquiéter *to worry*
naviguer *to navigate*
prêter *to lend*

Autres mots et expressions

à l'instant *at once*
au lieu *instead*
dont *whose, of/from which*
lequel, lesquels, laquelle,
 lesquelles *who, whom, which,*
 that
mal à la tête *headache*

Terrasse de café ensoleillée (sunny) et acceuillante: quel plaisir de se reposer en buvant une tasse de thé!

PRÉPARATION 80

1. The subjunctive of *faire*

1. a. Write the subjunctive form of *faire* from this sentence.
   Nous voudrions que le journaliste fasse un reportage
   sur l'arrivée du président. |

   fasse

   b. The subjunctive stem of *faire* has only one form. It is _____. |

   fass-

2. Use these expressions with *faire* to complete a–f logically. Write
   the whole *que* clause.

faire la cuisine	faire des bêtises
faire des économies	faire attention à
faire beau	faire des courses
faire le tour du monde	

   Modèle: Quand ma mère n'est pas là, il faut que je _____. |

   que je fasse la cuisine

   a. Il faut que je _____. Il n'y a rien à manger à la maison. |

   que je fasse des courses

   b. Si tu veux acheter un bateau, il faut que tu _____. |

   que tu fasses des économies

   c. Pour visiter tous les pays francophones, il faut que nous
   _____. |

   que nous fassions le tour du monde

   d. Quand ils naviguent la nuit, il faut que les marins _____ aux
   étoiles (*stars*). |

   que les marins fassent attention

   e. Cet examen est important. Il ne faut pas que vous _____. |

   que vous fassiez des bêtises

   f. Je suis content qu'il _____. Je peux me promener. |

   qu'il fasse beau

À Propos!   Express an opinion about someone else's ability to save money (*faire des économies*), and give a reason: *Je (suis content/e) que tu fasses des économies, parce que... .*

2. Practice with the subjunctive expressing emotions

1. Use the expressions listed below in French equivalents for sentences a–b. Remember to use the subjunctive.

> être content que   être ravi que
> être triste que   être surpris que

  a. I'm surprised she understands this book. |
     Je suis surpris/e qu'elle comprenne ce livre.
  b. My parents are glad that I don't go out every night. |
     Mes parents sont contents que je ne sorte pas tous les soirs.
  c. Michèle is sad that Pierre is leaving. |
     Michèle est triste que Pierre parte.
  d. We're delighted that you *(vous)* are coming to see us. |
     Nous sommes ravis (ravies) que vous veniez nous voir.

2. Rewrite the following statements, starting each sentence with the phrase in parentheses. (See key.)
   > *Modèle:* Nous aimons ce programme de télévision. (Il est surpris...) |
   > Il est surpris que nous aimions ce programme de télévision.

  a. Vous faites des fautes. (Nous regrettons...)
  b. Tu ne fais pas attention aux voitures. (Je suis furieuse...)
  c. Vous ne voyagez pas cet hiver. (Il est content...)
  d. Nous habitons ici. (Ma mère est ravie...)
  e. Ils ne connaissent pas bien les États-Unis. (Nous sommes surpris...)
  f. Elle part demain. (Il est très heureux...)
  g. Tu quittes Paris. (Je suis triste...)

À Propos!

Express (with the subjunctive) a strong feeling about a current news item.

3. Review of *y*

1. The word *y* is used in several different ways as shown in the following sentences. Write the English equivalent of each French sentence.
   a. *Y* can represent a place: *Nous n'allons pas à la plage aujourd'hui, mais nous y allons demain.* |
      We're not going to the beach today, but we're going (there) tomorrow.

b. *Y* is used instead of *lui* or *leur* as an indirect object pronoun, replacing *à* + an inanimate noun: *Marie a compris les questions, mais elle n'y a pas répondu.* |

Marie understood the questions, but she didn't answer them.

c. *Y* can represent abstract ideas, especially with verbs that express thought: *Je ne comprends pas la situation économique, et je n'aime pas y penser.* |

I don't understand the economic situation and I don't like to think about it.

d. *Y* occurs in certain idiomatic expressions: *Si vous êtes prêts, allez-y!* |

If you're ready, go ahead! (Go to it!) (Other expressions containing *y* are: *il y a*—there is, there are; *ça y est*—all set, ready; *on y va?*—shall we go ahead?)

2. Rewrite the following sentences, using *y*.
   a. Je voudrais aller à la bibliothèque. |

   Je voudrais y aller.

   b. Il faut qu'il aille en Afrique. |

   Il faut qu'il y aille.

   c. Tu n'es pas allé à Tunis l'année dernière? |

   Tu n'y es pas allé l'année dernière?

   d. Peux-tu répondre à ces questions? |

   Peux-tu y répondre?

   e. Il faut que tu fasses attention à ta prononciation. |

   Il faut que tu y fasses attention.

   f. N'allez pas au supermarché maintenant. |

   N'y allez pas maintenant.

À Propos!   Êtes-vous jamais allé/e à New York? à Londres? Si oui, à quelle occasion?

4. Relative pronouns after a preposition

1. Relative clauses can be introduced by a preposition. Look at the sentences below:

   La jeune fille *à qui* tu parlais hier est ma cousine.
   La jeune fille *à laquelle* tu parlais hier est ma cousine.

   a. What relative pronoun follows the preposition *à* in the first sentence? |

   qui

   b. What relative pronoun follows the preposition *à* in the second sentence? |

   laquelle

c. What word is represented by *qui* and by *laquelle?*
> la jeune fille

d. Write an English equivalent for both sentences.
> The girl you were speaking to (the girl to whom you were speaking) yesterday is my cousin.

2. a. Look at this sentence: *Le bureau dans lequel tu es entré est le bureau du doyen* (dean). What is the relative pronoun and what word does it represent?
> lequel; le bureau

b. Write an English equivalent for the French sentence in *d.*
> The office (that) you entered (in which you entered) is the dean's office.

Qui is used after prepositions when the antecedent (the word replaced by *qui*) is a person only. *Qui* has only one form. *Lequel (laquelle,* etc.) is used after prepositions when the antecedent is a person or a thing; it must match the antecedent in gender and number.

> C'est la personne *à qui/à laquelle* j'ai écrit.
> Ce sont les gens *avec qui/avec lesquels* il a parlé.

3. Complete each of the following sentences with *qui* or a form of *lequel.*
   a. C'est la personne à _____ le message a été envoyé.
   b. C'est la chaise sur _____ elle s'est assise.
   c. C'est le fruit dans _____ elle a mordu.
   d. C'est la porte par _____ elle est sortie.
   e. Ce sont les routes sur _____ elle a couru.
   f. Ce sont les gens avec _____ elle a parlé.
   g. C'est la rivière dans _____ elle s'est jetée.
   > a. qui/à laquelle   b. laquelle   c. lequel   d. laquelle   e. lesquelles   f. qui/auxquels   g. laquelle

4. *Quoi:* You have seen that *quoi* is used for things when no antecedent has been mentioned. Compare:

> Voici deux poèmes. Lequel préférez-vous?
> *Avec quoi* avez-vous fait ce gâteau?

Quoi is also used as a relative pronoun with no specific antecedent:

> Je ne sais pas *à quoi* il pense.
> Je ne sais pas *avec quoi* on ouvre cette boîte.
> Je ne sais pas *par quoi* commencer.

Dont: When the preposition *de* is used to introduce persons or things, relative constructions such as these are possible:

> Voici le poète *de qui* je parlais.
> Voici le poète duquel je parlais.

Voici le poème *duquel* je parlais. (Remember that *qui* cannot be used when the antecedent is a thing.)

Dont is another relative pronoun, which may be used instead of *de qui* or *duquel, de laquelle, desquels, desquelles*:

> Voici le poète *dont* je parlais.
> Voici le poème *dont* je parlais.

Dont may be used for persons and for things. It has only one form. It is strictly a relative pronoun, and cannot be used as an interrogative pronoun.

4. Complete the sentences with *dont*, or *de qui, duquel, de laquelle*, etc.

  Modèle: Ce n'est pas le livre _____ j'ai besoin. |

  dont, duquel

  a. Ce sont les poèmes _____ il est l'auteur. |

  dont, desquels

  b. Paul est l'ami _____ j'ai reçu cette carte. |

  dont, de qui, duquel

  c. Chicago est la ville _____ on m'a beaucoup parlé. |

  dont, de laquelle

  d. Ce sont les amis _____ je vous ai donné l'adresse. |

  dont, de qui, desquels

  e. Je ne sais pas le nom de la personne _____ j'ai reçu ce cadeau. |

  dont, de qui, de laquelle

Vocabulaire

Noms
l'arrivée   *arrival*

Adjectifs
urgent, -e   *urgent*

Verbes
faire attention à   *to pay attention to;*
  ~ des bêtises   *to act silly, to do something stupid;* ~ le tour du monde   *to travel around the world*

Note Culturelle
Les vacances des jeunes

Contrairement aux jeunes Américains, la plupart[1] des lycéens français ne travaillent pas pendant l'été. Beaucoup passent[2] leurs vacances en famille. Ils vont avec leurs parents au bord de la mer, à la campagne ou à l'étranger[3]. Ou bien ils vont chez leurs grands-parents ou cousins, souvent dans une autre partie de la France.

D'autres jeunes vont dans un pays étranger—surtout en Angleterre, en Allemagne et en Espagne—pour apprendre une langue étrangère, ou pour se perfectionner[4] dans la langue qu'ils étudient au lycée. Les familles font souvent des échanges[5]. Ainsi, un jeune Français va vivre dans une famille anglaise. Ensuite un des enfants anglais vient dans la famille française. D'autres jeunes

(au-dessus de 18 ans) peuvent être «au pair» dans une famille étrangère. Le plus souvent ce sont des jeunes filles; elles vivent dans une famille, s'occupent des enfants et font quelques heures de travail dans la maison. En échange, elles sont logées et nourries[6]. Si leurs parents le permettent[7], et s'ils ont assez d'argent, beaucoup de jeunes Français aiment voyager seuls ou avec des copains, en France ou à l'étranger. Certains utilisent leurs vélos ou leurs motos. D'autres font de l'auto-stop pour circuler[8] en France ou aller dans d'autres pays d'Europe. Beaucoup bénéficient de[9] tarifs réduits[10] dans les trains. Le soir, au lieu d'aller à l'hôtel, ils font du camping ou bien ils s'arrêtent dans des auberges de jeunesse[11].

1 most 2 spend 3 in foreign countries 4 to improve 5 make exchanges 6 they get food and lodging 7 permit 8 travel 9 benefit from 10 reduced fares 11 youth hostels

---

Quand on n'a pas assez d'argent pour aller sur la Côte d'Azur, on fait de l'auto-stop.

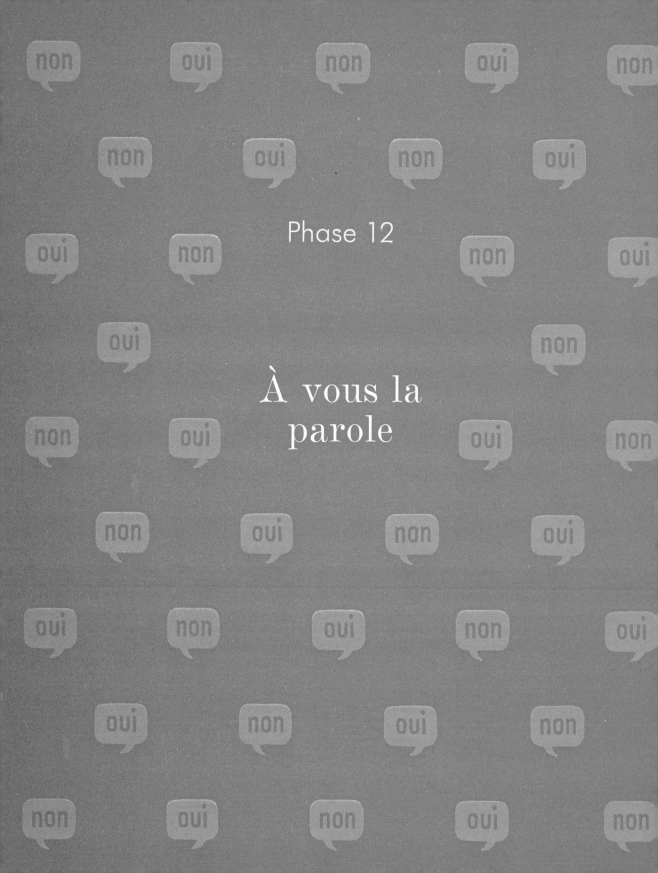

Phase 12

À vous la
parole

Qu'est-ce que vous allez apprendre?

In this Phase you will have the chance to conduct polls among your friends and classmates regarding such topics as travel, jobs, and parent-child relationships. You will discuss the response of French people to certain opinion questions, such as: what French girls think of their future and what professions and occupations their parents would like for them. You will also encounter another "language": *franglais*.

Communication

To help you with this task you will learn:
   Some impersonal expressions that express doubt.
   To express relationships between events by using conjunctions that require the subjunctive.
   The imperative of *avoir* and *être*.
   Uses of the past subjunctive, the past conditional, and the pluperfect to relate events in the past.
   The pronouns *celui* (the one) and *ce qui/ce que* (what...). The *passé simple* (literary past).
   Where to place adverbs in French sentences.
You will reinforce your competence with a number of the structures you have studied recently.

Culture

Vacations for French people; social behavior among young people in France.

PRÉPARATION 81

1. Impersonal expressions of certainty and doubt

Consider impersonal expressions that require the subjunctive, such as *il faut, il vaut mieux.*

1. Which is true?
   a. These expressions state that something is a fact or that it definitely will happen.
   b. These expressions give the speaker's opinion or wish about something that may or may not happen. |

   1. b

2. Look at the following sentence which states a fact: *Il est certain que la situation économique mondiale est instable.* Is the indicative or the subjunctive used after *Il est certain?* |

   2. indicative

3. Here are a number of other impersonal expressions which are generally followed by the indicative because they express certainty rather than doubt.

il est **certain** que	il **paraît** que
il est **évident** que	il est **clair** que + **indicative**
il **semble** que	il est **vrai** que
il est **probable** que	il est **sûr** que

   Negation: Il **n'**est **pas certain** que + **subjunctive**

Say that what is true today is likely to be true tomorrow. Use the expressions indicated, plus the future tense.
   a. Il fait beau. (il est probable) |
      Il est probable qu'il fera beau demain. (Note: *Il est possible* is treated as expressing a lack of certainty, and is followed by the subjunctive.)
   b. Thérèse aime beaucoup Paris. (il est certain) |
      Il est certain qu'elle aimera Paris.
   c. Elle visite le Louvre. (il est sûr) |
      Il est sûr qu'elle visitera le Louvre.

4. When these expressions are used in a negative construction, however, they are followed by the subjunctive:

   Il n'est pas certain que la situation économique mondiale redevienne stable bientôt.

Express doubts that Thérèse will be able to go to Paris. Use the expressions indicated, plus the subjunctive.

a. Elle a assez d'argent. (il ne semble pas) |

Il ne semble pas qu'elle ait assez d'argent.

b. Elle est riche. (il n'est pas vrai) |

Il n'est pas vrai qu'elle soit riche.

c. Elle n'ira pas à Paris. (il est possible) |

Il est possible qu'elle n'aille pas à Paris.

2. The demonstrative pronoun *celui*

The English pronoun *the one (pl.: the ones)* is used to refer to a specific thing or person. The French equivalent, like most French pronouns, shows gender as well as number; it therefore has four forms. This Préparation deals only with the masculine singular. The other forms are presented later.

1. Read this sentence.

> In that group of musicians, the one who is playing the violin is my cousin.

a. What noun phrase could replace *the one?* |

the musician (The pronoun the one refers to a specific person.)

b. The pronoun is followed by information that helps to distinguish or identify it. In the sentence above, what distinguishes the musician who is a cousin from the other musicians? |

He is playing the violin.

2. Write the phrase that tells exactly what person or thing is referred to. In other words, write *the one* plus the relative clause.

   We looked at several paintings, and we bought the one that our friend had painted. |

   the one that our friend had painted

3. The sentences in this frame show the masculine singular French equivalent for *the one*. After each sentence, write the pronoun and the relative clause, as you did for the English sentence in frame 2.

   Modèle: J'ai beaucoup d'amis; celui que je préfère s'appelle Jean-Pierre. |

   celui que je préfère

a. J'adore ces chats, surtout *(especially)* celui qui joue avec la balle. |

   celui qui joue avec la balle

b. Nous avons regardé beaucoup de vélos; celui que nous avons acheté n'était pas trop cher. |

   celui que nous avons acheté

Préparation 81

4. The French equivalent above for *the one* is _____. |
    celui

5. With a demonstrative adjective, *the one* becomes *this one* or *that one*.
   Compare the following French sentences with the English equivalents to see how *this one* and *that one* are expressed in French.

I like hats, but I don't like that one.   J'aime les chapeaux, mais je
                                             n'aime pas celui-là.
My camera is good, but this one is really terrific.   Mon appareil-photo est bon, mais
                                             celui-ci est vraiment formidable.

   a. What is added to *celui* to express the meaning *this one*? |
       -ci
   b. What is added to express *that one*? |
       -là

The words *-ci* and *-là* are also used after demonstrative noun
phrases when it is necessary to distinguish between *this* and *that*.

> Ce garçon-ci est français.   *This boy is French.*

6. In this frame you see English sentences followed by partial
   French equivalents. Write the completion of each French sentence.
   Modèle: *I've seen this dog before, but I've never seen that one.*
   J'ai déjà vu ce chien-ci, mais je n'ai jamais vu _____. |
       celui-là
   a. *These bikes are French; that one is Italian.*
      Ces vélos-ci sont français; _____ est italien. | a. celui-là
   b. *That boat is faster than this one.*
      Ce bateau-là est plus rapide que _____. | b. celui-ci
   c. *This book is more interesting than that one.*
      Ce livre-ci est plus intéressant que _____. | c. celui-là

7. *Celui* is also used to talk about possession. Give the English equivalent of the following example.

> Le cahier de Nancy est rouge, et celui de Serge est vert. |

   Nancy's notebook is red, and Serge's is green. (*Serge's* is short for *Serge's one,* but in
   English the pronoun is not expressed. *Celui* must be expressed in French.)

8. Possession is expressed with *celui* just as it is with a noun—by adding *de* plus the name of the owner. Give French equivalents:
   a. Roger's pencil and Paul's |
       le crayon de Roger et celui de Paul
   b. Alexandra's book and Victor's |
       le livre d'Alexandra et celui de Victor
   c. our record and our friend's |
       notre disque et celui de notre ami/e

Demonstrative pronouns are always followed by additional information that identifies them. The additional information may be a relative *qui* or *que* clause, *-ci* or *-là*, or a possession phrase with *de*.

9. Complete the following sentences, using one of these expressions: *celui qui, celui que, celui de,* or *celui-là.*

a. J'ai perdu mon stylo. J'ai pris ____ ma sœur. | a. celui de

b. Tu vois ces piétons? Je connais ____ porte une valise. | b. celui qui

c. Nous n'aimons pas beaucoup ce restaurant-ci, mais nous détestons vraiment ____. |

                                                          c. celui-là

d. Ce café-ci est ____ je préfère. | d. celui que

3. Noun subjects with inversion

1. If the subject is a noun or a name, not a pronoun, inversion can be used in questions that start with a question word.

Chantal va bien?	Comment va Chantal?
La table est vendue?	Où est la table?

When the subject of a *oui-non* question is a noun *(Chantal, la table)* there is a special interrogative pattern. Compare the informal and formal questions below.

Chantal va bien?	Chantal va-t-elle bien?
La table est vendue?	La table est-elle vendue?

What is added to the subject to permit inversion? |

a subject pronoun (of the same gender as the subject noun)

2. Rephrase these statements as *oui-non* questions, using inversion. After you check your answers, read them aloud.

a. Les voyages intéressent les jeunes. |

Les voyages intéressent-ils les jeunes?

b. L'auto est une manière agréable de voyager. |

L'auto est-elle une manière agréable de voyager?

c. Les représentants de commerce voyagent beaucoup. |

Les représentants de commerce voyagent-ils beaucoup?

d. *(Say this question before you write it.)* Un coopérant travaille dans un pays étranger. |

Un coopérant travaille-t-il dans un pays étranger?

3. Marcel is answering questions that his friend from the United States asked him in a letter. Write the question that corresponds to each answer, using inversion whenever possible.

Modèle: Oui, je suis en vacances. |

Es-tu en vacances?

a. Non, je ne vais pas en Suisse cette année.

b. Mes parents vont bien, merci.

Note Culturelle

Les vacances des Français

En France les personnes qui travaillent ont droit à[1] cinq semaines de congé payé[2] par an. Cela veut dire que[3] tous les Français—ou presque[4] tous—prennent un mois de vacances pendant l'été. Le mois favori pour les vacances est le mois d'août, et le premier août, le grand départ commence. Il y a alors des embouteillages[5] sur toutes les routes principales et les villes deviennent presque désertes.

Beaucoup de familles partent au bord de la mer. Certains vont sur la Côte d'Azur à cause de ses belles plages et de son soleil. D'autres préfèrent la Bretagne, avec ses rochers[6] et son eau plutôt[7] froide. D'autres encore aiment le camping et ils partent dans leurs caravanes à travers[8] la France. Et enfin, il y a les familles qui vont chez les grands-parents ou chez les oncles et tantes qui habitent à la campagne.

Mais les Français ne restent pas tous en France. Beaucoup vont à l'étranger[9], surtout[10] en Espagne où les hôtels ne sont généralement pas trop chers et où il fait chaud. L'Italie attire[11] les personnes qui s'intéressent à l'art et l'architecture. La Suisse et l'Autriche attirent ceux qui aiment l'alpinisme ou qui veulent respirer l'air pur des montagnes.

Certains organismes offrent un autre moyen de passer des vacances à l'étranger. On a établi dans plusieurs pays, à la plage ou à la montagne, des petits «villages» avec toutes les distractions possibles[12]. Au Club

Méditerranée, par exemple, on paie tout à l'avance[13], et pendant son séjour on n'utilise pas d'argent parce que tout est compris[14] dans le prix global[15]. Si on est au bord de la mer, on peut faire de la voile, de la plongée sous-marine[16], du ski nautique, du tennis, sans payer de supplément[17].

1 are entitled to 2 paid vacation 3 means that 4 almost 5 traffic jams 6 rocks, boulders 7 rather 8 throughout 9 to foreign countries 10 especially 11 attracts 12 with every possible activity 13 in advance 14 included 15 overall price 16 scuba diving 17 additional charge

Plage à la Grande-Motte, près de Montpellier.

c. Oui, ma sœur aime son travail.
d. Oui, elle parle anglais.
e. Oui, elle voudrait visiter les États-Unis.

a. Vas-tu en Suisse cette année?   b. Comment vont tes parents?/Tes parents vont-ils bien?   c. Ta sœur aime-t-elle son travail?   d. Parle-t-elle anglais?   e. Voudrait-elle visiter les États-Unis?

À Propos!

Using inversion, prepare a couple of questions to ask your class-mates about a course, their families, a TV program, etc.

Vocabulaire

Expressions de certitude

il est certain   *it is certain*
il est évident   *it is evident, obvious*
il me semble   *it seems to me*
il est probable   *it is probable, likely*
il paraît que   *it appears, seems*
il est clair   *it is clear*
il est vrai   *it is true*
il est sûr   *it is sure, certain*

Expressions de doute

il n'est pas certain/évident, etc.   *it is not certain, obvious, etc.*
il est possible   *it is possible (but not certain)*

PRÉPARATION 82

1. More on the subjunctive: *avant de* vs. *avant que*

1. Compare these two sentences.

> Je veux partir.
> Je veux que vous partiez.

When is the infinitive construction used—when each action has a different subject or one subject? |

one subject (je)

2. Read the two sentences below:

Jeanne prend son petit déjeuner *avant de quitter* la maison.
Jeanne prend son petit déjeuner *avant que nous quittions* la
  maison.

a. Give the English equivalents of the italic phrases in the sentences above. |

before leaving, before we leave

b. Which form follows *avant que*—infinitive or subjunctive?

the subjunctive (because the second action of the sentence has a second subject)

3. Use *avant que* to indicate what the second group of people will do, as in the model.

Modèle: Mes parents iront à Londres avant d'aller à Paris.
  (nous) |

Mes parents iront à Londres avant que nous allions à Paris.

a. Achetez les billets avant d'aller au théâtre. (nous) |

Achetez les billets avant que nous allions au théâtre.

b. Suzanne ferme les fenêtres avant de sortir. (la famille) |

Suzanne ferme les fenêtres avant que la famille sorte.

c. Ta mère fait-elle une liste avant de faire le marché? (tu) |

Ta mère fait-elle une liste avant que tu fasses le marché?

d. Je m'en vais avant de dire des bêtises. (vous) |

Je m'en vais avant que vous disiez des bêtises.

e. Il partira avant de finir le dessert. (nous) |

Il partira avant que nous finissions le dessert.

f. Allons à la banque avant d'acheter ces meubles. (tu) |

Allons à la banque avant que tu achètes ces meubles.

2. The past subjunctive

1. Look at the following sentences:

   Je suis ravi que Martine *ait aimé* l'Italie.
   Je ne suis pas surpris qu'elle y *soit retournée* pour ses vacances.

   a. Is the narrator expressing an opinion about an event in the future, present, or past? |
      in the past
   b. How is the past subjunctive formed? |
      with the present subjunctive form of avoir or être + the past participle

2. Mme Nouvelles is gossiping with a neighbor. Use expressions of opinion (*je suis désolé, il est possible,* etc.) and the past subjunctive to write what Mme Nouvelles said about her targets. (See key.)
   a. M. Boitout who returned late last night.
   b. Mlle Froide who caught a cold (*attraper un rhume*).
   c. Mme Avare who stole 100 francs from a neighbor (*voler quelque chose à quelqu'un*).
   d. M. Gauche who fell down in his garden.

3. Reading comprehension

Sondage: les jeunes filles d'aujourd'hui

This part contains a recent *sondage°* on the opinions of young French   opinion poll
girls. What follows will prepare you for a class discussion on the
sondage. The italicized words are discussed in the frames.
(This poll is adapted from a poll by Jacqueline Remy in *L'Express,*
June 14–20, 1976, and is used by permission of the author.)

Comment vous sentez-vous en pensant à votre avenir?	
Enthousiaste	14,4%
Optimiste	40,8
Indifférente	7,3
Inquiète	32,4
Résignée	2,6
Ne sait pas	2,5

1. The word *avenir* is made up of two words: *à* and *venir*—literally,

(that which is) to come. The English equivalent for *l'avenir* is the
_____. |

future

2. *Comment vous sentez-vous* contains the verb *sentir*. An easy cognate related to *sentir* is *le sentiment*. Using *le sentiment* and the context clues, can you guess what *Comment vous sentez-vous* means? |

How do you feel?

3. Look at the adjectives in the *sondage*. Which adjective means *anxious*? Which means *having given up*? |

inquiète *(unquiet)*; résignée *(resigned)*

4. Answer the question with a complete French sentence: *Quel pourcentage des jeunes filles se sentent optimistes?* |

40,8% (quarante virgule huit pourcent) des jeunes filles se sentent optimistes.

Quel métier—ou profession—souhaiteriez-vous le plus° exercer si cela vous était possible?		
		most of all
Éducatrice (pour délinquants ou inadaptés), assistante sociale°, puéricultrice°	13,7%	social worker / early childhood specialist
Hôtesse d'accueil, hôtesse de l'air, secrétaire	12,7	
Professeur, institutrice°	11,6	elementary school teacher
Professions manuelles, vendeuse, coiffeuse	10,3	
Médecin, chirurgien, dentiste, pharmacienne, psychiatre, psychanalyste	7,7	
Théâtre, cinéma, arts	6,4	
Vétérinaire	5,7	
Décoratrice, étalagiste°	2,9	window dresser
Ne rien faire («Vivre et respirer»)	2,5	
Profession juridique	2,0	

8. *Souhaiteriez* is a conditional form of *souhaiter*. On January 1st, friends say: *Je te souhaite une bonne année.* What do they mean? |

I wish you a good year. *(Le métier souhaité* is the "wished-for" job.)

9. In Phase 7 you read *Les Sénégalais sont accueillants. Accueillant* comes from *accueillir,* to welcome. Is an *hôtesse d'accueil* a secretary, a flight attendant, a receptionist, or a travel agent? |

a réceptionist (usually in a large company)

10. a. *«Vivre et respirer»,* as it's used here, means the same thing as *ne rien faire*—to do _____. |

nothing

*Au Centre Pompidou.
Déjeuner entre amies.*

b. If you don't recognize the verb *vivre,* think of the expression
Vive la France—Long _____ France. |
live

c. What is a literal translation of *vivre et respirer?* |
to live and breathe

Quel métier—ou profession—vos parents souhaitent-ils que vous exerciez?		
«Ils me laissent° faire ce que je veux»	41,8%	allow
Profession libérale (médecin, pharmacienne, avocate, ingénieur, etc.)	9,8	
Secrétaire, hôtesse	8,9	
«Je ne sais pas ce qu'ils veulent»	8,7	
Professeur, institutrice	7,6	
«Ils s'en moquent»	5,4	
Professions manuelles, vendeuse	5,1	
N'importe quoi, «pourvu que° ce soit un bon métier»	3,8	as long as
Infirmière, laborantine°	3,2	lab assistant
Autres réponses	3,7	

12. Give the English equivalent of *Ils me laissent faire ce que je veux.* |
They let me do what I want.

13. If *ils s'en moquent* means *they don't care,* how would you say *I don't care?* |

4. The pluperfect and indirect speech

1. Here are a few sentences where Jacques tells a bit about his family. Use indirect discourse to report what the speaker says. Begin each of your sentences with *Il dit que (qu')...*
   a. J'ai peu connu mon père.
   b. Mon père et mon grand-père étaient des marins.
   c. Avant d'embarquer pour les pays lointains, ils ont tracé le chemin sur les cartes.
   d. Moi, je déteste faire de la voile parce que ça me fait peur. |

   a. Il dit qu'il a peu connu son père.   b. Il dit que son père et son grand-père étaient des marins.   c. Il dit qu'avant d'embarquer pour les pays lointains, ils ont tracé le chemin sur les cartes.   d. Il dit que, lui, il déteste faire de la voile parce que ça lui fait peur.

2. We may wish to use the past rather than the present to report the same statements, and we would say:

   Il a dit qu'il avait peu connu son père.

   What is the English equivalent of this sentence? |

   He said that he had known his father very little.

3. The tense *had known* is called *the pluperfect.* In French, the corresponding tense is called *le plus-que-parfait* and it is formed in the same way:

   il avait connu   *he had known*

   In English, the auxiliary verb is in the past *(had),* whereas in French, the auxiliary verb is in the imperfect *(avait).*
   Give the meaning of *Le train était parti quand nous sommes arrivés.* |
   The train had left when we arrived.

Le Plus-que-parfait

j'avais ⎫	j'étais tombé(e)	je m'étais levé(e)
tu avais ⎪	tu étais tombé(e)	tu t'étais levé(e)
il/elle/on avait ⎬ oublié	il/elle/on était tombé(e)	il/elle/on s'était levé(e)
nous avions ⎪	nous étions tombés (ées)	nous nous étions levés (ées)
vous aviez ⎪	vous étiez tombés (ées)	vous vous étiez levés (ées)
ils/elles avaient ⎭	ils/elles étaient tombés (ées)	ils/elles s'étaient levés (ées)

4. Say that you didn't go to the movies because you had already seen the film. |

Je ne suis pas allé(e) au cinéma parce que j'avais déjà vu le film.

Say that you were furious because you had lost your keys. |

J'étais furieux(-euse) parce que j'avais perdu mes clés.

5. Madame Pipelet loves to report what the tenants of the apartment house did, and her friends enjoy repeating the news. Be one of her friends, according to the model. (See key.)

   Modèle: Les Thomas ont eu beaucoup d'invités hier soir. |

Ce matin, Mme Pipelet a dit que les Thomas avaient eu beaucoup d'invités hier soir.

   a. Les Roland sont rentrés de leurs vacances en Suisse hier.
   b. Le jeune Dupont a perdu sa bicyclette hier.
   c. M. Dupuis a acheté une nouvelle auto la semaine dernière.
   d. M. Lebrun est rentré à trois heures du matin dimanche dernier.
   e. La fille Dupont s'est mariée la semaine dernière.
   f. Elle a reçu des douzaines de cadeaux.
   g. Les Dupuis n'ont pas fait de cadeau de mariage.

Vocabulaire

Noms

un/une anthropologue *anthropologist*
une civilisation *civilization*
un emploi *job*
un invité, une invitée *guest*
une raison *reason*
une coutume *custom*
le luxe *luxury*
une auberge de jeunesse *youth hostel*
une caravane *camper-trailer*
l'auto-stop *(m.) hitchhiking*
une hôtesse de l'air *airline stewardess*
un steward *steward*
un astronaute *astronaut*
un représentant de commerce *sales representative*
le commerce *business, trade*
un homme d'affaires *businessman*
un militaire de carrière *a military man*
un routier *long-distance truck driver*
un diplomate *diplomat*
un consultant *consultant*

Verbes

faire du ski nautique *to water-ski*
pratiquer *to practice*

Adjectifs

local, -e, -aux *local*
modeste *unassuming*

PRÉPARATION 83

Ce que pensent les jeunes

Les Voyages

1. Pensez-vous que tous les jeunes devraient faire des voyages à l'étranger°?   abroad
   a. oui   b. non
2. Pour quelles raisons? (indiquez par ordre d'importance)
   a. pour visiter des pays différents
   b. pour rencontrer des personnes différentes
   c. pour apprécier des coutumes différentes
   d. pour apprécier des nourritures différentes
   e. pour apprendre des langues étrangères
   f. pour connaître d'autres formes d'art (musées, musique, etc.)
   g. pour connaître des climats différents

h. pour pratiquer des sports différents
   i. pour se reposer° dans un cadre° différent   to rest / setting
   j. pour mieux se connaître eux-mêmes°   to know themselves better
3. Si vous aviez seulement deux semaines pour faire un voyage à l'étranger, est-ce que vous préféreriez visiter:
   a. plusieurs pays.   c. un seul pays.
   b. deux pays.   d. une seule région.
4. Si vous voyagiez à l'étranger, iriez-vous:
   a. dans des hôtels de luxe.
   b. dans des hôtels modestes.
   c. dans des auberges de jeunesse.°   youth hostels
   d. dans un camping.
5. Quelle est la manière la plus agréable de voyager?
   a. l'avion   d. l'auto   g. le cheval°   horse
   b. le bateau   e. la moto   g. la caravane°   trailer
   c. le train   f. le vélo   i. l'auto-stop°   hitchhiking
6. Aimeriez-vous avoir un métier qui vous permettrait de voyager?
   a. oui
   b. non
7. Lesquels des métiers suivants choisiriez-vous? (par ordre de préférence)
   a. marin   k. missionnaire
   b. pilote   l. routier°   truck driver
   c. hôtesse de l'air/steward   m. chauffeur
   d. astronaute   n. diplomate
   e. représentant de commerce°   o. consultant en droit international°   traveling salesperson / consultant in international law
   f. employé dans une agence de voyage°   p. acteur   employee in a travel agency / stage or movie director
        q. metteur en scène°
   g. journaliste   r. avocat
   h. homme d'affaires°   s. médecin   businessman
   i. militaire de carrière°   professional military man
   j. coopérant°   French Peace Corps member

Échange d'idées   Avez-vous fait des voyages à l'étranger? Si oui, dans quels pays? Lequel de ces pays préférez-vous? Si non, quel(s) pays étranger(s) aimeriez-vous visiter?

1. *Ce qui, ce que*

1. Consider the interrogative pronouns in this dialogue:

     —Suzanne, qu'est-ce qui vous intéresse dans ce film?
     —Ce qui m'intéresse, c'est l'histoire.

—Et vous, Paul, qu'est-ce que vous aimez dans ce film?

—Ce que j'aime, c'est la musique.

Give the English equivalent of *qu'est-ce qui?* and *qu'est-ce que?*

what?

2. *What* is the English interrogative pronoun used to refer to things. It can also be used as a relative pronoun. Translate Suzanne's and Paul's responses to the questions in frame 1.

What interests me is the plot. What I like is the music.

	Subject	*Object*
Interrogative	qu'est-ce qui?	qu'est-ce que?
Relative	**ce qui...**	**ce que...**

These relative forms are used whenever the thing referred to has yet to be expressed or is of a vague, indefinite nature. In other words, they are used in the same way as the relative pronoun *what*.

Docteur, je ne sais pas *ce que* j'ai, mais je suis malade.
Doctor, I don't know what *is wrong with me, but I'm sick.*

3. Choose between *ce qui* and *ce que* to complete these sentences.
   a. Dis-moi _____ tu aimerais avoir pour le petit déjeuner.
   b. Savez-vous _____ est arrivé à la cafétéria aujourd'hui?
   c. Je ne comprends rien à _____ vous dites.
   d. Elle ne sait jamais _____ elle va acheter au marché.
   e. Moi, j'achète toujours _____ coûte le moins cher.

a. ce que   b. ce qui   c. ce que   d. ce qu'   e. ce qui

À Propos!

Qu'est-ce qui vous intéresse le plus dans la vie?
Qu'est-ce que vous aimez faire le dimanche?
(Use *ce qui* or *ce que* in your answers.)

2. Conjunctions requiring the subjunctive

1. Some conjunctions are followed by the indicative.

Je mange *parce que* j'ai faim.   *I eat because I am hungry.*
Puisque tu en as le temps,   *Since you have time, come and see me.*
 viens me voir.

Other conjunctions must be followed by the subjunctive. You already know *pour que* and *avant que*. Some others are:

quoique = *although*
Quoiqu'elle travaille beaucoup, elle n'a pas de bonnes notes.

bien que = *although*
Pierre est en classe aujourd'hui, bien qu'il n'aille pas bien.

afin que = *so that, in order that*
Je vais parler plus lentement afin que vous compreniez mieux.

en attendant que = *until*
En attendant que nous arrivions, elle a nettoyé sa chambre.

jusqu'à ce que = *until*
Nous avons attendu à l'aéroport jusqu'à ce que l'avion atterrisse.

pourvu que = *provided that, as long as*
Je te pardonnerai pourvu que tu me dises la vérité.

sans que = without (+ verb)
Ils sont partis sans que nous les ayons vus.

2. In formal writing, you might see a sentence like this:

Avant qu'on ne puisse être généreux envers *(towards)* les autres,
il fait qu'on soit bien nourri.

a. Here is the English equivalent of the sentence.

Before one can be generous toward others,
it is necessary that one be well-fed.

b. Is the *ne* in the phrase *qu'on ne puisse* a negative? |

no

This pleonastic (redundant or unnecessary) *ne* is often found after the following conjunctions, especially in formal or literary style.

avant que... (ne) = *before*
Avant que vous ne fassiez ce voyage, préparez bien votre
  itinéraire.

à moins que... (ne) = *unless*
L'inflation va continuer à moins que le président ne prenne des
  mesures strictes.

de peur que... (ne) = *for fear that*
L'armée protégeait la ville de peur que l'ennemi n'attaque.

3. Write the appropriate forms of the verbs in parentheses to com-

plete the following paragraphs, using *ne* where it could be used in formal style. (See key.)

Les magasins ont fermé *pour que* clients et employés (1. *pouvoir*) regarder passer le Tour de France. *Avant que* les cyclistes (2. *faire*) leur apparition, les spectateurs s'installent pour les attendre. Tous bavardent, mangent et boivent *jusqu'à ce qu*'ils (3. *voir*) les coureurs arriver.

Les personnes aux balcons sont très contentes *parce qu*'elles (4. *pouvoir*) voir facilement. Dans la rue, les gens se sont assis par terre, *à moins qu*'ils (5. *avoir*) des chaises pliantes. *Bien que* les heures d'attente (6. *être*) longues, personne ne veut partir, *de peur que* les coureurs (7. *arriver*) *sans que* leur passage (8. *être*) annoncé.

3. More on demonstrative pronouns

This section introduces the other forms of the demonstrative pronoun *celui* (the one).

1. One of these sentences contains a feminine demonstrative *article*. The other contains a feminine demonstrative *pronoun*.

> Je voudrais cette revue.
> Je voudrais celle qui est sur l'étagère.

Write the demonstrative *pronoun.* |

celle (Remember that a pronoun replaces a noun. *Cette* does not replace a noun, it only helps to identify a noun.)

2. Write the demonstrative pronouns from these sentences overheard in a bike shop. Also write the English equivalents.

a. Ces roues sont plus grandes que celles de mon vélo. |

celles; *Those wheels are bigger than the ones on my bike.*

b. Mes freins sont assez bons, mais ceux de Philippe sont meilleurs. |

ceux; *My brakes are pretty good, but Philippe's are better.*

	Masculine	Feminine
Singular	**celui**	**celle**
Plural	**ceux**	**celles**

A demonstrative pronoun is always followed by information about the noun it replaces and can be followed by *de* to show possession.

4. A *moniteur* at a summer camp is trying to sort out his campers' things and one camper is telling him to whom the things belong. Use demonstrative pronouns to write his statements.

Modèle: Ce chandail? (Bernard) |
               C'est celui de Bernard.

a. Cette chemise? (David) |

b. Ces chaussettes? (Jean) |

c. Ces pulls? (Guy) |

d. Ce pantalon? (Thierry) |

a. C'est celle de David.

b. Ce sont celles de Jean.

c. Ce sont ceux de Guy.

d. C'est celui de Thierry.

5. A group of cycling fans are discussing the Tour de France. Write the demonstrative pronoun plus the relative pronoun *qui* or *que* to complete their sentences.

    Modèle: Le coureur qui porte le maillot jaune est ＿＿ a gagné l'étape. |
           celui qui

a. Les meilleurs vélos sont ＿＿ sont légers *(lightweight)* mais solides. |

b. Alain a pris beaucoup de bonnes photos du Tour; elles sont meilleures que ＿＿ il a prises l'an dernier. |

c. Le coureur belge est ＿＿ a gagné l'étape d'aujourd'hui. |

d. La prochaine étape est plus longue que ＿＿ nous avons vue aujourd'hui. |

a. ceux qui

b. celles qu'

c. celui qui

d. celle que

6. Customers in a bike shop are comparing the merchandise offered for sale. Write sentences based on the cues, completing each comparison with a demonstrative pronoun plus *-ci* or *-là*.

    Modèle: Ce vélo-ci/moins confortable |
           Ce vélo-ci est moins confortable que celui-là.

a. ces roues-là *(wheels)*/plus solides |
           Ces roues-là sont plus solides que celles-ci.

b. ce guidon-ci *(handlebar)*/moins lourd *(heavy)* |
           Ce guidon-ci est moins lourd que celui-là.

c. ces freins-ci *(brakes)*/meilleurs |
           Ces freins-ci sont meilleurs que ceux-là.

d. cette bicyclette-là/plus jolie |
           Cette bicyclette-là est plus jolie que celle-ci.

Vocabulaire

Noms

les freins *(m.pl.)*   brakes
le guidon   handlebar
le metteur en scène   movie director
la roue   wheel

Conjonctions

afin que   so that
avant que (ne)   before
bien que   although
de peur que (ne)   for fear that

en attendant que   while waiting,
    until
jusqu'à ce que   until
à moins que (ne)   unless
pourvu que   provided that
quoique   although
sans que   without

Note Culturelle

Les jeunes entre eux

Comme partout[1] dans le monde, les jeunes en France aiment sortir avec leurs amis. Ils aiment sortir en bande, c'est à dire avec cinq ou six copains. Très souvent il y a plus de garçons que de filles ou vice versa, car la bande est une unité; elle n'est pas formée de couples. On va au café, au cinéma, au théâtre, au musée, en bande. On peut faire des promenades en ville ou aller à la plage, à la campagne, en bande. On se retrouve[2] aussi chez des copains, tous ensemble. Bien sûr, il y a aussi des couples. On peut avoir son petit ami ou sa petite amie[3]; mais généralement on reste quand même[4] avec ses copains.

Si les jeunes Français aiment être en petits groupes, ils n'aiment pas beaucoup les clubs, ni[5] les organisations. Depuis quelques années[6] il existe cependant des Maisons de jeunes et de la culture[7]. Mais même là, les jeunes vont le plus souvent pour y retrouver leurs copains.

1 like everywhere 2 get together 3 boy friend or girl friend 4 just the same 5 nor 6 since a few years ago 7 youth centers and culture centers

Fête d'étudiants: ambiance sympathique de jeunesse (youth) et de gaieté.

PRÉPARATION 84

Sondage

Parents et Enfants, **Part A**

1. À votre avis, les parents devraient être stricts:
   a. tout le temps.   c. quelquefois.
   b. souvent.   d. jamais.
2. À votre avis, vos parents sont stricts:
   a. tout le temps.   c. quelquefois.
   b. souvent.   d. jamais.
3. À votre avis, qu'est-ce qui est le plus mauvais°:   which is worse
   a. trop de contrôle° de la part des parents   too much control
   b. pas assez de contrôle de la part des parents
4. Est-ce que les parents ont le droit d'exercer leur autorité sur leurs enfants?
   a. oui   b. non
5. Les jeunes devraient avoir la permission de leurs parents pour:
   a. acheter des vêtements.
   b. regarder la télévision.
   c. choisir leurs amis.
   d. être dehors° après une certaine heure.   to be out
   e. passer le week-end chez des amis.
   f. avoir un emploi°.   have a job
   g. acheter quelque chose de très cher°.   something very expensive
   h. partir en vacances quelque part°.   somewhere
6. Les parents ont le droit de contrôler:
   a. la façon de s'habiller de leurs enfants.
   b. le langage de leurs enfants.
   c. la correspondance de leurs enfants.
   d. les conversations téléphoniques de leurs enfants.
7. À votre avis, les jeunes devraient participer aux décisions suivantes:
   a. achat d'une voiture.
   b. déménagement.
   c. changement d'emploi du père ou de la mère.
   d. lieu de vacances.
   e. budget familial.
   f. installation d'un parent âgé à la maison.

Campagne électorale.

Échange
d'idées

After selecting the answer which best represents your own opinion, guess what your neighbor in class selected. How well do you know him/her?

1. *C'est un* vs. *il est*

1. Read the following pairs of sentences.

>   Il est boulanger. *(baker)* Ils sont boulangers.
>   C'est un boulanger. Ce sont des boulangers.

a. Do the sentences in each pair mean the same thing? | a. yes
b. Do all four sentences contain articles? | b. no
c. When the name of a profession is introduced by *être*, it usually takes no article. But the noun does take an article when the subject of *être* is _____. | c. ce (c')

Frames a–f describe various people. Refer to the list below and write sentence saying what each person's occupation is, according to the model.

dentiste   marin   diplomate   avocat
vendeur   photographe infirmier   professeur

Modèle: M. Legrand va souvent au tribunal *(court)*. |
> M. Legrand est avocat. C'est un avocat.

a. Ces garçons traversent l'Atlantique en bateau tous les mois. |
> Ces garçons sont marins. Ce sont des marins.

b. Julie travaille avec plusieurs appareils-photos. |
> Julie est photographe. C'est une photographe.

c. Gérard aide les clients dans un magasin de vêtements. |
> Gérard est vendeur. C'est un vendeur.

d. François et Louis travaillent dans un hôpital. |
> François et Louis sont infirmiers. Ce sont des infirmiers.

e. Il explique une leçon à ses élèves. |
> Il est professeur. C'est un professeur.

2. The past conditional

1. You are familiar with sentences that express a condition and its results.

> Si j'en avais le temps,   If I had enough time,
> je finirais ce livre.   I would finish this book.

What tenses are used in this sentence? |
> The *imparfait* is used in the phrase beginning with *si;* the conditional is used in the main
> clause.

2. In *Si j'en avais le temps, je finirais ce livre,* the condition may still be brought about—there may still be enough time for me to finish the book. Sometimes, however, one can think back and reflect on events that did not take place because the conditions were *not* met.

> Si j'en *avais eu* le temps, j'*aurais fini* ce livre.

a. What is the English equivalent of *si j'en avais eu le temps?* |
> if I had had time (In English this tense is called the *pluperfect* or *past perfect.* In French,
> it is the *plus-que-parfait.*)

b. Look at the result clause: *j'aurais fini ce livre.* Give the English equivalent. |
> I would have finished this book.

3. *J'aurais fini* is a compound tense. What verb forms is it made of? |
> the conditional + the past participle (The auxiliary may be *avoir* or *être.*)

Take a moment to study the charts of the past conditional *(conditionnel passé).*

j'aurais		**je serais**		**je me serais**	
tu aurais		tu serais		tu te serais	
il/elle/on aurait	**fini**	il/elle/on serait	**allé/e/s**	il/elle/on se serait	**habillé/e/s**
nous aurions		nous serions		nous nous serions	
vous auriez		vous seriez		vous vous seriez	
ils/elles auraient		ils/elles seraient		ils/elles se seraient	

4. Complete these sentences according to the model.

> *Modèle:* Albert n'a pas appris le russe. Si Albert était allé en Russie,... |
>
> <small>Si Albert était allé en Russie, il aurait appris le russe.</small>
>
> Tu es tombé. Si tu avais fait attention,... |
>
> <small>Si tu avais fait attention, tu ne serais pas tombé.</small>

a. Jean n'a pas acheté une télévision. Si Jean avait eu 2000 francs,... |

> <small>Si Jean avait eu 2000 francs, il aurait acheté une télévision.</small>

b. Nous n'avons pas appelé la police. S'il y avait eu un hold-up,... |

> <small>S'il y avait eu un hold-up, nous aurions appelé la police.</small>

c. Nous ne sommes pas allés au concert. Si nous avions eu des billets,... |

> <small>Si nous avions eu des billets, nous serions allés au concert.</small>

d. Je ne me suis pas habillée en jean toute l'année. Si cela avait été possible,... |

> <small>Si cela avait été possible, je me serais habillée en jean toute l'année.</small>

e. Il ne s'est pas amusé pendant le week-end. S'il avait fini son travail,... |

> <small>S'il avait fini son travail, il se serait amusé pendant le week-end.</small>

3. Practice with expressions of emotion

When you began using the subjunctive with *vouloir,* you saw that the choice of subjunctive or infinitive depends on whether the subject wants to do something or wants somebody else to do something.

1. The same choice must be made between subjunctive and infinitive after expressions of emotion. Compare these examples:

Je suis contente de partir.   Je suis contente que tu partes.

a. Write the sentence that contains an infinitive, and say the English equivalent. |

> <small>Je suis contente de partir. (I'm glad to be leaving.)</small>

b. Write the sentence in which *partir* is in the subjunctive, and say the English equivalent. |

Je suis contente que tu partes. (I'm glad you're leaving.)

2. An expression of emotion is not immediately followed by an infinitive. In the following sentence, what word links the expression of emotion to the infinitive? *Nous sommes tristes de partir.* |

de

3. The sentences below tell you how certain people feel, and why. Combine the paris of sentences as in the model.

Modèle: Je suis heureux. Mon ami anglais vient me voir. |

Je suis heureux que mon ami anglais vienne me voir.

a. Michèle est ravie. Nous allons au match de football. |

Michèle est ravie que nous allions au match de football.

b. Pierre est furieux. Serge sort avec Nicole. |

Pierre est furieux que Serge sorte avec Nicole.

4. In the subjunctive, negation follows the usual pattern: *ne* before the verb, *pas* after the verb: *Mes parents regrettent que je n'apprenne pas l'anglais.* But look at what happens when an infinitive is made negative: *Elle est heureuse de ne pas travailler cette semaine.*

a. What is the English equivalent? |

She's happy not to work (not to be working) this week.

b. Where do *ne* and *pas* occur? |

Both *ne* and *pas* precede the verb. (This is always the case when an infinitive is made negative.)

5. Combine the sentences below as you did for frame 5.

Modèle: Je suis triste. Je ne vois pas mon ami. |

Je suis triste de ne pas voir mon ami.

a. Nous sommes contents. Nous n'allons pas à la fac aujourd'hui. |

Nous sommes contents de ne pas aller à la fac aujourd'hui.

b. Les enfants sont enchantés. Ils vont au cinéma. |

Les enfants sont enchantés d'aller au cinéma.

c. Le chien est malheureux. Son maître n'est pas avec lui. |

Le chien est malheureux que son maître ne soit pas avec lui.

d. Papa est furieux. Mon frère ne travaille pas. |

Papa est furieux que mon frère ne travaille pas.

À Propos!

Pensez à ce que vous avez fait cette année.
De quoi êtes-vous heureux/heureuse? De quoi êtes-vous fier/fière?

Vocabulaire

Noms

le boulanger   *baker*
l'emploi *(m.)*   *job*
le lieu   *place*

Autres expressions

quelque part   *somewhere*

PRÉPARATION 85

1. *Être* and *avoir* in the imperative

1. The command forms of *être* are not the same as the present tense forms. Read the following.

> Mme Péret veut que vous soyez sages. Alors, elle
> vous dit: «Soyez sages!»

a. Write the command that Mme Péret gives. |

    a. Soyez sages!

b. The imperative form *soyez* is the same as the *vous* form of the
_____. |

    b. subjunctive

The command forms of *être* are the same as the corresponding subjunctive forms.

2. Give commands with these cues.

a. (toi) gentil |

    a. Sois gentil.

b. (nous) tranquilles *(quiet)* |

    b. Soyons tranquilles.

c. (vous) ne... pas/paresseux |

    c. Ne soyez pas paresseux.

3. For *avoir*, as for *être*, the imperative forms are the same as those of the subjunctive (except that -*s* is dropped from the *tu* form): *aie; ayons; ayez.* Supply appropriate commands to follow the sentences below. Use these expressions:

> avoir confiance   avoir du courage
> avoir un peu de patience   avoir pitié

a. Tu attends le train et il est en retard. |

    a. Aie un peu de patience!

b. La route est dangereuse mais il faut que nous continuions. |

    b. Ayons du courage!

c. Vous hésitez à croire cet homme, mais il est très honnête.

    c. Ayez confiance!

d. Regarde ce pauvre enfant qui pleure et demande ton aide!

    d. Aie pitié!

À Propos!   Tell two pieces of advice you would give a particular person, and why.

> Je dirais à ma sœur «Aie un peu de patience!» parce
> qu'elle n'est pas très patiente.

2. Giving directions

1. Below is a list of useful vocabulary for giving directions. Choose among them to give the French equivalents of the sentences in frames a–g. Use the *tu*-form of verbs.

aller tout droit
traverser la rue/l'avenue/
  le boulevard
tourner à droite
tourner à gauche

être à gauche/à droite/
  devant/derrière
être près de/à côté de/
  en face de
la prochaine rue/avenue

a. You are near the library. |
    Tu es près de la bibliothèque.
b. Cross the street. |
    Traverse la rue.
c. Turn left. |
    Tourne à gauche.
d. Cross the avenue. |
    Traverse l'avenue.
e. Take the next street on the right. |
    Prends la prochaine rue à droite.
f. Go straight ahead. |
    Va tout droit.
g. You will find my house on the right, next to the shoe store. |
    Tu trouveras ma maison à droite, à côté du magasin de chaussures.

À Propos!   Write the directions someone would need to begin at your front door and drive to the library.

4. The pluperfect and past conditional in *si*-clauses

1. You have seen on p. 584 how the past conditional is formed:

j'aurais fini   *I would have finished*
je serais entré   *I would have entered*

Which tense is used in *si*-clauses that accompany these conditional phrases? |
    the pluperfect
2. Write *je faisais, j'allais,* and *je me promenais* in the pluperfect. |
    j'avais fait, j'étais allé(e), je m'étais promené(e)
3. Complete the following sentences with the correct form of the verb.

a. Si vous aviez pu faire un voyage n'importe òu *(anywhere)*, òu
   _____-vous _____? (aller) | a. seriez-vous allé(e)
b. Nous _____ l'avion si nous étions allés en France. (prendre) | b. nous aurions pris
c. J'aurais eu chaud si je _____ ce manteau. (mettre) | c. j'avais mis
d. Tu aurais été fatigué si tu y _____ à pied. (aller) | d. tu y étais allé

À Propos!

Be prepared to ask and answer:

Si vous n'aviez pas décidé de faire des études universitaires,
qu'est-ce que vous auriez fait?

Départ en vacances:
Des kilomètres de
voitures, parechoc
(bumper) contre pa-
rechoc, essaient de
traverser la frontière
franco-espagnole au
col *(pass)* du Perthus.

Vocabulaire

Noms

l'administrateur *m.*   *administrator*
le banquier   *banker*
le dessinateur   *designer*
l'explorateur *m.*   *explorer*
l'observateur *m.*   *observer*

Verbes

servir (à) (ser-, serv-, *p.p.* servi)   *to
   be used for, to serve as*
voler   *to steal; to fly*

PRÉPARATION 86

Sondage

Parents et Enfants, Part B

8. D'où vient votre argent de poche°?   pocket money
   a. vos parents vous le donnent quand vous en avez besoin
   b. vos parents vous le donnent régulièrement et sans obligations
   c. vos parents vous le donnent en échange de° travaux à la   in exchange for
      maison
   d. vous le gagnez°   earn
9. Quelles obligations faut-il que vous remplissiez quand vous êtes
   chez vos parents?
   a. mettre et débarrasser la table
   b. faire votre lit

c. mettre votre chambre en ordre
   d. faire la vaisselle
   e. nettoyer le garage ou le jardin
   f. faire les courses
   g. sortir les ordures°   garbage
   h. vous occuper du chien
   i. surveiller vos frères et sœurs
   j. faire votre travail de classe comme il faut
   k. étudier votre piano (ou autre instrument) régulièrement
10. Pensez-vous que les étudiants devraient travailler à l'extérieur°:   have an outside job
   a. après les cours.
   b. le week-end.
   c. pendant les vacances.
   d. jamais.
11. Est-ce que vous travaillez:
   a. après les cours.
   b. le week-end.
   c. pendant les vacances.
   d. jamais.
12. Quelles sont les raisons pour lesquelles les étudiants devraient
   travailler?
   a. pour avoir de l'argent de poche
   b. pour apprendre la valeur de l'argent
   c. parce que c'est une expérience utile
   d. pour faire des voyages
   e. pour payer leurs études
   f. pour être indépendants des parents
   g. pour faire un achat° important   a purchase
13. En moyenne°, combien d'heures par jour—en dehors des heures   On the average
   de cours—un étudiant devrait-il consacrer à ses études?
   a. 2 heures   c. 6 heures
   b. 4 heures   d. plus de 6 heures
14. Combien d'heures par semaine voudriez-vous pouvoir consa-   give
   crer° à vos loisirs°?   leisure activities
   a. 4–6 heures
   b. 6–10 heures
   c. plus de 10 heures
15. Préféreriez-vous avoir:
   a. un emploi intéressant et mal payé.
   b. un emploi ennuyeux° et bien payé.   boring

*Échange
d'idées*

Demandez à un(e) camarade s'il (si elle) travaille à l'extérieur. Si oui,
quel genre de travail fait-il (fait-elle)?

1. Statements with two object pronouns

In statements with two object pronouns, you find that the pronouns are divided into the three groups shown below.

me, te, nous, vous   le, la, les   lui, leur

1. The sentences below will remind you of the word order patterns for object pronouns.

Il me la demande.   Il te le donne.
Il la lui demande.   Il le leur donne.

What determines whether *le, la,* and *les* come first or second? |

It depends on which other pronoun is used. (*Le, la,* and *les* precede *lui* and *leur,* but they follow *me, te, nous,* and *vous.*)

2. M. Lambert, after an active and happy life, has died at the age of 102. His relatives have gathered for the reading of the will. Below are some of the things they say to one another about the will. Rewrite each sentence with two object pronouns.

Modèle: Il vous donne ses skis? |

Oui, il nous les donne.

a. Il te donne son vélo? | a. Oui, il me les donne.
b. Il donne ses disques de rock à Lucie et à Jean-Philippe? | b. Oui, il les leur donne.
c. Il te donne sa raquette de tennis? | c. Oui, il me la donne.
d. Il vous donne ses albums de photos? | d. Oui, il nous les donne.
e. Il lui donne son bateau à voile? | e. Il le lui donne.
f. Il donne sa caméra à tante Hélène? | f. Il la lui donne.

3. Answer these questions in the negative. Use object pronouns.
   a. Est-ce qu'elle lui donne ses vieux vêtements? |

   Non, elle ne les lui donne pas. (Remember that *ne* precedes the object pronoun, *pas* follows the verb.)

   b. Tu me donnes tes vieilles bottes? |

   Non, je ne te les donne pas.

   c. Elle leur donne sa vieille commode? |

   Non, elle ne la leur donne pas.

4. In the *passé composé*, object pronouns come before the auxiliary verb. Remember, also, that the past participle agrees with a preceding direct object.

   Rewrite the following sentences with two object pronouns.

   Modèle: Il m'a montré sa voiture. |

   Il me l'a montrée.

   a. Je leur ai indiqué la route de Paris. |

   Je la leur ai indiquée. (The direct object is *la. Indiquée* must be feminine singular.)

b. Le professeur nous a donné les livres. |
> Le professeur nous les a donnés.

c. Ton cousin ne t'a pas vendu ce vélo? |
> Ton cousin ne te l'a pas vendu? (Remember that *ne* precedes the object pronoun, and *pas* follows the auxiliary verb.)

d. Jean-Pierre ne m'a pas montré sa caméra. |
> Jean-Pierre ne me l'a pas montrée.

5. In double verb constructions, object pronouns precede the infinitive—not the first verb.

   Say that Paul is going to give the following things to the people indicated. Use two object pronouns in each sentence.

   Modèle: à toi: cette carte postale |
   > Paul va te la donner.

   a. à moi: ce roman |
   b. à Mireille: ces revues |
   c. à vous: cette photo |

   a. Paul va me le donner.
   b. Paul va les lui donner.
   c. Paul va vous la donner.

6. Rewrite these sentences with two object pronouns. (See key.)
   a. Nous allons dicter cette lettre à la secrétaire.
   b. Elle va m'envoyer sa carte d'Europe.
   c. Ne raconte pas l'histoire à tous tes amis.
   d. Je t'ai chanté ma chanson préférée. *(Remember to make the past participle agree with the direct object.)*
   e. Tu n'as pas annoncé la nouvelle à tes amis?
   f. Il faut que nous vous donnions ces résultats.
   g. Ne donne pas ton argent à Bertrand.

2. *Depuis = il y a...que*

1. To express that something started some time ago and has been going on for a given length of time, you know that French uses *depuis* and the present tense.

   > Son père *travaille* dans cet hôpital *depuis* trois ans.

2. There is another construction that has exactly the same meaning and is also frequently used: *il y a* at the beginning of the sentence, followed by *que* + the present tense.

   > *Il y a trois ans que* son père *travaille* dans cet hôpital.

   Give the English sentence that is equivalent to both of the French sentences above. |
   > His/her father has been working in this hospital for three years. (Did you remember to switch to the progressive past tense in English?)

3. Write a new sentence with the same meaning as each of the sentences on the next page.

Modèle: Je suis malade depuis quinze jours. |

Il y a quinze jours que je suis malade.

a. Nous avons cette voiture depuis deux ans.
b. Ils sont mariés depuis 25 ans.
c. Le repas est servi depuis 10 minutes.
d. J'attends l'autobus depuis au moins une heure.
e. La France est une république depuis plus d'un siècle. |

a. Il y a deux ans que nous avons cette voiture.   b. Il y a 25 ans qu'ils sont mariés.
c. Il y a 10 minutes que le repas est servi.   d. Il y a au moins une heure que j'attends
l'autobus.   e. Il y a plus d'un siècle que la France est une république.

4. Compare the meanings, word order, and tenses of these two *il y a* constructions.

Passé composé: Elle a appris à jouer de la guitare il y a trois ans.
Présent: Il y a trois ans qu'elle joue de la guitare.

Write English equivalents of each sentence above. |

She learned to play the guitar three years ago. She has been playing the guitar for
three years.

À Propos!

Il y a combien de temps que vous travaillez à cette Préparation?

3. *Le passé simple* of regular verbs

François et Catherine Bucher ont voyagé tout l'été et ont visité l'Angleterre, la Belgique, l'Espagne et le Portugal. Ils ont rencontré beaucoup de personnes intéressantes. Ils sont allés dans des restaurants sympathiques et ont apprécié des nourritures différentes. Ils n'ont pas perdu leur temps et ils ont fini leur voyage fatigués mais contents.

This little story is written in the *passé composé.* It could also have been written in another past tense called the *passé simple,* generally used in formal writing.

François et Catherine Bucher voyagèrent tout l'été et visitèrent l'Angleterre, la Belgique, l'Espagne et le Portugal. Ils rencontrèrent beaucoup de personnes intéressantes. Ils allèrent dans des restaurants sympathiques et apprécièrent des nourritures différentes. Ils ne perdirent pas leur temps et finirent leur voyage fatigués mais contents.

The verb forms *voyagèrent, visitèrent, rencontrèrent, allèrent, apprécièrent, perdirent,* and *finirent* are the *ils* form of the *passé simple* (unlike the *passé composé* it is made up of only one word). This tense has the

same meaning as the informal *passé composé*. *François et Catherine voyagèrent* = *ont voyagé* = François and Catherine traveled.
Here are the *passé simple* forms for all regular verbs.

Parler			Finir			Perdre		
je	parl	**ai**	je	fin	**is**	je	perd	**is**
tu	parl	**as**	tu	fin	**is**	tu	perd	**is**
il/elle	parl	**a**	il/elle	fin	**it**	il/elle	perd	**it**
nous	parl	**âmes**	nous	fin	**îmes**	nous	perd	**îmes**
vous	parl	**âtes**	vous	fin	**îtes**	vous	perd	**îtes**
ils/elles	parl	**èrent**	ils/elles	fin	**irent**	ils/elles	perd	**irent**

Every verb has only one stem—that is, there are no stem changes in the *passé simple*—and the endings follow a set pattern.

The *passé simple* of verbs ending in -*ir* or -*re* is based on the stem of the infinitive minus the ending. The endings are the same for both groups.

Young Paul is writing a composition on Napoléon. He can't help using the conversational past, which is not approved by his teacher. Write the teacher's corrections of the verbs.

1. Napoléon est parti de Corse pour chercher fortune à Paris où il a trouvé des amis influents. |
2. Il y a rencontré Joséphine de Beauharnais, dont il est tombé amoureux et qu'il a épousée en 1796. |
3. Quand l'occasion s'est présentée, il a saisi le pouvoir et il a choisi le titre d'Empereur. |
4. Il a envahi (invaded) de nombreux pays et il a gagné beaucoup de batailles, mais il a perdu la dernière, Waterloo. |

1. partit, trouva

2. rencontra, tomba, épousa

3. se présenta, saisit, choisit

4. envahit, gagna, perdit

Vocabulaire

Noms

l'argent de poche *m.*   *pocket money; allowance*
l'achat *m.*   *purchase*
le genre   *kind, type*
les loisirs *m.pl.*   *leisure activities*
la raquette   *(sports) racket*
le résultat   *result*

Verbes

mettre/débarasser la table   *to set/ clear off the table*
épouser   *to marry*
sortir les ordures   *take out the garbage*

s'occuper de   *to take care of, charge of*
surveiller (enfants)   *to look after (children)*
indiquer   *to indicate*

Autres expressions

comme il faut   *in the proper way, as it should be*
à l'extérieur   *outside*
en moyenne   *on the average*

PRÉPARATION 87

1. *Le passé simple* of irregular verbs

You have seen that regular *-er, -ir,* and *-re* verbs use the infinitive stem to form the *passé simple.* Some irregular verbs use a less predictable stem (which has to be learned), then the same consonant ending as the *-ir* and *-re* verbs.

Vivre			*Prendre*		
je	vécu	s	je	pri	s
tu	vécu	s	tu	pri	s
il/elle	vécu	t	il/elle	pri	t
nous	vécû	mes	nous	prî	mes
vous	vécû	tes	vous	prî	tes
ils/elles	vécu	rent	ils/elles	pri	rent

For some irregular verbs, like *vivre* and *prendre* above, the *passé simple* stem is similar or identical to the past participle.

avoir	j'ai eu	**j'eus**	*dire*	j'ai dit	**je dis**
croire	j'ai cru	**je crus**	*mettre*	j'ai mis	**je mis**
pouvoir	j'ai pu	**je pus**			
vouloir	j'ai voulu	**je voulus**			

Other irregular verbs have irregular stems.

être	j'ai été	**je fus**	*mourir*	il est mort	**il mourut**
faire	j'ai fait	**je fis**	*naître*	je suis né	**je naquis**
venir	je suis venu	**je vins**	*voir*	j'ai vu	**je vis**
écrire	j'ai écrit	**j'écrivis**	*tenir*	j'ai tenu	**je tins**

1. A few of these irregular verbs are used frequently. Study the examples above for a few minutes, then write the *passé composé* for each of the forms on the next page.

a. il fit
b. je fus
c. nous eûmes

d. ils furent
e. elle naquit
f. il vit |

a. il a fait b. j'ai été c. nous avons eu d. ils ont été e. elle est née
f. il a vu

2. Rewrite the verbs in each sentence in a more familiar style.

Modèle: Molière naquit à Paris en 1622. |

est né

a. Il commença sa carrière dramatique en province, puis il revint à Paris. |

a commencé, est revenu

b. Il obtint un énorme succès à la cour de Louis XIV quand il écrivit des comédies pour amuser le roi. |

a obtenu, a écrit

c. Par contre, certaines de ses comédies firent scandale et il fut sévèrement critiqué par ses contemporains. |

ont fait, a été

d. Il eut une vie difficile, mais il mourut en pleine gloire en 1673. |

a eu, est mort

2. Using indefinite adjectives and pronouns

Expressions such as *beaucoup, quelques, d'autres,* and *aucun* are similar to numbers, in that they answer the question *how many?* Because they don't express exact numbers, they are called *indefinite adjectives.*

1. Read the sentences below, then write the indefinite adjectives and their English equivalents.

J'ai beaucoup d'amis étrangers.
Je connais plusieurs Marocains.
Je ne connais aucun Tunisien.

Je connais quelques Algériens.
J'aimerais rencontrer d'autres
étrangers. |

beaucoup: *a lot;* plusieurs: *several;* aucun: *no, not any;* quelques: *a few, some;* d'autres: *some other*

2. Give the French equivalents of these sentences.

a. I have a lot of detective books. |

J'ai beaucoup de romans policiers. (Did you remember to write *de* after *beaucoup?*)

b. I have a few science fiction books. |

J'ai quelques livres de science-fiction.

c. I have several dictionaries. |

J'ai plusieurs dictionnaires.

d. I just bought some other French magazines. |

Je viens d'acheter d'autres revues françaises.

3. These indefinite adjectives can also be used as pronouns. Read the answers to the question *Tu as vu combien de films cet été?*

—J'en ai vu dix.   —J'en ai vu beaucoup.

a. In both answers, *films* is replaced by ＿＿＿. |
       en

b. The structure of the two sentences is the same: *en* comes ＿＿＿ the verb; the number or the indefinite pronoun comes ＿＿＿ the verb. |
       before; after

c. Write the English equivalents of the two answers. |
       I saw ten (of them). I saw a lot (of them). (Remember that in English you don't have to say *of them/of it*, but in French you must use *en*.)

4. Notice what happens with *quelques* when it is used as a pronoun.

—As-tu rencontré quelques Belges à Paris?   *Did you meet some Belgians in Paris?*
—Oui, j'en ai rencontré quelques-uns.   *Yes, I met a few.*

a. *Quelques,* when used as a pronoun, is followed by ＿＿＿. |
       -uns (Notice the hyphen: *quelques-uns.* It is pronounced with liaison between *s* and *uns* /kɛlkəzœ̃/.)

b. If the noun is feminine, the form changes slightly:

Des Canadiennes? Oui, j'en connais quelques-unes.

The feminine form of *quelques-uns* is ＿＿＿. |
       quelques-unes

c. Answer affirmatively, without repeating the noun *matchs:*

Est-ce que Philippe a vu quelques matchs de football l'hiver dernier? |
       Oui, il en a vu quelques-uns.

5. Use *en* plus *beaucoup, plusieurs, d'autres,* or *quelques-uns* to complete the French sentences below.

a. *I saw a lot of them.* J'＿＿＿ ai vu ＿＿＿. |
       J'en ai vu beaucoup.

b. *They showed us several.* Ils nous ＿＿＿ ont montré ＿＿＿. |
       Ils nous en ont montré plusieurs.

c. *She looked at some.* Elle ＿＿＿ a regardé ＿＿＿. |
       Elle en a regardé quelques-uns.

d. *Then she looked at others.* |
       Ensuite, elle en a regardé d'autres.

6. Write affirmative answers to these questions, using *en.*
a. Est-ce que Maurice voit beaucoup de pièces de théâtre? | a. Oui, il en voit beaucoup.
b. Avez-vous lu plusieurs romans anglais? (Answer with *je.*) | b. Oui, j'en ai lu plusieurs.

c. Est-ce qu'elle a d'autres sœurs? | c. Oui, elle en a d'autres.

d. Tu as quelques amies françaises? | d. Oui, j'en ai quelques-unes.

7. Compare these French and English sentences.

> Mon frère connaît plusieurs coureurs, mais moi, je n'en connais aucun.
> *My brother knows several runners, but I don't know a single one/any at all.*

   a. What expression is the equivalent of *not a single one* or *not any at all?* | a. ne... aucun

   b. Write the French equivalent of *I don't see a single one.* Je _____ en vois _____. | b. Je n'en vois aucun.

8. When *aucun* refers to a feminine word, you use the form *aucune*. Answer using *ne... aucun/aucune*.

   a. Tu connais des villes suisses? | a. Non, je n'en connais aucune.

   b. Tu connais des pays européens? | b. Non, je n'en connais aucun.

9. Liliane is very near-sighted and really should not be driving. Luckily she has Étienne with her and she keeps asking him if he can see various people and things. Write Étienne's answers, using the correct form of *aucun* or of *quelques-uns.*

   Modèle: Est-ce qu'il y a des piétons dans la rue? (Non) |

       Non, il n'y en a aucun.

   a. Est-ce qu'il y a des voitures devant moi? (Oui) | a. Oui, il y en a quelques-unes.

   b. Est-ce que tu vois un agent? (Non) | b. Non, je n'en vois aucun.

   c. J'entends un klaxon. Il y a une voiture à côté de moi? (Non) | c. Non, il n'y en a aucune.

   d. Est-ce qu'il y a des passages cloutés dans cette rue? (Oui) | d. Oui, il y en a quelques-uns.

À Propos!

Écrivez deux phrases, une avec *aucun* et une avec *quelques-uns,* pour dire que vous avez ou que vous n'avez pas de cousins, ou de frères, ou de sœur ou de petit ami ou petite amie. Par exemple: *Des cousins, je n'en ai aucun.*

3. Practice with ce qui, ce que

Write the relative pronouns *(qui, que, ce qui, ce que)* that fit in the following sentences.

1. Tu ne m'as pas dit _____ tu voulais boire, alors prends le jus d'orange _____ est sur la table. | 1. ce que; qui

2. Je ne comprends pas _____ vous plaît dans cet acteur. Il a une personnalité _____ je déteste. | 2. ce qui; que

3. _____ vous préférez n'est pas nécessairement _____ est le meilleur pour vous. | 3. ce que; ce qui

4. Le produit bon marché _____ vous achetez n'est pas celui _____ dure *(lasts)* le plus longtemps. | 4. que; qui

4. *Lequel* and *celui*

1. You are asking a friend her opinion on various things. Write your questions. (See key.)

   Modèle: Voilà deux motos. (la plus rapide) |
   —Laquelle est la plus rapide?

   a. Voilà des vélos. (les moins chers)
   b. Voilà deux voitures de sport. (la plus élégante)

2. Sharon is telling her friends about her vacation in France. Write the form of *lequel* that correctly completes each conversation. Notice that a question with *lequel* is often answered with a form of *celui.*

   a. –J'ai visité une très belle cathédrale. –_____? –Celle de Rouen.
   b. –J'ai vu deux beaux châteaux. –_____? –Ceux de Chambord et de Blois.
   c. –J'ai visité un très beau musée. –_____? –Celui de Cherbourg.
   d. –J'ai vu de très belles plages. –_____? –Celles qui sont près de Biarritz. |

   a Laquelle?   b Lesquels?   c Lequel?   d Lesquelles?

3. Gilles is pointing out some famous athletes in the lobby of a hotel. His friend doesn't always know to whom he's pointing, so she asks for more information. Write her questions and complete Gilles' responses, using interrogative and demonstrative pronouns.

   Modèle: —Ce jeune homme est champion de ski.

   —_____?

   —_____ porte un chapeau rouge. |

   Lequel: Celui qui

   a. —Cette jeune fille là-bas est championne de ski.
   —_____?
   —_____ est à côté de la porte. |
   Laquelle; Celle qui

   b. —Ces garçons sont d'excellents nageurs.
   —_____?
   —_____ sont assis près de la fenêtre. |
   Lesquels; Ceux qui

   c. —Cet homme-là est entraîneur *(coach).*
   —_____?
   —_____ parle aux deux garçons blonds. |
   Lequel; Celui qui

   d. —Ces trois petites filles sont excellentes en gymnastique.
   —_____?
   —_____ parlent au moniteur. |
   Lesquelles; Celles qui

Emblème de l'équipe des Expos de Montréal (baseball).

À Propos!

Lequel des poèmes que vous avez lus dans la Phase 11 vous a le plus touché/e? Pourquoi?

PRÉPARATION 88

Le français tel qu'on le parle

—Je meurs de faim, dit-elle. J'ai fait du shopping toute la journée. À midi, j'ai pris un sandwich dans un snack, c'est tout.

—Si on va faire du bowling, dit-il, on n'a pas le temps d'aller au
restaurant.

5   —Ça ne fait rien, dit-elle. Allons au drugstore. J'adore leurs
hamburgers avec du ketchup.

—Moi aussi! dit-il. Mais je crois que je préfère leurs club-sand-
wiches et, bien sûr, leurs banana-splits.

Philippe et Régine étaient habillés de façon identique: jeans et
10 pulls de laine par dessus leurs tee-shirts. C'était leur «uniforme»
favori quand ils n'étaient pas à leur travail.

Philippe travaillait dans une grosse entreprise d'engineering,
dans la section de marketing. Son job l'intéressait beaucoup mais
ne lui laissait pas beaucoup de temps pour son hobby préféré:
15 les sports.

Pendant les week-ends il allait parfois au club jouer au golf et
se relaxer au club-house en prenant un drink avec ses amis.

Régine avait un petit job dans une station de radio. Elle espé-
rait devenir reporter, un jour. Elle avait toujours aimé le journa-
20 lisme, les mass media. Ses parents étaient très riches et très
snobs. Ils habitaient un magnifique appartement dans un immeuble de grand standing et passaient une grande partie de leur
temps à jouer au bridge. Ils auraient voulu que leur fille épouse
un garçon riche et élégant, un de ces playboys qui vivent dans
25 les jets et les palaces, en tenue de ski ou de tennis dans la journée, en smoking dans la soirée.

Mais Régine préférait la compagnie de Philippe, les soirées à
écouter du jazz avec des amis, les discothèques où se retrou-
vaient les «fanas» de rock et de pop.

30 —Tu veux autre chose? dit Philippe, finissant son énorme ba-
nana-split.

—Non, merci, dit-elle, je n'ai plus faim... Oh zut! Je savais bien
que j'avais oublié quelque chose...

35 —Quoi? dit-il.

—Un gadget, pour ouvrir les boîtes de conserves... Je ne peux
plus retrouver celui que j'avais.

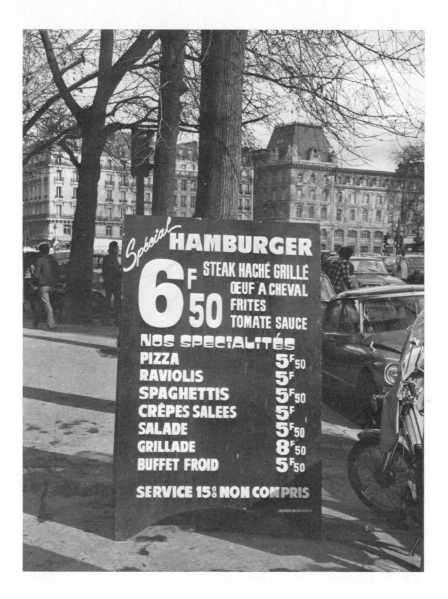

—Et moi, j'ai oublié d'acheter du détergent pour laver mon chandail de ski.

—Allons prendre la voiture au parking. On peut passer au shop-
40 ping-center, c'est ouvert tard.

—O.K.

*Échange
d'idées*

Trouvez trois expressions de franglais que vous pourriez remplacer par du français normal. (Exemple: J'ai fait du shopping = J'ai fait des courses.)

1. *Le futur antérieur*

1. You have already seen three compound tenses. Write the English equivalent of each compound verb phrase from these sentences.

    a. The *passé composé* has an auxiliary verb in the *présent:*

    Je mange mon dessert.   *J'ai mangé* mon dessert.
    Je me lève à six heures.   *Je me suis levé* à six heures. |

    I ate (I have eaten); I got up (I have gotten up)

    b. The *plus-que-parfait* has an auxiliary verb in the *imparfait:*

    Je mangeais mon dessert.   *J'avais mangé* mon dessert.
    Je me levais à six heures.   *Je m'étais levé* a six heures. |

    I had eaten; I had gotten up

    c. The *conditionnel passé* has an auxiliary verb in the *conditionnel:*

    Je mangerais mon dessert.   *J'aurais mangé* mon dessert.
    Je me lèverais à six heures.   *Je me serais levé* à six heures. |

    I would have eaten; I would have gotten up

2. The future of an auxiliary verb can also be used with a past participle.

    > Quand vous viendrez, j'aurai fini de préparer le dîner.
    > *When you come, I will have finished preparing dinner.*

    This compound tense is called the *futur antérieur* (future perfect), because it refers to events that *precede* (are anterior to) a future occurrence expressed by another verb in the future.

3. In frames *a–e*, restate the series of events. Use the *futur antérieur* to show which action will have taken place first.

    Modèle: Il fera son travail, et ensuite il sortira. |

    Quand il aura fini son travail, il sortira.

    a. Tu recevras ma lettre, et ensuite tu me répondras. |

    Quand tu auras reçu ma lettre, tu me répondras.

    b. Ils arriveront, et ensuite nous sortirons ensemble. |

    Quand ils seront arrivés, nous sortirons ensemble.

    c. Le Président terminera son discours, et ensuite il sera applaudi. |

    Quand le Président aura terminé son discours, ils sera applaudi.

    d. Le soleil se couchera, et ensuite nous regarderons le clair de lune. |

    Quand le soleil se sera couché, nous regarderons le clair de lune.

    e. Nous déjeunerons, et ensuite tu feras la vaisselle. |

    Quand nous aurons déjeuné, tu feras la vaisselle.

À Propos!

Que ferez-vous quand vous aurez terminé cette préparation?

2. Vocabulary practice

What's involved in these jobs?

garagiste   maître-nageur   pêcheur   serveuse
journaliste   ouvreuse   routier

1. Complete each sentence with the appropriate job titles, and conditional verb forms. (See key.)
   a. Si tu aimais les voitures, tu (être) ———.
   b. Si j'étais ———, j'(aimer travailler dans un restaurant français).
   c. Il (devenir) ——— s'il savait bien nager.
   d. Si vous étiez ———, vous (avoir) beaucoup de journaux dans votre bureau.
   e. Nous (passer) de longues heures en bateau si nous étions ———. *(Remember to make the noun plural.)*
   f. Si j'étais ———, j'(aller) dans tous les états des États-Unis.
   g. Si elles étaient ———, elles (pouvoir) voir tous les nouveaux films.

2. Refer to this vocabulary list from *Parents et enfants, Part B* to give the French equivalents of the sentences that follow.

   mettre la table   s'occuper du chien
   faire la vaisselle   débarrasser la table
   faire les courses   surveiller ses frères et sœurs
   faire son lit   mettre sa chambre en ordre
   sortir les ordures

   a. In the morning, I make my bed. |
      Le matin, je fais mon lit. (Did you use the correct possessive adjective?)
   b. Then I straighten up my room. |
      Après/Ensuite, je mets ma chambre en ordre.
   c. I do the shopping. |
      Je fais les courses.
   d. I take care of the dog and watch my brothers and sisters. |
      Je m'occupe du chien et je surveille mes frères et sœurs.
   e. Before dinner, I set the table. |
      Avant le dîner, je mets la table.
   f. After dinner, I clear the table and do the dishes. |
      Après le dîner, je débarrasse le table et je fais la vaisselle.
   g. At night, I take out the garbage. |
      Le soir, je sors les ordures.

À Propos!

Imaginez que vous êtes le/la propriétaire d'un grand château. Votre maître d'hôtel *(butler)* vous demande ce qu'il faut qu'il fasse aujourd'hui. Dites-lui trois choses essentielles.

RÉVISION

Vive le cyclisme!

Échange d'idées

1. Est-ce que vous pensez que les cyclistes doivent obéir au code de la route? Devraient-ils avoir leur permis de conduire?
2. L'automobile ou la bicyclette sont-ils des dangers publics? Donnez vos raisons.
3. Questionnez un partenaire sur un accident qu'il a eu ou qu'il aurait pu avoir.
   Où l'accident est-il arrivé? Dans quelles circonstances? Quels était ses sentiments? Quelles ont été ses réactions? Quelles ont été les conséquences?

1. Le passé composé

1. When does the past participle agree with the verb? |

> when the direct object precedes the verb (—Elle a aimé ces disques? —Oui, elle les a
> aimés.); when the verb is an intransitive verb of motion or a reflexive and is conjugated
> with *être:* elle *est* rentrée, elle *s'est* promenée.

2. The police have finally captured M. Raoul, head of a large spy ring in Paris. M. Raoul tries to confuse the police by contradicting all their evidence. Complete the dialogue, using the *passé composé.*

a. *Police:* Vous _____ au bar du Dôme. (aller)

   M. Raoul: Non, c'est Madame Auger qui _____ au bar St.-Michel. (aller) |

> êtes allé; est allée

b. *Police:* Madame Auger et Madame Tanet _____ deux heures à l'hôtel. (rester)

   M. Raoul: Non, elles en _____ après une heure. (partir) |

> sont restées; sont parties

c. *Police:* Vous et M. Calmar, vous _____ à Pigalle à minuit. (revenir)

   M. Raoul: Non, M. Calmar _____ avec moi. (ne pas revenir) |

> êtes revenus; n'est pas revenu

3. Say what the following people did during their vacation, according to the cues.

   Modèle: Moi, Jeanne (s'ennuyer) |

> Je me suis ennuyée.

a. Moi, Charles (bien s'amuser à la discothèque) |

> Je me suis bien amusé à la discothèque.

b. Eric et Claudine (se marier) |

> Ils se sont mariés.

c. Sylvie (s'entraîner pour le tournoi de tennis) |

> Elle s'est entraînée pour le tournoi de tennis.

d. Toi, Monique (s'installer dans un grand appartement) |

> Tu t'es installée dans un grand appartement.

4. M. Toulouse's students hardly ever hand in their homework. Here are some of the excuses he hears today. Complete the sentences, using the *passé composé* of the verbs in parentheses. Then rewrite your sentences, replacing the direct object with pronouns.

a. J'_____ mon livre de français. (perdre)

b. Je _____ les exercices. (ne pas finir)

c. Pierre et moi, nous _____ le match de football à la télé hier soir. (regarder)

d. Le chien _____ la main de mon frère. (mordre)

e. Je _____ la leçon. (ne pas comprendre) |

> a. ai perdu; je l'ai perdu   b. n'ai pas fini; je ne les ai pas finis   c. avons regardé;
> nous l'avons regardé   d. a mordu; l'a mordue   e. n'ai pas compris; je ne l'ai pas
> comprise

5. Several students brought back souvenirs from France. Complete these sentences with the *passé composé;* remember that past participles agree with the nouns represented by *que*.

a. Voilà les souvenirs que j'_____. (rapporter) |
     ai rapportés

b. Voici des billets de théâtre que nous _____. (ne pas utiliser) |
     n'avons pas utilisés

6. François has been neglecting his share of the household duties. When his roommates check up on him, he is forced to reply in the negative. Write their questions and François' answers. (See key.)

     Modèle: faire la vaisselle |
         —As-tu fait la vaisselle? —Non, je ne l'ai pas faite.

a. nettoyer la cuisine
b. faire la lessive
c. faire les courses
d. écrire la lettre à la propriétaire
e. mettre la table

7. Isabelle is going to Bordeaux for two weeks and has made a list of things she has to do before she leaves. But she's badly organized and only manages to do the first five things on the list. Say what she has done, using the *passé composé* and direct- and/or indirect object pronouns.

     Modèle: Envoyer les photos à mes parents |
         Elle les leur a envoyées.

a. Rendre visite à Paula et Jean |
         Elle leur a rendu visite.

b. Nettoyer le réfrigérateur |
         Elle l'a nettoyé.

c. Donner son adresse à la concierge |
         Elle la lui a donnée.

Now say that she has not done the following things.

d. Prêter sa mobylette à Odile |
         Elle ne la lui a pas prêtée.

e. Arroser *(water)* les plantes |
         Elle ne les a pas arrosées.

f. Envoyer mon numéro de téléphone à Michel |
         Elle ne le lui a pas envoyé.

g. Donner la clé à Pierre |
         Elle ne la lui a pas donnée.

8. Rewrite the following sentences, replacing the italic portion by a pronoun *(y or en).* (See key.)

a. Sylvie a visité *beaucoup de pays* l'année dernière.
b. Elle est allée *dans tous les pays d'Europe.*
c. Elle s'est beaucoup amusée *en Suisse.*
d. Elle n'est pas allée *en Afrique.*

À Propos! Write three brief statements about things you should have done but have not found the time to do.

La composition—je ne l'ai pas encore écrite.

2. *L'imparfait* vs. *le passé composé*

In frames 1–2, match each French sentence with the correct English description of the conversation.

Modèle: Elle réparait son vélo. Elle a réparé son vélo.

a. The speaker is telling how his sister cut her finger. |

Elle réparait son vélo.

b. The speaker is saying what his sister did in the afternoon. |

Elle a réparé son vélo.

1. J'écrivais des lettres. J'ai écrit des lettres.
   a. The speaker is answering a question about how she used to spend her lunch hour. |

   J'écrivais des lettres.

   b. The speaker is telling how he expressed his opinion of a proposed law. |

   J'ai écrit des lettres.

2. Nous parlions anglais ensemble. Nous avons parlé anglais ensemble.
   a. The speaker is remembering her favorite uncle, an English teacher, who died recently. |

   Nous parlions anglais ensemble.

   b. The speaker is telling about a brief conversation he had after class with the new American exchange student. |

   Nous avons parlé anglais ensemble.

3. David is telling a friend what happened when he drove over to Nathalie's house yesterday. Give the French equivalents of all the sentences.
   a. I saw Patricia. She was going into a store. |

   J'ai vu Patricia. Elle entrait dans un magasin.

   b. She didn't see me because I was in my car. |

   Elle ne m'a pas vu parce que j'étais dans ma voiture.

   c. Then I saw Max, who was crossing the street. |

   Ensuite, j'ai vu Max qui traversait la rue.

   d. When he saw me, he said hello to me. |

   Quand il m'a vu, il m'a dit bonjour.

   e. I asked him if he wanted to go to her house with me. |

   Je lui ai demandé s'il voulait aller chez elle avec moi.

   f. When we arrived at Nathalie's house, she was not there. |

   Quand nous sommes arrivés chez Nathalie, elle n'était pas là.

À Propos! Imagine that you are a famous detective. In three sentences, using the *imparfait*, describe what the criminal was doing when you caught him/her.

3. The recent past and the near future

1. Answer the following questions, using *aller* + infinitive and an object pronoun. (See key.)

   Modèle: Tu vas à l'épicerie? |

     Je vais y aller.

   a. Vous êtes allés à la poste?
   b. Est-ce que Marc a fini toutes ses lettres?
   c. Est-ce que vous écrivez à vos amis belges?
   d. Vous téléphonerez à vos parents?
   e. Béatrice et Paul iront au supermarché tout à l'heure?
   f. Tu as parlé à ton professeur aujourd'hui?

2. Answer the questions below, using *venir de* and an object pronoun.

   Modèle: Tu as reçu la lettre de ton père? (Oui,...) |

     Oui, je viens de la recevoir.

   a. Est-ce que vous avez réservé les places? (Oui, nous...) |

     Oui, nous venons de les réserver.

   b. Est-ce qu'ils achèteront des billets demain? (Non,...) |

     Non, ils viennent d'en acheter.

   c. Tu vas à la bibliothèque avec eux? (Non,...) |

     Non, je viens d'y aller.

   d. Ils vont prendre leur petit déjeuner? (Non,...) |

     Non, ils viennent de le prendre.

3. Robert has just joined the crowd of spectators waiting for the Tour de France. To find out what's going on, he talks to Alice, who is standing next to him. Use the context to complete each line with the correct form of *venir de* or *aller*.

   Modèle: Robert: Le maire _____ commencer son discours bientôt? |

     va

   Alice: Non, il _____ le terminer. |

     vient de

   a. *Robert:* Je _____ arriver. Et toi, tu es là depuis longtemps? | viens d'
   b. *Alice:* Non, moi aussi, je _____ arriver. Tu _____ rester longtemps? | viens d'; vas
   c. *Robert:* Tout l'après-midi. Je _____ apprendre que les coureurs arriveront dans deux heures environ. C'est vrai? | viens d'
   d. *Alice:* Oui, ils _____ arriver vers cinq heures. | vont
   e. *Robert:* En attendant, on _____ prendre un café? | va
   f. *Alice:* Non, si nous partons, nous _____ perdre nos places. | allons

4. The conditional, present and past

1. a. For most verbs, the conditional/future stem is the same as the _____ form of the verb. |

   infinitive (If the infinitive ends in -e the -e is dropped.)

   b. The verbs below have irregular stems for the future and the conditional. Write the _je_-form of the conditional of these verbs: _avoir, être, voir, venir, aller, faire, vouloir, pouvoir._ |

   j'aurais, je serais, je verrais, je viendrais, j'irais, je ferais, je voudrais, je pourrais

2. The conditional is often used when making a request or expressing a wish. Rewrite the following requests, replacing the italicized verbs with verbs in the conditional. (See key.)

   Modèle: Pouvez-vous nous donner le menu, s'il vous plaît? |

   Pourriez-vous nous donner le menu, s'il vous plaît?

   a. Je _veux_ encore de l'eau, s'il vous plaît.

   b. Nous _voulons_ du poulet et des frites.

   c. _Pouvez_-vous nous apporter une bouteille d'eau minérale?

   d. Les enfants _veulent_ encore du pain.

3. Say what the following people would do if it were Sunday. Si c'était dimanche...

   a. Michèle _____ toute le journée. (dormir)

   b. Henri et Yves _____ aux échecs. (jouer)

   c. Tu _____ à tous tes amis. (téléphoner)

   d. Brigitte et moi, nous nous _____ au Quartier latin. (promener) |

   a. dormirait   b. joueraient   c. téléphonerais   d. promènerions

4. Write what _would have happened,_ using the cues below. Give English equivalents of your answers.

   Modèle: si nous/être sur la place du Marché, nous/voir passer le Tour de France |

   Si nous avions été sur la place du Marché, nous aurions vu passer le Tour de France. _If we had been at the Place du Marché, we would have seen the Tour de France pass by._

   a. si je/avoir un poste de télé, je/pouvoir voir la course |

   Si j'avais eu un poste de télé, j'aurais pu voir la course. _If I had had a TV set, I would have been able/I could have seen the race._

   b. si tu/avoir de la chance, tu/avoir une place à un balcon |

   Si tu avais eu de la chance, tu aurais eu une place à un balcon. _If you had been lucky, you would have had a place on a balcony._

   c. si vous/apporter des provisions, vous/pouvoir manger |

   Si vous aviez apporté des provisions, vous auriez pu manger. _If you had brought some provisions/food, you could have eaten._

   d. si je/voir un marchand ambulant, je/acheter des cacahuètes |

   Si j'avais vu un marchand ambulant, j'aurais acheté des cacahuètes. _If I had seen a street vendor, I would have bought some peanuts._

En quoi votre vie aurait-elle été différente si vous aviez appris le français à l'âge de six ans? si vous étiez le fils ou la fille du Président des États-Unis? si vous n'aviez jamais eu de télévision?

5. The future

1. The following people are going on a bicycle tour in Brittany and have to do several things before they leave. Say what each person will do, using the future tense.

   a. Paul: écrire une lettre à un ami breton |

   Paul écrira une lettre à un ami breton.

   b. nous: trouver une tente |

   Nous trouverons une tente.

   c. moi: emprunter *(to borrow)* un sac de couchage *(sleeping bag)* |

   J'emprunterai un sac de couchage.

   d. toi: réparer ta bicyclette |

   Tu répareras ta bicyclette.

   e. Anne et Julie: acheter des provisions |

   Anne et Julie achèteront des provisions. (Did you remember the accent grave?)

2. Read the French and English sentences below.

Quand je serai en vacances, je me reposerai.	*When I am on vacation, I will rest.*

   In French, the _____ tense is used after *quand*. The English equivalent uses the _____ tense. |

   future; present

3. Here are some of the things the people will do when they are in Brittany. Rewrite the sentences in the future tense. Give the English equivalent of the first two sentences.

   Modèle: Quand il fait beau, nous allons à la plage. |

   Quand il fera beau, nous irons à la plage. When it's nice, we will go to the beach.

   a. Quand il fait mauvais, nous restons dans des auberges de jeunesse. |

   Quand il fera mauvais, nous resterons dans des auberges de jeunesse. *When it's bad weather, we'll stay in youth hostels.*

   b. Quand Danièle est en Bretagne, elle mange beaucoup de poisson. |

   Quand Danièle sera en Bretagne, elle mangera beaucoup de poisson. *When Danièle is in Brittany, she will eat a lot of fish.*

   c. Quand vous êtes fatigué, vous vous levez tard le matin. |

   Quand vous serez fatigué, vous vous lèverez tard le matin.

   d. Quand il fait beau le soir, je me promène. |

   Quand il fera beau le soir, je me promènerai.

4. Complete the sentences below to say what will happen if certain conditions are met. Use the future tense. (See key.)

a. S'il ne pleut pas, nous _____ demain matin. (partir)
b. S'il y a trop de circulation sur les routes, ils _____ le train. (prendre)
c. Si Paul prend le train, nous _____ le chercher à la gare. (aller)
d. Si les magasins sont encore ouverts, tu _____ acheter un pneu pour ta bicyclette. (pouvoir)
e. Si j'en ai le temps, je _____ quelques courses ce matin. (faire)
f. Si le métro est toujours en grève, Danièle et Julie _____ plus tard. (venir)

6. Review of *le futur antérieur*

1. In English, conjunctions of time are rarely followed by the future or future perfect. It is understood that your being older, your getting ready, will take place in the future and not in the present.

> When you *are* older, you will understand.
> As soon as you *are* ready, we'll leave.

In French in such cases, the verb must be in the future after conjunctions of time, such as *quand, lorsque* (when), *dès que* (as soon as), *après que* (after) and *aussitôt que* (as soon as).

Translate the two sentences above into French, using the proper tense after the conjunctions. |

Quand vous serez plus âgé/e vous comprendrez (tu seras... tu comprendras).

Dès que vous serez (tu seras) prêt/e/s, nous partirons.

If the action introduced by the conjunctions of time precedes the future action of the main verb, the *futur antérieur* is used:

> Je me marierai *après que j'aurai terminé* mes études.
> I'll get married *after I (will) have completed* my studies.

2. Complete the following sentences with the proper verb form.
a. Elle t'écrira dès qu'elle _____ ton adresse. (recevoir)
b. Tu prendras ton bain après que je _____ de la salle de bains. (sortir)
c. Elle me prêtera son livre quand elle le _____. (lire)
d. Nous irons acheter ce disque aussitôt que nous _____ au magasin. (arriver)
e. Vous étudierez la trigonométrie lorsque vous _____ l'algèbre. (apprendre) |

a. aura reçu   b. serai sorti(e)   c. aura lu   d. seront arrivé/e/s   e. aurez appris

7. Practice with the subjunctive

1. By now, you know quite a few structures that require the use of the subjunctive. This frame will help you review them.

a. Il faut que vous finissiez votre dîner. |
   The subjunctive is used after _____.

b. J'aimerais que tu viennes avec moi chez le docteur.
   The subjunctive is used after verbs that express a _____. |

c. Elle vient ici pour que nous puissions discuter ensemble. |
   The subjunctive is used after _____. |

d. Ils sont ravis que nous aimions leur pays.
   The subjunctive is used after expressions of _____. |

a. an impersonal expression

b. wish (aimer, préférer, vouloir, etc.)

c. a conjunction

d. emotion

2. Most verbs have a regular subjunctive formation.
   a. Forms with silent endings have the same stem as the _____ -form of the present indicative. *(que je prenne)* |
   b. Forms with pronounced endings have the same stem as the _____-form of the present indicative. *(que vous preniez)* |

   a. ils/elles

   b. nous

3. Complete these sentences with the subjunctive forms of the verbs in parentheses. Write the whole *que*-clause.
   a. Je voudrais que tu _____ ces disques. (acheter)
   b. Il ne faut pas que vous _____ tous ces romans maintenant. (lire)
   c. Nous sommes désolés que Michèle ne _____ pas ce soir. (venir)
   d. Le maître-nageur est furieux que ses élèves _____ pendant la leçon. (parler)
   e. Je suis contente que vous _____ chez moi demain. (venir)
   f. Il faut que vous _____ la table maintenant. (débarrasser)
   g. Nous étions ravis que le Tour _____ par notre ville. (passer)
   h. Écris-moi pour que je _____ ce que tu fais. (savoir)
   i. Je t'expliquerai cette leçon pour que tu _____ faire ton travail. (pouvoir) |

   a que tu achètes   b que vous lisiez   c que Michèle ne vienne pas   d que ses élèves parlent   e que vous veniez   f que vous débarrassiez   g que le Tour passe   h que je sache   i que tu puisses

4. Pierre is having a few friends over tomorrow. Write complete sentences below with the verbs in parentheses. (See key.)
   a. Pierre aimerait que tu / à la pâtisserie en allant chez lui. (aller)
   b. Il voudrait que vous / une tarte aux fraises. (acheter)
   c. Il est content que ses amis / chez lui. (venir)
   d. Il aimerait qu'il / beau pour que nous / faire une belle promenade dans la forêt. (faire, pouvoir)

5. The following people have been asked what they regret most about living in a big city. Write their answers. (See key.)
   Modèle: M. Poireau: les gens sont toujours pressés |
   M. Poireau regrette que les gens soient toujours pressés.
   a. Mme Julien: les voitures font tellement de bruit
   b. les Leduc: la vie est si chère
   c. vous: on ne peut pas facilement se garer
   d. moi: les rues sont sales
   e. nous: il y a tellement de bâtiments modernes

6. Read the instructions given to race driver Jean-Marie Ragier by his team manager, before the Monte Carlo Grand Prix races.

D'abord il est important que tu restes derrière le chef de file presque jusqu'à la fin de la course. C'est alors qu'il faut que tu accélères. Les autorités viennent de m'informer qu'il ne faut pas que nous fassions trop de bruit—les propriétaires du château désirent que les moteurs tournent au régime (operation) le plus bas possible. Et surtout, laisse-moi te rappeler un point capital; il est essentiel que tu aies les yeux fixés sur la route et que tu ne regardes pas les jolies filles qui seront sur la terrasse de l'usine de parfum.

Jean-Marie Ragier won the race and his manager is praising him for having followed instructions to the letter. Write what he says, using the following expressions and the past subjunctive. (See key.)

Modèle: Je suis content: rester derrière le chef de file |

Je suis content que tu sois resté derrière le chef de file.

a. Je suis enchanté: accélérer au bon moment
b. Je suis heureux: ne pas faire trop de bruit
c. Je suis ravi: avoir les yeux fixés sur la route
d. Je suis satisfait: ne pas regarder les jolies filles
e. Je suis très fier: gagner

8. The placement of adverbs

In simple tenses such as present, conditional, or subjunctive, an adverb generally comes right after the verb it modifies. It comes after *pas* if the verb is negative. Some adverbs may come at the beginning of a sentence, especially if they indicate time.

1. Rearrange the words below to form logical sentences.
   a. mal   chien   nage   mon |

   Mon chien nage mal.

   b. chasse   ton   mes   toujours   chien   chats |

   Ton chien chasse toujours mes chats.

   c. aime   cheval   vite   mon   courir |

   Mon cheval aime courir vite. (*Vite* comes after the verb *courir*, not *aime*, because it describes how the horse runs.)

In compound tenses (such as the *passé composé*), adverbs are usually placed between the auxiliary and the past participle. They usually come after *pas* if the verb is negative.

2. Rewrite these sentences, adding the adverbs provided.
   a. Je suis allée en Europe. (souvent) |

   Je suis souvent allée en Europe.

   b. Patrick n'a pas aimé ce disque. (beaucoup) |

   Patrick n'a pas beaucoup aimé ce disque.

   c. Catherine s'est habillée pour le bal. (déjà) |

   Catherine s'est déjà habillée pour le bal.

d. Eric dormait en classe. (quelquefois) |

Eric dormait quelquefois en classe.

3. The absent-minded professor mutters to himself as he leaves his office. Among other things, he forgets his adverbs, and leaves them out of his sentences. Put them in for him.

   a. Zut! J'ai oublié mon adresse! (complètement) |

   Zut! J'ai complètement oublié mon adresse!

   b. Bon! Je vais téléphoner à mon amie Mme Aigle. (immédiatement) |

   Je vais immédiatement téléphoner à mon amie Mme Aigle.

   c. Elle me la donnera. (certainement) |

   Elle me la donnera certainement.

   d. Tiens! J'ai oublié son numéro. (aussi) |

   Tiens! J'ai aussi oublié son numéro.

   e. Je le trouverai dans l'annuaire. (facilement) |

   Je le trouverai facilement dans l'annuaire.

   f. Pas de réponse chez Mme Aigle! Elle est allée chez sa fille. (probablement) |

   Pas de réponse chez Mme Aigle! Elle est probablement allée chez sa fille.

   g. Demain elle sera chez elle. (certainement) |

   Demain elle sera certainement chez elle.

   h. Alors, ce soir je dormirai dans mon bureau. (confortablement) |

   Alors, ce soir je dormirai confortablement dans mon bureau.

   i. Zut! J'ai perdu la clef de mon bureau! (encore) |

   Zut! J'ai encore perdu la clef de mon bureau!

9. The passive voice in various tenses

1. All tenses of the auxiliary *être* can be used to form the passive. The verb *être* carries the tense for the passive verb form.

   je suis accepté(e)
   j'étais _____
   j'ai été _____
   je serai _____   } à l'université
   je serais _____
   que je sois _____

2. Supply the verbs in the second half of the sentences below. Be sure to put the auxiliary *être* into the same tense as the original transitive verb.

   a. La souris n'est pas assez rapide et elle _____ *(is caught)* par le chat. |

   a. elle est attrapée

   b. La souris n'a pas été assez rapide et _____. |

   b. elle a été attrapée

   c. La souris ne sera pas assez rapide et _____. |

   c. elle sera attrapée

3. Translate the following passage into French, using the passive voice and the tense indicated. (See key.)

When I was kidnapped *(kidnapper, p.c.)*, I was thrown *(jeter, p.c.)* into the back seat *(sur le siège arrière)* of a car. My hands were tied together *(lier, p.c.)*, my eyes were covered *(couvrir, p.c.)*, and a handkerchief *(un mouchoir)* was put *(mettre, p.c.)* into my mouth. The car was *(imparfait)* equipped *(équiper)* with a loud-speaker *(un haut-parleur)* and a voice said *(p.c.):* "Will he be transported to the boss *(le patron)* right away or will he be taken *(emmener)* to *la chambre noire* first?" Meanwhile *(Pendant ce temps)*, I was tortured *(imparfait)* by the thought *(la pensée):* Will I ever be released *(relâcher, future)*, or would I be killed *(tuer, future)?*

10. Inversion with *quel*

1. Consider this sentence: *Quels gants a-t-il trouvés?*
   a. Two words agree with *gants*. One is *quels*. The other is
      ——. |
      trouvés
   b. Why does *trouvés* agree with the direct object *gants?* |
      Because the participle must agree with a preceding direct object.
2. Write the forms that are correct for the following questions.
   a. (Quel, Quelles) devoir as-tu (faits, fait) ce soir? | a. Quel; fait
   b. (Quels, Quelle) girafe ont-ils (achetée, achetés)? | b. Quelle; achetée
   c. (Quel, Quels) disques avez-vous (écouté, écoutés) avec Sté-
      phanie? | c. Quels; écoutés
   d. (Quels, Quelles) lettres as-tu (écrites, écrite) ce week-end? | d. Quelles; écrites
3. Bernard is telling a friend all of the latest news, but he doesn't give any details. Write the friend's questions asking for more precise information. Use inversion. (See key.)
   Modèle: Guy et Robert ont perdu des disques. |
   Quels disques ont-ils perdus?
   a. Sophie a acheté une voiture.
   b. Marc a vu deux films.
   c. Christophe et Anne ont rencontré deux amies.
   d. Nicolas a choisi un métier.
   e. Nathalie et Bernadette ont vendu des meubles.

11. Relative pronouns

1. Read these sentences, with attention to the relative pronouns.

   Villemétrie est un village *qui* est près de Paris.
   Villemétrie est le village *où* je suis né.

Villemétrie est un village *que* j'aime beaucoup.
Villemétrie est un village *dont* on ne parle pas souvent.
Villemétrie est un village *dans lequel* j'ai beaucoup d'amis.

	Personnes	*Choses*
Sujet:	qui	qui
Objet direct:	que	que
avec *de:*	dont, de qui, duquel etc.	dont, duquel, etc.
avec une autre préposition:	prep. + { qui / lequel	prep. + lequel
lieu ou temps:		où

1. Say that Nadia doesn't like the following things, using *qui*.
   Modèle: les automobilistes/klaxonner *(to honk)* |
   Elle n'aime pas les automobilistes qui klaxonnent.
   a. les films/être tristes |
   Elle n'aime pas les films qui sont tristes.
   b. les réveils/sonner trop fort |
   Elle n'aime pas les réveils qui sonnent trop fort.
   c. les gens/mâcher *(to chew)* du chewing-gum |
   Elle n'aime pas les gens qui mâchent du chewing-gum.
   d. les téléphones/ne pas marcher |
   Elle n'aime pas les téléphones qui ne marchent pas.

2. Etienne is showing Julie various people and places he used to know. Rewrite the sentences with *que*.
   Modèle: Je préférais cette boulangerie. |
   C'est la boulangerie que je préférais.
   a. J'adorais ce parc.   c. J'admirais beaucoup cette
   b. Je préférais ce café.   maison.
                                  d. Je voyais souvent cet ami. |
   a. C'est le parc que j'adorais.   b. C'est le café que je préférais.   c. C'est la maison
   que j'admirais beaucoup.   d. C'est l'ami que je voyais souvent.

3. Michel, who is traveling through Europe, is telling a new acquaintance about himself. Rewrite his statements, using the relative pronoun *où*.
   Modèle: Je vais en Espagne et puis au Maroc. *(les pays)* |
   Ce sont les pays où je vais.
   a. J'habite à l'avenue de Corbéra, à Paris. *(l'avenue)* |
   C'est l'avenue où j'habite.
   b. Je suis né à Lille. *(la ville)* |
   C'est la ville où je suis né.
   c. J'étais à l'hôtel Miramar hier soir. *(l'hôtel)* |
   C'est l'hôtel où j'étais hier soir.

4. Use the pronoun *dont* to complete the following sentences:
   a. J'ai besoin de ce livre. Voici le livre... |

      dont j'ai besoin.
   b. Le professeur nous a parlé de cet auteur. C'est l'auteur... |

      dont le professeur nous a parlé.
   c. Il est l'auteur de romans historiques. Voici les romans histo-
      riques... |

      dont il est l'auteur.

   In French after *dont* the word order must always be *subject, verb, object,* which contrasts with the English word order of object, subject, verb.

   > Voilà le chien dont j'aime beaucoup le propriétaire.
   > *There is the dog whose owner I like a lot.*

5. Use the pronoun *dont* to combine the following sentences.
   a. Le professeur fait une conférence. Je suis son ami.
   b. Le jeune homme frappe à la porte. Tu as son livre.
   c. Cette dame est riche. Nous connaissons son mari. |

      a. Le professeur, dont je suis l'ami, fait une conférence.   b. Le jeune homme, dont tu
      as le livre, frappe à la porte.   c. Cette dame, dont nous connaissons le mari, est riche.

6. Write the pronoun phrase to complete each of these sentences:
   a. Le cyclisme est le sujet sur _____ nous allons présenter ce re-
      portage.
   b. Les cyclistes sont les sportifs à _____ les automobilistes disent
      des insultes.
   c. Nous recherchons tous l'air pur _____ nous avons besoin.
   d. «Le cheval blanc» est le restaurant devant _____ les cyclistes
      passent.
   e. Les automobilistes sont les voyageurs pour _____ les cyclistes
      sont un dar |

      a sur lequel   b à qui; auxquels   c duquel; dont   d devant lequel   e pour qui;
      pour lesquels

7. You and your friends have just flown to a wonderful faraway vacation spot. Unfortunately, the airline sent some of your luggage
   by mistake to other faraway places. Using possessive pronouns,
   make an inventory of your possessions. (See key.)

   Modèle: Mes valises ne sont pas là. Et les tiennes? |

      Les miennes non plus.
   a. Nos raquettes ne sont pas là. Et les vôtres?
   b. Ma caméra n'est pas là. Et la caméra de Patrick?
   c. Nos clubs de golf ne sont pas là. Et les clubs de François et
      Richard?
   d. La guitare de Sophie n'est pas là. Et la tienne?
   e. Notre tente n'est pas là. Et la tente de Bernard et Laurent.

12. Superlatives

1. A Parisian friend of yours is showing you around her city. She uses superlatives for everything. Use the cues below to write what she is saying. Write the English equivalent of frame *a.*

   Modèle: ville/merveilleux/monde |
   > C'est la ville la plus merveilleuse du monde! It's the most marvelous city in the world!
   > (Remember that the preposition *de* is the only one used after a superlative.)

   a. avenue/élégant/Paris |
   > C'est l'avenue la plus élégante de Paris! It's the most elegant avenue in Paris!

   b. quartier/joli/ville |
   > C'est le plus joli quartier de la ville! (*joli* usually precedes the noun)

   c. pâtissier/bon/monde |
   > C'est le meilleur pâtissier du monde!

2. Five French friends spent the summer driving around the United States. Now they are looking back on the trip and commenting on each other's habits and reactions. Rewrite the following comments, using the superlative forms of the adverbs.

   Modèle: Henri se perdait souvent. |
   > De tout le groupe, Henri se perdait le plus souvent.

   a. Claude écrivait régulièrement à sa famille. |
   > De tout le groupe, Claude écrivait le plus régulièrement à sa famille.

   b. Jérôme comprenait facilement les panneaux indicateurs. |
   > De tout le groupe, Jérôme comprenait le plus facilement les panneaux indicateurs.

   c. Robert comprenait bien l'anglais. |
   > De tout le groupe, Robert comprenait le mieux l'anglais.

   d. Gilles se levait toujours tard. |
   > De tout le groupe, Gilles se levait toujours le plus tard.

   e. Luc tolérait mal le soleil en Floride. |
   > De tout le groupe, Luc tolérait le plus mal le soleil en Floride.

Jeu de mots (pun): Apprendre par cœur = learn by heart. Ici, cela signifie que, pour les Québecois, le français est la langue du cœur.

L'ANGLETERRE

Londres ☆

LA MANCHE

Calais

Lille

Amiens

☆ Bruxelles

LA BELGIQUE

Charleroi

L'ALLEMAGNE

Cherbourg

Le Havre

Rouen

la Seine

Reims

☆ Le Luxembourg
Luxembourg

NORMANDIE

☆ Paris

Versailles

LORRAINE

Nancy

Strasbourg

LES VOSGES

le Rhin

Brest

BRETAGNE

Chartres

ALSACE

Douarnenez

Rennes

Le Mans

Orléans

CHAMPAGNE

Fribourg

Angers

Blois

la Loire

Nantes

Tours

Dijon

Besançon

Beaune

BOURGOGNE

Berne
☆

LA SUISSE

LE JURA

La Rochelle

la Saône

Genève
Chamonix

L'OCÉAN ATLANTIQUE

Limoges

LE MASSIF CENTRAL

Clermont-Ferrand

Lyon

0   50   100   150 km

0   50   100 mi

AUVERGNE

Grenoble

L'Alpe d'Huez

LES ALPES

L'ITALIE

Bordeaux

le Rhône

Avignon

PROVENCE

Nice

la Garonne

Montpellier

Cannes

GASCOGNE

Toulouse

LANGUEDOC

Marseilles

Pau

L'ESPAGNE

Vitoria

LES

PYRÉNÉES

Perpignan

LA MER MÉDITERRANÉE

ANDORRE

LA FRANCE

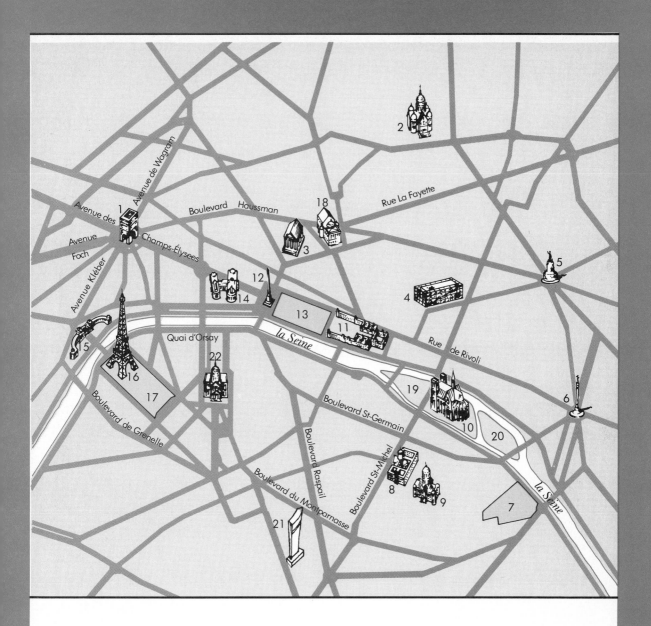

1	l'Arc de Triomphe	8	la Sorbonne	15	le Palais de Chaillot
2	le Sacré-Coeur	9	le Panthéon	16	la Tour Eiffel
3	la Madeleine	10	Notre-Dame	17	le Champ de Mars
4	le Centre Pompidou (Beaubourg)	11	le Louvre	18	l'Opéra
5	la Place de la République	12	la Place de la Concorde	19	Île de la Cité
6	la Place de la Bastille	13	le Jardin des Tuileries	20	Île St-Louis
7	le Jardin des Plantes	14	le Grand Palais	21	la Tour Montparnasse
				22	les Invalides

PARIS MONUMENTAL

1 l'Algérie
2 la Belgique
3 le Bénin
4 le Burundi
5 le Cambodge
6 le Cameroun
7 le Congo
8 la Corse
9 la Côte d'Ivoire
10 Djibouti
11 la France
12 le Gabon
13 la Guadeloupe
14 la Guinée
15 la Guyane française
16 Haïti
17 la Haute-Volta
18 le Laos
19 la Louisiane
20 le Luxembourg
21 Madagascar
22 le Mali
23 le Maroc
24 la Martinique

25 la Mauritanie
26 le Niger
27 la Nouvelle-Angleterre
28 la Nouvelle-Calédonie
29 la Polynésie française
30 le Québec
31 la République Centrafricaine
32 la Réunion

33 le Rwanda
34 le Sénégal
35 la Suisse
36 le Tchad
37 le Togo
38 la Tunisie
39 le Vietnam
40 le Zaïre

LE MONDE FRANCOPHONE

Regular verbs

	-ER	-IR	-RE
Infinitif	parl **er**	fini **r**	répond **re**
Participes	parl **é**	fini	répond **u**
	parl **ant**	finiss **ant**	répond **ant**

Indicatif

Présent

-ER		-IR		-RE	
je **parl e**	nous parl **ons**	fini **s**	finiss **ons**	répond **s**	répond **ons**
tu parl **es**	vous parl **ez**	fini **s**	finiss **ez**	répond **s**	répond **ez**
on/il/elle parl **e**	ils/elles parl **ent**	fini **t**	finiss **ent**	répond	répond **ent**

Imparfait

je **parl ais**	nous parl **ions**	finiss **ais**	finiss **ions**	répond **ais**	répond **ions**
tu parl **ais**	vous parl **iez**	finiss **ais**	finiss **iez**	répond **ais**	répond **iez**
on/il/elle parl **ait**	ils/elles parl **aient**	finiss **ait**	finiss **aient**	répond **ait**	répond **aient**

Passé composé

j' **ai parlé**	nous avons parlé	**ai fini**	avons fini	**ai répondu**	avons répondu
tu as parlé	vous avez parlé	as fini	avez fini	as répondu	avez répondu
on/il/elle a parlé	ils/elles ont parlé	a fini	ont fini	a répondu	ont répondu

Plus-que-parfait   j'avais **parlé**   j'avais **fini**   j'avais **répondu**

Futur

je **parler ai**	nous parler **ons**	**finir ai**	finir **ons**	**répondr ai**	répondr **ons**
tu parler **as**	vous parler **ez**	finir **as**	finir **ez**	répondr **as**	répondr **ez**
on/il/elle parler **a**	ils/elles parler **ont**	finir **a**	finir **ont**	répondr **a**	répondr **ont**

Futur antérieur   j'aurai **parlé**   j'aurai **fini**   j'aurai **répondu**

Conditionnel

Présent

je **parler ais**	nous parler **ions**	**finir ais**	finir **ions**	**répondr ais**	répondr **ions**
tu parler **ais**	vous parler **iez**	finir **ais**	finir **iez**	répondr **ais**	répondr **iez**
on/il/elle parler **ait**	ils/elles parler **aient**	finir **ait**	finir **aient**	répondr **ait**	répondr **aient**

Passé   j'aurais **parlé**   j'aurais fini   j'aurais **répondu**

Subjonctif

Présent

que je **parl e**	nous parl **ions**	**finiss e**	finiss **ions**	**répond e**	répond **ions**
tu parl **es**	vous parl **iez**	finiss **es**	finiss **iez**	répond **es**	répond **iez**
on/il/elle parl **e**	ils/elles parl **ent**	finiss **e**	finiss **ent**	répond **e**	répond **ent**

Passé   que j'aie **parlé**   que j'aie fini   que j'aie **répondu**

Impératif

parl **e**	fini **s**	répond **s**
parl **ez**	**finiss ez**	répond **ez**
parl **ons**	finiss **ons**	répond **ons**

Passé simple

je **parl ai**	nous parl **âmes**	fini **s**	fin **îmes**	**répond is**	répond **îmes**
tu parl **as**	vous parl **âtes**	fini **s**	fin **îtes**	répond **is**	répond **îtes**
on/il/elle parl **a**	ils/elles parl **èrent**	fini **t**	fin **irent**	répond **it**	répond **irent**

Reflexive verbs

Infinitif   se laver

Indicatif

Présent

je	**me**	**lave**
tu	te	laves
on/il/elle	se	lave
nous	nous	lavons
vous	vous	lavez
ils/elles	se	lavent

Passé composé

je	**me**	**suis**	**lavé/e**
tu	t'	es	lavé/e
on/il/elle	s'	est	lavé/e
nous	nous	sommes	lavé/e/s
vous vous	êtes	lavé/e/s
ils/elles	se	sont	lavé/e/s

Négatif

je	**ne**	**me**	**suis**	**pas lavé/e**
tu	ne	t'	es	pas lavé/e
on/il/elle	ne	s'	est	pas lavé/e
nous	ne	nous	sommes	pas lavé/e/s
vous	ne	vous	êtes	pas lavé/e/s
elles	ne	se	sont	pas lavé/e/s

Imparfait   je me lavais

Plus-que-parfait je m'étais lavé/e

Futur   je me laverai

Conditionnel
Passé   je me laverais
                     je me serais lavé/e

Subjonctif
Présent   que je me lave
Passé   que je me sois lavé/e

Impératif   **lave-toi**
                     lavez-vous
                     lavons-nous

Passé simple   je me lavai

Auxiliary verbs

Indicatif	**Être**	**Avoir**
Présent	je **suis**	j'**ai**
	tu es	tu as
	il est	elle a
	nous sommes	nous avons
	vous êtes	vous avez
	ils sont	elles ont
Passé composé	j'ai été	j'ai eu
Imparfait	j'étais	j'avais
Conditionnel	je serais	j'aurais

Subjonctif

Présent	que je **sois**	que j'**aie**
	que tu sois	que tu aies
	qu'il soit	qu'il ait
	que nous soyons	que nous ayons
	que vous soyez	que vous ayez
	qu'ils soient	qu'ils aient

Participes

Présent	étant	ayant
Passé	été	eu
passé simple	je **fus**	j'**eus**
	nous fûmes	nous eûmes

Irregular Verbs

Infinitif	Participe présent	Indicatif présent		Passé composé	Imparfait
aller	allant	je **vais** tu **vas** il **va**	nous **allons** vous **allez** ils **vont**	je **suis allé/e**	j'allais
boire	buvant	je **bois** tu bois il boit	nous **buvons** vous buvez ils **boivent**	j'ai **bu**	je buvais
battre	battant	je **bats** tu bats il bat	nous **battons** vous battez ils **battent**	j'ai **battu**	je battais
connaître	connaissant	je **connais** tu connais il **connaît**	nous **connaissons** vous connaissez ils connaissent	j'ai **connu**	je connaissais
croire	croyant	je **crois** tu crois il croit	nous **croyons** vous croyez ils **croient**	j'ai **cru**	je croyais
devoir	devant	je **dois** tu dois il doit	nous **devons** vous devez ils **doivent**	j'ai **dû**	je devais
dire	disant	je **dis** tu dis il dit	nous **disons** vous **dites** ils disent	j'ai **dit**	je disais
écrire	écrivant	j'**écris** tu écris il écrit	nous **écrivons** vous **écrivez** ils **écrivent**	j'ai **écrit**	j'écrivais
envoyer	envoyant	j'**envoie** tu envoies il envoie	nous **envoyons** vous envoyez ils **envoient**	j'ai **envoyé**	j'envoyais
faire	faisant	je **fais** tu fais il fait	nous **faisons** vous **faites** ils **font**	j'ai **fait**	je faisais
falloir	fallant	il **faut**		il a **fallu**	il fallait
lire	lisant	je **lis** tu lis il lit	nous **lisons** vous lisez ils lisent	j'ai **lu**	je lisais

Plus-que-parfait	Conditionnel Futur	C. passé F. antérieur	Subjonctif présent	Subjonctif passé	Passé simple
j'étais allé/e	j'**irais** j'irai	je serais allé/e je serai allé/e	que j'**aille** que nous allions	que je sois allé/e que nous soyons allé/e/s	j'allai
j'avais bu	je **boirais** je boirai	j'aurais bu j'aurai bu	que je boive que nous buvions	que j'aie bu que nous ayons bu	je bus
j'avais battu	je **battrais** je battrai	j'aurais battu j'aurai battu	que je batte que nous battions	que j'aie battu que nous ayons battu	je battis
j'avais connu	je **connaîtrais** je connaîtrai	j'aurais connu j'aurai connu	que je connaisse que nous connaissions	que j'aie connu que nous ayons connu	je connus
j'avais cru	je **croirais** je croirai	j'aurais cru j'aurai cru	que je croie que nous croyions	que j'aie cru que nous ayons cru	je crus
j'avais dû	je **devrais** je devrai	j'aurais dû j'aurai dû	que je doive que nous devions	que j'aie dû que nous ayons dû	je dus
j'avais dit	je **dirais** je dirai	j'aurais dit j'aurai dit	que je dise que nous disions	que j'aie dit que nous ayons dit	je dis
j'avais écrit	j'**écrirais** j'écrirai	j'aurais écrit j'aurai écrit	que j'écrive que nous écrivions	que j'aie écrit que nous ayons écrit	j'écrivis
j'avais envoyé	j'**enverrais** j'enverrai	j'aurais envoyé j'aurai envoyé	que j'envoie que nous envoyions	que j'aie envoyé que nous ayons envoyé	j'envoyai
j'avais fait	je **ferais** je ferai	j'aurais fait j'aurai fait	que je **fasse** que nous fassions	que j'aie fait que nous ayons fait	je fis
il avait fallu	il **faudrait** il faudra	il aurait fallu il aura fallu	qu'il **faille**	qu'il ait fallu	il fallut
j'avais lu	je **lirais** je lirai	j'aurais lu j'aurai lu	que je lise que nous lisions	que j'aie lu que nous ayons lu	je lus

Infinitif	Participe présent	Indicatif Présent		Passé composé	Imparfait
mettre	mettant	je **mets** tu mets il met	nous **mettons** vous mettez ils mettent	j'ai **mis**	je mettais
ouvrir	ouvrant	j'**ouvre** tu ouvres il ouvre	nous ouvrons vous ouvrez ils ouvrent	j'ai **ouvert**	j'ouvrais
partir	partant	je **pars** tu pars il part	nous **partons** vous partez ils partent	je **suis parti/e**	je partais
pouvoir	pouvant	je **peux** tu peux il peut	nous **pouvons** vous pouvez ils **peuvent**	j'ai **pu**	je pouvais
prendre	prenant	je **prends** tu prends il prend	nous **prenons** vous prenez ils **prennent**	j'ai **pris**	je prenais
recevoir	recevant	je **reçois** tu reçois il reçoit	nous **recevons** vous recevez ils **reçoivent**	j'ai **reçu**	je recevais
savoir	savant	je **sais** tu sais il sait	nous **savons** vous savez ils savent	j'ai **su**	je savais
suivre	suivant	je **suis** tu suis il suit	nous **suivons** vous suivez ils suivent	j'ai **suivi**	je suivais
venir	venant	je **viens** tu viens il vient	nous **venons** vous venez ils **viennent**	je **suis venu/e**	je venais
vivre	vivant	je **vis** tu vis il vit	nous **vivons** vous vivez ils vivent	j'ai **vécu**	je vivais
voir	voyant	je **vois** tu vois il voit	nous **voyons** vous voyez ils **voient**	j'ai **vu**	je voyais
vouloir	voulant	je **veux** tu veux il veut	nous **voulons** vous voulez ils **veulent**	j'ai **voulu**	je voulais

Verb Appendix

Plus-que-parfait	Conditionnel Futur	C. passé F. antérieur	Subjonctif Présent	Subjonctif Passé	Passé Simple
j'avais mis	je **mettrais** je mettrai	j'aurais mis j'aurai mis	que je mette que nous mettions	que j'aie mis que nous ayons mis	je mis
j'avais ouvert	j'**ouvrirais** j'ouvrirai	j'aurais ouvert j'aurai ouvert	que j'ouvre que nous ouvrions	que j'aie ouvert que nous ayons ouvert	j'ouvris
j'étais parti/e	je **partirais** je partirai	je serais parti/e je serai parti/e	que je parte que nous partions	que je sois parti/e que nous soyons parti/e/s	je partis
j'avais pu	je **pourrais** je pourrai	j'aurais pu j'aurai pu	que je **puisse** que nous puissions	que j'aie pu que nous ayons pu	je pus
j'avais pris	je **prendrais** je prendrai	j'aurais pris j'aurai pris	que je prenne que nous prenions	que j'aie pris que nous ayons pris	je pris
j'avais reçu	je **recevrais** je recevrai	j'aurais reçu j'aurai reçu	que je reçoive que nous recevions	que j'aie reçu que nous ayons reçu	je reçus
j'avais su	je **saurais** je saurai	j'aurais su j'aurai su	que je **sache** que nous sachions	que j'aie su que nous ayons su	je sus
j'avais suivi	je **suivrais** je suivrai	j'aurais suivi j'aurai suivi	que je suive que nous suivions	que j'aie suivi que nous ayons suivi	je suivis
j'étais venu/e	je **viendrais** je viendrai	je serais venu/e je serai venu/e	que je vienne que nous venions	que je sois venu/e que nous soyons venu/e/s	je vins
j'avais vécu	je **vivrais** je vivrai	j'aurais vécu j'aurai vécu	que je vive que nous vivions	que j'aie vécu que nous ayons vécu	je vécus
j'avais vu	je **verrais** je verrai	j'aurais vu j'aurai vu	que je voie que nous voyions	que j'aie vu fque nous ayons vu	je vis
j'avais voulu	je **voudrais** je voudrai	j'aurais voulu j'aurai voulu	que je **veuille** que nous voulions	que j'aie voulu que nous ayons voulu	je voulus

Answer Key

Phase 1

Préparation 2

4 3a. Jeanne est de Chicago.
b. Nous sommes d'Ivry.
c. Tu es très en retard.
d. Jeanne et Paul Dupont sont d'Ivry.
e. Vous êtes Monsieur Chardin?
f. Je suis très pressé.

Préparation 3

2 1. C'est un crayon.
2. C'est un bureau.
3. C'est une bande.
4. C'est un morceau de craie.
5. C'est un écran.
6. C'est une table.
7. C'est une feuille de papier.
8. C'est un tableau noir.
9. C'est une cassette.

5 1a. Marie est une fille.
b. Nous sommes derrière Marc.
c. Tu es pressé.
d. Robert et Marie sont de New York.
e. Je suis Stéphanie Romain.
f. Vous êtes en retard!
2a. Je suis de Paris.
b. Vous êtes devant le tableau.
c. Où est le crayon d'Alice?
d. Nous sommes en retard aujourd'hui.
e. La bande et le livre sont là.
f. Tu es de Chicago?

Préparation 4

1 5a. Le professeur est derrière la table.
b. Le morceau de craie est sous la table.
c. Le professeur est devant l'affiche.
d. L'écran est entre l'homme et la table.
e. La feuille de papier est sur la chaise.
2 4a. C'est la caméra de Marc.

b. C'est le transistor de Valérie.
5a. C'est un stylo. C'est le stylo de Mme Depardieu.
b. C'est un magnétophone. C'est le magnétophone de M. Guggenheim.
c. C'est une bande. C'est la bande de Mlle Simon.
d. C'est un cadeau. C'est le cadeau de Mme Langeais.
3 4a. Non, ce n'est pas une cassette. C'est une bande.
b. Non, nous ne sommes pas très en retard. Nous sommes seulement un peu en retard.
c. Non, la jeune fille n'est pas belge. Elle est française.
6 7a. Je cherche Jacqueline.
b. Il cherche un stylo?
7 3a. *to guide;* guid- ; je guide
b. *to resist;* résist- ; je résiste
c. *to remark;* remarqu- ; je remarque
d. *to verify;* vérifi- ; je vérifie
8 3a. Non, ils ne dansent pas le tango.
b. Non, nous ne dansons pas le tango.
c. Non, elle ne danse pas le tango.
d. Non, vous ne dansez pas le tango.

Préparation 5

2 3a. Je ne mange pas aujourd'hui.
b. Nous mangeons à midi.
c. Tu manges en classe?
d. Christine et moi, nous mangeons beaucoup.
e. Mon grand-père mange peu.
f. Vous mangez avec nous aujourd'hui?
2 6a. Vous commencez la leçon. Nous ne commençons pas la leçon.

b. Vous remplacez le cadeau. Nous ne remplaçons pas le cadeau.
c. Vous menacez le professeur. Nous ne menaçons pas le professeur.
5 1a. caméra, présent, pressé, télévision
b. français, garçon, ça alors!, ça va?
c. mathématiques, étudiante, géometrie, américaine
d. Bien sûr, vous êtes, bête, fenêtre
e. où est?, règle, très bien, à demain
f. élève, Hélène
2a. C'est le stylo de Philippe.
b. Ce n'est pas une gomme.
c. Je cherche l'affiche de Marie.
d. Tu parles français.
e. Nous travaillons beaucoup.
f. Hélène regarde Jeanne.
g. Vous écoutez le professeur?

Préparation 6

2 1. Vous
2. Je
3. Tu
4. Elle
5. Nous
6. Elles/Ils
3 1a. cherche
b. cherchons
c. cherchent
d. cherches
e. cherchez
f. cherche
g. cherche
h. cherche
i. cherchent
2a. vérifie
b. admires
c. réparez
d. accepte
e. travaille
f. parlez
g. aident
h. plaçons

3a. Thierry ne parle pas beaucoup en classe.
   b. Toi et Luc, vous ne
   parlez pas beaucoup en
   classe.
   c. Toi et moi, nous ne
   parlons pas beaucoup en
   classe.
   d. Lucie et Georges ne
   parlent pas
   beaucoup en classe.
4 1a. Tu es en retard.
   b. Nous sommes en retard.
   c. Danielle est en retard.
   d. Nous deux, nous sommes
   en retard.
   e. Eric et Jean sont en retard.
   f. Je suis en retard.
   2a. Mme Chenaud n'est pas
   pressée.
   b. Philippe n'est pas poli.
   c. Jean et Jacques ne
   sont pas de Versailles.
   d. Tu n'es pas bête!
5 1a. un b. une c. un d. une
   e. un f. une g. une h. une
   i. un j. un k. un l. une
   2a. le b. l' c. le d. le e. la f. l'
   g. le h. la i. la j. l' k. la l. la
   m. l' n. l' o. l'
7   a. L'homme est grand.
   b. Anne est française.
   c. M. Martelli n'est pas
   pauvre.
   d. Mme Martelli est riche.
   e. La fille est petite.
   f. Elisabeth n'est pas présente
   aujourd'hui.
   g. La femme est laide.
   h. Le monsieur est élégant.
   i. L'étudiant est intelligent.
   j. L'affiche est belle.
8 1a. C'est l'affiche de Martine.
   b. C'est le disque d'Annick.
   c. C'est l'enfant de M.
   Marteau.
   d. C'est la caméra de
   Bernard.
   2a. Où est la gomme de
   Jacques?
   b. Je cherche la caméra de M.
   Teyssier.
   c. Tu n'écoutes pas la
   cassette de Mme Legrand?
9 1. c 2. c 3. b 4. b 5. b

10 1. vous 2. tu 3. vous 4. tu
   5. vous 6. vous 7. vous
   8. tu 9. vous 10. vous
   11. vous

Phase 2

Préparation 7
2 7a. Ils n'aiment pas l'histoire.
   b. Georges n'aime pas la
   géographie.
   c. Anne et moi, nous
   n'aimons pas
   l'espagnol.
   d. Vous n'aimez pas tricoter,
   Madame?
3 5a. Monique aime le tennis,
   mais elle déteste le golf.
   b. Jean et moi, nous aimons la
   biochimie,
   mais nous détestons
   l'histoire.
   c. Antoine et Michel aiment la
   physique,
   mais ils détestent la
   sculpture.
4 5a. Vous regardez la télévision?
   b. Il n'écoute pas.
   c. Tu n'aimes pas le golf?

Préparation 8
1 4a. vous chantez
   b. Elle habite
   c. Nous n'écoutons pas
   d. aimez habiter
   e. Je ne chante pas
   5a. Jean-Claude et Philippe
   écoutent la radio.
   b. Richard et Martine ne dansent pas le rock.
   c. Tu aimes danser?
   d. Marc déteste le jazz.
   6a. Non, elles n'aiment pas la
   vie à la campagne.
   b. Non, nous n'habitons pas à
   Saint-Louis.
   c. Oui, il aime habiter à Ivry.
   7a. nages
   b. ne dansent pas
   c. ne mange pas
   d. patiner
   e. tricotez
   f. regardes
4 5a. Tu as un cahier?

   b. Le professeur a un
   magnétophone?
   c. Vous avez un livre?
   d. Pierre et Robert ont deux
   stylos?

Préparation 9
3 3a. Où est Philippe?
   b. Qui chante?
   c. Qu'est-ce que vous mangez?
5 10a. Cet homme qui habite à
   Munich est allemand.
   b. Cette femme qui habite à
   Wichita est américaine.
   c. Cette femme qui habite à
   Aix est française.

Préparation 10
2 6a. Sylvie Duval est très belle
   et très célèbre.
   b. Mme Lesage est très vieille
   et très intelligente.
   c. Christine est grosse, laide
   et jalouse.
4 3a. Cette b. Cet c. Cette
   d. Ce e. Ce f. Cette
   g. Cet h. Ce
5 7a. attendent
   b. descendent
   c. défend
   d. perdons
   e. rend
6 1. a 2. ont 3. J'ai
   4. avez 5. avons

Préparation 12
1 6a. J'attends Marianne.
   b. Jean-François répond au
   professeur.
   c. Jacques et Anne rendent la
   radio à Sophie.
2 2a. Ils parlent allemand?
   b. Il attend?
   c. Il entend le téléphone?
   d. Robert habite à New York?
   e. Pierre et Jean aiment
   patiner?
   f. La voiture marche
   maintenant?
   g. Ils admirent le président?
   h. Elle écoute la radio?
3 1a. Mardi, j'écoute la radio
   avec Gabrielle.
   b. Jeudi, je regarde la télévision avec Jean-François.

c. Dimanche, je patine avec Daniel et Sylvie.
2a. Je ne danse pas.
b. Je ne patine pas.
c. Je ne tricote pas.
3a. Non, il est dentiste.
b. Non, elle est comptable.
c. Non, il est photographe.
d. Non, elle est ingénieur.
e. Non, je suis écrivain.
4. Cette jeune fille est martiniquaise. Elle est grande, mince, élégante et elle est intelligente.
5. Ce garçon est anglais. Il est petit, roux, beau et il est gentil.
3 6. infirmière/actrice
musicienne/chanteuse
ouvrière/danseuse
7. canadien
belge
italien
suisse
anglais
4 1. b 2. a 3. b

Préparation 13

1 5a. Georges et François choisissent ce disque comme cadeau.
b. Marc et moi, nous choisissons ce livre comme cadeau.
c. Marie et toi, vous choisissez ce stylo comme cadeau.
d. Alain choisit cette radio comme cadeau.
9a. Je sors b. Je sors
c. Je pars d. Je pars
2 6a. La fille suisse n'aime pas les maths.
b. Le garçon allemand aime patiner.

Phase 3

Préparation 14

1 9a. Non, ce sont les chaises de M. Roger.
b. Non, ce sont les soeurs d'Henri.

3 3a. finissent, finissons
b. choisis, choisissez, choisis
c. vieillit, vieillissons
d. maigris, maigrissent
e. réussit, réussissez
f. obéissons, obéit
4 5a. Il y a des cahiers au bureau.
b. Il y a des gommes au bureau.
5 4a. Non, il n'y a pas de crocodiles dans le tiroir.
b. Non, il n'y a pas de lion sous la chaise.

Préparation 15

4 1a. Mme Perrier a un grand bureau.
b. J'ai des soeurs.
c. M. et Mme Victor ont deux enfants.
d. Vous avez quel âge?
2a. Mais nous n'avons pas de feuilles de papier!
b. Mais nous n'avons pas de crayons!
c. Mais nous n'avons pas de gomme!
3a. Nous n'avons pas de grands-parents.
b. Tu n'as pas de chien.
c. Guy et Henri n'ont pas de soeur.
d. Je n'ai pas de chat.

Préparation 16

1 5a. ne sont pas vieux.
b. ne sont pas jalouses.
c. ne sont pas ambitieux.
d. ne sont pas sérieux.
7a. sont belles.
b. sont beaux.
c. sont beaux.
5 1. Il y a 55 chiens en tout.
2. Il y a 36 lions en tout.
3. Il y a 69 personnes en tout.
4. Il y a 6 instruments en tout.

Préparation 17

1 6a. Je n'aime pas ces magnétophones.
b. Je n'aime pas ces électrophones.
7a. Ça alors, je ne trouve pas cet article!

b. Ça alors, je ne trouve pas ces photos!
c. Ça alors, je ne trouve pas ces notes!
4 2a. Tu trouves le magnétophone.
b. Je porte une grosse boîte.
c. Nous aidons M. et Mme Peyre, qui sont très vieux.
d. Hélène et Lucie ferment la porte.
e. Vous lavez la voiture.

Préparation 18

1 4a. mon b. ta c. son
d. mes e. ton
5 J'aime son humour, son intelligence, ses qualités artistiques, sa voiture et ses parents.
3 2a. Angélique et Jeanne connaissent cet avocat.
b. Tu connais cette ville?
c. Paul ne connaît pas ma tante?
d. Je connais cette mécanicienne.
5 5a. Je vois quatre serpents.
b. Marc et Robert voient trois souris.
c. Georges et moi, nous voyons une voiture.
d. Ils voient deux vélos.
e. M. Lafayette voit quatre saxophones.
f. Les enfants voient deux pianos.
6 Hélène: Tu connais ce garçon là-bas?
René: Bien sûr! C'est mon cousin Jean-Pierre.
Hélène: Il est médecin, n'est-ce-pas?
René: Mais non, il est ingénieur.
Hélène: Ah oui. Où est-ce qu'il travaille?
René: Chez Renault.

Préparation 19

4 2a. votre dentiste est
b. Notre médecin
c. Leur professeur
3a. leur b. sa c. leurs d. sa

Phase 4

Préparation 20

4 1a. Je le vois.
   b. Je les vois.
   c. Je les vois.
   d. Je la vois.
   2a. Vous connaissez cet homme? Oui, nous le connaissons (je le connais).
   b. M. et Mme Vincent cherchent cette caméra? Oui, ils la cherchent.
   c. Madeleine voit ce serpent? Oui, elle le voit.
   d. Son père aime ce garçon? Oui, il l'aime.
   e. Vous écoutez ces disques? Oui, nous les écoutons.
5 1a. nos b. votre c. mon
   d. Leurs e. Leur f. ma
   g. sa, ma h. ton
6 1a. Vous voyez une vieille moto.
   b. Jean-Paul voit une vieille chaise.
   c. Nous voyons une vieille voiture.
   d. Mes parents voient un vieux piano.
   e. Moi, je vois un vieux vélo.
   2a. Je vais voir mon petit ami.
   b. Jacques et toi, vous allez voir les Depardieu à Rome.
   c. Charlotte et Yves vont voir le cousin d'Yves.
   d. Tu vas voir tous tes amis.
   e. Mon mari et moi, nous allons voir notre avocate.

Préparation 22

4 1a. veux
   b. veulent
   c. voulez
   2a. Qui veut faire une promenade?
   b. Est-ce que Paul et Marie veulent jouer au volley-ball demain?
   c. Nous ne voulons pas habiter à New York.

Préparation 24

4 1a. Vous allez passer l'après-midi chez Jean.
   b. Elle va sortir avec ses amis dimanche.
   c. Les ouvriers vont travailler à l'usine.
   d. Je vais regarder un vieux film à la télé.

Préparation 25

1a. Il neige.
   b. Il fait beau.
   c. Il fait du vent.
   d. Il pleut.
   e. Non, il neige./(il fait mauvais).
   f. Il fait chaud.
1 2a. le piano
   b. l'accordéon (m.)
   c. le violon
   d. la batterie
   e. la flûte
   f. la trompette
2 5a. Tu sais compter de zéro à cent.
   b. Vous savez faire du ski.
   c. Ces enfants savent leurs leçons.
   d. Nous ne savons pas où est l'aéroport.
   e. Je sais jouer de la batterie.
   f. Elles savent ton numéro de téléphone.

Préparation 26

2 10a. chez eux.
   b. chez nous.
   c. lui.
   d. chez elles.

Préparation 27

1 2a. On te trouve généreux.
   b. On me trouve sympathique.
   c. On ne nous trouve pas du tout sérieux.
   d. On ne les trouve pas timides.
3 1a. Vous savez où cet homme habite?
   b. Albert veut savoir si vous avez un cadeau pour lui.

   c. Je sais qu'il ne neige pas à la Martinique.
   d. Tu sais quelle heure il est?
   e. Ma tante et ma mère savent patiner.
4 5a. Marguerite a lu un bon livre.
   b. Mes parents ont lu le journal au bureau.

Préparation 28

1 5a. Nous avons fait une promenade.
   b. Elles ont parlé avec leurs copains.
   c. Il a lu son magazine préféré.
   d. Vous avez vu un film à la télévision.
   e. J'ai dîné à neuf heures.
2 1a. savoir b. connaître
   c. savoir d. connaître
   e. savoir f. savoir
   2a. savent
   b. sais
   c. connaissez
   d. connaît
   e. savez
3 1a. Nicole et Martine jouent du piano.
   b. Je joue de l'accordéon.
   c. Tu joues des cymbales et de la batterie.
   d. Le petit Maurice joue du violon.
   e. Vous jouez de la trompette.
   f. Françoise joue du saxophone.
   2a. L'auto de l'ingénieur marche bien.
   b. L'auto de l'étudiante est rouge.
   c. L'auto du médecin n'est pas très grande.
   d. L'auto de la famille Gérard est grande et vieille.

Phase 5

Préparation 30

4 3a. Nous voulons habiter en France, mais nous ne pouvons pas./Nous ne

voulons pas habiter
en France et nous ne pou-
vons pas./Nous
voulons habiter en France
et nous pouvons habiter
en France.
  b. Tu veux chanter à l'opéra,
mais tu ne
peux pas./Tu ne veux pas
chanter à l'opéra
et tu ne peux pas./Tu veux
chanter à l'opéra
et tu peux chanter à
l'opéra.
  c. Elles veulent visiter Hawaii,
mais elles ne
peuvent pas./Elles ne veulent pas visiter
Hawaii et elles ne peuvent
pas./Elles
veulent visiter Hawaii et
elles peuvent visiter Hawaii.

Préparation 32

2 4a. Nous avons faim.
  b. Je n'ai pas soif.
  c. Patricia a raison.
  d. Ils ont très froid.
4 4a. C'est sa maison.
  b. C'est son vélomoteur.
  c. Ce sont leurs enfants.
  d. C'est sa guitare.
  e. C'étaient ses disques.
  f. C'était sa trompette.
  g. C'était leur restaurant.
5 1a. Les étudiants vont à l'université à dix-neuf
heures trente.
  b. Le médecin va à l'hôpital à
dix heures cinquante-cinq/
onze heures moins cinq.
  c. Nous allons à la maison à
dix-sept heures.
  d. Les ouvrières vont à l'usine
à cinq heures quarante-
cinq/six heures moins le
quart.
  e. L'acteur va au théâtre à
dix-huit heures quinze/
dix-huit heures
et quart.
  f. Le comptable va au bureau
à huit heures vingt.

6 4a. Il y a des petits pois! Passez-moi les petits pois, s'il
vous plaît.
  b. Il y a du jambon! Passez-
moi le jambon, s'il vous
plaît.
  c. Il y a de la glace! Passez-
moi la glace, s'il vous plaît.

Préparation 34

3 5a. Anne n'a pas joué de
violon.
  b. Je ne suis pas allé voir mes
amis.
  c. Ma mère n'a pas lu le
journal.

Préparation 35

4 1. b 2. c 3. b 4. a

Préparation 36

2 1a. du b. des
  c. une d. de
2a. moi b. lui
  c. elles d. eux
4a. B b. C
5 (1) a décidé
  (2) est montée
  (3) pesait
  (4) fallait
  (5) a pris
  (6) allait
  (7) allait
  (8) a pris
  (9) a mangé
  (10) a pris
  (11) est montée
  (12) pesait
  (13) était
  (14) pouvait
  (15) avait

Phase 6

Préparation 38

3 5a. Pour le dessert, vous pré-
férez/tu préfères
la glace au café, n'est-ce
pas?
  5b. Nous devons acheter ce
beau pull pour Marc!

Préparation 40

2 4a. Il mettait un costume.
  b. Nous mettons un maillot
de bain.
  c. Vous mettiez des
chaussettes.
  d. Ils mettent un
imperméable.
  e. Hier tu as mis un short et
une chemise.
3 2a. non, jamais
  b. rarement
  c. oui, quelquefois
4 10a. Marie dit que ma voiture
est belle.
  b. Marcel dit que je dois
travailler.
  c. Jacques dit que Pierre et
moi, nous pouvons aller
à la plage.

Préparation 43

3 4a. mangeons
  b. mangeais
  c. mangions, mangiez; because the i softens the g
  5a. commençons
  b. commençais; commençait,
commençaient;
the cédille is added to
soften the c before o and a
  6. préfère, préfère
préférons, préfèrent
  7. amène, amenons
me lève, nous levons
espère, espérons
exagère, exagérons
  8. jète, jetons, jètent
m'appelle, nous appelons,
s'appellent
5 1a. Non, nous n'achetons rien
aujourd'hui.
  b. Non, il n'y avait personne
chez moi.
  c. Non, elle ne connaissait
personne à Paris.
  d. Non, je n'ai vu personne
là-bas.
  e. Non, il n'y a rien dans
cette boîte.
  f. Non, elle n'a rien acheté.
  2a. Rien.
  b. Jamais.
  c. Personne.

Préparation 44

2 4a. Je te dis que je n'aime pas le café.
   b. On nous dit qu'il fait beau aujourd'hui.
3 1a. Elle me donne son appareil-photo.
   b. Il lui donne un cadeau.
   c. Oui, nous lui téléphonons à 7 heures.
  2a. Non, je ne leur donne pas de fraises.
   b. Non, elle ne te téléphone pas.
   c. Non, ils ne nous montrent pas les photos de leurs vacances.

Phase 7

Préparation 49

1 4a. Janine vient de Montpellier.
   b. Hervé vient d'Arles.
  5a. va en Allemagne.
   b. va aux Etats-Unis.
   c. va au Canada.
  6a. Mme Joly arrive d'Allemagne à 17h30.
   b. M. Clément arrive des Etats-Unis à 15h.
   c. Michel Bertrand arrive du Sénégal à midi.

Préparation 50

1 2a. Hier soir ma soeur et ses amis ont vu un très bon film.
   b. Tu as vu les clowns hier?
   c. Vous avez vu toutes les autos sur la route ce soir?

Préparation 51

  4a. Tu dois lui écrire.
   b. Tu dois lui répondre tout de suite.
   c. Tu dois leur donner ton adresse.
5 1. C'est un vélomoteur.
  2. C'est une voiture.
  3. C'est un avion.
  4. C'est un vélo.
  5. C'est une moto.

6. C'est un bateau.
7. C'est un autocar.
8. C'est un train.

Phase 8

Préparation 52

1 3a. Les pays d'Afrique que tu viens de visiter sont fascinants.
   b. Cette jeune fille qui va venir vous voir est professeur à Paris.
   c. Les diapos que vous montrez aux étudiants sont excellentes.
   d. Mon père, qui est assez vieux, aime faire des promenades en auto.
   e. Ma tante Lucie, qui habite à Marseille, ne m'écrit pas souvent.
3 2a. Oui, je vais lui donner ce disque.
   b. Oui, il veut leur dire bonjour.
   c. Oui, elle va les voir au restaurant.
   d. Non, je ne veux pas l'acheter.
  3a. Non, je ne peux pas lui écrire.
   b. Non, je ne peux pas leur envoyer ces cadeaux.
   c. Non, je ne peux pas lui donner ce transistor.

Préparation 53

2 3a. Il n'a jamais acheté de chapeau jaune.
   b. Il n'a jamais acheté de chaussures rouges.
   c. Il n'a jamais acheté de chemise rose.
   d. Il n'a jamais acheté de gants gris.

Préparation 54

2 5 1. à 2. à 3. d' 4. de
    5. de 6. d' 7. à 8. de

Préparation 55

1 3a. Non, je n'y vais pas.

   b. Oui, elle y va.
   c. Si, elles y vont.
   d. Oui, il y est.
2 2a. Vous dites que les gens courent toujours à Paris.
   b. Sa mère et sa tante disent que les prix sont astronomiques.
   c. Tu dis qu'il y a beaucoup de musées.
   d. Nous disons que c'est une belle ville.
   e. Je dis que c'est une ville moderne.
3 7a. Tu voudrais du poulet?— Oui, j'en voudrais.
   b. Tu ne prends pas de thé?— Non, je n'en prends pas.

Préparation 56

3 6a. Jean-Marc aimerait étudier le latin de nouveau.
   b. Les Bouvier aimeraient aller à la plage de nouveau.
   c. Tu aimerais collectionner des timbres de nouveau.
   d. Vous aimeriez écrire des chansons de nouveau.

Préparation 57

1 5a. Non, il ne doit pas te donner de l'argent.
   b. Non, elle ne veut pas nous voir demain.
   c. Oui, ils sont venus leur dire au revoir.
2 1a. Oui, j'y vais la semaine prochaine.
   b. Oui, il y est allé comme toujours.
   c. Non, je n'y mange jamais.
  2a. —Est-ce qu'Anne va au cours aujourd'hui?
    —Non, elle n'y va pas aujourd'hui.
   b. —Comment allons-nous à ce musée?
    —Nous y allons en autobus.
   c. —Tu vas au cinéma avec Gisèle?
    —Non, elle ne peut pas y aller.
  3a. Roger en a.

b. Nous n'en avons pas.

c. J'en veux.

d. Vous n'en avez pas pris?

e. Tu n'en a pas acheté?

3 1a. J'ai mangé trop de frites.

b. Vous n'avez pas acheté as-sez de sandwichs.

c. J'ai fini les devoirs.

d. Nous avons choisi des chaussures.

e. Mme Drouin n'a pas vendu la jupe.

f. Vous avez répondu à l'a-gent de police.

2a. Paul et Gérard ont fait du camping.

b. Nous avons dit au revoir aux voisins.

c. Julie a vu M. Lille ce matin.

d. On n'a pas mis de sel dans la soupe.

3a. Non, nous n'avons pas pris de petits gâteaux.

b. Non, je n'ai pas mangé de glace.

c. Non, je n'ai pas pris de jus d'orange.

d. Non, je n'ai pas fait d'omelette.

4a. Oui, je leur ai écrit.

b. Oui, elle lui a donné un cadeau.

c. Si, je l'ai envoyé aux Drouin.

4 2a. Un sofa est plus comforta-ble qu'une chaise.

b. Le céleri est moins riche en calories que le chocolat.

c. Un avion est plus rapide qu'un train.

d. Je crois que Roméo était aussi amoureux que Juliette.

e. Un ordinateur calcule plus rapidement qu'une personne.

f. On voyage plus comforta-blement en première classe qu'en classe touriste.

g. On vit plus agréablement à la campagne qu'à la ville.

h. Le Canada est plus peuplé que le Sahara.

i. Un vélo est moins cher qu'une auto.

j. Le temps paraît plus long quand on travaille que quand on est en vacances.

Préparation 58

1   —, de, de, de
      —, de, de, à, à
      —, de, de

4 7a. m'appellerais
      b. achèteriez c. parlerait
      d. aimerais e. donnerais

Phase 9

Préparation 59

1 7a. Je lui ai dit que je voudrais bien aller voir ce film de science-fiction.

b. Oui, je lui ai parlé de mes expériences de chimie.

c. Elle m'a rendu mon dic-tionnaire français-anglais.

Préparation 60

2 3a. Elle fait une promenade.

b. Nous faisons la cuisine.

c. Ils font du ski.
      Vous faites le marché/les courses.

3 1. Voilà sa vache.
      Voilà son chien.
      Voilà ses poissons.

   2. Voilà sa robe.
      Voilà son bateau.
      Voilà ses admirateurs.

   3. Voilà notre université.
      Voilà notre piscine.
      Voilà nos copains.

   4. Voilà leur salle de classe.
      Voilà leur professeur.
      Voilà leurs stylos.

Préparation 61

1 1a. Nos amis décident de nous offrir leur aide.

b. Nos amis hésitent à. . .

c. Nos amis continuent à. . .

d. Nos amis refusent de. . .

e. Nos amis commencent à. . .

2a. Il veut le finir ce matin.

b. Il espère le finir. . .

c. Il oublie de le finir. . .

d. Il essaie de le finir. . .

e. Il réussit à le finir. . .

2 2a. Avec quoi avez-vous fait le gâteau?

b. Où l'as-tu acheté?

c. Avec qui est-ce que tu y es allé?

d. Lequel (de ces hommes) était le criminel?/Laquelle (de ces photos) a montré le criminel?

3 1a. C'est la leur.

b. C'est la sienne.

c. C'est le sien.

d. Ce sont les leurs.

e. Ce sont les siennes.

f. Ce sont les siennes.

g. Ce sont les siens.

h. Ce sont les siennes.

2a. Oui, tu le vois, c'est le tien.

b. Oui, vous le voyez, c'est le vôtre.

c. Oui, je la vois, c'est la mienne.

d. Oui, je les vois, ce sont les miens.

e. Oui, je les vois, ce sont les miennes.

f. Oui, nous le voyons, c'est le nôtre.

g. Oui, je les vois, ce sont les miens.

h. Oui, vous la voyez, c'est la mienne.

4 5a. Oui, je les aime tous. Non, je ne les aime pas tous.

b. Oui, je les ai toutes visitées. Non, je ne les ai pas toutes visitées.

c. Oui, je les connais toutes. Non, je ne les connais pas toutes.

d. Oui, je les connais toutes. Non, je ne les connais pas toutes.

Préparation 62

2 2a. Oui, toutes sont chères.

b. Oui, tous sont très chers.

c. Oui, tout est de bonne qualité (tous sont de bonne qualité).

d. Oui, je les achète toutes ici.

3 4a. achetais, vaudrait
   b. veniez, sauriez
   c. voulais, devrais
   d. donnions, mourraient
4 2a. connais
   b. sais
   c. connais
   d. connaissons
   e. connaître
   f. connaît
   g. savez
   h. sais
   i. Connaissez

Préparation 63
2 1. Oui, c'est le mien.
   2. Oui, c'est la nôtre.
   3. Oui, ce sont les leurs.
   4. Oui, c'est le sien.
   5. Oui, c'est la sienne.
   6. Non, ce ne sont pas les siennes.
   7. Oui, ce sont les leurs.
   8. Oui, c'est la leur.
   9. Non, ce n'est pas la mienne.
   10. Oui, c'est le sien.

Préparation 64
2 7a. Nous prendrons la voiture de mon père.
   b. À midi, nous ferons un pique-nique.
   c. Jeannette achètera des provisions.
   d. J'emporterai un poulet froid.
   e. Vous préparerez un gâteau au chocolat.
4 1. Elle a demandé une cigarette. Il lui a répondu qu'il est interdit de fumer au musée.
   2. Non, il ne le croit pas.
   3. Le Musée d'Art moderne a, peut-être, des statues qui parlent.
   4. Elle a voulu faire une promenade.
   5. Il pense que quelqu'un a volé la statue.
   6. Elle vient d'Italie.
   7. Un des portraits pense que la statue est très gentille.

Préparation 65
1 4a. La famille Calvet a perdu son chien.
   b. Ma tante est arrivée à la gare.
   c. Tu as refusé de manger des épinards.
   d. Ils sont descendus pour le petit déjeuner.
   e. Les gangsters ont terrorisé les clients.
   f. Mes copains sont venus chez moi cet après-midi.
   6a. Suzanne n'a pas écouté ses disques.
   b. Votre copine n'est pas allée à la poste.
   c. Ils n'ont pas vendu leur maison.
   d. Nous n'avons pas mangé.
2 4a. Robert leur téléphone.
   b. Il y pense.
   c. Il ne lui donne pas le cadeau.
   d. Nous n'y répondons pas.
   6a. J'y ai répondu hier.
   b. J'y suis allé/e hier.
   c. Je vous ai raconté ce film hier.
   d. Je leur ai dit au revoir hier.
   8a. Elles y sont arrivées.
   b. Nous vous avons demandé de chanter.
   c. Ils n'y sont pas allés.
   d. Je ne lui ai pas répondu.
3 1a. depuis
   b. pendant
   c. pendant
   d. depuis
   e. pendant
   f. pendant
   g. depuis
   h. pendant
   i. depuis

Phase 10

Préparation 68
2 3a. Oui, il y en a.
   b. Non, il n'y en a pas.
   c. Oui, il y en a.

Préparation 69
3 5a. Philippe est le garçon le plus grand de la classe.
   b. Jeanne est la fille la plus intelligente de la famille.
   c. Les chiens sont les animaux les plus gentils (sympathiques) du monde.

Préparation 72
3 2a. Je lui écris souvent.
   b. J'y vais demain.
   c. Nous leur parlons.
   d. Il leur téléphone.
   e. Tu y penses?
   3a. Nous n'y allons pas.
   b. Je ne leur demande pas de m'aider.
   c. Tu ne lui donnes pas de bonbons.
   d. Albert lui a téléphoné.
   e. Nous n'y avons pas pensé.
   f. Vous ne leur avez pas parlé?
   4a. Téléphone-leur.
   b. Allez-y.
   c. Parle-lui.

Phase 11

Préparation 74
1 8a. Je voudrais que vous vous habilliez.
   b. Je voudrais que vous vous laviez.
   c. Je voudrais que nous nous reposions.

Préparation 76
3 a. (Il est mauvais) que tu regardes la télé.
   b. (Il est essentiel) que tu finisses ton travail.
   c. (Il est regrettable) que tu vendes ton livre de français.
   d. (Il est nécessaire) que tu apprennes cette leçon.
   e. (Il est mauvais) que tu sortes avec tes amis.
   f. (Il est juste) que tu répondes à cette lettre.
   g. (Il est malheureux) que tu lises cette bande dessinée.

h. (Il est important) que tu prennes ton petit déjeuner.

Préparation 77
2 3 a. aller/infinitive
   b. prendre/infinitive
   c. prendre/infinitive
   d. partir/infinitive
   e. arrive/subjunctive
   f. regarde/subjunctive
   g. alliez/subjunctive
   h. dise/subjunctive
   i. vais/indicative
   j. prenez/indicative
   k. quitte/indicative
   l. arrivez/indicative
   m. revienne/subjunctive
   n. revenir/infinitive
   o. part/indicative
   p. arrive/indicative
   q. prépare/subjunctive
   r. réfléchisse/subjunctive
   s. écrive/subjunctive

Préparation 78
3 4 a. Il les lui montre.
   b. Il la lui montre.
   c. Il la lui montre.
   d. Il les lui montre.
   e. Il les leur montre.

Préparation 79
2 4 a. Jean la lui a montrée.
   b. Le boulanger les lui a vendus.
   c. Henri et Catherine le leur ont donné.
   d. Je le lui ai rendu.
3 1 a. qu'on regarde
   b. que tu te reposes
   c. que nous prenions
   d. que les enfants prennent
   e. qu'on aille
   f. que je lise
   g. que tu ailles
   h. que tu sortes
   2 a. aller
      que nous allions
   b. qu'il aille
      qu'il finisse
   c. venir
      qu'elles viennent
   d. prendre
      que nous prenions

qu'ils prennent
3 a. devenir
   b. décrive
   c. apprennes
   d. parte
   e. travaillent
   f. braver
   g. craindre
   h. aime

Préparation 80
2 2 a. Nous regrettons que vous fassiez des fautes.
   b. Je suis furieuse que tu ne fasses pas attention aux voitures.
   c. Il est content que vous ne voyagiez pas cet hiver.
   d. Ma mère est ravie que nous habitions ici.
   e. Nous sommes surpris qu'ils ne connaissent pas bien les États-Unis.
   f. Il est heureux qu'elle parte demain.
   g. Je suis triste que tu quittes Paris.

Phase 12

Préparation 82
2 2 a. (Il est possible) que M. Boitout soit rentré tard hier soir.
   b. (Je suis désolée) que Mlle Froide ait attrapé un rhume.
   c. (Je suis surprise) que Mme Avare ait volé cent francs à un voisin.
   d. (Il est regrettable) que M. Gauche soit tombé dans son jardin.
4 5 a. Ce matin, Mme Pipelet a dit que les Roland étaient rentrés de leurs vacances en Suisse hier.
   b. Ce matin, Mme Pipelet a dit que le jeune Dupont avait perdu sa bicyclette hier.
   c. Ce matin, Mme Pipelet a dit que M. Dupuis avait

acheté une nouvelle auto la semaine dernière.
   d. Ce matin, Mme Pipelet a dit que M. Lebrun était rentré à trois heures du matin dimanche dernier.
   e. Ce matin, Mme Pipelet a dit que la fille Dupont s'était mariée la semaine dernière.
   f. Ce matin, Mme Pipelet a dit qu'elle avait reçu des douzaines de cadeaux.
   g. Ce matin, Mme Pipelet a dit que les Dupuis n'avaient pas fait de cadeau de mariage.

Préparation 83
3 1. puissent
   2. ne fassent
   3. voient
   4. peuvent
   5. n'aient
   6. soient
   7. n'arrivent
   8. soit

Préparation 86
1 6 a. Nous allons la lui dicter.
   b. Elle va me l'envoyer.
   c. Ne la leur raconte pas.
   d. Je te l'ai chantée.
   e. Tu ne la leur as pas annoncée?
   f. Il faut que nous vous les donnions.
   g. Ne le lui donne pas.

Préparation 87
4 1 a. Lesquels sont les moins chers?
   b. Laquelle est la plus élégante?

Préparation 88
2 1 a. serais garagiste
   b. serveuse, j'aimerais travailler dans un restaurant français
   c. deviendrait maître-nageur
   d. journaliste, auriez
   e. passerions, pêcheurs

f. routier, j'irais

g. ouvreuses, pourraient

Révision

1 6a. —As-tu nettoyé la cuisine?
    —Non, je ne l'ai pas
    nettoyée.
  b. —As-tu fait la lessive?
    —Non, je ne l'ai pas faite.
  c. —As-tu fait les courses?
    —Non, je ne les ai pas
    faites.
  d. —As-tu écrit la lettre à la
    propriétaire?
    —Non, je ne l'ai pas écrite.
  e. —As-tu mis la table?
    —Non, je ne l'ai pas mise.

  8a. Sylvie en a visité beaucoup
    l'année dernière.
  b. Elle y est allée.
  c. Elle s'y est beaucoup
    amusée.
  d. Elle n'y est pas allée.

3 1a. Je vais y aller.
  b. Marc va les finir.
  c. Je vais leur écrire.
  d. Je vais leur téléphoner.
  e. Béatrice et Paul vont y
    aller tout à l'heure.
  f. Je vais lui parler.

4 2a. Je voudrais encore de l'eau,
    s'il vous plaît.
  b. Nous voudrions du poulet
    et des frites.

  c. Pourriez-vous nous ap-
    porter une bouteille d'eau
    minérale?
  d. Les enfants voudraient en-
    core du pain.

5 4a. partirons
  b. prendront
  c. irons
  d. pourras
  e. ferai
  f. viendront

7 4a. ailles
  b. achetiez
  c. viennent
  d. fasse, puissions

  5a. Mme Julien regrette que
    les voitures fassent telle-
    ment de bruit.
  b. Les Leduc regrettent que la
    vie soit si chère.
  c. Vous regrettez qu'on ne
    puisse pas facilement se
    garer.
  d. Je regrette que les rues
    soient sales.
  e. Nous regrettons qu'il y ait
    tellement de bâtiments
    modernes.

  6a. Je suis enchanté que tu aies
    accéléré au bon moment.
  b. Je suis heureux que tu
    n'aies pas fait trop de
    bruit.
  c. Je suis ravi que tu aies eu

des yeux fixés sur la route.
  d. Je suis satisfait que tu
    n'aies pas regardé les jolies
    filles.
  e. Je suis très fier que tu aies
    gagné.

9 3. Quand j'ai été kidnappé, j'ai
    été jeté sur le siège arrière
    d'une voiture. Mes mains
    ont été liées, mes yeux ont
    été couverts, et un mouchoir
    a été mis dans ma bouche.
    La voiture était équipée d'un
    haut-parleur et une voix a
    dit: "Sera-t-il transporté au
    patron immédiatement ou
    sera-t-il d'abord emmené à
    la chambre noire?" Pendant
    ce temps, j'étais torturé par
    la pensée: Serai-je jamais re-
    lâché, ou serai-je tué?

10 3a. Quelle voiture a-t-elle
    achetée?
  b. Quels films a-t-il vus?
  c. Quelles amies ont-ils
    rencontrées?
  d. Quel métier a-t-il choisi?
  e. Quels meubles ont-elles
    vendus?

11 7a. Les nôtres non plus.
  b. La sienne non plus.
  c. Les leurs non plus.
  d. La mienne non plus.
  e. La leur non plus.

Vocabulaire français-anglais

à to, in, at; **à (moi)** mine; my turn

abandonner to give up, to abandon

abattre (like *battre*) to knock out, shoot down

l'abeille *f.* bee

aboli/e abolished

l'absence *f.* absence

absent/e missing, absent

absolument absolutely

l'acajou *m.* mahogany

accepter to accept

l'accident *m.* accident

l'accord *m.* agreement; **d'accord** ok (let's do it)

l'accordéon *m.* accordion

accourir (like *courir*) to rush, to run to

l'accueil *m.* reception, welcome

accueillant/e welcoming, friendly

accuser to accuse

l'achat *m.* purchase

acheter to buy; **acheter qqch à qqn** to buy something for someone

l'acrobate *m.* acrobat

l'acteur *m.* actor

actif/active active

l'action *f.* act

l'activité *f.* activity

l'actrice *f.* actress

l'addition *f.* addition; bill

l'administrateur administrator

l'admirateur/admiratrice admirer

admirer to admire

adorer to adore, to love

l'adresse *f.* address

adroit/e skillful

aérien/ne aerial, airy, elfin

l'aéroport *m.* airport

les affaires *f.* business

l'affiche *f.* poster

affreux/affreuse terrible

afin que so that

africain/e African

l'Afrique *f.* Africa

l'agacement *m.* annoyance

l'âge *m.* age; **quel âge as-tu?** how old are you?

âgé/e elderly, old

l'agent *m.* agent; **agent de police** police officer

agile agile, nimble

agité/e agitated

agréable pleasant

agressif/agressive aggressive

ah non, alors! certainly not! forget it!

l'aide *f.* help, aid

aider (à) to help (in)

ailleurs elsewhere

aimable pleasant, amiable

aimer to like; **aimer bien** to like well

l'aîné/e oldest child

l'air *m.* air; melody

l'album (de photos) *m.* (photo) album

l'algèbre *f.* algebra

alimentaire having to do with food

l'alimentation *f.* food

l'allée *f.* alley; ~ **privée** private driveway

l'Allemagne (*f.*) Germany

allemand/e German

aller (*irreg.*) to go; ~ (+ inf.) to be going to (+ inf.); ~ **à** go to (a place); ~ **voir** visit (people); **s'en aller** to go away; **allez-vous-en! va-t'en!** go away!; **aller-retour** round-trip

allons bon! oh, no!; **allons-nous-en!** let's go!; **allons-y** let's go

allô hello (on telephone)

allumer to light, to set fire to

alors so

les Alpes Alps

ambitieux/ambitieuse ambitious

améliorer to improve

amener to bring (someone)

américain/e American

l'ami/amie friend; **petit/e ami/e** boy/girlfriend

l'amour *m.* love; **lettre d'amour** love letter

amoureux/amoureuse in love

amusant/e amusing, funny

s'amuser to have fun, to have a good time

l'an *m.* year

l'année *f.* year

les ancêtres *m.f.pl.* ancestors, forebears

ancien/ne old, antique; former

l'âne donkey

anglais/e English

l'angle *m.* corner

l'animation *f.* liveliness

l'anniversaire *m.* birthday

l'annonce *f.* newspaper ad; announcement

annoncer to announce, to foresee

l'annuaire *m.* telephone book

l'anorak *m.* ski jacket, windbreaker

l'anthropologie *f.* anthropology

l'anthropologue *m./ f.* anthropologist

l'antilope *f.* antilope

antipathique unpleasant, disagreeable

l'antiquaire *m.* antique dealer

août August

apparaître (like *connaître*) to appear

l'appareil-photo *m.* camera

les appareils ménagers *m.* appliances

l'apparence *f.* appearance

apparition; faire son ~ to make one's first appearance

l'appartement *m.* apartment

appartenir à (like *tenir*) to belong to

appeler to call; **s'appeler** to name/ call oneself; **il/elle s'appelle** his/ her name is

apporter to bring, to supply

apprécié/e appreciated

apprécier to appreciate

apprendre (like *prendre*) to learn

après after; **après-demain** the day after tomorrow; **après-midi** *f.* afternoon; ~ **tout** after all

l'arbre *m.* tree

l'arc-en-ciel *m.* rainbow

l'architecte *m.f.* architect

l'argent *m.* money; ~ **de poche** pocket money, allowance

aride arid, dry

l'arme *f.* arm

l'armée *f.* army; **armée de l'air** air force; **armée de mer** navy; **armée de terre** land army

l'armoire *f.* wardrobe, free-standing closet

arranger to arrange

arrêter to stop; **s'arreter de** to stop (doing)

l'arrivée *f.* arrival

arriver to arrive; (with impersonal subject) to happen; **qu'est-ce qui est arrivé?** what happened?

arroser to water

l'article *m.* article, item

artistique artistic

l'ascenseur *m.* elevator

l'aspect *m.* aspect, characteristic

l'aspirateur *m.* vacuum cleaner

s'asseoir to sit down; **asseyez-vous/assieds-toi** sit down

assez enough; ~ **de** enough of; **en avoir assez** to have enough, to be fed up

l'assiette *f.* plate

l'assistant/e social/e social worker

assurer to assure

l'astronaute *m./f.* astronaut

astronomique astronomical

l'atelier *m.* studio, workshop

l'athlète *m.* athlete

attendre (pp. **attendu**) to wait (for)

attentif/attentive attentive

attention: faire attention à to pay attention to

attirer to attract; ~ **l'attention de qqn** to catch somebody's attention

attraper to catch, to trap

au (**à** + **le**) to the, in the; **au revoir** good-by

l'auberge de jeunesse *f.* youth hostel

aucun/e no; **ne...aucun** not any, none

l'augmentation *f.* increase

aujourd'hui today

aussi too; **aussi** (+ adj.) **que** as...as; **aussi bien** as well as

l'Australie *f.* Australia

autant de as much, as many

l'auto *f.* car

l'auto-stop *m.* hitchhiking

autobiographique autobiographical

l'autobus *m.* municipal bus

l'autocar *m.* long-distance bus

l'automne *m.* fall, autumn

l'automobiliste *m./f.* driver

autoriser authorize, permit

l'autorité (*f.*) authority

autre other; **un/e autre** another; **l'un à l'autre** to each other

autrefois formerly, in the past

avancé/e advanced, progressive

l'avancement *m.* advancement, promotion

avancer to go ahead; **ma montre avance** my watch is fast

avant before

l'avant garde *f.* avant garde, vanguard

avant-hier day before yesterday

avec with

l'avenir *m.* future

l'aventure *f.* adventure

l'avenue *f.* avenue

l'aviation *f.* air force

l'avion *m.* plane

l'avis *m.* opinion; **à mon avis** in my opinion

l'avocat/e lawyer

avoir (*irreg.*) to have; **avoir...ans** to be...years old; ~ **besoin de** to have to, need to; ~ **de la chance** to be lucky; ~ **chaud** to be hot; ~ **confiance** to trust; ~ **le droit** to have the right; ~ **faim** to be hungry; ~ **froid** to be cold; ~ **honte** to be ashamed; ~ **lieu** to take place; ~ **mal (à)** to have a pain, be sick; ~ **de la patience** to be patient; ~ **peur** to be afraid; ~ **du piston** to have connections, to have "pull"; ~ **pitié** to pity; ~ **raison** to be right; ~ **rendez-vous** (avec qqn) to have a date or appointment (with someone); ~ **soif** to be thirsty; ~ **sommeil** to be sleepy; ~ **tort** to be wrong; **il y a** there is/are; **il y a eu** there is, there was, there has been; **il n'y a pas de...** there is no...

avril April

les bagages *m.* luggage

se baigner to go swimming, to have a swim

le bal ball, dance

balayer to sweep

le balcon balcony

le ballon ball

la banane banana

le banc bench

la bande tape

la bande dessinée comic strip

la banlieue suburbs

la banque bank

le banquier banker

la barbe beard; **quelle** ~ ! how boring!

bas: à bas...! down with...!; **en bas** downstairs

le base-ball baseball

le basket-ball basketball

la bataille battle

le bassin pond

le bateau boat; ~ **à voile** sailboat; **bateau-mouche** sightseeing boat; **faire du** ~ to go boating

la batterie drums

bavard/e talkative

bavarder to chat

beau/bel/belle beautiful

le beau-père/frère father/brother-in-law

beaucoup very much, a lot; ~ **de** a lot of

les beaux-parents in-laws

belge Belgian

la Belgique Belgium

la belle-mère/soeur mother/sister-in-law

la besoin need; **avoir besoin de** to need

la bête animal, creature

bête stupid, silly

bêtises: faire des bêtises to act silly, to do something stupid

le beurre butter

la bibliothèque library

le bien good

bien well/good; **bien que** although; **bien sûr!** of course!, naturally!; **très bien** very well/good

bientôt soon

la bière beer

le bifteck haché hamburger

le billet ticket, bill; **billet aller-retour** round-trip ticket

la biochimie biochemistry

la biologie biology

bizarre strange, odd

la blague joke; **quelle** ~ ! what a joke!

le blanc white man

blanc/blanche white
blessé/e wounded, hurt
bleu/e blue
blond/e blond; blond cendré ash-blond; blond doré golden blond
le blond/la blonde blond man/woman
le bœuf beef
bof! oh, well...
boire (irreg.) to drink
les bois m. woods; en bois wooden
la boisson drink
la boîte box; boîte aux lettres mailbox
le bol bowl
bon/bonne good; bon O.K.; bon appétit! enjoy your meal!; bon marché (inv.) inexpensive, cheap
le bonbon candy, sweets
le bonheur happiness
bonjour hello, good morning, good afternoon
bonne chance! good luck
bonsoir good evening
bord: au bord de at the edge of; au bord de la mer at the seaside
les bottes f.pl. boots
la bouche mouth
la bouillie porridge
le boulanger baker
le boulevard boulevard
le boulot work
la boum surprise party
bout: à bout at the end of one's rope
la bouteille bottle
le boycottage boycotting
boycotter to boycott
la branche branch
le bras arm
braver to dare, to defy
bref/brève brief
brésilien/ne Brazilian
briller to shine
la brioche sweet bun
se brosser (les dents/les cheveux) to brush (one's teeth/one's hair)
le bruit noise
brûler to burn
brun/e brown, brown haired; tanned
le brun/la brune brown haired man/woman

le budget budget
le buffet buffet, china cupboard
le bureau office

c'est (Valérie) it's (Valérie); ce sont they/these are; c'est ça that's right; c'est la vie! that's life!; c'est que... it means that..., the reason is; c'est tout that's all
ça (indefinite pron.) that; ça alors! good grief!; ça fait combien en tout? how much is the whole thing?; ça m'est égal I don't care, it's all the same to me; ça va?; ça va bien? how's it going?
la cabine (téléphonique) phone booth
le cabinet de toilette bathroom, powder room
cacher to hide; se cacher to hide oneself
le cadeau present
le cadet/la cadette the younger brother/sister of the family
le cadre framework, setting
le café coffee; café
le cahier exercise book
la caméra movie camera
la caisse cash register
le/la caissier/caissière cashier
calculer to calculate
calme calm
calmement/e calmly
le/la camarade buddy, friend, companion; camarade de chambre roommate
le caméraman cameraman
la campagne countryside
le campeur/la campeuse camper
camping: faire du camping to go camping
le Canada Canada
canadien/ne Canadian
le canapé couch
le canard duck
le cancre lazy student, dunce
capable (de) able (to), capable (of)
le capitaine captain
la capitale capital
capitaliste capitalist
la caravane camper-trailer
caresser to caress, to stroke
la carotte carrot

la carrière career
la carte map
la carte postale postcard
la cassette cassette
la cathédrale cathedral
catholique Catholic, a Catholic
la cause cause; à cause de because (of)
causer to cause
la cave cellar
ce n'est pas it isn't
ce, cet, cette this, that
ce que, ce qui (ind. pron.) what
célèbre famous
le cendrier ashtray
cent 100; une centaine (de) about a hundred (of)
le centimètre centimeter
le centre center; centre ville center of town
cependant however
la cerise cherry
ces these, those
cesser to stop, to cease
la chaîne chain (of stores); TV channel
la chaise chair
la chambre bedroom; ~ à coucher bedroom
le champagne champagne
le champion/la championne champion
la chance luck; avoir de la ~ to be lucky
le changement change
changer to change
la chanson song
chanter to sing
le chanteur/la chanteuse singer
le chapeau hat
charmant/e charming
chasser to chase, to kick out, to hunt
le chat cat
châtain (inv.) chestnut (hair); châtain clair light brown
le château castle
le chauffeur driver; ~ de taxi cab driver
la chaussure shoe
le chef chef; head; le/la ~ comptable head accountant
le chemin path, way
la cheminée chimney, fireplace

la chemise man's shirt

la chemise de nuit nightgown

le chemisier woman's blouse or shirt

cher/chère expensive; dear

chercher to look for

le cheval/les chevaux horse/s; **à cheval** on horseback; **deux chevaux** low-horsepower car

les cheveux *m.* hair

la chèvre goat

chez (qqn) at someone's house, office, store

chic smart, in fashion

le chien dog

le chiffre digit

la chimie chemistry

la Chine China

chinois/e Chinese

le chirurgien surgeon

le chocolat chocolate; **~ chaud** hot chocolate

choisir to choose

le chômage unemployment

le chèque check

la chose thing

chouette great

chut! sh!

le cidre cider

le ciel sky

la cigarette cigarette

le cinéma movie theater; films

la circonstance circumstance

la circulation traffic

circuler to get around; to move along

la civilisation civilization

clair/e clear; **le clair de lune** moonlight

la clarinette clarinet

la classe class; **en ~** in class; **première ~** first class; **~ touriste** tourist class

classique classical

la clé/clef key

le client/la cliente customer

le climat climate

le clown clown

le cocker cocker-spaniel

le code de la route traffic laws

le cœur heart

se coiffer to fix one's hair

le coiffeur/la coiffeuse hairdresser

le collant pantyhose

la collection collection

collectionner to collect

le/la collègue colleague, co-worker

la colline hill

colombien Columbian

combattre to fight

combien de how many, how much

la comédie comedy

comme like, as; **comme tu es gentil!** how nice you are!; **comme il faut** in the proper way, as it should be

le commencement beginning

commencer (à) to start, to begin (to)

comment? how? what do you mean?; **~ allez-vous?** how are you?; **~ ça va?** how is it going; **~ dit-on...en français?** how do you say...in French?; **~ est...?** what is...like?; **~ t'appelles-tu?** what is your name?; **~ vas-tu?** how are you?; **~ vous appelez-vous?** what is your name?

le commerçant/ la commerçante shopkeeper

le commerce business, trade

la commode chest of drawers

la communication communication

communiquer to communicate

la compagnie company, firm

complet/complète complete

compliqué, -e complicated

composer to compose, to write

comprendre (like *prendre*) to understand

le/la comptable accountant

compter to count

le compte rendu report

le concert concert

la conclusion conclusion

la condition condition

conduire (*irreg.*) to drive a car; to conduct

la conférence lecture; **~ de presse** press conference

la confiance confidence, trust

la confiture jam

le confort comfort

confortable comfortable

congeler to freeze

connaître (*irreg.*) to know, to be acquainted with; **se connaître** to know each other, oneself

connu/e well-known, famous

consacrer to devote

la conscience conscience

consciencieux conscientious

les conseils *m.* advice

considérer to consider

constamment constantly

le conte tale, story

content/e happy, satisfied; **être ~ de** to be happy with/doing

coûter to cost; **ça coûte cher** that's expensive

contraire: au contraire on the contrary

le contraste contrast

contre against

le contrôle control, checking

la conversation conversation

le coopérant Peace Corps worker

coopérer to cooperate

le/la copain/copine pal, friend

le coq rooster

le corps body

la correspondance correspondence

le/la correspondant/e pen pal

corrompu/e corrupted

la Corse Corsica

le costume man's suit, costume

la côte coast; **la ~ Atlantique** the Atlantic coast

le côté side; **à côté de** near

se coucher to go to bed

le coucou cuckoo (bird)

coudre (*coud-, cous-, cousu*) to sew

la couleur color

le coup blow; **porter le ~** deliver the (final) blow

le courage courage

courir (*irreg.*) to run

le coureur runner, racer

le courrier mail

le cours class subject; class

la course race; **faire des ~** to do errands, go shopping

le cousin/la cousine cousin

la coutume custom

craindre (*irreg.*) to fear

le crayon pencil

le crayon-feutre felt-tip pen

créer to create

la crème cream

la crêpe French pancake

crépu: cheveux crépus very curly hair

le creux hollow, cavity

crier to shout, to cry out

le/la criminel/criminelle criminal

critiquer to criticize

le crocodile crocodile

croire (*irreg.*) to believe, think; **je crois** I think

le croissant crescent roll

cruel/le cruel

la cuiller spoon

la cuisine kitchen; **faire la ~** to cook

la cuisinière cook; stove

cultivé/e cultured

curieux/curieuse curious

le cycliste cyclist

les cymbales *f.* cymbals

le Danemark Denmark

le danger danger; **en danger** in danger

dangereux/dangereuse dangerous

dans in; **dans la vie** in life

danser to dance

le danseur/la danseuse dancer

davantage more

de of; **d'abord** first; **d'accord** O.K.; **d'habitude** usually; **d'où...?** where...from?; **d'une part...d'autre part** on the one hand...on the other hand; **de la part de** from; **de ma part** from/for me; **de nouveau** again; **de qui?/de quoi?** about whom?/about what?; **de rien** it's nothing, you're welcome, not at all; **de temps en temps** once in a while, sometimes; **de toute façon** anyhow, at any rate

débarrasser to get rid of; **~ la table** to clear off the table

debout standing up; **debout!** get up!

décembre December

décider to decide; **se décider** to decide; **décidez-vous** make up your mind

la décision decision

le décorateur, la décoratrice decorator

découvrir (like *ouvrir*) to discover

défendre to defend, forbid

la défense defense; **défense de fumer** no smoking

le défilé parade

les dégâts *m.* damages

dégeler to thaw

le degré degree

dehors outside; **en ~ de** outside of

déjà already

le déjeuner lunch

déjeuner to have lunch

délivrer to deliver

demain tomorrow; **à demain** see you tomorrow; **demain matin** tomorrow morning; **demain soir** tomorrow evening

la demande request

demander to ask; **demander qqch à qqn** to ask someone for something; **se demander si** to wonder if

le déménagement moving out (of a house)

le demi/la demie half; **dix heures et demie** ten-thirty

démonter to take down, disassemble

le/la dentiste dentist

les dents teeth

le départ departure

dépasser to pass

dépêcher: se dépêcher to hurry

les dépenses *f.* expenses

depuis since

dernier/dernière last

derrière behind

des some

désagréable unpleasant

la descendance posterity

descendre (de) to go down; to get out of (a vehicle)

la description description

le désert desert

se déshabiller to get undressed

désolé/e sorry

le désordre disorder

le dessert dessert

le dessin drawing

le/la dessinateur designer, graphic artist

dessiner to draw

dessous, au-dessous de below

dessus, au-dessus de above

détester to detest

deuxième second

devant in front of

devenir (like *venir*) to become

devoir (*irreg.*) to owe, to have to, must, should, ought to

les devoirs homework; **faire des ~** to do homework

le dialecte dialect

le dictateur dictator

la dictature dictatorship

la dictée dictation quiz

le dictionnaire dictionary

diététique dietetic

la différence difference

difficile difficult

difficilement with difficulty

la difficulté difficulty, trouble

dimanche Sunday

le dîner dinner

dîner to have dinner

le diplomate diplomat

dire (*irreg.*) to say, tell; **dis,...** say,...; **dis donc** by the way; **tu veux dire...?** you mean...?

le directeur/la directrice chief administrator; principal (of a school)

la discothèque discotheque

le discours speech; **faire un ~** give a speech

la discussion discussion

discuter (de quelque chose) to discuss (something)

disperser to scatter

le disque record

la dissertation academic paper

distingué/e distinguished

distraitement absent-mindedly

le divan sofa

diviser to divide

le docteur doctor

dodo baby-talk for *sleep* (from *dormir*)

le doigt finger

le domaine field, area of interest

donc thus

donner to give; **~ le bonjour** say hello

dont whose, of which/whom, from which/whom

dormir (like *sortir*) to sleep

le dos back

la douche shower

la douzaine a dozen

droit/e right; **à droite** to the right; **tout droit** straight ahead

le droit right; profession of law; **je fais mon** ~ I study law

drôle funny, strange

drôlement really, very, quite (*fam.*)

l'eau water; **eau minérale** mineral water

éblouissant/e dazzling

l'échange *m.* exchange

s'échapper to escape

l'école *f.* (elementary) school

l'économie *f.* economy; **faire des** ~ to save money

économique economical

écouter to listen to; **à l'écoute** tuned in; **rester à l'écoute** to remain listening

l'écran *m.* screen

écraser to run over

écrire (à) (*irreg.*) to write (someone)

l'écrivain *m.* writer

s'écrouler to collapse, to crumble

l'éducation *f.* education

effacer to erase

l'effort effort, endeavor

également also equally

égoïste selfish

eh bien well

s'élancer to rush, to dash

l'électrophone *m.* record player

l'élégance *f.* elegance

élégant/e elegant

l'éléphant *m.* elephant

l'élève *f.m.* pupil

élever to raise

s'embarquer to embark

embarrassé/e embarrassed, awkward

s'embrasser to hug, kiss, embrace one another

emmener to take (someone) along

émouvant/e moving (emotionally)

l'emploi *m.* job

l'employé/e employee

employer to use, to employ

emprunter to borrow

en in; **en attendant que** while waiting, until; **en avance** early, ahead of time; **en avion** by plane; **en bas** downstairs; **en bois** wooden; **en bonne santé** in good health; **en ce moment** right now; **en classe** in class; **en danger** in danger; **en forme** in form, in (good) shape; **en général** generally, usually; **en haut** upstairs; **en (juin)** in (June); **en moyenne** on the average; **en ordre** in order; **en retard** late; **en route!** let's go; **en tout** in all; **en vente** on sale; **en voyage** on a trip; **en France** to/in France

en some; **en avoir assez!** to have enough, be fed up; **j'en ai marre!** I've had it!

enchanté/e delighted (to meet you)

encore again, still, more; ~ **de** still some; ~ **un peu** a little more

l'encre *f.* ink

l'encyclopédie *f.* encyclopedia

l'endroit *m.* location, place

l'enfant *m./f.* child; **enfant prodige** *m.* bright child

enfin at last

enlever to take off (something)

ennuyer to annoy, bore

ennuyeux/ennuyeuse boring

énormément enormously

l'enquête *f.* investigation

ensemble together

ensoleillé/e sunny

ensuite then

entendre to hear; ~ **parler de** to hear about; ~ **dire que** to hear that

l'enthousiasme *m.* enthusiasm; **avec enthousiasme** enthusiastically

enthousiaste enthusiastic

l'entracte *m.* intermission

s'entraîner to train for

entre between

l'entrée *f.* entrance

l'entreprise (d'alimentation) *f.* (food) firm

entrer enter, come in, go in

entretenir (like *tenir*) to take care of; converse

l'entretien *m.* maintenance; conversation

envers toward

l'envie *f.* envy, longing, desire

environ approximately

s'envoler to fly away

envoyer (à) to send (to)

épeler to spell

l'épicerie *f.* grocery store

les épinards *m.* spinach

épouser to marry

l'équipe *f.* team

équipé/e equipped, furnished

l'escalier *m.* stairs

l'esclave *m.f.* slave

l'Espagne *f.* Spain

espagnol/e Spanish

espèce d'idiot you idiot!

espérer to hope

l'espion/espionne spy

l'esprit *m.* mind; wit

essentiel/le essential

essuyer to wipe

l'est east; **à l'est de** to the east of

est-ce que...? (introduces a question)

et and; **et quart** quarter past (the hour)

l'établissement *m.* institution, building

l'étage *m.* floor; **deuxième** ~ 3rd floor

l'étagère *f.* shelf

l'étalagiste *m./f.* window-dresser

l'état *m.* state, condition; **coup d'**~ overthrow of government

les États-unis *m.* United States; **aux** ~ in the U.S.

l'été *m.* summer

l'étiquette *f.* label

l'étoile *f.* star

étonner to astonish; **s'étonner** to be surprised

étranger/étrangère foreign; **à l'étranger** overseas, abroad

l'être *m./f.* being; **l'être humain** human being

être (*irreg.*) to be; ~ **d'accord** to agree; ~ **de** to be from; ~ **en train de** to be in the process of; **il était une fois** once upon a time there was

l'étudiant/e university student

étudier to study

eux them; **eux-mêmes** themselves

l'événement *m.* event

évidemment obviously

évident/e obvious, evident

l'évier *m.* kitchen sink

exagérer to exaggerate, to go too far

l'examen *m.* exam
examiner to examine
excellent/e excellent
excepté except
excusez-moi excuse me
exercer to practice, exercise; ~ **de l'influence sur** to exert influence on
l'exercice *m.* exercise
exotique exotic
l'expérience *f.* experience; experiment
l'expert *m.* expert
expliquer to explain
l'explorateur explorer
l'explosion *f.* explosion
l'exposé *m.* report
l'exposition *f.* exhibit
l'extérieur *m.* outside; **à l'extérieur (de)** (on the) outside (of)
extrêmement extremely

f (*abbr.*) francs (French monetary unit)
fabriquer to build, make
la fac (faculté) university; department; ~ **de droit** law school
fâché/e angry, upset
facile easy
facilement easily
la faim hunger
faire (*irreg.*) to do, to make; ~ **attention à** to pay attention to; ~ **des bêtises** act silly, do something stupid; ~ **du bateau/camping** go boating/camping; ~ **des courses** do errands, go shopping; ~ **des crêpes** make crêpes; ~ **la cuisine** cook; ~ **des devoirs** do homework; ~ **un discours** make a speech; ~ **des économies** save money; ~ **une petite fête** organize a small party; ~ **la grève** go on strike; ~ **l'idiot** act silly; ~ **du latin** study latin; ~ **la lessive** do the laundry; ~ **le marché** do the marketing; ~ **peur à qqn** frighten someone; ~ **le pitre** to act silly; ~ **des projets** to make plans; ~ **une promenade** to take a walk; ~ **son service militaire** serve time in the military; ~ **du ski** to ski; ~ **du sport** to

practice sports; ~ **le tour du monde** to travel around the world; ~ **la vaisselle** wash dishes; ~ **de la voile** go sailing; ~ **un voyage** go on a trip; **il fait beau/chaud/frais/froid/mauvais** the weather is beautiful/hot/cool/cold/bad; **il fait du vent** it's windy out
fais voir! let me see!
le fait /fɛt/ fact; **les faits** /fɛ/ **divers** local news
la falaise cliff
familial/e of the family
la farine flour
fatigué/e tired
le fauteuil armchair
faux/fausse wrong; fake
félicitations congratulations
la femme woman; wife
la fenêtre window
fermer close to
la fête party; **faire une petite** ~ organize a small party
le feu fire; **feu rouge/vert** traffic light
la feuille de papier sheet of paper
la feuilleton serial story
février February
ficher le camp (slang) to leave; **s'en ficher** not to care at all
fier/fière proud
la figure face
la fille daughter, girl; **fille unique** only daughter
le film movie; **film d'épouvante** horror movie
le fils son; **fils unique** only son
la fin end
finir to finish; **finir de faire** stop doing
la fleur flower
le fleuve river
la flûte flute
la fois time; **deux fois** twice; **fois** times (math)
la folie madness, extravagance; **aimer à la folie** to like immensely
font equals (math)
le football soccer
forcer to force
la forme form; **en forme** in (good) shape **formidable** great, terrific

fort/e strong; ~ **en quelque chose** good at something; **c'est trop fort!** that's going too far!
fou/folle crazy, mad
la foule crowd
le four oven
la fourmi ant
fournir to provide
frais/fraîche fresh, cool
la fraise strawberry
français/e French
la France France
les freins *m.* brakes
le frère brother
les frites *f.* French fries
le fromage cheese
le fruit fruit
la fumée smoke
fumer to smoke
furieux/furieuse furious

gagner to earn, to win
gai/e merry
le galet pebble
le gangster gangster
le gant glove
le garage garage
le/la garagiste garage mechanic, service-station proprietor
le garçon boy
la gare train station
gaspiller to waste
le gâteau cake
gaulliste Gaulliste (a Gaullist)
geler to freeze
la gendarmerie small-town police station
général: en général generally, usually
généralement/e generally
généreux/généreuse generous
le genre kind, type
les gens *m./f.* people
gentil/gentille nice, kind
gentiment nicely
la géographie geography
la géométrie geometry
le gérant/la gérante manager
le gigot leg of lamb
le gilet vest
la glace ice; ice cream; mirror
le glacier glacier
la gloire glory
le golf golf

Vocabulaire français-anglais

la gomme eraser
le gouvernement government
gouvernemental/e governmental
le gramme gram
le grand magasin department store
la grand-mère grandmother
le grand-père grandfather
grand/e tall, large, great
la grande surface shopping mall
les grands-parents grandparents
grave serious, dangerous
le grenier attic
la grenouille frog
la grève strike; **faire la** ~ to go on strike
gris/e grey
gros/se fat
grossir to put on weight, to get fat
groupé/e grouped
le groupe group
la guerre war
guider to guide
la guitare guitare
la gymnastique physical education; gymnastics

habillé/e dressed
s'habiller to get dressed
l'habitant *m.* inhabitant
habiter to live in; ~ **à** ~ a city; ~ **dans** ~ a building
s'habituer à to get used to
le hall hall
les haricots verts *m.* green beans
haut/e tall; **en haut** upstairs
hein? don't you think?; what?
l'héritage *m.* inheritance
hésiter to hesitate
l'heure *f.* time; **à l'heure** on time; **à quelle heure** at what time?; **à tout à l'heure** see you later; **quelle heure est-il?** what time is it?
heureusement happily, fortunately
heureux/heureuse happy
le hibou owl
hier yesterday; ~ **c'était...** yesterday was...
l'histoire *f.* history; story
historique historical
l'hiver *m.* winter
le hockey hockey
le hold-up hold-up

l'homme *m.* man; **homme d'affaires** businessman
honnête honest
l'hôpital *m.* hospital
l'horaire *m.* timetable
l'horizon *m.* horizon
horrible horrible
l'hôtel *m.* hotel
l'hôtesse hostess; **hôtesse d'accueil** receptionist; **hôtesse de l'air** airline stewardess
la huée *f.* hoot, jeer
humain/e human; **l'être humain** *m.* human being
l'humeur *f.* mood **de bonne/mauvaise humeur** in a good/bad mood
l'humour *m.* humor

ici here
idéal/e ideal
idéaliste idealist
l'idée *f.* idea
idiot/e stupid, idiotic
il faut (+ inf.) it is necessary, you/one must; **il faut que je me sauve** I've got to run
l'île *f.* island
imaginer to imagine
immédiat/e quick, immediate
immédiatement immediately
immense immense
l'immeuble *m.* building
l'impatience *f.* impatience
impatient/e impatient
impeccable impeccable
l'imperméable *m.* raincoat
impoli/e impolite
l'importance *f.* importance
important/e important
importe: n'importe quel no matter which; **n'importe où/qui/quoi** anywhere/one/thing
impossible impossible
impressionnant/e impressive
imprudent/e careless
inadapté/e mentally handicapped
inconnu/e unknown
l'incrédulité *f.* disbelief
indépendant independent
indien/ne Indian
indifférent, -e indifferent, unconcerned
indiquer to indicate, show

industriel/le industrial
l'infirmier/infirmière nurse
influent/e influential
les informations *f.* news
l'ingénieur *m.* engineer
inquiet/inquiète uneasy, disturbed
inquiéter to worry
l'installation *f.* moving in; establishment
s'installer to get settled
instant: à l'instant at once
l'instituteur/institutrice elementary school teacher
l'institut *m.* institute
intellectuel/le intellectual
l'intelligence *f.* intelligence
intelligent/e intelligent
intéressant/e interesting
s'intéresser à to be interested in
l'interview *f.* interview
invité/e guest
inviter to invite
Israël *m.* Israel
l'Italie *f.* Italy
italien/ne Italian

jaloux/jalouse jealous
jamais ever, never; **jamais de la vie!** not on your life!
la jambe leg
le jambon ham
janvier January
japonais/e Japanese
le jardin garden; **jardin public** public garden, park
jaune yellow
le jazz jazz
jeter to throw
le jeu game
jeudi Thursday
jeune young; **les jeunes gens** young people
la jeunesse youth
la Joconde Mona Lisa
la joie joy
joli/e pretty
jouer to play; **à** + sport: ~ **aux boules** play *boules;* ~ **à cache-cache** play hide-and-seek; ~ **aux cartes** play cards; ~ **aux échecs** play chess; ~ **au tennis** play tennis; **de** + instrument: ~ **des cymbales/de la flûte/du piano** to play cymbals/flute/piano

le joueur/la joueuse (de tennis) (tennis) player
jouir de to enjoy
le jour day; ~ de congé day off
la journée day
le journal newspaper
le/la journaliste journalist
juillet July
juin June
les jumeaux twins; le jumeau *m.*; la jumelle *f.*
juridique judicial (profession)
le jus de fruit fruit juice
jusqu'à until ~ + locative as far as, up to
jusqu'à ce que until (*conj.*)
justement exactly; in fact

kidnapper to kidnap
le kilogramme (kilo) kilogram
le kilomètre kilometer
le klaxon car horn

là there; là-bas over there
la laborantine lab assistant
le laboratoire laboratory
le lac lake
laid/e ugly
la laine wool
laisser to let, to leave, to allow; laisser tomber to drop
le lait milk; ~ en poudre powdered milk
la laitue lettuce
le langage language, speech
la langue language, tongue; ~ étrangère foreign language
latin Latin; faire du ~ to study Latin
le lavabo bathroom sink
le lave-vaisselle dishwasher
laver to wash; se laver (la figure) to wash (one's face)
le mien/la mienne mine
la leçon lesson
la lecture reading
légal/e legal
léger/légère light, lightweight
les légumes *m.* vegetables
lentement slowly
lequel/lesquels/laquelle/lesquelles who, whom, which, that
la lessive laundry
la lettre letter; ~ d'amour love

letter; ~ de félicitations congratulatory letter
le/la leur theirs
lever to raise; se lever to stand up, get up
la librairie bookstore
la license batchelor's degree
le lieu place; au ~ de instead of; avoir lieu to take place, happen; les lieux scene
le lion lion
lire (*irreg.*) to read
la liste list
le lit bed; lit deux places double bed
le litre liter (about 1 quart)
la littérature literature
le livre book
local/e, locaux local
le logement place to live ; lodgings
logique logical
loin away, far; ~ de far from
lointain/e far away
les loisirs *m.* leisure time
Londres London
long/ue long
la loterie lottery
louer to rent
le Louvre art museum in Paris
lui to her/him;
lundi Monday
la lune moon
les lunettes *f.* glasses
le luxe luxury
luxueux/se luxurious
le lycéen/la lycéenne high school student

la machine machine; machine à calculer calculator; machine à laver washing machine
madame (Mme) ma'am; Mrs.
mademoiselle (Mlle) Miss
le magasin store; ~ de disques record store
le magazine magazine
le magnétophone tape-recorder
magnifique magnificent
mai May
maigre thin
maigrir to lose weight, get thinner
le maillot de bain bathing suit; maillot jaune yellow jersey (worn by first-place bicycle racer)

la main hand; à ~ by hand
maintenant now
mais but; mais si yes, on the contrary; mais non! no! (emphatic)
la maison house
le maître teacher (elementary school); master
mal poorly, badly, pas mal not bad, pretty good; ~ à la gorge/la tête/aux jambes sore throat/ headache/sore legs (my legs hurt)
malade sick, ill
malgré in spite of
le malheur unhappiness, misery
malheureusement unfortunately
malheureux/malheureuse unhappy
la maman mother
manger to eat
le/la manifestant/e demonstrator
la manifestation demonstration
manquer to miss; tu me manques I miss you
le manteau woman's coat
manuel/le manual, by hand
se maquiller to put on makeup
le marchand dealer, merchant
le marché market; bon marché (inv.) inexpensive; faire le ~ do the food shopping
marcher to walk; to work (machinery); ça marche it's working
mardi Tuesday
le mariage wedding
se marier (avec) to get married (to)
le marin sailor
la marine navy
le Maroc Morocco
marocain/e Moroccan
la marque brand
marrant/e fun, funny
marre: j'en ai marre! I've had it!
marron (inv.) brown
mars March
martiniquais/e from Martinique
la Martinique Martinique
le match game
le matelas mattress
les mathématiques *f.* mathematics
le matin morning; in the morning; le samedi ~ on Saturday mornings
la matinée morning; en matinée afternoon show

Vocabulaire français-anglais

mauvais/e bad, evil
la mécanique machinery
le singe monkey
méchant/e bad, nasty
mécontent/e dissatisfied, discontent
le médecin doctor
le médicament medication
médiocre mediocre
méditerranéen/ne Mediterranean
meilleur/e better; **le/la ~ (de)** the best (in/of)
mélanger to mix
le membre member
même same; **en même temps** at the same time **(moi)-même** (my)self
mémorable memorable
la menace threat
menacer to threaten
merci thanks, thank you; **merci beaucoup** thanks a lot
mercredi Wednesday
la mère mother
merveilleux/se marvelous, wonderful
le message message; **~ publicitaire** commercial
la mesure measure
mesurer to measure; to be...tall
la météo forecast
le métier skilled occupation, specialty
le mètre meter
le métro subway; **métro-boulot-dodo** subway-work-sleep; "nine-to-five grind"
le metteur en scène movie director
mettre *(irreg.)* to put; to put on; **~ la table** to set the table
le meuble piece of furniture
mexicain/e Mexican
le Mexique Mexico
mi-temps: à mi-temps part time (work)
le micro microphone
microscopique microscopic, tiny
midi noon
mieux better; **le mieux** best
le militaire soldier, member of the Armed Forces; **militaire de carrière** a military man
mille 1000; **deux mille** 2000
un milliard billion

un million million
mince slim, slender
minuit midnight
la minute minute
le miroir mirror
le mistral fierce cold wind in Southern France
moche ugly
la mode fashion; **à la ~** in fashion, fashionable
modéré/e moderate, temperate
moderne modern
modeste unassuming
moi aussi me too; **moi non plus** me neither
moins less, minus; **moins (+ adj.) que** less...than; **à moins que (ne)** unless; **au moins** at least; **moins le quart** quarter to (the hour); **plus ou moins** more or less
le moment moment; **en ce moment** right now
le monde world
le moniteur/la monitrice camp counselor, sports instructor
monotone monotonous, dull
monsieur (M.) Mr.
la montagne mountain
monter to go up, climb
la montre watch
montrer to show; **~ qqch à qqn** to show something to someone
le monument monument
se moquer de to make fun of; **s'en moquer** not to care at all, not to give a hoot
le morceau de craie piece of chalk
le moteur motor
la moto (motocyclette) motorcycle
la mouche fly
mourir *(irreg.)* to die
la moustache moustache
le mouton sheep
la moyenne average **en moyenne** on the average
la mule mule
multiplier to multiply; **multiplié par** multiplied by
le mur wall
le musée museum
le musicien/a musicienne musician
la musique music
musulman Moslem (a Moslem)

nager to swim
le nageur swimmer
la naissance birth
naître *(irreg.)* to be born
le narrateur narrator
national/e national
la nature nature; **nature humaine** human nature
naturel natural
naturellement/e naturally
naviguer to navigate
n'est-ce pas? isn't it? don't you? etc.
né/e born
ne pas de (+ nom) not any; no; none; **ne jamais (de)** never (any); **ne pas non plus** not either, neither; **ne personne** nobody, not anybody; **ne rien** nothing
nécessaire necessary
nécessairement necessarily
la neige snow
neiger to snow
nerveusement nervously
nettoyer to clean
le neveu nephew
le nez nose
ni...ni neither...nor/either...or
la nièce niece
noir/e black; **le noir/la noire** black man, woman
le nom name; noun
le nombre number
le nord north; **au nord de** (to the) north of
normal/e, normaux normal
norvégien/ne Norwegian
la note note, grade; **bonnes notes** good grades; **mauvaise notes** bad grades
nourrissant/e nourishing
la nourriture food
nouveau/nouvel/nouvelle new
la nouvelle news
novembre November
le numéro number; **numéro de téléphone** telephone number

obéir à to obey
l'objet *m.* object
l'obligation *f.* obligation
obligatoire compulsory
obliger to compel

l'obscurité *f.* darkness
l'observateur *m.* observer
obtenir to get, to obtain
occuper to fill, occupy; être (très) occupé to be (very) busy; s'occuper de to concern oneself with, to take care of
l'océan *m.* ocean
octobre October
l'oeuf *m.* egg
officiel/le official
l'offre *f.* offer
offrir to offer
oh là là oh my!
oh, ça va! that's enough!
l'oiseau bird; oiseau-lyre lyre-bird
on one, we, you, people
l'oncle *m.* uncle
l'ongle *m.* nail (finger- or toe-)
l'opéra *m.* opera
l'opérette *f.* operetta
l'opinion *f.* opinion
optimiste optimistic
l'or *m.* gold en or made of gold
l'orage *m.* storm
orange (inv.) orange
l'orange *f.* orange
ordinaire ordinary
l'ordinateur *m.* computer
l'ordre *m.* order; en ordre in order
les ordures *f.* garbage; sortir les ordures to take out the garbage
l'oreille *f.* ear
organisé/e organized
l'orient *m.* east, the Orient
original/e original
ou or; ou bien or else
où where; n'importe ~ anywhere le moment ~ the moment when
oublier to forget
l'ouest west; à l'ouest de (to the) west of
l'ours *m.* bear
ouvert/e open
l'ouvreuse *f.* usherette
l'ouvrier/ouvrière manual worker, blue-collar worker
ouvrir (*irreg.*) to open

le pain bread; pain grillé toasted bread
la paix peace

le pamplemousse grapefruit
la pancarte placard
le panneau indicateur road sign
le papa daddy
le paquet package
par by; through; (fois) par an (times) per year, in a year; par exemple for example; par la fênetre through the window par rapport à in relation to; par terre on the floor, on the ground; passer par to pass by, to go by
le paragraphe paragraph
paraître (like *connaître*) to appear, to seem; il paraît que it seems that
le parapluie umbrella
le parc park
parce que because
parcourir (like *courir*) to travel over
le pardessus men's overcoat
les parents parents, relatives
paresseux/paresseuse
parfait/e perfect
parler to speak, to talk; parler à qqn to speak to someone; se parler to speak with each other
parmi among
la parole word
part: de ma part for me, on my behalf
participer to participate
le particulier individual, private party
la partie part
partir (*irreg.*) to leave, depart
partout everywhere
pas not; ~ du tout not at all; ~ mal not bad; pretty good; ~ possible! unbelievable!; ~ tellement not so much, not really
le passe-temps pastime
le passeport passport
passer (deux heures) to spend (two hours); passer par to pass by, go by; se passer to happen
passif/passive passive
passionnant/e fascinating, exciting
le pâté meat spread, pâté
patient/e patient
patiner to skate
le patron/la patronne boss
pauvre poor

le pavillon large house
payer to pay, pay for
le pays country
la pêche peach
le pêcheur fisherman
se peigner to comb one's hair
peindre (*irreg.*) to paint
le/la peintre painter
la pelouse lawn
pendant during, for
la péninsule peninsula
penser to think; ~ à to be thinking of
perdre to lose; perdre la tête to go crazy
le père father
permettre to allow, permit
la permission permission
le perroquet parrot
la perruque wig
le personnage character
la personne person; les ~ people; personne...ne nobody
personnel personal
personnellement personally
la pesanteur gravity
peser to weigh
pessimiste pessimistic
le petit déjeuner breakfast
le petit pain small bread roll
petit/e small; le/la petit/e ami/e boyfriend/girlfriend
les petites annonces classified ads
les petits pois peas
peu little, few; un peu a bit; un peu de a little bit of
peuplé/e populated
peupler to populate
la peur fear; avoir ~ to be afraid; de peur que (ne) for fear that; faire peur à qqn to frighten someone
peut-être maybe
le pharmacien, la pharmacienne pharmacist
la philosophie (philo) philosophy
le/la photographe photographer
la photographie (photo) photograph, photography
la physique physics
le/la pianiste pianist
le piano piano
la pièce coin; play
le pied foot; à pied on foot

le piège trap
le piéton pedestrian
le/la pilote pilot
le ping-pong table tennis
le pique-nique picnic
la piscine swimming pool
le pitre clown, buffoon; **faire le pitre** to act silly
pittoresque picturesque
le placard cabinet, closet
la place seat; **à la place de ...** in...'s place
placer to place
la plage beach
plaindre: se plaindre (like *craindre*) to complain
la plaine meadow
plaire à to please
plaisanter to joke
plaît: s'il vous/te plaît please
le plan plan; drawing
la planche à voile windsurfing board
le plancher floor
plancher to work hard
le plat dish (food); **plat principal** main dish, entrée
le plateau plateau
plein/e full, complete
pleurer to cry
pleuvoir to rain; **il pleut** it's raining
la pluie rain
plus more; **~ de** more of; **(le) ~ ...de** the most...of all; **plus (+ adj.) que** more...than; **plus ou moins** more or less; **plus tard** later; **ne...plus** no more, not any more, no longer; **ne...plus de** no more of
plusieurs several, a few, some
plutôt rather
la poche pocket
le poème poem
le poète/la poétesse poet
le point point; **point de vue** point of view, standpoint; **les points cardinaux** the points of the compass
la pointure size (shoe, glove)
la poire pear
pois: les petits pois *m.* peas
le poisson fish
le poivre pepper

poli/e polite
la police police; **l'agent de ~** police officer
poliment politely
la politique politics
la pollution pollution
la pomme apple
la pomme de terre potato
le porc pork
la porte door
le portefeuille wallet
le porte-plume penholder
porter to carry; to wear; **porter le coup** to deliver the final blow
le portrait portrait
portugais/e Portuguese
poser to put (something) down; **poser une question** to ask a question
la possibilité possibility
possible possible; **pas possible!** unbelievable!
la poste post office
le poste de télé TV set
le poster poster
la poubelle garbage; garbage container
la poule hen
le poulet chicken
pour for; in order to
le pourcentage percentage
pourquoi why
pourrait: on pourrait we could
pourvu que provided that; as long as
pouvoir *(irreg.)* can, may, to be able to
les poux *m.* lice
pratique practical
la pratique practice, experience
précipiter: se précipiter to rush
précis/e precise
préférable preferable
préféré/e preferred, favorite
préférer to prefer
premier/première first
le premier étage 2nd floor
prendre *(irreg.)* to take; **prendre une décision** to make a decision; **prendre rendez-vous avec** to make an appointment with; **se prendre trop au sérieux** to take oneself too seriously; **prendre un verre** to have a drink

préoccuper to preoccupy
préparer to prepare; **se préparer** to get ready
prés de close to, near; **près d'ici** nearby
présent/e present
présenter to introduce, to present
le/la président/e president
pressé/e in a hurry
le prêt-à-porter ready-to-wear
prêt/e ready
prétendre to claim
prêter to lend
le prêtre priest
le printemps spring
le prisonnier prisoner
privé/e private
le prix price, prize
le problème problem
prochain/e next
proche near, close
les produits laitiers dairy products
le professeur teacher, professor
la profession profession; **les professions libérales** professions requiring advanced study
profiter de to take advantage of
le programme program
le projet plan; **faire les projets** to make plans
projeter to project, to hurl; to plan
la promenade walk; **faire une promenade** to take a walk
se promener to take a walk, to wander about
proposer to suggest, to offer
propre clean; **mon/ma propre** ...my own...
le/la propriétaire owner, landlord/landlady
la propriété property, estate
la protestation protest
la province region
les provisions food supplies
prudemment cautiously
prudent/e careful
le psychanalyste psychoanalyst
le psychiatre psychiatrist
le public public, audience
la publicité advertising
le puériculteur/la puéricultrice early-childhood specialist
puis then

puisque because, since
puissant/e powerful
le pull sweater
punir to punish
le pupitre pupil's desk
pur/e pure
purement purely
le pyjama pajamas

qu'est-ce qui? who? (subject)
qu'est-ce qu'elle/il a dit? what did she/he say?
qu'est-ce qu'il y a? what's the matter?
qu'est-ce que? what? (object)
qu'est-ce que c'est what is it?
la qualité quality
quand when; **quand même** still, anyway
le quartier district
quatre-vingt-dix 90
quatre-vingts 80
que (conjunction) that; (interrog.) what?; (comparison) than
quel/quels/quelle/quelles which, what; **quel jour est-ce aujourd'hui?** what's today?; **quel temps fait-il?** what's the weather like? **quelle heure est-il?** what time is it? **quel dommage!** what a pity!; **quelle barbe!** what a drag; **quelle chance!** how lucky!; **quelle horreur!** how horrible!
quelqu'un someone
quelque chose de (+adj.) something (+adj.)
quelque part somewhere
quelquefois sometimes
quelques a few, some
la question matter, question; **poser une question** to ask a question
le questionnaire questionnaire, interrogation
qui who, which; **à qui?** to whom?; **qui est-ce que/qui?** whom? who?; **qui est-ce?** who is it?; **qui sait...?** who knows...?; **qui suis-je?** who am I?
quitter to leave; **ne quittez pas** please hold (telephone)
quoi? what?; **à quoi ça sert?** what good is it?, what is it used for?
quoique although

raconter to tell (a story)
la radio radio; **à la ~** on the radio
raffiné/e refined
rafraîchissant/e refreshing
raide straight
la raison reason
raisonnable reasonable
ranger to put in order
rapide fast, quick
rapidement quickly
rappeler to remind; **se rappeler** to remember
rapporter to bring back, to return
la raquette (sports) racket; **raquette de tennis** tennis racket
rarement rarely
se raser to shave
se rassembler to gather
ravi/e delighted
ravissant/e lovely, ravishing
le rayon department (of a store); shelf
la réaction reaction
réaliste realistic
réapparaître to reappear
récemment recently
le recenseur census taker
recevoir (*irreg.*) to get, receive
rechercher to look for
réduire to reduce
la référence reference
refermer to close again
réfléchir to think, to reflect
la réflexion reflection
le réfrigérateur refrigerator
refuser to refuse
regarder to look, to watch; **se regarder** to look at oneself, each other
le régime diet; **être au régime** to be on a diet
la région region
la règle ruler
regrettable regrettable
regretter to regret
régulièrement regularly
la reine queen
rejeter to reject, to throw back
se réjouir to rejoice
remarquer to remark
le remplacement replacement
remplacer to replace
remplir to fill up, fill out (a form)

la rencontre meeting, encounter
rencontrer to meet, run into
le rendez-vous appointment
rendre à to give back to
se rendre compte to realize, take into account
renouveler to renew
rentrer to go back inside, to return home
renverser to overturn
réparer to repair
répéter to repeat
répondre (à) to answer (someone, a letter, etc.)
la réponse answer
le reportage report (radio, TV, or newspaper)
le reporter reporter
se reposer to rest
le représentant representative; **représentant de commerce** sales representative
reprocher (à) to reproach, accuse
réservé/e reserved
les réserves énergétiques *f.* energy resources
résidentiel/le residential
résigné/e resigned to
résister to resist
la résolution resolution
respirer to breathe
la responsabilité responsibility
responsable responsible
la ressemblance resemblance
ressembler à to look like
le restaurant universitaire university cafeteria
le reste the rest, remaining part
rester to stay, to remain
le résultat result
retard: en retard late
retarder: ma montre retarde my watch is slow
le retour return
retourner to return, to go back
la réunion meeting, reunion
réussi/e successful
réussir (à) succeed (in)
la réussite success
le rêve dream, daydream
le réveil alarm clock; awakening
se réveiller to wake (oneself) up
revenir (like *venir*) to come back
la révision review

Vocabulaire français-anglais

revoir (like *voir*) to see again; **au revoir** good-by

le/la révolutionnaire revolutionary man/woman

le revolver gun

la revue magazine

le rez-de-chaussée lst floor, ground floor

riche rich, wealthy

le rideau curtain

rien nothing; **rien de (sérieux)** nothing (serious); **rien du tout** nothing at all; **ne...rien** nothing

le rire laughter

la rivière river, stream

le riz rice

la robe dress

le rock rock and roll

le roman novel; **roman policier** detective novel

le rond circle, round

rond/e round

rose pink

la roue wheel

rouge red

la route road, highway; **en route!** let's go!

le routier long-distance truckdriver

roux/rousse red-haired

royal/e royal

la rue street

le rugby rugby

russe Russian

rustique rustic

le sac bag, handbag; **sac de couchage** sleeping bag

sage well-behaved, wise

saisir to seize

la saison season

la salade salad; lettuce

le salaire salary

sale dirty

la salle room; **salle à manger** dining room; **salle de bains** bathroom; **salle de séjour** living room

le salon living room

salut hi, hello (informal)

samedi Saturday

le sandwich sandwich

sans without; **sans doute** proba-

bly; **sans faute** without fail; **sans qu'il me voit** without him seeing me

la santé health; **en bonne santé** in good health

la saucisse sausage

le saucisson salami

sauf except for

sauter to jump

sauver to save

savoir (*irreg.*) to know

le savon soap

le saxophone saxophone

la science fiction science fiction

les sciences économiques *f.* economics

les sciences naturelles *f.* life sciences

les sciences politiques *f.* political science

la sculpture sculpture

secret/secrète secret

le/la secrétaire secretary

le séjour stay, visit

le sel salt

selon according to

sembler to seem

sénégalais/e from Senegal

sensationnel/le fantastic, wonderful

sensible sensitive

le sentiment feeling

sentir (like *sortir*) to feel (an object or reaction); **se sentir** (+ emotion) to feel (an emotion)

septembre September

la série series

sérieusement seriously

sérieux/sérieuse serious

le serpent snake

le service militaire military service; **faire son service militaire** to serve time in the military

la serviette briefcase, attaché case; napkin

servir (like *sortir*) to serve; **servir à** to be used for

seul/e alone

seulement a little; only; **si seulement...** if only...

le short shorts

le siècle century

le silence silence

silencieux/silencieuse silent

la situation situation

le ski skiing; **ski nautique** water skiing; **faire du ski** to ski

sociable sociable, friendly

socialiste socialist

la société society

la sociologie sociology

le/la sociologue sociologist

la sœur sister

le sofa sofa

la soie silk

soigneusement carefully

le soir evening

la soirée evening (affair)

le soldat soldier

solitaire lonely

la solution solution

sombre dark

le sondage poll, survey

sonner to ring

la Sorbonne (part of the University of Paris)

la sorcière witch

sortir (*irreg.*) to go out; **sortir les ordures** to take out the garbage

soudain suddenly

souffrir (like *ouvrir*) to suffer; **souffert** suffered

souhaiter to wish

soulever to raise, to lift

la soupe soup; **soupe à l'oignon** onion soup

sourd/e deaf

le sourire smile

la souris mouse

sous under

le sous-sol basement

souvent often

spacieux/spacieuse spacious

spécial/e special

le spectacle de variété variety show

le spectateur/la spectatrice member of the audience, spectator

splendide beautiful, splendid

le sport sports; **faire du sport** to practice sports

sportif/sportive athletic

le stade stadium

la station-service gas station

la statue statue

le steward airline steward

strict/e strict

la strophe stanza
studieux/studieuse studious
stupide stupid
le stylo pen
le succès success
le sucre sugar
le sud south; **au sud de** (to the) south of
suggérer to suggest
la Suisse Switzerland
suisse Swiss
la suite continuation, following part, rest
suivre (like *vivre*) to follow
super super
superbe superb, beautiful
superficiel/le superficial
le supermarché supermarket
sur on
sûr/e sure, certain; **bien sûr!** of course!
sûrement surely
surprendre (like *prendre*) to surprise
la surprise surprise
surtout above all
surveiller (enfants) to keep an eye on, to look after (children)
sympathique nice, pleasant, likeable
la symphonie symphony
le syndicat union

la table table; **table de nuit** bedside table
le tableau painting; chalkboard
la taille size
le tailleur woman's suit
tais-toi/taisez-vous be quiet
tant de... so many...
la tante aunt
le tapis rug
taquiner to tease
tard late
la tarte pie
la tartelette small fruit pie
la tasse cup
le taxi taxi
le technicien technician
technique technical
tel/telle such; **un tel/une telle** such a
le télégramme telegram
le téléphone telephone

téléphoner (à) to call (someone)
la télévision television
tellement so; ~ **de** so much
la température temperature
la tempête storm, tempest
le temps weather; time; **à plein temps** full time; **quel temps fait-il?** what's the weather like?
tenir to hold
le tennis tennis; **faire du tennis** to play tennis
tentant/e tempting
la tentation temptation
la tente tent
la tenue: en tenue in uniform
terminer to finish, to end
le terrain piece of land
la terrasse terrace
terroriser terrorize
la tête head
têtu/e stubborn
le thé tea
le théâtre theater
la théorie theory
le thermomètre thermometer
tiens! oh, look! wait! well!
le tigre tiger
le timbre stamp
timide shy, timid
tirer to shoot
le tiroir drawer
le titre title
tolérer to tolerate
la tomate tomato
tomber to fall down; **laisser tomber** to drop
tôt early
total/e complete, total
toujours always, still
le tour turn; tour; **à leur tour** in turn, one after the other; **faire le tour du monde** to travel around the world
le/la touriste tourist
tourner to turn; **tourner à gauche/droite** turn left/right
le tournoi tournament
tout/tous/toute/toutes all, everything; **à tout à l'heure** see you later; **à tout prendre** on the whole; **en tout** in all; **tout confort** with all modern conveniences; **tous les jours** everyday; **partout** everywhere; **pas du**

tout not at all; **rien du tout** nothing at all; **sans rien du tout** without anything at all; **tout à fait** exactly, entirely; **tout au plus** at the most; **tout de suite** right away; **voilà tout** that's all; **tout à l'heure** later; **toute l'année** all year; **toute la journée** all day; **toutes les fois** every time
tracer to trace
le train train
la tranche slice
tranquille quiet, calm
le transistor portable radio
transporter to carry, to transport
le travail/les travaux work
travailler to work
travailleur/travailleuse hard-working
traverser to cross
très very
le tricot sweater
tricoter to knit
la trigonométrie (trigo) trigonometry
triste sad
se tromper to make a mistake
la trompette trumpet
trop too; too much; ~ **de** too much of; ~ **peu de** too little of
tropical/e tropical
trouver to find, to think; **tu ne trouves pas?** don't you think?
le truc thing
la truite trout
le type guy, fellow
typique typical

un/e a, an
l'université *f.* university
urgence: en cas d'urgence in an emergency
urgent/e urgent
l'usine *f.* factory
utile useful
utiliser to use

les vacances *f.* vacation, holidays
vaisselle: faire la vaisselle to do the dishes
la valeur value
la valise suitcase
la vallée valley
valoir (*irreg.*) to be worth
la vanille vanilla

Vocabulaire français-anglais

la **vanité** vanity
varié/e varied
vaut: il vaut (valoir) it's worth
le **vélo** bicycle
le **vélomoteur** moped
le **velours** velvet
le **vendeur, la vendeuse** salesman/ saleswoman
vendre (à) to sell (to)
vendredi Friday
venir (*irreg.*) to come; **venir de** to have just (done something)
la **vente** sale; **en vente** on sale
le **ventre** stomach
vérifier to verify
la **vérité** truth
le **vers** line of poetry; **les vers** verses, poetry
vert/e green
la **veste** jacket
les **vêtements** clothes
le **vétérinaire** veterinarian
la **viande** meat
la **victime** victim
le **vieillard** old man
vieillir to grow old
vieux, vieil/vieille old; **mon vieux** old fellow, my friend

la **villa** country house
le **village** village; **village de pê- cheurs** fishing village
la **ville** city, town
le **vin** wine; **vin rouge/blanc** red/ white wine
une **vingtaine** about twenty
violet/te purple
le **violon** violin
visiter to visit (places)
la **vitamine** vitamin
vite fast; quick! (exclamation)
la **vitre** pane of glass
vivre (*irreg.*) to live
voilà here is/here are; there is/ there are; **le/la voilà** there it/he/ she is
la **voile** sail; **faire de la voile** to go sailing
voir to see; **voyons** let's see; oh, come on, now!
le **voisin/voisine** neighbor
la **voiture** car
la **voix** voice
voler to steal; to fly
le **volley-ball** volleyball
le/la vôtre (*irreg.*) yours
vouloir to want

vouloir dire to mean; **que veut dire...en anglais?** what does ...mean in English?
le **voyage** trip; **en voyage** on a trip; **faire un voyage** to take a trip
voyager en to travel by (a means of transportation)
le **voyageur/la voyageuse** traveler
le **voyant/la voyante** seer, sooth- sayer, fortuneteller
vrai/e true
vraiment truly
la **vue** view
vulgaire vulgar
les **w.c./vese/** toilet
le **week-end** weekend
le **western** western movie
le **whisky** wiskey, liquor

y there (replaces preposition + noun phrase referring to a place, thing, or idea); **il y a** there is/are
le **yaourt, le yogourt** yogurt

le **zèbre** zebra
le **zoo** zoo
zut! darn!

Index

Credits

Illustrations by Bascove 2, 17, 26, 27, 35, 36, 47, 58, 80, 102, 103, 112, 117, 118, 121, 125, 153, 154, 162, 166, 168, 177, 187, 201, 202, 216, 220, 227, 228, 234, 235, 244, 245, 252, 257, 276, 303, 321, 322, 330, 340, 362, 363, 381, 423, 434, 435, 457, 458, 470, 486, 487, 511, 543, 560.

Illustrations by Devera Ehrenberg 4, 32, 34, 60, 77, 114, 148, 180, 194, 222, 239, 278, 293, 332, 373, 394, 413, 432, 444, 461, 472, 483, 518, 548, 552, 574, 589, 604, 605.

Archive Pictures Joan Liftin 138. Philip Jon Bailey 371. *Canadian Government Office of Tourism* 75. Stuárt Cohen 15; 553; 571; 202; 254; 306; 399; 417; 438. *Editorial Photocolor Archives* Alain Keler 601. *French Embassy Press & Information* 41; 110; 191; 477. *Global Focus* Ted Cordingley 302; 431; 481; M.L. Thomas 422. *Liaison Photo Agency Inc.* Gamma 588; Sipa 292; 433; Olivier Villeneuve 430. *Magnum Photos* Martine Franck 230; 566; Leonard Freed 527; 566; Erich Hartmann 118; Richard Kalvar 198; 324; 502; Guy LeQuerre 129; 580; Dennis Stock 11. *Monkmeyer Press Photo Agency, Inc.* Michael Kagan 496; Hugh Rogers 496. *New Orleans Tourist Office* 49. *The Picture Cube* Read D. Brugger 69; Foto du Monde 559; Richard Wood 344; 353. Tito Simboli 99; 211. *Stock, Boston* Mark Antman 507; 582; Owen Franken 60; 268; 522; Franklin Wing 275; Cary Wolinsky 179. *Taurus Photos* Karen Collidge 163; Eric Kroll 7; 283; 532; Richard Wood 351; 379. Derrick TePaske 83; 104; 105; 122; 146; 163; 184; 384; 412; 463; 546.